Blessed Thessaly

Liverpool Studies in Ancient History

LIVERPOOL STUDIES IN ANCIENT HISTORY

Blessed Thessaly

The Identities of a Place and Its People from the Archaic Period to the Hellenistic

EMMA ASTON

First published 2024 by
Liverpool University Press
4 Cambridge Street
Liverpool
L69 7ZU

British Library Cataloguing-in-Publication data
A British Library CIP record is available

ISBN 978-1-83553-001-6 paperback

Typeset by Carnegie Book Production, Lancaster
Printed and bound by CPI Group (UK) Ltd, Croydon CR0 4YY

Contents

List of illustrations

Maps

Figures

Tables

Abbreviations

AB	Austin, C. and G. Bastianini eds. 2002. *Posidippi Pellaei Quae Supersunt Omnia*. Milan: LED.
AD	*Αρχαιολογικόν Δελτίον*
AE	*Αρχαιολογική Εφημερίς*
BICS	*Bulletin of the Institute of Classical Studies*
BNP	Cancik, H., H. Schneider and C.F. Salazar eds. 2002–10. *Brill's New Pauly: Encyclopaedia of the Ancient World. Antiquity*. 15 vols. Leiden: Brill.
Chron.	*Χρονικά*
CID	*Corpus des Inscriptions de Delphes*
DK	Diels, H. and W. Kranz 1952. *Die Fragmente der Vorsokratiker*. 6th ed. Berlin: Weidmann.
DVC	Dakaris, S., I. Vokotopoulou and A.-F. Christidis. 2013. *Τα χρηστήρια ελάσματα της Δωδώνης των ανασκαφών Δ. Ευαγγελίδη*. 2 vols. Athens: Η εν Αθήναις Αρχαιολογική Εταιρεία.
Epigr. tou Or.	Petrakos, B.Ch. 1997. *Οι Επιγραφές του Ωροπού*. Athens: Η εν Αθήναις Αρχαιολογική Εταιρεία.
FD	*Fouilles de Delphes*
FGrH	Jacoby, F. 1923–59. *Die Fragmente der griechischen Historiker*. Berlin: Weidmann; Leiden: Brill.
FHG	Müller, K.W.L. 1841–70. *Fragmenta Historicorum Graecorum*. Paris: Firmin Didot.
I.Atrax	Tziafalias, A., R.A. Bouchon, L. Darmezin, J.-C. Decourt, B. Helly, G. Lucas and I. Pernin. 2016. *Corpus des inscriptions d'Atrax en Pélasgiotide (Thessalie). Études épigraphiques, 7*. Paris: de Boccard.
IACP	Hansen, M.H. and T.H. Nielsen eds. 2004. *Inventory of Archaic and Classical Poleis*. Oxford: Oxford University Press.
IG	*Inscriptiones Graecae*

I.Magn.	Kern, O. 1900. *Die Inschriften von Magnesia am Maeander.* Berlin: W. Spemann.
I.Thess.	Decourt, J.-C. 1995. *Inscriptions de Thessalie I: Les cités de la vallée de l'Énipeus.* Athens: École Française d'Athènes.
KA	Kassel, R. and C. Austin. 1983, 1991. *Poetae Comici Graeci.* 2 vols. Berlin: de Gruyter.
LGPN	*Lexicon of Greek Personal Names*
L-P	Lobel, E. and D.L. Page. 1955. *Poetarum Lesbiorum Fragmenta.* Oxford: Clarendon.
LSJ	Liddell, H.G., R. Scott and H. Stuart Jones. 1940. *Greek-English Lexicon.* Oxford: Oxford University Press.
MDAI(A)	*Mitteilungen des deutschen archäologischen Instituts in Athen*
MW	Merkelbach, R. and M.L. West. 1967. *Fragmenta Hesiodea.* Oxford: Clarendon.
PAE	*Πρακτικά της εν Αθήναις Αρχαιολογικής Εταιρείας*
PCPS	*Proceedings of the Cambridge Philological Society*
PMG	Page, D.L. 1962. *Poetae Melici Graeci Fragmenta.* Oxford: Clarendon.
SEG	*Supplementum Epigraphicum Graecum*
SIG	*Sylloge Inscriptionum Graecarum*
SNG	*Sylloge Nummorum Graecorum*
TGrF Adespota	Kannicht, R. and B. Snell. 1981. *Tragicorum Graecorum Fragmenta (TrGF),* Vol. 2: *Fragmenta adespota, testimonia volumini I addenda, indices ad volumina I et 2.* Göttingen: Vandenhoeck & Ruprecht.

Acknowledgements

The creation of this book began and ended with fellowships. In 2009 I was Early Career Fellow at the British School at Athens, and began research in its excellent library. During my stay, several people in the School, in particular the Director Catherine Morgan and the Assistant Director Robert Pitt, gave me their generous assistance and advice. With them I travelled to Thessaly, where numerous members of the Thessalian Ephorates gave their time to show me round sites and museums. There could have been no better start to what became a very long-drawn-out project, and I am grateful to everyone who made my stay so fruitful and enjoyable.

I finished writing this book as a Margo Tytus Fellow at the University of Cincinnati in spring term 2022. I should like to thank Steven Ellis, Rachel Schwerdtfeger and Joe Katenkamp for co-ordinating the process, including the postponement of my stay because of the coronavirus pandemic. The staff of the peerless Blegen Library, in particular Shannan Stewart and Rebecka Lindau, looked after me with infinite patience as I blundered around in the stacks; Mike Braunlin also gave generous hospitality, including access to dogs and a horse. Without the time and academic resources that my stay in Cincinnati offered, the book would never have been finished.

In the closing phase of the book's production, Rosanagh Mack and Una Markham accompanied me on a trip to central and northern Greece to gather some final photographs; their comradeship and support were much appreciated, as were the many other forms of help they offered as the book reached its completion.

Within the University of Reading, I would like to thank Roberta Gilchrist, Research Dean for Heritage and Creativity, for allocating funds to relieve me of teaching and administrative duties twice: first in 2016–2017 and again in spring term 2021, when Covid delayed my Tytus Fellowship. If she ever felt she might be throwing good money after bad, she never showed it. Her patience was much appreciated, and I hope is now rewarded. I am extremely grateful to Liverpool University Press for their efficiency and support, in particular senior commissioning editor Clare Litt, series editor Fiona Hobden and senior production editor Sarah Davison. The two anonymous readers of the manuscript provided extensive, detailed and helpful suggestions for its improvement, and Rosanagh Mack gave invaluable feedback on the sections dealing with coinage. Remaining errors and examples of downright perversity can be laid at no door but mine.

Finally, it is a joy to acknowledge the contribution of my parents. My mother Rosey created the maps and several images (one for the front cover); as many of my colleagues have remarked over the years, I am lucky to have an artist in the family. My father John proofread drafts, helped compile the index and discussed the whole thing with me on many occasions. Both parents provided endless support and encouragement. The book's title *Blessed Thessaly*, in addition to quoting Pindar, is meant to evoke a touch of the exasperation they must occasionally have felt when the region and its inhabitants were once more inserted into conversation. They never showed anything but enthusiasm, however. This book is dedicated to them, with love and gratitude.

Introduction

Shortly after the fall of Troy, a new group entered the land we call Thessaly, in northern Greece. They came from the west, over the Pindos mountains, though Epeiros may not have been their original home. They were the Thessaloi, and they would come to dominate Thessaly, giving it its historical name – Thessalia, land of the Thessaloi – and enslaving its indigenous population as an agricultural workforce.

Such, in essence, is the story that Greeks from the fifth century onward told about the origins of the Thessalians and their presence in the land they inhabited. There are two ways of looking at the tradition. For some scholars past and present it encapsulates elements of historical truth: post-Mycenaean migration, the arrival of a new ethnic element in the region, the step by step subordination of pre-existing communities.[1] Alternatively, one can regard it as deriving from 'intentional history', as Gehrke has called it:[2] stories the Thessalians told about themselves to create a sense of shared origin and therefore of collective identity, and to justify the inequality of power between themselves and various subaltern groups such as the Penestai (enslaved agricultural workers). The sheer prevalence of migration narratives in the origin-stories of *ethnē* strongly suggests the

[1] For the most part, migration theories are a feature of somewhat older scholarship, such as Sordi (1958), 1–31, and Larsen (1968), 13–14. Sordi sees the origin of the Thessaloi as coming from Kos and adjoining areas; for Larsen, they arrived over the Pindos from the west, a position also taken, and developed in a great deal more detail, by Corvisier (1991). The migration of the Thessaloi is sometimes embroiled in the theory of the Dorian invasion: see, for example, Hammond (1931–1932), 147–55 (cf. Hammond [1967], 393). The historicity of the arrival of the Thessaloi has, however, significant current exponents, chief among them Bruno Helly, who explains intra-regional variations in the Thessalian dialect by reference to the arrival and expansion of the Thessaloi over the Pindos. See Helly (1991), 144–47; Helly (2007); Bouchon and Helly (2013), 210–11; cf. Helly (2013), which proposes a model for the gradual displacement of the Magnetes by the Thessaloi. For a sceptical view of the historical reality of the arrival of the Thessaloi and the displacement of the Boiotoi, by contrast, see Morgan (2003), 188. For discussion of the Dorian invasion and its role in historiography and archaeology see Middleton (2010), 41–48.

[2] Gehrke (1994).

potency of the motif as a way of unifying populations on the symbolic level, however diverse and indeed conflicted they were in other modes of life.[3] These two perspectives are not mutually exclusive, and 'no smoke without fire' is in general a sound historical principle: probably trans-Pindos and trans-Aegean population movements were part of the upheavals in Thessaly that occurred between the Bronze and the Early Iron Age. To that extent, this book abnegates membership of the 'école hypercritique' that presents the traditions of the Thessalian migration as wholly imaginary, a position lambasted by Sakellariou.[4] In fact the reality of population movements is simply not its subject. The real question is why certain memories, real or not, are preserved, while others fall by the wayside; this book considers the stories told, and their significance, without making an assumption either way about their basis in shreds of reality from the very distant past. It focuses on when, how and why certain stories were told about who the Thessalians were and where they came from; why those stories and not others (since migrations will have been various and multidirectional); and why it became desirable to promote them at certain times and through certain channels of symbolic communication.

As Luce has remarked, 'L'identité est donc avant tout un fruit de la parole. En effet, c'est par les mots que l'on peut se nommer et que l'on peut nommer les autres, c'est par la parole que l'on peut raconter l'histoire de son groupe.'[5] Recovering Thessalian stories, and how they described themselves, will be the core purpose of this book, though the speech is often indirect; we rarely have the words of the Thessalians themselves, used in explicit self-definition, but we can build up some understanding of their symbolic language from myth, cult, iconography and certain significant material choices.

1. The structure of the book

This book follows a largely chronological trajectory, both within and between chapters, in order to chart the discernible phases of Thessalian ethnic articulation. Chapters 1 and 2 examine the place and significance of Thessaly within Archaic Greece; first its role within the political and

[3] As Kaplan observes (2014, 306), 'Virtually every Greek community located its origins in a story of immigration.'

[4] Sakellariou (2009), 75. It is striking that in his treatment of the proto-history of the Thessalian *ethnos* (749–58) he makes no mention of the theories of Helly, despite some elements of compatibility.

[5] Luce (2014), 37. ('Identity is above all a product of speech. In effect, it is through words that one can name oneself, and name others; it is through speech that one can recount the history of one's group.')

religious landscape of central Greece, and then, in Chapter 2, in the production of epic verse. As these two chapters establish, most of our surviving Archaic sources show little or no desire to emphasise the unity of Thessaly or its identity as sharply separated from that of other Greeks. This is not because texts such as the Iliadic Catalogue of Ships predate the presence of the Thessaloi in Thessaly, but because they reflect different priorities of self-expression within Thessaly and different ways of seeing Thessaly from the outside. Around the end of the sixth century, this starts to change. Chapter 3 charts the development of the origin-myth of the Thessaloi, from its beginnings as a 'wandering heroes' tale designed to assert the privileged ethnic standing of a west-Thessalian elite to its gradual extension and adaptation, culminating in the first half of the fifth century, as a charter-myth for the Thessaloi as a whole *ethnos*. Chapter 4 shifts the focus to cult and examines the development, again in the late sixth and earlier fifth century, of a complex of ritual and myth connected with Poseidon and designed to express a suite of Thessalian characteristics to do with the land, its abundance and its natural products, especially horses and grain. While the late Archaic period did not see the creation *ex nihilo* of ethnic terms and consciousness in Thessaly, it did see the start of a project, led by polis elites, to find ways of articulating what the Thessalians had in common and what set them apart from other Greeks.

This development coincided with the first attested stages of Thessalian political co-operation, in particular the creation of the tetrads, the four districts of Thessaly with their highly significant names, Pelasgiotis, Thessaliotis, Hestiotis[6] and Phthiotis. However, as Chapter 5 asserts, to read this co-operation as the creation of a fully fledged federal state is to imagine the conditions of the late fifth century and the fourth back into the late sixth. Thessalian political and military unity should not be regarded – as some have regarded it – as somehow primordial, inherent in the warrior identity of the invading Thessaloi and in the geographical unity of the Thessalian plains.[7] Rather, over the course of the Classical period various models of political co-operation seem to have been tried, ranging from *philia*-ties between polis elites, through various paradigms of pan-Thessalian rule, to the formal *koinon* mechanisms discernible from the 360s BC. Chapter 5 follows this political evolution of Thessaly on the regional level, tracing its phases without trying to smooth over the massive rifts in our available evidence and therefore our understanding.

The story thus far may be seen as, in effect, the creation of Thessaly, first as a mythological entity, then as a ritual one and finally as a political

[6] This spelling is preferred to the more usual Hestiaiotis/Histiaiotis because it is attested in Thessalian inscriptions. See Chapter 3.

[7] E.g., Larsen (1968), 12–26; cf. Tziafalias (1994), 154–56.

one. In this process, the role of the external perspective should not be ignored. We may regard it as a necessary inconvenience to have to rely so often on non-Thessalian sources in our quest to understand how the Thessalians themselves regarded their own identity. In some ways it is, but in fact non-Thessalian sources are not just a cracked and faulty lens through which one peers dimly at realities beyond; they are themselves part of the picture. The formation and expression of regional identity in ancient Greece always had a dialogic element, as ingredients of external perception, even pejorative stereotyping, were co-opted and incorporated within how a community regarded and presented itself. Arkadia is a good example of this: other Greeks regarded it as primitive and primordial, and while in fact the isolated untouched Arkadia was very far from historical reality, this characterisation of the region and its people was built into the cults and myths most salient to the articulation of its shared identity from the fourth century BC onwards.[8] Sparta, too, affords examples of a community 'playing up' to external perceptions, of internal and external perspectives informing each other.[9] This dialogic process is fully in play in Thessaly too, and cannot be written out of the picture.

The external perspective takes centre stage in Chapter 6, which discusses the increasingly hostile treatment of the Thessalians and the perceived Thessalian character, especially in the Athenian sources, from the later fifth century, and the climax of criticism occasioned by the close association between the Thessalians and Philip II of Macedon. This sees the traits traditionally regarded as positive – wealth, hospitality, an old-fashioned political system – turned more and more into modes of disparagement. Thessalian voices are not, however, lost to hearing, and we see signs of Thessalians trying to enhance their collective standing in the eyes of other Greeks. This is even more visible in Chapter 7, in which the conditions of the Hellenistic world offer new opportunities both for interaction with other communities across the Greek world and for collective representation in myth and religion. In many ways these new opportunities were used by Thessalians – groups and individuals – to control the narrative about their character, their deeds and their identity. We see a return to some of the themes prevalent in the Archaic period: a close connection between Thessaly and the origins of Hellenism, a positive association between Thessaly and natural wealth, horses and horsemanship, traditional aristocratic values. But between the Archaic and the Hellenistic

[8] Jost (2007), 264–69; Roy (2011) discusses especially the relationship between the Arkadians' reputation for 'backwardness' and themes of conservatism and primordiality in their self-representation.

[9] Hellenistic and Roman Sparta embellishing and advertising famous Spartan traditions: Kennell (2017). See also Flower (2002).

periods so much has happened: the *idea* of Thessaly has achieved potency, in a way that is not visible in Archaic sources, and has become freighted with cultural, ethical and political associations in the eyes of other Greeks. Hellenistic Thessalians, while reclaiming Archaic myths in particular, did so in the light of centuries of such cumulative discourse-building.

Before commencing this exploration, however, it is necessary to consider some key preliminary aspects of method and approach, and to set the stage by discussing some of the basic manifestations of Thessaly as a natural, political and linguistic entity. It will be shown that no one measure reveals Thessaly to us as having inherent or straightforward regional unity; rather, such factors – landscape, political co-operation, language, material culture – all played a part in the process by which Thessalians deliberately shaped and articulated their shared identity, the subject of this book.

2. Studying regional identity in ancient Greece

One of the most significant advances in ancient history since the 1980s has been the reassessment of the *ethnos*. The word itself was used in various ways by the Greeks to denote a range of groups, categories and communities, one of which was a tribe seen as bound together by consanguinity, kinship and shared origins.[10] It is in this specific sense that the present book, in keeping with most modern scholarship, uses the term, while retaining awareness of its relative flexibility in ancient usage. Even in the tribal sense, *ethnos* could, for the Greeks, denote a geographically diffused group, such as the Dorians, the Ionians, or even the Hellenes. A Hellene did not have to live in Hellas to be a Hellene; long before the cultural expansion of the Hellenistic period, Hellenes identifying themselves as such were to be found in western Asia, in north Africa, in Magna Graecia. There was, however, a second tier of *ethnos*, smaller, more land-based (though still potentially mobile). The Thessaloi were one such; to the south of them there were others, not only large and important ones such as the Phokians and Boiotians but also a patchwork of micro-*ethnē* in and around the Spercheios valley, such as the Oitaians, Malians, Ainianes, Dorians of the Metropolis. Unlike Hellenes, such *ethnē* were firmly grounded in the reality of territory and territorial possession; land and its occupation dominated their lives, but also their myth-histories.

Stories of arrival were especially significant; *ethnē* (including the Thessaloi) move from one region to another, finally to take up residence in their historical homeland. The alternative is autochthony, the claim that a group is so absolutely indigenous as to have been sprung from the very land in which it lives. Myths of migrating *ethnē* used generally to be considered

[10] Hall (1997), 34–40; Fraser (2009), 1–5; McInerney (2001), 55–56.

records of historical reality, in particular the movements of peoples after, or accompanying, the decline of Mycenaean civilisation.[11] As a consequence, it was thought, the *ethnos* was a primordial unit.[12] The tribe predated the polis. It was the earliest component of social organisation. It had inherent coherence. These assumptions have been challenged from two main angles. First, Catherine Morgan's *Early Greek States Beyond the Polis* dispelled the easy assumption that the *ethnos* was always an earlier, indeed a primitive, phenomenon, supplemented and effectively supplanted (except in certain 'backwaters') by the innovation of the polis. Thessaly is one of the regions she examines in detail to demonstrate that, if we set aside the conviction that only the polis (defined according to rather narrow Aristotelian criteria) is the true measure of political maturity and cohesion, we can recognise the many tiers of identity operating in Early Iron Age society.[13] Second, regional studies have identified the importance of ethnogenesis as the process by which a sense of ethnic belonging within a certain group is forged through reference to shared myths, cults and customs.[14] Salient examples of this latter approach are McInerney's *The Folds of Parnassos: Land and Ethnicity in Ancient Phokis*, Luraghi's *The Ancient Messenians: Constructions of Ethnicity and Memory*, and Larson's *Tales of Epic Ancestry: Boiotian Collective Identity in the Late Archaic and Early Classical Periods*. What such regional studies have in common – and what this book also shares – is that *ethnos*-identity is approached as a process, rather than an inherent reality. Societies – diverse in landscape, stories, cults, material culture – build a sense of collective belonging.

As well as establishing the *ethnos* as the product, in part at least, of a process of manufacture, this trend in scholarship has had the crucial effect of enhancing our understanding of the role of the *koinon*, or federal state. Political institutions used to be given the prime role in how a community beyond the polis – or across poleis – interacted. The federal state was implicitly or explicitly valorised: when an *ethnos* united in this fashion, often for military purposes, it was seen as successful; an apparent lack of formalised political co-operation was regarded as a sign of weakness or decline. This narrative is pervasive in the past scholarship on Thessaly, and will be encountered and challenged at various junctures. The apex of

[11] E.g. Hammond (1931–1932); discussion of the approach in Hall (1997), 41–42.

[12] See, for example, Snodgrass (1980), 86–87; he uses Thessaly as his main example of the 'primitive *ethnos*'.

[13] Morgan (2003), 4–16, 85–104, 135–42.

[14] Among the many studies of ancient Greek ethnicity and ethnogenesis see, for example, Ulf (1996), McInerney (2001), Hall (1997 and 2002), Lund (2005), Freitag (2007) and the articles in McInerney ed. (2014), especially those of Reger, Luraghi and Ganter.

the Thessalian achievement is typically located in the sixth century BC, when the Thessalians had formed a federal state under the leadership of Aleuas Pyrrhos, and when – partly as a consequence – they had been able to assert military dominance over the adjoining *ethnē* and their neighbours to the south. The current book does not remove the *koinon* from the picture altogether, but political co-operation is situated alongside developments in religion and myth to create a diverse understanding of regional co-operation in all its discernible forms.

The ethnogenetic process does not happen *ex nihilo*, but it does cut across some aspects of the tangible daily reality of Thessalians' lives. It is important that those of us studying communities from the regional perspective do not unconsciously come to see our view as more important on the practical level than it actually was. Two caveats have to be made and kept in mind. The first is that the discernible production and consumption of myths and cults expressing Thessalian identity happen among elites. The project of Thessalian ethnogenesis in its active form cannot be claimed to be truly shared by all Thessalians. This is not to deny a degree of organic diffusion within Thessalian communities, occasionally visible. But most of the material we are able to assess – coins, inscriptions, non-Thessalian historical writing – reflect decisions made on the civic level and among relatively narrow groups of influential individuals. The second caveat is that the polis, so far from being weak and under-developed in Thessaly as used to be claimed,[15] was actually the prime unit of religious, civic and political life. Citizenship was citizenship of the polis, not of 'the Thessalians'. Cults served, and reflected the priorities of, poleis or parts of poleis. Unlike the *ethnos*, the polis involved regular face-to-face contact, within public spaces and for the purposes of practical daily life. We have no evidence that even a truly representative sample of 'the Thessalians' ever gathered together for political or religious reasons, such as would ground their shared identity in physical interaction. The greatest achievement of Mili's *Religion and Society in Ancient Thessaly* is to have examined cult on different levels – households, poleis, groups of poleis, the region – and the interaction between these levels. Archaeological and epigraphic work in Thessaly in the later twentieth and the twenty-first century have shed more and more light on the unique societies of specific settlements in all periods.[16]

[15] For example by Westlake (1935), 31–33.

[16] A few examples among many: Doulgeri-Intzesiloglou (1994, 1996, 1997) on Pherai; *I.Atrax.* (Tziafalias et al. 2016) on the inscriptions of Atrax; and the Canadian–Greek Kastro Kallithea Project directed by Sophia Karapanou and Margriet Haagsma (see Haagsma 2014 for an overview; a recent report in Haagsma et al. 2015). An important forerunner to such sub-regional studies is the work of Béquignon on Pherai (1937a) and on the Spercheios valley (1937b).

The present book focuses chiefly on the *ethnos*/regional level, while frequently examining its intersection with the local. After all, expressions of *ethnos*-identity normally took place on the local level, when a group or an individual chose to espouse the pan-Thessalian perspective for reasons driven by the particular conditions of the time and place. And the formation of *ethnos*-identity stimulated divergence and dissent, as communities chose to emphasise an alternative myth-history, such as an origin before the Thessaloi arrived. The regional focus will reveal, not obscure, these divergent voices wherever they may be discerned. Nonetheless, it is important constantly to recognise the superficiality of the project of ethnogenesis, at any rate many of its ingredients, compared with routine realities of Thessalian lives. An example is the hero Thessalos himself; for all that he and his descendants are pivotal in the development of the Thessalian story, for most Thessalian communities he would have been a figure of fleeting importance (if any), compared with the heroes and deities of their own local area.

3. Thessaly as a natural and political space

So ethnogenesis in Thessaly as elsewhere was a project, a process of intentional manufacture. But the land of Thessaly was entirely real, and from the bird's eye perspective of the Barrington Atlas seems to have its own inherent coherence. Historians have attributed to the distinct and distinctive Thessalian landscape a key role in promoting political unification in the Archaic period.[17] However, this simple equation requires critical examination. As Chapter 1 establishes, Thessaly was by no means precocious in either ethnogenesis or *koinon*-formation, seeming to engage in these processes a little after regions with far less geographical unity. Moreover, borders and border conflicts are important stimuli behind a community's desire to articulate its distinct identity, and the sheer size of Thessaly meant that many poleis would not have been near the boundary between Thessaly and not-Thessaly; rather, the edges they would have experienced routinely were those between the *chōra* of one polis and that of the neighbouring one, and we know – albeit largely from later sources because of the dating of most inscriptions – that territorial disputes between poleis were a reality of Thessalian life.[18] It is instructive to compare the vast expanse of the Thessalian plains with the micro-*ethnē* of

[17] See, for example, McInerney (1999), 173: 'Although Thessaly in the fifth and fourth centuries was eclipsed by the poleis of southern Greece, in the Archaic period it achieved a degree of unity and organization unmatched elsewhere in Greece. This was the result of a variety of factors. Environmentally, Thessaly is well suited to unification … .'

[18] See, for example, Chandezon (2003), 75–91, nos 16–18.

the Spercheios valley and central Greece, where grazing land, passes and routes were frequently contested and identities forged in the crucible of endemic low-level conflict. Such a geopolitical environment was as likely to stimulate ethnogenesis as was Thessaly's extensive land, perhaps more so. Moreover, Thessaly's geographical unity is in part the product of the kind of map-gazing that is a staple of the modern historian's craft but which the ancients did not often do.

From the bird's eye view, Thessaly takes the form of two large interlinked plains (see Map 1). For convenience, these will be referred to as the east and west plains, though because their alignment is diagonal the terms are somewhat inexact.[19] Most of the eastern plain consisted of the tetrad of Pelasgiotis, comprising poleis (such as Larisa, Atrax, Krannon and Pherai) that bulk disproportionately large in ancient literary accounts, in the production and the modern publication of inscriptions and in the amount of archaeological excavation and publication. The western plain – which has tended to be far less explored and understood by historians,[20] though this imbalance is diminishing[21] – comprises Hestiotis, in the north-western corner (whose most famous polis is Trikka, home of an important Asklepios-cult); Thessaliotis, comprising the poleis of Kierion and Metropolis and the sanctuary of Athena Itonia at (modern) Philia; and Phthiotis. Phthiotis, whose foremost polis was Pharsalos, occupies the south-eastern corner of the western plain; east of it, across a chain of hills projecting north from Mount Othrys, is the coastal plain of Achaia Phthiotis, one of the perioikic regions of Thessaly.

At this point it is necessary to stop and consider the terms tetrads and *perioikis*. As we shall see, the tetrads were created in the late sixth century

19 The region's geology consists of two zones, their shared boundary running diagonally NW–SE: see Schneider (1979), 47.

20 Through most of the twentieth century western Thessaly benefited far less, and more slowly, from advances in economics, education and agriculture entering Thessaly from the eastern side, and this broader difference is certainly a factor in its historiographical obscurity. See Sivignon (1979), 40–41. In fact, however, it was the attempt in the 1970s to boost its agricultural productivity and economic importance that did most harm to the preservation of archaeological material: in this process, ancient mounds (settlement and burial) were levelled and land cleared and drained. See Orengo et al. (2015).

21 Some recent archaeological projects have started to redress the balance somewhat, illuminating both individual sites (see, for example, the report on striking new discoveries at Vlochos, in Vaïopoulou et al. 2020), and the area more widely (e.g. Orengo et al. 2015; Krahtopoulou et al. 2018). The IGEAN project (*Innovative geophysical approaches for the study of early agricultural villages of Neolithic Thessaly*) applies new archaeological methods to recovering lost landscapes in Thessaly, across the region. See https://igean.ims.forth.gr/.

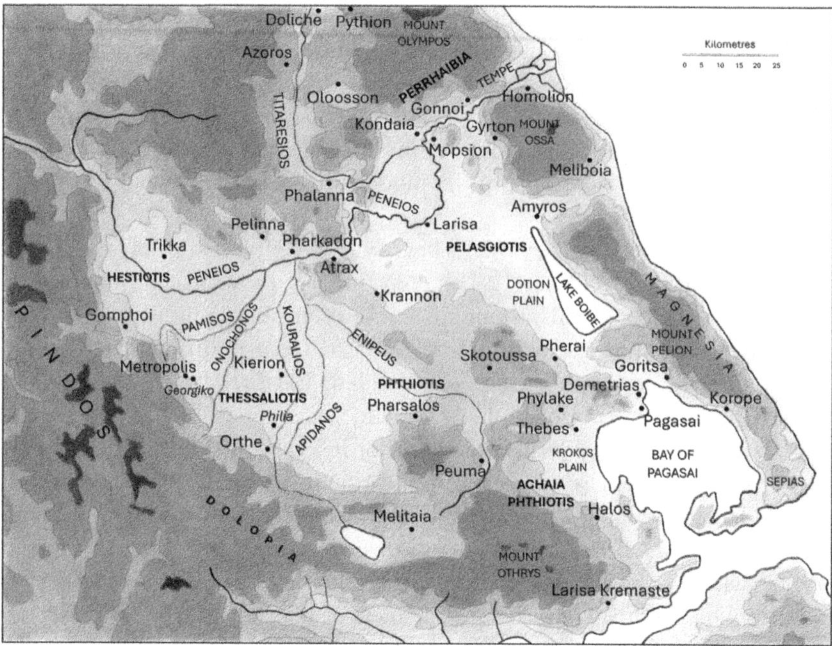

Map 1. Thessaly. © Rosemary Aston 2023

BC, an event of great significance for this study; thereafter, they appear with reasonable frequency in non-Thessalian texts and occasionally in Thessalian inscriptions. However, their practical importance appears to have been slight. Chapter 5 will identify some of their functions within Thessalian political organisation, but their impact on the daily lives of ordinary Thessalians was probably limited. They are the cornerstone of Aleuas' military reforms as envisaged by Helly, but, as we shall see, there is good reason for scepticism in that regard. In this book they will be used rather as Strabo and his ilk used them, as convenient ways of referring to sub-regional zones. This convenience reflects the fact that they do mirror, and must have emerged out of, the interaction of certain settlement clusters, as will be discussed below. However, it was possible for a community on the boundary between tetrads to belong to one or the other depending on the date and the source, and which side of the line it was considered to fall would have made little difference to life within the polis in question.

The picture is comparable when we consider the *perioikoi*. This term was not in common usage in this sense in antiquity,[22] but in modern historiography it is routinely used to designate the immediate neighbours of the

[22] The term is only used, in fact, by Xenophon (6.1.19): discussion in Sprawski (2008), 131–35.

Thessalians: the Perrhaiboi to the north, the Phthiotic Achaians to the south-east, the Magnetes along the eastern seaboard and the Dolopes on the southern fringe of the Pindos, adjoining Thessaliotis. This book will, for practical purposes, refer to '*perioikoi*' and 'perioikic *ethnē*', in contrast with the tetrads, or 'tetradic Thessaly', the home of the Thessaloi. The ancients recognised a difference: the Perrhaiboi, Magnetes, Achaioi and Dolopes were not Thessaloi. At times, this ethnic distinction was extremely important to the process of defining and demarcating the Thessalian *ethnos*. However, in practical terms the distinction was shaky. People travelled freely between tetrads and *perioikoi*; with them went livestock, goods, customs, speech patterns. Thessaly may look on the map like a bifurcated bowl with steep and definite sides, but those sides were in fact highly permeable, pierced by passes through which armies (famously) and herdsmen (more obscurely) moved into and out of the region.[23]

4. Thessaly as a linguistic area

The permeability of Thessaly's boundaries is amply reflected in the linguistic tendencies of the Thessalians, in as much as they can be reconstructed from the epigraphic record, scant as it is before the Hellenistic period. Handbooks of ancient Greek dialects will invariably supply a list of forms in use in Thessaly, as revealed by inscriptions.[24] Behind this list, however, various complexities lie. When we talk of the Thessalian dialect, what we chiefly mean is the dialect found in the inscriptions of Pelasgiotis, especially Larisa; this is in part because this area is disproportionately represented in the available epigraphic record, but it is also the case that when one moves into west Thessaly one encounters some differences, especially influence from North West Greek.[25] Even at the level of individual poleis there were probably local variations in usage. All in all, to speak of the Thessalian dialect as if it were a homogeneous and immutable thing is, of course, misleading.

[23] See Kilian (1975). More recently, the work done by Pikoulas on the passes linking Thessaly with neighbouring regions to the north and west has emphasised the permeability of the region's boundaries. See Pikoulas (2008, 2009 and 2012). Hammond (1931–1932), 139–47, retains its value: the discussion is old, but based on a great deal of personal observation, including of early twentieth century pastoralism. See also Helly (1973, vol. I, 8–12) on routes between Thessaly and Macedon in the area of Gonnoi; Reinders and Prummel (1998) on pastoral mobility in the territory of Hellenistic New Halos.

[24] Buck (1955) retains its essential utility; see also, however, García-Ramón (1975); Blümel (1982).

[25] On the dialect variations of Hestiaiotis see Helly (1970), 164–82.

Nonetheless, as long as one bears in mind the inevitable shades of variation on the subregional level, it is possible to describe the region's linguistic tendencies as distinct from those of other regions.[26] There is enough consistency across the region to make it clear that certain forms – such as, for example, ου for ω and the patronymic adjective[27] – would have had a 'Thessalian flavour'.[28] There are also forms that would have caused some challenge of comprehension for, say, an Athenian visitor, and would have left him or her with the clear sense of having been in a region with its own linguistic character.[29]

This is enhanced by the fact that on the whole the use of dialect in the adjoining perioikic *ethnē* was relatively slight once the Hellenistic koine was in circulation.[30] The difficulty underlying this observation is that the vast majority of available inscriptions from these areas are Hellenistic and later, so

26 Helly (2018) supplies an important collation and reconsideration of the key documents that illustrate Thessalian forms and their shades of variation across the region, interacting with 'the diffusion of the same type of alphabet across all parts of Thessaly' (p. 352).

27 Morpurgo-Davies (1968).

28 Surely features such as ου for ω tell us about the Thessalian accent; however, it is interesting that Thessalian speech is not 'spoofed' in Attic comedy, as Boiotian and Laconian are. There is, however, a possible sign of Athenian awareness of the Thessalian dialect in the form of the famous dinos from Pharsalos, painted by Sophilos (Athens NM 15499). The chariot-race scene on the pot (or, rather, on a large surviving fragment) is labelled by the painter ΠΑΤΡΟϘΛΥΣ ΑΤΛΑ, 'games of/for Patroklos'. Baurain-Rebillard (1998) observes that Sophilos was probably perfectly capable of writing the 'correct' Attic *Patroklous* (*Patrokleos*, contracted), and suggests that he was trying to capture the Thessalian dialect to match the linguistic tendencies of the pot's destination. If so, Sophilos was intriguingly wrong: vowel shifts to υ are somewhat more noticeable in Boiotian. Would his attitude have been 'Well, it's all Aeolic'? Finally, it is worth mentioning Parthenios' *Erotica Pathemata* 24, in which a man wishing to hide his identity puts on a Thessalian accent (θετταλίζων τῇ φωνῇ), indicating not only an external awareness of the Thessalian linguistic character but also perhaps a perception that Thessalian speech was distinctive enough to be a useful vocal disguise.

29 For example, δαύχνα for δάφνη ('laurel'), or βέλλομαι instead of βούλομαι ('I wish/want'). The same Athenian, visiting Larisa for example, might have been baffled by an apparent reference to the harbour, λιμήν; surely Larisa had no access to the sea? Walking confusedly thither he would have found himself in the market-place, for Thessalians in Pelasgiotis sometimes used λιμήν where an Athenian would say ἀγορά. (See, for example, *IG* IX.2 517, line 40.)

30 Alternatives to dialect did exist before Alexander the Great, as Niehoff-Panagiotidis reminds us (1994, 197–222). However, for the most part, it is only from the Hellenistic period that we have sufficient Thessalian inscriptions to be able to observe the patterns at work. It should be noted that the relative scarcity of dialect inscriptions from Hellenistic Magnesia and Achaia Phthiotis surely reflects the high degree of Macedonian involvement in those areas (on which see Chapter 7), rather than purely linguistic factors.

that we cannot accurately gauge their linguistic habits before the establishment of the koine; nonetheless, from the third century onwards we can see a clear disinclination on their part to adopt the dialect forms used so frequently by their Thessalian neighbours, especially for public documents.[31] Nowhere is this more starkly visible than in the dossier of third-century *asylia* inscriptions from Kos. The communities granting *asylia* passed decrees to that effect at home; the texts of these decrees were then displayed by the Koans in the Asklepieion itself. On one large block were inscribed decrees from Gonnoi (Perrhaibia), Phthiotic Thebes (Achaia Phthiotis), Homolion (Magnesia) and Megara.[32] Each records the favourable decision of the community in question; there are some repeated formulae and phrases, but apart from that a different wording is used in each. The whole text is in koine, without obvious dialect variation according to place. As Helly remarks, this use of koine 'est conforme aux habitudes de chancellerie de ces cités au 3e s. av. J.-C.'[33] A different situation is encountered in *SEG* 53.851[1], which contains two further decrees from Thessalian poleis, unfortunately unidentifiable. Here the dialect throughout is Thessalian, and this takes us from the *perioikis* into (probably) Pelasgiotis. It seems very likely that Larisa was one of the cities, since she was especially energetic in prosecuting trans-Aegean connections at this time (see Chapter 7). Thus we have a clear and deliberate distinction between perioikic *ethnē* and 'Thessaly proper', a distinction that is also indicated through language (koine for the *perioikoi*, dialect for the Thessalians).

The ethnic significance of dialect is enhanced rather than reduced by the practice of code-switching of which Thessalians, in certain circumstances, were perfectly capable.[34] Dialect – like material culture, as the next section will discuss – does not have to be automatic and unthinking: it can

[31] Perrhaibian Gonnoi illustrates this especially clearly because of its copious and well-published epigraphic record. All of its public inscriptions from the third century are in pure koine. In the second century some dialect forms are allowed to creep into a small number of public inscriptions. On the other hand, dialect usage is far more strongly represented in private texts such as dedications. For the figures and discussion see Bubeník (1989), 146–47.

[32] *SEG* 53.850. See Rigsby (1996), nos 19–22; however, no. 21 could be identified as a decree of Gonnoi only with the discovery of a new fragment of the stone: see Bosnakis and Hallof (2003), 229–31.

[33] 'In keeping with the practices of the administration of these cities in the third century BC': Helly (2004a), 89; *contra* Rigsby (1996), 132, who finds the koine surprising (but without good reason).

[34] There is scope for a far more extensive analysis of this topic than this book can undertake; moreover, such a study could also take into account variations in the use of epichoric letter-forms, now that much of the relevant material has been collated in Doulgeri-Intzesiloglou (2000); see also Jeffery (1990), 96–99; Johnston (2021), 115–17. Jeffery's broad conclusion concerning the material she examined (which was in itself a limited and unrepresentative corpus) was that Thessaly had a regional repertoire of

be employed to make statements about identity. It is fascinating to observe that the Thessalians maintained the co-existence of dialect and koine with relative tenacity. Bubeník's comparison of Thessalian with Boiotian habits in this regard is illuminating, despite some problematic aspects of his data.[35] In the two regions, both using a form of the Aeolic dialect, the adoption of koine followed quite different patterns. Boiotia was far slower to adopt it than Thessaly; however, pure dialect was retained in Thessalian usage into the first century BC in public documents at the polis level, whereas in Boiotia it had ceased to be used for public documents by the end of the second century. Therefore, the ready adoption of koine in Thessalian public documents did not spell the swift eradication of dialect across the board. In Boiotia, the rise of koine, though slower to start, was more rapid than in Thessaly, in both public and private texts. And the trajectory is different in shape as well as in velocity: in Thessaly, the use of koine for public documents actually peaked in the second century BC; in Boiotia the peak was in the first. Also noteworthy is the fact that a far larger proportion of Boiotian inscriptions than Thessalian are in dialect with some koineisation. The Boiotians resisted pure koine, and retained their dialect, more assiduously than the Thessalians in the third and (to a lesser extent) second centuries; however, they allowed a greater 'contamination' of dialect with koine. In Thessaly, there was a greater tendency to keep dialect and koine apart; when creating an inscription, a clearer choice was made between dialect and koine, and less mingling of the two occurred.[36] This shows a strong awareness of the linguistic distinction, and a desire to maintain it.

The operation of code-switching is especially striking on the rare occasions when shifts between dialect and koine are made within a single inscription.[37] The famous Thessalian example of an inscription of this type is from Larisa and dates to the late third century BC.[38] It records two letters sent consecutively to the polis by the Macedonian king Philip V; both letters are quoted in full. The first letter instructs the Larisaians to overcome their economic troubles and population depletion by enrolling new citizens from among the other Thessalians and Greeks of other areas who are living in

letter-forms, but one that showed strong affinities with regions to the south, especially Phokis. On this see also Helly (2018).

35 Bubeník (1989), 138–47. He appears to classify Gonnoi as Pelasgiotic, whereas in fact it was a Perrhaibian town and its dialect profile is rather different from those of the other poleis he examines. See Bubeník (1989), 142–43. However, the effect of this error is actually to exaggerate koine use rather than dialect use, and it does not invalidate his basic findings, merely the actual figures. Further on the co-existence of dialect and koine see Niehoff-Panagiotidis (1994), 247–72. Specifically on the Boiotian situation: Vottéro (1996).

36 As noted by Bubeník (1989), 161.

37 For an instructive non-Thessalian example, see Minon (2009).

38 *IG* IX.2 517. For the dating of the letters see Habicht (1970), 273–79.

the city. This is followed by the text of a decree of the city, passed in 217 BC, essentially doing as the king instructed. Next comes the text of the second letter, rebuking the Larisaians for having erased the names of the newly enrolled citizens and so essentially transgressing the terms of their first decree. Finally there is a second decree, passed in 215 BC, that the city should carry out the terms of the king's second letter and re-enrol the citizens. As far as we know, Philip's instructions were adhered to thereafter.

That the letters are in koine is of course natural. However, koine is not used for the preamble or for the two decrees; these are in full Pelasgiotic dialect. This serves to differentiate the two types of document that the stone carries; however, Bubeník is surely right to see it as a gestural decision as well. In the face of ultimate and undeniable Macedonian power, the polis of Larisa chooses its local mode of language to assert its separate identity and preserve something of its cultural autonomy, even if its political autonomy is largely fictional at this point. Because the decrees follow the wording of the letters very closely in places, the visual and linguistic effect is very striking: we find the bland koine of the king transformed – translated, almost – into a very different mode of language. To give one small sample: 'Πετραῖος καὶ Ἀνάγκιππος καὶ Ἀριστόνους ὡς ἀπὸ τῆς πρεσβείας ἐγένοντο,' writes Philip, 'ἐνεφάνιζόν μοι ὅτι καὶ ἡ ὑμετέρα πόλις διὰ τοὺς πολέμους προσδεῖται πλεόνων οἰκητῶν.' ('Petraios and Anankippos and Aristonous, when they returned from their embassy, made clear to me that your polis, because of the wars, is seriously short of inhabitants.')[39] The decree coverts this to: 'Πετραῖος καὶ Ἀνάγκιππος καὶ Ἀριστόνοος, οὖς ἀτ τᾶς πρεισβείας ἐγένονθο, ἐνεφανίσσοεν αὐτοῦ, πὸκ κί καὶ ἁ ἀμμέουν πόλις διὲ τὸς πολέμος ποτεδέετο πλειόνουν τοῦν κατοικεισόντουν'.

The same linguistic contrast continues throughout. Did the Larisaians choose to mirror the text of the letters so closely, or did the king actually stipulate that his letters be quoted in full? Or was it simply customary practice? Although royal letters abound from the Hellenistic period, this is our only surviving example of letters and decrees inscribed together, so we cannot ascertain what was usual. If the arrangement of the inscription – letter, decree, letter, decree – was decided by the Larisaians rather than by Philip, as seems likely, the effect is very striking: it comes across as an assertion of loyalty, of taking the king's words *very seriously indeed*, while all the time dialect is used to turn the situation into a matter of local decision-making. The king's words become the words of the Larisaian leaders.[40] Using koine for the decrees would not have achieved this effect.[41]

[39] Note that, throughout this book, translations are my own unless otherwise specified.

[40] Brixhe and Vottéro (2004), 18–20.

[41] The well-known historical circumstances of this example make the code-switching relatively easy to understand. Motivations are more obscure in cases where context

Code-switching is one form of deliberate and significant linguistic usage; another is the avoidance of dialect. In Thessaly, as indeed elsewhere, verse inscriptions adopted a literary register from which epichoric elements are deliberately excluded despite their prevalence in prose inscriptions of the time.[42] And, indeed, it is noteworthy that the content of the verse inscriptions also sometimes stresses the non-local, as in the following two examples.

> You have in no way disgraced the glory of the city to lie here,
> the glory of broad-landed Atrax,
> Theotimos son of Menyllos, together with the best men
> of the Greeks in the plain of Tanagra.[43]

And:

> This earth hides Menon, the son of Pothon, who
> Hellas hoped would decorate Thessaly with
> garlands. Orestes honoured his grave, and all
> his city feels grief because of the dead man's moderation.[44]

is wholly lacking. Such a case is the late fourth- or third-century dedication by one Tolemaios, in Larisa (*IG* IX.2 598). The white marble statue-base of the votive carries on one side Τολεμαῖος/ἀνέθηκε, while on the other side is Τολεμαῖος/Λεόντειος/ὀνέθεικε. Hence, one side speaks in koine, the other in dialect (complete with patronymic adjective). It is interesting that no patronymic is included in the koine text; this might indicate non-citizen status. Was the dialect inscription carved in later than the koine one, after citizenship was formally conferred, as a celebration of that elevation? We cannot know. Overall, Tolemaios seems to have wanted to signal a certain duality of affiliation: he was both a Thessalian and part of the wider Greek world that koine represented. See Kontogiannis (1985), 115–16.

42 That is not to say that epichoric touches cannot be discerned: see Helly (2019) for examples. For the occasional mixture of dialect elements in verse inscriptions see also Lorenz (2019), 100; *I.Atrax* 161, 162 (later fifth and early fourth century BC respectively). Such inclusions are surely accidental, and would have occurred naturally when the local dialect was being deliberately suppressed to achieve a literary tone.

43 Lorenz (2019), no. G51; *I.Atrax* 160 (discussion in Helly 2004b):

> οὔ τι καταισχύνας πόλεōς κλέος ἐνθάδε κεῖαι
> Ἄτραγος εὐρυχόρō Θεσσαλίᾱ στέφανον
> τεύχōν, ὃ Θεότιμε, Μενύλλου παῖ, σὺν ἀρίστο<ι>ς
> ἀνδρ<ά>σιν Ἑλλε̄́νōν ἐν Τανάγρας πεδίōι.

(trans. Osborne and Rhodes, adapted).

44 Peek (1960), 76–77, no. 81; Lorenz (2019), no. G34:

> κρύπτει μὲν χθὼν ἥδε Μένωνα Πόθωνος, ὃν̣
> Ἑλλὰς | ἤλπισε κοσμήσειν Θεσσαλίαν στεφ[ά]-
> νοις· | οὗ τύμβον τίμησεν Ὀρέστης, σωφρο̣-
> σύνης δὲ | οὕνεκα πένθος ἔχει πᾶσα πό̣-
> λις φθιμένου.

This is the standard language of funerary inscriptions;[45] moreover, in keeping with the linguistic register, the dead men in both instances are cast as valued members not only of their respective poleis but also of the wider Greek community. It is quite predictable, and in line with Greek epigraphic practice more generally, to find this type of text shunning epichoric language in favour of the panhellenic language of praise and accomplishment, though, as Morpurgo-Davies points out, some Aeolic elements would have resembled epic and so would potentially have been quite suitable for a lofty tone of praise-verse.[46] Nonetheless, they are generally excluded.

The deliberate avoidance of dialect in verse inscriptions of a certain gravity is made more apparent by the case of Astioun son of Souos and his religious and poetic activity in Atrax in the early third century. Astioun signs himself as the composer of an elegant verse recording the creation of a nymph-sanctuary near the Peneios at Atrax:

> 'Do tell: who laboured over this structure and everything which stands in front of it,
> setting up votives with many sacrifices,
> below a flowering hill along the banks of the Peneios,
> where Naiads in delicate dress twirl with their feet?'
> 'To the Naiad Nymphs, in a beautiful-looking place,
> eagerly Arneklos erected a rock-made structure and
> silver horns(?), as soon as he pushed away
> his illness and regained his health.
> Elevating it with honours appropriate to immortals,
> the son of Souos gave splendour to the Naiads' precinct'.
> Astioun.[47]

[45] Helly finds faint shades of Thessalian linguistic colouring in the Theotimos epitaph, overlaid with panhellenic language and themes: Helly (2004b), 19–20. A further example of banal funerary language in a Thessalian epitaph is discussed by Santin (2008).

[46] Morpurgo-Davies (1987), 10–11.

[47] *I.Atrax* 83:

> [εἰπόν, τίς τόδε δῶμ]α̣ καὶ ἀ̣[ντί]α πᾶν ἐπόνη̣[σεν],
> [στήσας σὺν πολλ]οῖς θύμασιν ἀνθέματα,
> [ὄχθαισιν Πηνειοῦ ὑ]πὸλ̣ λόφον ἀνθεμ[ό]ε̣[ντα],
> [ἧι ποσὶ δινοῦντ]α̣ι Να̣ΐδε̣ς ἁβρόπεπλοι.
> Ν[α]ϊά̣[σ]ιν Νύμφαισι κατ̣’ ἀγλαοε̣[ι]δ̣έ̣α̣ χῶρον
> [δ]ῶ̣[μά] τ̣ε̣ ἵδ̣ρ̣[υ]σ[ε π]έ̣τ̣ρ̣οις καὶ [κέρατ’ ἀρ]γυρ̣έ̣α̣
> Ἄ̣ρ̣νεκλος προφρόνως, ἐκλυομ̣[ένην ὄθ’] ὑγείαν
> ἐξα̣[ῦτις] λά̣[χ’] ἐ̣ή̣ν, νοῦσον ἀπω̣σ[άμενος]·
> αἷς πρέπει ἀθανάτους αὔξων τιμαῖσιν ὁ Σούου
> υἱὸς ἐπηγλάϊσεν Ναϊάδων τέμενος.
> Ἀστίουν.

The poem itself is in the high register of formal verse, and almost dialect-free, including the patronymic genitive on line 9.[48] When it comes to signing his own name, however, Astioun maintained the 'ou for ō' tendency of his region, and did not convert his name to Astiōn.[49] In a way, this fits in with a general tendency – not, however, without exceptions – that occurs when an artist signs a sculpture commissioned, as a dedication, by someone from a different region.[50] In such cases, the words of the dedication tend to be in the dialect of the dedicator, whereas the artist's signature is in the artist's own dialect. However, our cases do not mark ethnic separation, but rather the verse/prose distinction.[51]

This section has shown that to treat Thessaly simply as an undifferentiated linguistic area – or, to put it another way, to treat dialect as a simple indicator of ethnicity – is misleading. Instead, Thessaly would have been a patchwork of subregional linguistic variations, much of it now lost to view, all of it also subject to change over time. Moreover, though linguistic usage could be a matter of unthinking habit, it was not always so. Thessalian stonecutters, or the authorities behind them, quite often used language to emphasise or to play down their Thessalian identity. The picture is just as nuanced when we consider the relationship between identity and material culture.

(trans. Wagman, adapted). Wagman (2015, 92–93) suggests that Astioun was a local Pharsalian poet.

48 A shade of dialect exists in the form Souos, rather than Soös.

49 Note that in the same area of his city's land the same man put up a short text to accompany a dedication to the nymphs and Dionysos (*SEG* 45.554; *I.Atrax* 75): Νύμφαις: Διοννύσου/Ἀστίουν Σούειος ὀνέθεικε. Here the patronymic adjective is employed, as is the dialect form ὀνέθεικε and the geminated *nu* in the god's name.

50 Buck (1913).

51 That we are not dealing with a situation particular to authors'/artists' signatures is, furthermore, indicated by an example from third-century BC Larisa, where a grieving woman commissioned a white marble funerary stele for her dead son (*SEG* 42.522); here the deceased is named Thersōn in the metrical text, but underneath is the name Θέρσουν Θερσούνδαιος (Thersoun son of Thersoundas). Who is this Thersoun son of Thersoundas? Is the name of the deceased being repeated, extra-metrically? Or is it a family member who commissioned the monument or perhaps even composed the verse? That it is the deceased is strongly suggested by a comparable example in which the name and key signifiers of the deceased appear in dialect as a heading: (Πουτάλα Πουταλεία κόρα,/Τιτυρεία γυνά); under that are four lines of verse – elegiacs – in which the deceased reappears in koine, as Pōtala. *IG* IX.2 638; Lorenz (2019), no. 56 (Larisaian, third century BC). Plainly it is the verse/prose distinction that governs the dialect usage in such instances. For more juxtapositions of metrical koine and non-metrical dialect see Santin and Tziafalias (2013), 269. For further discussion of this feature of the Thersoun and Poutala texts, and the cultural context of Hellenistic Larisa see Santin (2018), 228–30.

5. Landscape, identity and material culture

We can identify some regional pottery styles and region-wide artefact distribution, but material culture is as likely to divide the region as to unite it, as likely to connect Thessalians with other Greeks as to tie them in to each other.[52] It would, of course, be simplistic to assume that we might locate Thessalian identity through an obvious regional coherence of object types and styles. A straightforward relationship between material culture and ethnicity has long since been dealt a fatal blow by the work of such as Jonathan Hall.[53] Nonetheless, it is interesting to observe the flourishing of certain sub-regional material trends, combined with others whose scope is, on the face of it at least, more regional. A separate book would be required to analyse them all (and such a volume would have great merit). Here, however, two examples will suffice to make the point.[54]

The first relates to Thessaliotis. This area seems to have had and fostered a strongly demarcated identity from a very early period. In it was the sanctuary of Athena Itonia at (modern) Philia, which, though much later accorded a federal role, in the Early Iron Age served a more local network of worshippers with ritual probably centred round dining in an open-air sacred space. Within the ambit of this important religious site, between the eighth and the fifth century BC, archaeologists have identified a distinctive material habit: the construction of apsidal houses.[55] These are known from sites elsewhere in the Greek world, such as Lefkandi,[56] and exist at other Thessalian sites in the Bronze Age,[57] but in the Early Iron Age and Archaic period their Thessalian distribution forms a strong cluster within

[52] See, for example, Coldstream (2003), 40–41: even here, however, the number of artefacts particular to Thessaly is significantly outnumbered by those shared with adjoining and connected places. For the pitfalls of trying to read ethnicity from the material record in any simplistic way based on the distribution of material homogeneity or trends see Morgan (2009a), 19–21.

[53] See esp. Hall (1997), 111–42: he argues that the true value of artefacts to the study of ancient ethnicity is not as an indication of ethnic identity in some absolute sense but as potentially involved in the ancient process of expressing ethnic affiliation or separation. Cf. Morgan (2001), 84–91; at p. 91 she observes that 'it is plain that artifact study must not mean ascribing ethnic significance to cultures – understanding material patterning (or assemblages) is useful only insofar as it reveals the symbolic resources available to those making strategic selections and the inherited burden of selections on which the next generation must act'. See also Luraghi (2014), 215–17.

[54] See now Canlas (2021), who analyses in detail the self-consciously archaising trends in Thessalian sanctuary and funerary architecture, especially in the later Classical and the Hellenistic periods.

[55] Karagiannopoulos (2017–2018).

[56] Lemos (2002), 140–50.

[57] For Middle Bronze Age examples in the vicinity of Pherai see Agnousiotis (2014).

the south-western part of the region, being found at Philia itself, Orphana, Neo Monastiri (ancient Proerna), Ermitsi (ancient Peirasia) and Anavra.[58] Strikingly, Pharsalos – on the eastern edge of the area and in a different tetrad – also had apsidal houses. Within this group of sites, the ceramic record also displays some consistencies. In addition to the geographical coherence of the group, we see a remarkable continuity of the apsidal house type over several centuries, the maintenance of a material tradition against the backdrop of wider political and historical change. Such patterns in the archaeological record are unsurprising, and reflect in part practicalities such as the circulation of craftsmen. However, the presence of strongly interrelated cult sites – the sanctuary of Athena Itonia, that of Apollo at Lianokokkala near Metropolis and the probable *heroön* of Aiatos at Georgiko – suggests the more self-conscious development and maintenance of shared culture. As we shall see in Chapter 3, this area had a special role in the formation of Thessalian origin-mythology; it was part of the development of regional identity, but was careful to maintain its own place within it.

A very different picture is given when we turn to patterns in burial types across Thessaly. On the one hand, Early Iron Age Thessalian communities were marked by the diversity of their funerary preferences, with cist graves, pits graves, tholos tombs and chamber tombs all in use.[59] On the other hand, a regional specificity is discernible in the prevalence and the remarkable persistence of the construction and use of corbel-vaulted tombs covered by earth mounds and containing round (tholos) or rectilinear chambers.[60] Even in the Early Iron Age, the distribution of these tombs in Thessaly was significant enough for them to constitute a regional practice. Interestingly, Thessaly is one of the regions that do not fully accord with Luce's observations concerning the overlap between the dialect map of Greece and the map of tomb types and funerary practices.[61] It shares some funerary features with Boiotia, with whom its linguistic affinities are clearly discernible, but not sufficient to create a definite continuum between the two regions; at the same time, the use of tholos tombs is clearly widespread enough in Thessaly – given the variations of archaeological excavation and publication – to justify Stamatopoulou's description of it as 'a diagnostic trait of Thessalian funerary archaeology'.[62] The complete absence of tholos-tombs in adjoining regions is also significant.

58 In general in Thessaly the apsidal building habit endures from the ninth to the fifth century BC: Karagiannopoulos (2017–2018); Stamatopoulou (2019), 32.

59 Georganas (2009); Panagiotopoulou (2020), 7.

60 Tholos tombs were made in Messenia until the ninth century BC, and there are examples also from Crete. However, on the Greek mainland Thessaly was unique in retaining the tholos type so long. Luce (2007), 44–47.

61 Luce (2014).

62 Stamatopoulou (2016), 182.

Their use was not a material practice that flowed over the edges of Thessaly by simple processes of influence and diffusion; it was obviously cultivated by the Thessalians as a marker of their shared regional character.

Whether in the Early Iron Age this diagnostic trait really amounts to *ethnic* self-consciousness, as Luce argues, we cannot say with any certainty. But the element of the intentional becomes more marked with the passage of time, as Thessalian communities maintained the tholos type long after their use had been abandoned elsewhere in Greece. By adapting Mycenaean burial structures, the tomb type recycled tradition in a way that would have become more and more striking as the Archaic period advanced into the early Classical.[63] Not only did the tomb type persist, but individual tholoi – at least, the larger earlier examples – were used for multiple burials over large periods of time.[64] Recent scholarship has rightly seen this not as an unthinking adherence to conservative practices, symptomatic of the artistic and technological sluggishness of the Thessalians,[65] but as the deliberate cultivation of links to the past and the status those links could bring.[66] The visibility of the structures made them ideal as declarations of status, and would have encouraged their competitive diffusion.[67] Especially at Krannon and Pharsalos, the later sixth and earlier fifth centuries seem to have seen a deliberate revival of the tomb type, and the fact that this coincides with the

[63] Georganas (2000); Georganas (2009), 197–98; Georganas (2011); Karouzou (2017), 354; Knodell (2013), 242–43; Knodell (2021), 168. A recent summary of the material is provided by Stamatopoulou and Katakouta (2020). For a detailed examination of an important example, at Chloe to the north of Pherai, see Arachoviti (1994). The date range of the tombs' production is extended if we accept the suggestion of Stamatopoulou and Katakouta (2020, 154) that the built chamber tomb with a corbelled pyramidal roof is essentially an adaptation of the tholos tomb; this type was in use at Krannon as late as the fourth century BC.

[64] Georganas (2009), 198.

[65] Thessalian backwardness: e.g. Westlake (1935), 17–18, 22; Larsen (1968), 13. While this perception no longer has currency among those working in the field, it is remarkable how prevalent it remains on the fringes of Classical scholarship; the entry on Thessaly in the *Encyclopedia of the Ancient Greek World* (Sacks 2005) is a good example. It is of course such mainstream publications aimed at a general readership that carry most weight beyond the narrow confines of academia, so if non-specialists have any view of Thessaly at all it is probably the old-fashioned one of the 'self-contained, horse-ranching aristocracy' and the land that 'remained politically and culturally backward'.

[66] Stamatopoulou (2016). See also Canlas (2021), 329–46: he makes an important connection with styles of sanctuary and temple in Thessaly, in which he detects a comparable preference for traditional and modest forms as a persistent and pervasive trend in Thessalian material culture.

[67] As Karouzou observes (2018, 170–71), there was a significant tendency to situate tholoi in flat areas with extensive sight-lines, and/or on major road-ways, thus ensuring their visibility.

period in which, for the first time, the Thessalian *ethnos* was being energetically articulated in Thessaly is surely not coincidental.[68] Therefore we can see that a material habit present in the Early Iron Age was perpetuated for ideological reasons amid a steady accumulation of archaising significance. As the custom persisted, it became an ever-stronger mode of signalling Thessalian identity.

At the same time, the tomb-type was neither universal nor unvaried. Even within specific cemeteries, the tholos tombs and their rectilinear-chambered counterparts were combined with very different burial modes; clearly the relatives of the dead had a range of possibilities to choose from, and there was no single mode for the expression of identity. Exactly why they chose as they did we cannot fully know, but, as Stamatopoulou has argued, the tholos type with its evocation of the myth-historical past can plausibly be connected with the activities of competing elite families.[69] The tholos and chamber tombs with earth mounds were widespread enough through the region to serve as a statement of Thessalian identity, while at the same time showing considerable local variation in their form. Thus even a clear regional style is shot through with a far more nuanced local aspect, constituting a competitive gesture. This combination of regional and subregional material tendencies is discernible also in the archaeological traces of cult.[70] We shall see, throughout this book, a very similar pattern pertain to the development of mythic traditions: stories about being Thessalian co-existed with stories allowing individual groups to strike out on a limb and claim a somewhat divergent identity.

Geography and landscape clearly have a part to play in shaping such tendencies in the material record, by shaping patterns of settlement and travel. In general, rivers are powerful agents of connectivity in Thessaly. From a map – or indeed from reading Strabo[71] – we might see rivers as borders in Thessaly, and therefore imagine that they limited movement and interaction; but in fact they are just as likely to draw together different communities living on opposite banks and along their course. The Spercheios and the Peneios exemplify this cogently. In Chapter 1 we shall see that the Spercheios sat at the heart of an area of transit between

68 Kravaritou (2012), 510.

69 Stamatopoulou (2016), 191–95; cf. Morgan (2006), 246–47.

70 Stamatopoulou observes (2021), 687: 'The similarities in both dedicatory practices and votives among the known Archaic Thessalian sanctuaries hint at the existence of a "koine" irrespective of the various population groups that are recorded as inhabiting the respective regions. Differentiations, such the deposition of weapons and tripods and the concentration of imported "valuable" goods at Philia and, to a lesser extent, Pherai, are related to the specific role of each site.'

71 Strabo 9.5.1: Thessaly as bracketed by the Peneios in the north and the Spercheios to the south.

northern and central Greece, where a patchwork of small *ethnē* shared passes, grazing lands and religious sites. As for the Peneios, it might seem a clear boundary between Thessaly and Perrhaibia, but in fact it probably heightened interaction between those ethnic groups. In addition to its importance as a pastoral resource, for watering livestock, it supplied fish for human consumption.[72] That it linked Thessalian communities on the east–west axis is clear from the co-operative coinage of the early fifth century, produced chiefly by poleis on or near the Peneios and its major branches.[73] So the Peneios, flowing from the north-west corner of Hestiotis (Fig. 1) to its debouchment east of Tempe, breaks down the divide between west and east.

The Peneios has numerous tributaries, one of which, the Enipeus, flows near Pharsalos; the settlements around the Enipeus were strongly interconnected, Pharsalos being especially prominent in the grouping from the Early Iron Age.[74] Key aspects of its material culture pull Pharsalos westward and suggest contact with the poleis of Thessaliotis.[75] At the same time, important aspects of its mythology reveal a design to align itself eastwards and southwards, and its archaeological remains from the Early Iron Age also reveal links with eastern Thessaly and, further afield, with the area of the so-called Euboian koine.[76] The name Phthiotis ensured the preservation of its connection with the Homeric kingdom of Phthia, realm of Achilles, and it maintained an important cult of Achilles' mother Thetis within its territory. Achilles' contingents at Troy included also the Phthiotic Achaioi and the peoples of the Spercheios valley. Its epic credentials angled Pharsalos in this direction. Thus it was genuinely liminal; geography shaped behaviour and connections but was not the only factor in the formation of political and cultural alignment.

Another striking example of variation and flexibility is the polis of Pherai. In the Bronze Age Pherai was part of a network of settlements otherwise focused on the Bay of Volos.[77] It was one of the major centres

[72] See, for example, *IG* IX.2 521 (esp. lines 30–37) – this late 3rd-century BC boundary record mentions *keletrai*, a word that Helly plausibly argues to refer to fish-traps: Helly (1999); Chandezon (2003), 129.

[73] As Kaczmarek observes (2015, 68–76), pre-Classical settlements in Thessaly tend to be distributed near rivers and in the prime cultivable land of their alluvial basins. In the Classical period a 'prolific building phase' (80) sees settlements established in less prime farmland as population growth necessitates fuller exploitation of the region's natural resources.

[74] Katakouta (2012): she emphasises the place of Pharsalos within a local landscape in which the river shapes herding and travel practices.

[75] Apsidal buildings have been noted above; coinage is also significant in this regard: see Georgiou (2015), 58–60.

[76] Stamatopoulou (2012–2013), 45–46.

[77] Pantou (2010).

Fig. 1. The Peneios in north-western Thessaly, looking east, near Kalambaka. Photograph: author's own

of Bronze Age Thessaly and its significance received no discernible check when the Mycenaean culture ended in the region, despite a slight temporary diminution of the site.[78] Its importance was largely the result of a highly favourable position with sea access and connection to major roads, and these factors did not lose their importance.[79] Signs of civic significance in the late Archaic period include the construction of the Doric temple of Ennodia in the sixth century, a major project to enhance an existing cult site of local

[78] Apostolopoulou-Kakavoyanni (1990); Georganas (2008), 279; Doulgeri-Intzesiloglou (1994), 77–79; Doulgeri-Intzesiloglou and Arachoviti (2009); Adrymi-Sismani (2012), 120–21; Karouzou (2017), 346–47. The fact that the modern town of Velestino is located exactly on the ancient site has hampered archaeological investigation of the ancient urban space. Geophysical survey techniques have recently identified interesting features such as a rectilinear street pattern, but the dating of this arrangement is not elucidated (Donati et al. [2017]).

[79] Di Salvatore (1994); Georganas (2008), 274; Knodell (2021), 94. Pagasai is called the harbour of Pherai by Theopompos (*FGrH* 115 F 53) but this connection was a longstanding one. Whereas the settlements on the Bay of Volos itself diminished in their independent power, Pherai expanded its dominance in that zone.

importance.[80] As well as being archaeologically attested, this situation is reflected in mythology, such as in the family relationship between Iolkian Jason and the Pheraian family of Admetos. In later centuries, Pherai retained its maritime connection, unusual in Thessaly, controlling the port at Pagasai.[81] Politically, however, it was part of Pelasgiotis, and it was an active part of the group of poleis minting the first Thessalian coinage in the early fifth century BC. This exemplifies the way in which the landscape of Thessaly is cross-hatched in different ways by different forms of association, with political organisation, myth-history and topography connecting communities in different directions and configurations.

So geography did not create a simple primordial unity in Thessaly. It was, however, a vital part of the process of articulating the shared identity of the Thessalian *ethnos* from the early fifth century. The myth-cult bundle promoted on early fifth-century coinage minted by several Thessalian poleis is strongly related to landscape. It presented Thessaly as the birthplace of the first horse, because the region's ability to produce excellent horses was well recognised by this time – had been, in fact, as early as the *Iliad*. It presented the fertile Thessalian plains as the work of divine engineering, and it gave the Peneios and its tributaries a starring role too, distributing vital waters but also preventing their harmful accumulation. It advertised arable wealth through the grain motif. When Thessalian poleis sought clear emblems of what Thessaly was and meant, it was to the natural landscape and its fruits that they had recourse. They were able, too, to contrast their land with that of the perioikic *ethnē*. Their land produced horses, Magnesia produced centaurs. Centaurs were not universally rejected by the tetradic Thessalians; Cheiron, in his cave home on Mount Pelion, was the lynchpin of early Thessalian mythology, linking west-Thessalian Asklepios with Iolkian Jason and south-Thessalian Achilles. The *phēr theios* retained his potency as a way of thinking about the past of the region through the childhood of its heroes. But rowdier specimens of the centaur race could provide an antithesis to the world of settled and prosperous agriculture, and they lived in the mountainous fringe, sometimes under the control of the Thessaloi but representing a very different symbolic space.

6. A note on beginnings and endings

Broad as it is in its chronological range, this book may still seem to raise questions about its time parameters. Why does it cover this particular span of time, beyond the sheer necessity of keeping it within manageable bounds?

[80] On the earlier importance of the sanctuary see Georganas (2008); Karouzou (2018), 126–27. It was an important metallurgical centre: Orfanou (2015).

[81] Theopompos *FGrH* 115 F 53.

Its starting point is governed by the material itself, in effect, because it is only in the Archaic period that the Thessaloi as an idea actually appear in our surviving textual sources. To this an obvious rejoinder is that regional identity need not depend on a shared name, and that Bronze Age (even, for that matter, Neolithic) Thessaly repay just as amply the study of how the region operated as a unit and how its sense of collective being was articulated through material culture. It is indeed true that Thessalian society in these periods emerges fascinatingly from the archaeological record and that the study of interactions between groups and communities in Neolithic and Bronze Age Thessaly has produced some especially important recent scholarship.[82] However, this is not really the *version* of Thessaly, of Thessalian identity, that this book pursues. As stated above, my theme is the manufacture and subsequent adaptation of the entities Thessaloi and Thessalia as political mechanisms for achieving a new kind of regional coherence from the sixth century onward. At no point do I mean to claim that this Thessaly is the only one, or even the most important. That said, it will be essential at various points to consider the legacy of Bronze Age culture in later Thessalian society, especially in mythology.

Where the book should end is, if anything, a thornier question. On the one hand, the arrival of strong Roman involvement after Flamininus' declaration of Greek freedom in 197 BC is obviously a significant juncture, and the dedicated study of Roman Thessaly is a very valuable strand in recent and current scholarship;[83] stopping at that point of major change is sensible. And yet the cut-off cannot be complete. Some aspects of third-century Thessaly can only make sense when we look forward to developments in the second century; and of course some crucial ancient sources are later still. Of these, the most significant is obviously Strabo. Steeped as Strabo is in the Homeric depiction of Thessaly,[84] nonetheless he is a product of his own Augustan age, and that perspective must be taken into account. To sum up, the chief focus of this book reaches up to the beginning of the second century BC, but there will be many points at which it will be necessary to look past that terminus.

82 For example: Pentedeka (2012) on the production, circulation and exchange of pottery in Neolithic Thessaly; Eder (2009) re-evaluating Thessaly's role as a northern frontier region in the Mycenaean world; Pantou (2010) and Adrymi-Sismani (1999–2001, 2006) on the Mycenaean settlements around the Pagasitic Gulf.

83 For example, Graninger's treatment (2011a) of the post-196 Thessalian *koinon* is a seminal contribution to this area. To this should be added, in particular, several important articles by Bouchon (esp. Bouchon 2008) and the doctoral thesis of Kaczmarek (2015).

84 On the place of Homer in Strabo's work and the connection with the key theme of ἔκλειψις, extinction, see Wallace (1979), 171; Clarke (1999), 248–49; Biraschi (2005); Lightfoot (2017).

1

Thessaly and the *ethnos* in Archaic central Greece

The early articulations of the Thessalian *ethnos* cannot be studied in isolation. Of course its development over centuries was subject to a range of influences, some reaching across wide geographical distances; nonetheless, it is particularly important to view Thessaly in relation to the *ethnē* to the south, in central Greece – in particular, those of the Spercheios valley, and the Phokians, Lokrians and Boiotians (see Map 2). There are several reasons for the particular importance of this context. First, the geography of southern Thessaly facilitates interaction with those *ethnē*. Second, this interaction was further increased by membership of the

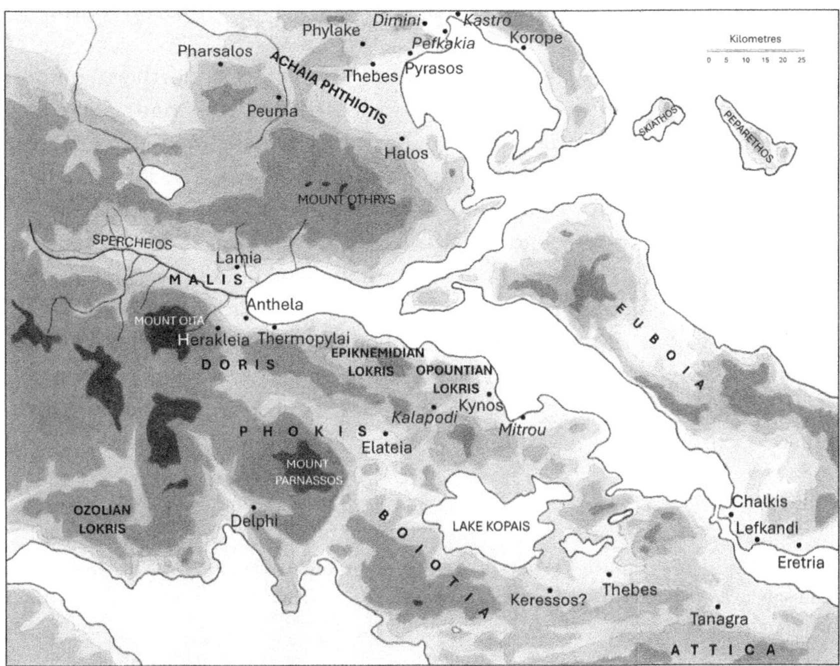

Map 2. Central Greece. © Rosemary Aston 2023

Delphic Amphiktyony. Third, relations between Thessaly and her southern neighbours – especially Phokis and Boiotia – have formed a significant strand in the modern historiography of the regions involved, as will be discussed in the final section of this chapter.

Typically, relations between Thessaly and the *ethnē* to the south are characterised in terms of unease and – by the late sixth century – open conflict. This chapter will end with a critical analysis of this theme; however, its aim on the whole will be to break free from traditional narratives of war and invasion to consider inter-*ethnos* relations in a more holistic way. In the first section Thessaly's relations with its southern neighbours in the Early Iron Age will be examined, to show the limited importance of the *ethnos* boundaries we later see articulated. In the second, the focus moves into the second half of the sixth century, a time when Thessalian aggression is considered to have been a major catalyst to political co-operation and the expression of collective identity among her southern neighbours; this long-standing theory is treated to a critical scrutiny to reveal the extent to which the ancient evidence has been manipulated to fit our modern expectations.

1. Thessaly and central Greek connectivity

a) Southern Thessaly and her neighbours in the Late Bronze and Early Iron Age

Traditionally, Thessaly has been seen as the furthest northern outpost of Mycenaean civilisation, a place in which that culture had taken only relatively scanty root in a small number of sites in or near the Pagasitic Gulf.[1] This picture has been challenged in a number of ways. First, whereas it used to be thought possible to identify Mycenaean sites as peripheral, or belonging to a kind of second rank in terms of importance, by reference to certain key elements in their material remains, we now have a far greater appreciation of the amount of variation between sites and the inadvisability of working with a universal template.[2] The second major challenge to the traditional view of Thessaly's status within the Mycenaean world is the identification of more Mycenaean material from even further north, in Macedon and in the march-lands between Thessaly and Macedon,[3] and

[1] See, most importantly, Feuer (1983); he reiterates in Feuer (2016) his belief that Thessaly was peripheral and subject to a process of 'Mycenaeanization' rather than being truly integrated into the Mycenaean world.

[2] Papadimitriou (2008). For a useful overview of Mycenaean settlements in Thessaly see Adrymi-Sismani (2008); Karouzou (2020), 884–94.

[3] The site of Aiani is especially important in this regard as a junction-point between

even into modern Albania.[4] This material does not include clear evidence of palace and administrative centres, and it is certainly true that the nature of the Mycenaean presence changes once one moves north of Thessaly.[5] Nonetheless, to see Thessaly as the very edge of the Mycenaean sphere of influence is plainly unrealistic; instead, it was part of a broader network, and – as so often in its history – a significant zone on the north–south axis.[6]

It also managed to withstand, as a region, the sharp decline that befell other areas at the end of the Mycenaean period. Pantou (2010) has suggested that the sites in the Volos area, connected also with Pherai inland,[7] interacted so closely that, instead of analysing each site individually, we should consider them as a co-operative settlement group without a clear central-place hierarchy; this disrupts in an interesting way the normal approach of historians approaching a single site armed with a 'checklist' of key ingredients.[8] There is a striking lack of site fortifications

Thessaly, Macedon and Albania: Karamitrou-Mentessidi (2011), providing also a list of excavation reports.

[4] Krapf (2018).

[5] Eder (2009), 115–18: she argues for a 'cultural border' between Thessaly and Macedon. Cf. Karouzou (2018), 196–97.

[6] There was also a greater Mycenaean presence in western Thessaly than has traditionally been appreciated. The site at Dranista (Ano Ktimeni) in south-west Thessaly is especially significant because, as Galanakis and Stamatopoulou (2012) observe, it would have controlled a key route between Thessaly and the western Spercheios valley, thereby challenging the impression (for which see, for example, Feuer 2016, 109–16) that western Thessaly in the Mycenaean period was either isolated or reliant on east Thessaly for its wider connections. It also shows signs of connection with the Georgiko tholos tomb, suggesting an interconnected west Thessalian elite in the Late Bronze Age, though there are also some affinities with the Kapakli tomb at Volos: Galanakis and Stamatopoulou (2012), 208–11. East–west contacts in Late Bronze Age Thessaly are also suggested by affinities between the rural sanctuary at Mavromati Karditsas (north-west of Metropolis and Georgiko) and House K at Dimini, and by evidence of fire-rituals in tholoi in the Karditsa and Volos regions: Karouzou (2018), 133, 170. Increasing numbers of Late Bronze Age discoveries in west Thessaly generally: Stamatopoulou (2011–2012), 88–89.

[7] Pherai as an important site in the Late Bronze Age and Early Iron Age: Apostolopoulou-Kakavoyanni (1992); Georganas (2008), 279; Doulgeri-Intzesiloglou (1994), 77–79; Doulgeri-Intzesiloglou and Arachoviti (2009); Adrymi-Sismani (2012), 120–21; Karouzou (2017), 346–47. Its importance was largely the result of a highly favourable position with sea-access and connection to major roads, and these factors did not lose their importance: Di Salvatore (1994); Georganas (2008), 274; Knodell (2021), 94. Pagasai is called the harbour of Pherai by Theopompos (*FGrH* 115 F 53) but this connection was a longstanding one. Whereas the settlements on the Bay of Volos itself diminished in their independent power, Pherai expanded its dominance in that zone.

[8] Pantou (2010). Her approach differs somewhat from that of Adrymi-Sismani, whose reading of the remains at Dimini lead her to identify it as a dominant palace

in Mycenaean Thessaly, suggesting a largely co-operative relationship between communities and a relative absence of inter-site conflict;[9] in fact, this 'networked' system – within Thessaly, but with wider connections also – may be a factor behind the relatively high level of continuity in Thessaly between the Late Bronze and the Early Iron Age.[10] The fortunes of each site fluctuated on a different trajectory; the decline of the Mycenaean culture affected them in different ways and at different rates, with Dimini and Pefkakia falling into disuse after LH IIIC Early,[11] whereas Kastro endured beyond that,[12] while inland areas such as that around Pharsalos saw an especially high level of site abandonment as the Bronze Age drew to its close.[13]

The same pattern of relative endurance and resilience applies to the area on and around the Euboian Gulf and the Spercheios valley (but not to Boiotia, where the destruction of the palaces seems to have triggered a sharp wholesale decline).[14] Though by no means immune to the destructive events that accompany the end of the Mycenaean palatial period, with the destruction by fire of several sites in LH IIIB, a relatively high proportion of coastal settlements around the Euboian Gulf continued to be occupied in LH IIIC. Crielaard paints a picture of LH IIIC in this area as a period of prosperity and technological innovation, the latter especially in seafaring.[15] While involvement was most intense in areas with good access to the sea,[16] maritime and coastal prosperity fed inland to sites such as Kalapodi

centre, though she accepts the co-operative relationship with other sites: see Adrymi-Sismani (2006), 476–79; see also Knodell (2013), 140–41 and Karouzou (2018), 63–64.

9 In fact the only securely dated fortified site from the Late Bronze Age in Thessaly is Palamas, north-east of Karditsa: Karouzou (2018), 177–78. There are no known fortifications of the Protogeometric and Early Archaic periods: Karouzou (2017), 344.

10 Karouzou (2018), 197; Archibald (2009), 304.

11 The state of preservation of the remains at Dimini in particular allow for the reconstruction of a detailed picture comprising an initial disaster at the end of the thirteenth century, after which a 'new administration' made a determined effort to reorganise and maintain the settlement. Complete depopulation occurred at the end of the first half of the twelfth century. See Adrymi-Sismani (2006), 474–75; Adrymi-Sismani (2020), 27–30.

12 Karouzou (2017), 344–46; Karouzou (2018), 58–64. Abandonment of Pefkakia: Adrymi-Sismani (2006), 476; Middleton (2010), 14–15.

13 Knodell (2021), 127; Middleton (2010), 110.

14 Mycenaean culture in the Spercheios Valley: see Karantzali (2013), who notes, p. 151, that 'The evidence … shows a chronological correspondence with the destruction/abandonment horizon at Dimini and Pevkakia near Volos.' For an overview of the Late Bronze Age–Early Iron Age transition in Phokis, Lokris and surrounding areas see Livieratou (2012, 2020); Kramer-Hajos (2016, 2020).

15 Crielaard (2006); see also Kramer-Hajos (2016), 149–65.

16 Lemos (2002), 212–17; Lemos (2011–2012), 22; Livieratou (2012), 104–05. Lokrian

and Elateia in Phokis.[17] Thessaly had a role in this important network, in particular the Volos area and the shore of Achaia Phthiotis to the south of Mount Othrys,[18] though more inland Thessalian sites were not wholly excluded.[19] In LH IIIC, for example, Elateia in northern Phokis reveals in its pottery styles influences from Thessaly and Euboia throughout, as well as from the Argolid, Crete, Achaia and the Kyklades (LH IIIC Middle) and from Skyros (LH IIIC Late).[20] To some extent, Thessalian inclusion in the 'Euboian koine', as it has been termed, was a continuation of her connectivity in the Late Bronze Age, but also built on population movements in the wake of the Mycenaean collapse.[21] As in the Late Bronze Age, coastal Thessaly will have functioned as a staging post between central Greece and the northern Aegean.[22]

Scholars debate exactly how far the significance of the archaeological similarities can be taken: does the koine amount chiefly to trading routes and to the distribution of artefacts which that produced, or does it suggest a greater degree of cultural affinity, at least within the core area around the Euboian Gulf, including Phthiotis and south-eastern Thessaly?[23] In

Kynos, for example, had a significant harbour, probably from the Bronze Age: see Kounouklas (2018).

17 Lemos (1998), 56; Crielaard (2006); cf. Middleton (2010), 111–12; Kramer-Hajos (2016), 149–65; Kramer-Hajos (2020), 81–82. For Kalapodi's position near major routes between the coast and eastern Phokis and between northern Boiotia and Thessaly as early as the Late Bronze Age, see Livieratou (2012), 82. She observes (91–92) that after the palatial collapse Kalapodi seems to take on the role of prime meeting-place for local elites.

18 Kastro is especially significant in this regard, since it seems to have functioned as an entrepot for imports into Thessaly during the Late Bronze Age; as Karouzou argues, this role transformed into participation in the Euboian koine in the Early Iron Age. Karouzou (2018), 62–63.

19 Lemos (1998), 202–17.

20 Livieratou (2009), 954; Deger-Jalkotzy (2004).

21 Kalligas (1992); Lemos (1998), 51–52; Morgan (2009b), 46–49.

22 Leone (2012), 237; Knodell (2013), 112–13, 228–29, 288; Papadopoulou (2017), 306–07.

23 Although the idea of the koine goes back to the work of Desborough (1972), its most energetic current exponent is Lemos (see, for example, Lemos 1998), who argues for significant cultural affinity by identifying, among other things, the role of religious sites such as Kalapodi as places of congregation and shared cult within the network. For a critical reassessment of the koine theory see Papadopoulos (1997 and 2011), and more recently Donnellan (2017); she does not, however, argue against a high degree of connectivity and mutual influence among the members of the grouping, rather that by using the term koine (and by making less use of burial remains than is warranted) we risk overlooking the complexity of the interrelationships at work between the different communities. As long as we do not try to make the koine model work too hard as an explanation and description of the communities involved, it retains great utility.

fact it was probably both. As we shall see, the world conveyed in the *Iliad*'s Catalogue of Ships is certainly one in which the later political boundaries between Thessaly and her southern neighbours were weak, unimportant or non-existent. And the Lefkandi Centaur (Fig. 2), found split between two graves at Euboian Lefkandi, seems to suggest that the Centaur-lore so central to the mythology of Thessaly – perhaps even more specifically the stories of Cheiron – moved across the water along the same routes as the material objects.[24]

One very significant illustration of some of these connections is provided by the sanctuary at Kalapodi in north-eastern Phokis. The identification of the site is still not wholly beyond debate, but the inscriptions found at the site make its identification as the oracle of Apollo at Abai very likely.[25] What is wholly clear is that the remains from Kalapodi confirm a general picture emerging in many areas of central Greece: the lack of any significant rupture at the end of the Mycenaean age.[26] On the contrary, we see continuous usage from the Middle Helladic period, with a peak of cult activity in what we would traditionally call the late Dark Age, in the ninth century.[27] Though the orientation of its external relations was different from that of Delphi,[28] Kalapodi was no rustic backwater; the finds attest to connections with the Aegean Islands and the Dodekanese, and the use of roof tiles from a Lakonian workshop that also supplied the temple of Aphaia on Aigina. It was also a node in a regional network in central Greece, one in which Thessaly played a significant part, as the ceramic finds especially reveal.[29] While historians understandably tend to focus on the activities

Knodell (2017) argues for the use of network theory to plot connections while acknowledging the diversity of microregions within the network.

[24] On the dating of the Lefkandi Centaur see Desborough et al. (1970), 22–24; on the significance of its physical details see Arrington (2016), 23; Gregory (2018), 42.

[25] Niemeier (2013), 3–5. The identification of the site as the sanctuary of Artemis Elaphebolos at Hyampolis underpinned its publication under the direction of Felsch (2007). Of the many reasons evinced by Niemeier in favour of Abai, the most persuasive is that inscriptions from the site record dedications to Apollo. On these see Prignitz (2014).

[26] Niemeier (2017), 323–26. For the pattern of change and continuity across central Greek sites in this period see Papadopoulou (2017).

[27] In the part of the site called the South Temple, in particular, a sequence of eight temples dating from the Mycenaean to the Archaic period testifies to both the early inception and the remarkable longevity of Kalapodi's religious significance. For an overview of the temple phases see Felsch (2007), 4–27; Niemeier (2013), 10–21.

[28] Morgan (1990), 116–17, 122–26; Morgan (2003), 120–24, 213–18; McInerney (2011), 98.

[29] For example, ceramic links between Thessalian Pefkakia and Lokrian Mitrou in the Middle Helladic period: Lemos (2011–2012), 21. On the important role of Lokris in the seafaring around the Euboian Gulf and up to Thessaly see Arjona (2013).

Fig. 2. Terracotta statuette of a centaur, perhaps Cheiron, from Lefkandi, Euboia; tenth century BC. Archaeological museum of Eretria, Greece. Ink-wash drawing by Rosemary Aston. © Rosemary Aston 2021

of the Delphic Amphiktyony, which makes a far greater impression on the ancient textual record, Kalapodi is the other great component in the interaction between the Thessalians and the *ethnē* to the south, especially (but not only) Phokis.[30] The nature of the finds from the sanctuary, including armour and horse trappings, suggests a strong element of military display, such as may have been cultivated and espoused by the elites of the various communities that participated in the cult.[31] Their interaction also took the form of communal dining.[32]

The chief difference was that the Thessalian presence at Kalapodi was not, as far as we know, enacted on the *ethnos* level, unlike at the Amphiktyonic meetings at Delphi and Anthela. Indeed, none of the interaction described in this section involves any activity by Thessaly as an *ethnos*, or any representation of the Thessalian *ethnos*. Instead, the Euboian koine and its predecessor slice Thessaly up, incorporating Achaia Phthiotis and the Volos area – areas that looked southward and outward – far more than any other part of the region. This is partly a matter of the type of evidence available: archaeological material never, in any period, hives Thessaly off neatly from its neighbours while unifying it seamlessly within. However, this theme of early Thessaly divided, of its different cultural zones, is not purely a feature of the material record: it will reappear when we look at its depiction in Archaic epic in Chapter 2. The continuing involvement of the Volos area in maritime activity after the Late Bronze Age may well have played a role in the development and dissemination of the myth of Jason and the Argo, as will be discussed. Even more notably, the high degree of connection between Thessaly's southern fringe and the Malian Gulf and Spercheios valley[33] chimes strongly with the distribution of Achilles' contingents at Troy, contingents which straddle that ethnically mixed region. While it is notoriously problematic to connect the Catalogue of Ships to any single historical – or indeed archaeological – setting, we can see its general relevance. There are no signs of Thessaly's southern border sharpening up, becoming stricter or more clear-cut, at any stage before the sixth century. The Catalogue of Ships, probably composed in the seventh century, would reflect a centuries-old situation in which southern Thessaly, the Spercheios valley and the Malian Gulf, as well as Lokris and parts of Phokis, formed, with Euboia, a melting pot of interlocking local identities. The geographical vagueness of Achilles' Hellenes, of his Phthia, may derive

[30] Finds from Kalapodi revealing Thessalian influence: Franchi (2016), 78–79.

[31] Lemos (2011–2012), 20. On the votive weapons from the site see Schmitt (2007), 423–551.

[32] Morgan (2003), 113–20; Niemeier (2017), 327–27.

[33] Karouzou (2017), 344; for Thessalian influence on the Protogeometric pottery of the Spercheios valley see Dakoronia (1994), 236–37.

not (or not only) from a poet's patchy knowledge, nor even only from the poet's desire to universalise the cradle of Hellenism, as will be discussed in Chapter 2, but also from the reality of a region where the lived experiences of trade, travel and religion easily overrode the boundaries of *ethnē*, even once those were in place. This picture is amply confirmed as we leave behind the focus on the Euboian Gulf and examine long-lasting overland routes of connection.

b) Passes and pastures

Connections within central Greece and between central Greece and Thessaly were also facilitated by a chain of passes, with a considerable ancient road system, that led south from the Spercheios river valley (into which various north–south paths through the Othrys range led) to the Gulf of Krisa, with loops and branches projecting out somewhat.[34] This series of land routes, through what has been termed the Great Isthmus Corridor, went through or near, and therefore linked, the lands of a number of *ethnē*: Malis, Doris, Phokis, Ozolian Lokris.[35] It adjoined major river systems, themselves axes of connectivity. Along the banks of the western reaches of the Spercheios lay the Dolopes, the Oitaioi and the Ainianes. About a third of a way down from its northern end, the Corridor skirted the western edge of the Kephissos valley, which led down to Lake Kopais and Boiotia generally. In sum, we can see Thessaly, central Greece and Euboia (this last forming a conduit to more distant maritime connections) as criss-crossed by land routes and further linked by sea routes allowing for a near-constant network of mutual influence and interaction from the Late Bronze Age onwards.[36]

Interactions between *ethnē* in central Greece, with its patchwork of tribal communities, were by no means frictionless. Political and ethnic boundaries had to be negotiated, emphasised, sometimes adjusted, while the pastoral focus of the economies meant that herdsmen and flocks moved through the landscape, crossing border areas between poleis and *ethnē*.[37] Competition for grazing was one of the causes of friction between the *ethnē*,[38] but in

[34] Stählin (1924), 180–91; Béquignon (1937b), 21–48; Fossey (1986), 115–19.

[35] Kase et al. (1991), with trenchant reassertion of key views in Szemler et al. (1996). Debate about precise routes and locations is possible – see, for example, MacKay's critical discussion of the 'Dyo Vouna Gap' (2002) – and many have taken issue with the claim that Thermopylai was not a viable pass before the fifth century; see, for example, Sánchez-Moreno (2013), 346–47, n. 24. Nonetheless, the importance of the zone as a place of transit is certain. See Dakoronia (1994), 241.

[36] For a detailed study of routes through Epiknemidian Lokris see Sánchez-Moreno (2013).

[37] For pasturing and liminal political zones see McInerney (2006). See also Chandezon (2003), 332–46, referring chiefly to later epigraphic evidence.

[38] E.g. *Hell. Oxy.* 21.3: 'ἔστι τοῖς ἔθνεσιν τούτοις ἀμφισβητήσιμος χώρα περὶ τὸν

general terms, too, their border lands were often contested. This climate of contact and sporadic friction (largely minor but with occasional flare-ups) would have been fertile ground for the articulation of tribal distinctions, since antagonistic encounters are a crucial ingredient in the awareness of ethnicity and the difference between in-group and out-group.[39]

Therefore Thessaly was in frequent contact with an area where the definition of *ethnē* was especially complex and significant. Her own experiences would have been quite different. While the ethnic consciousness of the perioikic communities – Magnetes, Perrhaiboi, Phthiotic Achaians, Dolopes – will no doubt have fed into the development of Thessalian *ethnos* identity, life in one of the towns on the expansive plains will have provided very different natural and political conditions from those to the south. The boundaries between one's home polis and the polis next door will have been felt and recognised, with occasional friction, as documented land disputes reveal. Contact with non-Thessalians will have occurred frequently, for Thessaly was not a place of unbroken isolation. But the kind of near-constant awareness of adjoining *ethnē* that a great proportion of central Greeks will have experienced will have been alien to the daily lives of the Thessalians, except those on the region's peripheries.[40]

Παρνασσόν, περ[ὶ] ἧς καὶ πρότερόν ποτε πεπολεμήκασιν· ἣν πολλάκις ἐπινέμουσιν ἑκάτεροι τῶν τε Φωκέων καὶ τῶν Λοκρῶν, ὁπότεροι δ' ἂν τύχωσιν αἰσθόμενοί ποτε <τοὺς> ἑτέρους συλλεγέντες πολλοὶ διαρπάζουσι τὰ πρόβατα.' ('There is a territory near Mt. Parnassos that is disputed between these peoples, concerning which they had already made war in the past. Men from both sides, from the Phokians and from the Lokrians, would often use it for grazing, and whichever side noticed the others doing this would gather together many men and carry off the sheep' (trans. Billows). This dispute is clearly chronic, though it is mentioned in the context of events of 395 BC: see Buckler and Beck (2008), 44–58. On pastoral interactions in this region: Howe (2008), 71–73. A striking Hellenistic illustration of the need to regulate the use of upland grazing in Lokris to prevent overuse and conflict may be found in *IG* IX.1^2 3.748 (discussion in Bousquet 1965).

[39] See Morgan (2006), 235, 245: she observes the importance of the articulation of difference in the formation of ethnic groups and their development into political entities, observing moreover that 'Boundary negotiation was generally a late seventh- or sixth-century phenomenon' (235). The importance of borders and the presence of the outsider has been recognised as fundamental to the development of collective identity since the seminal work of Fredrik Barth: discussion in Reger (2014); see also Feuer (2016), 83–87.

[40] It is significant that we do hear of the kind of herding-related conflict described above, *between* Thessalian poleis – in other words, part of the negotiation of space and identity between subregional communities rather than formative on the collective identity as a whole. *IG* IX.2 521, Chandezon (2003), no. 18; further discussion in McInerney (2010), 218–19.

This may well have been one cause behind the fact that the Thessaloi, under that name, are not mentioned in the Homeric poems at all. The Boiotians, Phokians and Lokrians all appear in those terms, as *ethnē*, in the *Iliad*'s Catalogue of Ships.[41] To put this in context, apart from the Euboian Abantes and the Aitolians they are the only groups to be presented in this way. Other contingents are presented with the names of individual sites,[42] of islands, or – occasionally – a more expansive region containing several settlements.[43] The Boiotians, Phokians, Lokrians and Aitolians stand out as having the usual lists of sites, but under *ethnos*-headings of a sort not found elsewhere in the Catalogue. Boiotia, Phokis and Lokris all had eponymous heroes too, attested in Archaic verse; by contrast, as we shall see, Thessaly's eponym Thessalos receives only oblique reference in the *Iliad* and is otherwise absent from Archaic texts. Admittedly, the identification of the eponym Boiotos in the *Ehoiai* rests partly on some ingenious argumentation by Larson,[44] discussed in Chapter 3; Lokros is certainly present, however, and Phokos appears in the *Theogony*. It is plausible that the high degree of interaction – sometimes tension – in central Greece stimulated the deployment of such ethnic expression to an extent not, for the most part, felt in Thessaly at the time.

Another catalyst in the cases of Lokris and Phokis may also have been a degree of territorial complexity Thessaly did not have. Lokris especially may have needed solidifying figures more than most *ethnē* because of its geographical peculiarity, entirely divided by the Parnassos range into East (or Hypoknemidian) Lokrians and West (or Ozolian) Lokrians.[45] It is the East Lokrians who feature in the Catalogue of Ships[46] but their western

[41] They form a block, in the order Boiotians – Phokians – Lokrians, at *Il.* 2.494–535; this is the start of the Catalogue, which then leaps over to Euboia and the Abantes. Then the poet moves to Athens and Salamis, Korinth, the Peloponnese, the Ionian Islands and over into Aitolia. Then there is a big leap into nesiotic territory: Crete, Rhodes, Syme, Kos and adjacent areas (under the sons of Thessalos). Finally the Thessalian contingents are listed, and there – apart from a brief summing-up and 'catalogue of horses' – the Catalogue ends. On the Boiotian contingents see Schachter (2016), 11–12.

[42] Most of the Peloponnese falls into this category. Adjectives and epithets convey a sense of the natural topography of the site and its surrounding area. See, for example, 2.581–82: οἳ δ' εἶχον κοίλην Λακεδαίμονα κητώεσσαν,/Φᾶρίν τε Σπάρτην τε πολυτρήρωνά τε Μέσσην ('And they that held hollow Lakedaimon with its many ravines, and Pharis and Sparta and Messe, the haunt of doves … ').

[43] E.g. 2.603: 'οἳ δ' ἔχον Ἀρκαδίην ὑπὸ Κυλλήνης ὄρος αἰπὺ' ('Those who held Arkadia under the steep mountain of Kyllene … ').

[44] Larson (2007), 41–46.

[45] Domínguez (2015); Domínguez Monedero (2008); Nielsen (2000).

[46] Kramer-Hajos (2012), 88–91, argues that the sites included in the Lokrian portion of the Catalogue fit closely with the Late Bronze Age and Early Iron Age.

counterparts were not insignificant, participating in the cult of Athena Ilias and also in the establishment of the colony in south Italy, Lokroi Epizephyrioi,[47] in which also the cult of Athena Ilias and the figure of Aias were important.[48] The role of this colony in shaping how the Lokrians saw themselves and their myth-history cannot be overstated; it galvanised their collective identity through myth and cult. A great deal of this process occurred within the colony and represents a distanced perspective, but it fed back into the mother-land. At the same time, a more localised identity was forged through the figure of Lokros, son of Physkos and grandson of Amphiktyon, and father of Opous. Opous was in East Lokris and Physkeis in West, so Lokros' family tree served to pull the two halves of the *ethnos* together, while also tying it firmly to the Amphiktyony.[49]

Phokis too, though in a less extreme way, comprised two main geographical 'compartments', one to the north of Parnassos and the other to the south and east. Its process of ethnogenesis was both spurred on and made more complex by this division.[50] While, as the Introduction argued, we have to avoid simplistic forms of geographical determinism, such factors must be considered significant. The error in some past treatments has been to assume that a geographically coherent landscape produces functional unity and co-operation as a matter of course. The truth may be almost the reverse: that a fragmented landscape energises the explicit articulation of shared ethnicity in the face of physical barriers. These observations apply to the perioikic *ethnē* around Thessaly, as well as to her southern near-neighbours, reminding us that they appear *qua ethnē* in the Catalogue of Ships. In particular, the Perrhaiboi to the north and the Phthiotic Achaians to the south were in regions of transit, of geographical intersection, of transhumant and more general mobility. Frequent inter-ethnic encounters and conflicts would have been formative in their own identity development.[51]

However, the main way in which the small *ethnē* of central and northern

47 Redfield suggests (2003, 253–63) that in fact the reality of the *apoikia* is suspect or at least irrecoverable; what we see instead is an accretion of tradition at Lokroi in Italy that served to anchor the community to the Greek heartland and to its myths.

48 Daverio Rocchi (2015), 180–81. For discussion of the myth and cult see Hughes (1991), 166–84.

49 Daverio Rocchi (2013), 179–80. For a nuanced reading of how the Lokros stemma was adapted over time to meet changing political conditions see Franchi (2020a).

50 McInerney (1997), 193–95; Daverio Rocchi (2011).

51 In their 1998 article, Reinders and Prummel examine evidence for transhumance in the territory of Hellenistic New Halos. While they argue for relatively short-distance movements of flocks, Othrys emerges as a destination for herders in the summer months. In the Archaic period, too, it would surely have had this function, and on it herders of the Achaioi would have met inhabitants of the Spercheios communities, approaching the grazing areas from the mountain's other flank, rather as the Theban

Greece enter into our larger histories is through their membership of the Delphic Amphiktyony, which – though of course the surviving Amphiktyonic membership lists are of fourth-century date – must have been early.[52] Taking part in gatherings of the Amphiktyonic council under their *ethnos*-banners, so to speak, will have been crucial to their sense of *ethnos* identity, even if actual representation on the council is likely to have favoured particular poleis, in some cases and periods perhaps exclusively. This makes the near-invisibility of the Thessaloi in Archaic literature all the more striking, and is one reason for thinking critically about their role at Delphi, as the next section proceeds to do; while we cannot plausibly suggest that their membership of the Amphiktyony was any later in inception than that of the Perrhaibians or the Magnetes, we have to be cautious in reading far back into the Archaic period the kind of importance that Delphi certainly had for the Thessalians from the late sixth century onwards. Two aspects of the topic will be considered: first, whether we should give credence to the widely held modern view that Thessaly dominated the Amphiktyony in the Archaic period; and, second, the more general question of how Thessaly was characterised in her dealings within the sanctuary.

2. The aggressive Thessaly

a) Delphic dominance

Thessaly's role in the Amphiktyony

The difficulty attending all study of the early stages of the Delphic Amphiktyony, including its composition, is the late date of much of the evidence. However, such as we have permits the following basic schema, the subject of a general scholarly consensus. There are signs that by the early sixth century the Apollo-sanctuary at Delphi was under a form of governance beyond the local; this is hinted at in the *Homeric Hymn to Apollo*, and the likelihood is that the poem refers to the establishment of Amphiktyonic control. As Davies comments,

> City and Amphiktyony had plainly established a *modus vivendi* by 548 at the latest. Only thus could it have been an Amphiktyonic responsibility to draw up a specification for a new temple of Apollo after the fire of 548, to

and Korinthian shepherds meet on Kithairon, as described in Soph. *Oid. Tyr.* 1132–38.

52 For the rather patchy inclusion of the Oitaians, however, see Lefèvre (1998), 92. The Oitaians may also have had a composite ethnicity originally, being composed of Dryopes, Malians and Ainianes: see Béquignon (1937b), 168–69; Baladié (1996), 177.

cost it at 300 T., to allot to Delphi City the task of raising one quarter of that sum, and to let the building contract to one Athenian family.[53]

However, Delphi seems not to have been the Amphiktyony's first religious centre; that role belonged with the sanctuary of Demeter at Anthela, near Thermopylai, signalled as an important site by Herodotos and always the location of the autumn meetings of the Amphiktyonic synedrion.[54] In all likelihood, the Amphiktyony in its earliest form comprised the *ethnē* around the Anthela shrine:[55] that is, those in and around the Spercheios valley.[56] The extension of the grouping to include less local members probably coincided roughly with its assumption of control over Delphi in the early sixth century BC. A further reflection of this expansion may well be the inclusion of the hero Amphiktyon as a son of Deukalion in the *Ehoiai*;[57] this hero had a shrine at the Anthela site, according to Herodotos, and this may date from the same period. By this time Delphi had long since stopped serving a local catchment and had become a wealthy node in a wide interregional network. It is in the early sixth century that Athenian and Spartan involvement in the Amphiktyony probably began, perhaps along with the inclusion of the Phokians and Boiotians.[58] It is indeed quite possible that the Perrhaiboi, Magnetes and Thessalians joined around this time, since to assume that these *ethnē* were members *ab initio* disrupts the geographical integrity of the earliest organisation.[59] Our earliest lists of

[53] Davies (1998), 2.

[54] Hdt. 7.200.2: 'ἐν δὲ τῷ μεταξὺ Φοίνικος ποταμοῦ καὶ Θερμοπυλέων κώμη τε ἐστὶ τῇ οὔνομα Ἀνθήλη κεῖται, παρ' ἣν δὴ παραρρέων ὁ Ἀσωπὸς ἐς θάλασσαν ἐκδιδοῖ, καὶ χῶρος περὶ αὐτὴν εὐρύς, ἐν τῷ Δήμητρός τε ἱρὸν Ἀμφικτυονίδος ἵδρυται καὶ ἕδραι εἰσὶ Ἀμφικτύοσι καὶ αὐτοῦ τοῦ Ἀμφικτύονος ἱρόν.' For discussion of the Amphiktyonic meetings, their timing and locations see Lefèvre (1998), 193–204.

[55] 'Those living around' is the most plausible translation of the word *amphiktyones/amphiktiones*, though it has not gone uncontested: for an alternative see Hall (2002, 148–49), who suggests that the hero Amphiktyon was very early, and may have been the genuine etymological source.

[56] Sánchez-Moreno (2013, 322–23 and 341) argues for Anthela's 'omphalic' nature: that is, that it stood at a crucial juncture of interregional routes and therefore provided the perfect meeting-place for the Amphiktyony in its early stages.

[57] Fowler (2013), 143.

[58] Lefèvre (1998), 14.

[59] Hall (2002), 134–38. Sordi argues that the early manifestation of the Amphiktyony, based at Anthela before its incorporation of Delphi in the early sixth century, was initially hostile to the Thessalians – indeed, one of its functions was to guard the passes, and the Pylai themselves, against encroachment from the north. Sordi (1958), 35–37; cf. Guillon (1963, 100), who argues that the communities of the Spercheios valley formed the Amphiktyony to protect themselves from the competing expansion of the Thessalians and Boiotians; cf. Tausend (1992), 36–47 and 58–59, who takes Thessalian

Amphiktyonic members are fourth century in date and do not perfectly agree with each other;[60] reconstructions of the early membership, its growth and change at key junctures, is perforce somewhat conjectural.[61]

It has often been asserted that in effect the Amphiktyony was an instrument of Thessalian control.[62] The dating of this varies: for Hall it is a seventh-century phenomenon, whereas Sordi places it in the sixth.[63] This approach has had a number of bases:

1. the supposition that the Thessalians in the Archaic period came to dominate a number of other Amphiktyonic *ethnē* and so would have been able to steer the voting in the synedrion through the application of behind-the-scenes pressure;
2. the apparent prominence of Thessaly in the traditions concerning the First Sacred War, conventionally dated to ca. 590 BC;
3. the idea that when Philip II conferred the presidency of the Amphiktyonic synedrion on the Thessalians he was restoring something that had been theirs before.

expansion as a given but challenges the idea that the Amphikyony was formed to counter it.

60 Aisch. 2.116; Theopompos *FGrH* 115 F 63; see also Paus. 10.8.2. There is a degree of variation and uncertainty in these membership lists. Aischines' list actually comprises only eleven *ethnē*, plainly an accidental omission from the manuscript since he himself says that he will list twelve. It is most usual to insert 'Dolopians', though Daux (1957, 102–03) prefers 'Delphians'. Theopompos also seems to have omitted one name (since 'Αχαιοί Φθιῶται is a single *ethnos*, not two), and in this case it must be the Thessalians. However, the error must surely be that of Harpokration, who is quoting him (*Lexicon* s.v. Ἀμφικτύονες). Theopompos, all too aware of the importance of the Thessalians at Delphi in the fourth century, would not have left them out.

61 Sánchez (2001), 32–41.

62 See, for example, Forrest (1956), 42: 'it is a fair guess that by the end of the seventh century the Amphiktiony was no more than an instrument of Thessalian policy'. Cf. Wade-Gery and Morrison (1942), 59: 'In the seventh century Thessaly was the most considerable military power in Greece. Under her direction the Amphictyony which centred in Anthela, near Thermopylae, spread its influence widely among the northern peoples and ultimately brought Delphi under its control.'

63 Hall argues that by the early sixth century Thessaly influenced or even controlled the *ethnē* in and around the Spercheios valley, having begun its encroachment into the Great Isthmus Corridor in the seventh, further observing that 'since it is highly unlikely that Thessaly would have granted equal seats on the Amphiktyony to those *ethne* it had subjugated … we should probably infer that the Amphiktyony, with the number of its twelve members chartered and maintained by religious authority, was already in existence by the seventh century' (Hall 2002, 144). Sordi, by contrast, sees the original Anthelan Amphiktyony as a coalition against Thessalian aggression: Sordi (1958), 35–37.

This encapsulates much of the traditional historiographic stereotype of Thessaly, found in particular in the works of Larsen and Sordi: as a major regional power of the Archaic period that lost its influence in the fifth century because of fragmentation and internal conflict, before recovering at least some of it under Jason and subsequently under Macedonian influence in the fourth. However, the three suppositions listed above are all problematic.

First, point 1 rests upon the claim that the Thessalians – or powerful individual Thessalian poleis – controlled adjoining *ethnē* who were also Amphiktyonic members in their own right. The starkest such claim comes from Sordi in an article of 1979, repeating theories from her 1958 monograph,[64] but it also lies behind the more recent discussions of Hall and Fowler.[65] Scholars have tried to fix the date of the Thessalian subjection of the *perioikoi*,[66] but in fact the veracity of the whole situation before the fourth century is in doubt. The key ancient evidence for Thessaly's control over her *perioikoi* is in Xenophon's *Hellenika*: describing the assumption of pan-Thessalian rule by Jason of Pherai, Xenophon says that he προεῖπε δὲ τοῖς περιοίκοις πᾶσι καὶ τὸν φόρον ὥσπερ ἐπὶ Σκόπα τεταγμένος ἦν φέρειν ('commanded all the *perioikoi* also to bring the tribute as it had been fixed in the time of Skopas').[67] This is a vulnerable source in many ways, however. First, Jason is evoking a precedent that is vague and murky in the extreme; attempts to fix Skopas in time and context are highly conjectural.[68] Second, the idea that Jason was following a well-established Archaic tradition is doubtful (see Chapter 5); and Xenophon wished to emphasise the power at Jason's disposal and therefore the risk he posed to southern Greece. More broadly, Sprawski has levelled a sensible challenge to the picture of the Thessalians imposing control over their neighbours by military force, pointing out that no ancient authors describe it in those terms.[69] Only

[64] 'Il controllo dei Tessali su Delfi fu sempre in diretto rapporto con il controllo dei Tessali sulla maggioranza anfizionica: solo quando i Tessali ebbero ridotto sotto il loro dominio i Perieci (Perrebi, Magneti, Achei Ftioti, Dolopi, Eniani, Mali, Etei) e poterrono dei loro voti nel sinedrio degli ieromnemoni, essi rivendicarono la presidenza di diritto sull' Anfizionia e sui giochi pitici ed esercitarono un controllo fatto sul santuario e sull' oracolo.' Sordi (1979), 157.

[65] Hall (2002); Fowler (1998).

[66] Sánchez (2002), 42–44.

[67] Xen. *Hell.* 6.1.19.

[68] Sordi considers Aleuas to have been Tagos of all Thessaly, the successor of Skopas in that role, in the closing years of the sixth century: see Sordi (1958), 59–84. For a contrary view, Helly (1995), 185–87; Helly does not, however, reject the idea of Thessalian control over the *perioikoi*, but merely adjusts it to fit his own reconstruction of the Thessalian federal state.

[69] Sprawski (2008).

Thucydides uses the term *hupēkooi* – subordinates – to describe some neighbouring *ethnē*, the Perrhaibians and the Phthiotic Achaians, and his use of the term serves his authorial interest in violent expansionism.[70] Before the rule of Jason, as Sprawski shows, the relationship between Thessaly and her *perioikoi* was more typically characterised as *summachia*. Such a relationship may well have allowed Thessaly to exert a degree of influence in the decision-making of the Amphiktyony, but before the fourth century we have no attested instances of this at work, so are unable to turn the plausible suggestion into measurable reality.

As for Thessaly's role in the First Sacred War (point 2), this is especially prey to the long-recognised difficulties in ascertaining the historicity of the conflict in the form described.[71] A comparable situation applies to the Lelantine War, the other large-scale early conflict in which Thessaly supposedly played an important role. In this event, a contingent of Thessalian cavalry under Kleomachos of Pharsalos supposedly aided Euboian Chalkis in a war against neighbouring Eretria for control of the Lelantine Plain. While faint traces of both the Lelantine and the First Sacred War may be discernible in Archaic texts,[72] full accounts come much later, and in neither case is Thessalian involvement attested before the fourth century BC.[73] We are dealing here neither with blatant fiction

[70] E.g. Thuc. 8.3.1, describing events in 413 BC.

[71] The most sceptical treatment of the war's historicity is that of Robertson (1978), whose doubts are largely shared by Hall (2002, 146–48); for an opposing view see Lehmann (1980). A balanced overview is provided by Davies (1994); see also Sánchez (2002), 58–77, for cautious partial credence. McInerney (1999, 171) reasserts its reality (overlaid, he grants, by centuries of embellishment and distortion), but argues that 'it was essentially … a local affair arising from the disparity of wealth between Delphi and its neighbors, which prompted an attempt to take control of the sanctuary'. Scott (2010), 51–53, takes a similar line, emphasising the role of local power-wrangling. Howe (2003; 2008, 89–93) relates the conflict to the control of vital pastoral resources; on this see further Rousset (2002), 283–86. A recent nuanced treatment of the evolving ancient traditions of the conflict, situated within a discussion of Phokian ethnopoiesis, considers their further development in Hellenistic as well as mid-fourth-century sources: Franchi (2016), 199–230.

[72] For example, the funeral games of Amphidamas of Chalkis mentioned in the *Works and Days* of Hesiod are thought to relate obliquely to the Lelantine War, since Amphidamas was believed in antiquity to have died in the conflict: see, for example, Plut. *Seven Sages* 10; Stamatopoulou (2014). In the case of the First Sacred War, some scholars consider that the threat in the *Homeric Hymn to Pythian Apollo*, that Delphi would be controlled by men from outside Delphi itself, refers to the establishment of Amphiktyonic administration there after the defeat of the Krisaians. *HH* 3.542–43; see Richardson (2010), 151–52. For a justly scathing treatment of this approach see Clay (2006), 87–91.

[73] On the ancient sources for Thessalian participation in the conflict see Parker

nor with unmixed historical fact, but rather with a complex layering of traditions cherished by particular communities.[74] Kleomachos of Pharsalos, for example, whose role in the Lelantine War is described by Plutarch, seems to have been a figure of genuine veneration in Chalkis, where his tomb was a prominent local landmark;[75] stories would have been told about his deeds and of the friendship between Chalkis and Thessaly, a friendship made more plausible by the emphasis both societies placed on horses and horsemanship;[76] for the Euboian aristocracy, links to horse-rearing Thessaly may have been a powerful consolidation of status. Certainly the tradition in Plutarch goes back to the third-century Chalkian scholar–poet Euphorion, who seems to have included the Lelantine War in a prose work about the Larisaian Aleuadai (which must have discussed Thessalika more generally).[77] Euphorion himself probably drew on generations of local history in Chalkis focused round Kleomachos' tomb and the stories woven and embellished around it.[78] Interestingly, Euphorion is also one of the authors – Aristotle being the earliest, as far as we know – who wrote about Thessalian leadership of the Amphiktyonic forces in the First Sacred War.[79] Emphasising the prominence and utility of Thessalians on the wider Greek stage seems to have been one of his purposes.

(1997), 145–47; pages 11–24 on the sources for the conflict more generally. Howe (2008, 82–84) discusses the role of the Lelantine Plain as prime contested grazing land.

[74] As for the Lelantine War itself, Walker (2004, 164) identifies a 'series of wars involving Eretria and Khalkis and their allies' from around the mid-eighth century. The tendency of ancient traditions to turn periods of on-and-off hostility into single epic wars may very well have been at work in this case.

[75] Plut. *Amat.* 17.

[76] Hippobotai and Hippeis in Chalkis and Eretria respectively: Kôiv (2016), 311–16. Hippobotai of Chalkis as the ruling oligarchic elite: Strabo 10.1.8; cf. Aristotle, *Pol.* 4.1289b. Athens forcibly instals *klerouchoi* on the lands of the Hippobotai, ca. 507 BC: Hdt. 5.77.2–3.

[77] Euphorion fr. 29 Meinecke; see Acosta-Hughes and Cusset (2012), 114–15. He does not mention the war specifically, but Kôiv (2011, 368–69) argues that elsewhere in the work he did so to substantiate his argument that Homer and Archilochos were contemporaries at the time of the conflict.

[78] These traditions may be dated back to the social status of leaders in Archaic Euboia (as argued by Kôiv 2016, 314: 'We can be therefore pretty sure that both Amphidamas of Chalkis and the anonymous warrior of Eretreia were outstanding men in their communities, honoured posthumously as heroic benefactors of their poleis'); however, it is impossible to disentangle when and how successive elements of the tradition as it existed by Plutarch's day were added to the mix.

[79] Fr. 165 Meinecke.

Table 1 Ancient literary sources related to the First Sacred War

Source	Date	Context and account	Individuals and groups involved
Homeric Hymn to Pythian Apollo	Early 6th c.	The Hymn seems to refer to the imposition of outsider control on the Delphic sanctuary, perhaps the take-over by the Amphiktyony that supposedly happened after the First Sacred War.[80]	The war and its participants are not directly alluded to.
Speusippos, *Letter to Philip* (*Epistula Socratica* 30) 8	343/2[81]	Philip's acquisition of the Amphiktyonic votes confiscated from the Phokians is likened to the reallocation of the votes of the Krisaians after the First Sacred War.	Just 'the Amphiktyons'.
Aischines 3.107–109 (*Against Ktesiphon*)	Speech delivered in 330	Aischines is giving an account of his own role in the outbreak of the Fourth Sacred War in 339 BC. He mentions the First Sacred War by way of background: how the Kirrhaian[82] plain was first made sacred land.[83] He says that the plain was inhabited by the Kirrhaians and the Kragalidai, but that these committed sacrilege against the sanctuary of Apollo and transgressed the rules of the Amphiktyons (in ways unspecified), so the Amphiktyons waged war against them, confiscated their land and dedicated it to the god.	Aischines emphasises Athenian involvement to encourage Athenian participation in the Fourth Sacred War of his own day. In his account, Solon of Athens proposes the motion to make war on the Kirrahaians and Kragalidai.

80 Chappell (2006), 331–34; Richardson (2010), 151–52.

81 For the date and context of this work see Pownall (1998), 50.

82 For the names Kirrha and Krisa, and their relationship, see Rousset (2002), 32–33 (summarising earlier scholarship).

83 On the pastoral significance of the Delphic sacred land see Howe (2003).

Source	Date	Context and account	Individuals and groups involved
Kallisthenes, *On the Sacred War* (*FGrH* 124 F 1)	4th c. BC	The war lasts ten years and seems to be occasioned by the Krisaians' capture of a Phokian woman and some Argive girls.	No details of participants or leaders preserved in the Athenaios citation (*Deipn.* 13.10.560b–c)
Aristotle and Kallisthenes, *Pythionikai*[84]	4th c. BC	The list of Pythian victors inscribed and displayed at Delphi began with an account of the First Sacred War. In this account, the Krisaians are attacked and defeated by the Amphiktyons because they have assaulted visitors to the sanctuary and were generally transgressive. After their victory the Amphiktyons re-establish and enlarge the Pythian games.	The Amphiktyonic forces are led by Eurylochos of Thessaly, who was called the 'new Achilles'. Another Thessalian, Hippias, helps to mop up some of the Kirrhaians who held out on Mount Kirphis. However, Solon is an important advisor, urging the Amphiktyons to undertake the war.[85]
Hippocratic *Presbeutikos Logos*[86]	3rd c. BC	Nebros helps the Amphiktyons by poisoning the water-supply of the Krisaians with Hellebore.	Thessalian Eurylochos; Koan Asklepiad Nebros and his son Chrysos.

[84] I follow the view, now widely accepted, that this text was the chief source for the Hypotheses in the scholia on Pindar's Pythians. See Robertson (1978), 55–56; Christesen (2007), 191–95. For a sceptical discussion of the dating of the Hypotheses' source material see Davies (2007b), 51–52.

[85] This detail is supplied by Plut. *Sol.* 11, quoting the *Pythionikai.*

[86] On this text see Smith (1990), 4–6, and the discussion in Chapter 7.

Source	Date	Context and account	Individuals and groups involved
Euphorion, *Poetic fragment* 116 (quoted in the *Hypotheses* b and d of Pindar's *Pythians*)	3rd c. BC	Brief mention of the sacking of Krisa.	Thessalian Eurylochos has sole responsibility for the campaign; he is called the new Achilles.
Diod. 9.16	1st c. BC	The Kirrhaians are defeated after a long siege; their offence is trying to plunder the oracle.	Not specified: just 'the Greeks'.
Strabo 9.3.4	1st c. BC–1st c. AD	The Krisaians levied taxes on imported goods and on visitors to the sanctuary, against the decrees of the Amphiktyony, and so were defeated and Krisa destroyed.	Sole agency in the destruction of Krisa is attributed to 'Eurylochos the Thessalian'.
Plut. *Sol.* 11	1st–2nd c. AD	The Amphiktyons make war on the Krisaians because they are 'ὑβρίζοντας εἰς τὸ μαντεῖον'.	It is Solon who persuades the Amphiktyons to go to war; however, the Athenian forces are commanded by Alkmaion.
Paus. 10.37.5–8	2nd c. AD	In addition to unspecified transgression, the Kirrhaians have appropriated sacred land, and so are besieged by the Amphiktyons. Tricks are used to defeat them: their water supply is diverted, and then, when that fails, it is poisoned with hellebore.	Kleisthenes of Sikyon heads the Amphiktyonic forces. Solon of Athens is brought in to advise, and it is he who diverts and then poisons the Krisaians' water supply.

In the particular case of the First Sacred War, a summary of the traditions concerning the conflict (Table 1) reveals one fundamental fact: that in no way is Thessaly actually singled out as the sole, or even the main, player on the Amphiktyonic side, at any time. Overall, it is important to note that Thessalian involvement in the War is by no means universal in the accounts summarised here. Other communities also inserted their legendary representatives into the narrative. If the First Sacred War was indeed a Thessalian-led enterprise, part of Thessaly's ambitious programme of expansion in the sixth century BC, as has been claimed, then that fact is absolutely not emphasised by any of the ancient accounts. There is no reason to believe that the Thessalian dimension of the story is any earlier, or any more authentically reflective of Archaic events, than the Athenian involvement.

No less problematic is the third point, the idea that Philip II restored Amphiktyonic privilege the Thessalians had previously held at some undefined earlier time. It is certainly the case that Thessalians achieved unparalleled visibility at Delphi under the aegis of Philip and then Alexander; at this time the Thessalian *hieromnēmones* were Kottyphos and Kolosimmos from 346 to 338 BC, thereafter Daochos and Thrasydaios, who were noted supporters of Philip;[87] and their names head lists of Amphiktyonic representatives so consistently that it has been suggested that they, or one of the pair perhaps, held a formal presidential role within the synedrion. The office of Amphiktyonic president, however, is not substantially attested as a routine position in its own right, and we should probably content ourselves with seeing the primacy of the Thessalian Amphiktyons as a clear sign of their high status and influential positions within the Macedonian-steered Amphiktyony of the times.[88] Was this, however, a return to a state of affairs that prevailed in the Archaic period? Much rests on the language in which Demosthenes phrases his brief descriptions of Philip's Delphic interaction with the Thessalians, and this is ambiguous. Twice he uses the phrase τὴν Πυλαίαν ἀποδοῦναι or a form thereof.[89] The verb ἀποδίδωμι is significant. It can mean 'to give back', 'to restore', and it is in this sense that the

[87] See, for example, *CID* 2.76 (335 BC).

[88] A formal presidency – held by Kottyphos – is only really attested once, in Aischin. 3.128: in the context of the Amphiktyonic decision to attack the Amphissians in 339 BC, Aischines says that 'στρατηγὸν εἵλοντο Κόττυφον τὸν Φαρσάλιον τὸν τότε τὰς γνώμας ἐπιψηφίζοντα' ('they chose as general Kottyphos the Pharsalian, who was then in charge of the voting process').

[89] This form of the phrase is used at 8.65 (*On the Chersonese*), delivered in 341, in which the orator attributes the popularity of Philip in Thessaly to the fact that he expelled tyrants and 'τὴν Πυλαίαν ἀποδοῦναι'. At 6.22 (the *Second Philippic*, delivered in 344) we have τὴν Πυλαίαν ἀποδόντα, and the rhetorical context is similar: the Thessalians were seduced, Demosthenes says, with favours, and before they knew it, Philip had started to manipulate their political system and appropriate their revenues. On the sense of 'the Pylaia' see Bowden (2003), 68–70: he argues that it chiefly refers not only to the meetings of the Amphiktyony but also to the festival gatherings that accompanied them.

Demosthenic phrase has tended to be translated, meaning 'to give back [control over] the Amphiktyonic meetings'. However, this sense is not the only one; the verb can also mean 'to assign', 'to deliver'. Relevant literary parallels exist for both options, and the fact that 'give back' and 'restore' are so often preferred probably reflects a widespread unconsidered assumption that the Thessalians dominated Delphi in the Archaic period. But in fact Demosthenes may just as well have been describing – in shocked tones – the unprecedented, namely a disgraceful new coalition between two northern regions to overturn long-standing Delphic tradition.

Even if the sense 'give back', 'restore' is correct, the reference may not be to a time and a situation in the distant past. We must take into account how much Delphic influence Thessaly had lost in the 360s and early 350s, to the advantage especially of Thebes. As Hornblower has pointed out, when the Thebans detached Magnesia and Achaia Phthiotis from the domination of Alexandros of Pherai in 364 BC, those regions passed into Boiotian rather than Thessalian control.[90] This greatly enlarged the Theban influence on the Amphiktyonic Council. In 360/59 the Thebans were given the right of *promanteia*; and in 357 they used their Amphiktyonic clout to charge the Spartans with the capture of the Kadmeia, a charge that resulted in the Amphiktyons fining Sparta 500 talents.[91] In 363 it seems that the Thessalians were still prominent on the Council: a man from Krannon, Andronikos, led a vote to banish eleven Delphians and to confiscate their property, in circumstances that remain mysterious; this suggests that the Thessalians held the formal presidency of the Council.[92] But by the outbreak of the Third Sacred War this situation had changed. Demosthenes, describing Thessalian motives for their involvement in the war, says that they 'τῆς Πυλαίας δ' ἐπεθύμουν καὶ τῶν ἐν Δελφοῖς ... κύριοι γενέσθαι' – 'longed to control the Pylaia and affairs at Delphi'.[93] This indicates that by this time they no longer had the position at Delphi they wished to hold.[94] So Philip may merely have been restoring Thessalian influence to its earlier fourth-century levels.

It is highly significant that no mention is made of a background of Amphiktyonic dominance when Xenophon describes the ambitions of Jason

90 Diod. 15.80.6; Hornblower (2011), 263.

91 Buckler (1989), 14–16.

92 *IG* II² 109; Buckler (1989), 10–15; Sánchez (2001), 168–73; Hornblower (2009), 45–46.

93 Demosth. 5.23. ἡ Πυλαία denotes an Amphiktyonic gathering; in Delphic inscriptions (e.g. *CID* 2.4) it is normally qualified with 'spring' or 'autumn', which makes it clear that, though originally referring to Thermopylai, it had come to designate either meeting-place, Anthela or Delphi, depending on the time of year.

94 Buckler (1989, 14) has suggested that their alliance with Athens in 361/0 BC may have contributed to her loss of status at Delphi, since Athens was out of favour with the Delphians at that time.

of Pherai, who at the time of his death was apparently planning a significant move at the time of his assassination: 'παρήγγειλε δὲ καὶ ὡς στρατευσομένοις εἰς τὸν περὶ τὰ Πύθια χρόνον Θετταλοῖς παρασκευάζεσθαι· διενοεῖτο γάρ, ὡς ἔφασαν, καὶ τὴν πανήγυριν τῷ θεῷ καὶ τοὺς ἀγῶνας αὐτὸς διατιθέναι.'[95] In Xenophon's account, Jason frequently uses tradition – real or manufactured – to reinforce the legitimacy of his own position, citing Aleuas as a precedent for the pan-Thessalian ruler and Skopas for the tribute paid by the *perioikoi*. At no point, however, are his Delphic plans described in terms of a return to past Thessalian dominance. If, when Xenophon was writing, there had been a widespread belief that the Thessalians used to dominate the Amphiktyony, whether through influence or actual or threatened force, that fact would surely have been brought into the narrative. Overall it is astonishingly difficult to find a single ancient source that attests unequivocally to the reality of a dominant Thessaly in the Delphic Amphiktyony before the fourth century BC.[96]

Thessaly and the motif of Delphic distrust

Several Archaic myths have been interpreted as reflecting conflicts for control of Delphi, or as attempts by communities to cast themselves as Delphic saviours while their rivals appear as would-be plunderers of the sanctuary and its treasures. These myths are sometimes read as 'anti-Thessalian', and yet doing so risks ignoring the flexibility and ambiguity of their meaning. Particularly tendentious in this regard are the myth of Herakles' fight against Kyknos, that of his struggle with Apollo over the Delphic tripod and that of Neoptolemos and the circumstances of his death.

The fight between Herakles and Kyknos was the subject of the *Aspis*, probably composed in the early sixth century BC;[97] Stesichoros also composed a poem on the subject, at a not too dissimilar date. Herakles in the *Aspis* is strongly characterised as a Theban figure; that much is clear. As for Kyknos, he appears to be at home in Thessaly; that, at least, is where the fight takes place – vaguely located near Arne, Iolkos, Anthea, Helike and 'the polis of the Myrmidones' – and where Kyknos is eventually buried. While some well-known Thessalian topographic details are brought in – such as the river Anauros obliterating Kyknos' tomb – there is no sense that the poet had a precise and realistic location in mind; rather, he is conjuring

[95] Xen. *Hell.* 6.4.30: 'Furthermore, he gave orders to the Thessalians to make preparations for taking the field at the time of the Pythian festival; for he was intending, it was said, to organise, himself, both the festal assembly in honour of the god and the games' (trans. Brownson, adapted).

[96] See also Bowden (2003), arguing for caution in interpreting the Amphikyony as exercising a powerful political or military role, especially before the time of Philip.

[97] Janko (1986).

a generalised mythic Thessaly. Largely on the basis of the final three lines of the poem, Kyknos is seen as a Thessalian threat to Delphi[98] and Herakles an emblem of the Theban desire to pose as the sanctuary's champion. The Boiotian origin of the poem is very probable, and it has therefore been seen as a work of pro-Theban anti-Thessalian propaganda.[99] The overwhelming tendency to seek a political interpretation probably arises from modern dissatisfaction with the poem's literary merit – artistic motives alone are considered inadequate to explain the creation of such a *peculiar* piece of work.[100]

However, a closer examination of the poem rapidly brings to light inconvenient complexities. For one thing, Kyknos' aggression against Apollo is by no means straightforward. At first it seems so: when Herakles finds him, Kyknos is in Apollo's sanctuary, with his father Ares, plotting the slaying of Herakles and the despoiling of his corpse. However, on lines 70–71 we discover that the scene is not Delphi:

> The whole grove and altar of Apollo Pagasaios
> shone from the armour and body of the terrible god.[101]

From the *epiklesis* it would seem that we are in the sanctuary of Apollo in Pagasai.[102] This muddies the waters: now Kyknos is threatening a god who is – in this poem at least – as much Thessalian as Delphic, and the sacred precinct in danger of witnessing sacrilegious violence is a Thessalian one. Only at the end of the poem (lines 479–80) does the motif of the threat to Delphi enter the frame, to explain the obliteration of Kyknos' tomb at Apollo's orders:

98 E.g. Mackil (2013), 23: 'the Thessalians have corrupted the cult of Apollo, and the Thebans are its true defenders.'

99 See Kühr (2006), 180–82; Larson (2007), 195. Further political interpretations are various. For Guillon (1963), the poem reflects Theban claims on northern hegemony, at Thessaly's expense, in the seventh century. Ducat (1964) places the poem in the sixth century but sees it as reflecting Theban desire to claim the sanctuary of Apollo at Pagasai. Sordi (1966) argues that the poem reflects Theban attempts to control Delphi and present Thebes as Apollo's champion against Thessalian aggression; cf. also McInerney (2015b), 205, for a similar view.

100 For a fuller understanding of its literary qualities see Martin (2005).

101 'πᾶν δ' ἄλσος καὶ βωμὸς Ἀπόλλωνος Παγασαίου/λάμπεν ὑπαὶ δεινοῖο θεοῦ τευχέων τε καὶ αὐτοῦ.'

102 The sanctuary of Apollo at Soros (Pagasai) seems to have flourished in the sixth century with the construction of a cella; however, earlier ritual activity on the site, both open-air and associated with an older structure (Building E, to the north-west), is clearly indicated by the finds. See Mazarakis Ainian (2009) and (2012), and Mili (2015), 343–45.

… because whoever drove rich hecatombs
to Pytho, Kyknos would observe and plunder them with force.[103]

Some scholars have deemed these lines a later interpolation;[104] even if we reject that drastic expedient, they do form an awkward element and feel superficial. Their superficiality is perhaps enhanced if we compare other versions of the story. Stesichoros', as summarised by a scholiast on Pindar, did not contain the Delphic element: 'Kyknos, a son of Ares, who lived on the road through Thessaly, used to cut the heads off passing strangers, wishing to build a temple to Phobos from the skulls.'[105] Euripides seems to think in the same vein, calling Kyknos ξεινοδαΐκταν, the murderer of guests or strangers.[106] Pindar merely says that Herakles was defeated by Kyknos, which again seems to echo Stesichoros.[107] The two elements that the poet of the *Aspis* seems to have added are the strongly Theban character of Herakles and the final mention of the threat to Delphi.[108] These were, in all likelihood, grafted onto a rather different myth, one about attacks on passing travellers through Thessaly, inversions of good *xenia* rather like the Attic predators, Sinis, Skiron and Kerkyon, whom Theseus tackles. The peril he seems to represent most of all is to travellers through Thessaly – since he sits in the *parodos* – rather than travellers to Delphi. He may also be compared with other transgressive figures in Thessalian myth who threaten the very gods – Ixion, for example, or the Aloadai – but who have no association with Delphic aggression.

[103] '… ὅτι ῥα κλειτὰς ἑκατόμβας/ὅστις ἄγοι Πυθοῖδε βίῃ σύλασκε δοκεύων.'

[104] E.g. Andersen (1969), 14: 'they sound very much like a second consideration superficially pasted on the rest.' Cf. Russo (1950), 33–35, 191–92: an old myth is rather clumsily fitted to events in the poet's own day.

[105] Schol. Pind. *Ol.* 10.19: 'ὁ Κύκνος υἱὸς ὢν τοῦ Ἄρεος ἐν τῇ παρόδῳ τῆς Θεσσαλίας οἰκῶν τοὺς παριόντας ξένους ἐκαρατόμει, ἐκ τῶν κεφαλῶν ναὸν τῷ Φόβῳ ποιῆσαι βουλόμενος.'

[106] Eur. *Her.* 389–90.

[107] The Pindaric scholion (see n. 105 above) says that Herakles was defeated by Kyknos when the latter had Ares' help, but later caught him alone and killed him. See Andersen (1969), 14–16.

[108] Herakles had an Archaic cult near Sesklo, approximately half-way between Pagasai and Pherai (see Stamelou and Doulgeri-Intzesiloglou, 2010, 167–68), and this prompts one to wonder whether the author of the *Aspis* was manipulating a myth that originally was purely Thessalian, about a Herakles with strong Thessalian connections fighting a Thessalian villain to secure the Thessalian sanctuary of Apollo Pagasaios. The poet Thebanised Herakles and rather clumsily anchored Apollo to Delphi as well as to Pagasai. That said, Archaic connections between Delphi and Pagasai are suggested by the role of Pagasos, a Hyperborean, in one tradition of the creation of the Delphic oracle (Paus. 10.5.8), and perhaps also by Strabo's obscure and otherwise unsubstantiated reference to a *pylaikē panēguris* – 'Pylaic festival' – in the area of Iolkos (Strabo. 9.5.15). For discussion of this 'Pylaic festival' see Boehm (2018), 156 and n. 43.

This leaves us with the possibility, of course, that the *Aspis*' manipulation of the myth was intended to turn it into one with a Delphic message, casting the Thessalians as aggressors and the Thebans as saviours of the sanctuary. But nothing in the poem really supports this antagonistic reading, since the Apollo who benefits from Herakles' action is both Delphic and Thessalian. Nor does Kyknos represent all of Thessaly, since the very landscape – the Anauros that washes away his grave monument – works against him. Overall, there is simply no need to read into it a hostility between Thessaly and Thebes; the fact that scholars have done so illustrates the lingering desire to find traces of conflict between Thessaly and her southern near-neighbours. This desire is also apparent in the interpretations of the next myth to be considered, that in which Herakles and Apollo fight for possession of the Delphic tripod.

The struggle for the tripod was a popular subject in art of various media, especially in the sixth century BC,[109] but not a popular theme in our surviving literature.[110] Though we have a mention of the myth in Pindar,[111] Apollodoros supplies our fullest account, telling us that Herakles grew angry when the Pythia would not give him an oracle, and decided to steal the tripod so that he could set up an oracular sanctuary of his own.[112] Historians have sometimes read Herakles as a metaphor for a Thessaly-dominated Amphiktyony, once more casting the Thessalians as the would-be plunderers of Delphi.[113] The Phokians themselves may have used the myth in this way: they set up a statue group of the episode in Delphi and at Abai, apparently in celebration of a military victory over the Thessalians (see below); if the myth was metaphorical in this instance, then Herakles may have stood for Thessaly, the defeated aggressor, and Apollo for the Phokians. When the myth appears in other contexts, however, other interpretations prevail: it has been suggested that the myth makes reference to the First Sacred War and that Herakles represents the Kirrhaians/Krisaians, themselves Phokians.[114] Or is the tripod-snatching Herakles actually Thebes, a reflection of anti-Theban sentiment at Delphi, as Sordi

[109] Parke and Boardman (1957), 278–79.

[110] Even when Pausanias recounts the Delphic story about the struggle, he does so in explanation of an image of the myth in the sanctuary of Apollo: Paus. 10.13.7–8; cf. Hdt. 8.27.5. The literary sources, none earlier than the third century BC, are collated by Defradas (1954), 126–32.

[111] Pind. *Ol.* 9.29–36.

[112] Apollod. *Bibl.* 2.6.2.

[113] For Defradas the myth reflects the take-over of Delphi by the Amphiktyony of Thermopylai/Anthela, with Herakles representing the Amphiktyony. Defradas (1954), 144–45.

[114] Parke and Boardman (1957).

argues?[115] Clearly in a Delphic context – such as on the Siphnian Treasury[116] – the myth was a powerful endorsement of Apollo's power and the authority of his oracle, but determining the coded identity of his attacker is subject to many pitfalls. As to the tripod, does it really represent control over the Delphic sanctuary or the Amphiktyony?

Neer, in his analysis of the decoration on the Siphnian Treasury, in which the struggle over the tripod was a prominent element, suggests a much more subtle range of meanings and resonances, to do with the role of tripods as prizes in contests and as votive objects associated with aristocratic display.[117] While reading such myths in a symbolic and political sense can have value, their extreme versatility, and the likelihood of multiple interpretations by those viewing, hearing or reading them at different times, should discourage us from focusing on single meanings.[118] Moreover, singling out Thessalian aggression as a dominant factor is plainly impossible. Rather, we should see Thessaly as one community implicated in a far more general climate of mutual suspicion that hung over Delphi and involved, in varying ways and degrees, all its constituent groups: the various Amphiktyonic communities and the Delphians themselves. Certainly this climate pervades the mythology of our third significant figure, Neoptolemos.

On the face of it, Achilles' son Neoptolemos – also called Pyrrhos – seems to encapsulate perfectly the use of myth as claim and counter-claim among conflicting groups.[119] On the one hand, he can be brought in, and has been brought in, to serve arguments in which myth expresses the possibility of Thessalian aggression: in some sources he has come to pillage Apollo's rich shrine, or is thought to have this intention.[120] His father Achilles is also presented in the *Iliad* as a potential threat to Delphi.[121]

115 Sordi (1966, repr. 2002), 273: she posits a back-and-forth of accusation and counter-accusation, with the *Aspis* promoting the Theban role at Delphi and the tripod myth refuting that favourable characterisation. Cf., however, Sordi (1958), 36: here she suggests that Herakles stands for the Amphiktyony before Thessaly joined and dominated it.

116 Parke and Boardman (1957), 279. It should be noted that the myth also appears in architectural contexts, where its Delphic significance would have been faint, such as in the sanctuary of Demeter and Despoina at Lykosoura, Arkadia (see Paus. 8.37.1).

117 Neer (2001), 292–97.

118 Larson (2019) argues that, rather than seeing Herakles as allegorically representing a particular group or *ethnos*, we should view the tripod struggle as expressing the hero's claim on Olympian status.

119 See, for example, Kowalzig (2007), 197–200.

120 Defradas (1954), 146–56. For a general collation and discussion of the sources on Neoptolemos at Delphi see Suárez de la Torre (1997).

121 Hom. *Il.* 9.404–07. Homer presents the sacking of Troy as the alternative to the plundering of Delphi. This may be another reason why, symbolically, Achilles' *nostos* cannot be accomplished (see Chapter 2): he represents a threat to Delphi, a threat his

On the other hand, in some texts Neoptolemos dies in the sanctuary at the hands of greedy and unscrupulous Delphian priests after a quarrel concerning the distribution of sacrificial meat; does this element of the story derive from a Thessalian attempt to push back against their hero's negative characterisation? Subtler approaches see him as not so much Thessalian as Amphiktyonic, representing less specifically Thessalian aggression than the imposition of (unwelcome) Amphiktyonic management at Delphi: 'Neoptolemos' ancestry is wholly Thessalian and stems from the land of the intruding amphiktyony.'[122] Even here, however, it is striking that Thessaly is presented as the dominant power within the Amphiktyony, by no means verifiable as we have seen.

On the whole, however, scholars have moved beyond this view of the myth as expressing local rivalries. On the one hand, Nagy has demonstrated that Neoptolemos' connection with the division of sacrificial meat is part of a wider association between the Aiakidai and the motif of *daís*, feasting, and quarrels attached to that practice. Delphi is an evocative focus for this theme because the wealth of its sanctuary from the eighth century onward naturally engendered a concern about misappropriation, but the *daís* theme is anything but local; it sprawls across the overtly panhellenic canvas of epic.[123] More than that: Neoptolemos' Delphic actions and death have also been shown to form an important part of ancient literary and philosophical discourse concerning correct and incorrect religious behaviour. For Kurke, Neoptolemos combines with Aesop (another Delphic disrupter) to challenge elite religious authority in the form of Apollo's greedy and self-serving priests.[124] This complex and wide-ranging theme does not, of course, negate local meanings and local readings, especially pre-dating the (largely Classical) material Kurke examines. However, the sources simply do not allow us to uncover a single original meaning (such as Thessalians *versus* Delphians) that the myth had in its pristine form before the accretion of literary manipulations, especially since its significance is already complex in Homer.

In addition, the idea of accusation and counter-accusation is disrupted by the ritual dimension of Neoptolemos' role. The former depends on two opposing sides, each deploying the hero to suit its own propagandist purpose. But in fact the cult of Neoptolemos was all about ritual reconciliation. True, his burial at the threshold of the temple was described by

son comes closer to fulfilling, and must therefore be killed at Troy and tethered to the Hellespont and the Black Sea through cult, his menace neutralised and held in check by ritual observance.

122 Kowalzig (2007), 198.

123 Nagy (1999), 118–41.

124 Kurke (2012), 53–94.

Euripides as a 'reproach to the Delphians';[125] true, Pausanias claims (with very dubious veracity) that the Delphians started to worship Neoptolemos only after he aided them against the invading Gauls in 279/8 BC.[126] But he also presided over the festival of the Theoxenia, at which the gods were ritually feasted and in which visiting *theoroi* also participated, whose centrepiece was the carefully regulated allocation of shares of the sacrificial meat. The Delphians appear to have controlled participation in this ritual; so, while in myth and folklore[127] they could be characterised as greedy and unscrupulous, they were by no means excluded or marginalised. The myth of Neoptolemos' death seems to have expressed tensions between the Delphians and the various incomers using and involved in the sanctuary, but his ritual role worked to resolve those tensions. Those seeing Neoptolemos as an instrument of specific accusation (rather than generalised anxiety) should also recall that heroes tend by their very nature to be problematic figures, their cult intended to harness and control their aggressive potential.

Finally, to call Neoptolemos Thessalian is as problematic as seeing Herakles as always Theban. As has been discussed above, Achilles' Phthian kingdom did not sit neatly within the boundaries of the historical Thessaly, but sprawled down into the Spercheios valley; moreover, in most ancient accounts Neoptolemos himself never set foot there. The Molossians and the Aiginetans claimed him much more energetically than the Thessalians did, before the fourth century BC at least. A comparable geographical indeterminacy attends other mythological aggressors at Delphi, such as the Phlegyai, and this prevents their interpretation as coded references to Thessalian aggression against the sanctuary.

The Phlegyai refuse to be pinned down to a single geographical location: instead, they are variously located according to circumstances and the context of a particular retelling. The earliest mention is in the *Iliad*, and while it does not allocate them to a specific settlement it does give an impression of basic geographical range. The lines come from a simile in which the hero Idomeneus is compared with Ares, sallying forth to battle with his son Phobos:

> These two would go armed out of Thrace with the Ephyrans
> Or with the great-hearted Phlegyai; they did not pay heed to
> Both equally, but gave glory to one side or the other ...[128]

125 Eur. *Andr.* 1241: Δελφοῖς ὄνειδος.

126 Paus. 1.4.4; cf. 10.24.6.

127 There existed a proverb that those sacrificing at Delphi did not themselves get to eat any of the meat (sc. because the sacrificial personnel took it all): see Plut. *Quaest. Conv.* 7.6.3.

128 Hom. *Il.* 13.301–03:

The fact that Ares and Phobos are coming out of their Thracian haunts already suggests a northern location; several places called Ephyra were known in antiquity, one of them in Thessaly later associated with the polis of Krannon, and a northern Ephyra seems most likely here, either that in Thessaly or that in Epeiros. By the early fifth century the name 'Ephyraioi' is used by Pindar of the Thessalians around the Peneios,[129] and it is quite possible that the Thessalian Ephyra was known in Homer's day, especially given the strong ties between Thessaly and Epeiros in the Archaic period (as reflected in Achilles' particular connection with Dodona: see Chapter 6). In any case, this Homeric passage seems to place the Phlegyai in the north of Greece; their conflict with the Ephyrans makes little sense if the two peoples are not neighbours. The other indubitably early link between the Phlegyai and Thessaly comes in the form of the family connection between Phlegyas, the eponym of the tribe, and Koronis the mother of Asklepios, who lived on the Dotion Plain in Thessaly.[130]

However, placements of the Phlegyai further south, especially in Phokis or Boiotia, are not flimsy late graftings onto the mythological tradition. For example, the *Homeric Hymn to Apollo* locates them on the shore of the Κηφισίς λίμνη – that is, Lake Kopais near the river Kephissos on the border between Phokis and Boiotia[131] (and indeed there was a town called Phlegya near Orchomenos, indicating a local Boiotian appropriation of the Phlegyan connection).[132] A tradition surely Theban in origin held that Thebes had been fortified by Amphion and Zethos, but that this did not ultimately protect it from capture by the warlike tribe.[133] The rule of the Phlegyai is fitted in before the arrival of Kadmos, and is presented as a dark time: apparently Pherekydes wrote that ἔρημον γενέσθαι τὴν πόλιν μέχρι τῆς Κάδμου ἀφίξεως ('the polis became a wasteland before the arrival of Kadmos').[134] Sordi has argued that this account derives from the Thebans' desire to cast Orchomenos, linked with the Phlegyai, as villains. This role of Orchomenos has a Delphic dimension: the hero Orchomenos was the grandfather of Tityos who tried to rape Leto.[135] Pherekydes is also our

τὼ μὲν ἄρ' ἐκ Θρῄκης Ἐφύρους μέτα θωρήσσεσθον,
ἠὲ μετὰ Φλεγύας μεγαλήτορας· οὐδ' ἄρα τώ γε
ἔκλυον ἀμφοτέρων, ἑτέροισι δὲ κῦδος ἔδωκαν…

129 Pind. *Pyth.* 10.55–56; see Mili (2015), 185.

130 Koronis as daughter of Phlegyas: *Ehoiai* fr. 60 MW. Koronis and the Dotion Plain: *Ehoiai* fr. 59 MW.

131 *HH* 3.278–80; Richardson (2010), 122.

132 Steph. Byz. s.v. Φλεγύα.

133 Pherekydes, *FGrH* 3 F 41b–e.

134 Pherekydes, *FGrH* 3 F 41d.

135 Apollod. *Bibl.* 1.4.1; Sordi (1966); Fowler (2013), 365.

earliest source for the story that the Phlegyai attacked Delphi, apparently being punished severely by Apollo as a result.[136]

In addition to noting the geographical variability of the Phlegyai, we should also not overlook the fact that ancient communities could actually choose to *claim* Phlegyan connections in particular circumstances. McInerney has argued that the Phokian polis of Panopeus adopted such a strategy: it espoused Phlegyan origins in order to articulate its antagonism with Delphi as that sanctuary's growth became more and more of a threat to the economic and religious balance of the region.[137] In addition to identifying themselves as a Phlegyan settlement, the Panopeans also claimed to have been the location of the attempted rape of Leto by Tityos, another act of impious aggression against Apollo.[138] So we should not assume that Phlegyan links are always imposed from outside by a hostile agency trying to use myth to denigrate a competitor or enemy. What was the situation with regard to Thessaly's Phlegyan aspects? The sources do not allow for a reconstruction of political circumstances that may have underpinned the myth-making, being late and detached from such conditions. Strabo's claim that the people of Thessalian Gyrton used to be called Phlegyai is interesting. Did the Gyrtonians consider themselves as erstwhile Phlegyai, or was this identification simply imposed on them by others? The various connections in myth between Gyrton and Phlegyas/Phlegyai suggests the former, that the Gyrtonians themselves espoused this mythic identity. Whether their doing so, however, was related to Delphi and to the Phlegyan role as Delphic aggressors is another matter. Phlegyas was connected with the Lapith Ixion and, as has been said, the story of Koronis and (by extension) Asklepios, and so plugged into the network of Thessalian mythology concerning the Lapiths and their territorial conquests within Thessaly and its environs. We cannot assume that the Gyrtonian link with the Phlegyai related directly to Delphi.

There is a tendency, then, for Delphic aggressors to refuse to be limited to a single location according to the *ethnos* boundaries prevailing from the Archaic period. Their extent can spill between *ethnē*; they can also be relocated in different texts and traditions. The latter pattern may perhaps reflect ancient mud-slinging ('You're Phlegyai!' 'No, you are!'). However, crucially, to see Thessaly as more consistently accused in this way than other groups or regions is simply not in keeping with the evidence. Rather, Delphi – with its wealth and its important interregional participants – was at the centre of a nexus of disquiet and a penumbra of mutual suspicion,

136 Pherekydes, *FGrH* 3 F 41e: 'οὗτοι δὲ ἐνέπρησαν καὶ τὸν ἐν Δελφοῖς ναὸν τοῦ Ἀπόλλωνος. ἡ ἱστορία παρὰ Φερεκύδει.' (Schol. Hom. *Il.* 13.302).

137 McInerney (1999), 169–70.

138 Ephoros, *FGrH* 70 F 31b. Myth of Panopeans at war with Phokians: Paus. 8.4.4.

sometimes focused briefly on a particular group or individual,[139] but rarely retaining that focus long. Like the tripod pulled between Apollo and Herakles, the wealth of the sanctuary was, because of its immense material and symbolic value, always potentially subject to contestation and misappropriation.

The Amphiktyony was, in a way, set up to hold fractious communities in balance, their voices equally represented on the synedrion, outrageous violence between them prevented, the interests of the sanctuary protected. It did not prohibit war between members, but rather war's most extreme manifestations. The ancient Amphiktyonic oath that Aischines quotes in *On the Embassy* prohibits the total destruction of settlements and the cutting off of their water supplies.[140] Rather than seeing the Amphiktyony as a simple instrument by which Thessaly – or any other *ethnos* – could exert control over her neighbours, it is perhaps better to consider how it sought to achieve some measure of peaceful co-existence between the interconnected *ethnē* of central Greece who had to share through-routes, passes and grazing lands. This is not to say, however, that their co-existence was without a high degree of mutual suspicion; without such suspicion, measures to limit actual violence would not have been considered necessary. But the view of the Amphiktyony as essentially serving the interests of Thessaly as the single most powerful and aggressive force in Archaic central Greece is not born out by the material at our disposal. Moreover, as we shall now see, equal caution must accompany the wider theme of which Thessaly's supposed Delphic dominance is a part: the widely held view among historians that the Thessalians operated an aggressive policy of southward expansion in the Archaic period.

139 Jason of Pherai, for example, was seen as a potential threat to the treasures of Delphi before his assassination. Xenophon (*Hell.* 6.4.30) recounts a brief anecdote to illustrate the possible menace: 'λέγεται δὲ ἐπερομένων τῶν Δελφῶν τί χρὴ ποιεῖν, ἐὰν λαμβάνῃ τῶν τοῦ θεοῦ χρημάτων, ἀποκρίνασθαι τὸν θεὸν ὅτι αὐτῷ μελήσει.' ('It is said that when the Delphians asked him what they should do if Jason should take the god's money, Apollo replied that he himself would take care of the matter.') If Jason's assassination was the workings of divine will, presumably he did constitute a real threat (in Xenophon's view). For discussion of Jason's possible intentions see Shrimpton (1991), 158–59. One further case of legendary Thessalian aggression should be noted: Diodoros' story (16.26.6) of a Pythia at some unspecified date being raped by a Thessalian named Echekrates.

140 Aischines 2.115: 'μηδεμίαν πόλιν τῶν Ἀμφικτυονίδων ἀνάστατον ποιήσειν, μηδ' ὑδάτων ναματιαίων εἴρξειν μήτ' ἐν πολέμῳ μήτ' ἐν εἰρήνῃ' ('that they would raze no polis of the Amphiktyons nor cut it off from spring-water either in peace or in war'). The phrase ἀνάστατον ποιήσειν suggests destroying a settlement so completely that its population are driven to find another home. For discussion of the Delphic oaths see Lefèvre (1998), 147–51; Funke (2013), 457; Raaflaub (2015), 438–39.

b) Thessalian invasions

> During the first half of the sixth century enlightened administration of their national state so united the Thessalians that they formed the strongest military power in Greece. Moreover, by their control of the Amphictyony at Anthela they were enabled to exert a wide influence over the lesser peoples of the north. After the First Sacred War the Amphictyony was transferred to Delphi, and its reorganisation welded almost the whole of northern Greece into a Thessalian empire. Phocis was now subject, and it seemed that Boeotia too must soon be conquered. But here the tide of success turned. An aggressive foreign policy was continued throughout the half-century which preceded the Persian Wars, but the scanty notices of Thessalian affairs in this period present a catalogue of almost uninterrupted set-backs. This remarkable change in the course of Thessalian imperialism must be attributed to internal decay within the national state.[141]

It may seem unfair to hold Westlake up as an example of erroneous approaches to Thessalian history. After all, his work, published in 1935, did not benefit either from the considerable archaeological and especially epigraphic discoveries that have transformed our knowledge of Thessaly in recent decades, or from recent advances in the understanding of ancient state-formation, ethnicity and the federal state (to name but a few influential branches of the discipline). Few could read the passage above without immediately identifying it as obsolete in several key aspects. In particular, Catherine Morgan's *Early Greek States beyond the Polis* dealt a lasting blow to the assumption that success, in early Thessaly, must be bound up with, and measured by, a certain type of unity, a proto-federalism, variously referred to by historians using such terms as 'tribe' and 'nation'.[142] In places like Thessaly, it used to be thought, regional identity was strong because individual sites were weak; the backwardness of such regions retarded urbanisation and the political evolution of the polis, and therefore the tribe or nation flourished in the vacuum thus left. Therefore Thessaly was a model for both success (tribal unity) and failure (the tardy development of the polis). None of this picture has survived Morgan's nuanced analysis of the interplay between *ethnos* and 'big sites', the latter just as influential and developed in Thessaly as elsewhere. None of it has survived the emerging archaeological picture in which sanctuaries such as those at Philia and Pherai were major sub-regional religious hubs with rich votive records. The picture of the backward and isolated Thessaly has evaporated in the face

[141] Westlake (1935), 28–29.

[142] On the modern preoccupation with the theme of regional unity as a measure of Thessalian success see Mili (2015), 213–15.

of growing evidence for the region's connections, not only with adjoining regions but on a far larger scale, in both the Bronze and the Early Iron Age. So Westlake's text might seem a mere straw man, easily – and pointlessly – knocked down.

However, in fact certain aspects of his approach, and of the traditional scholarship generally, linger on in current historiography to a surprising extent, having taken on the status of orthodoxies, implicitly accepted.[143] The model of the aggressively expansionist Thessaly underpinned the region's treatment in Larsen's still-influential 1968 book *Greek Federal States: Their Institutions and History*; it received a largely positive reframing by Lehmann in 1983. While few Thessalographers would openly espouse the model now, and while it has received several significant challenges from Sprawski in particular, it continues to exert influence, especially among historians of state-formation in adjoining and nearby regions for whom Thessalian aggression supplies a useful catalyst to political co-operation elsewhere.[144]

It has been established by various scholars, most recently Elena Franchi, that the conflicts on which the model of the aggressive Thessaly are based come to us through centuries of elaboration, adaptation and embellishment, and that they tell us more about the operation of collective memory in Phokis and Boitoia than they do about historical fact.[145] Nonetheless, this major advance in scholarly understanding has not really prevented the aggressive Thessaly from being treated as essentially factual, and from being woven into the wider understanding of Archaic central Greece, even its material remains.[146] We have already seen the weaknesses in some aspects of this belief, in particular Thessaly's use of Delphi as an instrument of expansion and control in central Greece. Now it is time to confront

143 For example, Keaveney, in his 1995 treatment of Thessalian medism, comments in his opening paragraph: 'This, *of course* [my emphasis], took place at a time when Thessalian power had waned and she had received rough treatment at the hands of the Phocians.' Cf. Rop (2019), 429: 'north and east Phocis had chafed under Thessalian rule in the sixth century'.

144 As observed by Mili (2015), 271. McInerney's analysis of Phokian development is a clear example of this trend: 'Taken together, these colourful stories [of Thessalian invasion] reveal how the domination of Phokian territory by Thessaly in the course of the sixth century cemented the loose ties that had existed previously between the communities of the region. A common enemy provided the communities of the Parnassos district with the impetus to unite' (McInerney 1999, 177). For a comparable description of the role of Thessalian aggression in Boiotian political formation see Buck (1972); Mackil (2013), 23.

145 Franchi (2016).

146 For example, traces of fire that apparently destroyed the North and South Temples at Kalapodi ca. 580 BC have been attributed to Thessalian attack: Niemeier (2013), 18; Niemeier (2017), 329. Fossey, too (1990, 140), reads new fortifications in sixth-century Lokris as responses to Thessalian incursions.

directly the ancient traditions concerning the Thessalian invasions of regions to her south. While there are some scanty testimonies concerning Thessalian activity in Boiotia, it is in Phokis that we find the most detailed and elaborate accounts, and it is with Phokis that we begin.

Three ancient authors describe Thessalian aggression against the Phokians in the Archaic period. First, Herodotos: he tells us of two battles in which the Phokians defeated the invading Thessalians; the first is against infantry, and involves a ruse in which the Phokians paint themselves with white chalk to terrify their opponents (hereafter, the Battle of the Chalk), and the second, against cavalry, also involves trickery, this time a trap of buried earthenware vessels to lame the Thessalian horses (hereafter, the Battle of the Amphorai). Later and more elaborate accounts are supplied by Pausanias and Plutarch, with a brief description also in Polyainos.[147] The significant new or changed elements in the accounts of Pausanias and Plutarch are as follows.

- Pausanias changes the order of the battles, so that the Battle of the Amphorai comes before the Battle of the Chalk. Between the two he inserts a dusk attack on the Thessalians by a picked Phokian force under one Gelon; the contingent is massacred, and trampled by the Thessalian horses. This disaster provokes the Phokians to a desperate gambit known thereafter as *aponoia Phōkikē*, 'Phokian despair', in which they placed all their women, valuables, goods and cult effigies onto a great pyre, to be set alight – with the addition of all surviving men – should the Thessalians ultimately defeat them. Finally, Pausanias tells us that, whereas the Thessalians use as their rallying-cry 'Athena Itonia', the Phokians call on the hero Phokos.
- Plutarch also includes the 'Phokian despair', but presents the gambit slightly differently: only the women and the children are placed on the pyre, and both groups are given a vote to ensure their willingness. Thereafter there is one battle, near Hyampolis, in which no ruse is included. There is elaboration on the threat posed by the Thessalians: they had previously installed governors and despots in the Phokians' poleis; these had been killed, and in reprisal the Thessalians had killed 150 Phokian hostages and invaded Phokis πανστρατιᾷ, with their whole army. The war between the two sides is called ἄσπονδος: no truce is possible; and the Thessalians have also sworn in advance to kill every man and enslave all the women and children.

Overall, the two accounts change the impression given by Herodotos in two main ways. First, the sense of jeopardy is heightened: in Pausanias' account through the inclusion of the Gelon disaster – whereas in Herodotos' we

[147] Paus. 10.1; Plut. *Mul. Vir.* 2; Polyain. *Strat.* 8.65.

have only Phokian victories – and in Plutarch's account by the revelation that the Thessalians intend to eradicate the Phokians entirely as an *ethnos* and will not agree to a peaceful resolution. In both, the motif of 'Phokian despair' is a crucial element, highlighting that for the Phokians the situation is one of all or nothing; if they cannot defeat the Thessalians then they will destroy everything that will otherwise fall into Thessalian hands. Second, the scale of the Thessalian enterprise is increased, especially by Plutarch. The background to the conflict is a period of military occupation, its duration unspecified.

There are extremely good reasons for distrusting the historical veracity of these accounts. It has long been recognised that they constitute a 'Phokian national myth'.[148] The symbolic expression of shared values and the manufacture of a positive shared identity shines from every element. Both treat the Phokians and Thessalians as primordial foes, locked in their hatred, a hatred that can be resolved only through the decisive defeat of the Thessalians or by the total annihilation of the Phokians. The Thessalians are everything the Phokians are not: tyrannical, greedy, slave-makers, putting aside the honour codes of war. They are the Adversary, which allows self-definition to crystallise. The courage of the Phokian men and the self-sacrifice of their women (and, in Plutarch, children) represents moral idealisation of the most extreme kind. Their character is forged through an image of possible extermination; their being comes from potential non-being. Such intense symbolism in the accounts is undeniable, as is their Phokian origins, for all that the authors turn them to their own authorial account.

More recently, another element has been emphasised: the fourth-century context in which the elaboration of these traditions would make most sense. Franchi has observed the various ways in which the circumstances of the Third and Fourth Sacred Wars would have encouraged expressions of Phokian solidarity.[149] Not only were Thessalians and Phokians largely on opposite sides of the conflict, but the Phokians suffered a devastating penalty upon their defeat,[150] and their opponents (Thessalians and Macedonians combined under Philip's leadership) would have been able to commandeer the moral advantage, depicting them as greedy plunderers of Delphi's treasures and as enemies of the gods (especially Apollo).[151] We have seen

[148] See esp. Ellinger (1993).

[149] Franchi (2016), 99–167; Franchi (2020b).

[150] See, for example, Demosthenes 19.65 for a vivid description of the destruction and depopulation of Phokian settlements – just the kind of disaster which, in the legends of the First Sacred War, they triumphantly averted. On the context of this episode see Harris (1995), 98–101.

[151] Justin reports that Philip dressed his soldiers in laurel chaplets, so that they fought as Apollo's representatives: Just. *Epit.* 8.2.3. Diod. 16.60.4 conveys a similar tone.

above that the legends of the First Sacred War were augmented, if not created, in this same climate, and depicted the Thessalians as instrumental in protecting Delphi against Krisaian aggression; this would have stimulated the Phokians to emphasise accounts of their own past courage and integrity.

However, this persuasive theory can account for only the expansion and elaboration of the episodes, not their fabrication; and so we return to Herodotos, and to his account of the Battle of the Chalk and the Battle of the Amphorai. The context is Xerxes' invasion of Greece in 480 BC. The Thessalians try to extort fifty talents of silver from the Phokians in return for persuading the Persians not to ravage Phokis; interestingly, the extreme threat the Thessalians represent is here depicted as the result of their collusion with the Persians. 'In the past, we were preferred to you by the Greeks, as long as we were on their side. Now, alongside the Persians, we are so powerful that we have the means to have you deprived of your land and enslaved.'[152] It is the combination of Thessalians and Persians that is so deadly. And so it proves: the Thessalians, their offer rejected, direct the Persians to go through Phokis on their way south and to do as much harm as they can, burning towns and sanctuaries and raping women. Fascinatingly, there are elements of this account that the later accounts of the Thessalian occupation of Phokis seem to wish to 'correct': in Herodotos, most of the Phokians leave, fleeing into West Lokris while a minority take refuge on Mount Parnassos; the fugitives leave behind a party of women, who are raped to death by the Persians. This seems the antithesis of the Phokians' devotion to saving their womenfolk from such disgrace in Plutarch and Pausanias. We shall return below to the ways in which the traditions of the early hostility between Thessaly and Phokis may have been shaped by memories of the Persian invasion. Returning to the course of Herodotos' account, the historian explains why the Thessalians send their unpleasant message to the Phokians in 480 BC: 'since they always nursed anger against them, especially since the latest disaster. For the Thessalians and their allies had invaded the Phokians with their whole force [πανστρατιῇ] not many years before the Persian King's campaign, and were defeated by the Phokians and treated roughly.'[153]

[152] Hdt. 8.29.2: 'πρόσθε τε γὰρ ἐν τοῖσι Ἕλλησι, ὅσον χρόνον ἐκεῖνα ἡμῖν ἥνδανε, πλέον αἰεί κοτε ὑμέων ἐφερόμεθα· νῦν τε παρὰ τῷ βαρβάρῳ τοσοῦτο δυνάμεθα ὥστε ἐπ' ἡμῖν ἐστι τῆς γῆς ἐστερῆσθαι καὶ πρὸς ἠνδραποδίσθαι ὑμέας.'

[153] Hdt. 8.27.1–2: 'ἅτε σφι ἔχοντες αἰεὶ χόλον, ἀπὸ δὲ τοῦ ὑστάτου τρώματος καὶ τὸ κάρτα. ἐσβαλόντες γὰρ πανστρατιῇ αὐτοί τε οἱ Θεσσαλοὶ καὶ οἱ σύμμαχοι αὐτῶν ἐς τοὺς Φωκέας, οὐ πολλοῖσι ἔτεσι πρότερον ταύτης τῆς βασιλέος στρατηλασίης, ἑσσώθησαν ὑπὸ τῶν Φωκέων καὶ περιέφθησαν τρηχέως.'

There follows the account of the two battles, of the Chalk and of the Amphorai. On the face of it, his account, as well as being earlier, seems brisker and less morally weighted; neither side emerges with much glory, and there is a strong flavour of *Realpolitik* in the whole episode, culminating in the cynical assertion that the Phokians resisted the Persians only because the Thessalians, their hated foe, did not. Moreover, we seem to be dealing with quite recent history, rather than events lost in the mists of time, if οὐ πολλοῖσι ἔτεσι πρότερον is anything to go by. Finally, Herodotos goes on to say that after the Battle of the Chalk the Phokians dedicated the spoils of the battle at Abai and Delphi and commissioned celebratory statue-groups in each sanctuary. This seems to anchor the story in the reality of what visitors to Abai or Delphi would have been able to see there, so verifying the essential truth of the events.

Nor is it necessary in fact to dismiss altogether the military realism of the battles themselves. There is a long-standing scholarly interest in the symbolic dimension of the Battle of the Chalk in particular.[154] Most recently, Franchi has argued that the tradition, with its irresistible resemblance to *rite de passage* motifs, serves to articulate the coming into being of the Phokian *ethnos* through imagery of the coming into being of individual young men (parallel concepts she terms ethnopoiesis and anthropopoiesis).[155] What is generally agreed is that, unlike the amphorai ruse, which would be a perfectly plausible booby-trap for cavalry, the chalk ruse is less easy to explain purely by reference to military expediency. However, while the chalk ruse clearly has some affinity with myth and ritual, and while its power within the 'Phokian national myth' probably drew on, and fed into, its symbolic properties, dismissing it entirely as a military stratagem is unwarranted. Herodotos himself identifies its basic utility. While the effect it has on the Thessalians – terror at the uncanny – is a useful side-effect, its main purpose is to allow the Phokians to tell friend from foe during a night raid, a very valuable expedient given the danger that, in the dark, an army might harm as many of its own as of the foe.[156]

Nor is it entirely impossible to imagine concerted Thessalian military action at such a time. If we take οὐ πολλοῖσι ἔτεσι πρότερον to suggest a date late in the sixth century then, significantly, this takes us into the period that also saw the formation of the tetrads, which shows a degree of

154 The most developed analysis of the traditions is that of Ellinger (1993). For a summary of past scholarship see Franchi (2017), 182–84.

155 Franchi (2016).

156 Hdt. 8.27.3: Tellias of Elis, advising the Phokians, has them smear their bodies with chalk or gypsum, and tells them 'τὸν ἂν μὴ λευκανθίζοντα ἴδωνται, τοῦτον κτείνειν' ('to kill anyone they saw who wasn't whitened'). For a reconstruction of the battle's tactical realities see Blome (2020), 9–28.

regional co-ordination that might, just possibly, have produced a πανστρατιῇ incursion into Phokis. If so, then a striking parallelism emerges between the two regions, a kind of ethnopoietic symbiosis: not only does Phokis experience events that prompt it to build on its *ethnos*-solidarity, but those events stem from increased *ethnos*-solidarity on the Thessalian side. καὶ οἱ σύμμαχοι αὐτῶν has sometimes been taken to indicate that by this time the Thessalians were already able to direct their *perioikoi*, but nothing in the Greek supports or requires such a grandiose interpretation: the Thessalians could merely have cultivated alliances with those *ethnē* whose co-operation would have been especially useful in the context of a southward incursion, the Dolopes and the Phthiotic Achaians in particular. And yet Herodotos' account certainly has a heavy admixture of symbolism alongside a probable kernel of historical reality.

The relationship between the Thessalian invasion of Phokis and the Persian invasion of Greece seems crucial to our understanding of Herodotos and his sources, and also resurfaces significantly in the later accounts. In Herodotos, the theme of the aggressive Thessaly leads to a remarkable compression of chronology. In his description of the pass at Thermopylai and the so-called Phokian Wall, he says:

> The Phokians built the wall in a state of fear when the Thessalians came from Thesprotia [lit. 'the Thesprotians'] to settle the land of Aiolis which they now possess. Since the Thessalians were trying to subdue them, the Phokians took measures to prevent this, and then directed the hot water toward the pass so that the area would become a water-course, contriving everything [they could] so that the Thessalians would not invade their country. The now ancient wall had been built long ago, and most of it lay in ruins because of the passage of time …[157]

The meshing of myth and history here is very intricate. It is as if the arrival of the Persians and the new threat faced by all of Greece reanimates a set of long-standing traditions about dangerous invaders and draws them into the present consciousness.[158] In the fifth century the Thessaloi were thought to have come over the Pindos two generations after the end of the Trojan War,

[157] Hdt. 7.176.4–5: 'ἔδειμαν δὲ Φωκέες τὸ τεῖχος δείσαντες, ἐπεὶ Θεσσαλοὶ ἦλθον ἐκ Θεσπρωτῶν οἰκήσοντες γῆν τὴν Αἰολίδα τήν νῦν ἐκτέαται. ἅτε δὴ πειρωμένων τῶν Θεσσαλῶν καταστρέφεσθαι σφέας, τοῦτο προεφυλάξαντο οἱ Φωκέες, καὶ τὸ ὕδωρ τὸ θερμὸν τότε ἐπῆκαν ἐπὶ τὴν ἔσοδον, ὡς ἂν χαραδρωθείη ὁ χῶρος, πᾶν μηχανώμενοι ὅκως μή σφι ἐσβάλοιεν οἱ Θεσσαλοὶ ἐπὶ τὴν χώρην. τὸ μέν νυν τεῖχος τὸ ἀρχαῖον ἐκ παλαιοῦ τε ἐδέδμητο καὶ τὸ πλέον αὐτοῦ ἤδη ὑπὸ χρόνου ἔκειτο … '

[158] As Franchi (2016, 305) observes, Herodotos creates an implicit analogy between Thessalians and Persians and between Phokians and resisting Greeks. She also suggests (305–27), persuasively, that the traditions surrounding the Thessalian invasion

so the episode is placed in remote myth-history, and yet this first incursion foreshadows, in Herodotos' account, that in the late sixth century. The idea that the Phokians would have been afraid at the arrival of the Thessaloi into Thessaly is clearly not historically true; even leaving aside the complete lack of historical or archaeological corroboration for the arrival of the Thessaloi in the manner here imagined – as a single violent inrush – the earlier versions of the story were in fact very different, wandering heroes rather than invading horde. The latter version arises only in the fifth century as far as we can tell. Returning to the Thermopylai description, we observe how Herodotos infuses that charged location, scene of the desperate stand under Leonidas' leadership, with apparent mementoes of the first incursion of the Thessaloi: the Phokian Wall, built to repel them (Fig. 3),[159] and even the shape of the watercourses, apparently diverted by the frightened Phokians.

On the one hand, Herodotos is retrojecting more recent Thessalian incursions into the distant past, and seeing Thermopylai as the potential pinch-point for both.[160] On the other hand, the influence between the two stories of Thessalian aggression may have gone both ways. If, after the Persian Wars, the Thessalians came to be characterised as warlike invaders, seizing land by force (Thessaly and then potentially Phokis) and enslaving resident populations (the Penestai and then potentially the Phokians), might this motif not have been just as influential on how the sixth-century events were depicted and viewed? In other words, might not small-scale raids by some Thessalians have been converted into the image of the terrifying πανστρατιῇ invasion of the whole Thessalian force? It seems more than likely.

If we return to how the Phokians in the fifth century may have wished these matters to be viewed, we can develop the idea further. The Phokians were the only Amphiktyonic *ethnos* in central Greece – and west of Athens – who did not medise wholesale. While Herodotos belittles this fact and

of Phokis may have arisen in Thessaly and been co-opted by the Phokians in the development of their myth-history.

159 The ancient wall discovered by Marinatos at Thermopylai is unlikely to be the one (apparently) built by the Phokians. See Marinatos (1940); Pritchett (1958), 211–13; Domínguez-Monedero (2015), 882. However, it is, as Sánchez-Moreno notes (2013, 346), a strong suggestion that 'in the Archaic period, Thermopylae was a point of defence and control'. Szemler et al. (1996), 49–54, argue that the Wall described by Herodotos would in fact have controlled the Dhema Pass.

160 A striking further example of the Thessalians/Persians analogy in Herodotos is the fact that the narrow track by which the Persians circumvented the pass at Thermopylai was the very one the Malians had earlier shown to the Thessalians, facilitating their invasion of Phokis (Hdt. 7.215). All in all, Thermopylai and its surroundings are imbued with local 'memories' of Thessalian aggression, traditions that are embellished and exaggerated in the aftermath of Xerxes' invasion.

Fig. 3. A section of the 'Phokian Wall' above Thermopylai, looking north towards the Malian gulf. Photograph: author's own

generally slights their contribution to the resistance, and while a shadow of doubt hangs over their general loyalty to the cause,[161] we can imagine them wishing to capitalise as much as possible on this decision once the Persians had been successfully repelled. They had stood firm while the Thessalians capitulated; moreover, the Thessalians co-opted Persian aggression to strike a savage blow by proxy at their fellow Greeks. Presenting Thermopylai as the place where they had stopped the Thessalian onrush the first time would have sent a powerful message: we helped to save Greece this time, and we did it before, on the very same spot. Explaining landmarks of Thermopylai as relics of their first victory would have tallied well with the intense memorialisation of the site in the aftermath of the battle against

[161] Questionable Phokian motives: Hdt. 8.30.2. Some Phokians fight on the Persian side at Plataia: Hdt. 9.31.5; Paus. 10.2.1. Rop (2019) argues that the ineffectual Phokian contribution at Thermopylai resulted from actual treachery rather than incompetence. As Williams remarks (1972, 8), 'It cannot be denied that the part played by the Phokians during the invasion of Xerxes was an equivocal one.' Such ambiguity is especially ripe for subsequent 'correction' through myth-making: compare the energetic self-exculpation by Alexandros I of Macedon that seems to be reflected in Herodotos' account. Of course, Herodotos is himself especially interested in these case of divided loyalties.

Xerxes' forces. As part of this, the Battle of the Chalk and the Battle of the Amphorai make perfect sense: further emphasis of the Phokians' ability to defend their northern border and triumph over the mighty Thessalian army, especially its cavalry. While total invention is implausible, exaggeration and mythologisation are absolutely plausible in the highly charged climate of self-advertisement that prevailed in the aftermath of the Persian Wars.[162]

The very things that seem to promise the most tangible proof of the Thessalian invasions of Phokis are themselves susceptible to the greatest scepticism: the Phokian dedications of Thessalian spoil and the riches of battle at Delphi and Abai. Herodotos records that the spoils from the Thessalian dead were dedicated at Abai and Delphi; a few chapters later, however, he reports that Abai was sacked and burned by the Persians in 480 BC, and its treasures looted.[163] What battle-spoils had been placed there were surely lost in this conflagration, leaving the memory of their existence and nature ripe for reworking and adaptation. Herodotos himself may have had imperfect information on this score, not having been able to view the commemorative dedications himself,[164] but by the fourth century BC, as Franchi has shown, the matter had become more complex still, with new monuments set up at Delphi to celebrate Phokian victories against the Thessalians in the context of the Third Sacred War and its aftermath.[165] In other words, while it is not plausible to deny absolutely that Abai and Delphi may have been used by the Phokians in the Archaic period to advertise victories against *some* Thessalians, physical monuments are just

[162] On the interleaving of Thessalian invasion and Persian invasion in the fourth-century formation of Phokian traditions see Londey (2020), who emphasises the extent to which the Phokians wished to rehabilitate, by reference to glorious successes of the past, both their conduct in the Third Sacred War and their rather mixed record in the Persian War.

[163] Hdt. 8.27.4–5 and 8.33. Kalapodi, the best candidate for identification with Abai, shows clear signs of this destruction: Felsch (2007), 16. As McInerney observes (1999, 60), there seems to have been a deliberate choice not to rebuild the burned temple on the same spot; instead, the charred ruins were left as a memorial. Oddly, a few months after the destruction, Mardonios apparently sent an envoy to consult several Greek oracles, Abai included (Hdt. 8.133–34.) This indicates that the oracle itself resumed functioning very quickly, despite the destruction of the temple. However, valuable and highly lootable dedications would surely have been removed from the sanctuary. See Funke (2007), 26–27.

[164] At 8.27.5, Herodotos uses the present tense – ἀνακέαται – of the dedications at Abai, as if they were still there to view in his own day, but this is misleading.

[165] Franchi and Proietti (2015), 239–42; Franchi (2016), 254–67; Paus. 10.13.4, 6–7. As Franchi notes, the existing remains at Delphi identified as the Phokian offerings mentioned by Pausanias are in fact late fourth or early third century in date. (*FD* III 3.150.)

as likely as the textual tradition to become woven into a shifting discourse founded upon a tradition of triumph over the Thessalian foe.[166]

Ultimately, we can ask ourselves *why* the Thessalians would have used their combined armed forces to invade Phokis. The answer may seem obvious, but the Thessalians were not short of rich land and other resources. Were their ambitions truly imperialist, directed at annexing and controlling all of central Greece? The only evidence we have that their sights were set even further is the highly debatable battle of Keressos, in which the Thessalians supposedly tried and failed to capture the Boiotian town of Keressos, near Thespiai, an event that may or may not have occurred earlier in the sixth century. Historians have tried to weave together this Boiotian adventure with the Phokian one and to connect the defeat at Keressos with the moment at which the Phokians rose up against their Thessalian overlords and chased the occupiers back north of the Spercheios.[167] But the only attestation of the event in ancient sources takes the form of two brief and mutually contradictory[168] mentions in Plutarch and one description in Pausanias; there is nothing about it in Herodotos.

As has been noted, both Plutarch and Pausanias were plainly in receipt of post-Archaic Phokian myth-making, and the Keressos episode seems very much to belong to the same basic discourse. The defeat of Thessaly is presented as securing the freedom of Greece, a rallying cry at home after the Persian Wars and in a sequence of later contexts.[169] As with the Phokian narratives, there is a great sense of jeopardy: the Thessalians have taken 'all of Greece up to Thespiai' and are all set to keep going, a near-unstoppable

[166] McInerney (1999, 178) believes that Abai/Kalapodi was indeed used as a locus of Phokian resistance to wholesale Thessalian aggression in the sixth century, but in fact I would argue that this represents a later accretion of Phokian tradition. The sense of competitive monument-positioning in the context of the Third Sacred War is conveyed by Diodoros' account (16.33.1–2) of the dream of Onomarchos that he was remodelling and enlarging with his own hands a statue set up by the Amphiktyons to celebrate the Phokians' punishment. Onomarchos takes the dream as a good omen for him, but it proves otherwise. For the Amphiktyons' statue see also Paus. 10.15.1.

[167] Sordi (1958), 85–91, dating Keressos and the defeats in Phokis to the years between 491 and 486 BC; cf. Morgan (2006), 235; Larsen (1968), 113–14; Mackil (2013), 23–24. For a more sceptical approach see Van Wijk (2017), 15; Tufano (2019), 41–42.

[168] The divergence is chronological: in his *Life of Camillus* (19.4) Plutarch dates the battle to 'more than two hundred years before' the battle of Leuktra in 371 BC, but in the *de Her. Mal.* (33) he suggests it took place shortly before the invasion of Xerxes. The latter is more likely to be skewed by the rhetorical needs of the text (proving that relations between Thebes and the Thessalians were anything but friendly in 480 BC), but the earlier date is far from secure. Pausanias (9.14.2) is vague on the date: πάλαι ποτέ (in the old days').

[169] Plut. *Cam.* 19.2: Leuktra and Keressos are the two battles in which the Boiotians 'τοὺς Ἕλληνας ἠλευθέρωσαν'.

force.[170] The Boiotians are thus cast as heroes who save Greece from northern marauders, a motif certainly coloured by the Persian invasions and also resembling somewhat Xenophon's characterisation of Jason of Pherai as a man who, had he not been assassinated, might have gone on to annex Greece wholesale.[171]

This is not to say that the battle of Keressos simply did not occur.[172] It would be odd for the sources to invent it *ex nihilo*. Yet its omission from earlier historians' work strongly suggests that its symbolic importance developed over time, as did the stories of the Thessalian attacks on Phokis – perhaps in their train, in fact, to supplement the increasing characterisation of Thessaly as a threat to the south. Such a characterisation was no doubt fuelled both by the Persian Wars and by fourth-century events, in particular the career of Jason and the alliance between Philip and Thessaly, which would foster the sense of Thessaly as a minatory presence on the fringe of Greece. What seems most likely is that a contingent of Thessalians fought a battle for some very much more specific purpose than a wholesale regional take-over. Scholars have long suspected that internal Boiotian politics may have been involved. If we should in fact place Keressos at the end of the sixth century, opting for something approximating Plutarch's earlier date, then we might conjecture some link with Thessalian – that is, Aleuad – support for Peisistratos and the Peisistratids at that time. Larson has argued strongly for a close relationship between the Peisistratos (and his sons) and the Thebans;[173] perhaps Peisistratos brokered an alliance by which the Thessalian cavalry would help to subdue a Boiotian polis resisting Thebes' attempt to secure regional domination.[174] That Thessalian armies were willing to undertake such ventures to enhance their influence abroad is born out by their aid to Hippias in 510 BC. However, it should be noted that that seems to have been enacted not on the level of the whole *ethnos* but as a matter of personal *xenia* and its obligations, obligations that may have extended to helping their friends' friends, the Thebans.

[170] Plut. *de Her. Mal.* 33: 'τῆς Ἑλλάδος αὐτοὺς κρατοῦντας ἄχρι Θεσπιέων.'

[171] Xen. *Hell.* 6.4.30–32. Indeed, there is a striking analogy between Xenophon's depiction of Jason and how Plutarch presents the outcome of Keressos. Xenophon casts both Jason and the Spartans as dire threats to Greece's liberty, which is then heroically saved; Plutarch sees Keressos and Leuktra, the latter a Spartan defeat, as milestones in the preservation of Greek freedom. On this aspect of Jason's portrayal see Dillery (1995), 173–74; Sprawski (1999), 12.

[172] Beck and Ganter (2015), 136–37.

[173] Larson (2000).

[174] Thespiai, near (and controlling) Keressos, took a different stance when the Persians invaded, siding with the Hellenic League; this suggests some resistance to Theban hegemony.

Overall, though, we should follow the cautious maxim of Van Wijk: 'The ambiguity surrounding this position and extremities in dating prevents any plausible argument to be made to regard the Thessalians as catalysts in the political landscape of central Greece at the end of the sixth century.'[175] It is astonishing how much has been made, and continues to be made, of an event as insubstantial and obscure as Keressos in reconstructing great swathes of Archaic political history and casting the Thessalians as the perennial aggressors. Given also that none of the military actions covered here can be shown to have been a pan-Thessalian venture, we would also be very ill-advised to follow the dictum of Westlake and others that an aggressive Thessaly is a unified Thessaly, operating with the benefit of a full federal army. Instead, we should envisage specific Thessalian communities pursuing their own specific aims, such as the Aleuadai's cultivation of friends in Athens and – perhaps – Thebes.

3. Conclusions

The chief aim of this chapter was to challenge the formula linking unity to strength and dominance in Thessaly's relations with the other *ethnē* of central Greece in the Archaic period. This cast serious doubt on the traditional narrative by which the Thessaly of the fifth century represents a serious falling-off of power and prestige; in fact, that power and prestige was shown to be posited on the slimmest and most problematic of evidence. The cherished image of the Thessalian cavalry sweeping south down the Great Isthmus Corridor, threatening the lives and freedom of the Phokians and others, did not generally stand up well to critical scrutiny.

The implications of challenging the model are considerable, not only for our understanding of early Thessaly but for other Archaic institutions as well. The Delphic Amphiktyony, so far from being the means by which the Thessalians enacted their dominance among their southern neighbours, was in fact a far more complex political environment in which different groups regarded each other with suspicion but found a vital mode of co-operation through religious observance, and were prevented from carrying out the worst excesses of military oppression. The Amphiktyony was also crucial in supplying a context where *ethnos* identity really mattered, where Thessalians were represented *qua* Thessalians, as well as facilitating contact with other *ethnē* whose *ethnos*-expression was undergoing its own processes of articulation and development, especially in the sixth century. The collective nature of this process, testing and reinforcing borders and discrete identities in the crucible of religious collaboration, should not be overlooked in favour of seeing the Amphiktyony as a Thessalian empire thinly disguised under

175 Van Wijk (2017), 15.

a layer of religion. Myth, too, was shown to be collaborative rather than conflictual; the *Aspis* presents Apollo as both Delphic and Thessalian, and Kyknos as the enemy of Thessaly as well as of Delphi.[176]

In general, the role of large-scale conflict in processes of ethnogenesis needs to be approached with circumspection. Larsen saw Thessaly as the Sparta of the north, building a land empire through concerted force and the subjugation of neighbours, just as Sparta did in the Peloponnese.[177] This neat Greek symmetry, on the horizontal axis, may no longer be overtly espoused, but it continues influential, as historians of Phokis and Boiotia use Thessaly to explain their regions' ethnogenesis or formation of political cohesion. And the role of an external aggressor in fostering collective identity cannot be overlooked; to give one example, the influence of Spartan aggression on the development of Messenian identity has been analysed in detail by Luraghi.[178] The present chapter, however, urges caution in applying that model to the north. As section 1 of this chapter outlined, Thessaly was by no mean precocious in her own ethnogenetic process, nor able early to generate military excursions on a regional basis. Instead, therefore, of seeing a unified Thessalian *ethnos* as the catalyst to *ethnos*-formation in central Greece, we should envisage a situation of mutual influence and low-level border conflicts over the course of the seventh and sixth centuries.

As we move into the next chapter, these themes will be further explored. The importance of Thessaly in Archaic epic has often been seen as a manifestation of her cultural and political dominance. However, close examination of the material reveals a very different picture, one in which the priority seems not to be to pit the Thessalians against other *ethnē* but rather to express their connectedness within the wider (aristocratic) Greek world. In this process, Thessaly is not united but is rather divided up into sub-regional zones, local heroic dynasties and separate nodes within an interregional network of myth.

[176] We might also consider the fact that the hero Phokos, son of Peleus, seems to represent a Phokian desire to forge or emphasise a connection with Thessaly. The belief in longstanding hostility between Thessaly and Phokis causes Franchi (2017) to develop the ingenious idea that the Phokians were trying to be *equal* to Thessaly, because they were threatened by them. But if we consider the myth as arising in the conditions of the Early Iron Age or even earlier, when Thessalians and Phokians met at Kalapodi and may have enjoyed reasonably harmonious relations, such a claim is not actually needed. As with interpretations of the *Aspis*, a preoccupation with armed conflict can cause a distorted reading of ambiguous mythology.

[177] Larsen (1968), 14, 108, 111.

[178] Luraghi (2002) and (2009).

2

Thessaly and Archaic epic

> Thessaly makes up in the realm of mythology for its shortcomings in history.[1]

At first glance, this statement seems to be at odds with the historiographic tendency identified in the preceding chapter: the persistent and ill-founded claim that Thessaly was a dominant power in the Archaic period. In fact, however, both that idea and Brown's remark arise from the same basic motive: to compensate for a perceived deficiency in Thessaly's historical achievements. In Chapter 1 that compensation took the form of the ingenious revelation of traces of past glory in the face of sparse and problematic evidence. Here we find a slightly different suggestion: that *at least mythology* gives us the Thessaly we think we ought to find, one with a strong record of dynamism and influence.

Though we may reject the discontent and problematic assumptions at work in both forms of compensatory scholarship, Brown's comment does identify a truth: that while Thessaly cannot be claimed to feature particularly prominently – though there are exceptions – in most of our ancient narratives of major historical events, its appearance in mythology is apparently substantial. Thessalian mythological figures stand at some of the most important junctures in Greek myth and epic. One has only to think of the wedding of Peleus and Thetis to see the force of this. Thetis' maternal role is obviously central to the *Iliad*; her reluctant marriage to Peleus featured in the *Kypria* and can be identified in art as early as the seventh century, becoming popular in the sixth.[2] Thetis is a figure of cosmic import: she is the instrument of fate, being destined to produce a son greater than his father, and she is even accorded cosmogonic powers in a fragment of Alkman (seventh century).[3] Her son, Phthian Achilles, dominates the

[1] Brown (1986), 387, n. 1.

[2] *Kypria* frs 1 and 2 West. The wedding itself is most famously depicted on the early sixth century dinos by Sophilos (London BM 1971,1101.1). For scenes of the wrestling of Peleus and Thetis see Aston (2011), 61–64.

[3] Alkman fr. 5 *PMG*. See Detienne and Vernant (1978), 140–42; Slatkin (1991), 53–84.

Iliad and all the works it influenced. Add in Jason and his crew of heroes from across Greece, voyaging to the Black Sea and back, the healer hero/god Asklepios and many other significant heroes, and it may very well be thought that Thessaly was one of the major crucibles of Greek myth and epic.

Interpreting this trend, however, is not straightforward. Two basic questions present themselves. The first concerns agency: does a significant role in epic necessarily mean that the active Thessalian participation in the production and transmission of epic was also significant, or might non-Thessalians have adopted – perhaps even invented – Thessalian mythological figures? As part of this, was Thessaly perhaps 'good to think with' for non-Thessalian poets, charged with symbolic meaning extending far beyond the region's own myth-making in the active sense? Second, even if Thessalian agency was involved, how does this relate to the conscious development and articulation of Thessalian *ethnos* identity?

1. Thessaly in Homer

a) Thessaly behind the Iliad *and* Argonautika*: the 'Iolkos Cycle'*

No poem raises the agency question more cogently than the *Iliad*. Several scholars from the nineteenth century onward[4] developed the theory that the poem evolved out of Thessalian prototypes.[5] A version of this approach has been pursued by Martin West in an article of 1988 and more recently in his book *The Making of the* Iliad (2011). In the article he posited the existence of what he called the 'Iolkos cycle', which would have included 'the Lapiths and Centaurs, whose Thessalian designation φῆρες survives in Homer; the story of Pelias, Jason, and the Argonauts who sailed from Pagasai; the funeral games for Pelias; the exploits of Peleus'.[6] This early epic cycle he situates in the late Mycenaean period. In his more recent monograph he draws back somewhat from suggesting that Thessaly had a rich epic tradition of this kind, and instead posits story-telling traditions that fed into the production of epic verse elsewhere. It is doubtful how helpful the distinction between stories and epics really is; tales of heroes may have naturally been couched in hexameters in a culture so steeped in

[4] See Drews (1979), 111–12 for a review of earlier theories.

[5] Cf. Nagy (2011b), who argues on the basis of dialect forms in the poems that Homer was Aiolian – from the eastern Aiolian zone rather than the Greek mainland, but receptive to mythological traditions from Thessaly. On the linguistic evidence for an (eastern) Aiolian branch of epic composition see Jones (2012). Janko suggests that the Aeolic elements reflect the incorporation into the Homeric poems of verse from both Aiolis and Thessaly: Janko (1982), 91–92.

[6] West (1988), 160.

traditions of verse composition. However, the major contribution of West's book is to show how non-integral Achilles is to the *Iliad*; so far from being a direct rehash of an earlier Thessalian poem, the *Iliad* attaches to the non-Thessalian Trojan War story a hero from northern Greece who does not really belong there.

West draws attention to the several mentions in the poem of Achilles' raids, conducted independently, on various sites on and around the island of Lesbos. On this he remarks: 'The ancestors of these Aeolians had come from Thessaly in the late second or early first millennium. Achilles' unfocused marauding makes him appear as their forerunner. He establishes no colonies, he leaves no descendants, but he takes control of the region and paves the way for the later immigrants.'[7] Leaving aside the question of whether the Aiolian migration ever actually occurred,[8] West's observation challenges Thessalian poetic agency head-on. If Achilles' 'unfocused marauding', part of the earlier myth that the poet of the *Iliad* takes over and incorporates in his epic, was intended to commemorate travel and contact between Thessaly and the Aiolian lands of western Asia Minor, from which side of the Aegean did the stories arise? Quite possibly the Thessalian side, originally. In the tenth and ninth centuries, as has been seen, southern Thessaly in particular was part of the trans-Aegean network of trade in which Euboia played a pivotal role, and such contacts may well have fed into Thessalian myth-making, encouraging the development of stories in which their heroes roamed and raided far afield.[9] Indeed, as early as LH IIIC there is evidence of trading connections between Thessaly, Phokis, Euboia and Skyros, the last of these especially interesting given the myth of Achilles' adolescent spell on that island.[10] Euboian influence is also a strong possibility.[11] And yet there is no evidence that Thessalian connectivity in

[7] West (2011), 43.

[8] Parker (2008) argues against using the theory of the migration to explain the distribution of the Aeolic dialect; he builds on Rose (2008), who emphasises the lack of archaeological corroboration for a substantial settlement of Aiolis by migrants from northern Greece, and argues that the tradition of the Aiolian migration arose in the aftermath of the Persian Wars. In general there has been a justified turning aside from models of large-scale, systematic population movements at certain key junctures in early Greek history; see, for example, Hall (2002), 71–73; Beck (2019), 390–91; Bernstein (2019). For criticism of Parker's views, however, see Nagy (2011b); summarising and reconsidering the linguistic evidence for the relationship between Thessalian and Lesbian: Finkelberg (2018).

[9] For 'decentralised maritime trading activity' as a phenomenon increasing after the end of the Mycenaean period see Sherratt and Sherratt (1991), 373; Lis and Ruckl (2011), 164–65.

[10] Deger-Jalkotzy (1999), 195 and (2004); Livieratou (2012), 94–97.

[11] This idea is espoused by West (1988); see, however, the critical discussion of Cassio

the Early Iron Age was especially focused on Lesbos and its environs. This specific geographical dimension of Achilles' freebooting activities seems to be shaped by an early awareness of shared Aiolian identity between the two zones, and, as we shall see below, other groups – especially the Athenians and the Aiolians of Asia Minor – are the ones deliberately cultivating Achilles as a figure to link northern Greece with the Troad.

Thessaly's most famous travelling hero, however, is Jason. This lands us in a situation very similar to that of Achilles: the recognition that early Thessalian myths find their lasting and accessible form in the mouths of non-Thessalian poets.[12] The story of Aison, Pelias and Jason probably has its roots in the Mycenaean age; this is strongly suggested by the fact that Iolkos, at its heart, a rich prize fought over, a local power, was not in fact a particularly significant site after that period. This is not to say that identifying Jason's Iolkos is straightforward. One strong contender is modern Dimini. Not only was Dimini a major Neolithic and Bronze Age site, but recent excavations have also revealed a picture of continuous – though not of course uniform – habitation and importance throughout those periods. The Mycenaean phase commenced in the late fifteenth century but reached its peak, according to the archaeological material, in LH IIIB2.[13] However, Pantou has challenged the traditional view of Dimini as a dominant regional centre, suggesting that if we look collectively at Dimini and the nearby Bronze Age settlements of Kastro and Pefkakia we find no clear evidence that any one achieved a position of hierarchical superiority over the others;[14] rather, their equality of status and lack of fortifications suggest a non-hierarchical co-operative relationship. So it is not the case that Dimini supplies us, in simple fashion, with Iolkos the home of King Pelias or King Jason. It may even be that 'Iolkos' was the way in which Thessalians after the Mycenaean age nostalgically described the interlocking triad of Dimini, Pefkakia and Kastro, and that they simplified the power structure of 'Iolkos' to a single ruler. We cannot be sure. However, it is also significant that the three sites on the Bay seem to have been in a condition of close interdependence with those of the interior, especially Pherai. That this relationship should form the basis of the interlocking family trees of Aison and Jason with Pheres and Admetos is highly likely.

If the Jason myth emerges from this crucible of Bronze Age sites on and inland from the Bay of Pagasai, however, it does not remain limited to that

(1998), who argues that, though Euboian myths may well have found their way into epic verse, there is no linguistic evidence for a Euboian context for epic composition.

[12] For a discussion of the various stages of the myth's transmission and adaptation see Green (1997).

[13] Adrymi-Sismani (2006), 467.

[14] Pantou (2010); see also Morgan (2006), 239.

region for very long. While we do not have a surviving Archaic epic treating Jason's adventures, it is clear that one lies behind the *Odyssey*, supplying Homer with various elements of Odysseus' voyage such as the Symplegades.[15] It has also been convincingly argued that this earlier Argonautic poem reflects a Milesian perspective and was designed to valorise and legitimate Miletos' exploration and colonisation of the Black Sea.[16] We should not go so far as to say that a Milesian poet grafted a story of maritime adventure onto a Thessalian original that dealt solely with events within Thessaly. In the later Mycenaean period the Thessalian sites mentioned above were by no means insular backwaters, and it is even possible that they imported gold from the Black Sea, something which historians and archaeologists have inevitably tried to make the basis for the Golden Fleece.[17] Even if that is far-fetched, the Fleece does take us east; it has been persuasively argued that it has its origins in the Anatolian ritual object the *kurša*, a bag of hide that stood for kingship and plenty; Jason's dragon-killing may have Hittite origins as well.[18] It need not be imagined that these Anatolian elements entered the story only after it had passed from Thessalian hands to Milesian ones; they are likely to have been integral to its original composition, not least because the role of the *kurša*/Fleece as an embodiment of a king's authority fits well with the Iolkian part of the myth and the need for Jason to win his rightful throne through trial. And the cult of Zeus Laphystios at Halos in Achaia Phthiotis, though first attested in Herodotos,[19] was probably much older; in the mythology surrounding this cult the figure of

15 West (2005), 39–43; West (2014), 30 and 39–43; Dowden (2006), 197. N.b. – Jason's quest is also mentioned in Mimnermos (seventh century): fr. 11 and 11a W; Allen (1993), 87–93.

16 Epic composition against a backdrop of Archaic Greek expansion and colonisation: Crielaard (1995), 224–39. Active participation in the Jason myth by Greek communities around the Black Sea: Braund (1996). For an overview of the colonisation in the Black Sea region: Tsetskhladze (1998). A Milesian, Arktinos, was thought to have composed the *Aithiopis*, in which Achilles, after death, is carried to the Island of Leuke by Thetis.

17 The ancients themselves suggested that the Fleece originated in the historical practice of sifting alluvial gold from rivers: *TGrF* Adespota fr. 37a; Strabo describes the practice without linking it to the Jason myth at 11.2.19. For discussion see Bremmer (2007), 14–15; Lordkiparidze (2001). A Kolchian origin tentatively suggested for gold in a Bronze Age tomb in Thessaly: Adrymi-Sismani et al. (2009). On gold extraction in and around Kolchis in antiquity: Hauptmann (2011); Stöllner and Gambashidze (2011). Lordkiparidze (1996, 43) is sceptical of the idea that Mycenaean sailors travelled from Greece all the way to Kolchis; cf., however, Thomas (2005), 79–82, who asserts the feasibility of such a journey, based in part on its reconstruction by Timothy Severin (see Severin 1986).

18 Bremmer (2007) and (2008, 310–17); for a more sceptical discussion see Rutherford (2020), 95–97.

19 Hdt. 7.197.

Phrixos (integral to the story of the Fleece's origins) was central. As with Achilles, it seems most likely that early Thessalian myth-making supplied the Jason story, if not in its entirety, then with its two key elements – Iolkian power struggle; voyage to Kolchis – in place, but that the form in which we receive this – via the *Odyssey* – comes through, and was shaped by, a Milesian intermediary.

It should be stressed that none of the above discussion is intended to argue that the Thessalians stopped telling their own stories once others had started to make use of them. Probably they went on as before, cultivating the myths that had resonance and traditional power within specific sub-regions: stories of Peleus, Thetis, Cheiron and Achilles in Phthiotis and Pelion, stories of Pelias, Aison and Jason around the Bay of Pagasai, stories of Asklepios and his sons in Hestiotis and so on; moreover, these stories will have circulated and developed. We shall meet them again at various stages over the chapters of this book and over the centuries of Thessalian history. However, there are two important points we can make. The first is that when we meet the stories in their developed and fixed form, as famous epics, they are not of Thessalian manufacture. The second is that in the form we have them they tend to serve non-Thessalian purposes. They legitimate processes in which other Greeks were involved. The sense of direct Thessalian agency is very hard to identify. Thessaly lies behind the major epics, a shadowy presence, its involvement belonging chiefly to an earlier stage.

b) The impossibility of nostos

However, it is not only the case that the poets of our surviving epics drew on earlier Thessalian material that does not now survive. More than that, the poet of the *Iliad* in particular cultivates a certain view of Thessaly that is very far from that of a dynamic, active region. If the *Iliad* was in any way intended to serve the cultural interests of the inhabitants of southern Thessaly in the poet's own time, by enhancing their prestige and the heroic credentials of their elites, then it may be quickly observed that he did a poor job of it. (In fact, of course, we shall see that that was anything but his intention.)

As Mackie has shown, building on the work of Nagy,[20] Phthia – part of Achilles' contingent at Troy, and his homeland – plays a peculiar role in the *Iliad*. It is not just that its relative obscurity seems a poor match for the eminence and fame of Achilles; that had been noted long before.[21] It is more that the poet of the *Iliad* actually cultivates that obscurity. Up to Book 18, Phthia is named by Achilles as the place to which, in his

20 Mackie (2002); Nagy (1999), 174–89.
21 Kirk (1985), 186.

disgruntlement with Agamemnon, he might decide to return. From Book 18, Mackie detects a shift: returning to Phthia becomes wholly incompatible with winning *kleos aphthiton*, unwithering renown, and the poet actively encourages the linguistic echo of the *phthi-* element in both words. φθίω means 'I wither away, I die', and Phthia is cast as the land of obscurity and reputational death.[22] In a sense, I would suggest, Achilles inherits this theme from his mother. For Thetis, Phthia means marriage to a mortal, Peleus, a state she abhors. It means a contamination of her divinity and the production of mortal children, of which the most famous is of course Achilles. Her dissatisfaction with this situation is certainly present in Archaic epic: *Iliad*, *Kypria*, *Aigimios*. In the *Iliad*, of course, it is channelled rather differently, as grief for the fate of her all-too-mortal son, but even there her own resentment finds some mention.[23] For Achilles, Phthia means the death of renown; for Thetis, it means contaminating involvement in the lives, and indeed the creation, of mortals. I would go so far as to suggest that, though it found historical usage in the form of Phthiotis, in origin the name Phthia was devised – by whom we cannot say – as an element in the storytelling, to explore the central theme of the hero, his relationship with death.[24] The opposite of Phthia is Leuke, the White Island: here Achilles (in the *Aithiopis*, not in the *Iliad*)[25] finds a kind of eternal luminescent semi-divinity. It is surely no coincidence that Achilles actually received cult honours on the Black sea, at Olbia and present-day Smeinÿi. This cult was founded and tended by Milesian colonists, a world away from the lives and

[22] As Sammons (2010, 184–94) argues, this theme is prefigured in the arrangement of the Thessalian part of the Catalogue of Ships. Both Protesilaos and Achilles fall into the pattern of the 'absent leader'; both have powerful death associations; and even the seemingly irrelevant mention of the Styx, within the contingent of Gouneus, is meaningful: 'The image of a river from the Underworld flowing into a river of the earth, but failing to mix with it, reflects the uneasy mixture of the living and the dead peculiar to the Thessalian section of the catalogue' (p. 194).

[23] Hom. *Il.* 18.432–33. In the *Kypria* Thetis rebuffs Zeus' advances and her marriage to Peleus is her punishment for this; in the *Aigimios* we find a totally un-Iliadic story in which she boils her children to ascertain their mortality and to rid herself of the perishable ones, only just stopping short of inflicting this treatment on the baby Achilles.

[24] What of Achaia, which Nagy argues (1999, 69–93) to have chimed with *achos*, grief (an element also present in the name Achilleus)? In this case we cannot plausibly consider the name a poetic fiction; rather, it may be assumed that the poet exploited fortuitous linguistic resonances.

[25] *Apud* Procl. *Chrest.* 4; for an overview of the text see Rengakos (2015). While Homer does not send Achilles home to Phthia, he does consign him to the underworld and to a condition of murky impotence. On the relationship between *Iliad* and *Aithiopis* and their different treatment of Achilles' afterlife see Edwards (1985).

preoccupations of the people of southern Thessaly.[26] The Thessalians seem not to have a major hero-cult of Achilles in their own territory, though they were interested in Thetis: see below.

Achilles also had a tomb-cult at Sigeion in the Troad, and as Nagy shows this is likely to be the historical basis for the references in the *Iliad* and the *Odyssey* to the hero's tomb. Homer may not have allowed Achilles to escape his mortality, but he did allow him a significant burial whose site is actually signalled as a place of future cult:

> Then over them both we put up a great and faultless
> Tomb, we the holy army of Argive spearmen,
> On a promontory jutting out over the broad Hellespont,
> So that it would be visible from afar to men from the sea
> Both for those who live now and for those who will come in the future.[27]

The cult at Sigeion was a major religious and maritime landmark, of interest not only to the local Aiolian population but also, from the time of the Peisistratidai, to the Athenians.[28] Nagy also suggests Thessalian pilgrimage, based on the famous account in Philostratus' *Heroikos* of Thessalian *theoriai* to Achilles' tomb. However, that work is extremely problematic as evidence for Thessalian cult practice (see further pp. 350, 391 n. 184, 393, 421–23), and we lack other evidence of Thessalian activity in the area before the Hellenistic period. While we cannot posit Thessalian inactivity purely from the silence of the sources, it is safe to say that their involvement in the cult of Achilles in the Troad, or for that matter on the Black Sea,[29] is far less visible than that of other communities – locals or Greeks with an interest in maritime trade and expansion. As in the case of the Milesian worship of Achilles on the Black Sea, the hero in this zone appeals to those whose ships ply along the shores of the area and for whom Achilles can provide a heroic precedent of

[26] Ostroverkhov and Okhotnikov (1996), 272–73, noting that the earliest architectural remains of the temple of Achilles on the island are mid-seventh century, and that the first graffiti of Achilles' name from the site are from the middle of the sixth century or slightly earlier.

[27] Hom. *Od.* 24.80–84. Cf. *Il.* 23.125–26:

> ἀμφ' αὐτοῖσι δ' ἔπειτα μέγαν καὶ ἀμύμονα τύμβον
> χεύαμεν Ἀργείων ἱερὸς στρατὸς αἰχμητάων
> ἀκτῇ ἔπι προὐχούσῃ ἐπὶ πλατεῖ Ἑλλησπόντῳ,
> ὥς κεν τηλεφανὴς ἐκ ποντόφιν ἀνδράσιν εἴη
> τοῖσ', οἳ νῦν γεγάασι καὶ οἳ μετόπισθεν ἔσονται.

See Nagy (2010), 147–51.

[28] Nagy (2010), 147–77.

[29] For the cult of Achilles in the Black Sea see Hedreen (1991); Rusyaeva (2003). For a useful overview of his various cult sites see Burgess (2009), 111–31.

their own ventures. As for the Aiolians worshipping Achilles at Sigeion, for them Thessaly was the motherland, the starting point of their *ethnos*.[30] By possessing Achilles' tomb they had secured a vital product of their mythical homeland, and this signalled Achilles' departure from Thessaly forever.[31] This meshes with the theme of his non-*nostos* in the *Iliad*; in Book 23 (lines 138–51), when he dedicates his shorn hair to the dead Patroklos, he says that this is the very hair he would have given to the river Spercheios upon his return. By consecrating it to Patroklos' shade he redirects his allegiance from Thessaly to the Troad and prefigures the way in which that land will claim his own body, cult and *kleos*. Thessaly has lost him, and seems to have made no move, through an Achilles-cult of its own, to reclaim him.

The non-*nostos* of Achilles is part of a more general tendency to cast Thessaly as a place left behind and not returned to. Achilles is not the only hero who does not go back to Thessaly. Another example is Neoptolemos, who takes part – an especially bloody and disruptive part – in the final phase of the siege of Troy. It might be argued, quite reasonably, that we should not expect Achilles' son to regard Thessaly as his home, as a suitable destination for *nostos*; after all, he was not born there. However, after Achilles' death he was Peleus' heir; moreover, Achilles' departure and death had left the old man sorely vulnerable and in need of the support of his friends and relations, especially when embroiled in a feud with Akastos, son of Pelias and king of Iolkos. The *Odyssey* is very rare in allowing Neoptolemos to make his way to Phthia, leading his father's Myrmidones; most authors, including the poet of the *Nostoi*, have him journeying from Troy to Molossia, more or less directly.[32] There he obtains a kingdom by force of arms and establishes a dynasty, producing a son, Molossos, by Hektor's widow Andromache, before dying violently at Delphi. The key driving force behind the development of this myth is obviously the ruling family of the Molossians, who claimed descent from Neoptolemos' son Molossos.[33] It is unlikely to be the case that they diverted to themselves the figure of Neoptolemos who had previously been thought to return to, and rule, in Phthia; the *Odyssey*'s version does not support that idea. There are no signs of early Thessalian interest in Neoptolemos.[34] Rather, we should see his *nostos* as essentially of Molossian manufacture.

[30] Nagy (2010), 149. On Aiolian assertion of Thessalian origins see Beck (2019), 385–86 and 393–95.

[31] On the origin of the concept of the Aiolian tribe in Asia Minor rather than mainland Greece: Ulf (1996), 250.

[32] Hom. *Od.* 3.188–90.

[33] Kittelä (2013), 36–40.

[34] Nor can we follow Fontenrose (1960) in believing that both Neoptolemos and Achilles were primordial Thessalian fertility deities.

Achilles dies; Neoptolemos goes to Molossia (and then dies); Peleus too leaves according to Euripides' *Andromache*, in which the Aiakid diaspora from Thessaly is at its fullest:

> [Thetis speaks to Peleus:] As for yourself, in order that you may feel gratitude for your marriage to me, [1255] I shall set you free from mortal woe and make you a god, deathless and exempt from decay. And then you shall dwell with me in the house of Nereus, god with goddess, for all time to come. From there, walking dry-shod out of the deep [1260] you will see your beloved son and mine, Achilles, dwelling in his island home on the strand of Leuke in the Sea Inhospitable. But go to the god-built city of Delphi with the body of this man, and when you have buried him in earth, [1265] go to the hollow cave on the ancient promontory of Sepias and sit. Wait there until I come from the sea with a chorus of fifty Nereids to escort you.[35]

No-one is left in Thessaly. Instead, the departing Aiakidai form a network: Neoptolemos has his hero-tomb at Delphi, and has left his line in Molossia; Achilles is on the White Island in the Black Sea, a site of genuine cult of the hero from the Archaic period;[36] Thetis returns to her watery abode, having lived very little in Thessaly; and Peleus goes to join her. Who rules in Phthia? It is not made clear. A strange vacancy is produced. Pharsalos is left with Thetis' cult – a real one – but the heroes have decamped.[37]

[35] Eur. *Andr.* 1254–69:

σὲ δ', ὡς ἂν εἰδῇς τῆς ἐμῆς εὐνῆς χάριν,
κακῶν ἀπαλλάξασα τῶν βροτησίων
ἀθάνατον ἄφθιτόν τε ποιήσω θεόν.
κἄπειτα Νηρέως ἐν δόμοις ἐμοῦ μέτα
τὸ λοιπὸν ἤδη θεὸς συνοικήσεις θεᾷ·
ἔνθεν κομίζων ξηρὸν ἐκ πόντου πόδα
τὸν φίλτατον σοὶ παῖδ' ἐμοί τ' Ἀχιλλέα
ὄψῃ δόμους ναίοντα νησιωτικοὺς
Λευκὴν κατ' ἀκτὴν ἐντὸς ἀξένου πόρου.
ἀλλ' ἕρπε Δελφῶν εἰς θεόδμητον πόλιν
νεκρὸν κομίζων τόνδε, καὶ κρύψας χθονὶ
ἐλθὼν παλαιᾶς χοιράδος κοῖλον μυχὸν
Σηπιάδος ἵζου· μίμνε δ', ἔστ' ἂν ἐξ ἁλὸς
λαβοῦσα πεντήκοντα Νηρῄδων χορὸν
ἔλθω κομιστήν σου· τὸ γὰρ πεπρωμένον
δεῖ σ' ἐκκομίζειν…

(Trans. Kovacz.)

[36] Hedreen (1991), 319–22.

[37] On the cult of Thetis near Pharsalos see Pherekydes *FGrH* 3 F1a and 1c; Eur. *Andr.* 19–20; Strabo 9.5.6; Livy 33.6.10. *Pace* Ghisellini (2017), there is no very solid evidence of a significant cult of Achilles himself in Thessaly.

To return to the Jason story that lies behind parts of the *Odyssey*, we find there further examples of the motif of the Thessalian diaspora. Jason himself does return to Thessaly, with Medea, and it may be that the earliest version has them settling peacefully there; in the *Theogony* their son Medeios was brought up by Cheiron on Pelion, maintaining the family tradition.[38] From the mid-sixth century, however, vase paintings allude to the story of Medea boiling Pelias to death,[39] and this gruesome act may belong to an alternative version in which she and Jason, unable to remain in Thessaly after the murder, hand the throne of Iolkos to Akastos and leave for Korinth, where Jason dies. Euripides gives him an inglorious end, struck on the head by a falling timber from the Argo. (Is the implication that the ship itself is disintegrating?)[40] Jason creates no lasting lineage, in Thessaly or elsewhere: his children by Medea die in Korinth, and the closing section of Euripides' *Medea* seems to suggest that Korinthian religion included some hero-cult for the dead children.[41] Again, a Thessalian hero seems to have been diverted from *nostos*, his mythology fed into the myth-history of a different community (here, Korinth). The absence or removal of descendants is closely allied with the failure of *nostos*. Achilles too left no family, no possibility of a subsequent line of heroes, in Thessaly, since Neoptolemos was conceived and born on Skyros. In this regard he is like Protesilaos, who, though he does marry in Thessaly, leaves and dies at Troy before he can father a child. At *Iliad* 2.701, Homer remarks that Protesilaos left behind a distraught new wife and a δόμος ἡμιτελής, a half-finished house, not in the sense of half-built, but rather incomplete because of the marriage cut short before it could bear fruit.

The very name of the Hellespont – location of Achilles' *sema* – is itself relevant to this theme of Thessaly as the land left behind. Here Helle, daughter of Athamas and sister of Phrixos, drowned when she fell from the magical ram that carried the young people away from their murderous stepmother Ino. Phrixos reached Kolchis safely and there sacrificed the golden ram to Poseidon, installing the Fleece Jason would later take, but Helle, dying, gave her name to the straits of the Dardanelles.[42] Whether we should consider Phrixos and Helle as Thessalian or Boiotian is an unnecessary dilemma; the story had links with both regions, and

[38] Hes. *Theog.* 1000–01.

[39] For example, the famous neck-amphora attributed to the Leagros Group, ca. 530–520 BC, showing Medea 'rejuvenating' a ram to deceive the daughters of Pelias: Harvard Art Museums 1960.315.

[40] This is not made clear in Eur. *Med.* 1386–88, but the scholion *ad loc.* says as much.

[41] Eur. *Med.* 1381–83. The Pheraians – probably – tried to rectify this lack of lineage by creating the figure of Thessalos son of Jason and Medea: see Chapter 3.

[42] For the early traditions, verse and prose, surrounding this story see Fowler (2013), 195–205.

establishing primacy with any certainty is impossible.[43] As Fowler remarks, 'The split location mirrors many other points of contact between these two regions', including a cult, in each, of Zeus Laphystios, the deity to whom Phrixos and Helle narrowly escape being sacrificed.[44] Herodotos' account of the cult of Zeus Laphystios at Halos, in which the figure of Phrixos plays an important role, gives a strong impression of a religious institution deeply embedded in the community's civic life, rather than a recent innovation. Like Achilles later (later in myth-time, that is), Helle travelled across the Aegean from Thessaly/Boiotia and established a permanent landmark on its eastern shore.[45] As Nagy observes, the Hellespont, with its dangerous shipping conditions, is central to the perceived character of Achilles and of his tomb, the former as a son of the marine Thetis, the latter as a beacon for imperilled sailors. Neither Helle nor Phrixos ever perform the journey in reverse; like Achilles, they leave Thessaly behind them for ever.

At this point one has to step back and consider in more general terms how the *nostos* motif really works in Greek culture, and what it was for. As scholars have remarked, to translate the word as 'return' or 'return home' is to overlook how rarely, in the spread of Greek *nostos*-stories, that actually happens.[46] Fowler calculates that, of forty-six heroes setting out from Troy after its fall, only seven certainly reach their homelands.[47] This is not because Greek poets loved heroic failure, as modern British authors and audiences arguably do. Instead, two purposes are achieved. The first is to emphasise a major watershed in myth-historical time: the Trojan War and its aftermath signal the end of the age of the *hēmitheoi*.[48] Second, *nostos* allows new players to insert themselves into the picture, by claiming or creating heroes whose journey takes them to a new land, to found a new dynasty. Stories of travelling heroes were particularly used to confer solid credentials upon newly established *apoikiai*, and Thessalian poleis did not take part in the Archaic city-foundations. Newly established communities quite often claimed a Thessalian ancestor or founder, while Thessalian communities did not make equivalent claims for themselves. The one major exception to this pattern – the arrival in Thessaly of the founder-hero Thessalids – appears in the late Archaic period and in the next chapter of

43 Bremmer (2008), 304–05 (noting that even within the *oeuvre* of Euripides there is indecision in the matter). See also Schachter (2016), 181–82.

44 Fowler (2013), 200.

45 In addition to the Hellespont itself, there was a supposed grave of Helle nearby: see Hdt. 7.58.2; for discussion of the site and its significance in Herodotos' account of Xerxes' march see van Rookhuijzen (2019), 86–89.

46 Stewart (2017), 141; Malkin (2018), 88–89.

47 Moreover, 'The lines of the three major heroes who return home, Polyxeinos, Menelaos and Nestor, run into the sand.' Fowler (2018), 53.

48 Fowler (2018), 43–44.

this book. Before then, Thessaly was a net loser of heroes, not a net gainer. Its diasporic role will also be observed in Section 2, below, when we turn to the *Ehoiai*.[49]

However, in addition to this practical reason for the trend, we can discern a wider tendency – surely both its cause and its result – for Thessaly to be associated with past time. The figure of Cheiron exemplifies this. In the *Iliad* he has taught healing to both Achilles[50] and Asklepios;[51] later texts (but not necessarily later traditions) add Jason, Herakles and others.[52] He epitomises the age of the *hēmitheoi* and its values.[53] His charges grow up and go off to wars and adventures and death; he remains. Even Cheiron, however, does not endure for ever, and Pindar's *Pythian* 3 begins with the 'common prayer' that Cheiron might be alive again, since mankind misses his 'mind friendly to man'; as I have argued elsewhere, death and loss are Leitmotifs in Cheiron's character.[54] His seniority casts him as 'before'; his death casts him as absent.[55] Just as Phthia is left without Aiakid heroes, Pelion is left without its Best of Centaurs (until he is restored to the religious landscape of Magnesia in the third century BC: see Chapter 7).

c) New uses for old stories

The Molossian rulers' claim on Aiakid lineage was achieved through *nostos* and heroic descent,[56] in a way that connected them with the *nostos*-traditions of epic as well as with the illustrious myth-history of Thessaly.[57] However,

[49] A further example of this trend from the fifth century is the myth of Melanippe, who, raped by Poseidon (the main event of the *Melanippe Sophe*), leaves Thessaly and goes to Metaponton with her twin sons by the god. This was part of the myth-history of the city of Metaponton, and drew both on Thessalian and on Boiotian mythology (on which see Chapter 3). Stewart (2017), 144–51. The hero Gouneus also fails to accomplish his *nostos*, and is implicated in the foundation of Kyrene, in post-Homeric sources: Helly (1973), vol. I, 64–65.

[50] Hom. *Il.* 11.830–32.

[51] Hom. *Il.* 4.217–19.

[52] A sort of 'snowball effect' seems to have led to more and more heroes being attached to Cheiron's tutelage by ancient authors, but Jason's case is certainly early: see above.

[53] Cheiron the teacher of traditional heroic values: Gregory (2018), 57–84.

[54] Aston (2006).

[55] Gregory (2018), 28, 36; she further observes (88) that the *Iliad* presents Cheiron as displaced by Phoinix from the prime role of Achilles' teacher.

[56] The heroic lineage is summarised by Plut. *Pyrrh.* 1.2.

[57] The clearest indication of this is Euripides' *Andromache*, probably composed in part to please King Tharyps of Molossia. Recent scholarship confirms the importance of Tharyps' rule to the political and cultural development of Epeiros: see Domínguez (2018), esp. 11–13. In addition to establishing Neoptolemos as ancestor of the royal line, the play is chiefly set in and around the sanctuary of Thetis near Pharsalos. For

sometimes the appropriation of Thessalian heroes was carried out not through *nostos* but by a more basic process of transfer. The community that focused its self-representation on the Aiakidai with unparalleled energy was the Aiginetans, and it is their behaviour in the early fifth century that gives the clearest picture of how old myths and rituals could be adapted to serve the particular conditions of the post-Persian War age.

It seems likely that the figure of Aiakos was of Thessalian origin; as West remarks, 'Homer has the short and apparently complete genealogy Zeus – Aiakos – Peleus – Achilles', and he notes also the ways in which the story of Aiakos creating the Myrmidones out of ants (*murmikes*) seems to fit well with the *Märchen* quality of early Thessalian myth, in which he identifies a particular concentration of 'fabulous' elements such as human/animal transformation.[58] By the time of the *Ehoiai*'s composition, however, Aiakos is placed instead on the island of Aigina, and this does seem to be one instance among many of other communities appropriating myths of Thessalian origin. However, the Aiginetan tradition is no flimsy add-on;[59] in that sphere the myth of Aiakos and his progeny takes on a depth of integration into collective self-projection that it never appears to have, as far as our evidence will take us, in any Thessalian community.[60] And what the Aiginetans do with the Aiakidai in the early fifth century gives us a powerful model of how old myths may be adapted to meet changing conditions, conditions far from favourable to the maintenance of Thessalian influence on the formulation of the stories.[61]

the play's political context see Stevens (1971), 15–18; Allan (2000), 149–60; Easterling (1994), 79; Stewart (2017), 139–44. Taplin argues for performance at the Pylaia at Anthela, followed by a tour of Thessalian towns: Taplin (1999), 44–48. This would make Thessalian interests more significant than Molossian ones, but the play itself – in which, as noted above, Thessaly is the origin-point of a wholesale diaspora – does not really support such a view.

58 West (1985), 162–65.

59 Nagy, indeed, argues that West's emphasis on Thessalian primacy ignores the 'contractual' nature of the myths: 'It is not that the Aeginetans made the gesture of relocating from Thessaly a native Thessalian myth about Aiakos and a mother named Aegina by linking this myth with their own native Aeginetan myth about their own nymph named Aegina. From the standpoint of the Hesiodic *Catalogue*, the pathway for the relocation of myths must have been a two-way street, as it were, not one-way from Thessaly to Aegina.' Nagy (2011a), 53–62.

60 For a detailed analysis of the development of the myth of the Aiakidai and its incorporation into Aiginetan self-representation see Polinskaya (2013), 422–36. She makes the important point (520–31) that we should not see the Aiginetans as 'stealing' the myths from Thessaly; rather, they deliberately maintain their Thessalian origins, enshrined in Homer, and Thessalian connections are a key part of the myths' valency.

61 Prinz (1979), 34–55. For the Aiakid myths against the backdrop of sporting competition and its celebration see Beck (2020), 118–20.

At the battle of Salamis in 480 BC, the Aiakidai joined the Greek naval effort. How exactly this occurred – perhaps in the form of their cult statues conveyed on board ship – is debated.[62] However, the import, especially in Herodotos' account, is clear: they, Aiginetan heroes par excellence, assist the cause of Greek resistance and help to turn the tide of battle in the Greeks' favour. The special duality of Greek allegiance in the Persian Wars is in evidence: on the one hand, the Aiakidai favour the cause of Greece; on the other, their Aiginetan identity allows Aigina to compete with Athens in claiming the key role in the battle and in the defeat of Persia more generally. It is worth noting that they dedicated a nautical votive – a ship's mast ornamented with stars – at Delphi in celebration of the battle, their moment of collective *aristeia* in the wider conflict. This should be seen against the backdrop of accusations of Aiginetan medism; the justice of these claims is uncertain, but the way in which Herodotos presents them is significant, since the Athenians interpret it as just a new parry in Aigina's long-standing antagonism with them.[63] Deploying the Aiakidai on Hellas' behalf allowed the Aiginetans to live down their own questionable allegiance while maintaining the assertion of their superior Hellenic credentials.

Kowalzig has argued that the incorporation of the Aiakidai in the panhellenic rhetoric of the salvation of Hellas goes far beyond the battle of Salamis.[64] Particularly interesting is its Delphic dimension, whose enactment would of course have come to the attention of the Thessalians and all the other medising Amphiktyonic *ethnē*.[65] The key source for this process is Pindar, whose poems for Aiginetan patrons are especially numerous and utilise a striking quantity of Aiakid mythology.[66] As well as numerous *epinikia*, Pindar's *Paian* 6 is highly significant. The poem is likely

62 Nagy (2011a), 50. See also Irwin (2010), 397–423, for discussion of Herodotos' depiction of the Aiginetans at the battle of Salamis.

63 Hdt. 6.49.3: 'ποιήσασι δέ σφι ταῦτα ἰθέως Ἀθηναῖοι ἐπεκέατο, δοκέοντές τε ἐπὶ σφίσι ἐπέχοντας τοὺς Αἰγινήτας δεδωκέναι ὡς ἅμα τῷ Πέρσῃ ἐπὶ σφέας στρατεύωνται, καὶ ἄσμενοι προφάσιος ἐπελάβοντο, φοιτέοντές τε ἐς τὴν Σπάρτην κατηγόρεον τῶν Αἰγινητέων τὰ πεποιήκοιεν προδόντες τὴν Ἑλλάδα.'

64 Kowalzig (2007), 181–223. A more nuanced picture is given by Polinskaya, who modifies Kowalzig's claim in two important ways: first, by asserting the influence, on our view, of ancient authors (especially Herodotos and Pindar), who had their own conceptions of panhellenism; and, second, by claiming that 'saviours of Greece' was only one of many symbolic personae that the Aiginetans sought to project. Polinskaya (2013), 528–31.

65 Aiginetan celebratory dedications at Delphi after Salamis: Scott (2010), 84–85.

66 For discussion of Aiginetan propaganda in epinikian see Burnett (2005), 13–28; Fearn (2007), 96–105; Hornblower (2007), 294–97. On the importance of the Aiakidai in the work of Aiginetan local historians see Figueira (1991), 87, n. 21.

to have been composed, probably in the 470s BC,[67] for performance at the festival of the Theoxenia at Delphi, a ritual occasion on which the hero Neoptolemos, despite his own association with problematic sacrifice, was thought to preside over the sacrificial meal offered to both gods and humans at the festival.[68] Part at least of the poem was composed, apparently, 'for the Delphians', and reflects Pindar's crucial role in contributing to what Rutherford has called a 'programme of Delphic propaganda';[69] certainly it suited Delphi, in the earlier fifth century, to find channels through which to assert its utility and value to Greece, after the somewhat patchy record of its behaviour during the second Persian invasion, the medism of most of the Amphiktyons and the rather lukewarm rhetoric of the oracle. However, *Paian* 6 also lauds Aigina, and is a good example of another trend Rutherford observes: the role of Pindar in helping to mesh together Delphi and local Greek communities in presenting both as working for collective Hellenic ideals.[70]

The first Triad of the poem establishes the context of the Theoxenia (the poet describes himself as ἀγῶνα Λοξίᾳ καταβάντ' εὐρὺν ἐν θεῶν ξενίᾳ, 'having come to the broad gathering for Loxias on the occasion of the guest-festival of the gods'). The second opens with a statement that the sacrifice is being conducted 'on behalf of glorious Panhellas, which the *ethnos* of the Delphians prayed (to save from) famine', and goes on to recount the sack of Troy by the Aiakid Neoptolemos, and his death at Delphi in a quarrel with sanctuary attendants. The third heaps praise on Aigina – the Διὸς Ἑλλανίου φαεννὸν ἄστρον[71] – and recounts the ravishing of Aigina by Zeus and the 'boundless virtues of the Aiakidai'. A bundle of associations is at work here: Aigina's close connection with Neoptolemos, the guarantor of good sacrificial procedure at Delphi on behalf of Greece; the Aiginetan cult of Zeus Hellanios, a god of rain-bringing and drought-prevention; and Aiakos himself, who – according to myth – interceded with Zeus on behalf of all the Greeks and so brought a drought (and resulting famine) to an end.[72] The proper provision of food is at the centre of this bundle: sacrificial meat properly shared among gods and all Greeks; and grain, its successful production guaranteed by Aiakos as mankind's champion. Especially in

67 Rutherford (2001a), 331 n. 95.

68 Nagy (1999), 59–61 and 118–27; Suárez de la Torre (1997), 168–72; Hedreen (2010). On Aiginetan *theōriai* to Delphi and the link with Neoptolemos see Polinskaya (2013), 246–59.

69 Rutherford (2001a), 179.

70 Rutherford (2001a), 181; see also Hedreen (2010).

71 'Bright star of Zeus Hellanios' – lines 25–126.

72 On the cult of Zeus Hellanios see Polinskaya (2013), 336–43, who observes that the cult was not actually panhellenic, but epichoric; a subtle evocation of panhellenism was, however, central to its character.

the fifth century,[73] when the aftermath of the second Persian invasion had threatened to tarnish their credentials, the Aiginetans had the perfect incentive to advertise their local myths and cults as being dedicated to the common weal.[74] Hellenism had been the subject of competitive display in the Archaic period, of course: witness, for example, the Hellenion at Naukratis, signalling the shared Greekness of various communities of Asia Minor and adjoining islands, and plainly saying that Eastern Greeks had just as strong a claim on Greek identity as their mainland counterparts.[75] But a special urgency and a new set of priorities arose in the decades following the defeat by the Hellenic League of the invading forces of Xerxes.

Nor was the appropriation of the Aiakidai in this new context apparently limited to Aiginetan self-presentation. In the verses of the 'New Simonides', the figure of Achilles plays a prominent role in the so-called Plataia Elegy, in which the hero, to whom a hymn is addressed, seems to have served as a paradigm of martial valour and self-sacrifice.[76] Considerable discussion surrounds the place of first performance and the specific community or communities with which Achilles might have been implicitly associated.[77] It has even been argued that, since Achilles was strongly associated with Thessaly, the poem was attempting to rehabilitate the Thessalian character, blotted by their recent medism.[78] This does not, however, convince; Achilles' links with Thessaly at this time were not particularly robust, and nothing in the surviving portions of the poem seems to be trying to give Achilles a Thessalian identity. In fact – although a Delphic performance context might have pleased the Aiginetans, given their involvement in the cult of Neoptolemos there – Kowerski is surely right to emphasise the panhellenic tone and purpose of the poem, and of Achilles. The hero stood for all

[73] Needless to say, the religious institutions were of earlier origin: the archaeological remains of the sanctuary of Zeus Hellanios on the island go back at least to the sixth century. Kowalzig (2007), 204–07.

[74] Another prime motivation was the longstanding rivalry with Athens; in the late sixth century the Athenians had established their own cult of Aiakos, which Figueira plausibly interprets as a political gambit: Hdt. 5.89.2; Figueira (1991), 104.

[75] Kowalzig (2007), 198.

[76] For a reconstruction of Achilles' presentation in the poem see Rutherford (2001b), 42–45.

[77] For a summary of the places proposed see Rutherford (2001b), 40–41. Especially interesting is Shaw's argument (2001), that the poem was performed at the Isthmian Games, and that – while its audience and perspective were panhellenic – it evoked two religious networks, that of Achilles' cult sites and (connected through maritime associations) that of the worship of Poseidon. While Thessaly had, of course, a share in both Achilles and Poseidon, there is no sense in which the poem appears to be favouring the region in any way.

[78] Bearzot (1997).

Greeks who fought against the Persians, and in many cases lost their lives, gaining ***kleos aphthiton*** in the manner of the doomed hero.[79] The fact that Achilles could be used in this way conveys his lack of strongly epichoric associations. He was ripe for appropriation. Once again, non-Thessalian agency is most visible, as it was in the composition of the *Iliad*.

This is not to say that the mythological figures made famous by epic lost all their importance in Thessalian religious life. Phrixos was important in Halos, Thetis in Pharsalos; there were games in honour of Protesilaos at Phylake in Achaia Phthiotis;[80] Jason's sandal turns up on Larisaian coins in the fifth century.[81] But there is no sign of these institutions being used to assert a privileged role for Thessaly within the discourse of Hellenism; they seem merely to have maintained their local importance, no doubt of long standing, within specific Thessalian communities.

d) Thessaly in the Iliad*'s Catalogue of Ships*

Though ultimately the Trojan War stripped Thessaly of many of its heroes, the *Iliad* itself serves to immortalise their origins, especially in the great muster-roll of contingents and heroes, the Catalogue of Ships in Book 2. Few parts of the *Iliad* have generated more scholarly interest and disagreement than this section, discussion tending to focus on three particular aspects: first, whether the Catalogue records a particular historical reality of places and *ethnē* (and, if so, which one); second, why the places and peoples included are listed in the order they are; and third, its role within the poem as a whole and whether it may be considered integral and born out of

79 Kowerski (2005), 96–107.

80 Stamatopoulou (2007a), 333–34; the key ancient evidence is Pind. *Isth.* 1.58 and school. *ad loc.*, and – even more striking – a later fifth-century bronze hydria from Pelinna whose inscription identifies it as a prize from the games (Athens NM 13792). See also Bouchon and Helly (2013), 211, n. 17. However, there is a slight puzzle over the provenance. The inscription identifies the vessel as coming from 'Aia of Phthia'. Is this the Aia in Malis, as Helly argues (1995, 137–40)? If so, the hydria, rather than confirming the contests at Phylake, would suggest that another location was involved in the hero's cult, and was also claiming an association with the realm of Achilles. It is certainly perfectly feasible to find such an elision of the two heroes' spheres of influence. Perhaps Aia was on the border between Malis and Achaia Phthiotis, its identity somewhat labile? On the other hand, as Doulgeri-Intzesiloglou points out (2000, 156–60) there is mention of an Aia in Thessaly, Steph. Byz. s.v. Αἶα, and it is possible that this one was in Achaia Phthiotis. Note also Paus. 6.11.5: Theogenes of Thasos wins a running race in a festival ἐν Φθίᾳ τῇ Θεσσαλῶν, 'in Phthia of the Thessalians' (or 'Thessalian Phthia'). Nielsen (2014, 114) takes this as evidence of a fifth-century festival in Thessaly, 'presumably in honour of Achilles', but it is more likely that Pausanias is using 'Phthia' for 'Achaia Phthiotis', and the occasion referred to was the festival in honour of Protesilaos.

81 See, for example, *Triton* XV, 80–83.

the same time and context of composition.[82] As regards the first question, the Thessalian section represents no one time-period or cultural moment exactly; indeed, of all parts it is arguably the hardest to make fit with any particular historical context, as Sprawski notes.[83] Moreover (and this draws in the second aspect), which places are included, and how, goes beyond any geopolitical reality because it also relates to how the poet worked, the emphases he wished to create and also, more fundamentally, systems of memorisation and performance.[84] All in all, while Morgan seems justified in identifying the Archaic period as the age whose realities the Catalogue most closely resembles,[85] the resemblance should still not be overstated, and I am not persuaded that we can identify in the Catalogue a clear reflection

[82] The following serve as a few salient examples of influential and significant views. Among those claiming Mycenaean origins for the Catalogue, Hope Simpson and Lazenby (1970) certainly deserve mention; they reinforce a position held by earlier scholars such as Allen (1921), and the Bronze Age focus certainly did not end with them: cf. Latacz (2004), 219–38. In fact, the Bronze Age basis of at least the Boiotian material has received further corroboration, he argues, from a Linear B tablet found in Thebes in 1993, which names many of the sites included in the Catalogue of Ships. An eighth-century date, on the other hand, is proposed by Anderson (1995) and by Visser (1997).

[83] Sprawski (2014b), 86; cf. also Kullmann (2012), 218–19. Kullmann believes that the place-names in Thessaly are for the most part identifiable and that the confusion lies in their distribution among the relevant heroes, which is done rather haphazardly 'in order to give each of them a kingdom without always knowing precisely the geographical situation' (219). Compare Gounaris (2012), who argues that no attempt to draw a map of the territories apparently described in the Thessalian portion of the Catalogue is ultimately convincing, because we are not dealing with neat, fixed blocks of land under stable monarchic control; instead, he posits a highly nomadic and mobile society. This is an attractive suggestion, but ultimately unpersuasive.

[84] Memorisation: Clay (2011), Minchin (2001). The particular challenge of memory in the Catalogue is signalled by Homer himself at *Il.* 2.488–92. Theories concerning the order of the Catalogue include considerations of the identity and therefore the perspective of the Catalogue's composer (e.g. as a Boiotian: Kirk 1985, 178–79; Anderson 1995), as well as stylistic analysis, connecting it with the themes and characters of the wider poem (e.g., Sammons 2010, 135–96; Marks 2012), relating it to the mnemonic processes of oral poetry (Minchin 2001) and examining the relationship between geography and syntax (as applied to Boiotia by Jasnow et al. 2018). Giovannini's argument that the content and order of the Catalogue reflected the theoric routes of Delphic envoys may be hard to accept in every detail, but we cannot discount the possibility of a strong Delphic dimension to the Catalogue, for example in the inclusion of northern *ethnē* such as the Perrhaiboi and Magnetes who appear in the Catalogue (Perrhaiboi: 2.748–50; Magnetes: 2.756–59) and who had Amphiktyonic membership but almost no narrative significance in the rest of the *Iliad.* See Giovannini (1969); cf. Kullmann (2012), 220–21. As Kirk observes (1985, 185), the difficulty lies in the claim that the theoric routes attested in Hellenistic inscriptions existed in exactly that form in the Archaic.

[85] Morgan (2003), 103–05; cf. Morgan (2006), 237, who suggests that 'the Thessalian

of how Thessalian communities saw themselves, or wanted to be seen by others, at that time. Clearer, I think, is the sense of a poet drawing on tangled skeins of myth and heroic genealogy and loosely applying them to the territories and toponyms with which the oral tradition associated them.

The idea that the Catalogue had origins independent from the rest of the *Iliad* is based on some notorious mismatches between it and the rest of the poem, most strikingly in the warriors featured in the former but not, or barely, mentioned in the latter, or *vice versa*, and the fact that the Boiotians bulk so large in the Catalogue while their contribution to the actual action of the poem is slight.[86] However, to infer from this that the Catalogue is not really integral to the *Iliad* is unnecessary when one considers its true purpose. On the one hand it is logical – by the criteria of ancient epic – to list the participants in a major war.[87] On the other hand, we can see a further purpose beyond the requirements of the narrative, what might loosely be termed a political value to the Catalogue. Like the *Ehoiai* discussed below, the Catalogue serves as a muster-roll of Greekness. Whereas the source material on which he drew was probably much more localised, a Peloponnese-centred Trojan expedition teamed with the northern raider Achilles, the poet of the *Iliad* is creating a panhellenic story, a *grande geste* of boundary-setting and community-definition. And so we may ask ourselves what role Thessaly – the Thessalian block – plays in such a project. It was argued above that in the composition of the poem as a whole Thessaly was rather passive: Homer used early epic, but bound it into a new form whose purposes were anything but Thessalian, taking Achilles to the Troad and leaving him there. And yet the Catalogue of Ships seems to put Thessaly back into the frame. With what import?

Famously, Thessaly is not Thessaly in the *Iliad* – it is never named as such, nor its people called Thessaloi. This will be discussed further in Chapter 3, where it will be argued that the poet of the *Iliad* did indeed know of Thessaloi and Thessalia, but that these names were omitted partly in order to maintain chronological integrity: Thessaly did not become Thessaly until the sons of Thessalos arrived there after the Trojan War. However, is Thessaly really wholly absent as an entity? In fact, it is possible that Homer does use a collective name for the northern third of

section seems to offer a highly abbreviated insight into what was probably a dynamic picture of interlocking tiers of political affiliation and identity.'

86 Hom. *Il.* 2.493–510: the Boiotians have fifty ships; see Kirk (1985), 178–79. Heroes mentioned in the Catalogue but nowhere else include the Magnesian Prothoos: 2.756–58. Cf. Aias, 2.557–58: a brief entry for a warrior whose role elsewhere in the poem is considerable.

87 This was a standard component of martial epic, as West (2011, 111–12) observes. He, however, espouses the view that the poet of the *Iliad* drew on a pre-existing poetic account of the muster at Aulis.

his Catalogue. Strabo,[88] and some modern scholars,[89] suggested that τὸ Πελασγικὸν Ἄργος, with which the Thessalian block begins, is an umbrella term for what follows – that is, for all of Thessaly (probably including what would we would call the *perioikis*).[90] This has linguistic logic: line 681, 'νῦν αὖ τοὺς ὅσσοι τὸ Πελασγικὸν Ἄργος ἔναιον', does signal a major shift rather than just the start of the next contingent,[91] and while it may at first seem just to belong to Achilles' command, the first in the block, this impression derives much from the punctuation, which would not have been part of the poet's own composition.

Of course, there is a different explanation: that the scholiasts – and Strabo – who saw Pelasgian Argos as denoting all of Thessaly were influenced by a desire to find unity and cohesion in the northern Greek section that would have matched the political conditions of their own ages but not those of the poem. Moreover, the flourish of νῦν αὖ τοὺς ὅσσοι may reflect the massive spatial jump that the poet has just performed, across the Aegean from the Koan and adjoining contingents with which he has previously been dealing. However, on balance and especially because of the τοὺς, it is very tempting to see Pelasgian Argos as Homer's deliberately archaising name for Thessaly, his alternative to the anachronism of the name Thessalia. The thematic unity of the northern block may also be suggested by the fact that the poet, having closed the Catalogue of human participants on the Greek side, appends a short but significant section on the horses that went with them: 'τίς τὰρ τῶν ὄχ' ἄριστος ἔην σύ μοι ἔννεπε Μοῦσα / αὐτῶν ἠδ' ἵππων, οἳ ἅμ' Ἀτρεΐδῃσιν ἕποντο.'[92] The horses of Eumelos son of Pheres are singled out as best, but only as long as those of Achilles are kept out of the fray by their master's wrath. No non-Thessalian horses are even mentioned.

It seems plausible to detect a 'Thessalian flavour' in such equestrian focus, and to consider that the 'Catalogue of horses' is intended to close,

[88] Strabo 5.2.4: 'καὶ τὸ Πελασγικὸν Ἄργος ἡ Θετταλία λέγεται, τὸ μεταξὺ τῶν ἐκβολῶν τοῦ Πηνειοῦ καὶ τῶν Θερμοπυλῶν ἕως τῆς ὀρεινῆς τῆς κατὰ Πίνδον, διὰ τὸ ἐπάρξαι τῶν τόπων τούτων τοὺς Πελασγούς.'

[89] See, for example, Loptson (1981). *Contra*, taking the phrase to refer to part of Achilles' domain: Sourvinou-Inwood (2003), 109.

[90] Strabo (5.2.4) thought that the term just denotes the Thessalian plains (as is implied also in Steph. Byz. s.v. Ἄργουρα), but in fact Homer does nothing to suggest a distinction between plains and mountainous fringes; quite the reverse, since many of the contingents include portions of both.

[91] West (2011), 119. As scholiasts on the line suggest, the τοὺς requires an implied verb, which must be something meaning 'Tell me, Muse, of … ' or 'I shall sing of … '; it is as if the poet is starting the Catalogue afresh.

[92] Hom. *Il.* 2.762–63: 'But tell me, Muse, who was far the best among them – best of the warriors and of the horses that followed with the sons of Atreus.'

appropriately, a coherent regional block within the larger Catalogue. However, it is undeniable that the poet's chief focus is on the separate contingents, in which a key connecting principle is kinship on the level of individual heroic genealogies. Moreover, crucially, while they are grouped programmatically, they are not described as a single *ethnos*; 'Pelasgian Argos' seems to be a territorial rather than ethnic designation, and includes non-Thessalian *ethnē* such as the Magnetes and the Perrhaiboi. The contingents of Achilles are perhaps the most striking example of the complexity of the contingents and the non-alignment of their edges with the political and ethnic boundaries we see in operation from the late Archaic and early Classical period.

> And, as for those who dwelt in Pelasgian Argos:
> those who inhabited Alos, Alope and Trechis,
> and those who held Phthia and Hellas of the lovely women –
> these were called Myrmidones and Hellenes and Achaioi,
> and Achilles commanded their fifty ships.[93]

This raises a number of questions. Are the Myrmidones, Hellenes and Achaioi essentially the same people, or three separate groups? If the latter, how do they map onto the toponyms? Which toponyms designate settlements and which broader regions? Which are historically attested? Are the others wholly imaginary? We must be resigned to sharing some of the palpable confusion of Strabo when he says

> As for Phthia, some say that it is the same as Hellas and Achaia, and that these constitute the other, the southern, of the two parts into which Thessaly as a whole was divided; but others distinguish between Hellas and Achaia. The poet seems to make Phthia and Hellas two different things when he says, 'and those who held Phthia and Hellas … '.[94]

Regarding the groups listed, it seems that only 'Achaioi' had any real valency in the historical period. As has been said, they are included as an

[93] Hom. *Il.* 2. 81–685:
νῦν αὖ τοὺς ὅσσοι τὸ Πελασγικὸν Ἄργος ἔναιον,
οἵ τ' Ἄλον οἵ τ' Ἀλόπην οἵ τε Τρηχῖνα νέμοντο,
οἵ τ' εἶχον Φθίην ἠδ' Ἑλλάδα καλλιγύναικα,
Μυρμιδόνες δὲ καλεῦντο καὶ Ἕλληνες καὶ Ἀχαιοί,
τῶν αὖ πεντήκοντα νεῶν ἦν ἀρχὸς Ἀχιλλεύς.

[94] Strabo 9.5.6: 'Φθίαν τε οἱ μὲν τὴν αὐτὴν εἶναι τῇ Ἑλλάδι καὶ Ἀχαΐᾳ, ταύτας δ' εἶναι διατεμνομένης τῆς συμπάσης Θετταλίας θάτερον μέρος τὸ νότιον· οἱ δὲ διαιροῦσιν. ἔοικε δ' ὁ ποιητὴς δύο ποιεῖν τήν τε Φθίαν καὶ τὴν Ἑλλάδα ὅταν οὕτως φῇ 'οἵ τ' εἶχον Φθίην ἠδ' Ἑλλάδα,' ὡς δυεῖν οὐσῶν …' (trans. Jones, adapted).

ethnos in the Delphic Amphiktyony; by contrast, Myrmidones and Hellenes have the nebulous quality of legend.[95] As for the place-names, Phthia came to be strongly identified with Pharsalos (see Chapter 3), and it is quite possible that Achilles' part of the Catalogue should be imagined as including a portion of the later tetrad of Phthiotis, even though the name Phthia is itself not a real town or area, but a symbolic idea, as discussed above.[96] Of the other toponyms, Alos is a settlement, probably to be identified with the polis of Alos/Halos described by, for example, Herodotos.[97] Alope has been somewhat tentatively located on the coast to the south of Mount Othrys,[98] looking towards the western end of Euboia and, beyond that, the coast of Lokris (where, intriguingly, is the well-attested polis of Alope and another called Halai).[99] Trachis was also a settlement, later satisfying the criteria for inclusion in the *IACP*; its post-Homeric identity is Malian. Despite the uncertainty of locations and identifications, it is clear that we are dealing with a diverse sprawl of territory and groups ranging across southern Thessaly, Achaia Phthiotis and the Spercheios valley. The patchwork of *ethnē* discussed in Chapter 1 is not wholly absent from the Catalogue, but they plainly do not constitute the poet's chief way of ordering territory, nor are they coterminous with the contingents under the heroes' command.

As suggested above, we have to exercise caution in assuming historical reality behind the Catalogue; nonetheless, Achilles' mixed command cannot but remind us of the conditions prevailing in the region in the Early Iron Age: the network of inland and maritime connections linking southern Thessaly with Lokris, Phokis, Euboia and beyond. We noted above Achilles' role as a 'freebooting hero', in keeping with the seafaring of the Early Iron Age, and probably integral to his origins, drawn by the poet of the *Iliad* into his epic, from central and northern Greek story-telling origins. This

95 Finkelberg (2005), 30, n. 18.

96 That said, cf. *Il.* 9.447, 478–84: Phoinix' father Amyntor rules Hellas, which seems to be adjacent to Phthia; when Phoinix as a young man has to flee his home he escapes into Phthia, where Peleus gives him refuge. He ends up 'on the edge of Phthia, ruling over the Dolopes'. This suggests that Phthia, if it was ever an actual region, stretched westward along the Spercheios rather than north to Pharsalos.

97 No rough breathing in Hdt. (7.173.1 and 197.1); Halos, however, seems to become standard from Demosthenes (19.163) onwards.

98 Helly (1995, 87) describes its placement as 'approximative mais suffisante'.

99 Kirk (1985) states that these two Lokrian place-names have been displaced into Achilles' contingent (taking Alos as Halai). However, this would surely not have the effect he suggests, 'to magnify a small and peculiar contingent' (i.e. the Lokrians), since in fact it enhances Achilles' at their expense. Strabo notes the conundrum at 9.5.8. It seems most likely that, given their geographical proximity, the Thessalian shore south of Othrys and the northern coast of East Lokris genuinely did share place-names, close cognates if not identical.

essential historicity cannot, however, extend in any straightforward manner to one particular element of his contingents: the Hellenes, and their home Hellas.

The location of the 'original Hellas' on Thessaly's southern margins has piqued the interest of scholars both ancient and modern.[100] Given that the *Iliad* seems so intimately connected with the articulation of shared Greek identity, to find Hellas as a toponym somewhere in the mishmash of territory and people led by Achilles cannot fail to seem significant. Working out where exactly Homer imagined Hellas to be is impossible; historians have tended to place it in the Spercheios valley,[101] but even if Homer had a precise location in mind he did not relay it and guesswork is futile. It is amply possible that Homer had no intention of placing 'Hellas' realistically, because (even) when the *Iliad* was composed the name was not attached to any real region or site. In general, the occurrence of Hellas and Hellenes in the *Iliad* is susceptible to two basic explanations.

1. When the *Iliad* was composed, the names Hellas and Hellenes really did attach only to a portion of southern Thessaly or the Spercheios valley. This theory allows scholars to postulate a process by which, over time, the names achieved wider and wider geographical scope.[102] In the *Odyssey*, Hellas seems to denote central and northern Greece; by the *Works and Days* it seems to have spread to include all of Greece in the historically familiar sense.[103] The *Ehoiai* in the sixth century works to

[100] Ancient interest: see, for example, Strabo 8.6.6, which suggests wider debate and a recognition of Thessaly's special place in the matter – 'περὶ δὲ τῆς Ἑλλάδος καὶ Ἑλλήνων καὶ Πανελλήνων ἀντιλέγεται. Θουκυδίδης μὲν γὰρ τὸν ποιητὴν μηδαμοῦ βαρβάρους εἰπεῖν φησι διὰ τὸ μηδὲ Ἕλληνάς πω τὸ ἀντίπαλον εἰς ἓν ὄνομα ἀποκεκρίσθαι. καὶ Ἀπολλόδωρος δὲ μόνους τοὺς ἐν Θετταλίᾳ καλεῖσθαί φησιν 'Μυρμιδόνες δὲ καλεῦντο καὶ Ἕλληνες' ('But there is disagreement about the terms "Hellas", "Hellenes" and "Panhellenes". For Thucydides says that Homer nowhere speaks of barbarians, "because the Hellenes had not as yet been designated by a separate name". And Apollodoros says that only the Greeks in Thessaly were called Hellenes: "and were called Myrmidons and Hellenes".') On Greek ethnicity in Strabo see Dandrow (2017).

[101] E.g. Béquignon (1937b), 126; Hall (2002), 127. The inclusion of the Spercheios in Achilles' realm, at least, is certain, thanks to Homer's reference to his planned hair-offering to the river: *Il.* 23.140–48.

[102] By the time Bury (1895, 224) was writing, this basic progression could be presented as an orthodoxy. Among its subsequent exponents: Wathelet (1975), 119–21; Lévy (1991), 57–64; Hall (2002), 125–34.

[103] Even the term *panhellenes*, in the *Iliad*, does not necessarily seem to denote more than north/central Greece. It occurs at 2.530 – the poet asserts that the Lesser Aias, though small of stature and poorly equipped, 'ἐγχείῃ δ' ἐκέκαστο Πανέλληνας καὶ Ἀχαιούς ('outdid with the spear the *panhellenes* and the Achaioi'). But Aias' merit may be being judged not against the whole Greek army but against the Hellenes of the Spercheios

integrate the newer names through the creation of the eponym Hellen, son of Deukalion, manufacturing a heroic origin for the Hellenes when in fact the name itself is a retrojection.

2. When the *Iliad* was composed Hellas already applied to all of Greece, and Hellenes to all Greeks, perhaps even those outside Greece proper. This rests upon the idea that Homer is conducting substantial and sustained archaism. He calls the Greek force at Troy Achaioi, Danaoi and Argeioi because he regards those as the correct names for the Greeks of the heroic age. 'Hellenes' he regards as a relatively modern term, whose inclusion would constitute a clashing anachronism. The myth of the 'Hellenic stemma' – the descent of all Hellenes from the hero Hellen, son of Deukalion – has not been developed yet. It is, by contrast, the core of the *Ehoiai*, a century or so later; the poet of that work does not wish to omit 'Hellenes' as anachronistic, but to weave them, and the name, into the heroic age by means of a new eponym.

The implications of the second theory are interesting. Here, Homer's Hellas is all of Greece, and yet he does not wish to show it as such, so he creates – or the tradition on which he builds creates – a proto-Hellas, a little local version, on Thessaly's southern fringe. Why would he choose to locate it here? We have seen already that Achilles' homeland Phthia has a certain quality in Homer, as the land left behind, a backwater associated with the loss of *kleos* and strongly at odds with the vitality of the cultic landscape of the Troad and the Black Sea, where Achilles' worship maintained something of his presence and his involvement in the lives of local inhabitants and travelling Greeks. At first glance this Thessalian obscurity may seem to make the location of the 'original Hellas' more puzzling than ever. However, from the point of view of a Greek in the Aiolian Troad, say, it might make a great deal of symbolic sense.[104] Thessaly was the source of the Aiolian tribe, and of the hero Achilles; what better place to be the source of Hellenism also? Their own credentials as Hellenes would be greatly enhanced by the idea that Hellas began roughly where the Aiolians began, and exactly where Achilles began; the effect would be to reduce their peripherality and make them the direct recipients of the original Greekness. Thessaly as the original Hellas seems to make sense from a trans-Aegean perspective, just as the name Graikos/Graikoi has been shown to reflect the perspective of those to the west, across the Ionian

region and the Achaioi of Thessaly's southern margin; as Tronson (2000, 18) suggests, the *pan-* could be an intensifier.

[104] East Greek influence on the development of Hellenic identity and its articulation in myth: Ulf (1996), 268.

Sea.[105] The cultivation of certain sites as the cradle of Greek identity often appears to be the work of relative geographical outsiders, who have a strong incentive to assert their inclusion within Greece and Greekness. We have seen the importance of Achilles to such communities; the work of Malkin has established a corresponding importance, on Greece's western side, for Odysseus, another wandering hero used to forge ties between periphery and centre. If we see Achilles' Hellas and Hellenes in such a light, Thessaly itself has little active part to play. In fact, its passivity may have helped, laying it open for appropriation as *fons et origo*.[106] That Homer would be capable of, and perhaps inclined toward, deliberate archaism is not implausible. We have seen that Homer deliberately avoids calling Thessaly by that name (or its people Thessaloi), chiefly for this reason; a similar motivation may underpin the omission of Ionians and Dorians,[107] and the use of 'Maionia' for Lydia.[108]

If, however, we prefer the first theory, this must mean that the names Hellas and Hellenes began as locally limited and subsequently spread out like ink seeping from the original drop, first through central and northern Greece and then into the Peloponnese and beyond. This process of diffusion is unlikely to have happened in the minds and mouths of Greeks across the Aegean, but on the very doorstep of the original Hellenes, who are very likely to have been actively involved, a contrast with their passivity in the case of the alternative explanation, discussed above. The fact that communities of relative obscurity, in many ways, could have exerted such influence over the expression of Greek identity must surely, as has been recognised, relate to their membership of the Delphic Amphiktyony.[109] The Amphiktyony will reappear, again connected with the discourse of Hellenism, as we turn to consider the representation of Thessaly in another Archaic poem, the *Ehoiai* or *Catalogue of Women*. First, however, let us sum up the discussion of the *Iliad*'s Catalogue of Ships. It was found that the region of Thessaly was not without a presence, as a whole, in the Catalogue; however, its extent

[105] Bury (1895), 236.

[106] The same observation has been made about the ancient myth of the migration of the Dorians: the very obscurity of the Dorian metropolis in central Greece was useful to those claiming it as their homeland, since it did not compete or interfere with their own importance (Robertson 1980, 3). On Spartan involvement in the creation of the idea of the Dorian metropolis: Ulf (1996), 259–64. He dates the inception of the concept to the time of Pindar (cf. Vanicelli 1989, who detects in the Catalogue of Ships an oblique allusion to 'proto-Dorians' in the lands controlled by Achilles.)

[107] West (2011, 31) suggests that the stories of the Return of the Herakleidai and the Dorian invasions may be obliquely alluded to at *Il.* 4.50–52, when Hera gives Zeus permission to destroy Argos, Sparta and Mykene, but this suggestion seems far-fetched.

[108] E.g. Hom. *Il.* 3.400–01.

[109] Hall (2002), 134–54.

overspills the boundaries of Thessaloi and Thessalia in the Classical sense. This reflects two things: first, the organisation of the Catalogue according to heroic commands rather than single territorial or political units; second, in all probability, the influence of historical circumstances of inter-regional connectivity – trade, travel and religious congregation.

2. Thessaly in the *Ehoiai*

a) Thessaly divided and connected

There is a reasonable scholarly consensus that the *Ehoiai* was composed some time between 580 and 520 BC,[110] though one can never be sure that the stories such works contain were not in existence long before;[111] it is most plausible that individual myths were of long-standing circulation in their several homelands, but that the real innovation of the poem as a whole was to draw them together, gathering regional traditions into a single massive work united by a basic theme: the creation of heroic lineages in – and linking – different parts of Greece, derived from the unions of gods and heroines. How massive the work was we cannot be sure because we have only fragments, which for the most part are very slight and pose the usual challenges of interpretation, such as determining just what [Hesiod] did say and what may have been introduced by the later author who quotes him. But we have enough to recognise its overall significance, as an attempt not only to collate disparate traditions but to connect them with a single stemma: that of Deukalion, his son Hellen, and Hellen's sons Aiolos, Doros and Xouthos (the ancestors of the Aiolian, Dorian and Ionian tribes). It is probable, though not certain, that the flood, which Deukalion and his wife Pyrrha survived, was included in the poem;[112] if so, then this episode provided the poet with a 'clean slate' – at least in central Greece where the flood occurred – on which to (re)draw the family trees of the many heroic families, signalling that truly Greek myth-history started at that point of rupture.[113]

The view of Thessaly given to us by the *Ehoiai* may be summed up as follows. In the surviving portions at least, the places most strongly represented were Iolkos and Pherai, with perhaps a special link between Hellen and the Hellenes of Thessalian Hellas in the south of the region.

[110] Ca. 580 is favoured by Fowler (2013, 127); West (1985, 136) prefers the end of the range. Note also the useful overview of his theories concerning the dating of epics in West (2012).

[111] As Fowler (1998, 1–2) maintains.

[112] Clay (2005), 28–29, *pace* West (1985), 55–56.

[113] Ulf (2015), 40–42. The other great rupture is the Trojan War, signalling the end of the age of *hemitheoi*: Scodel (1982), 39; Ormand (2014), 196–216.

Phrixos is mentioned, and Helle, and the Golden Fleece;[114] Jason is raised by Cheiron;[115] surely something of the Argo's voyage was described.[116] A second bundle appears to have concerned the Lapiths: Kaineus, and Ischys who angered Apollo by sleeping with Koronis daughter of Phlegyas, the mother of Asklepios.[117] Koronis was located on the Dotion Plain, and 'bathed her foot in Lake Boibeis'.[118] These are the surviving Thessalian myth-clusters; there must have been others.

Was Thessaly viewed and presented as Thessaly in the *Ehoiai*? That is, was it named as such, or treated in any way as a united entity distinguished from other *ethnē*? Consideration of ethnic terminology is especially vulnerable to the fact that we rely on later quoters for our snippets of the poem. Take, for example, fragment 6 MW, a scholion on Apollonios' *Argonautika*: '"Nor did the glorious descendants of Deukalion rule the Pelasgian land at that time." The descendants of Deukalion ruled over Thessaly, as Hekataios and Hesiod say. Thessaly used to be called Pelasgia after Pelasgos, who was its king.'[119] We cannot take from this the conclusion that the poet of the *Ehoiai* used the word Thessaly, or even that he referred to Thessaly as a whole as the land ruled by the descendants of Deukalion. Hekataios almost certainly did;[120] by the fifth century it was routine to use the Thessalian ethnic, and by that time also the idea that all of Thessaly was once Pelasgian was well established. It is not impossible that Thessaly was mentioned in the poem as such, but we certainly have no evidence that it was. That said, Phokos, the eponymous hero of the Phokians, is included in the surviving fragments, as is Lokros,

114 Frs. 68–69 MW.

115 Here we actually have a direct quotation, from the scholion on Pind. *Nem.* 3.92:

Αἴσων, ὃς τέκεθ' υἱὸν Ἰήσονα ποιμένα λαῶν,
ὃν Χείρων ἔθρεψ' ἐνὶ Πηλίωι ὑλήεντι.

116 This is suggested by the mention of Phineus' blinding in fr. 157 MW.

117 Kaineus: fr. 87 MW. Ischys: fr. 60 MW; however, note that some doubt surrounds the attribution of the fragment to the *Ehoiai*: West (1985), 69–72. He also argues that there probably was not a whole 'Koronis-Ehoie'. For a survey of Kaineus' appearances in ancient texts see Decourt (2011).

118 Fr. 59 MW. On early settlement around Lake Boibeis (modern Karla) see Karouzou (2018), 890–91.

119 'οὐδὲ Πελασγὶς χθὼν τότε κυδαλίμοισιν ἀνάσσετο Δευκαλίδηισιν] οἱ ἀπὸ Δευκαλίωνος τὸ γένος ἔχοντες ἐβασίλευον Θεσσαλίας, ὥς φησιν Ἑκαταῖος καὶ Ἡσίοδος. ἡ Θεσσαλία δὲ Πελασγία ἐκαλεῖτο ἀπὸ Πελασγοῦ τοῦ βασιλεύσαντος.'

120 As Fowler shows, prose mythographers of the late sixth and the fifth century drew heavily on the *Ehoiai* for their accounts of the descendants of Deukalion: see Fowler (2013), §4. However, the stories will surely have been adjusted in language and presentation to suit the new contexts and purposes of the prose works.

eponym of the Lokrians.[121] Of course, the missing portions may possibly have encompassed the hero Thessalos; however, when later authors of an antiquarian disposition list earlier traditions concerning Thessalos, Hesiod is never among the sources they cite. The Thessalos tradition does not seem to belong in the world conjured up by the *Ehoiai*, but that is not because it was not in circulation; Thessalos' sons did not arrive in Thessaly until after the Trojan War, and so their activities do not fall within the chronological range of the poem.

Does the *Ehoiai* differentiate between Thessaly and the perioikic regions? Yes, to some extent: the eponym of the Magnetes, Magnes, features in a surviving fragment as the son of Zeus and Thyia.[122] However, genealogies are not generally used to create sharp brackets between the *ethnē*. If the Catalogue of Ships is anything to go by, the Magnetes in the Archaic period were thought to occupy a somewhat more restricted geographical range than in the Classical, because they do not encompass the Bay of Pagasai, Magnesian from the fifth century; in the *Ehoiai* there is certainly no suggestion that Iolkos and its heroes are of a different *ethnos* from that of the Pheraian dynasty, even though from the Classical period Iolkos was Magnesian and Pherai Thessalian (part of Pelasgiotis). And the Lapiths who feature in the poem have a tendency to spread between the later boundaries of Thessaly and Perrhaibia.[123] While Magnetes, Thessaloi and Perrhaiboi were surely considered distinct when the poem was composed – and would after all have been represented separately in the Delphic Amphiktyony – the myths it contains do not seem to have been deployed in order to police and emphasise the boundaries, apart from identifying the different parentage of Magnes.

And indeed, while the poem's surviving fragments are not ignorant of historical *ethnē*, in the case of Thessaly in particular the tone and purpose of the poem seem to have been quite differently constructed. Rather than uniting Thessaly and distinguishing it from other *ethnē*, the poem seems to weave Thessalian dynasties into a wider network of Aiolid identity. The way in which genealogies are constructed in the poem emphasises connections and the role of heroic lineages as shared possessions. An especially clear example is provided by the offspring of Tyro and Poseidon.

Tyro is the daughter of the Aiolid Salmoneus, who seems to have moved from Thessaly to the north-western Peloponnese; his daughter, however, marries her paternal uncle Kretheus, who had remained in Thessaly

[121] Phokos: fr. 58 MW.

[122] Hall (2002, 168–70) argues that the fact that Magnes is not descended from Hellen indicates that the Magnetes were being subtly excluded, by the Thessalians, from the roll-call of the truly Greek.

[123] Aston (2017).

and founded Iolkos.[124] Her strong connection to the Thessalian land is reinforced by the fact that she falls in love with the river Enipeus, in whose guise Poseidon seduces her.[125] To Poseidon she bears twins, Pelias and Neleus, whose paths diverge through the will of Zeus:

> Neleus and] Pelias, [lords] of many people;
> and these] the father [of men and of gods] settled separately;
> apart] from each other they dwelt in cities [
> For the one] possessed Pylos and founded a [lovely] land,
> Neleus,] and the daughter of Iasos' son Amphion,
> Chloris,] he made his well-girdled vigorous [wife.[126]

There follow fragments concerning Neleus and his progeny.[127] Smaller fragments survive to show us that the *Ehoiai* would have followed the Thessalian dynasty too, Pelias' half-brothers Aison and Pheres (sons of Kretheus rather than Poseidon), and Aison's son Jason. Jason's upbringing by Cheiron was included.[128] No doubt Pheres' son Admetos and grandson Eumelos, rulers of Pherai, would have been included also.[129] The way the poem works is to establish the heroic lineages of Pylos and Iolkos (and Pherai) as having shared northern Greek origins, but this should not be seen as somehow diluting the importance of Thessaly because the stories extend far from her boundaries. Heroic genealogy is not a zero-sum game; the status of regions is enhanced by their interregional connections. The importance of this bundle of interregional mythology is reinforced by the occurrence of the Tyro myth in the *Odyssey*. When in Book 11 Odysseus travels to the land of the dead, the first shade he sees and speaks with is Tyro's. The poet – with Odysseus as his mouthpiece – devotes quite a substantial digression to the story of Tyro's seduction by Poseidon in the guise of Enipeus, and to the resulting heroic lineages:

[124] It seems as good as certain that this foundation was mentioned in the *Ehoiai*; however, this part does not survive, and we need to resort to later sources, such as Apollod. *Bibl.* 1.9.7–11.

[125] *Ehoiai* fr. 30 MW.

[126] Fr. 33a MW:

> Νηλέα κα]ὶ Πελίην πολέσιν λαοῖσι[ν ἄνακτας·
> καὶ τοὺς] μὲν διένασσε πατὴρ ἀν[δρῶν τε θεῶν τε,
> νόσφιν δ'] ἀλλήλων ναῖον πτολίεθρα [
> ἤτοι ὁ μ]ὲν Πύλον εἶχε καὶ ἔκτισε γῆν [ἐρατεινὴν
> Νηλεύς,] καί ῥα θύγατρ' Ἀμφίονος Ἰασίδα[ο
> Χλῶριν ἐ]ΰζωνον θαλερὴν ποιήσατ' ἄκ[οιτιν.

[127] Frs 34 and 37 MW.

[128] Fr. 40 MW.

[129] Certainly the story of Apollo's servitude to Apollo seems to have been: frs 54 b and c MW. Alkestis is mentioned in fr. 37 MW.

She conceived and bore Pelias and Neleus,
Who both became strong servants of mighty Zeus.
Pelias lived in Iolkos with its spacious land, and was
Rich in sheep; Neleus lived in sandy Pylos.
But Tyro, queenly among women, bore other children to Kretheus:
Aison, Pheres, and Amythaon who fought from a chariot.[130]

So, once again, the Thessaly–Pylos connection is paramount. However, if we look beyond the surviving portions of Archaic epic we can reconstruct the lines and lives of the Aiolids further. Apollodoros, whose *Library of Greek Mythology* closely mirrors and certainly drew on the *Ehoiai*, fleshes out the picture and enhances our sense of the complex network of regional connections which the stemma facilitates. In their most basic form these may be summed up as follows:

Sons of Aiolos
Kretheus: ruled in Iolkos, fathered Aison.
Sisyphos: ruled in Korinth; while in Homer his location is a little ambiguous,[131] the *Ehoiai* seems to have contained the Korinthian story of Sisyphos' grandson Bellerophon and the taming of Pegasos.[132]
Athamas: ruled in Boiotia, normally at Orchomenos.[133]
Salmoneus: left Thessaly to found Elis.[134]
Deion: ruled Phokis;[135] however, his son Phylakos is sometimes connected with Phylake in southern Thessaly.[136]
Magnes: here Apollodoros and the *Ehoiai* seem to part company. In the former Magnes is an Aiolid whose sons settle on Seriphos; in the *Ehoiai*

[130] Hom. *Od.* 11.254–59:
ἡ δ' ὑποκυσαμένη Πελίην τέκε καὶ Νηλῆα,
τὼ κρατερὼ θεράποντε Διὸς μεγάλοιο γενέσθην
ἀμφοτέρω· Πελίης μὲν ἐν εὐρυχόρῳ Ἰαωλκῷ
ναῖε πολύρρηνος, ὁ δ' ἄρ' ἐν Πύλῳ ἠμαθόεντι.
τοὺς δ' ἑτέρους Κρηθῆι τέκεν βασίλεια γυναικῶν,
Αἴσονά τ' ἠδὲ Φέρητ' Ἀμυθάονά θ' ἱππιοχάρμην.
On the relationship between the *Odyssey*'s Catalogue and the *Ehoiai* see Rutherford (2012), 161–64.
[131] Hom. *Il.* 6.152–54: 'Ephyra' may be Korinth.
[132] Fr. 43a MW, lines 70–91. Actually, while Sisyphos' son Glaukos is considered the father of Bellerophon, Poseidon is the true father (and gives him Pegasos).
[133] Hellanikos *FGrH* 4 F 126.
[134] Apollod. *Bibl.* 1.9.7.
[135] Apollod. *Bibl.* 1.9.4.
[136] In the *Iliad* Phylakos' grandson Podarkes commands the contingents of Protesilaos, Phylake, Pyrasos, Iton and Antron: see *Il.* 2.703–07. See also Steph. Byz. s.v. Φυλακή and schol. Hom. *Il.* 2.69: Phylakos as founder of Phylake.

he is the son of Zeus and Thyia and brother of Makedon, and both Magnes and Makedon live in Pieria and Olympos, that is the marches on Macedon's southern border close to northern Thessaly.[137]
Perieres: left Thessaly to rule Messenia.[138]

Daughters of Aiolos
Kanake: lay with Poseidon, bore the impious giants the Aloadai, who piled up Ossa and Pelion to attack Olympos.[139] Another son is Triops or Triopas, father of Erysichthon and variously associated with Thessaly and Knidos; Erysichthon is not situated in Thessaly by the poet of the *Ehoiai*.[140]
Alkyone: famous for the transformation of her and her husband Keyx into kingfishers; they are not geographically located.
Peisidike: married Myrmidon, *Stammvater* of the Myrmidones.[141] Their son Aktor and grandson Eurytos ruled the Myrmidones in Phthia before Peleus.[142]
Kalyke: with Aëthlios, mother of Endymion and grandmother of Aitolos. Produces an Aitolian dynasty closely interlocking with that derived from Perimede.[143]
Perimede: has intercourse with the river Acheloios and generates a segment of the ruling family of Kalydon in Aitolia.[144]

In sum, few of these heroic lines remain long based in Thessaly. Thessaly is a place of origins in the Aiolid stemma, but to refer to the stemma as Thessalian is deeply misleading. The substantial role of the Aiolids within Aitolian myth-history is especially significant. Thucydides calls Aitolia, not Thessaly, the original Aiolis,[145] and this is an identity the Aitolians cultivated at the time of the *Ehoiai*'s composition as part of their active role in the trade and traffic through the Korinthian Gulf.[146] Thessalian

137 Apollod. *Bibl.* 1.9.6; *Ehoiai* fr. 7 MW.

138 Apollod. *Bibl.* 1.9.5. It is interesting to note that the son of Perieres, Leukippos, is the father of Arsinoe, mother of Asklepios: the Arsinoe variant is an alternative to the role of Thessalian Koronis as Asklepios' mortal mother. Koronis does feature in the *Ehoiai*, plainly situated in Thessaly in the Dotion Plain (see fr. 59 MW), but perhaps was not considered mother of Asklepios, since the Messenian version of the story seems to have been included.

139 *Ehoiai* fr. 19 MW; Apollod. *Bibl.* 1.9.4.

140 *Ehoiai* fr. 43a MW.

141 *Ehoiai* fr. 10a MW.

142 In Pherekydes (*FGrH* 3 F 1b) we find the story that Peleus is received and purified by Eurytos (sometimes spelled Eurytion) after the murder of Phokos.

143 *Ehoiai* fr. 10a MW, lines 58–74.

144 *Ehoiai* fr. 10a MW, lines 35–57.

145 Thuc. 3.102.5.

146 Bommeljé (1988); Beck (2019), 394–96. Note, however, that Bommeljé evinces some

domination of the *Ehoiai*, its formation and its geographical organisation, is by no means evident from the surviving fragments.

b) Thessaly and Hellenism

So far I have tried to show that the effect of the *Ehoiai* is not to single Thessaly out but to integrate its heroes and heroines within the Aiolid network of which Thessaly is an important starting point. We can speak of Thessalian heroes in the poem, but Thessaly is not really Thessaly; nothing was done by the poet to emphasise its boundaries or its shared myth-historical identity. Instead, it was given a place – an important one – within a more expansive project, the formulation of the origin and extension of the Hellenes. The fact that Thessaly's place in this process does appear to be important has drawn attention and requires discussion here. We shall ask what this importance amounts to, and whether it may reflect a background to the poem in which Thessaly was actively influential, as some have claimed.

Past assertions of the importance of Thessaly in the poem rest upon two elements: first, the particular weight placed on the Aiolids; and, second, the position of Thessaly within the Aiolid stemma. In an influential 1998 article, Fowler made the following claim:

> The stemma Deukalion → Hellen → Doros/Aiolos … has Thessaly stamped all over it. If we now ask who were the most significant power in north-central Greece in the seventh century, when this stemma was established, the answer is again 'Thessaly'. They dominated the amphictyony first headquartered at Anthela, in Malis just west of Thermopylae, and then at Delphi after the First Sacred War, which was their entrée into the south.[147]

scepticism – without strong justification – about the prominence of the Aitolians in the *Ehoiai* (p. 315), and identifies significant confusion and contradiction in the later accounts of Aiolian settlements in Aitolia (301–04).

[147] Fowler (1998), 11. Cf. Kowalzig (2007), 197: 'The Sacred War is increasingly considered to be the context for the pseudo-Hesiodic Catalogue of Women and its genealogical constructions. These reflect a world-view where Thessalians shape the stemmata of the Greeks, supporting the claim to Thessalian domination of Delphi through the Amphiktyony. Together with that, however, the poem advertises a notion of "Hellas" as extended from a small part of Thessaly, a region called Ἑλλάς, into something which strikingly coincides with the boundaries of the sixth-century Amphiktyony.' Note, however, that in later publications Fowler has somewhat adjusted his earlier view. See for example Fowler (2018), 44: here he argues that the *Iliad* and the *Ehoiai* represent two quite distinct perspectives and traditions concerning the origins of the Greeks. While the *Iliad* – with its Hellas and Hellenes in the contingents of Achilles – was the product of east Greek communities, in the *Ehoiai* 'the Thessalians propagated the story of descent of all Greeks from Hellen and his sons. They slotted themselves in

In similar vein, Hall's argument concerns the prime role played by Delphi and Olympia in the development of Archaic concepts of Greek identity; he accords a key place to Thessaly as the dominant power within the Delphic Amphiktyony, and influential at Olympia, in the sixth century.[148] He argues that 'There are … good reasons for supposing that the filial succession Deukalion-Hellen-Aiolos constitutes the oldest element of the "Hellenic Genealogy" and was first created on the initiative of the Thessalians.'[149]

Chapter 1, however, asserted the impossibility of establishing Thessalian dominance at Delphi – or indeed in central Greece generally – in the relevant period. Moreover, consideration of the poem itself reveals the difficulties of reconstructing Thessalian agency behind its creation. For a start, Hall suggests that Aiolos is signalled by the poet as the most important of the three sons of Hellen because he is given an epithet and they are not;[150] however, metrical and stylistic considerations may have carried just as much weight in this formulation. More noteworthy is the relative weight of the Aiolid stemma within the poem. By their very nature, the *Ehoiai*'s surviving 'shreds and tatters', not only incomplete but probably unrepresentative, provide very poor material for any statistical analysis of the relative amounts of coverage afforded to different genealogical lines. However, it has long been recognised that the basic structure of the poem is mirrored by Apollodoros' *Library of Greek Mythology*. Compared with the Aiolid coverage in this work, Doros, Ion and Achaios feel empty and slight;[151] but this should be interpreted with caution; it may simply reflect the fact that the myths encompassed within the Aiolian umbrella were of great antiquity and available to the poet in large quantity. Finkelberg has argued that the myths of the Aiolids and their travels derive ultimately from southward migrations of northern tribes in the Bronze Age;[152] they are part of the oldest stratum of collective myth-history, and therefore constitute, as she puts it, the 'bushiest' family tree. However, while this original Bronze Age context is convincing, we cannot ignore the way in which the Aiolid mythology has drifted away from that base. Thessaly had the major

as Aiolians, an ethnos that claimed practically all of central Greece, and even the west Greek Aitolians as their own.'

148 Hall (2002), 159–61.

149 Hall (2002), 161–62.

150 Hall (2002), 161.

151 Actually, as Hard comments (2004, 409), 'Aiolos himself is little more than a cipher', for all the abundance of the lineages he generates. He is obviously chiefly a device for grouping certain old interlocking myths under a new ethnic heading.

152 Finkelberg (2005), 40: 'As far as I can see, this pattern only makes sense if we assume that the translocations of the descendants of Aiolos as described in Greek tradition were meant to commemorate the process of their gradual infiltration into the Bronze Age Peloponnese.'

Mycenaean site of Iolkos, strongly implicated in Aiolid beginnings, but the *Ehoiai* contains another important element: the roots of Hellenicity are located not exclusively in Thessaly but more generally in the ethnically mixed area of southern Thessaly and the Spercheios valley.

The surviving fragments make this clear, and caution us against singling Thessaly out as the sole point of Hellenic origins. Fr. 6 MW, it is true, says that Deukalion's descendants ruled Thessaly; however, as suggested above, it is unlikely that the poet of the *Ehoiai* really presented the matter in such a pan-Thessalian way. The reference may have been to Deukalion's son Hellen as ancestor of the Hellenes, and this first generation of Hellenes may well have been the geographically restricted group that we find in the *Iliad*, the Hellenes whom Achilles led to Troy; this would allow the *Ehoiai* to dovetail with the Catalogue of Ships.[153] So the *Ehoiai* may have inherited and reinforced the *Iliad*'s positioning of the 'original Hellas' just beyond Thessaly's southern edge. What about Deukalion himself? By the fifth century, when we have our first explicit narratives of the flood story, opinion is divided about where the 'ark' of Deukalion and Pyrrha first made landfall: was it on Othrys or on Parnassos?[154] Obviously there was some contestation between regions for ownership of the story or part of it – Lokris cherished the story of the Leleges, for example, while the Athenians claimed to possess Deukalion's tomb (but Kynos in Lokris claimed Pyrrha's!).[155] Doubtless, Thessalian communities in later centuries staked claims on these myths in a spirit of competition, by which time the association between Deukalion and Thessaly had outstripped other regions in non-Thessalian sources.[156] But there is no evidence that the *Ehoiai* promoted any one community or region as owning Deukalion. In fact, the contest between places in the later texts may have been facilitated by a certain vagueness, the same vagueness that attends 'Hellas' and prevents any one *ethnos* from achieving sole possession.

Rather than seeing Thessaly as singled out for special status in the poem, we should recognise two trends. First, its role in the Aiolid stemma was as the

[153] Cf. Thuc. 1.3.2–3: Hellen and his sons rule in Phthia specifically, and the πρῶτοι Ἕλληνες are the Hellenes of Achilles' command, the descendants of Hellen on Thessaly's southern margin.

[154] Othrys: Hellanikos *FGrH* 4 F 117; cf. F 6 (Deukalion as king of Thessaly and establishing an altar of the twelve gods in Phthiotis). Parnassos: Pind. *Ol.* 9.41–45.

[155] Tomb of Pyrrha: Strabo 9.4.2.

[156] See, for example, Strabo 9.5.6: both Pharsalos and Melitaia claim that Hellas is in their respective territories. The Melitaians elaborate on the claim: their polis used to be called Pyrrha, and the tomb of Deukalion and Pyrrha is located in their agora. They also say that they were settled by Hellenes from the nearby Hellas, giving themselves a primordial association both with the Homeric place-name and with its key position in the theme of Hellenicity.

place of origin, but one from which many heroes departed. This reinforces the sense given by the *Iliad* – see above – of Thessaly as the land left behind. This gives a certain prestige, but also a peculiar vacuum. Second, Deukalion and Hellen are attached to the southern fringe of Thessaly, but not – as far as one can tell – in such a way as to debar them from other associations; look at the Leleges, for example. The *Ehoiai* contained the story by which Deukalion created the tribe of the Leleges from thrown stones, after which they somehow came under the leadership of Lokros.[157] Hall argues that he was in origin a Lokrian hero, appropriated by the Thessalians as an act of competitive self-aggrandisement, levering themselves into a core position within the Hellenic discourse the poem fosters.[158] Such a view, of myths being pulled away from one *ethnos* by another, is, however, unnecessarily bleak and combative. Given that Deukalion is attached, in the poem, *both* to southern Thessaly (fr. 6 MW) *and* to Lokris (fr. 234 MW),[159] it is best to see his role as forming a connection between the two regions, which were, in any case, closely interrelated in the Catalogue of Ships (see above). The possibility that the hero Amphiktyon was already present in the *Ehoiai* as the brother of Hellen reinforces this sense that the poem articulated not only the shared genealogical belonging of the Hellenes but also, as a crucial component of that, the shared identity of Amphiktyonic membership.[160] This is not significantly affected by the various possibilities of the poem's composition. A northern Greek location, suggested by Fowler, is tempting, but is based on the importance of Thessaly in the poem, which, as argued here, is not in fact possible to establish as a simple certainty.[161] If, as West believed, the poem was composed in Athens,[162] that would in no way militate against the importance of the Amphiktyonic theme in the work, since Athens was probably part of the Amphiktyony in the sixth century and using its Delphic involvement to boost its panhellenic visibility.[163]

157 Fr. 234 MW.
158 Hall (2002), 169. Cf. also Fowler (2013), 127–30.
159 Cf. Pind. *Ol.* 9.44–46, in which the stone-throwing takes place in Lokris itself, though elsewhere – e.g. Apollod. *Bibl.* 1.7.2 – it is placed on Mount Parnassos.
160 Fr. 4 MW; cf. Apollod. *Bibl.* 1.7.2.
161 Fowler (1998), 11–12; cf. Finkelberg (2005), 30.
162 West (1985), 130. It has also been suggested that the prominence of the Neleid element, both in the *Ehoiai* and in *Odyssey* 11's Catalogue of Women, reflects the influence of the Peisistratidai, who claimed Neleid ancestry: see Lavelle (2005), 18–29; Larson (2000) argues that the Peisistratidai used the mythology to assert their affinities with both the Thessalians and the Boiotians. A certain amount of ingenuity is required to make the dating fit; Lavelle argues that Peisistratos co-opted much earlier Athenian mythology; Larson accepts West's dating of the *Ehoiai* to the mid- to late sixth century, and further posits revision of the *Odyssey* at that time.
163 Lefèvre (1998), 65–66. Rutherford (2005, 117) suggests an attractive compromise: 'I

Other, more distant forces may also have been at work. We saw above Nagy's observation that in the time of Peisistratos both the Athenians and the Aiolians of Asia Minor were interested in epic verse as a way of emphasising the status of the eastern Aiolians as an *apoikia* of the original Aiolians of central and northern Greece. Might the composition of the *Ehoiai* too have been stimulated by such motivations, just as the cultivation of Achilles' hero-cult at Sigeion was? The Thessalians are unlikely to have objected to the flattering presentation of their region as an important origin-point, but we have here another reason to treat cautiously any claim that Thessaly actively dominated the themes and formulations of Archaic epic.[164]

Finally, the *Ehoiai* has a place in the theme of implicit Thessalian obsolescence that we identified as operating in the *Iliad* and more widely.[165] It is not only the departure point of stemmata then rooted elsewhere; it is associated with a value system the poem itself subtly signalled as outmoded. Ormand has argued that the rise of so-called 'middling discourse' provides a crucial backdrop to the composition of the *Ehoiai* in particular. For him, 'we should understand the *Catalogue of Women* as an aristocratic text at the end of the aristocratic era.'[166] The poem itself signals this juncture by heralding the end of the Age of Heroes. Women are central to this shift: the heroines in the poem derive their merit from noble lineage, beauty and being singled out by gods as mothers of heroes. By contrast, good women in the texts of the new climate are good because of their behaviour: thrifty, virtuous, keeping a tidy and well-stocked home. So value shifts from lineage to conduct; whereas the former is available only to the nobly born, the latter may be aimed at by any, from any family. How is this relevant to Thessaly?

prefer to think of the poet … not as an Athenian, but as a poet with an Amphictyonic or panhellenic perspective, concerned to represent Athenian mythology as linked to the mythology of the rest of Greece.'

164 Cf. Ulf (1996, 270), who posits a transplantation of key elements of the Hellenic stemma from Asia Minor to Thessaly, but without identifying Thessalians as active agents in the process. Instead, the new location is a useful one because the location has a certain convenience: 'Deukalion und Pyrrha können leicht in den Norden der Balkan-Halbinsel, am Fuß von Ossa und Olymp angesetzt werden, wodurch – am Rand der von Griechen bewohnten Zone – ein praktikabler Konflikten mit älteren Sagentraditionen ausweichender Ausgangspunkt für die "Ethnogenese" aller Griechen gewonnen wird.'

165 As Fowler notes with regard to prose mythography, 'Despite its importance in the general construction of Hellenism, Thessaly is not much represented in our corpus' (2013, 147). Rather than seeing this as the result of Thessaly's importance falling away at the end of the Archaic period, I would suggest that in the *Ehoiai* too Thessaly's significance was consigned to the realm of origins.

166 Ormand (2014), 217.

It adds another strand of explanation to the importance of the region in the poem. Not only is it the heartland of the myth-historical past – it is the heartland of the political past as well, of the *ancien régime*. In other words, there is a political dimension to its fairy-tale quality.[167]

3. Conclusions

In this chapter, Thessaly has been shown to lie at the very heart of the stories and genealogies on which some of the major surviving epic poems of the Archaic period are founded. However, it has been shown that this core position cannot necessarily be taken to reflect active Thessalian involvement in, and influence on, the processes of epic composition in this time. Thessaly has been shown to have supplied some important 'raw material' for Homeric epic, and this indicates that as far as the *Iliad* in particular is concerned its period of importance is earlier, probably in the late Mycenaean or submycenaean period. Homer reflects the appropriation of Thessalian heroes, chief among them Achilles but also Jason and other figures of the Iolkos Cycle, as exemplars of travel, colonisation and exploration, in which activities the Thessalians of the Archaic period seem not to have been engaged. Probably as a result of this role as source of pre-existing mythology,[168] Thessaly in Homer is the land left behind, Achilles' home to which he may never return if he wishes to fulfil his heroic destiny and achieve *kleos aphthiton*. This is part of a wider tendency for Thessaly to be the launching point of journeys and departures, few of which entail a successful *nostos*.

In the *Ehoiai*, Thessaly is once again the place of origins: the origin of the massive Aiolid stemma which was by far the poem's largest and probably oldest component. Heroes from Thessaly tend to leave, and their journeys and families form a spreading mesh of heroic lineages across Greece. Unlike with Homer, however, we do have a distinct possibility, even probability, of active Thessalian involvement in the milieu that underpinned the poem's production if we believe the commonly held and plausible view that Delphi and its Amphiktyony were formative entities, and that the view of Hellenism which the poem projects is one strongly shaped by Delphi. It is very likely that in the sixth century Thessaly was a member of the Amphiktyony. However, it is a step too far to say that the

[167] This is not to say, of course, that the message of the poem maps onto the reality of heroes' roles in Greek communities, in Thessaly and elsewhere; as ancestor-figures and recipients of cult, they increased in importance, if anything. Ormand's reading of the poem, however, highlights the *Ehoiai*'s strong element of nostalgia, in keeping with Thessaly's more widespread presentation as belonging to past time.

[168] It is also possible that Thessaly's massive importance in the Neolithic period (on which see Feuer 2016, 109) contributed to the *topos* of past Thessalian glories: Neolithic culture would have left enduring marks on the Thessalian landscape (especially the *magoules*), of which all subsequent inhabitants would have been aware.

role of Thessaly in the poem – as Aiolid homeland and especially closely tied to Deukalion and Hellen – represents the imposition by Thessaly of a formula for Hellenicity that suits its political interests. As Chapter 1 made clear, we have no good grounds for thinking that Thessaly dominated the Amphiktyony at this time, and our whole view of that organisation needs to shift from a focus on manipulation to one of collective enterprise. Crucial figures such as Deukalion and Hellen can never be pinned down as belonging to, and owned by, any single state; it was a prime function of the Amphiktyony to share them, just as it worked to share influence in the Apollo-sanctuary. This picks up on the Homeric Catalogue of Ships: the 'original Hellas' and the 'original Hellenes' were never meant to give Thessaly (or any one place) an unchallenged cultural ascendancy. Their very location is vague and does not in any way conform with the political boundaries that are clear to see from the fifth century onwards. Whether this means that those boundaries were not in place earlier, or whether the myths were deliberately allowed to ignore them as an expression of collective identity, is uncertain. As seems most likely, when the *Ehoiai* was composed the process of ethnogenesis for central Greek *ethnē* – Lokrians and Phokians especially – was a current and dynamic process in which the poetry itself played a part; however, the recipe for primordial Hellenism is not accorded to any one *ethnos* but rather emphasises the shared ethnicity of Greekness. This is completely incompatible with the idea of an aggressive Thessaly using the myths of epic to claim a prestige others therefore could not have.

Moreover, Archaic epic is not interested in reinforcing the collective identity of the Thessaloi as an *ethnos*; instead, epic slices Thessaly up, according specific significance to sub-groups and sub-regions, whether as contingents in the Catalogue of Ships or as supplying key figures in the Aiolid stemma. It must be emphasised that this was not because the idea of Thessalian identity did not exist before it came into widespread usage and reference at the end of the Archaic period. In the seventh century, Alkman could say:

> He was no rustic man, nor
> a fool, not even among [i.e. as judged by?] clever
> people, nor a Thessalian by *genos*, nor an
> Erysichaian shepherd – no,
> he was from lofty Sardis.[169]

[169] Alkman fr. 16 L-P:

> οὐκ ἦς ἀνὴρ ἀγρεῖος οὐ-
> δὲ σκαιὸς οὐδὲ † παρὰ σοφοῖ-
> σιν † οὐδὲ Θεσσαλὸς γένος,
> Ἐρυσιχαῖος οὐδὲ ποιμήν,
> ἀλλὰ Σαρδίων ἀπ' ἀκρᾶν

(Erysiche is in Akarnania.)

This reveals the existence not only of the ethnic but also of a strong sense of a Thessalian regional character – rustic, unsophisticated, an early manifestation of a stereotype ingredient that would reappear centuries later. The epic poets could have referred to Thessaly as Thessaly, and the Thessalians as the Thessalians, had they wanted to; instead, they preferred to focus on distinguished lineages within the region, which tended to connect to others in Greece and beyond.

When in the next chapter we turn to the development, in the late sixth century and the earlier fifth, of myths that explicitly told of the origins of the Thessaloi as an *ethnos*, we shall see that this new development marks a significant departure from the visible Archaic material with which we have dealt in this chapter. In formulating their charter-myths, the Thessalians did not, primarily, draw on the stories that might strike us as suitable because of their far-reaching fame and importance, those of the house of Achilles and the house of Jason. Instead, they adapted and elaborated the traditions surrounding a previously obscure and localised personage, Thessalos son of Herakles. The power and utility of an eponym is obvious, but there is more to the choice than that. Thessalos and his family supplied a myth of arrival, when Archaic epic had made Thessaly into primarily a place of departure. Herakles, only slightly connected with the Trojan saga, was the perfect progenitor of a new heroic lineage whose arrival in Thessaly would constitute a major myth-historical watershed. For the first time, myth would be used not primarily to establish links between Thessalian and non-Thessalian elites, as in the *Ehoiai*, but to draw *ethnos*-boundaries between Thessalians and other Greeks, in the process binding the Thessalians together with a newly emphasised shared identity.

3

The creation of Thessaly in the late Archaic and early Classical period: myths of origin and arrival

The period from the later sixth century and the early fifth was a time of major change in how the Thessalians used myth to formulate identities. Archaic epic never identified Thessaly as Thessaly. Instead, it divided it up by heroes: in the Catalogue of Ships, the contingents led to Troy; in the Catalogue of Women and the *Odyssey*'s list of heroines, the lines of descent linking local elites with the gods. Thessaly was thus divided rather than unified; moreover, it was not clearly separated from its immediate neighbours. The little kingdoms in *Iliad* 2 spill over between 'Thessaly proper' and *perioikis*. The *Ehoiai*'s chief purpose was to articulate connections beyond all political borders, whatever they were at the time of its creation, forging – or expressing and mapping – a network of heroic clans. This, as we shall see, starts to change in the second half of the sixth century with a new strand of mythology aimed at simultaneously binding Thessaly together internally and setting it apart from other Greek *ethnē*. This was a radical shift, creating a myth-historical moment in which Aiolid Thessaly (or, rather, Aiolis, as it would later be thought to have been called) is acquired, controlled and renamed by Heraklid invaders.

The approach in this chapter will be to attempt to separate this mythology into different phases and different strands, resisting the tendency to treat it as a synthetic whole.[1] This is achieved through a largely chronological structure: over a series of necessarily generous time-chunks we shall see different places and different actors swim in and out of view, each developing the myths in a particular way as prompted by driving circumstances. Though advisable, this strategy is vulnerable. A single new archaeological discovery, or indeed a persuasive redating of a known artefact or text, could disrupt the schema entirely. However, the same applies to most historical theories to some extent, and it is better to produce

[1] For discussion of the pitfalls of trying to stitch mythological variants into a single ethnic 'story', using Theban origin-myths as a case study, see Ganter (2014).

a differentiated framework whose meaning is open to future contestation than a homogenised amalgam that lacks real meaning in the first place.

Before untangling the myths in this way, however, it may be helpful briefly to combine them to provide an artificial summary of all the surviving components, leaving out for the moment diverging side-shoots,[2] so that the ingredients of the story are all known. Thessalos was the son of Herakles by the Koan princess Chalkiope. He had two sons, Pheidippos and Antiphos, who led the Koan contingent fighting for the Greeks at Troy. After the fall of Troy Pheidippos and Antiphos travelled to Thesprotia; in a sense this is a *nostos*, since Greek warriors returning from Troy seldom went back to their original home. From Thesprotia, the migration into Thessaly was conducted, either by Antiphos and Pheidippos themselves,[3] or by Aiatos and Polykleia, the children of Pheidippos, who formed an incestuous marriage,[4] or – finally – by their son, another Thessalos.[5] This story is what we may term, for convenience, the Thessalids tradition. There is another, closely related but with some essential differences, in which the incursion is made not by a family but by a whole *ethnos*, the Thessaloi. In this version, which we might call the Thessaloi tradition, no mention is made of Koan origins. The fullest sources for this version are Herodotos and Thucydides, whereas that for the Thessalids tradition is much later, passages from Polyainos' *Strategemata*, a work on military stratagems and ploys.

1. The Catalogue of Ships again

On the face of it, Thessalia and the Thessaloi are absent from Homer. However, their presence is obliquely suggested. Thessaly is not yet Thessaly, and its people are not yet the Thessaloi; instead, they are the inhabitants of a patchwork of kingdoms, geographically proximate and sometimes interlocking but having no shared identity as an ethnos. But Thessalianity, so to speak, is waiting in the wings. The poet knew it was coming, and prefigured it fleetingly in the Catalogue of Ships.

> Those who held Nisyros and Krapathos and Kasos,
> and Kos the city of Eurypylos, and the Kalydnian
> islands, those were led by Pheidippos and Antiphos,

[2] For a useful summary of all the variants in circulation from Homer to Velleius Paterculus see Sprawski (2014a), 267–70; see also Bouchon and Helly (2013), 206–09; Mili (2015), 220–23.

[3] Strabo 9.5.23.

[4] Polyain. *Strat.* 8.44.

[5] Polyain. *Strat.* 1.12. For convenience, I shall refer henceforth to the family of Thessalos as the Thessalids, though I know of no ancient use of *Thessalidai*.

the two sons of the *anax* Thessalos son of Herakles.
And with them were ranged thirty hollow ships.[6]

Here is mention of Thessalos, who can only be the eponymous ancestor of the Thessalians (or of some Thessalians, as we shall see). But his sons do not lead Greek contingents. They lead the men of Kos and nearby island communities. They are not themselves identified as Koan but it is perverse to detach them from the later tradition of Thessalos as son of Herakles by the Koan princess Chalkiope; the poet further encourages the association by locating the Thessalian contingents immediately after the lines about Pheidippos and Antiphos.[7] Therefore we have here an early manifestation of the myth of Thessaly being 'founded' (that is, conquered and renamed) by Koan heroes. We know that that foundation took place sixty years after the fall of Troy, that instead of going home to Kos, Pheidippos and Antiphos would travel to Thessaly, perhaps via Thesprotia, and that either they or their son, a second Thessalos, would lead the invasion of Thessaly. So Homer may well be taking pains to adhere to proper myth-historical chronology. Thessaly is not Thessaly in the *Iliad* because the Thessalids have not arrived there yet. That is all to come. Homer sets his poem in the days when Thessaly was the homeland of Achilles, of Protesilaos, of Machaon and Podaleirios, of Eumelos, of other local princes. In his own day, Thessaly probably *was* called Thessaly and its people Thessaloi; however, this contemporary reality was not of interest to him, nor to his listeners.

There is another side to the *Iliad*'s acknowledgement of the tradition of the Thessalids' arrival in the land. This is that a curious gap in the Catalogue's coverage exists in the very location in which the new arrivals would primarily settle, roughly equating with the tetrad of Thessaliotis. There are two chief ways of explaining this omission. One, that of Sprawski for example, is to argue that the poet of the *Iliad* had a patchy knowledge of Thessaly – for example, one limited to 'places located along communication

[6] Hom. *Il.* 2.676–80:
οἳ δ' ἄρα Νίσυρόν τ' εἶχον Κράπαθόν τε Κάσον τε
καὶ Κῶν Εὐρυπύλοιο πόλιν νήσους τε Καλύδνας,
τῶν αὖ Φείδιππός τε καὶ Ἄντιφος ἡγησάσθην
Θεσσαλοῦ υἷε δύω Ἡρακλεΐδαο ἄνακτος·
τοῖς δὲ τριήκοντα γλαφυραὶ νέες ἐστιχόωντο.

[7] The placement of the northern Greek contingents at the end of the Catalogue (*Il.* 2.681–759) has caused some scholarly puzzlement; see Kirk (1985), 184–86; Sprawski (2014b), 88–89. Sammons (2010, 184–94) argues in detail that the order, including the seemingly peculiar 'jump' to Thessaly, serves important literary purposes, chiefly contingent on placing Achilles at the end, as a culmination.

routes: the seacoast and the course of the Peneios'.[8] The second view sees the omission as deliberate: the poet is leaving Thessaliotis blank because that is the very zone that awaits its imminent new settlers. As in the teasing reference to Thessalos, Antiphos and Pheidippos, the effect would be to evoke the audience's knowledge of myth-history. The first theory is of course highly plausible, especially if we envisage the author as coming from the eastern Greek world and being far from steeped in the mythological geography of the Greek north.[9] However, ultimately it does not seem wholly to explain why some decidedly obscure parts of Thessaly and its adjoining regions *are* represented (as in Phoinix' Dolopian contingent, or the northern section of Polypoites' Lapith territory), while only Thessaliotis is omitted. After all, so far from being a negligible backwater, this area contained one of the significant sanctuaries of Early Iron Age Greece, that of Athena Itonia at Philia; on the whole, as noted in the Introduction, the relative obscurity of Thessaliotis today is largely the result of archaeological destruction carried out in the twentieth century.

The two views need not be wholly incompatible, however. It is quite likely that Homer has limited knowledge of the mythological traditions of western Thessaly. Had he known these, he might have sketched in some picture of the sub-region's previous heroes and given them contingents to lead. As it is, I suggest that the only tradition related to that region that he really knew was that of the arrival of the Thessalids; furthermore, we may conjecture that the reason he know that story in particular was that it was not, in fact, at the time of the *Iliad*'s composition, one of Thessalian making – or at least, not exclusively so. And this brings us to a fundamental question regarding the story of the Thessalids in its earliest manifestation: was it really a Thessalian myth at this date, or a Koan one?

We have to admit the possibility that the Koans, or an influential subset of them, cultivated by this time the myth that they were the founders of Thessaly. They certainly did so in the third century BC, in the context of the enhancement and inter-regional self-publicisation of their Asklepios-cult, and of course Hellenistic myths often pick up on and adapt much earlier ones. (On this, see further Chapter 7.) But while the third-century Thessaly–Kos association makes ample sense, it is hard to guess at their motives for connecting with Thessaly at the time when the Catalogue of Ships was composed. Affiliation with the Greek mainland might be being emphasised; it is striking that they are among only a few communities along

8 Sprawski (2014b), 94. He goes so far as to suggest that a maritime traveller's account (or accounts) may lie behind the Catalogue's apparent prioritisation of the view from the coast and the course of the Peneios. Given, however, that significant settlements did indeed cluster in those zones, this is perhaps an unnecessary elaboration.

9 West (2011), 20–27; Nagy (2011b).

the coast of Asia Minor who fight for the Greeks rather than the Trojans, and the poet of the Catalogue may have been reflecting their desire at that time to reinforce their inclusion within the Greek world by asserting their contribution, their loyalty, their utility. The most obvious way of doing so might have been to claim migration the other way round – to claim Thessalian origins for themselves. However, that might have been too much at odds with their plainly non-Aiolian identity.[10] Better, instead, to supply a Heraklid hero of their own to colonise previously Aiolian Thessaly.[11] Certainly in the Hellenistic period this device would allow them to emphasise their *syngeneia* with Thessaly alongside Aiolian poleis (that is, poleis for whom the migration was indeed west-to-east, since they claimed Thessaly as their original motherland). Therefore, Koan claims to have settled Thessaly, claims reflected in the Catalogue of Ships, cannot be ruled out.

An alternative is to posit a combination of Thessalian and Koan agency, and this relates to the geographical peculiarity of the tradition. By the time we have a complete narrative, in the work of second-century Polyainos, the Thessalids travel from Troy to Thesprotia and thence to Thessaly. On the one hand, expecting straightforward linear journeys in early myth is misguided: *nostoi* and migrations often involve wandering, as they serve to connect non-contiguous communities and map networks. However, in this case we are justified in wondering whether at an early stage there were in fact two traditions: one, of Koan creation, in which the sons of Thessalos simply went from Troy to Thessaly; the other, of west-Thessalian creation and entirely local, in which Thessalos son of Aiatios was Thesprotian, and simply migrated over the Pindos into Thessaly. The idea of two originally independent versions of Thessalos is by no means impossible, since the construction of an eponymous hero's name – a fairly widespread device in Greek mythology – does not allow much room for linguistic variation. The existence of other myths that linked Thessaly and Epeiros – not to mention the historical reality of movement across the Pindos – may well have prompted the development of a story of Thessalian origins in that quarter.[12]

[10] Fowler also makes the attractive suggestion that Pheidippos and Antiphos had to be made to 'vacate' Kos, to allow for the arrival of Dorian heroes from Epidauros: Fowler (2018), 49. This would reinforce Kos' assertion of Dorian, rather than Aiolian, identity.

[11] This is not to say that Herakles did not have a pre-existing presence in the religious and mythological life of Thessaly: his interactions with Admetos, Kyknos and Jason may well have very early roots, and his cult near Sesklo seems to have been active in the seventh century BC. See Stamelou and Doulgeri-Intzesiloglou (2010), 165–66; Stamelou and Doulgeri-Intzesiloglou (2019). This pre-existing cult would surely have facilitated his gradual adoption as a figure of regional importance in Thessalian myth-history.

[12] Examples of mythological figures/groups who cross the Pindos are Neoptolemos

As the previous chapter posited, the *Iliad* does not, *per se*, seem to represent a strongly northern Greek point of view, but rather a primarily Ionian one in which substantial pieces of Thessalian mythology (and probably some elements of an Amphiktyonic perspective) are incorporated. This applies, I think, as much to the Catalogue of Ships as to the rest of the poem. In this, I differ somewhat from Morgan, who argues that the organisation of sites and groups represented certain realities of Thessalian self-perception in the Archaic period, though not the physical reality of settlements and toponyms.[13] While this may be true in parts, in Chapter 2 I aimed to demonstrate the detached perspective at work in the poet's vision, one that treated Thessaly as a symbolic entity, incorporating Thessalian myths and traditions but moulding them to serve the presentation of the region as the land left behind. So also in the case of the Thessalids: rather than reflecting unmixed Thessalian traditions, the poet is forging his own world view, a world view in which a key purpose of south-western Thessaly is to be a space awaiting Heraklid arrivals of Koan origin.

Moreover, though active Thessalian engagement with the stories of the Thessalids is visible in the Archaic period, we should not assume that the tradition constituted, from the start, a charter-myth cultivated by the Thessalians collectively. There are no signs whatever that it enjoyed regional currency before the later sixth century; it seems a very limited and isolated strand of myth. It is easy to imagine, as scholars have tended to do, that Thessalos was the eponymous ancestor of all the Thessalians.[14] However, no ancient source describes him in such terms, and there is in fact a wholly different – and, I think, more accurate – way of looking at him.

It is well known that heroic lineage could be deployed by ancient Greek elites in order to assert an ethnic difference between them and their subjects. One might think, for example, of another Heraklid, Temenos, the supposed ancestor of the kings of Macedon up to Alexander III. At least from the early fifth century, these kings claimed that Temenos, the founder of their line, came from the Peloponnese and established his rule in Macedon.[15]

and the Ainianes. The migrations of the latter had accumulated several stages in the story-telling tradition by the time Plutarch wrote about it in *Quaest. Gr.* 13. Passes and passage across the Pindos: Pikoulas (2012).

13 Morgan (2003), 102–05.

14 See, for example, Molyneux (1992), 130; Sprawski (2014a), 267. The latter refers to Thessalos as the 'primogenitor of the Thessalians', but ancient texts do not couch the matter in those terms: instead, they speak only of the people being named after – rather than descended from – the hero.

15 This myth is first articulated in Herodotos' *Histories* (8.137–39), in connection with the claim to Hellenic descent of Alexander I of Macedon. However, the myth was further embellished and adjusted in the time of Archelaos, when Euripides wrote a play incorporating a new hero, Archelaos – clearly a flattering namesake of the ruling king

Temenos was not the ancestor of the Macedonians, but of their ruling family. Crucially, he did not articulate shared mythic identity, but rather a separation between rulers and ruled. The kings were distinguished by their Heraklid origins, and the difference – their ancestral superiority – validated their right to rule. To this it may be objected that a crucial linguistic distinction exists between Temenos and Thessalos: the latter is the eponym of the ethnos, so how can he be restricted in lineage to the 'ownership' of a sub-group? Does not his very name proclaim him pan-Thessalian? But this objection may be countered with another northern ancestor-hero, Molossos, the son of Neoptolemos and grandson of Achilles. Molossos is of course the eponym of the Molossians, but he is not their collective ancestor. Rather, like Temenos, he is the ancestor of a ruling clan. Their Aiakid descent gave the kings of Molossia a *special* status, one not shared by their subjects.[16] This is the other role of the eponymous hero: to articulate not the genealogical unity of an *ethnos* but rather the separation – and superiority – of a sub-group within it. Until the later sixth century, I think we should regard the Thessalids tradition in rather the same light. While a belief in Aiolid descent was widespread, as reflected in the *Ehoiai*, one group set themselves apart by claiming Heraklid origins. And by 'owning' Thessalos and his family they claimed a special connection with the *ethnos*. As the descendants of Thessalos, they were the *original* Thessalians – original and – by implication – best.

It is important to bear in mind, however, that, according to my argument, this exclusive ownership of the hero Thessalos does not indicate a limited spread of the ethnic/geographic designations Thessaloi and Thessalia. The existence (as reflected in the *Iliad*) of the eponymous hero presupposes the existence of the *ethnos*, and there is no reason – *pace* Helly[17] – to believe that the *ethnos* did not, in this early period, have the same geographical extent that it had in the fifth century or later. The restricted development of the hero Thessalos in the seventh and sixth centuries simply

– into the Temenid stemma. See Harder (1985), 125–39; Borza (1990), 80–83; Duncan (2011), 78–82; Ogden (2011), 57–70; Stewart (2017), 118–38; Müller (2016), 85–104; Müller (2017), 183–92; Pownall (2017), 220–21.

16 For example, in Euripides' *Andromache* (which may well have been intended for performance in Molossia; see Allan 2000, 152–57) it is prophesied that Molossos, the son of Neoptolemos, would become the ancestor of a line of kings in the region: see esp. lines 1247–49, at which Thetis proclaims: 'βασιλέα δ' ἐκ τοῦδε χρὴ/ἄλλον δι' ἄλλου διαπερᾶν Μολοσσίας/εὐδαιμονοῦντας' – 'It is fated that king after king in succession, descended from him [i.e. Molossos], should rule all of Molossia in prosperity.'

17 Helly has argued that the Thessaloi arrived in the region only in the early seventh century BC, and indeed that the extension of their influence and control over all Thessaly took 'deux ou trois siècles' (Helly 2007, 215), being still in progress in the Classical period.

reflects the fact that one sub-group had adopted a new way of articulating their privileged position within the wider *ethnos*, as the descendants of its founder and his family.

And who was this sub-group who took this interesting new step in identity-expression? This kind of question is always hard to answer in Archaic Thessaly, where agency is murky in the extreme, and it is most unlikely that we are dealing with a ruling clan in the Macedonian or Molossian sense – rather, a local elite. They may well have been the people who cultivated the *heroön* at Georgiko in western Thessaly (see Figs 4 and 5). Here a Mycenaean tholos tomb was, from the seventh century, treated as a cult site.[18] A small sanctuary was constructed just outside its dromos; animals were sacrificed, and votive objects dedicated.[19] In the same area was found also a tile incised with the letters AIATIIO or AIATIION.[20] The word probably identifies the site as a sanctuary of the hero Aiatios, who can only be the same as the Aiatos of Polyainos' account.[21] The date of the incised tile is hard to pinpoint exactly; Intzesiloglou places it in the seventh or sixth century, but in Helly's view the letter-forms could support a date as late as the beginning of the fifth.[22] But the seventh-century inception of the cult is certain, and it is unlikely to have been reallocated to a different hero after a century or so of use. The *heroön* was not very far from Philia and its early cult of Athena Itonia.[23] As Morgan demonstrates, the archaeological material from Philia suggests that the sanctuary served the articulation of a local identity rather than a regional one.[24] If it was associated with the Thessalids tradition at this time, that association was cultivated by

18 *AD* 52 (1997) *Chron.* 479–80; *AD* 53 (1998) *Chron.* 439; *AD* 54 (1999) *Chron.* 408–9. Karouzou (2017), 350–51 and 376, fig. 19.

19 Intzesiloglou (2002b), 292–93. Intzesiloglou says that Aiatios was worshipped on this site as 'le fondateur de la région qui était aussi le père de Thessalos et l'ancêtre de tous les Thessaliens'; however, as I have said, this view – that Thessalos was considered the ancestor of the whole *ethnos*, and that his cult in the early period was symbolically pan-Thessalian – is not really tenable.

20 For an image of the tile see *AD* 54 (1999) *Chron.* 409 Eik. 28; Intzesiloglou (2002b), 294.

21 The inscription is not unproblematic, because there are traces of an E at the beginning and a letter that is hard to distinguish at the end. An alternative is to take the EAIA as the tail end of a feminine patronymic adjective, and the ON?E as the start of ONEΘEIKE. However, this raises even bigger problems: what of the TII, for one thing? And would the tile really have been that much bigger in its unbroken state? All in all, AIATIION seems likeliest, as is supported by comparable sanctuary names in -eion/-ion.

22 *AD* 54 (1999) *Chron.*, 408; Helly (2007), 214.

23 Kilian-Dirlmeier (2002), 176.

24 Morgan (2003), 140–41, noting the prevalence of dining-related objects and weaponry among the finds from the site; cf. Mili (2015), 229.

Fig. 4. Entrance of the Late Bronze Age tomb at Georgiko. Photograph: author's own

west-Thessalian elites, and we are still not dealing with the collective use of the myth to express shared Thessalian origins on the regional level.[25]

[25] Given the striking similarity of the hero Molossos as the eponym of an *ethnos* 'owned' by a ruling elite, one may speculate that there was influence involved; since Thessalos has the earlier attestation, this is likely to have been Thessalian influence

Fig. 5. Late Bronze Age tomb at Georgiko (top left) showing *heroön* in the foreground. Photograph: author's own

Such collective use was not, in fact, long to emerge. Before discussing that stage, however, we must bring into the frame the other crucial group active within the development of these traditions: the Boiotians.[26] It is a perennial failing of historians researching one particular region to valorise the activities of that region's inhabitants at all costs and to play down those of other communities. But in fact the myths under discussion here are a prime example of the dialogic nature of myth-making, the fact that stories are rarely shaped exclusively within the bounds of a single group, but rather are passed back and forth between multiple interested parties, each of which adapts the story for its own particular purposes at a given time.[27]

on the Molossian rulers rather than the other way around. Thessalos and his family were known in Epeiros: in the Thesprotian town of Ephyra an inscription was set up recording the deeds of Antiphos and Pheidippos, who were thought to be buried there. Perhaps their awareness of the Thessalos tradition encouraged the Molossian rulers to develop an eponymous hero of their own, of a similar type.

26 Kravaritou (2012) provides a brief discussion of the interplay between Thessalian and Boiotian *ethnos*- traditions.

27 For another example of such 'contractual myth-making' see Nagy (2011a).

It is important to acknowledge that the Boiotians are more energetic in their contribution to the tradition of the Thessalian migration than are the Thessalians themselves, in most times and situations.[28]

2. Enter the Boiotians: the *Ehoiai* and the *Aspis*

In the Catalogue of Ships, the Boiotoi are plainly located in Boiotia. This puzzled Thucydides, because at that time they should not have been. By the time he was writing, all well-informed Greeks knew that the Boiotians – most of them, anyway[29] – moved into the region that took their name only after the Trojan War. They did so because the Thessaloi, arriving in Thessaly, ousted them and forced them to migrate south to their historical location. So why does Homer place them in central, rather than northern, Greece? Attempting to reconcile this apparent conundrum, Thucydides ingeniously posits two migrations: a first, smaller contingent of Boiotoi, an *apodasmos*, has already made the move south; it is these that fight at Troy.[30] The majority are still in Thessaly, and will later set out to join the advance party when displaced by the Thessaloi.

In fact, *contra* Thucydides, I would suggest a different solution: that the Boiotian ingredient of the myth was added on to a pre-existing myth of the arrival of the Thessalids in Thessaly. When the Catalogue of Ships was composed the Thessalian component was in existence, but the Boiotian addition was not; therefore, in Homer, the Boiotoi are in Boiotia, since the story of their arrival there from Thessaly was yet to be created. Homer scrupulously maintains mythic chronology by *not* locating the Thessaloi in Thessaly, but he has no such reason not to place the Boiotoi in Boiotia.

At first sight it may seem perverse to argue that the myth of the displacement of the Boiotoi was originally of Boiotian rather than Thessalian manufacture: surely it serves Thessalian interests better, since it presents them as the victors and the Boiotoi as displaced refugees? But, after all, we cannot always expect foundation myths to follow simple logic as we would conceive of it. In fact such stories are often couched in terms of trauma, conflict, the overcoming of inauspicious beginnings and dire odds. Here the Heraklid Temenos and his brothers are pertinent once again: not only were they, according to the legend, banished from Argos, but when they arrived in Macedon they were initially in a state of servitude to the king. Nonetheless, this was the story the ruling family of Macedon apparently

[28] For detailed discussion of various ways in which Thessalian and Boiotian mythology interleave see Tufano (2019).

[29] One always has to recognise the existence of divergent traditions within a region, such as the Theban claim of descent from Kadmos. On this see Kühr (2006).

[30] Thuc. 1.12.3.

chose to represent their identity and right to rule. As Ogden has shown, *oikistēs* figures are rarely 'straightforward' heroes: in fact they share some features with scapegoats – *pharmakoi* – in being driven out of their homes and forced to find new territory.[31] In various ways, Boiotos fits the complex discourse of the *oikistēs*.[32]

At what point, then, does the Boiotian component of the story first appear? Its earliest literary expression comes in the *Ehoiai*, though, as usual with that text, we have to contend with the challenges of fragments. Fr. 218 MW exemplifies this difficulty:

> ὁ γὰρ τοῦ Μενεσθίου πατὴρ ἀρηίθοος Βοιοτὸς ἦν κατοικῶν Ἄρνην. ἔστι δὲ αὕτη Βοιωτίας, ὡς καὶ Ἡσίοδός φησιν.

Larson translates this as follows:

> For the father of Menesthios, Boiotos swift in war, was an organizer/administrator of Arne. This is Boiotian Arne, as Hesiod says.

To arrive at this translation, Larson has had to do two things: first, decapitalise Areithoos so that it becomes an epithet, 'swift in war', rather than a personal name; and, second, argue for Boiotos as a personal name rather than an ethnic. Thus the traditional translation 'For the father of Menesthios, Areithoos the Boiotian, was … ' is rejected to substantiate Boiotos' appearance in the poem. Complex linguistic and historical reasoning lies behind this, which may not wholly convince, for all its ingenuity. However, Onchestos seems to turn up as the son of Boiotos in fr. 219 MW; moreover, we may find oblique evidence for the existence of the tradition in some form at this time in the *Aspis*. In this poem, a work of quite probably Boiotian (and certainly not Thessalian) creation, dated to the same early sixth-century period as the *Ehoiai*, we find Arne as a Thessalian place-name rather than a Boiotian one, and this is significant. From the fifth century we have sources that clearly identify Arne as the Thessalian metropolis the Boiotoi were forced to leave by the invading Thessaloi;[33] the idea of Boiotian Arne as the daughter-city of this Arne is attested only in later sources, but in this case may be assumed to have been in play from the fifth century if not earlier. Arne is a Boiotian site in the Catalogue of Ships; the fact that the Thessalian Arne has appeared in the *Aspis* may well suggest that between the composition dates of the two texts – that is,

31 Ogden (1997).

32 Larson (2007), 63–64.

33 Hellanikos may also have called a sub-region of Thessaly 'Arnaia' (see *FGrH* 4 F 14). However, this cannot be securely located. See Fowler (2013), 185–86.

between the seventh and the sixth centuries BC – the legend was developed in which the inhabitants of Boiotian Arne had founded that settlement after their migration south from their Thessalian homeland, from the original northern Arne.[34]

It is important to note at this point that neither Arne is very real.[35] In Boiotia Arne simply has not been located, but may have been a historical polis; in Thessaly the unreality of Arne is strongly suggested by the fact that Kierion could claim to be Arne (see below). In all likelihood the Thessalian Arne was fictional, created by Boiotians to provide the legendary metropolis of a (real) Boiotian polis, and this probably happened in the Archaic period, after Homer but before – or at the time of – the creation of the *Aspis*. In any case, the myth of the Boiotian migration from Thessaly was securely in place, and circulating widely, in the fifth century BC. Not only does Thucydides mention it, but various authors have started to elaborate on the parentage and deeds of Boiotos.[36] Significantly, the genealogy of the hero emphasises descent from Poseidon and from Aiolos. By the fifth century there are few if any signs that the Thessalians were actively promoting the Aiolid descent that had been so important to their representation in the *Ehoiai*. For the Boiotians of the fifth century and later, Aiolid descent was part of their unified identity as an *ethnos*, but it had never served that purpose for the Thessalians: instead, in the *Ehoiai*, it distinguished heroic lineages in individual Thessalian communities and linked them with others across the Greek world. The traditions of the Thessalids in the late sixth and fifth century allowed some Thessalians to turn aside from Aiolid roots and forge a new identity, to create a watershed in their myth-history. Shortly we shall look at how this process continued among new actors and in new contexts. First, however, we return to the Boiotoi to examine how the Thessalians themselves took up and developed the story from their side.

3. Thessalian interest in the migration of the Boiotoi in the Archaic period?

We have seen that, probably as early as the early sixth century BC, Thessalian origins were an essential component in the creation of a shared Boiotian myth-history and therefore identity. So far Thessaly herself has

[34] For discussion of these various Boiotian traditions see Tufano (2019), 96–100.

[35] Beck and Ganter (2015), 134. On the name and its etymology see Dubois (2014), 66–68.

[36] E.g. Euripides' *Melanippe Sophē* and *Melanippe Desmotis*, probably composed to reflect and advertise the foundation myths of Metaponton, but in so doing developing some earlier strands of Boiotian myth-history concerning the hero Boiotos as offspring of Poseidon and Arne. Stewart (2017), 147–48.

been rather passive in this. The myth of the arriving Thessalids was of Thessalian creation, but upon this stem the Boiotoi grafted their own ethnogenetic narrative. Did the two traditions continue separate, running along parallel tracks in the two regions? No: in fact we see clear signs that the Thessalians picked up and adapted the Boiotian arm of the story, from the end of the fifth century BC at least. To some extent, and for certain Thessalian groups and communities, being the origin of the Boiotian *ethnos* was a significant strand in their myth-historical identity. There are two ways of approaching this matter. First, we shall look at the Thessalian cult sites seen – by the Boiotians as well as by some modern scholars – as connected with Boiotian counterparts, and ask whether the Thessalians themselves seem to have treated them in this light. Second, we shall examine further signs – coins, toponyms and so on – that Thessalian communities wished to situate themselves as participants in the Boiotian story.

On the former aspect, the cult involved more than any other in both ancient and modern theories concerning connections between Thessaly and Boiotia is that of Athena Itonia. Both regions contained cult sites of this form of the goddess; in Boiotia her chief place of worship was Koroneia.[37] At some time hard to pin down, but certainly by the third century BC, the Koroneia sanctuary hosted the festival of the Pamboiotia, plainly signalling its crucial importance in the articulation of the *ethnos*;[38] well before that, however, it was of regional significance and considerable fame outside Boiotia. Alkaios mentions it (late seventh or early sixth century), and the goddess appears on Boiotian pottery of the sixth century.[39] Uncertainty over the identification of the site precludes the use of archaeological data to add to our understanding of the nature and date of the cult.[40]

Only in late sources, such as Strabo,[41] are we explicitly given the story that it was founded by refugees from Thessalian Arne; however, there are glimpses of this tradition in earlier texts, as reported here by the scholion on Apollonios' *Argonautika* 1.551:

> 'The work of Itonian Athena': There is a sanctuary of Itonian Athena in Koroneia in Boiotia. But Apollonios would not mention in connection

[37] Roesch (1982), 217–24.

[38] For an attempt to balance its importance alongside that of other cult sites in Boiotia, however, see Ganter (2013).

[39] Alkaios fr. 325 Campbell; he does not mention the *epiklesis* Itonia but casts her in a warlike light that chimes entirely with her characterisation across sources. The most relevant vase (London BM 1879,1004.1), a lekanis, dates to ca 550 and shows the goddess armed, spear raised and striding forward; it seems a cult statue is being depicted, because before her is an altar and a procession bearing offerings.

[40] Lalonde (2020), 105–10.

[41] Strabo 9.2.29.

> with the construction of the Argo Athena with her epithet in Koroneia, but rather her epithet in Thessalian Itonia, which Hekataios [*FGrH* 1 F 2] mentions in the first book of his *Histories*. Armenidas [*FGrH* 378 F 1] in his work on Thebes said that Itonos had been begotten by Amphiktyon in Thessaly … .[42]

This presents the usual unlovely patchwork of deracinated snippets. We cannot be sure that Hekataios said that the Thessalian sanctuary was the original of the Boiotian one, only that he mentioned the Thessalian cult. Armenidas, on the other hand, writing in the fifth century BC and one of the key early exponents of Boiotian historiography, seems to have told of a hero, Itonos son of Amphiktyon;[43] the fact that he is specifically said to have been born in Thessaly suggests that he left the region at a later stage of his life, presumably moving south to found the cult site at Koroneia.[44] The mention of Amphiktyon is significant, obviously referring to the Boiotian role within the Amphiktyony, weaving their *ethnos* into its mythical origins, and perhaps also connecting the Boiotian cult of Athena Itonia with the prime religious authority of Delphi.[45]

Did the Thessalians ever think of their Athena Itonia cult as the original, and the Boiotian counterpart as the offshoot? One might envisage this forming an important ingredient in their sense of regional self-importance, to have been the *fons et origo* of a cult of such wide fame – wider, indeed, than their own. Addressing that question, however, requires consideration first of the location and nature of the Thessalian sanctuary, and this has been the subject of decades of academic controversy, still ongoing. That said, some of the controversy has perhaps arisen from an unnecessary purpose, that of determining which of a number of candidates was *the* cult site of Athena Itonia in Thessaly. It is certainly misguided, as both Graninger (2011) and Mili (2015) have argued, to search for rigid centralisation of the cult within the region, especially before the development of the new *koinon* after 197 BC. Instead, we should consider a wide diffusion of the cult over Thessaly, with sanctuaries in a number of locations, two of them especially important on the supra-polis level: one in Thessaliotis, near modern Philia, and another in Achaia Phthiotis, at the ancient site actually called Iton or Itonos.

[42] 'ἔργον Ἀθηναίης Ἰτωνίδος] Ἰτωνίας Ἀθηνᾶς ἐστιν ἱερὸν ἐν Κορωνείαι τῆς Βοιωτίας. ὁ μέντοι Ἀπολλώνιος οὐκ ἂν λέγοι τὴν Ἀθηνᾶν ἐπὶ κατασκευῆι τῆς Ἀργοῦς ἀπὸ τῆς ἐν Κορωνείαι ἐπικλήσεως, μᾶλλον δε ἀπὸ Θεσσαλικῆς Ἰτωνίας, περὶ ἧς Ἑκαταῖος μὲν ἐν τῆι πρώτηι τῶν Ἱστοριῶν λέγει. Ἀρμενίδας δὲ ἐν τοῖς Θηβαικοῖς Ἀμφικτύονος υἱὸν Ἴτωνον ἐν Θεσσαλίαι γεννηθῆναι … '.

[43] Tufano (2019), 134–38.

[44] Fowler (2013), 64.

[45] Tufano (2019), 136.

To take Iton(os) first, it is by no means insignificant in terms of the Boiotian connection. Its very name, of course, suggests an early relationship with the goddess, and it is more likely that her *epiklesis* came from the toponym, though the reverse is possible. As Iton, it is included in the Catalogue of Ships, within the command of Protesilaos.[46] While we are, as so often, reliant upon Strabo for this detail, it appears to have been the site to which the Boiotian sanctuary harked back;[47] this would accord with the fact that, in the *Aspis* and the *Ehoiai*, Thessalian Arne was in the south-east of the region. In the early period it is probably not particularly relevant that, *sensu stricto*, the place was in the perioikic region of Achaia Phthiotis rather than in 'Thessaly proper', since a sharp division between tetrads and *perioikis* is expressed in our surviving sources only from the late sixth century onwards (on which see Chapter 1); the idea that the eastern sanctuary of Athena Itonia would therefore have been considered marginal or non-Thessalian would be anachronistic in the Archaic period. However, we are hampered by not having identified the site's physical remains,[48] and this contrasts strongly with the situation pertaining to the western sanctuary, near modern Philia, whose archaeological investigation has supplied one of the most striking landmarks on the religious map of Thessaly.

The Philia site used to suffer from scholars' determination to find the federal sanctuary of the Thessalians;[49] nothing discovered there provides evidence that it fulfilled this role any earlier than the second century BC, and once we have shed this unnecessary preoccupation we are free to see the place for what it was, not a place of formal pan-Thessalian congregation but a site whose wealth and importance from a strikingly early date would have given it a major role in west Thessaly and connections throughout Thessaly, including with other major early sanctuaries such as that of Ennodia at Pherai and perhaps that of Athena Polias at Phthiotic Thebes.[50] The earliest finds from Philia are centuries older than the first attestation of cult at Koroneia, and it is quite possible that it was the progenitor of the Boiotian and even of the Athenian cults of Athena Itonia, though simple linear transfer of a cult from site A to sites B and C may be a less judicious model than that of a central and northern Greek distribution of a cult-type whose origins *per se* are unknown.[51]

[46] Hom. *Il.* 2.696.

[47] Strabo 9.2.29 and 9.5.14.

[48] Graninger (2011a), 55–58.

[49] For example, this was the opinion of the first systematic excavator, Theocharis: see Theocharis AD 19 (1964) chron., 248–49; Lalonde (2020), 68–70.

[50] Karouzou (2018), 130–35; she observes the tendency for the major early sanctuaries in Thessaly to be located on important road-ways, ensuring their accessibility beyond the local area.

[51] Mili (2015), 229–32; Lalonde (2020), 9–10. The latter does on the whole, however,

The fact that the non-Thessalian literary sources do not mention it more is puzzling, but the attention of the early poets is chiefly focused on eastern Thessaly, especially the area around the bay of Pagasai; the only west-Thessalian contingent in the Catalogue of Ships, for example, is that of Podaleirios and Machaon, which extends as far south only as Ithome and, as noted above, leaves a strange and desolate gap with Philia where its centre would be. By contrast, places named in the Catalogue positively cluster around the Bay of Pagasai and around the course of the Peneios north of Larisa.[52] As has been said, the Catalogue does not depict how Greece actually was at any given time, but rather the places included within various networks of religious interaction; therefore, the omission of the Philia region cannot be taken to negate that site's importance, but might suggest that it was, culturally and religiously, somewhat off the beaten track at that time, though its finds certainly preclude a picture of complete isolation.[53] As Morgan argues, however, the archaeological record of the site, despite some striking imports from distant lands and from the other side of Thessaly among the votives, generally creates a picture of a sanctuary strongly rooted within the sub-regional level, its workshops producing not only votives but also weapons, its early ritual dominated by sacrifice and communal dining.[54]

The broad-brush picture of the site's fluctuating usage is instructive. The votive deposits at Philia appear to peak in the period 750–575 BC; thereafter there is a steady decline in their number, and a sharp decline after 350 (though a slight rise is discernible in the Roman period). This picture does not, however, map seamlessly onto the architectural and other remains. Part of an early fifth-century kouros was discovered, as were pieces of bronze statues from the sixth century and the Hellenistic period. In the later fifth or early fourth century the first monumental buildings are added; a third-century BC building is also attested. The Classical building is significant for this chapter, as it coincides with signs that this part of Thessaly was coming to be regarded – or, perhaps more accurately, to regard itself – as the original homeland of the Boiotoi. We shall return to this point later on; first, it is necessary to consider whether the Philia sanctuary, or any of the adjoining sites, seem to bear any connection with the myths under discussion.

The evidence available is not conducive to detailed argumentation on this point, and certainly it would be going too far to posit clear references to the

argue quite strongly for the primacy of the Thessalian cult.

52 See the map in Helly (1995), 90.

53 Mili (2015, 339–40) notes, for example, a bronze figurine from Luristan.

54 Morgan (2003), 141. The majority of the bronze votives seem to be of local manufacture, indicating a flourishing metalworking culture in the area, and the proportion of the votives that are of definitely non-Thessalian origin is very small, just 2 per cent in the eighth and seventh centuries: Karouzou (2018), 134.

Fig. 6. Bronze statue of Apollo from the temple at Lianokokkala, near Metropolis; sixth century BC. Photograph: author's own

displacement of the Boiotoi. However, it has been suggested that some aspects of Athena Itonia and of her cult at Philia are highly compatible with myths of invasion and territorial appropriation.[55] The character and iconography

55 Bouchon and Helly (2013), 214–18.

of Athena Itonia, though we have no representation of the goddess surviving from Philia itself, are consistently martial. The dedication of weapons (actual and miniature) was an important element of the votive record of the site, with 547 finds overall (many sadly undatable); the practice of dedicating weapons also underwent some interesting fluctuations. In the period between the late Geometric and the early Archaic weapons were the least well-represented offering-type, but their occurrence grows markedly between 625 and 500 BC (eighty-eight items) and continues to increase, with 102 dating to 575–350 BC. Only one item is securely dated after 350 BC. While we should not overlook the non-military nature of the large number of, for example, fibulae (737 items), the changing popularity of weapon dedications[56] is suggestive, not least when we compare it with, in particular, the highly unusual warrior type of the mid-sixth-century cult statue of Apollo at Liannokokala, some two kilometres to the west of Metropolis (see Fig. 6).[57]

However, while this military aspect of the Metropolis Apollo and of Athena Itonia is hard to deny, it is a big step from that to believing that it was, *ab initio*, intended to evoke the myth of the invading Thessalids, let alone – at this early stage – the displaced Boiotoi. It may possibly have worked the other way round: west-Thessalian elites constructed their shared identity in terms of military excellence, as expressed through their ritual attendance at the Philia sanctuary, and this encouraged the development or at least the adoption of invasion-myths as a secondary stage; of this development or adoption the *heroön* of Aiatios at Georgiko provides strong evidence. The evidence from the Archaic period is simply not sufficient to take the matter any further, however. It is in fact in Pelasgiotis that we find our next clear signs of Thessalian groups co-opting the myth of the Thessalids – though not of the Boiotian displacement – and it is to these that we now turn, before, in the next section, moving westward again to look at the mythological resonances of Metropolis and Kierion in the late fifth and the fourth century BC.

4. The appropriation of the Thessalids by the elites of Pelasgiotis

To sum up the picture so far: there are signs that in the seventh century the myth of the invading Thessalids was of interest to one group of Thessalians at least, those who cultivated the *heroön* at Georgiko. By the early sixth century a

[56] For the changing proportions in pie-chart form see Kilian-Dirlmeier (2002), 189–91.

[57] Initial detailed report of the excavation: *AD* 49 (1994) *Chron.* 331–33; follow-up excavation reports in *AD* 50 (1995) *Chron.* 375–76; *AD* 51 (1996) *Chron.* 347–48; *AD* 52 (1997) *Chron.* 475–76; *AD* 54 (1999) *Chron.* 410. Overview discussion: Intzesiloglou (2000) and (2002a).

secondary element had been grafted on to the story of the Thessalids crossing the Pindos into Thessaly; now, by doing so they displace a resident (in some traditions indigenous) *ethnos*, the Boiotoi, who thereupon migrate south to their historical homeland in central Greece. This part of the myth was of Boiotian rather than Thessalian manufacture, and we shall have to wait until the end of the fifth century at least to find signs that the Thessalians are aware of, and interested in, it. However, the incursion of the Thessalids remains visible: in the later sixth century there are signs that the myth was pulled away from its west-Thessalian roots[58] and incorporated into the self-presentation of Pelasgiotic elites, and also, crucially, into the reorganisation of the whole region.

By 498 BC, when Pindar composed his *Pythian* 10, he was able to flatter the Aleuadai of Larisa by describing them as of the *genos* of Herakles.[59] He does not explain the genealogical connection, but it would seem perverse to suggest that it was not via the figure of Thessalos and his sons Antiphos and Pheidippos, following the tradition established in the *Iliad*. Here, then, is a clear sign that by the early fifth century the Thessalids tradition had moved beyond its probable west-Thessalian origins and been espoused by the elite of Larisa, the polis that, by then, was firmly placed as dominant around the course of the Peneios (see Chapter 5). Note, also, that in the *Ode* Heraklid ancestry is plainly being used, as so often in Greek mythology, to legitimate the special standing of a ruling clan:

> Prosperous Lakedaimon,
> Blessed Thessaly: both are ruled by the race
> Of a single ancestor, Herakles excellent in battle.[60]

[58] That is not to say that its original 'owners' relinquished it: most of the finds from the Georgiko *heroön* are in fact fifth century in date. See Nikolaou (2012), 62.

[59] Herakles, without explicit connection to Thessalos, was the recipient of early cult in Thessaly. At the site now called Spartias-Latomeio, near Sesklo, there was a significant Archaic sanctuary of the hero, which continued to operate into the Hellenistic period. The earliest votives date from the seventh century, but the sixth century seems to have been a time of particular cult activity. See Stamelou and Doulgeri-Intzesiloglou (2010) and (2019). This may relate to the diffusion of the Thessalids myth. On the poem and its context see Stamatopoulou (2007a), 309–13. For a detailed analysis of how the myths included in the poem may have served the purposes of Aleuad self-promotion see Pavlou (2022).

[60] Lines 1–3:

> ὄλβια Λακεδαίμων,
> μάκαιρα Θεσσαλία: πατρὸς δ' ἀμφοτέραις ἐξ ἑνὸς
> ἀριστομάχου γένος Ἡρακλεῦς βασιλεύει.

The connection with Sparta reinforces the claim, since the Heraklid identity of Spartan kings was well established as the basis of their authority. So, as with our west-Thessalian clan tending the *heroön* of Aiatios, we have here the exclusive use of the eponym, to set an elite apart from those over whom they wielded inherited power.

There is a further suggestion of the Thessalids myth in the same poem. Later in the poem Pindar expresses the wish that the performance of his poem will enrich the life of the victor Hippokleas:

> And I hope that, when the Ephyraioi
> pour forth my sweet sound beside the Peneios,
> I shall, with my songs, make Hippokleas even more
> conspicuous for his garlands among his age-mates and older men,
> and the darling of young girls.[61]

Who are these Ephyraioi? Ephyra is a place-name found in various locations in the Greek world, including Elis[62] and Korinth.[63] However, its Thesprotian location is surely the most significant one here, in view of that site's connection with the Thessalids myth. In the pseudo-Aristotelian *Peplos*,[64] from which survives a collection of heroic epitaphs, the epitaph of Pheidippos and Antiphos describes them as buried in their *patris*, Ephyra. Though they are called Koans, Ephyra probably refers to the Thesprotian land that they occupied before entering Thessaly; while it is a slight stretch to call it *patris*, the fact that it was their first home after their journey from Troy may explain the use of the word. So calling a Thessalian group 'Ephyraians' seems to constitute a further link with the myth. But which Thessalians? Mili is surely right to identify them as either Pelinnaians – the

[61] Lines 55–59:
ἔλπομαι δ' Ἐφυραίων
ὄπ' ἀμφὶ Πηνεϊὸν γλυκεῖαν προχεόντων ἐμὰν
τὸν Ἱπποκλέαν ἔτι καὶ μᾶλλον σὺν ἀοιδαῖς
ἕκατι στεφάνων θαητὸν ἐν ἅλιξι θησέμεν ἐν καὶ παλαιτέροις,
νέαισίν τε παρθένοισι μέλημα.

[62] Strabo 8.3.5. on the sources and composition of Strabo's list of Ephyras see Starikova (2019), 10–11.

[63] Ephyra as an older name of Korinth: Paus. 2.1.1; Apollod. *Bibl.* 1.9.3.

[64] Gutzwiller (2010) has argued convincingly that this text is Classical rather than Hellenistic; the attribution to Aristotle, though erroneous, would suggest a fourth-century date. Gutzwiller further suggests that the *Peplos* in its full form was 'not … an anthology of epigrams, but a prose catalogue or handbook on events of the legendary past that included epitaphs' (p. 223). She argues that the burials included in the work actually corresponded closely with sites of hero-cult, suggesting that Antiphos and Pheidippos may have been accorded cult in Thesprotia.

victor's people – or the Larisaians who commissioned the Ode.[65] But the name may not have been used by a particular kinship group in one of the two poleis, as she suggests. Rather, it may be Pindar's way of flattering one or the other by subtly evoking the mythological past of the Thessalids from whom the Aleuadai – and perhaps also the leading families of Pelinna – claimed descent. In the third century BC, as we shall see in Chapter 7, the Thessalian authors Kineas and Souidas could build upon this association by claiming that Krannon, another Pelasgiotic polis, was previously called Ephyra, and its people Ephyraians. (However, in that context the drive was to reinforce the link between Thessaly and Dodona, as well as the link with Thessalos.)[66]

Pindar's *Pythian* 10 may not, however, have been the first epinikian poem to utilise the Thessalids in establishing the prestige of its honorand and his associates. In the closing decade of the sixth century the poet Simonides undertook some commissions from Thessalian patrons, though unfortunately the details are shrouded in anecdote and dating is difficult.[67] We have part of a poem for a Thessalian victor in the *keles* (horse-race) in the Pythian Games at Delphi. The name of the victor is unknown: the prescript reads 'for the sons of Aiatios', which probably indicated the family that commissioned the verse. The victor may have been a member of the family, but need not have been, as Pindar's *Pythian* 10 reminds us. The opening lines – the best-preserved portion, are as follows:

> In the *kelēs*.
> For the sons of Aiatios.
> The glorious son of Kronos Ouranidas
> [Protects] the race of Aiatios,
> And Apollo of the golden
> Lyre, the far-shooter,

65 Mili (2015), 96.

66 A comparison might be made with the identification of Thessalian groups as 'Lapiths'. When Simonides called some inhabitants of Pelasgiotis Lapiths (quoted in Strabo 9.5.20), we might assume he was just drawing on his knowledge of the area's myth-history; however, in a Hellenistic funerary inscription from Atrax the dead man calls his companions, from whose company he regrets being separated by death, 'Lapiths', suggesting that social groups could and did identify with mythological groups (*SEG* 34.498).

67 The most famous anecdote is the one in which Simonides has a lucky escape from the collapsing feasting hall of his patron Skopas of Krannon, and is afterwards able to use his prodigious spatial memory to identify the disfigured corpses of Skopas' family and friends. See Cic. *de Orat.* 2. 86. 351–53; Quint. *Inst.* 11. 2. 11–16. Thessalian feasting – especially to their detriment – is such a *topos* as to make one sceptical of the veracity of this tale; however, the association between Simonides and Thessaly is not *per se* in doubt: see Stamatopoulou (2007a), 327–28.

And shining Pytho distinguish them,
And the glory of the horse-race … .[68]

The reference to a 'race of Aiatios' is striking; here the name of an important Thessalid (in Polyainos' version, the grandson of one Thessalos and the father of another) is being used to label the members of a late sixth-century clan. There are two possible ways of reading this: either the *paides Aiatiou* are the sons of a man called Aiatios, or the family traced descent from the hero Aiatios. A combination of the two is possible, and in any case either is significant in its own way: the adoption of Aiatios as legendary ancestor would be especially interesting, but choosing Aiatios as a personal name within an aristocratic family has its own mythological resonance. But in either case, where was this family situated? Krannon would be a plausible suggestion in view of Simonides' well-established connections with the Skopadai in that polis. However, the tattered vestiges of the poem's second half refer to a *basileus* who is called *Pyrrhidas*, surely with the sense 'descendant of Pyrrhos'; this is most likely to refer to Aleuas Pyrrhos, the influential Larisaian. This does not necessarily mean that the 'race of Aiatios' were the same as the Aleuadai, since the Skopadai may have espoused the same genealogy, but it seems quite likely that they were: Heraklid descent via Aiatios would explain the mythological basis behind Pindar's description of them as descendants of Herakles.

So, by the end of the sixth century, the name Aiatios – with its Thessalid associations – had moved east into the dominant poleis of Pelasgiotis.[69] We cannot with any plausibility claim that Simonides 511 can have had a west-Thessalian patron; that region is not represented in what we know of Simonides' Thessalian range, nor indeed in the surviving names of Thessalian victors at the panhellenic festivals. Instead, what we may have here is an act of appropriation, aristocrats within a polis quite recently

68 Simonides fr. 511 *PMG*:
κέλητι
τοῖς Αἰατίου παισίν̣
Οὐρανίδ]α Κρόνοιο παῖς ἐρικυδ[ής
] Αἰατίου γενεάν
]ται καὶ χρυσοφ[όρ]μι[γξ
Ἀπόλλων ἑκαταβόλο[ς
σαμαίνει λιπαρά τε Πυθ[ώ
τό] θ' ἱπποδρ[ομίας κῦδος …

69 Further evidence of the Pelasgiotic adoption of Thessalos towards the end of the sixth century may lie in Peisistratos' choice of Thessalos as a name for one of his sons. This choice probably worked on two levels, chiefly signalling an affiliation with the region (since the Peisistratidai and the Aleuadai were *philoi* – but also evoking the hero Thessalos, as suggested by Morgan (2009a), 17.

grown to dominance taking on a mythical genealogy first developed elsewhere. This does not mean the original 'owners' gave the identification up; rather, as we shall see, it was losing its exclusivity, and by certain discernible stages moving to cover more and more of the land and people of Thessaly.[70] The myth's circulation beyond its original local origin-point is strongly suggested also by its occurrence in the work of Hekataios of Miletos in the later sixth or early fifth century BC.[71] In fact, by the time Simonides and Pindar were composing their poems for Thessalians, the myth of the incursion of the Thessalids had already passed out of the hands of a few families and become part of the exploitation of myth-history on a regional basis, through the naming of the tetrad Thessaliotis. We shall now go on to consider this process in more detail.

5. The invasion of the Thessaloi

When scholars discuss the origin-myths of Thessaly, they tend to overlook a very important distinction in the ancient traditions. Whereas most of the variants here discussed relate to the Thessalids – Thessalos and his family – there are two authors, Herodotos and Thucydides, who couch the matter in slightly different terms, speaking on an incursion not by members of a specific heroic family but by an undifferentiated *ethnos*, the Thessaloi.

We cannot dismiss the Thessaloi tradition as the product of rationalising historiography that prefers to avoid old-fashioned hero-tales; this may be true of Thucydides' style, but not of Herodotos'. We need instead to examine more closely the role played by the Thessaloi in the two texts. Herodotos first: the context is the historian's description of the area around Thermopylai, when the Greeks chose it (instead of Tempe) to make their defensive stand against the invading Persians in 480 BC, and his explanation of the so-called 'Phokian Wall'. As Chapter 1 established, the incident involves implicit mirroring between the Persians and the Thessaloi, both aggressors entering Greece from the north. However, the characterisation of the Thessalians as dangerous neighbours is not at all limited to Herodotos' narrative. Indeed, it also pervades Thucydides' version of the Thessaloi tradition. 'Sixty years after the capture of Troy the modern Boiotians were driven out of Arne by the Thessalians, and settled in the present Boiotia, the former Kadmeis; though there was a division of them

[70] This process of dissemination may have lain behind the creation of an Archaic sanctuary of Herakles in the chōra of Pherai: see Stamelou and Doulgeri-Intzesiloglou (2010).

[71] Hek. fr. 137A Fowler; see Fowler (2013), 314–15. Very little of the fragment survives, but the remaining portion includes traces of the names Aiatios (in that form), Pheidippos and Antiphos, and it is plain that the myth of the Thessalids was recounted.

there before, some of whom joined the expedition to Troy.'[72] So Thucydides brings in the other major element in this mythology: the displacement of the Boiotoi. But what both texts have in common is the replacement of individual heroes with an undifferentiated group, a proto-*ethnos*.

As suggested above, the impact of the Thessaloi tradition is completely different from that of the Thessalids. While the Thessalids initially allowed elites to establish themselves as separate from – and implicitly superior to – their fellow Thessalians, because of their privileged relationship with Thessalian identity, the Thessaloi version, a secondary development, seems on the face of it to be much more expansive, providing a charter-myth for the whole *ethnos*, for all Thessaloi. A very comparable progression from the singling out of elites to the drawing together of an *ethnos* has been discerned by Crielaard in the development of Ionian identity. The earliest traditions, he argues, reflect competition between elites, striving to establish their status through heroic descent. From this evolved a secondary process: 'stories of wandering 'heroes' were extrapolated to migratory stories that served as 'ancestor myths' for a large part of the polis population.'[73] It is exactly this distinction, between the wandering hero and the migrating *ethnos*, that I suggest we see in the Thessalian case.[74]

However, the evidence available to us, limited as it is, does not really allow us to posit a general adoption of the Thessaloi tradition at all levels of Thessalian society – a democratisation of the mythology, so to speak. What myths meant to non-elites is largely lost to view, and it may well be that the Thessaloi tradition remained the preserve of very limited sectors of society. Instead of imagining a widening demographic spread, perhaps we should rather consider that the difference between the Thessalids tradition and

[72] Thuc. 1.12.3: 'Βοιωτοί τε γὰρ οἱ νῦν ἑξηκοστῷ ἔτει μετὰ Ἰλίου ἅλωσιν ἐξ Ἄρνης ἀναστάντες ὑπὸ Θεσσαλῶν τὴν νῦν μὲν Βοιωτίαν, πρότερον δὲ Καδμηίδα γῆν καλουμένην ᾤκισαν (ἦν δὲ αὐτῶν καὶ ἀποδασμὸς πρότερον ἐν τῇ γῇ ταύτῃ, ἀφ' ὧν καὶ ἐς Ἴλιον ἐστράτευσαν).'

[73] Crielaard (2009), 53.

[74] Note that the argument that the invasion of the Thessaloi represents a secondary tradition goes against a claim that the theme of territorial acquisition is inherent in the etymology of their name. Bader (2009) includes them, and the toponym Thessalia, among a large number of names whose etymology supposedly contain the element of 'desire' or 'wish', which he argues with the theme of invading or appropriating a chosen land. However, to read into this the idea that the Thessaloi are 'those who wish to acquire the land' and that Thessalia is 'the desired land' (as do Bouchon and Helly 2013, 207) seems to risk importing the theme of invasion from the ancient narratives into decidedly ambiguous etymological associations. As Bader observes, the bundle of linguistic associations is not limited to invasion; it can encompass notions of 'willingness' and sexual desire as well. The original meaning in the case of the Thessaloi is not securely recoverable.

the Thessaloi tradition lies chiefly in that between internally and externally generated ethnic identity. Heroic genealogy does two basic things. First, as has been said, it confers elevated status upon specific sub-groups within an *ethnos*: one group of Thessalians could claim a superior form of Thessalianity than their peers. Second, it connects that group with elites of other regions. Heraklid ancestry is especially valuable in this regard: the hero's own travels and those of his offspring form a dense network over the imaginary map of the Greek world, and, by espousing the Thessalids, Thessalian families could link themselves into this network, establishing connections as much with Heraklid clans in other regions of Greece as with their fellow Thessalians. By contrast, the Thessaloi tradition unites the Thessalians *contra mundum*. And it is therefore no coincidence that the tradition arises in the mode of violence, conflict and defeat: the Thessaloi displacing the Boiotoi, the Thessaloi being defeated by the Phokians. We are not now dealing with inter-regional elite networks, but with the process by which neighbouring and near-neighbouring *ethnē* in the Archaic period used myth to establish their own internal unity and distinction vis à vis those around them.

In this, Thessalian agency must be seen as operating alongside that of the other groups involved; in fact, in the Thessaloi tradition external agency may at first be dominant. This is especially plain in the Herodotos text and the Phokian angle. We have already established that Herodotos, in all likelihood, drew upon Phokian traditions concerning their own heroic resistance to Thessalian incursions; the fabular quality of the Battle of the Chalk certainly suggests this. The story of the Thessaloi storming over the Pindos was probably added to a bundle of 'aggressive Thessaly' traditions. When the Phokians experienced some real Thessalian aggression at the end of the sixth century, they saw this in light of older stories of the Thessalids' arrival in Thessaly: the two incursions, mythical and real, could easily be bolted together to enhance the sense that they were facing a dangerous foe with a record of violent invasion. This purpose would not be served by myths of a heroic clan; what it required was a wave of faceless invaders. The creation of the traditions surrounding the battle of Keressos (see Chapter 1) extends to Boiotian territory this view of the Thessalians as a terrifying force pouring down into central Greece, their onrush only stopped with the greatest difficulty.

The internal perspective is not insignificant, however. Just as neighbouring *ethnē* were sharpening their sense of oppositional identity and the articulation of their own shared ethnicity by casting the Thessalians as defeated aggressors, so these narratives may well have fed into the Thessalians' own sense of internal coherence and shared identity. The Thessalids tradition is far easier to pin to active Thessalian myth-making than is the Thessaloi tradition. Nonetheless, we should not ignore the fact that the time when Herodotos and Thucydides wrote was not long after the first surviving internal use of the collective ethnic: the ΦΕΤΑ/ΦΕΘΑ legend ('Of the Thessalians') on coins around the middle of the fifth century (indeed, Herodotos' time of writing was roughly contemporary with this). Significantly, some of these coins carried Herakles on the reverse, either the hero's lion-skin-clad head in profile or else just his unmistakeable club, both with the letters of the ethnic in the field. While these coins cannot be taken to represent the whole Thessalian *ethnos* in any kind of federal capacity, the fact that Herakles was the image chosen – or one of them – to accompany this powerful declaration of *ethnos* identity, without a particular polis being signalled on the coins themselves, is striking, and suggests that by the mid-fifth century he could be regarded not only as the ancestor of select and exclusive elites but as the figurehead of all Thessaloi.

6. Thessalos variations

In no way did the Thessaloi version, for all that it seems to be a secondary development, stifle interest in the figure of Thessalos and his family. In fact, from the Classical period onward the figure of Thessalos was subject to various reworkings and adaptations, in particular regarding his parentage. By this means he was woven in a number of different ways into the mythical fabric of the region, intersecting with its other significant figures and stories. The late, non-Thessalian sources in play here prevent the identification and analysis of specific Thessalian motives and contexts behind the adaptations, and our observations must perforce be limited chiefly to recognising the way in which Thessalos, over time, became a way of reflecting on the different facets of Thessaly's myth-history among authors trying to weave the multiple strands of Greek myth into a smooth and coherent fabric; often they acknowledge the presence of more than one version of the hero's genealogy, and appear to revel in the uncertainty that surrounds him. The variants that survive are as follows:

1. Thessalos as son of Herakles and the Koan princess Chalkiope: in addition to the sources already cited, this seems to have been included in Pherekydes (*FGrH* 3 F 78). Slight variants on this version occur in the Tabula Albana, *IG* 14, 1293 (probably first century BC) and Charax, *FGrH* 103 F 6 (second century AD).
2. Thessalos as son of Haimon and grandson of Pelasgos: Rhianos of Bene, *FGrH* 265 F 30 (third century BC); cf. Strabo 9.5.23.
3. Thessalos as son of Jason and Medea: Diodoros 4.55.2–3.
4. Thessalos as father of Aleuas, perhaps: Hegemon, *FGrH* 110 F 1 (probably Hellenistic).

Of these, only 3 and 4 are of potential interest with regard to Thessalian involvement, on the face of it. Sprawski has made the plausible suggestion that weaving Thessalos into the myths of Jason and Medea may be read as a product of Pheraian self-aggrandisement in the late fifth and the fourth century BC;[75] this would constitute quite a bold step to rebrand the hero as a scion of their own key mythical dynasty, the extensive stemma that connected them with the ruling family of Iolkos.[76] 4 would seem to be a similarly audacious gesture, Thessalos as the *Stammvater* of the Aleuadai (and perhaps indeed the father of Aleuas Pyrrhos himself), but we are hampered by an uncertainty in the translation: Aleuas is described as Ἀλεύα τοῦ Θετταλοῦ, which is in fact just as likely, *pace* Helly, to mean 'Aleuas the Thessalian'.[77] However, Thessalos as the father of Aleuas raises an interesting possibility. By the Hellenistic period, Thessalos in his various forms had become widespread enough in ancient literature and awareness to have lost any especially strong connections with specific Thessalian poleis, and this may well have provoked Larisa's elite to try to create, or recreate, a sense of exclusive connection. As we shall see in Chapter 7, there are other signs of a Larisaian interest in Thessalos in the third and second centuries BC.

7. A return to west Thessaly in the later Classical period

a) Kierion as Arne

As has been said, locating a 'real' Arne in Thessaly is not easy; in Archaic verse it is somewhere in the south-eastern part of the region, but cannot be securely placed on a map, and certainly does not emerge as a historical polis from the literary, epigraphic or numismatic record. However, around 400 BC the west-Thessalian polis of Kierion (modern Pyrgos Kieriou)[78] started to mint coins with an intriguing reverse design: a young female figure kneeling and throwing knuckle-bones. Sufficient of these coins have

[75] Sprawski (2014a). It is a pity that we do not know the identity of the father of Jason, fourth-century ruler of Pherai, since the choice of name is obviously significant in this regard.

[76] Jason's line is a very early one, appearing in Homer: his uncle Pheres, father of Admetos, appears at *Il.* 2.763–64 and 23.376; Pheres and Aison, Jason's father, are mentioned in *Od.* 11.259.

[77] Helly (1995), 118–19. That said, Hegemon – or Aelian, who is paraphrasing him at this point – does not need to identify Thessalos as Thessalian here, because his location on Ossa, and beside the Haimonian spring, which the author says is in Thessaly, indicate that. On the other hand, if the hero were meant, one feels Aelian might have taken the trouble to avoid such an ambiguous phrasing.

[78] Chatziangelakis (2008), 316–19; *AD* 56–59 (2001–2004) *Chron.* B2 578. For a discussion of the settlements of Thessaliotis see Helly (1992), 82–91.

the figure labelled for us to identify her as Arne, surely, as historians have recognised, the eponymous nymph of the place. This gives local veracity to the late-attested fact that Kierion identified itself as the new name of the legendary Arne, thereby giving itself a key role in the myth of the displacement of the Boiotoi.

As for the nymph Arne, Hellanikos may well have made her the daughter of Aiolos and the mother of Boiotos by Poseidon;[79] Pausanias also calls her a daughter of Aiolos and says that she gave her name both to the Thessalian city (presumably Kierion, though he does not say as much) and to Boiotian Chaironeia.[80] However, it is worth noting that the coins themselves do nothing to make visible the Boiotian connection. We do not know why the nymph Arne casts knuckle-bones, whether in reference to a local oracular tradition, or simply as a game.[81] What we do know is that Kierion selected for its coins an exceptionally obscure and localised aspect of the mythology that connected them with the Boiotoi, one that would have been recognised and understood only by inhabitants of that particular polis and perhaps the surrounding area. Kierion was carving out its own unique aspect of the myth and fitting it to its own particular mythical and perhaps religious environment. In doing so it may have been influenced by a Larisaian coin type, first minted around the middle of the fifth century BC, in which their eponymous nymph bounces a ball.[82] While Larisa's identity as daughter of Pelasgos, and her Argive connections, give her a place within a wide and important mythological strand, her ball-playing and her drowning in the Peneios root her firmly within the local landscape and create a unique iconography. This is very comparable with the case of Arne, evoking a trans-regional myth-cluster but emphasising its local dimension through the use of epichoric imagery and myth.

[79] *FGrH* 4 F 52. See Fowler (2013), 188. The usual problem attends the attribution: knowing how much of the story told by the source, schol. Hom. *Il.* 2.494, was actually included in Hellanikos' narrative.

[80] Paus. 9.40.5: it is interesting that Chaironeia also claimed that Arne was its former name, like Kierion. Rather like Ephyra, Arne was sufficiently legendary, free from precise topographic anchoring, to be appropriated in the myth-histories of historical communities in this way.

[81] Hampe (1951) identified as *astragaloi* the objects held in the left hands of the women on the famous fifth-century funerary relief from Pharsalos, Louvre Ma 701. Even if this is correct, however, a connection with the Kierion Arne is unlikely: playing with knuckle-bones is widely attested across the Greek world.

[82] Larson (2001), 165–66.

b) The synoecism of Metropolis

Some time in the early fourth century BC, three 'insignificant' poleis in Hestiotis were combined into a single new settlement, called Metropolis.[83] The polis was recorded in 358 BC as contributing to the construction of the new Apollo temple at Delphi;[84] it minted coins showing Aphrodite,[85] who seems to have been their chief deity, along with Apollo and Dionysos.[86] It was in Metropolis' territory (at modern Moschato) that the important Apollo-temple stood whose remains include the bronze cult statue mentioned above, but that was built before the synoecism: in the sixth century BC, to be precise.[87] One reading of the highly significant name Metropolis relates to this proximity. As has been said, the highly unusual military iconography of that Apollo statue may refer to armed conquest and to the invasion of the region by the Thessaloi or Thessalids; given that the new polis was established in the vicinity of the cult site, should we take its name as a claim to be the mother-city of the Thessalians – that is, the first location of the invaders, the first place they settled before extending their control over the region? While the word *metropolis* can on occasion convey merely a central or dominant polis within a region, its normal usage is that of a place of origin, sometimes specifically the mother-city of a colony, but also more generally of a person's or group's original home.[88] But if we take the name of the Thessalian polis in this sense, as whose original home was it presenting itself? Can we be sure that the Thessaloi are the most plausible answer to that question?

In fact, if we are seeking a mythological group that fits the context, that may not be the best choice. After all, such a claim would run counter to the fact that Metropolis was in Hestiotis, not in Thessaliotis, and it was Thessaliotis that, from the late sixth century, was considered as the original base of the invaders from across the Pindos. This is not an insuperable obstacle, since Metropolis may have been trying to forge a link with the Thessaloi as a competitive gesture, to create a counter-claim; myth-history is always open to revision. Could it be that Metropolis was specifically positioning itself as a rival, in this regard, of Kierion, which at very much the same time was advertising its identity as Arne, the original – indeed the *metropolis* – of the Boiotian Arne? This is a tempting possibility.

But in fact a mythological group with a stronger link to Hestiotic origins were the Dorians. The Dorians have an exceptionally complex

83 Nikolaou (2012), 59.
84 *CID* 2.5.
85 E.g. *Triton* XV, 208, no. 475 (early to mid fourth century).
86 Nikolaou (2012), 60–61; Mili (2015), 116.
87 Mili (2015), 180–81.
88 For the range of meanings see examples in *LSJ* s.v. μητρόπολις.

migration-story, which differs from author to author, but north-east Thessaly is a fairly consistent ingredient. In Herodotos they do not belong there, but in Achaia Phthiotis;[89] Hestiotis is their second location, and they are driven thence by the Kadmeioi, briefly residing in Pindos; from Pindos they go to Dryopis, which Herodotos elsewhere equates with the historical Doris, north-west of Phokis.[90] Strabo says that Hestiotis was once called Doris, and seems to treat it as the first stage in the migration.[91] There is general agreement among sources that from northern and central Greece the Dorians then travelled down to the Peloponnese. So might the Thessalian polis Metropolis have been claiming to be the original homeland of the Dorians?

If so, it would be an interesting gesture vis-à-vis Doris in central Greece, which was itself seen, at least by Thucydides' day, as the *metropolis* of the Dorians. Was the foundation of the Thessalian polis of Metropolis a competitive move, asserting an earlier and more fundamental role in the story of the Dorian migration, thus placing Doris in a secondary position? The timing of the synoecism around the end of the fifth century is significant in this regard. Only a quarter-century or so earlier, the Spartans had founded Herakleia Trachinia, one of their aims being to assist the Dorians – whom, Thucydides says, they regarded as inhabitants of the Dorian homeland[92] – against the Oitaians, who were harassing them.[93] This move was extremely unpopular with the Thessalians, described by Thucydides as ἐν δυνάμει ὄντες τῶν ταύτῃ χωρίων ('being powerful in this area'), who subjected the settlement to constant attacks.[94] (The poor Herakleians never had an easy time of it, in fact: their town suffered serious

[89] Hdt. 1.56.3.

[90] Hdt. 8.31. It is interesting to observe the inclusion of the Kadmeioi, arriving in Hestiaiotis after their own displacement from Thebes by the Epigonoi (cf. Hdt. 5.61). This myth may have given Thessalian Metropolis its own Boiotian connection, an alternative to the myth of the displacement of the Boiotoi.

[91] Strabo 10.4.6. On these traditions see Vanicelli (1989), 37–46; Ulf (1996), 259–64; Hall (2002), 82–89.

[92] Thuc. 3.92.3; indeed, he uses the same formula at 1.107.2 when discussing another moment of Spartan involvement in the area, this one in 457 BC, when the Spartans move to protect the Dorians from Phokian incursions.

[93] Thuc. 3.92.4 on Sparta's ulterior motive: 'τοῦ πρὸς Ἀθηναίους πολέμου καλῶς αὐτοῖς ἐδόκει ἡ πόλις καθίστασθαι.' 'The town [Herakleia] seemed to be well placed for their war with the Athenians' – by offering, as he goes on to say, a base for a naval assault on Euboia, and a staging post on the road to Thrace.

[94] Thuc. 3.93.2: 'The reason was as follows: the Thessalians, who were the chief power in those parts, and within whose territory the settlement had been established, fearing to have a powerful neighbour, harassed and constantly attacked the new settlers.'

turbulence in 420–419,[95] 409,[96] ca. 399/8[97] and 375.[98]) The foundation was certainly a bid by Sparta for increased Delphic visibility. Herakleia was a mere forty stades from Thermopylai and the Amphiktyonic sanctuary at Anthela. Helping the Dorians was all the more important for Sparta because her own Amphiktyonic involvement derived from her putative kinship with them as the original Dorians.[99] So the Spartan involvement in the area fostered the presentation of the Dorians as the originals, and challenged Thessalian interests in the process. One can imagine no more conducive conditions to underpin a gesture on the part of the Thessalians to reclaim Dorian origins for their own region, and so diminish the importance of Doris and undermine Sparta's own self-presentation.[100] So it is more likely that the Thessalian polis Metropolis was named to refer not to the arrival of the Thessaloi but to the association of the area with the early wanderings of the Dorians.

8. Thessaly and pre-Thessaly: the naming of the tetrads

The naming of the tetrads has been left to the end of this chapter, but that is not because it is of least importance: rather the reverse. Whereas, as we have seen, the myths of the Thessalids in particular should be seen in terms of sub-regional claims and counter-claims, now we move into a different dimension: the inclusion of myths in a process of concerted regional reorganisation and the attempt, as part of that, to choose and deploy stories encapsulating the essential pre-existing strands of Thessaly's myth-history.

In Chapter 5 we shall confront the long-standing *communis opinio* that the tetradic reorganisation was the work of one man, Aleuas Pyrrhos. It will be shown that, in the late sixth century, the power to enact such changes actually lay in the hands of co-operative polis elites, strongly interlinked through marriage and *philia*-ties. Nothing in the creation of the tetrads requires the agency of one man, from a practical perspective, and in general scholars in recent decades have become more and more

[95] Thuc. 5.51–52: war between the Herakleians and surrounding *ethnē*, and an eventual occupation of the town by Boiotians. Cf. Diod. 12.77.4.

[96] Xen. *Hell.* 1.2.18: the Herakleians go to war with the Oitaians, and are betrayed by their supposed allies the Phthiotic Achaians; 700 of them are killed, as well as the Spartan harmost.

[97] Diod. 14.38.4, 14.82.6.

[98] Xen. *Hell.* 6.4.27; Diod. 15.57.2.

[99] Hornblower (2009), 49.

[100] This active Thessalian involvement in the myth of the Dorian invasion is all the more interesting in light of Robertson's suggestion (1980, 3) that myths of the Dorian migration follow a story-telling trope of 'obscurity to fame', and so deliberately cast Thessaly as a place of insignificance.

aware of the accretion of legend around ancient *nomothetai*, a process that saw complex and long-drawn-out political changes being attributed to a single heroic individual.[101] So while only Aleuas is visible, we can imagine others involved, and a degree of debate and collaboration. Moreover, we cannot assume a purely Larisaian perspective, the wholesale imposition on Thessaly of a schema devised within a single polis, however influential. Though the mechanisms are entirely obscure, we may conjecture that in each tetrad the influential men in the chief poleis would have had some say in how their area was named.

As to those names, we should not assume that they were necessarily based upon the adjectivisation of pre-existing names or, at least, not of names that represented real sites or communities. Phthiotis comes closest, but even Phthia seems to have been a mythological construct in the period covered in this book. As for Pelasgiotis, it is not plausible to suppose that any part of Thessaly was actually called Pelasgia by its inhabitants, even though some historians claim as much;[102] instead, the name is applied to several parts of Greece in ancient texts, and is a way of suggesting primordial origins and past time. Overall, the naming of the tetrads should be seen as a concerted ideological process, from whatever quarters it was driven, and one that reveals a commitment to the preservation of major sub-regional myths and myth-clusters, rather than to that of important pre-existing place-names.[103]

a) Thessaliotis

Whereas, as we have seen, elite clans could and did seek to boost their significance, and the legitimacy of their power, by presenting themselves as descendants of Thessalos, this exclusive and essentially competitive approach ran alongside, from the later sixth century, another more inclusive strand. The version of the invasion myth in which the incursion was performed by a whole *ethnos*, the Thessaloi, had the opposite effect from that of the Thessalids: it was a foundation-myth for the whole *ethnos*, and tended to arise in the context of conflict, to represent the antagonism between the Thessalians and their neighbours. This was the Thessalians as a whole closing ranks symbolically as a united *ethnos* against other *ethnē*; the Thessalids, on the other hand, began life as a way of allowing certain

[101] To cite just one particularly potent example, the Spartan Lykourgos has long been recognised as a figure more legendary than factual, the subject of myth-making from the fifth century BC if not earlier, and a figurehead for political development actually involving many actors and contexts. See, for example, Nafissi (2017) for a recent summary and discussion of ancient and modern sources.

[102] E.g. Larsen (1960), 230.

[103] On the names' actual form see Gschnitzer (1954).

groups of Thessalians to distinguish themselves from among their fellows by asserting a privileged relationship with the region's myth-history. We have argued that this was probably the older strand, but that by the end of the sixth century both – Thessalids and Thessaloi – were operating.

The naming of the tetrad Thessaliotis represents, in a sense, a third strand: the desire to give a particular sub-region its own inalienable place in the story of Thessaly. This was not a matter of elite genealogy, which could be claimed and moved depending on dynastic associations. This was the permanent branding of the southern part of west Thessaly as the place in which the Thessalids or the Thessaloi – and we cannot know which, here – first arrived. This will have encouraged the developments noted in section 7 above, by which Thessalians in Thessaliotis reaffirmed privileged connection with the origin-myth of the whole *ethnos*. In Chapter 4 we shall see how Thessaliotis also had a particular claim on the cult of Poseidon, which became central to the shared religious identity of the Thessalians and their land.

b) Pelasgiotis

Ancient authors from the fifth century BC onwards sometimes put forward the view that Pelasgia was an earlier name for Thessaly or for a part of Thessaly;[104] if this were true, then Pelasgiotis might be seen simply to incorporate a pre-existing place-name. However, this is unlikely to be historically accurate. The toponym Pelasgia is no more real than the ethnonym Pelasgoi, whose main function was as a tool for thinking through the different phases and facets of Greek identity. Therefore, we have various Greek communities claiming Pelasgian associations of one kind or another; of these, the creation of the tetrad name Pelasgiotis is an especially unambiguous gesture. Nonetheless, when we look in detail at the links between Thessaly and the Pelasgoi, the matter inevitably turns out to be complex.[105]

Even in our earliest surviving texts, the Pelasgoi are not limited to a single geographical location: one fragment, perhaps from the *Catalogue of Women*, calls Dodona a 'seat of the Pelasgoi';[106] in another, ascribed to the *Catalogue* with more certainty, Pelasgos is made father of Lykaon, and

[104] E.g. Hekataios *FGrH* 1 F 14 (all of Thessaly); Souidas *FGrH* 602 F 11a (part of Thessaly, around Skotoussa).

[105] For discussion of the Pelasgoi-myths of Greece see Sourvinou-Inwood (2003); Fowler (2013), 84–96. Helly (1991, 144) sees them as the pre-Mycenaean inhabitants of Thessaly.

[106] Hes. fr. 319 MW; this seems to echo the description of Dodonaian Zeus as Pelasgian in *Iliad* 16.233–34.

the Pelasgoi an Arkadian race.[107] The Arkadian location of the Pelasgoi finds supporters thereafter.[108] Sometimes they seem to extend over most of Greece.[109] Overall, many regions, Attica included, used them as a way of reflecting on their shared past.[110] But the majority of texts connect them with Thessaly, normally through myths of migration, with Peloponnesian Argos also strongly connected.[111]

Occasionally, the migration is into Thessaly, from some point of origin elsewhere.[112] More commonly, they are indigenous inhabitants of Thessaly who are driven out by some more powerful agent: by Deukalion, by Deukalion's sons, by Deukalion's flood, by Triopas, by the Lapiths – the range of aggressors is various and confusing.[113] As to where the Pelasgoi went once ousted, two traditions seem to predominate. The first is that they went to Tyrrhenia in Italy. This goes back to Herodotos at least: he says that the Pelasgoi used to be neighbours of the Dorians, when both groups lived in Thessaly, though he does not say who drove the Pelasgoi from their Thessalian homeland. Diodoros adds the detail that they were driven out by the flood. The second strong tradition is that the Pelasgoi went from Thessaly to Kyzikos and settled there: this version finds its earliest surviving expression in Hekataios,[114] and numerous mentions thereafter.[115] The frequency of these references, as well as those (including a Kyzikene author, Agathokles) describing a more general connection between Pelasgoi

107 Hes. fr. 161 MW.

108 For example Ephoros, *FGrH* 70 F 113. However, cf. Apollod. *Bibl.* 3.8.1: one of the many sons of Arkadian Lykaon, the son of Pelasgos, is Phthios, indicating that there were points of contact (now entirely obscure) between the Arkadian and Thessalian traditions.

109 Aisch. *Suppl.* 250–59: Pelasgos, king of (Peloponnesian) Argos, claims that his rule extends northwards, including Thessaly and Dodona and reaching as far as the river Strymon. Mitchell (2006), 212, sees his rule as covering all of Greece, whereas McInerney (2014, 45) suggests a twinning between Peloponnesian and Thessalian Argos. The former view, however, better suits the themes of the *Suppliants*, which include the distinction between Greek and non-Greek identity.

110 McInerney (2014).

111 Sourvinou-Inwood (2003), 113–16.

112 Travelling to Thessaly from Arkadia: Pherekydes F 12. From Argos to Thessaly: Staphylos of Naukratis, *FGrH* 269 F 10; Dion. Hal. *Ant. Rom.* 1.17 and 18. Pelasgos as king of Argos: Aisch. *Suppl.* 251.

113 Deukalion: Dion. Hal. 1.17.3. Deukalion's sons: Diod. 5.60. Deukalion's flood: Diod. 14.113.1–2. Triopas: Kallim. *Hymns* 6.25. The Lapiths: Strabo 9.5.22, quoting Hieronymos, *FGrH* 154 F 17.

114 Hekataios *FGrH* 1 F 14.

115 Hellanikos, *FGrH* 4 F 52, 91; Ephoros, *FGrH* 70 F 61; Konon, *FGrH* 70 F 61 (cf. F 113); Deiochos, *FGrH* 471 F 7.

and Kyzikos,[116] surely reflects the fact that the Kyzikenes themselves cultivated this account of their origins; and, indeed, the Pelasgoi were one way in which communities across the Greek world could assert northern Greek origins, a strategy we shall meet again in Chapter 7. All migration stories may be considered from both sides, and often had a collaborative or dialogic dimension, as we have seen in the case of the Boiotoi, above. Now, however, it may be asked whether we can identify among Thessalian communities any signs of active interest in Pelasgian associations.

There are the usual faint glimpses in various spots, such as Iolkos and Krannon (not the main city of that name, apparently), and the Dotion Plain, that cradle of early Thessalian myth-history. However, two places emerge most strongly in their Pelasgian connections. The first is the area called 'Pelasgian Argos'; the second is the city of Larisa. Our literary references to Pelasgian Argos begin with the Catalogue of Ships and the line discussed in detail in Chapter 2: 'Now as for all those who lived in Pelasgian Argos … '.[117] It has been suggested that *Pelasgikon Argos* was Homer's name for all of Thessaly, a sense also largely accepted by Strabo.[118] While some modern scholars accept this,[119] others seek to attach the phrase to a particular sub-region.[120] The reality is probably that, whatever Homer meant, several Thessalian communities laid claim to being *Pelasgikon Argos* and to having particular Pelasgian credentials.[121] However, the strongest association, as stated above, is with the city of Larisa. Helly argues that Larisa was a city whose dominance postdates the main composition period of the Homeric poems.[122] This argument is complicated, of course, by the Homeric dating question and by the early habitation evidence at the site of Larisa itself,[123] but it is certainly true that the polis receives no mention

116 Agathokles of Kyzikos *FGrH* 472 F 2; Lykophron, *Alexandra* 1364–65; Valerius Flaccus 2.657–62 and 3.45.

117 Hom. *Il.* 2.681.

118 Strabo 5.2.4: *Pelasgikon Argos* is the name for Thessaly 'μεταξὺ τῶν ἐκβολῶν τοῦ Πηνειοῦ καὶ τῶν Θερμοπυλῶν ἕως τῆς ὀρεινῆς τῆς κατὰ Πίνδον, διὰ τὸ ἐπάρξαι τῶν τόπων τούτων τοὺς Πελασγούς.' Cf. 9.5.5: here he introduces two slightly different theories, neither of which he definitely endorses: first, that *Pelasgikon Argos* was 'the plain of the Thessalians' (which is very vague – all of tetradic Thessaly, or just Pelasgiotis?), and the second that it was a 'polis near Larisa'. Plainly, different opinions abounded, some of which he tries to include.

119 Loptson (1981).

120 Helly (1991), 141–42. Further discussion in Mili (2015), 193–95.

121 For a possible third-century use of the term, seemingly to denote a part of Thessaly (or Achaia Phthiotis), see Rigsby (2004), 13.

122 Helly (1987); see also Mili (2015), 195–96.

123 As Karouzou observes (2019, 195) the discernible rise of Larisa – as well as Pherai and Pharsalos – from the Protogeometric period provides the background of the power and influence of the polis in later periods. It is of course unrealistic to imagine

in the Catalogue of Ships and is in general strikingly absent from Archaic epic. Its Pelasgian connections appear in no text before the fifth century:[124] the earliest and fullest account is in Pherekydes, in his retelling of Perseus' search for Akrisios, and the latter's death.

> When he arrived he did not find Akrisios in Argos. For having become afraid, he [*sc.* Akrisios] departed for the Pelasgians in Larissa. Having not caught him, he left Danaë behind with her mother Eurydike and Andromeda and the Kyklopes, and he went himself to Larissa. And having arrived, he recognized Akrisios and persuaded him to go with him to Argos. And when they were about to go, they chanced upon a contest for young men in Larissa, and Perseus stripped for the contest, and having taken a discus, he made a throw; for it was not a pentathlon, but they were contending <privately> for a prize in each one of the contests. The discus spun around onto the foot of Akrisios and injured him. Having fallen sick from this, Akrisios died there in Larissa, and Perseus and the Larissaians buried him in front of the city, and the locals created a hero-cult for him. And Perseus left Argos.[125]

The Pelasgian phase of Thessalian myth-history is thereby the setting for the relationship between Larisa and Akrisios, which finds frequent and various expression. Here Akrisios merely happens to be in Larisa

that Homer preserves only the Bronze Age picture of Thessaly, but less unfeasible to imagine that he was deliberately privileging Mycenaean source material, in which Larisa was unimportant: this archaising perspective was discussed in Chapter 2.

[124] A great puzzle in this regard is Hom. *Il.* 2.840–43: here Pelasgians from Larisa are among the allies of the Trojans. To argue that this is the Thessalian Larisa seems impossible: to include such a group among contingents from Thrace and Asia Minor would be so peculiar that the poet would surely accompany it with special remark. Plenty of more logical Larisas are available. However, the entry has a slight Thessalian 'flavour': Larisa is called *eribōlax*, fertile, and one of the leaders of the group is Pylaios. Did the poet import a separate tradition about Pelasgoi in Thessalian Larisa? See Bader (1999) for more detailed discussion of the linguistic connections between Thessaly and Pelasgians in the Catalogue.

[125] Pherekydes, *FGrH* 3 F 12: 'ἐλθὼν Ἀκρίσιον οὐχ εὑρίσκει ἐν Ἄργει. ὑπεχώρει γὰρ αὐτὸν δείσας εἰς τοὺς Πελασγοὺς εἰς Λάρισσαν. μὴ καταλαβὼν δὲ αὐτὸν τὴν μὲν Δανάην καταλείπει παρὰ τῆι μητρὶ Εὐρυδίκηι καὶ τὴν Ἀνδρομέδαν καὶ τοὺς Κύκλωπας, αὐτὸς δὲ ἔβη εἰς Λάρισσαν. καὶ ἀφικόμενος Ἀκρίσιον ἀναγνωρίζει καὶ σὺν αὐτῶι ἕπεσθαι εἰς Ἄργος πείθει. καὶ ὅτε δὴ ἔμελλον ἰέναι, συντυγχάνουσιν ἀγῶνι νέων ἐν τῆι Λαρίσσηι· καὶ ὁ Περσεὺς ἀποδύεται εἰς τὸν ἀγῶνα, καὶ λαβὼν τὸν δίσκον δισκεύει· τὸ γὰρ δὲ πένταθλον οὐκ ἦν, ἀλλὰ <ἰδίαι> ἕν' ἕκαστον τῶν ἄθλων ἤθλουν. ὁ δὲ δίσκος τροχαλισθεὶς ἐπὶ τὸν πόδα τοῦ Ἀκρισίου τιτρώσκει αὐτόν. καμὼν δὲ ἐκ τούτου Ἀκρίσιος ἀποθνήισκει αὐτοῦ ἐν Λαρίσσηι, καὶ αὐτὸν κατατίθεται Περσεὺς καὶ οἱ Λαρισσαῖοι πρόσθεν τῆς πόλεως, καὶ αὐτοῦ ποιοῦσιν ἡρῶιον οἱ ἐπιχώριοι. Περσεὺς δὲ ἀναχωρεῖ τοῦ Ἄργους' (trans. Morison). Note the similarity of Apollod. *Bibl.* 2.4.4. See Fowler (2013), 255–57.

when he is accidentally killed (so the role of Larisa is a rather incidental one), though he does receive a hero-cult in front of the city. In Pausanias' account he is living in the city in permanent retirement, rather than temporary refuge, when he is killed. In the near-undateable Antiochos,[126] the tomb of Akrisios is actually within the Larisaian Athena-temple, a location mentioned in the same sentence as the location of Kekrops' grave within the Athenian Athena-temple – the parallel may suggest that Akrisios was considered the founder of Larisa.[127] This is reinforced by the following scholion:

> 'Polyphemos son of Eilatos came to them having left Larisa.' He is referring to the Larisa of Thessaly, which Akrisios founded. This Larisa was named after Larisa the daughter of Pelasgos, as Hellanikos says. There are three Larisas: the oldest is the Argive one, which is actually the acropolis itself. The second is in the Pelasgic area of Thessaly. And then there is the Larisa of Gyrtone, which Apollonios makes mention of here.[128]

This text is both valuable and confusing. Akrisios appears as founder; moreover, he does so in connection with Pelasgos, whose daughter Larisa gives the city its name (this statement is attributed to Hellanikos). However, the scholion introduces a doubt as to which Larisa is being treated. According to him, the Larisa founded by Akrisios was 'the Larisa of Gyrtone', and is different from the Larisa in 'the Pelasgic part of Thessaly'. There must be some authorial confusion at work here, since 'the Larisa of Gyrtone' makes no sense; Gyrtone (also called Gyrton) is a separate polis from Larisa. Moreover, it is clear from evidence within Thessaly itself that Larisa in Pelasgiotis is the one linked with the Pelasgoi or with Pelasgos. The southern Larisa, Larisa Kremaste in Achaia Phthiotis, makes no real claims on Pelasgian origins. Larisa on the Peneios, on the other hand, certainly did consider itself 'Pelasgic': 'Pelasgian Larisa' became one of the standard ways of designating the city and its inhabitants, and of distinguishing them from other cities of the same name, chiefly Larisa Kremaste.[129] It is therefore advisable to suppose that the scholiast was mistaken, that Akrisios

126 Antiochos, *FGrH* 29 F 2.

127 Mili (2015), 195, 104.

128 Schol. Ap. Rhod. *Arg.* 1.40 = Hellanikos, *FGrH* 4 F 91: '[Λάρισανδ' ἐπὶ τοῖσι λιπὼν Πολύφημος ἵκανεν Εἰλατίδης] Λάρισαν τὴν Θεσσαλίας λέγει, ἣν ἔκτισεν Ἀκρίσιος. ἥτις ὠνομάσθη ἀπὸ Λαρίσης τῆς Πελασγοῦ, ὥς φησιν Ἑλλάνικος. εἰσὶ δὲ Λάρισαι τρεῖς· ἀρχαιοτάτη μὲν ἡ Ἀργειῶτις, ἥτις ἐστὶν αὐτὴ ἡ ἀκρόπολις· δευτέρα δὲ ἡ ἐν τῶι Πελασγικῶι τῆς Θεσσαλίας· καὶ Λάρισα Γυρτώνης, ἧς νῦν ὁ Ἀπολλώνιος μέμνηται' (trans. Pownall). See Fowler (2013), 242, 244.

129 See, for example, *IG* IX.2 528, 530, 534. For an earlier (third-century BC) epitaph with comparable language see *SEG* 47.735.

was thought to have been the founder of Larisa in Pelasgiotis, and that it was this Larisa also that was connected with Pelasgos through the figure of his daughter Larisa.[130] That this is a different Larisa from the nymph who was daughter of Peneios does not invalidate the argument; an ancient Greek city could certainly have two mythical figures with different identities but the same name at the same time.

The Akrisios tradition, then, fits an important episode (or series of episodes) in the myth-history of Larisa into the time before – long before, indeed – the arrival of Thessalos' tribe. The willingness, desire even, to identify Larisa especially as Pelasgian may in fact relate to the polis' status as a relative newcomer. Aware of their own scant showing, indeed general invisibility, in early Thessalian myth as represented in Homer and the *Ehoiai*, the Larisaians will have seen the advantage of characterising their polis as part of the earliest myth-historical stratum of Greece.[131] Further motivation to espouse the connection with Peloponnesian Argos through the figure of Akrisios may have been supplied, in the fifth century, by the alliance that connected Thessaly, Athens and Argos in 461 BC,[132] and perhaps even by the fact that Argos, though not as overt in its medism as Thessaly, did not join the Hellenic League in the resistance to Persia.[133] Herodotos relates a rumour that Xerxes had won the Argives' sympathy by reminding them of shared ancestry through the figure of Perseus.[134] Even though the relationship between Akrisios and his grandson Perseus was by no means straightforward, it is interesting to consider that Argives, Larisaians and Persians may have formed an understanding through their shared connection with a particular myth – or, at any rate, that they may have been thought to have done so.[135]

We therefore have two quite divergent strands of myth-historical identity operating in the polis. On the one hand, by asserting Heraklid/Thessalid origins at the start of the fifth century BC the Aleuadai seem to have cast themselves as descended from invaders, whose right to rule derived from their forceful acquisition of the land and whose ethnicity was

130 According to Pliny (*NH* 34.19), the Phokaian sculptor Telephanes made a statue of Larisa. Was this the daughter of Peneios or the daughter of Pelasgos? We cannot know, though Langlotz (1951, 165–66) suggests the former and that the statue may have been sent to Persia as part of the city's pledge of submission to Xerxes. He identifies Pliny's mention with a statue discovered at Persepolis, a tempting if unproveable theory.

131 Cf. Papadimitriou (2008), who posits Argive influence on Thessaly in the Mycenaean period. Early contact, however, would not eliminate the significance of Larisa's decision to emphasise the connection, through the figure of Akrisios, in the fifth century BC.

132 Thuc. 1.102.4.

133 Hdt. 7.148–50.

134 Hdt. 7.150.

135 Vannicelli (2012), 259–61.

different from many of those over whom they wielded power. On the other hand, the Pelasgian element is by no means consigned to an underclass, to the ruled; the foundation of Larisa by Argive Akrisios and the presentation of Larisa as a daughter of Pelasgos place Pelasgian identity at the heart of the polis. Of course, divergent myth-histories are a staple ingredient of any Greek community, and we may see this one as reflecting the articulation of difference between one elite clan and their home polis. While the naming of the tetrad Pelasgiotis, dominated by Larisa, denotes a widespread acceptance of the idea of Pelasgian origins and identity in that part of Thessaly, the Aleuadai may have deliberately cultivated a tradition that set them apart as descendants of the Koan invader Thessalos.

That said, there are clear signs of an attempt to weave Thessalos and Pelasgos together so as to reconcile, or at least connect, the two accounts. The evidence for this development is Rhianos, probably writing in the third century BC and supposedly the author of a *Thettalika* of which a short passage is quoted verbatim by a scholiast on Apollonios' *Argonautika*:

> In the old days, Thessaly was called Pyrrhaia, as Rhianos says: 'Once the ancients called it Pyrrhaie from Pyrrhe, the ancient bride of Deukalion; later, they called it Haimonie from Haimon, whom Pelasgos begot, his best son; and in turn Haimon begot Thessalos, and from this one the people changed the name to Thessalia'. But others say that it was called that from Thessalos son of Herakles, father of Pheidippides, after the Trojan War.[136]

The scholiast here explicitly identifies that there are two separate traditions about Thessalos: the 'Thessalos stemma' discussed above, and the version given by Rhianos: Pelasgos → Haimon → Thessalos.[137] We can tell nothing about the date of this variant – whether it predated Rhianos, or whether it represented an innovation of the third century, perhaps an invention of the author himself, who may have tried to stitch together and so reconcile the divergent Thessalian *aitia* of Thessalos' invasion and the indigenous Pelasgoi.[138] However, its implications are striking: Thessalos ceases to be

[136] Rhianos, *FGrH* 265 F 30a: 'ἡ Θεσσαλία ἐκαλεῖτο τὸ παλαιὸν Πυρρ<αί>α, ὡς Ῥιανός· «Πυρραίην ποτὲ τήν γε παλαιότεροι καλέεσκον/Πύρρης Δευκαλίωνος ἀπ᾽ ἀρχαίης ἀλόχοιο·/Αἱμονίην δ᾽ ἐξαῦτις ἀφ᾽ Αἵμονος, ὅν ῥα Πελασγὸς/γείνατο φέρτατον υἱόν· ὁ δ᾽ αὖ τέκε Θεσσαλὸν Αἵμων,/τοῦ δ᾽ ἄπο Θεσσαλίην λαοὶ μετηφημίξαντο». οἱ δὲ ἀπὸ Θεσσαλοῦ τοῦ Ἡρακλέους τοῦ Φειδιππ[ίδ]ου πατρὸς μετὰ τὰ Τρωικὰ κληθῆναί φασι.'

[137] Stephanos cites Rhianos in inserting an extra generation: Pelasgos → Chloros → Haimon → Thessalos (Rhianos, *FGrH* 265 F 30b = Steph. Byz. s.v. Αἱμονία). Since Stephanos does not quote Rhianos verbatim, his citation is of less value than that of the scholiast; moreover, his attribution to 'Rhianos and others' does not inspire confidence.

[138] As Latacz (2006) points out, Rhianos' work draws heavily on early Greek literature,

an outsider and instead becomes indigenous. Such a development would have served the interests of Larisa very well, as well as Rhianos' own urge to smooth out contradictions in the mythological traditions, and may well have been formulated within the polis. One has only to look to the Athenian case and to claims of autochthony, of being sprung from the very soil of Attica, to see this theme at work.[139] By making Thessalos a Pelasgian, the Larisaians involved would have been claiming a similar kind of primacy, of authenticity.

c) Phthiotis

In our ancient sources, the line between a Thessalian tetrad called Phthiotis and a perioikic region called Achaia Phthiotis was not always clearly drawn. This is not because the two were not considered different. That the Achaioi Phthiotides were thought of as a separate *ethnos* from the Thessalians is clear from their separate membership of the Delphic Amphiktyony.[140] At times a polis will be clearly identified as belonging to one *ethnos* or the other: for example, Thucydides refers to 'Meliteia [*sic*] Achaia' – Achaian Melitaia – at 4.78.1; Pharsalos, by contrast, was plainly a polis of the Thessaloi, within the tetrad of Phthiotis. The inhabitants of every polis would probably have been able to identify themselves as belonging to one *ethnos* or another, though in some cases there may have been room for contestation and debate.

However, there is no evidence that when the tetrads were named a sharp distinction was made between Achaia Phthiotis and [Thessalia] Phthiotis.[141] Phthiotis by itself in ancient texts is very often vague, covering both Achaian and Thessalian territory, and there is no reason to think that this is just a matter of non-Thessalian carelessness. Whereas the *ethnē*, Thessaloi and Achaioi, were at least theoretically distinct,[142] Phthiotis seems usually to have been used in the expansive sense. In non-Thessalian inscriptions the phrases *Achaia Phthiotis* and *Achaioi Phthiotes* occur frequently, but the force of the phrase is not to distinguish Achaian Phthiotis from Thessalian Phthiotis but rather to identify this Achaia as the

but he was by no means averse to innovation and revision. For more detailed discussion of Thessalian myth in Rhianos see Cuscunà (2009).

139 Loraux (1993); Forsdyke (2012). For tensions between autochthony and invasion in Theban foundation-myths see Fowler (2013), 354.

140 See also Hdt. 7.132.1: they are differentiated in a list of medizing *ethnē*.

141 On Phthiotis as presupposing the unexpressed 'Thessalia' see Gschnitzer (1954), 461.

142 The brief mention in Aristotle (*Politics* 1269b) of war between the Thessalians and the Achaians at some unspecified earlier time should, I suspect, be treated in the same way as the conflict between the Thessalians and the Phokians: that while the reality of fighting at some stage is likely, the persistence of its memory has more to do with the negotiation of *ethnos* distinction than with any substantial period of hostility.

northern rather than the Peloponnesian one. In Thessalian inscriptions, the phrases are virtually unattested.[143] Achaios/Achaioi appears on its own, in a substantive sense,[144] or describing a polis whose location would otherwise be ambiguous.[145] The adjectival form of *Phthiotēs* in singular or plural tends to describe Larisaians, to distinguish citizens of Larisa Kremaste from their counterparts in the (more famous) Larisa further north.[146] When *Phthiōtai* as a substantive is used by Aischines it means the Phthiotic Achaians (in the Amphiktyonic context once again); when it appears in a second-century BC Thessalian inscription it obviously refers to the Thessaloi of the tetrad Phthiotis, since the context is a set of decrees of the Thessalian *koinon* and the other tetrads are listed also.[147] So the word itself can designate either *ethnos* depending on context.

Obviously the name Phthiotis, whatever its geographical extent, evokes Phthia, part of Achilles' contingent in the Trojan War and, even in later literature, almost always used with regard to the mythological past,[148] normally in connection with Achilles and his family. Whether the poleis of Phthiotis had any real claim on the name as it appears in Homer is doubtful; as noted in Chapter 2, Phthia seems to be imagined (if the poet really had any specific placement in mind) too far south, along the western course of the Spercheios, near the Dolopes.[149] This makes it all the more intriguing that the name Phthiotis was deployed as, and where, it was. By the fifth century it had clearly been appropriated with particular energy by Pharsalos, as reflected in Euripides' *Andromache*, set in Pharsalos and its vicinity and concerning Achilles' son Neoptolemos and his mother Thetis, worshipped in the Thetideion. While Pharsalos is called a polis (line 16), Phthia seems to designate the surrounding area, its *chōra* in effect. It is part of the playwright's evocation of the myth-history of Pharsalos and its

[143] In *IG* IX.2 108 *Achaiōn* and *Phthiot* [...] seem to be within a few lines of each other, but the text is so fragmentary that their relationship is unclear, and in any case they do not form a phrase.

[144] E.g. in *IG* IX.2 1228 (third century BC, from Phalanna), citizenship is conferred on groups from a number of perioikic *ethnē*. Discussion in Mili (2015), 75–76.

[145] One example is Thebes, which requires clarification since the reader might expect that Boiotian Thebes is meant. See, for example, *SEG* 23.422, a fourth-century BC proxeny decree from Pherai in which the recipient is called a *Thebaios Achaios*, an Achaian Theban.

[146] However, surviving examples are late: e.g. *IG* IX.2 520, Augustan date.

[147] *SEG* 34.588 (from Larisa in Pelasgiotis; ca. 150–130 BC).

[148] When Phthia does occur in contexts of historical reality it does so as the qualifier of Achaia, as discussed above. See, for example, Xen. *Hell.* 4.3.9: Agesilaos marches into τὰ Ἀχαϊκὰ τῆς Φθίας ὄρη, 'the Achaian mountains of Phthia', really just another way of saying 'the mountains of Achaia Phthiotis'.

[149] Contesting the claim that Phthia was simply Pharsalos: Béquignon (1958).

environs, deliberately at odds with the political reality of the fifth century. This may be taken as straightforward literary archaism, but probably also reflects the desire by elite Pharsalians in the fifth century to give their polis a privileged claim on the region's Homeric links.[150]

The cult of Thetis near Pharsalos, though unattested in the epigraphic record,[151] is mentioned in a sufficiently diverse range of literary sources to be treated as a reality, though the date of its inception is unfortunately unknowable. This focus on Thetis is interesting: rather than consistently attempting to reclaim Achilles as a specifically Thessalian product and possession,[152] the chief polis in Phthiotis worshipped his mother, whose fame and cult were somewhat less widespread in the Greek world. If we bring in also the fact that from the third century at least Cheiron was an object of cult in Magnesia, while Thetis rather than Achilles has, at that time, a strong presence on the coins of Larisa Kremaste,[153] then we might be justified in detecting a Thessalian preference for the older generation in the story, and for figures without Achilles' unexampled panhellenic fame. If Taplin and Allan are right in suggesting that Euripides' *Andromache*, set chiefly at the Pharsalos Thetideion, was intended for performance in Thessaly, we have even stronger confirmation that in the later fifth century BC at least Pharsalos saw Thetis and her cult as a key ingredient in their polis' identity.[154] If we follow the earlier suggestion of a collaborative process of polis elites, it seems likely that the tetrad name Phthiotis was selected with the agreement, or perhaps even at the insistence of, the influential citizens of Pharsalos, who cultivated Aiakid associations through the figure of Thetis.

[150] Note also Strabo 9.5.6: both Pharsalos and Melitaia claim Hellas, further corroborating Pharsalos' appropriation of the territory commanded by Achilles; unfortunately we cannot know when the contestation began.

[151] Arvanitopoulos' identification of the name of Thetis as recipient of a dedication in an early fourth-century inscription from Pharsalos (see Arvanitopoulos 1929, 221) is not supported either by the later transcription of Decourt (1995, no. 77, 97–99) or by my own inspection of the stone in 2009.

[152] I say 'consistently' because we do have one intriguing exception, the well-known Pharsalian dedication to Apollo at Delphi of a statue-group showing Achilles on horseback and Patroklos on foot. See Paus. 10.13.5; Mili (2015), 176. I am unpersuaded by the dating of the statue-group to the fourth century on the grounds that a pair of warriors, one on horseback and one on foot, found on fourth-century Pharsalian coins are a depiction of the statue-group. While this identification is possible, of course, nothing on the coins actually suggests heroic or mythological identity.

[153] For these Hellenistic manifestations of the Aiakid theme see Chapter 7.

[154] Taplin (1999); Allan (2000), 155–58. For a more cautious approach see Easterling (1994), 79. See also the discussion in Chapter 2.

So the Thetis cult gives us our clearest suggestion that a strand of myth related to the Aiakidai was active and important in Phthiotis in the fifth century. It is interesting to note, however, a further strand of mythology in operation from the time of Pherekydes at least: the hero Phthios, clearly an eponym of Phthia (and by extension Phthiotis). In fr. 172 Pherekydes is cited as having explained the name of Thessaly's Dotion Plain in the following manner: Φερεκύδης δὲ ἀπὸ Δώτιος τοῦ Ἀστερίου καὶ Ἀμφικτυόνης τῆς Φθίου ('Pherekydes [says that it was named] after Dotis the son of Asterios and Amphiktyone daughter of Phthios'). So here we have a connection between the Dotion Plain, a mythological heartland of Thessaly, the Delphic Amphiktyony, and Phthia/Phthiotis. That this story is intended to slot in before the myth-time of the *Iliad* is suggested not only by the eponym function of Phthios but by the tradition that the Pelasgians, the region's earliest inhabitants, arrived in Thessaly under the command of Achaios, Phthios and Pelasgos.[155] Therefore, Phthios supplies a supplementary element in the myth-history of Phthia, before Achilles' birth and the area's Homeric fame. Phthia itself was rich in mythological associations, but the eponym anchors it firmly within the wider mythical landscape of Thessaly and its Delphic connections.

d) Hestiotis

Whereas the other tetrad names are redolent with myth-historical significance, Hestiotis is far harder to interpret. Indeed, even its form is uncertain. The difficulty is not the e/i spelling variation, since that is unlikely to have any bearing on sense (*hest-* and *hist-* being etymologically interchangeable in this context); rather, the problem is a complete lack of attestation of the -aiotis ending, usually used in ancient literary works and modern scholarship, within Thessaly itself. Admittedly, the internal evidence consists of a meagre two inscriptions, but in both the name shares a common essential form. In the fourth-century text the spelling is [Ἑ]στ[ι]ωτ[ῶ]ν (masculine, genitive plural);[156] in the second-century one, it is Ἱστιώτας (masculine, accusative plural).[157] Neither has the -ai- component. Scant as the evidence is, it discourages a glib assumption that the Thessalians ever used the name Hestiaiotis/Histiaiotis in either of

155 Dion. Hal. 1.17.2–3.

156 *IG* II² 175. Note that the *epsilon* is a restoration, and an *iota* cannot be absolutely ruled out. While I have not been able to inspect the stone myself, it should be said that the goddess' name Hestia is less well attested than the form Histia in Thessalian inscriptions. Histia is certain in *SEG* 45.645 (see below), whereas in *I.Thess.* I.68 the *epsilon* of Hestia is another restoration. That said, the Attic stone-cutter of *IG* II² 175 may have automatically slipped into the more normal Athenian usage.

157 *SEG* 34.558.

those forms. What does the nature of each inscription suggest to us about the reliability of their name-spelling, and its significance?

The fourth-century inscription (*IG* II^2 175) is not Thessalian, but Attic. It will be discussed in detail in Chapter 5. It is a shorter addendum to a long record of a treaty formed in 361/0 between Athens and 'the Thessalians', which is the earliest convincing evidence for any kind of formalised *koinon* structure in Thessaly.[158] In the inscription, names are given of the four *polemarchoi* of the Thessalians, one from each tetrad. The tetrad names are in the form of the masculine genitive plural: 'of the Pelasgiōtai', 'of the Phthiōtai', 'of the Thettaliōtai', 'of the Hestiōtai'. In this context it is especially significant to find the form Hestiōtai rather than Hestiaiōtai, because it means that the Athenian stone-cutter and those instructing him deviated from what was standard literary practice at the time. Why would they have done so? Surely the only answer must be that the Thessalians themselves, those participating in the treaty, influenced the spelling of the name. In other words, though not itself a Thessalian text, the inscription must reflect Thessalian usage.

As to the second relevant document, this is a famous decree – recorded in koine rather than dialect – of the Thessalian *koinon* from ca. 130 BC in which is recorded the decision to send grain to Rome to alleviate that city's severe shortage. The text stipulates the quantities of grain to be sent by, on the one hand, the Pelasgiōtai and the Phthiōtai (bracketed together as being from the region's eastern side, one supposes) and on the other hand by the Histiōtai and the Thessaliōtai (on the west).[159] It will be noted that, as in *IG* II^2 175, the other three tetrad names are spelled in a manner quite in keeping with non-Thessalian literary usage. Moreover, the text – as is the case with *IG* II^2 175 – is in general very error-free. In neither case is the spelling of the name likely to be the result simply of a stone-cutter's ignorance or error. A tangential corroboration may also be supplied by [Herodian.] *Gramm.* s.v. Ἑστίαια·

> Hestiaia: a polis of Euboia. Homer [*Iliad* 2.537] says: 'Hestiaia rich in grape-vines'. The Ionian spelling is with an 'i'. There is also a Histiaia of Thessaly. The citizen [of Thessalian Histiaia] is called 'Histiaieus'. Ephoros

[158] *IG* II^2 116.

[159] That stipulating contributions (of grain, perhaps also sometimes of money and troops) by each tetrad was in some way habitual, or at any rate a known practice (at least after 197 BC), is perhaps suggested by a joke in Plutarch (*Praecepta* 31) in which a man called Hermon tried to avoid public office by pleading poverty and the Thessalians voted him certain measures of food and wine ἀφ' ἑκάστης τετράδος. That this phrase referred to the tetrads was recognised by Larsen (1963).

says that the ethnic is 'Hestiaios'. And [the ethnic] of the Thessalian one is 'Histiōtēs.[160]

A great deal of confusion seems to lie within this entry. The Euboian polis is straightforward: this is a well-known site. The Thessalian polis of Histiaia, on the other hand, is otherwise unattested. Moreover, the ethnic Histiōtēs seems anomalous as describing someone from Histiaia. It has obviously been confused with the tetrad name: the -iotēs component is unmistakeable. Little, clearly, can be done with such a scant and unreliable source; however, it is interesting to see the same form Histiotēs turning up, rather than Histiaiotēs. Perhaps the unknown author of this grammatical work happened to have access to information on genuine Thessalian usage, but muddled it.

What difference does the spelling make? Actually, quite a lot. Hestiaiotis/Histiaiotis would be an adjectival form derived from the toponym Hestiaia/Histiaia. There is a well-known site of that name (Histiaia) in southern Euboia. A (now lost) Thessalian site of the same name in the north-west part of the region is of course eminently possible. But it is also possible that non-Thessalian authors took their spelling from the Euboian toponym, inaccurately as regards the Thessalian usage, and that this became habitual. This error may even lie behind Strabo's claim that the Perrhaibians attacked Euboian Histiaia and drove its inhabitants onto the Greek mainland, where many of them settled in north-western Thessaly, and that the tetrad took its name from them.[161] This pattern of Perrhaibian conquest – going over to Euboia, defeating the Histiaians and driving them towards your own homeland – seems entirely counter-intuitive and is surely a concoction by Strabo or one of his sources, intended to explain the apparent (though actually coincidental) resemblance between the names of the Euboian polis and the Thessalian tetrad.

So what would Hestiotis/Histiotis mean? It would be derived rather from Hestia (of which Histia is simply a variant), and mean 'the Hestian [tetrad/Thessalia]'. This is quite different, and the difference has to be considered seriously. Why might a tetrad be called 'Hestian'? What might that mean? The semantic cluster involved would be that of hearth, home, hospitality, communal eating and the goddess associated with such things. It could be argued that this cluster is of more potency in Thessalian self-perception than an obsolete toponym; the latter is a curious inclusion within the culturally charged naming process to which the tetrads were clearly

[160] '<Ἑστίαια> πόλις Εὐβοίας. Ὅμηρος (Β 537) «πολυστάφυλον Ἑστίαιαν». ἡ δὲ διὰ τοῦ <ι> Ἰωνικὴ γραφή ἐστιν. ἔστι δὲ καὶ Θετταλίας Ἱστίαια. ὁ πολίτης Ἱστιαεύς. Ἔφορος δὲ τὸ ἐθνικὸν Ἑστιαῖός φησι. καὶ Ἱστιώτης ὁ τῆς Θεσσαλικῆς.'

[161] Strabo 9.5.17.

subject. Each of the other names (Pelasgiotis, Thessaliotis and Phthiotis) is intensely evocative when seen within the mythological landscape of Thessaly. Hestiaiotis/Histiaiotis looks anomalous in this regard, whereas a link with the goddess might have real potency, given her prominence elsewhere in Thessaly. Cults of Hestia were of undoubted importance – including political and civic importance – in poleis in other areas of Thessaly;[162] Demetrias had a month named Hestios;[163] Hestia – or rather Histia – was included in the altar of the six goddesses at Pherai;[164] the theme of feasting and hospitality was a significant one in Thessalian religion, as the next chapter will show. However, a specific connection with the north-west tetrad is missing from view, and we must resign ourselves to a lacuna in our knowledge.

It is possible that we should consider Hestiotis as standing outside the concerted process in which the other tetrads seem to have been named, to evoke important aspects of early Thessalian myth-history. Such is certainly suggested by the third-century BC author Charax of Pergamon: 'Histiaiotis, which Charax recalls in his seventh book, writing about Thessalos the son of Aiatos who defeated the Boiotoi in Arne: "Thessalos did not change the name of the fourth part (lit. 'the fourth part of the naming'), but let it be called Histiaiotis as before."'[165] Charax differs significantly from Aristotle in attributing the naming of the tetrads to Thessalos rather than placing it in the time of Aleuas the Red; the suggestion is that Thessalos did not necessarily create the tetrads, but did rename them – except for Histiaiotis, apparently. The separateness of Hestiotis may be corroborated by the Hellenistic author Apollodoros of Athens, who gives the four parts of Thessaly as Pelasgiotis, Thessaliotis, Phthiotis and *Iolkitis*.[166] This is not historically plausible, but does highlight the way in which Hestiotis (unlike the evocative name of Iolkos) fails to chime with widely attested strands of Thessalian mythology. Instead, there may have been an agreement to preserve a long-standing local connection between north-western Thessaly and the goddess Hestia, one now otherwise lost to view.

162 Mili (2015), 131–34.

163 At least in the Roman period: see, for example, *IG* IX.2 1117d.

164 *SEG* 45.645. Discussion in Miller (1974); Graninger (2006), 192–93.

165 Charax *FGrH* 103 F 6: 'Ἱστιαιῶτις, ἧς μέμνηται Χάραξ ἐν ζ′ τῇδε γράφων περὶ Θεσσαλοῦ τοῦ Αἰάτου τοῦ νικήσαντος ἐν Ἄρνῃ Βοιωτούς «ὁ δὲ Θεσσαλὸς οὐδὲ τὴν τετάρτην μοῖραν τῆς ἐπωνυμίας μετέβαλεν, ἀλλ' Ἱστιαιῶτιν αὐτὴν ὡς πρὶν καλεῖσθαι εἴασε».'

166 Apollodoros *FGrH* 244 F 164. It is interesting that the mention is attributed to Apollodoros' work on the Catalogue of Ships: is Iolkos evoked because of its strong presence in early epic?

9. Conclusions

In this chapter we have followed the story of shared Thessalian origins through the main phases of its development. By the time Alexander the Great ascended to the Macedonian throne in 336 BC he was able to encourage the co-operation of the Thessalians by ὑπομνήσας τῆς ἀρχαίας ἀφ' Ἡρακλέους συγγενείας ('recalling their ancient *syngeneia* from Herakles').[167] By that time, Heraklid/Thessalid descent had obviously achieved regional currency. But it did not begin that way. It began as a much more limited phenomenon, probably in west Thessaly in the seventh or early sixth century, before being co-opted by Pelasgiotic elites in the late sixth and early fifth century. At the same time, an offshoot of the tradition, that of the invading Thessaloi, was developed, partly to cast the Thessalians as aggressors and to emphasise the *ethnos*-wide implications of the mythology. At various points these traditions generated, influenced and interacted with those promulgated by the Boiotians, and the Boiotian aspect of the stories was in its turn incorporated back into Thessalian myth-history through the identification of Kierion with Arne.

The tradition of the Thessalids/Thessaloi was itself multivocal and open to reinvention and adaptation, as we have seen. In addition, it had no discernibly suppressant effect upon alternatives. In fact, the very development of the tradition allowed for the generation of myths of ethnic difference within the region; the centralising narrative – we are Thessalians because we share this common origin – lay alongside, fuelled and shaped the formation of divergent myths, especially those about what we might call the 'pre-Thessaly Thessaly', the region's names and populations before the arrival of the Thessalids/Thessaloi. Sometimes this was a strategy employed by the Thessalians to denigrate subaltern groups. The key example of this is the Penestai: they were depicted as the *ethnos* (Boiotoi, Perrhaiboi, Magnetes – their putative identity varies from source to source)[168] who had occupied Thessaly's rich plains before the invaders displaced them. They were, in this discourse, the defeated, and their ethnic difference established their essential, their inherent inferiority and, therefore, the right of their owners to own them. However, this was not the only kind of use to which the myths

[167] Diod. 17.4.1. Patterson (2010), 86–90.

[168] The Penestai as Boiotoi who did not wish to leave Thessaly and who accepted servitude as the condition of remaining: Archemachos *FGrH* 424 F 1. The Penestai as enslaved Magnetes and Perrhaiboi: Theopompos *FGrH* 115 F 122. For discussion see Ducat (1994), 14–16, 52–53, 94–98. Van Wees (2003, 53–57) treats the conquest of the Penestai as a historical reality, but his argument rests on the historicity of the invasion and expansion of the Thessaloi, which in fact is chiefly mythological, as this book attempts to show.

of the pre-Thessaly Thessaly were put. As we saw, the tetrad names showed a centralised process of its incorporation, a concerted drive to capture and memorialise the vital aspects of Thessaly's distant legendary past, the rule of Achilles' family in Phthia, the existence of the Pelasgoi, whose presence in Thessaly reinforces its place as one of Greece's primordial realms. Such centrally driven processes, however, are only part of the picture. Individual poleis, and no doubt families, deliberately cultivated descent from different heroes: Lapiths, for example, as I have argued elsewhere.[169] At no point was the profusion of local origin-stories checked, or in obvious conflict with, the pan-Thessalian narrative.[170]

The steady accretion of such traditions over centuries led to such later descriptions as the following, by Strabo:

> But speaking of Thessaly as a whole, [I may say] that in earlier times it was called Pyrrhaia, after Pyrrha the wife of Deukalion, and Haimonia after Haimon, and Thessaly after Thessalos the son of Haimon. But some writers, dividing it into two parts, say that Deukalion obtained the portion towards the south and called it Pandora after his mother, and that the other part fell to Haimon, after whom it was called Haimonia, but that the former name was changed to Hellas, after Hellen the son of Deukalion, and the latter to Thessaly, after the son of Haimon. Some, however, say that descendants of Antiphos and Pheidippos, the sons of Thessalos the son of Herakles, invaded the country from Thesprotian Ephyra and named it after Thessalos, their own ancestor. And it has been said that the country too was once named Nessonis, like the lake, after Nesson the son of Thessalos.[171]

[169] Aston (2017). See also Decourt (2011), suggesting that the mythology surrounding the Lapiths and Kaineus reflects early conflicts between the Thessalians and other ethnic groups in the region.

[170] One might compare the way in which the formation of the 'Hellenic stemma' never worked against the survival, even the flourishing, of 'non-Hellenic' descent myths (that is, heroic genealogies without connection to Hellen) in various parts of the Greek world. See Finkelberg (2005), 39.

[171] Strabo 9.5.23: 'καθ' ὅλου δ' ὅτι Πυρραία πρότερον ἐκαλεῖτο ἀπὸ Πύρρας τῆς Δευκαλίωνος γυναικός, Αἱμονία δὲ ἀπὸ Αἵμονος, Θετταλία δὲ ἀπὸ Θετταλοῦ τοῦ Αἵμονος. ἔνιοι δὲ διελόντες δίχα τὴν μὲν πρὸς νότον λαχεῖν φασι Δευκαλίωνι καὶ καλέσαι Πανδώραν ἀπὸ τῆς μητρός, τὴν δ' ἑτέραν Αἵμονι, ἀφ' οὗ Αἱμονίαν λεχθῆναι· μετωνομάσθαι δὲ τὴν μὲν Ἑλλάδα ἀπὸ Ἕλληνος τοῦ Δευκαλίωνος, τὴν δὲ Θετταλίαν ἀπὸ τοῦ υἱοῦ Αἵμονος· τινὲς δὲ ἀπὸ Ἐφύρας τῆς Θεσπρωτίδος ἀπογόνους Ἀντίφου καὶ Φειδίππου, τῶν Θετταλοῦ τοῦ Ἡρακλέους, ἐπελθόντας ἀπὸ Θετταλοῦ τοῦ ἑαυτῶν προγόνου τὴν χώραν ὀνομάσαι. εἴρηται δὲ καὶ Νεσσωνὶς ὀνομασθῆναί ποτε ἀπὸ Νέσσωνος τοῦ Θετταλοῦ, καθάπερ καὶ ἡ λίμνη' (trans. Jones, adapted).

Fig. 7. View south-east into the north-western plain from the E92 road from Metsovo

Haimonia, Pandora, Hellas, Nessonis: many versions of the pre-Thessaly Thessaly, no doubt reflecting non-Thessalian mythographic sources as well as local traditions.[172] There is no disentangling most of them now, no tracing them back to their creators at the local level, though important strands – such as the link with Deukalion – may, as we have seen, be analysed with regard to their place within Thessaly's broader role in Hellenic mythology.

Wandering heroes and invading *ethnē* are both ancient strategies for describing and expressing interactions between regions and communities. Thessaly and Boiotia really did share toponyms, some religious features and dialect forms; these ancient affinities provided the basis and the stimulus for the story that the Boiotoi originated in the north. The Pindos was a place of frequent traffic, pierced by paths and passes (one of them on the

[172] Cf. Pliny, *NH* 4.28: 'Sequitur mutatis saepe nominibus Haemonia, eadem Pelasgis et Pelasgicon Argos, Hellas, eadem Thessalia et Dryopis, semper a regibus cognominata.' Pliny seems here to be talking about southern Thessaly and Achaia Phthiotis; the fact that the two are so indistinct probably relates to the fact that, by the time of his writing, the former *perioikoi* were included within the Thessalian League; indeed, Achaia Phthiotis was incorporated as early as the 190s BC. Graninger (2011a), 35–42. On the whole, however, Pliny's depiction of Thessaly is confused and inexact.

route of the present road from Metsovo to Kalambaka: see Fig. 7), routes used by transhumant pastoralists and no doubt also groups of migrants at different times; thus arose the various myths of incursions into Thessaly from Epeiros. Realities of travel underpin the myths, but are transformed, increasingly from the fifth century, into grandiose stories of mass population movement and forceful take-over. Such stories had always been a major part of Thessaly's place in Greek mythology, and for the most part cast the region as the point of departure. This trend was identified in Archaic epic in Chapter 2, but it did not stop in the Classical period; in fact, it was then that stories of mass movement from Thessaly by Dorians and Aiolians gained momentum, as far-flung communities showed a desire to anchor themselves to the original Greek homeland, the land of the Hellenes.

In the Classical material considered in this chapter there are some clear signs of the Thessalians recognising and claiming this aspect of primordiality, especially through the tetrad name Pelasgiotis and the highly charged name of the new polis of Metropolis, though Aiolian identity, interestingly, seems to have held little obvious appeal for them. Their *ethnos* charter-myth, however, took a different direction, literally. Thessalos may be *assez pâle*,[173] but his significance lies in how strongly he contrasts with other, older strands in Thessaly's mythic personality. From the Archaic period, as we have seen, Thessaly tended to be characterised as a point of departure, a land left behind, consigned to past time. This conferred on it the honour of originality, but left it oddly empty. For the first time, with Thessalos and the Thessaloi, the direction of travel is reversed, and departure is replaced by arrival. So far from being the place that other *ethnē* left, Thessaly becomes the place into which the Thessalians themselves have journeyed. The empty space is filled.

173 For the use of this phrase to describe the eponymous hero Lokros, see Franchi (2020a), 138.

4

The creation of Thessaly in cult

In the extensive scholarship of recent decades concerning the development and expression of *ethnos* identity in ancient Greece, the role of religion has been amply recognised and discussed.[1] Its importance could take two basic forms. Sanctuaries were places of congregation at which members of an *ethnos* met to achieve face to face interaction and affirm and reaffirm their mutual bonds, normally within the context of a festival. Secondly, cults could express themes central to how an *ethnos* saw its own identity and wished that identity to be projected. Both modes are discernible in Thessaly, and in the fifth century in particular we can see Thessalian communities participating in rituals whose form and related mythology formed an implicit commentary on what it meant to be a Thessalian, what the land of Thessaly was like, and its value and importance.

The Archaic period significantly failed to supply an obviously pan-Thessalian element, at least in terms of physical gatherings. Theocharis, the first to conduct serious excavations of the sanctuary of Athena Itonia at Philia, believed that the site was a pan-Thessalian sanctuary from an early period, but this was based largely on its later role and on the definite importance of the area to the mythology of the Thessalian *ethnos*.[2] The increasing archaeological illumination of western Thessaly in more recent years, and the discovery of a settlement at Philia itself,[3] suggests instead that the shrine served a local cluster of communities whose elites met there for

[1] See, for example, the papers in Funke and Haake (2013). However, this volume stresses the diversity of roles played by sanctuaries in the development and functioning of federal structures; as Freitag (2013) observes concerning Akarnania, for example, a central cult site – in the sense of a place of regional congregation associated with federal institutions – is absolutely not a pre-requisite of *ethnos*-consciousness.

[2] *AD* 19 (1964) *Chron.* 241–67, esp. 248–49; see also *AD* 18 (1963) *Chron.* 135–9; *AD* 20 (1964) *Chron.* 311–13; *AD* 22 (1967) *Chron.* 295–96. For a summary of the site and its excavation history see Nikolaou (2012), 88–98; Canlas (2021), 146–54. On the goddess and her cult: Mili (2015), 225–34.

[3] Karagiannopoulos (2017–2018); Stamatopoulou (2019), 39. It is significant that at the sanctuary itself there seems to have been some manufacturing activity, serving this local population beyond purely religious needs: Morgan (2003), 119, 149.

various cult observances, perhaps including ritual dining.[4] This activity seems to have been at its height between ca. 750 and ca. 575 BC.[5] Other important sanctuaries known to us from this period are those of Ennodia at Pherai[6] and Athena Polias at Phthiotic Thebes (Fig. 8).[7] Neither had an overtly pan-Thessalian character or scope. The Ennodia sanctuary, for all that it shared certain characteristics with Philia, has been shown to have quite a different character in both its votive record and the society it served; it really does seem to have been a Pheraian sanctuary first and foremost, although its situation on a major road network certainly made it accessible to travellers from other parts of Thessaly and beyond.[8] Though by the Classical period Ennodia will have struck non-Thessalians as a deity with an unambiguously Thessalian character, she was never truly pan-Thessalian in her cult;[9] instead, Pherai became increasingly energetic in asserting its primary claim on her, even as her worship spread to other parts of Thessaly.[10]

This does not reflect a general lack of energy or investment in religious life. The sixth century saw an increase, though not quite the beginning,[11] of temple construction in the region;[12] before then, cult at sites such as the sanctuary of Ennodia at Pherai was apparently carried out in the open air,

4 Morgan (2003), 141; Karouzou (2018), 133–37. Note that, although the numerous votive weapons – real and miniature – convey an elite warrior ideology, perhaps also suggested by the tripods also dedicated there (Karouzou 2020, 902), the majority of the votives are not especially lavish or costly. The military character of the cult should not be overstated, moreover: fibulae – suggesting dedications of textiles? – are the most numerous finds from the site.

5 Kilian-Dirlmeier (2002), 175–91.

6 Béquignon (1937a); Graninger (2006), 202–04; Mili (2015), 112, 147–58, 336–38.

7 This sanctuary has a cautionary quality for the historian regarding the perils of dating: only recent scrutiny of the notebooks of Arvanitopoulos and re-examination of material in the storerooms of the Ephoreia revealed that the site was in existence in the Early Iron Age. See Stamatopoulou (2004–2009), 635–37.

8 Morgan (2003), 135–39. In general, the location of important early sanctuaries in Thessaly on major routes ensured their accessibility beyond the immediate local area: Karouzou (2018), 133–35.

9 *Pace* Chrysostomou (1998), 262–67, who argues that, her cult diffused from powerful Pherai, she 'έγινε η εθνική θεά των Θεσσαλών πιθανότατα ήδη πριν από τά κλασσικά χρόνια' (p. 262). On the earlier importance of the sanctuary see Georganas (2008); Karouzou (2018), 126–27. It was a prominent metallurgical centre: Orfanou (2015).

10 Graninger (2009).

11 Possible earlier temples tend to be beset with near-insuperable uncertainties of dating, an example being the horseshoe-shaped structure at Gonnoi: Helly (1973), vol. I, 72–74 (arguing that the seventh-century structure was restored in the sixth); Mazarakis Ainian (1997), 86; Karouzou (2017), 349 and 373, fig. 16.

12 Morgan (2003), 140–44; Archibald (2009), 305; Karouzou (2017), 351. For further

Fig. 8. Part of the temple of Athena Polias at Phthiotic Thebes (in foreground); fourth century BC, but incorporating remnants of its Archaic predecessor. Photograph: author's own

or in structures that left less substantial archaeological traces.[13] Significant examples of temples from this period – marked out by their thorough and well-published excavation and by the volume of the finds – are found at Soros (Apollo) and at Lianokokkala, near Metropolis (also Apollo) (Fig. 9),[14] though further sites give evidence of new building at this time, as far as the vagaries of dating small finds and architectural fragments can reveal as much.[15] In addition, the sanctuary of Ennodia at Pherai received its first temple in the same period, though Philia seemingly did not.[16] Of course, new built spaces could accommodate pre-existing ritual practices, such as

significant trends in later Archaic material culture in Thessaly see Stamatopoulou (2019).

[13] Karouzou (2018), 133. For the relatively recent discovery of a Protogeometric/Geometric eschara and its probable connection with open air ritual see Arachoviti et al. (2012).

[14] Soros: Mazarakis Ainian (2009) and (2012), and Mili (2015), 343–45. Lianokokkala: Intzesiloglou (2000) and (2002a).

[15] For examples see Stamatopoulou (2021), 688.

[16] Mili (2015), 338.

Fig. 9. Temple of Apollo at Lianokokkala, near Metropolis (west end); sixth century BC. Photograph: author's own

food consumption, which seems to have occurred in the temple at Soros;[17] there the site encompassed a *hestiatorion*, a space for elite ritual dining practices.[18] But temple construction does suggest a significant new focus on the monumentalisation of sacred space. However, none of the monumentalised sites was a place of pan-Thessalian congregation on the *ethnos* level. In fact, rather than trying to find evidence of a pan-Thessalian cult within Thessaly in the Archaic period, it is more plausible to suppose that the process of ethnogenesis received a powerful religious stimulus *outside* the region's borders when Thessalians interacted with members of adjoining central Greek *ethnē* at Kalapodi and Delphi.[19]

[17] Mazarakis Ainian (2009 and 2012); Mili (2015), 343–44. It is interesting to note that the new temple at Pherai took care to incorporate within its structure the earlier altar: Karouzou (2018), 126–27.

[18] On the importance of the temple-*hestiatorion* in Early Iron Age religious building and its surviving into the Archaic period see Mazarakis Ainian (1997), 390–92.

[19] Sanctuaries that facilitated regular interaction with other communities had a particular potency in the formation of collective identity. For a discussion of the Argive Heraion as such a case see Hall (1995).

This is not to diminish in importance, however, the emergence of pan-Thessalian religious elements; indeed, it is all the more interesting to consider what they consist of, where they come from and why they are chosen over other available possibilities. The centrality of Poseidon in this process, though we cannot say it comes out of nowhere, certainly marks an apparent departure from our earlier view, and one major aspect we shall have to tackle concerns the sources and inspirations of this choice. It must be noted, however, that some of the apparent novelty of the fifth-century material derives from evidence type. For the first time we have coinage, and this lets in a great flood of light concerning how Thessalian poleis, operating with a high degree of collective action, wished to present themselves. A new technology, a new mode of expression, is bound to generate fresh images and themes, and so we have to exercise caution in speaking of change and innovation. Nonetheless, when the first coin series were minted, from ca. 475 BC,[20] a choice had to be made as to the deities and religious emblems to be placed upon them, and which were chosen – and which not (*not* Athena Itonia, *not* Ennodia)[21] – is a matter of the greatest significance. In the ensuing discussion we shall start with the main coin types, bringing in the textual sources that allow for their interpretation. We shall then consider aspects of background and context so as to illuminate the pre-existing material on which the die-cutters, the governing authorities and the poleis as a whole were drawing.[22]

[20] The most extensive and systematic analysis of this coinage is now that of Mack (2021).

[21] Athena Itonia came to dominate the federal coinage of the post-196 BC Thessalian *koinon*, by which time there is other evidence for her cult having a federal status. As for Ennodia, she does appear on the polis coinage of Pherai in the fourth century BC: for examples see *Triton* XV, 284–88.

[22] We are largely ignorant of the mechanisms through which coin imagery was chosen, and indeed of the minting process generally: see Howgego (1995), 26–28. While the location of the Athenian mint has been identified with relative certainty, in general minting may have been done in small or perhaps multi-purpose buildings and did not require extensive dedicated premises. In the case of Thessalian poleis, it seems very likely that the choice of imagery and legends on coins lay with the same narrow elites who steered other aspects of civic and political life. That said, Mili (2015, 238–39) makes the important point that the coins, in their circulation, would have brought key religious imagery to a far wider audience than the more restricted group able to participate directly in the rituals evoked.

1. The bull-wrestling

In the period 475–460 BC, a number of Thessalian poleis, and the Perrhaiboi,[23] established a closely co-ordinated repertoire of coin types, including the image of a young man wrestling with a bull[24] (for an example, see Fig. 10). This contest is now routinely referred to as the *taurokathapsia*, though we have no evidence that the Thessalians themselves would have used this term; inscriptions from the second century BC use instead the term *taurotheria*, bull-hunt.[25] Because we cannot know what term the Thessalians of the fifth century would have used, this study will tend to prefer the English 'bull-wrestling'. The largest denomination, the drachma, shows on the obverse a young man on foot, naked but for a short cloak and sometimes a *petasos*, gripping a bull's head with a restraining fabric band as the animal charges forward; on the reverse his horse, rein trailing, runs freely. Plainly the young man has pursued the bull on horseback and then dismounted to grapple with it. On fractional issues less of both scenes is shown: the horse is present as forepart or just head, and the wrestling scene focuses on the front end of the bull, the man restraining it by means of the fabric band stretched across its forehead.

This detail is clearly referred to in a sadly undatable[26] poem in the *Anthologia Palatina*:

> The well-horsed bull-driving band of men of Thessaly
> Fighting beasts with their bare [lit. 'unarmed'] hands,
> Harnessed their goad-driven colts for the leaping of bulls [or: combined it with],
> Eager to cast the plaited brow-straps around them;
> Bending the head and the free-sliding strap to the earth
> They overthrow the beast's [so] great might.[27]

[23] Liampi (2015, 5–6) suggests that Larisa, Krannon and the Perrhaiboi minted the bull-wrestling type earliest, with other poleis (Pherai, Skotoussa, Pharkadon, Pelinna, Trikka) quickly following suit; in fact, however, this relative chronology is impossible to determine with any certainty. For the Larisaian issues see Lorber (2008). There is no need to assume that the Larisaians compelled the Perrhaiboi to adopt a compatible currency as part of their subordination: as Mackil and van Alfen observe (2006, 205–10), various motivations could induce a minting community to copy the coins of another.

[24] Liampi (1996).

[25] The term *taurokathapsia* is found in inscriptions from various parts of the Greek world in the Roman period; as Robert (1940, 318–19) suggests, the Roman enthusiasm for the Thessalian contest led to its diffusion, perhaps under a different name, especially among eastern Greek cities.

[26] It is likely to have been composed some time in the first century AD: see Gow and Page (1968), suggesting ca. AD 40; Cameron (2004, 43–47), suggesting the reign of Claudius or Nero.

[27] *Anth. Pal.* 9.543:

Fig. 10. Silver drachma from Larisa; ca. 470–460 BC. Obv.: young man wrestling a bull; rev.: running horse. Private coll. Photograph: author's own

It is hard to imagine a better demonstration of a vital skill in a society where pastoral wealth was so important. Even if there was a competitive element – presumably not every man would manage to catch and subdue a bull – this is plainly a group event, and we should imagine a noisy, frantic mêlée of animals (equine, bovine and human) dashing hither and thither and forming pairs of combatants, riderless horses running freely, until the last bull had its brow to the ground. All this may vividly be imagined[28] and would have been an exciting spectacle.[29]

It is generally assumed that this contest, in the fifth century BC at least, took place at a festival of Poseidon called the Petraia,[30] which included an *agōn* mentioned by late sources.[31] This, however, demands some interrogation. The earliest attestation of the contests the festival entailed is a fragmentary epinikian of Bacchylides, whose final lines run thus:

Θεσσαλίης εὔιππος ὁ ταυρελάτης χορὸς ἀνδρῶν,
χερσὶν ἀτευχήτοις θηρσὶν ὁπλιζόμενος,
κεντροτυπεῖς πώλους ζεῦξε σκιρτήματι ταύρων,
ἀμφιβαλεῖν σπεύδων πλέγμα μετωπίδιον·
ἀκρότατον δ' ἐς γῆν κλίνας ἅμα κεῦροπον ἅμμα
θηρὸς τὴν τόσσην ἐξεκύλισε βίην.

[28] We also have an elaborate and vivid description of such a practice from the late antique novel *Aithiopika* by Heliodoros (10.41.4): on this text see the Epilogue.

[29] So much so that the emperor Claudius apparently made an attempt to add it to the repertoire of the Roman amphitheatre: Pliny, *NH* 8.182; Suet. *Div. Claud.* 21.3; the latter speaks of 'Thessalos equites, qui feros tauros per spatia circi agunt insiliuntque defessos et ad terram cornibus detrahunt'. As Cameron remarks (2004, 56–57), the author of the poem may actually have seen the event, either in Rome or in the Greek East.

[30] Fearn (2009), 24, n.13.

[31] Schol. Pind. *Pyth.* 4.138; Schol Ap. Rhod. *Arg.* 3.1244a.

> Now as a mark of favour to Kleoptolemos
> the sanctuary of Poseidon Petraios
> must be celebrated in song,
> and also the renowned son of Pyrrichos, victorious with his horses, who
> ... of hospitable and just ... (the rest is missing).[32]

What did the contest consist of? The heading of the poem in the manuscript is 'Κλεοπτολέμῳ Θεσσαλῷ Ἵπποις Πετραῖα', and the plural ἵπποις would seem to indicate a chariot race; we may therefore imagine the bull-wrestling and the chariot races taking place in the same ritual setting. Can we be sure that the bull-wrestling was part of the Petraia? Strong corroboration in the form of a close parallel comes from the programme of the Eleutheria, the Thessalian festival founded after 197 BC. This contained, in addition to several categories of horse and chariot race, a suite of equestrian contests of a highly local flavour, one of which was the *taurotheria*, a pursuit of bulls on horseback.[33] From the early first century BC come a number of inscriptions listing 'οἱ τὸν ταῦρον πεφειράκοντες' ('those having hunted the bull');[34] though the occasion of that bull-hunt is unknown, the fact that the participants are recorded in this way suggests a festival. The difficulty, of course, lies in tracing such practices back to the fifth century. The Eleutheria was in some ways a fundamentally different festival from the Petraia: it received participants from across the Greek world, though participation in the equestrian events seems to have been restricted to Thessalians.[35] However, it is probable that it encapsulated earlier customs within this new setting. It therefore seems highly likely that the bull-wrestling shown on the fifth-century coins (while it may well have been a widespread and popular custom more generally in the region) was enacted at the Petraia. The inclusion of Poseidon's trident in proximity with some of the bull-wrestling scenes on coins of Krannon and Pharkadon reinforces this probability.[36]

32 Bacchyl. *Ep.* 14.19–24; I use here the text of Maehler (1968).
Κλεοπτολέμῳ δὲ χάριν
νῦν χρὴ Ποσειδᾶνός τε Πετρ[αί-
ου τέμενος κελαδῆσαι,
Πυρρίχου τ' εὔδοξον ἱππόνικ[ον υἱόν,
ὃς φιλοξείνου τε καὶ ὀρθοδίκου...

33 Graninger (2011a), 78–79.

34 See, for example, *IG* IX.2 536. It is suggested by Decourt and Helly (2015, 516) that this inscription type goes back to the third century BC, which would suggest an interesting bridge between fifth- and second-century practice; however, I have been unable to locate an example from this earlier period.

35 Graninger (2011a), 81–84. He observes that in fact the equestrian victors were chiefly drawn from prominent families, active in political and civic life.

36 The tridents are always on the reverse, accompanying the horse, which is not

It is very significant that in the first half of the fifth century the Thessalians directed their competitive equestrian energies in this way. Their showing in the hippic contests of the panhellenic Crown Games in this period – indeed, until the third century BC – is not especially substantial.[37] Importantly, they chose to display their horsemanship not in the 'mainstream' contests of the Crown Games, where they would engage with wealthy Greeks from a host of regions, but instead in contests involving Thessalians alone.[38] Moreover, the bull-wrestling really was of a uniquely Thessalian type. Regional festivals were by no means rare at the time, and their importance in the articulation of an *ethnos*' shared identity is well established;[39] however, in a culture where remarkable similarity pervaded the nature of *agōnes* between regions, the sheer peculiarity of the Thessalian bull-wrestling is very striking. Even the chariot ritual at Onchestos – like the Petraia, in honour of Poseidon – does not really come close, because

insignificant; the horse is plainly being designated as the animal of Poseidon in a way that the bull rarely is in Thessaly. But since the two sides of these coins (bull-wrestling and horse) are closely connected in a narrative sense the trident may apply symbolically to both. See, for example, *Nomos* 4, 1266. For a rare juxtaposition of bull and trident see *Nomos* 4, 1082. On the obverse are a man's and a horse's head side by side, facing right, suggesting partnership; on the reverse a bull charges right, head and horns lowered. Thus the two sides of the coin hold the two sides of the combat, on the one hand man and horse in a state of co-operation, on the other the violent and dangerous bull. A trident is placed horizontally in the field over the bull's back, its tines at the bull's head-end, strongly suggesting that the two sets of sharp points (tines and horns) are to be considered analogous and that the bull stands for Poseidon's dangerous might.

[37] Aston and Kerr (2018), 3–6. There are attested Thessalian equestrian victories from the panhellenic Games in the Archaic and Classical periods, but not as many as the region's reputation for horses and horsemanship might lead us to expect; the Sicilians, Athenians and Spartans all produce more attested victors. Nor does this reflect a general Thessalian indifference to the Games *per se*; as Stamatopoulou (2007a) has shown, they were actively engaged in such fora of panhellenic elite display.

[38] It is significant in this regard that, among the *epinikia* of Bacchylides, the two surviving Thessalian honorands are the only ones celebrated not for victories in the panhellenic Crown Games but rather for local Thessalian successes. They did, however, commission a famous poet to commemorate the events, so were not immune to the opportunity for the wider dissemination of their achievements. Tantalising, too, is a fragment of Sophokles' *Larisaioi* referring to a πολὺς ἀγὼν πάγξενος, a 'big contest welcoming all foreigners'. (Fr. 378 Radt; see Nielsen 2014, 114.) Was this the Petraia? If so, πάγξενος probably implies that some at least of the contests were open to participation by outsiders; they need not all have been, however, as the later example of the Eleutheria (see above) makes clear.

[39] For example, fresh light was recently shed on Arkadian regional festivals by the recent publication of an early fifth-century inscription from Mount Lykaion or Methydrion: see Carbon and Clackson (2016).

it is not, *sensu stricto*, an *agōn*;[40] moreover, unlike the Onchestian rite, the Thessalian bull-wrestling seems to demonstrate practical skills. We know nothing of the realities of Thessalian herding practices, but it is hard to believe that the skills of pursuing and subduing livestock do not reflect, at root, the priorities of stock-breeding communities. As Mack observes, even elite Thessalians were not people who saw fit to leave the practicalities of horsemanship and herding to slaves and hirelings.[41]

There is another explanation of the bull-wrestling motif, and it is one that deserves serious consideration: the theory that the young man is a hero, either Thessalos or Jason.[42] While Thessalos would be tempting in view of the increasing importance of his mythology in the fifth century, there is nothing at all to link him to bulls; Jason, on the other hand (*pace* Liampi),[43] does seem a promising fit. Aietes king of Kolchis set him the task of yoking fire-breathing bulls as a condition of being allowed to take away the Golden Fleece and return triumphant to recover his Iolkian kingdom. It may be argued that the myth of Jason had no connection with the poleis of Pelasgiotis, being Iolkian (albeit with strong links to Pherai); however, there are other signs that myths connected with the area on and adjoining the Pagasitic Gulf were incorporated into the Thessalian bundle, so this would not represent a barrier to the identification. In particular, in the period 479–460 Larisa placed the empty sandal of Jason – the sandal he lost crossing the Anauros – on its coins, so it is clear that such myths were not restricted to a narrow geographical scope.[44] However, the evidence for the bull-wrestling as a historical custom is stronger than the link with Jason, and perhaps it would be safest to believe that both the custom and Jason's bull-fighting were ways of making reference to Thessaly's pastoral resources and their exploitation. In fact, the two interpretations of the images – as

[40] Schachter (1986), 219; Teffeteller (2001).

[41] Mack (2021), 83; ancient comments on this aspect of Thessalian culture: Eur. *El.* 815–17 and *Dissoi Logoi* 2.11.

[42] Moustaka (1983), 74–75; she rightly regards Thessalos and Achilles as unlikely candidates, but puts forward the suggestion of Jason based on artistic parallels with his depiction as a young, beardless man with *chlamys* and *petasos*. She notes the possibility of the hero being either Theseus or Herakles, but neither is in fact likely: Theseus would be thoroughly out of place in the Thessalian context, and Herakles, though important on Thessalian coins of the time, is likely to have been bearded (as *Stammvater*) and made recognisable through the inclusion of the lion-skin.

[43] Liampi (2015), 11–12.

[44] Kagan (2004) recognised the need to date the sandal issues, not to the years immediately preceding the invasion of Xerxes, as Herrmann (1925) thought, but to the period after it; cf. Liampi (2015), 7, 9–11. The sandal also appears as a motif within larger compositions: see, for example, Lorber (2008), Appendix nos 1, 2, 14–17, 19–22, 24, 26.

depicting a hero or a 'real' participant – may not be wholly separate: perhaps young men taking part in the contest were emulating the skill and courage of noted Thessalian heroes.

2. The first horse

When, around the mid-fifth century, the Thessalians – or some of them – minted a coin type in the name of the whole *ethnos*, bearing the abbreviation ΦΕΤΑ/ΦΕΘΑ, they deployed a highly significant combination of images.[45] The obverse almost always bears a horse leaping from a rock, as in Fig. 11, though occasionally we find a horse's head or the forepart of a horse instead. The reverse usually depicts a kernel of grain, though sometimes this is replaced by a head of Herakles, in lion-skin, or the hero's club. In a rare variation the reverse bears the trident of Poseidon;[46] as noted above, however, tridents do also appear on the bull-wrestling issues of Krannon and Pharkadon. The extent to which the rocks are depicted in the emerging horse motif varies from die to die, but the identification of the animal as a highly specific mythological character in myth is permitted by, once again, a scholion:

> 'Son of Poseidon Petraios': Poseidon is worshipped as Petraios among the Thessalians, because cutting through the Thessalian mountains – I mean Tempe – he made the river flow out through them; previously it had run through the middle of the polis and had destroyed many of the regions. … And others say that Poseidon, asleep upon a certain rock, ejaculated, and the earth received the seed and gave forth the first horse, whom they called Skyphios.
>
> Another: Petraios is an epithet of Poseidon. They say that a contest is conducted for Poseidon Petraios where the first horse sprang out of the rock. And because of this Poseidon is also called Hippios.[47]

[45] Mili (2015), 234–37.

[46] Berlin, Münzkabinett der Staatliche Museen 18213231. This remarkable and rare issue, ca. 470–450 BC, shows the emerging Skyphios on the obverse; the reverse is dominated by a trident-head with the letters ΦΕΘΑ arranged between its prongs. For another, very worn, example see Mack (2021), 122, fig. 86.

[47] Schol. Pind. *Pyth.* 4.138: '<παῖ Ποσειδᾶνος Πετραίου:> Πετραῖος τιμᾶται Ποσειδῶν παρὰ Θεσσαλοῖς, ὅτι διατεμὼν τὰ ὄρη τὰ Θετταλικὰ, φημὶ δὴ τὰ Τέμπη, πεποίηκε δι' αὐτῶν ἐπιτρέχειν τὸν ποταμὸν, πρότερον διὰ μέσης τῆς πόλεως ῥέοντα καὶ πολλὰ τῶν χωρίων διαφθείροντα. … οἱ δὲ, ὅτι ἐπί τινος πέτρας κοιμηθεὶς ἀπεσπερμάτισε, καὶ τὸν θορὸν δεξαμένη ἡ γῆ ἀνέδωκεν ἵππον πρῶτον, ὃν ἐπεκάλεσαν Σκύφιον.
'ἄλλως· ἐπίθετον Ποσειδῶνος ὁ Πετραῖος. φασὶ δὲ καὶ ἀγῶνα διατίθεσθαι τῷ Πετραίῳ Ποσειδῶνι, ὅπου ἀπὸ τῆς πέτρας ἐξεπήδησεν ὁ πρῶτος ἵππος· διὸ καὶ Ἵππιος ὁ Ποσειδῶν.'

Fig. 11. Silver hemidrachm minted in the name of the Thessalians. Obv.: the first horse, Skyphios, emerging from rocks; rev.: kernel of grain. Private coll. Photograph: author's own

To this we may add the *Etymologicum Magnum*, s.v. ἵππιος ὁ Ποσειδῶν: '[He is called Hippios] because it seems that he created the first horse, Sisyphos, in Thessaly, striking the rock with his trident; because of this the sanctuary of Poseidon Petraios was established in Thessaly.'[48] There is little doubt that the coin motif of the horse leaping from rocks must depict this event: the creation of the first horse, Skyphios, by Poseidon, either by a cleaving of the rocks or by their accidental insemination. It is interesting that, while by this time Thessalian elites were emphasising their identity as incomers, Heraklid invaders, a different discourse was chosen for their horses – that of autochthony. The horses of Thessaly were, fittingly, the product of the land itself.[49]

In the fifth century, only one polis mints the Skyphios type in its own name: Methylion, which lay in Thessaliotis; its precise location is not known for certain, but Decourt et al. suggest that it is 'probably to be located at the village of Myrina near Prodomos Karditsis, whence come C3 tiles stamped Μεθυλι/ων.'[50] In the later fourth century it was joined by another polis, Orthe in Thessaliotis, in a highly significant coin issue discussed further below. A few poleis also minted in their own names a type clearly similar to that showing Skyphios, but with a horse forepart or head instead of one unambiguously emerging from rocks. Can we also

[48] 'ὅτι δοκεῖ πρῶτον ἵππον γεγεννηκέναι Σίσυφον ἐν Θεσσαλίᾳ, τῇ τριαίνῃ πέτραν παίσας· ὅθεν ἱερὸν Ποσειδῶνος Πετραίου καθίδρυται ἐν Θεσσαλίᾳ.'

[49] For a comparison with the myth of Erichthonios in Athens see Graninger (2006), 212. The name 'Sisyphos' instead of 'Skyphios' is presumably a simple error.

[50] *IACP* s.v. Methylion (no. 402), 697. For an example of the Skyphios coins of this polis see, for example, *Triton* XV, 204, no. 462.

take the leaping horse forepart, minus rocks, as Skyphios?[51] If so, the die-engravers have done nothing to encourage that interpretation beyond doubt, and the horse forepart motif is known from other regions without, as far as we know, their own version of the Skyphios myth. Moreover, the horse forepart or head tends to deployed on the smaller denominations, and may therefore be seen as primarily driven by the space available (and perhaps a subtle joke about fractions of horses on fractions of drachmas). It is safest, therefore, to say that the Skyphios myth may have encouraged the popularity of the horse forepart type, and that the latter may well have evoked the myth subtly; however, there is a significant difference between this oblique evocation and the absolutely graphic depiction of horse-from-rock that we find on some of the ΦΕΤΑ/ΦΕΘΑ issues.

Who actually produced the ΦΕΤΑ/ΦΕΘΑ coins? Around the mid-fifth century we are unlikely to be looking at the output of a federal mint in the strict sense: as Chapter 5 will make clear, the first clear signs of federal institutions appear in the later fifth century. Theories about the identity of the minting polis or poleis have been various: Larisa, according to Liampi; for Kraay, a group of poleis in southern Thessaly competing with the bull-wrestling type dominated by Larisa.[52] As discussed below, Bouchon makes a strong case for associating the Skyphios myth with Orthe, which placed it on their polis issues in the fourth century; this might support a Thessaliot minting location. However, as has been said, not all the ΦΕΤΑ/ΦΕΘΑ coins depicted Skyphios; some, for example, show the club of Herakles, which, as Liampi observes, could also suggest a connection with Larisa, whose Aleuadai in particular cultivated Heraklid descent. We should, I think, envisage the coins as produced by more than one polis,[53] adjusting the iconography to reflect their own particular self-representation, rather as, in the bull-wrestling series, individual poleis could modify the standard pattern, either with their own stylistic variant or with a place-specific emblem such as the lion-head fountain-spout of Pherai.[54] Taken as a whole, the ΦΕΤΑ/ΦΕΘΑ coins built up, and circulated,

[51] Pendleton (2004), 28.

[52] Liampi (1996), 122–26; Kraay (1976), 116. See also Franke (1970), 92, who argues for a mint union controlled by Pherai and including Methylion and Skotoussa. In this he is tentatively followed by Martin (1985), 38.

[53] The likelihood of different minting poleis is enhanced by the fact that, as Mack observes, coins with the legend ΦΕΤΑ and those with ΦΕΘΑ do not bear identical or wholly interchangeable imagery: it is on the ΦΕΘΑ coins only that Herakles appears, for example. See Mack (2021), 122–24 and 142–43.

[54] Occasionally the lion's head spout appears on the fifth-century coins of Larisa as well, but their frequency and longevity on Pheraian coinage supports the theory of a special relevance in that case, surely connected with the famous Pheraian Hypereia spring. For an example of the Pheraian type see Münzkabinett der Staatliche Museen

a repertoire of images not restricted to a particular sub-region, whatever the circumstances of their production. This accords very strongly with a wider pattern: that the early fifth century was a time when, as we shall now see, various sub-regional religious themes and strands were being brought together to produce a set of myths and cults that embodied the region and the *ethnos* as a whole.

3. The sources and background of the 'Poseidon Bundle'

a) Bringing together east and west Thessaly?

The scholion on Pindar's *Pythian* 4, quoted above, strongly suggests that the emergence of the horse from the rock was the *aition* of the Petraia, at which, as has been said, the bull-wrestling was probably conducted. There was another *aition*, it would seem: Poseidon's cleaving of the rocks at Tempe, to release the waters that had previously made Thessaly an inland sea, revealing its fertile and extensive plains in the process. The antiquity of the tradition of the cleaving of Tempe is secured by its mention in Herodotos.[55] This cluster of myth and cult provides a perfect 'recipe' for Thessaly, its landscape and its natural resources: in one fell swoop, Poseidon generated the horse whose descendants would supply Thessaly's famous cavalry and form such an important part of its pastoral life, and also opened up the plains on which both arable and pastoral agriculture – the core of Thessaly's wealth – would take place. The cult of Poseidon Petraios, therefore, with its attendant mythology, would seem to amount to the creation of Thessaly, in essence, and also the creation of its most externally famous characteristics, since agricultural wealth and fertile land were the basis of its ancient stereotype.[56] However, there are signs that this apparently seamless thematic cluster was actually the result of a certain amount of deliberate synthesis, a process that we could imagine took place in the early fifth century.[57]

zu Berlin, 18213162. The Larisaian cases tend to show a female (the nymph Larisa?) carrying away water from the fountain in a hydria: see, for example, *Triton* XV 87, nos 159 and 160.

[55] Hdt. 7.129, mentioning a *logos* about the event, which surely suggests a longstanding local tradition.

[56] This stereotype will be considered in Chapter 6; key ancient texts, however, include Plato, *Men.* 70a–b and Theokritos, *Idyll* 16.34–39.

[57] Mili (2015, 235) suggests that the early fifth century may have seen a substantial reorganisation of the cult of Poseidon Petraios.

A recent discussion[58] of Poseidon Petraios has made the important point that the scholia on which our understanding unfortunately rests do not, in fact, constitute an undifferentiated whole. In fact, there are two alternative *aitia*: one, the cleaving of Tempe; the other, the creation of Skyphios. One might naturally assume that the two are compatible, for example if the god's trident, striking the rocks to release the waters through Tempe, also allowed Skyphios to leap forth. Certainly this is how the *Etymologicum Magnum* achieves a connection. However, the scholia do not say as much; instead, they seem to take pains to preserve the separation of the two variants ('ἄλλως'). In one, Poseidon creates Tempe and – by extension – the fertile plains; on the other, he inseminates a rock and engenders Skyphios. The linguistic argument for maintaining this distinction is very strong. Bouchon, however, goes further, and suggests that we have here not only mythological alternatives but traces of two different cults. The Poseidon who clove Tempe was, he argues, worshipped under the *epiklesis* Lytaios, connected with the verb λύειν and with the toponym Lytai, of which Stephanos of Byzantium says: 'Lytai: an area of Thessaly, called that because Poseidon *loosed* Tempe and released the flood-water.'[59]

As for the *epiklesis* Petraios, Bouchon argues that this was applied to the god in a different location: south-western Thessaly, where the myth of Skyphios' birth from the rock really belongs, specifically in the territory of the polis of Orthe. This argument is based on the late fourth-century coins of Orthe showing the emergence of Skyphios from the rocks.[60] In this later variant the rocks are quite differently depicted from those in the ΦΕΤΑ/ΦΕΘΑ coins of the fifth century, and the whole composition is surrounded by a wreath; nonetheless, the evocation of the Skyphios myth and the reuse of the earlier imagery is clear. Drawing largely on the fact that early Hellenistic bronze coinage in particular tended to advertise the minting community's own myths and cults, rather than region-wide ones or those of

[58] I am grateful to Richard Bouchon for generously sharing with me the proofs of his forthcoming paper, 'Lieux des cultes et concours de Thessalie en l'honneur de Poséidon', which will be published shortly in C. Morgan and M. Stamatopoulou eds, *Sanctuaries and Cults in Ancient Thessaly*. It has also been extremely helpful to be able to read the contribution, in the same volume, of Bruno Helly, entitled 'Poséidon Kouérios, "celui qui sort du creux du rocher"', and I am grateful to him for generously supplying a draft copy.

[59] 'Λυταί· χωρίον Θεσσαλίας, διὰ τὸ λῦσαι τὰ Τέμπη Ποσειδῶνα καὶ σκεδάσαι τὸ ἀπὸ τοῦ κατακλυσμοῦ ὕδωρ.' See Graninger (2006), 213. Larisa had a district called Lytai within its territory: see Helly and Tziafalias (2013), 205. While this is unlikely to be the same as the one noted by Stephanos, it is interesting to note what might be a sign of interest, in Larisa specifically, in the myth of the cleaving of Tempe.

[60] For a detailed analysis of the known coins of Orthe, the Skyphios type included, see Georgiou (2015).

other communities, Bouchon argues that Orthe was the location of the cult of Poseidon Petraios, whose *aition* was the birth of Skyphios. Not all of his supplementary evidence convinces: for example, the chance find of a bronze horse figurine[61] beside the Sophaditikos river, for example, is hardly enough by itself to prove an aspect of the area's religious character. On balance, however, we should probably accept the coins as depicting a locally situated cult, and consider it likely that Orthe was the site of the cult of Poseidon Petraios and of the Petraia.[62] This would perhaps explain why Orthe retained the Skyphios motif on her coins long after it had disappeared on the coins of the Thessalian *ethnos*: by the late fourth century the cult may have lost its importance as a regional religious institution, but remained significant to the specific polis that possessed it.[63]

A strong early presence of Poseidon in western Thessaly is indicated by the identification of an Archaic sanctuary of the god on the site of ancient Kierion (modern Pyrgos Kieriou).[64] In the Hellenistic period[65] Poseidon had the cult title Kouerios at Kierion. It might be supposed that the god's *epiklesis* is simply toponymic because of the nearby river (the modern Sophaditikos) called, by Strabo, the Kouarios. This would not be without significance, tying the god to another watercourse than the Peneios, albeit one that does eventually join that river. However, there is confusion over whether the river was actually called the Kouarios or the Kouralios, and Helly has argued persuasively for the latter, suggesting that it related to the Greek word *kōrallion* (coral) and referred to the reddish colour of the surrounding rocks. This leaves the *epiklesis* Kouerios to be accounted for, and Helly has put forward a striking suggestion: based chiefly on the argument that the *kou-* element conveys the sense of a hollow space – as in a hollow in a rock, or a cave – he argues that Kouerios is in fact the epithet of Poseidon as the one who leaps from the hollow rock. Presumably in this

61 Now on display in the museum at Karditsa. See Intzesiloglou in *AD* 54 (1999) *Chron.* 421.

62 This theory seems to be further strengthened by the coin type in which the wreath frames not the emerging Skyphios but an upright trident: this seems to evoke a contest (conveyed by the wreath) in honour of Poseidon (represented by the trident). See, for example, *Triton* XV, 218, nos 499.1–4.

63 We have one early fourth-century issue on which the emerging Skyphios accompanies the regional ethnic (here in full, ΠΕΤΘΑΛΟΝ) (*Nomos* 4, 28, no. 108; *Triton* XV, 22, no. 23). This suggests the final phase – or perhaps a brief renaissance – of the cult of Poseidon Petraios as an important emblem of the Thessalian *ethnos*. The location of the mint is of course wholly unknown.

64 Intzesiloglou in AD 36 *Chron.* 252; Karouzou (2017), 349–50.

65 *IG* IX.2 265: third or second century BC, with more precise dating sadly impossible. See Decourt (1995), no. 20, 26–28.

argument the god himself is the original leaper, in horse form, before this nature is transferred to a separate horse of the god's creation.[66]

So we have the myth of Tempe's cleaving, which belongs at or near the mouth of the Peneios in Thessaly's north-eastern corner, and the myth of Skyphios' birth, which probably belongs in the south-west.[67] Did the stitching together of these traditions happen among only the scholars of Alexandria and Byzantium,[68] or does it have its roots in Thessaly in the fifth century BC? I would suggest the latter, based on the synthesis of imagery on the coins themselves. On some of the ΦΕΤΑ/ΦΕΘΑ series, Skyphios is combined with the reverse type of Poseidon's trident, with which Tempe was cleft, subtly juxtaposing the two myths.[69] The other, more common obverse image is the kernel of grain; on the one hand this is plainly a simple advertisement of Thessaly's arable wealth, but grain production was facilitated by the exposure of the plains when Tempe was created. The desire to bring together on the coins the two sides of Thessaly's natural abundance, horses and grain, strongly suggests that the myths of Skyphios and of Tempe were considered as closely aligned.[70]

66 Helly (forthcoming b).

67 A third location is posited by Szidat (2001, 28–43), who argues that the Petraia took place at Armenion, between Pherai and Lake Boibe. However, this theory rests heavily on the idea that the cult was of Mycenaean origin, and therefore requires a location of attested Bronze Age habitation. She argues that, by the fifth century when coins depicted it, the bull-wrestling of the Petraia had declined in importance and devolved upon individual poleis rather than being practised at a single pan-Thessalian location. This is an interesting suggestion, but the lack of supporting evidence from the early period makes it impossible to accept.

68 Actually, a secure *terminus ante quem* is Philostratus, *Imagines* 2.14: the author describes a painting of the cleaving of Tempe by Poseidon, and has Thessalia herself, in anthropomorphic form, emerging from the receding waters on the plains. She holds a horse, and Philostratus explains that this refers to the next stage of the myth: Poseidon will go on to inseminate the Thessalian earth, now that the waters no longer cover it, and thus create the first horse (not named). Note, Szidat argues on the basis of this description that the Artemision god (Athens NM 15161) is Poseidon in the act of cleaving Tempe. The statue itself, however, does nothing to support such a specific identification.

69 See n. 62 above.

70 It is also significant in this regard that Pindar (*Pyth.* 4.138, on which see further below) uses the name Poseidon Petraios of the divine father of Pelias. There is no reason to connect Pelias with Orthe, and so for Pindar the *epiklesis* Petraios must have been considered one of generally Thessalian currency.

b) Poseidon's pre-existing character in Thessalian mythology

The fact that the Thessalians drew together subregional traditions to formulate a new religious identity in the fifth century constitutes a wholly logical development from the early political co-ordination whose first faint signs – the creation and naming of the tetrads – appear at the end of the sixth century. Which happened first is unknowable; certainly the religious developments here proposed cannot have begun with the commencement of coinage, but must have been in train and available for polis authorities and die-cutters to draw on when minting began and suitable emblems were considered. Setting relative chronology aside, however, we may see the creation of the tetrads and the development of Poseidon as the *ethnos*' main deity as highly comparable events, since both aimed to achieve a regional synthesis of previously separate traditions. The other feature of the tetrads, however – specifically their names – which we noted in the previous chapter was their incorporation of very old myths. In the case of Poseidon's cult, therefore, we must ask about parallel incorporation of earlier elements. Are there aspects of the cults and myths that we see attaining importance in the fifth century which may be shown to have drawn on known pre-existing themes?

Poseidon as supplier of horses

The idea of Poseidon as supplier of horses to humans does not begin with the first attestations of the Skyphios myth. In the *Iliad*, Achilles has acquired from his father divine horses given to Peleus by Poseidon himself.[71] For his part, the Pheraian hero Eumelos son of Pheres has horses reared (though not, surely, created) by Apollo in Pieria, and these have pride of place in the little 'catalogue of horses' attached to the end of the Catalogue of Ships in Book 2.[72] The poet takes the trouble to make it clear that Peleus' horses would be the best, except that, since Achilles is out of the fighting, they too are idle, eating and doing no work.

There are some intriguing differences in implications between this material and the Skyphios myth. First, in the *Iliad*, Poseidon does not have

[71] Hom. *Il.* 23.277–78. Cf. Apollod. *Bibl.* 3.13.5: Poseidon as donor of Balios and Xanthos.

[72] Hom. *Il.* 2.760–67:

οὗτοι ἄρ' ἡγεμόνες Δαναῶν καὶ κοίρανοι ἦσαν·
τίς τὰρ τῶν ὄχ' ἄριστος ἔην σύ μοι ἔννεπε Μοῦσα
αὐτῶν ἠδ' ἵππων, οἳ ἅμ' Ἀτρεΐδῃσιν ἕποντο
ἵπποι μὲν μέγ' ἄρισται ἔσαν Φηρητιάδαο,
τὰς Εὔμηλος ἔλαυνε ποδώκεας ὄρνιθας ὣς
ὄτριχας οἰέτεας σταφύλῃ ἐπὶ νῶτον ἐΐσας·
τὰς ἐν Πηρείῃ θρέψ' ἀργυρότοξος Ἀπόλλων
ἄμφω θηλείας, φόβον Ἄρηος φορεούσας.

a monopoly on the horse-providing role; he shares it with Apollo, and it is easy to imagine, in the early Archaic period, the elite families of Pharsalos and Pherai engaging in competitive story-telling about their respective studs, the Pharsalians claiming Poseidon as the ultimate source of their fine horses and the Pheraians issuing the counter-claim that their horses' line went back to the herds of Apollo. Nor is Apollo's own horse-association a trivial one; the god had sacred horse herds at Delphi, where of course horses raced on the Krisaian Plain from 582 BC, when equestrian events were introduced into the programme of the Pythian Games.[73] Moreover, Apollo's considerable pastoral associations come out especially strongly in the context of his spell of servitude at Pherai as punishment for his killing of the Kyklopes; while working as the king's herdsman, he increased the fecundity and number of his cattle.[74] Second, in the *Iliad*, Poseidon does not confer the benefit of horses on the whole of Thessaly, as he does in the Skyphios myth; rather, he distinguishes a particular heroic family through the gift of exceptional horses. This should be seen in the light of other, comparable stories from other parts of the Greek world, in which heroes obtain god-created or god-sent animals. The idea of Archaic elites across Greece competing to display the prowess of their horses and enhancing their credentials through divine connections is a very plausible one, given that these were the very elites who tended to take advantage of the opportunity for further equestrian display at the equestrian *agōnes* of the Crown Games. However, not all these stories work in the same way.

Areion and Pegasos are god-begotten horses that heroes are permitted to ride as a demonstration of their heroic excellence. The horses' father Poseidon[75] does not create them specifically as gifts for mortals; indeed, in the case of Pegasos, Bellerophon has to catch him, and the divine aid he receives is from Athena, not Poseidon. In the case of Areion, one late source has him given as a gift by Poseidon to Kopreus the king of Haliartos.[76] His next owner is Herakles (Iolaos drives him in the *Aspis*),[77] and from Herakles he passes to Adrastos, whom he saves (the only survivor) from the war of the Seven against Thebes.[78] The only other known heroic recipient of a gift of horses from Poseidon is Pelops; however, this story is in a slightly different vein from the other instances discussed. Poseidon gives Pelops horses and a chariot specifically so that he may win the race for Hippodameia's hand

[73] Sacred herds at Delphi: see Howe (2003), 142. The date of the evidence is Hellenistic, but there is no particular reason to detect an innovation.

[74] Apollod. *Bibl.* 3.10.4.

[75] For the myths of their begetting see below.

[76] Schol. Hom. *Il.* 23.346.

[77] [Hes.] *Aspis* 118–21.

[78] *Thebaid* fr. 11 W.

in marriage, rather than the more general gift of horses to enrich a hero's stud.[79] This seems likely to have been an *aition* of the chariot races at the Olympic Games, rather than a part of the self-promotion of a particular horse-breeding family.

Just because the story of god-given horses in Thessaly is attested earlier than the Skyphios myth does not mean, of course, that it existed earlier, or that the two were in any way incompatible. The poet of the *Iliad* may indeed have been aware of a myth that Poseidon created the first horse in Thessaly; in no way does this conflict with a belief that, later, he showed special favour to Peleus with a gift of fine horses. However, the differences between the two traditions reinforce the sense of the special emphasis that the Skyphios myth, placed on the coins minted in the name of all the Thessalians, achieved: to assert the role of the horse as a shared possession of the whole *ethnos* and a shared product of the Thessalian land in its entirety. No doubt specific Thessalian families continued to assert the unique quality of their particular equine strains. But, just as the hero Thessalos became a figurehead for the Thessaloi as a collective body, so the horse became the single most potent emblem of Thessalian regional identity. It was from the beginning, and remained, the dominant motif on the region's coinage, both on the *ethnos* and the polis level.

Poseidon as father of heroes

Although none of our evidence for the Petraia and its related myths pre-dates the fifth century, and although our earliest epigraphic attestations of the god's cult in Thessaly are also fifth century,[80] it should be recalled that, with regard to Thessalian mythology, Poseidon plays an important and early role, as illustrated by the *Ehoiai*. To recapitulate from Chapter 2: the fragments of the poem, read alongside the *Odyssey*'s 'Catalogue of Heroines' and Apollodoros' *Bibliotheke*, allow us to see that Poseidon fathers a heroic line, that of Pelias, the uncle of Jason. He takes the guise of the river Enipeus, with whom Tyro the daughter of the Aiolid Salmoneus has fallen in love, and in that form seduces her; she gives birth to Pelias and Neleus.[81] This places Poseidon in close relation not only to the ruling house of Iolkos but also to that of Pherai, since Aison and Pheres were the half-brothers of Pelias. That said, Aison and Pheres are the offspring of a mortal father, the Aiolid Kretheus, and so not actually descended from the god. But Pelias' own god-descended line is

79 Pind. *Ol.* 1.86–87.

80 An inscription from Vlochos (perhaps Limnaion): see Decourt (1995), 1–2, no. 1; Doulgeri-Intzesiloglou (2000), 16–17 and pls 8–9. One from Soros (Pagasai): *AE* 1932, 27.12.

81 *Ehoiai* frs 30 and 33a MW.

not without consequence: his daughter Alkestis[82] marries Admetos of Pherai, Pheres' son, and their son Eumelos leads a contingent at Troy;[83] Pelias' son Akastos rules Iolkos after the departure of Jason and Medeia, but comes into conflict with Peleus,[84] who sacks Iolkos in revenge.[85]

As we established in Chapter 2, the Aiolid stemma is ill-suited to the expression of *ethnos* identity because, instead of unifying the Thessaloi and distinguishing them from other *ethnē*, it singles out particular heroic lines associated with specific settlements and settlement groups, in particular Iolkos and Pherai. However, it is in the context of this mythology that our first attestation of the name Poseidon Petraios actually occurs: in Pindar's *Pythian* 4, the text that generated the scholion quoted and discussed above. The poem itself, though the source of our insight, tends not to be considered in detail, and yet it has interesting light to shed on how the god might have been thought to relate to the Archaic traditions of Thessalian heroic genealogy. It is especially interesting because Pindar composed *Pythian* 4 in 462 BC, when, according to our numismatic evidence, the cult of Poseidon Petraios was in full operation and of regional importance. While Pindar's own known acquaintance with Thessaly – through the commissioning and composition of *Pythian* 10 – was rather earlier, in the 490s, a reasonable knowledge of Thessalian myth and religion may be supposed; his work as a whole is suffused with Thessalian mythology, especially relating to the Aiakidai, Cheiron and Jason.

Of course, it should be acknowledged at the start that we cannot rule out substantial mythographic invention by Pindar in *Pythian* 4, and that we have to take into account the prime function of the poem, which was not to do with Thessaly; nonetheless, Pindar was obviously drawing strongly on the myths of Iolkos and Pherai included in the *Ehoiai*, and was doing so to ground his patron, King Arkesilas of Kyrene, in mainland Greek myth.

82 Mentioned in the *Ehoiai* (fr. 37 MW), though the fullest exposition of her actions is of course Euripides' play of that name.

83 Hom. *Il.* 2.711–15.

84 The story of Akastos' wife Hippolyte (sometimes called Astydameia) falsely accusing Peleus of rape, and of Akastos' attempt to engineer his death at the hands of centaurs on Pelion, is present in the *Ehoiai* (frs 208 and 209 MW) and is also told by Pindar (*Nem.* 4.54–68; *Nem.* 5.27–35).

85 *Ehoiai* fr. 211 MW. By the fifth century at least there was a tradition that eventually Peleus in his old age was attacked by Akastos or his family: see, for example, Eur. *Tr.* 1123–28, in which Neoptolemos is depicted as sailing to Peleus' aid. On the whole the chief function of this version of the myth seems to be to enhance the credentials of Neoptolemos as the one who restores Aiakid power in Phthia. As has been noted, ancient opinion was divided as to whether Neoptolemos ended up ruling in Phthia himself, an outcome denied by Pindar and in Euripides' *Andromache*, but present in the *Odyssey* (3.186–89; 4.5–9).

Thessaly was especially valuable in this regard because of its equestrian heritage: Arkesilas won the chariot race at Delphi in 462, and *Pythian* 4 is full of references to the hippotrophic excellence of his homeland.[86] As a Greek from the fringes of the Greek world, Arkesilas would have appreciated a connection with the traditional solidity of established myth, even if the precise applicability of the Jason story to his own life is notoriously hard to understand.[87] He claimed descent from one of the Argonauts, Euphamos, and Pindar – perhaps building on Battiad family traditions – elaborates the contribution of that particular character beyond what any Thessalian myth would have contained, but surely grafts this new or enlarged element onto the rootstock of the original Thessalian story. Moreover, Pindar is clearly trying to give the poem a strongly Thessalian flavour in a number of significant ways, including by the mention of Poseidon Petraios. Brief as it is, the reference to the god in that form is not without significance.

At the heart of the poem is Jason's return to Iolkos at the age of twenty to claim the throne from Poseidon's son Pelias. Immediately after his birth his father Aison – deposed but seemingly allowed to live in Iolkos in obscurity – sent him away to be raised by the centaur Cheiron and Cheiron's (fully human-form) wife and daughters on Mount Pelion, to protect him from Pelias should the latter decide that Aison's lineage needed to be curtailed by the removal of his son and heir. This decision would be motivated not only by the natural insecurity of the usurper but by an oracle Pelias had received that he would be killed by a descendant of Aiolos. Aison and Pelias were half-brothers, sharing Tyro as their mother but with different fathers. Pelias' father was Poseidon, while Aison's was Kretheus son of Aiolos; all Aison's descendants, therefore, would constitute a threat. Pindar gives us a vivid account of the young Jason arriving in Iolkos, strong and impressive and dressed in the garb of the Magnesian uplands in which he was reared. He comes steeped in the medicinal teaching of the wise centaur, announcing to Pelias that he will διδασκαλίαν Χείρωνος οἴσειν ('bring the teaching of

86 E.g. εὐΐππου … Κυράνας (line 2); εὐάρματον/πόλιν (lines 7–8). The equestrian focus of the Battiads is further emphasised by the prophecy concerning them spoken by Medea: 'ἀντὶ δελφίνων δ' ἐλαχυπτερύγων ἵππους ἀμείψαντες θοάς,/ἀνία τ' ἀντ' ἐρετμῶν δίφρους τε νωμάσοισιν ἀελλόποδας' ('Instead of short-finned dolphins they will have swift horses, and reins instead of oars, and they will drive storm-footed chariot teams', lines 17–18). This horses-not-ships theme is driven home when the anchor of the Argo is referred to as its bridle, *chalinos*, on line 25.

87 Pindar was undertaking the rather delicate process of praising Arkesilas of Kyrene, while at the same time encouraging him to recall from exile a Kyrenaian noble, Damophilos; Damophilos himself may have claimed descent from Jason, and his situation probably lies behind the sympathetic treatment of the hero and his mission to recover his home. See Robbins (1975), 207; Sigelman (2016), 111–36. On the Kyrenean context: Kurke and Neer (2019), 158–88.

Cheiron', line 102); to Cheiron also he attributes his name, Jason, which literally means 'healer' (119). His youth is signalled by his long hair, a certain rusticity explained by the fact that he has arrived ἀπὸ σταθμῶν (76) and is wearing an animal skin. His arrival further alarms Pelias because he is wearing only one sandal, and the king has been warned by a second oracle to beware of a one-sandalled man;[88] this pronouncement came from Delphi, and amounts to an oblique ratification by Apollo of Jason's right to the Iolkian throne.

So when Jason addresses Pelias as 'son of Poseidon Petraios', using the god's uniquely Thessalian *epiklesis*, a peculiar situation is created: Poseidon is associated with an unjust man whose right to rule is denied by the very gods; Aison's possession of the Iolkian throne, on the other hand, is described as ordained by Zeus (107–08). However, Pelias is not rejected outright; in fact, Jason proposes a rather surprising division:

> I leave you the flocks,
> and the tawny herds of cattle, and all the fields, which you keep,
> having stolen them from my ancestors, feeding fat your wealth;
> and it does not grieve me that they provide for your household beyond all measure.
> But as for the royal sceptre and the throne, in which Aison
> son of Kretheus once sat, and dispensed straight justice for a population of horsemen:
> without any distress between us,
> release these to me, lest some more disturbing evil arise from them.[89]

[88] Jason's monosandalism has encouraged scholars to see the myth as associated with rites of passage (also evoked by the spatial aspects, the hero's descent from the mountain and crossing of the river). See Vidal-Naquet (1986), 69–70, 108–09; Edmunds (1984), 71; Blundell (2019). The fact that Jason wears an animal skin also signals his connection with myths and rituals of maturation: see Buxton (1994), 81–96; for a wider range of initiatory motifs in the myth see Moreau (1994), 117–42. Though there is no evidence of the hero's involvement in Thessalian rites of passage in the fifth century or earlier, the fleece-wearing visitors to Cheiron's cave in the third century may well have been recalling, implicitly, the youth of Jason: see Chapter 7.

[89] Lines 148–55:

> μῆλά τε γάρ τοι ἐγὼ
> καὶ βοῶν ξανθὰς ἀγέλας ἀφίημ' ἀγρούς τε πάντας, τοὺς ἀπούραις
> ἁμετέρων τοκέων νέμεαι, πλοῦτον πιαίνων·
> κοὔ με πονεῖ τεὸν οἶκον ταῦτα πορσύνοντ' ἄγαν·
> ἀλλὰ καὶ σκᾶπτον μόναρχον καὶ θρόνος, ᾧ ποτε Κρηθεΐδας
> ἐγκαθίζων ἱππόταις εὔθυνε λαοῖς δίκας,
> τὰ μὲν ἄνευ ξυνᾶς ἀνίας
> λῦσον ἄμμιν, μή τι νεώτερον ἐξ αὐτῶν ἀνασταίη κακόν.

So the son of Poseidon Petraios is confirmed as possessor of his kingdom's pastoral wealth, but not its rightful ruler. Moreover, Poseidon seems to be directly responsible for this. The poem strongly suggests that Poseidon's intrusion into the stemma by his duplicitous seduction of Tyro has implications for the validity of Pelias' line. Pelias is fated to be killed by one of the Aiolidai; to the sons of Aiolos, we are told, Zeus granted the right to rule in Iolkos. Both these pronouncements imply that Pelias is not an Aiolid proper, whereas Jason is. And yet Pelias is descended from Aiolos: his mother Tyro was the daughter of Salmoneus, son of Aiolos. But for Poseidon's seduction of Tyro, however, his father would have been Kretheus, son of Aiolos – he would have had two Aiolid parents. So far, therefore, from granting distinction and status, having Poseidon as a father seems to have cut Pelias out of legitimacy as king of Iolkos.[90] He is allowed to keep the livestock so suited to his paternal identity, but the sceptre and throne he must, as Jason says, relinquish. There does not, therefore, seem to be, behind the poem, any nod towards a Thessalian elite clan who derived their descent and therefore their prestige from Poseidon; the god is not an effective *Stammvater* in the Thessalian context. It should be noted, however, that the sense of rupture applies also to Jason, as we observed in Chapter 2. Though he does recover his throne, having secured the Golden Fleece (perhaps itself an emblem of kingship), he does not establish a stable and long-lasting dynasty in Iolkos; Medea kills his sons by her, and when the Greeks fight at Troy the Iolkian contingent is under the command of the Pheraian Eumelos, son of Admetos and Pelias' daughter Alkestis.[91] Genuine continuity between myth-time and present time is only really conferred on the poem's honorand, Arkesilas, who claimed descent from the Argonaut Euphamos.

Did Poseidon's ancestral role have any application to the Thessalian ethnos as a whole? There survive Hellenistic attestations of two cult titles, Patroös and Patragenes, which may be relevant in this regard. Patroös is a fairly common *epiklesis* among Greek deities; however, only in Thessaly is it applied to Poseidon, as far as we know. This gives it, potentially, special meaning within the region, but care is needed in its interpretation; in particular, there are no good grounds for reading it as an assertion that Poseidon was somehow the forefather, in the strict sense, of all Thessalians.

[90] Beyond Pindar, is Pelias branded with the mark of Poseidon – and therefore set apart from his half-brother Aison – in the story of his face scarred by a kick from a horse? Hellanikos *FGrH* 4 F 123.

[91] Hom. *Il.* 2.712. Admetos is son of Pheres, the son of Kretheus and Tyro and full brother of Aison. While Iolkos lost its prominence after the end of the Bronze Age, Pherai, of course, continued to flourish, perhaps explaining the vigour of Pheres' line compared with Aison's.

In most known contexts it seems to refer not so much to a general sense of the old, the traditional or the ancestral, but more specifically to the phratries or kinship groups within a polis. The worship of the Patrooi Theoi in Thessaly seems to have a firm connection with kinship groups and the household, as Mili remarks, indicating the desire by certain subsets within a community to claim a privileged relationship with the god.[92] Similarly, the location of the shrine of Herakles Patroös within the palace complex at Aigai in Macedon[93] reflects the ruling family's desire to assert their descent from the god, not shared by the *ethnos* of the Macedonians as a whole. Less exclusive meanings are attested elsewhere, for example in the cult of Apollo Patroös at Athens; Cromey argues that there the *epiklesis* encompassed the broad concepts of age, tradition, genealogical primacy and the deity having played a key role in the early myth-historical formation of the polis.[94] So in Thessaly two possible meanings seem likely: either a claim by a particular clan or other sub-group that the god was their particular ancestor, or else the use of the term to evoke tradition and shared past of a particular community.

The Thessalian inscriptions bearing the *epiklesis* Patroös are from the polis of Pytheion, part of the so-called Perrhaibian Tripolis of Azoros, Doliche and Pytheion.[95] They are all fourth- or third-century BC in date. The chief deity of the polis was Apollo Pythios, but Poseidon Patroös may also have had a temple there, and was plainly of great importance within the polis. As for the *epiklesis* Patragenes, that is attested in both Atrax[96] and Kastri Agias (modern Kerkinion?)[97] in Pelasgiotis in the third century BC. As with Patroös, the identities and motives of the dedicators are unknown. The name is even harder to interpret because of a shortage of comparanda from elsewhere. Did it mean, essentially, the same as Patroös? Plutarch seems to hint that the name had a special relevance in Thessaly, but his explanation of its meaning is entirely unconvincing.[98] Overall, while these Hellenistic inscriptions may attest to a later characterisation of Poseidon as 'ancestral' in the broadest sense – that is, belonging to ancestral time and to collective

92 Mili (2015), 91. For further discussion of individual families having *theoi patrooi* see also Cromey (2006), 58.

93 Kottaridi (2011), 326–31. She argues that the palace, including the Herakles shrine, dates from the time of Philip II rather than the Antigonids.

94 Cromey (2006), 46–48. In fact the sense that he identifies as absent, contrary to the *communis opinio*, is that of Apollo as god of phratries.

95 Rakatsanis and Tziafalias (2004), vol. 2, 82–84, 91–92.

96 *SEG* 45.557.

97 *SEG* 40.472.

98 Plut. *Quaest. Conv.* 8.8. It is reasonably likely that by 'the descendants of Hellen' ('οἱ ἀφ' Ἕλληνος τοῦ παλαιοῦ') he means the Thessalians, but there seems little plausibility in his claim that man, like fish, was originally born ἐκ τῆς ὑγρᾶς, 'from moisture'.

tradition – it is unwise either to confer on them the specific theme of descent or to take them as reflecting the shared origins of the Thessalian *ethnos*. It is plausible to interpret them as highly localised evolutions of the fifth-century portrayal of Poseidon as creator-figure, but not as evidence that he was considered the shared ancestor of the Thessalians.

Poseidon and the manipulation of the Thessalian landscape

The idea of Poseidon as a mover and rearranger of landscapes – chiefly through earthquakes – is absolutely fundamental to his character across Greek religion and mythology, as we shall see below. However, it is interesting to note that his association with earth-moving in Thessaly, prior to the fifth century, takes a rather contrary form. So far from helpfully redistributing the landscape to produce cultivable land, Poseidon in one early tradition is associated with a far more destructive enterprise, as father of Otos and Ephialtes. Though called the sons of the Aiolid Aloeus, Otos and Ephiates were in fact the offspring of Poseidon; their mother Iphimedeia fell in love with Poseidon and contrived to have intercourse with him on the sea-shore.[99] Though not called *Gigantes*, the pair share some qualities with that group: they combine marvellous size[100] with impious intentions towards the gods; in particular, they threaten to storm the divine stronghold by piling Ossa on Olympos and Pelion on Ossa.[101] The sources for their actions are of the earliest, and their transgressions are on the face of it strongly localised within the landscape of eastern Thessaly through their planned moving of mountains. They therefore reinforce Poseidon's early links with Thessaly and its natural form, and their planned earth-moving somewhat resembles their father's seismic associations.

The planned actions of the Aloadai are interesting because they represent, as it were, an 'unmaking' of the Thessalian landscape. The piling up of mountains would represent an intolerable disruption of the natural order, as well as an attack on the gods' domain. In fact, in Apollodoros' account (*Bibl.* 1.7.4), the Aloadai constitute a transgressive inversion of Poseidon's powers: 'τὴν μὲν θάλασσαν χώσαντες τοῖς ὄρεσι ποιήσειν ἔλεγον ἤπειρον, τὴν δὲ γῆν θάλασσαν' ('and they said that by filling the sea with mountains they would turn it into land, and the earth into sea'). Poseidon

99 Apollod. *Bibl.* 1.7.4.

100 ἐννέωροι γὰρ τοί γε καὶ ἐννεαπήχεες ἦσαν/εὖρος, ἀτὰρ μῆκός γε γενέσθην ἐννεόργυιοι ('for when they were nine years old they were at least nine cubits wide; then they became nine fathoms tall'): Hom. *Od.* 11.311–312. Not every source emphasises their size: see Simon (1962) for a probable depiction on an Attic red-figure bell krater, in which they appear merely as youths of normal dimensions.

101 Hom. *Od.* 11.315–16. They also imprison Ares in a bronze jar: Hom. *Il.* 5.385–91.

turned sea to land to create the Thessalian plains; in this version, his sons threaten to undo that crucial act.[102]

Significant as this is within the mythological tradition as a whole, we have no real evidence that the myth had any active currency within Thessalian communities, and it may have been of substantially non-Thessalian devising; Pelion and Ossa were famous far and wide, and their proximity to Olympos may have been sufficient to draw them into the narrative – after all, Thessaly is a reasonable location from which to attack the home of the gods. If anything, active adoption of them as myth-historical figures is clearer in Boiotia, where they were associated with the foundation of Askre and the establishment of the cult of the Muses on Helikon,[103] and where their graves were apparently monuments one could visit.[104] Naxos, scene of their death, had a hero-cult of the pair, epigraphically attested.[105] The Boiotians and the Naxians no doubt thought of the Aloadai as Thessalian, and their impious behaviour is strikingly similar to that of Thessalian Ixion, who tried to rape Hera. But a true grounding in Thessalian myth or cult is impossible to prove. The Thessalians of the fifth century may well, however, have been aware of these myths, and it is interesting that their Poseidon had such a different effect on the landscape from that planned by his disruptive sons. This essential contrast will be revisited later in the chapter when we compare Poseidon's impact on the Thessalian landscape with his operations in other parts of Greece.

c) Poseidon, horses and water beyond Thessaly

Across Greece many communities maintained myths and cults of Poseidon in which water and horses were combined. Exactly why this combination occurs so frequently is unclear, but the pervasiveness of the juxtaposition encourages the belief that in Thessaly the Skyphios myth and the flood-removal myth had some original or at least early interconnection. Comparing these motifs in Thessalian culture with comparable instances in

[102] The Thessalian landscape as a scene of violent disturbance and upheaval, caused by or strongly associated with the involvement of gods and heroes, has a long and interesting *Nachleben*: see Ambühl (2016) for its exploitation in Latin verse.

[103] Paus. 9.29.1 presents some lines from an earlier author, Hegesinos (*FGrH* 331 F 1); how much earlier he was is wholly unknown, but Pausanias' assertion that his work was no longer wholly extant in his day suggests a not inconsiderable gap between them. In the lines of verse, the Aloadai collaborate in the foundation of Askre with another son of Poseidon, Oiokolos (whose mother is the nymph Askre).

[104] Paus. 9.22.6. They are supposed to have died, at Apollo's hand, on Naxos, taking us even further from Thessaly: Pind. *Pyth.* 4.88–89. Alternatively, they are killed by Artemis: Apollod. *Bibl.* 1.7.4. For detailed discussion of the Aloadai and their association with culture, order and the foundation of cities and cults see Hardie (2006).

[105] *IG* XII.5.56.

other parts of Greece is valuable in providing a wider context and opportunities for significant comparison that sheds light on the choices made by the Thessalians in their own characterisation and treatment of the god. There are also some instances of probable influence and interplay between Thessalian and non-Thessalian Poseidon-cults.

Poseidon as creator of horses outside Thessaly

It is easy simply to assume that because horses had great functional importance in Thessalian society this must have been reflected in religious life. We might therefore assume that horse-related Poseidon was part of a deep stratum of symbolism and significance in Thessalian religion.[106] So he may have been, but the evidence is wholly lacking, and the earliest attested cults, especially those of Athena Itonia, Zeus Thaulios and Ennodia, do not show any obvious horse associations.[107] Rather than assuming that the horse had a primordial dominance in Thessalian religion and myth, it is instead important to consider how and why it was chosen to play such an important role when, in the late Archaic or early Classical period, religion was deployed to assert *ethnos* identity with particular determination. Nor does Thessaly, for all its equestrian credentials, display a more pervasive or systematic horse aspect in its religion than do other regions not so famous for the cultivation and use of horses.

Arkadia is an instructive place to start. There, as in Thessaly, Poseidon was the creator of a special horse, Areion, but unlike in Thessaly the horse is the product of a union between two gods, Poseidon and Demeter.[108]

[106] See, for example, Rakatsanis and Tziafalias (1997), 52, stating that Thessalian Poseidon was one of the oldest and most important of the ancient chthonian pantheon.

[107] Ennodia comes to acquire some equine iconography in the fourth century: Pheraian coins of this period sometimes depict her on horseback, and from Krannon comes a famous relief (ca. 360–350 BC) showing her flanked by a horse and a dog (Mili 2015, 153). Her *epiklesis* Stathmia (e.g. in *IG* IX.2 577) may refer to stables, though the word can just as easily suggest byres or small farmsteads. It is true that this is extremely distinctive compared with the images of Artemis and Hekate, and certainly reflects a desire to enhance Ennodia's regional flavour by connecting her with Thessaly's famous animal. However, it does not appear to have been an early and fundamental aspect of her character.

[108] The full account of the mating of the two deities in equine form comes to us from a relatively late source, Pausanias, but Areion appears in the *Iliad* as the miraculously swift, divinely born horse who saves the hero Adrastos. Hom. *Il.* 23.346–347: 'Ἀρίονα δῖον [...] /Ἀδρήστου ταχὺν ἵππον, ὃς ἐκ θεόφιν γένος ἦεν' ('divine Arion, the swift horse of Adrastos, descended from the gods'). It is possible, even probable, that the *Iliad* passage about Areion does not relate in any way to the Thelpousa cult, but the Thelpousans seem to have proudly believed that it did. Paus. 8.25.8: 'ἐπάγονται δὲ ἐξ Ἰλιάδος ἔπη καὶ ἐκ Θηβαΐδος μαρτύριά σφισιν εἶναι τῷ λόγῳ' ('They adduce verses from the *Iliad* and the *Thebaid* as evidence in support of their tradition'). Note that a third source mentioned

Pausanias relates what appear to be very ancient stories from Arkadia,[109] in particular from the cult sites of Demeter Melaina at Phigaleia and Demeter Erinys at Thelpousa, in which the birth of Areion to Poseidon and Demeter Erinys is the cornerstone of the cult's aetiology.[110] In any case, the pairing of Poseidon and Demeter, their horse metamorphosis and their creation of the first horse (in circumstances characterised by Demeter's grief, anger and reluctance) seem to have been at the heart of the cults at Phigalia and Thelpousa, significant sites within the Arkadian religious landscape. The Arkadian polis of Mantineia also had Poseidon Hippios as its poliadic deity, and placed his trident on its coins in the fourth century BC. Pausanias relates a story that may be the *aition* of the Mantineian cult; its position in his text near descriptions of Mantineia and its surroundings suggests this. In the myth, Rhea gives Kronos a foal to swallow rather than the new-born Poseidon, a local variant on the *Theogony*'s account of Rhea's trick.

Although Arkadian horses were admired in antiquity, and although parts of Arkadia were highly suitable for horse-rearing, there is no evidence that the equine aspects of Poseidon and Demeter were strongly connected with the production or use of horses, or with the equestrian craft. A rather different picture in this regard comes from Korinth and from Attica. Korinth claimed not the first horse but certainly a wonder-horse, the winged Pegasos, offspring of Poseidon and Medousa. In some ways this bears close similarity to the Arkadian pairing of Poseidon and Demeter; while metamorphosis seems not to have been involved, Medousa's production of one equine and one human offspring does indicate some latent horse-quality in her,[111] as well as Poseidon's persistent horse-creating properties. As for Pegasos, while his wings single him out (at least from the fifth century BC), he certainly belongs with Areion in the category of god-begotten horses that only heroes

(Paus. 8.25.9–10), the late fifth-century BC poet Antimachos of Kolophon, made Areion leap out of the earth in a way strikingly reminiscent of Skyphios and obviously divergent from the story of his birth from Demeter.

[109] Jost argued that Arkadian horse-Poseidon evolved from a theriomorphic Mycenaean deity, *i-qo*. See Jost (1985), 283–84; however, as Balériaux (2019, 82) observes, Jost herself came to repudiate this theory (Jost 2007, 276–77). This does not, however, militate against the likelihood of the cult's early origins. On Poseidon as a Mycenaean deity, to whose nature the horse was fundamental, see Schachermeyr (1950); see also Palaima (2009) for a local case study of continuity.

[110] Paus. 8.25.5–7.

[111] While the monstrous form she was later given does not include equine elements, the snakes in her hair recall those of the Erinyes – cf. Demeter Erinys at Thelpousa. The word *gorgo* also has horse echoes: see Detienne (1971), 167–68. A small number of her early representations make her mare-headed; it is possible that a misunderstanding of these gave rise to the myth about Pegasos emerging, head first, from her severed neck. See Aston (2011), 101.

can ride. His taming by Bellerophon constitutes an important strand of Korinthian mythology, connected with the cult of Athena Chalinitis, Athena of the Bridle. Bellerophon's lineage places him at the heart of Korinthian myth-history:[112] as Glaukos says in the *Iliad* (using Korinth's alternative name, Ephyra): 'There is a polis, Ephyra, in the heart of horse-nourishing Argos; there Sisyphos lived, who was the wiliest of men – Sisyphos the son of Aiolos. He fathered a son, Glaukos, and Glaukos fathered blameless Bellerophontes.'[113] So we are in Aiolid territory, and Bellerophon is closely related to wily Sisyphos; as Detienne has shown, the capture of Pegasos is a celebration of Korinthian *mētis*, cunning intelligence, and their form of Athena is part of this complex. Athena supplies the golden bit with which Bellerophon is able to tame Pegasos. So this Korinthian myth-cult bundle celebrates not so much the horse as a natural resource but the ability of humanity, with divine aid, to control it.

Pegasos on Korinthian coins also subtly reinforces this theme of control and exploitation. On the silver coins of the earlier fifth century the flying Pegasos is often accompanied by a small *koppa* in the field, normally between his fore- and hindlegs. *Koppa* is not just the symbol for Korinth but was also used as a brand on the polis' most famous strain of racehorses, the *koppatiai*.[114] In the fifth century these became a by-word not only for equine excellence but for the ruinous expenditure involved in keeping racehorses, animals useful only for competitive elite display. Reckoning up his insuperable debts at the beginning of Aristophanes' *Clouds*, old Strepsiades reflects bitterly on his ill-judged purchase of a *koppatias*: 'If only I'd had my eye knocked out with a stone first!'[115] The *koppatias* is not an animal that people of moderate means can afford to own. The wide fame of the type, however, indicates their value as an export, and the coins therefore obliquely associate the magical horse Pegasos and his supernatural speed with the real racehorses of Korinth, which other Greeks might aspire, realistically or otherwise, to buy. Pegasos, therefore, signals not just the domestic value of the Korinthian horse but also its mercantile value, part of the export network of 'wealthy Korinth'.[116]

[112] For a detailed treatment of the role of Bellerophon and Pegasos in the early mythology of Korinth and its heroic dynasty see Ziskowski (2014).

[113] Hom. *Il.* 6.152–55: 'ἔστι πόλις Ἐφύρη μυχῷ Ἄργεος ἱπποβότοιο,/ἔνθα δὲ Σίσυφος ἔσκεν, ὃ κέρδιστος γένετ' ἀνδρῶν,/Σίσυφος Αἰολίδης· ὃ δ' ἄρα Γλαῦκον τέκεθ' υἱόν,/αὐτὰρ Γλαῦκος τίκτεν ἀμύμονα Βελλεροφόντην.'

[114] For discussion of the *koppatias*, including its depiction in Attic vase-painting – a further sign of its prestige – see Fritzilas (2019).

[115] Aristoph. *Clouds* 21–24.

[116] The Korinthians' association with racing was enhanced by the presence of the Isthmian Games in their territory, which included equestrian contests and were in

A similar connection with the theme of horses as the possessions of the elite is to be found at Kolonos, a deme in the northern suburbs of Athens. Kolonos had a cult of Poseidon Hippios and Athena Hippia[117] made famous by Sophokles' *Oidipous at Kolonos*, whose action takes place there. The hero Kolonos was the eponym of the deme, and is called a *hippotēs* in Sophokles' play, enhancing the already strong equestrian flavour of the site. It has been observed by scholars that in the fifth century BC this cult of Poseidon and Athena in their horse-related forms was especially associated with the Athenian cavalry and therefore with those of oligarchic disposition; this is one factor behind the choice of the sanctuary as the meeting place for the setting-up of the Four Hundred, the oligarchic regime instituted in 411 BC.[118] Kolonos also seems to have been the site of a myth so close to that of Skyphios' creation that in fact our sources – all late and cursory – have a tendency to confuse the two: for example, Tzetzes' scholion on Lykophron's *Alexandra* 766 says 'Others say that, having fallen asleep near the rocks of Kolonos in Athens, he ejaculated and the horse Skyphios emerged, who is also called Skironites',[119] seeming to suggest that the myth of Skyphios could be situated at Kolonos rather than in Thessaly, but that there the horse has the name Skironites instead.

An oblique reference to the myth of the horse leaping from the rock may be made in Alkman's *Partheneion*, a text probably of the late seventh century BC. The beauty of Hagesichora is illustrated in the poem by an equine analogy: among the other dancers she seems like an exceptional, prize-winning racehorse suddenly loosed among other herd animals. This wonderful horse is τῶν ὑποπετριδίων ὀνείρων, of, or out of, 'under-rock dreams'.[120] Through a complex series of comparisons, pursuing the theme of horses, sleep and sexual release in Greek poetry, Nagy explains the mysterious phrase as relating subtly to the myth of Poseidon's creation of the horse through his insemination of the rock.[121] This would certainly serve the purposes of the poem, creating an implicit contrast between normal horses (the other girls) and a god-made miracle, and combining

Poseidon's honour. Very little Thessalian participation in the Isthmia is attested, so this is unlikely to have been a significant channel through which horse-related mythological and cultic influence could have passed between the two regions.

117 Paus. 1.30.4.

118 Kolonos and oligarchy: Siewert (1979). In Aristophanes' *Knights* the cavalrymen have a tendency to evoke Poseidon in his horse-related form.

119 'ἄλλοι δέ φασιν ὅτι περὶ τοὺς πέτρους τοῦ ἐν Ἀθήναις Κολωνοῦ καθευδήσας ἀπεσπέρμηνε καὶ ἵππος Σκύφιος ἐξῆλθεν, ὁ καὶ Σκιρωνίτης λεγόμενος.' The name Skironites may be connected with the worship of Poseidon at Skiron in Attica, in the sanctuary of Demeter and Persephone. Paus. 1.37.2.

120 Alkman fr. 1 *PMG*, lines 45–49.

121 Nagy (1990), 223–62.

that with the suggestion of erotic desire and its potential release. For our discussion the striking element is the date (seventh century): no other source allows us to trace the myth so early. What it cannot do, however, is to link it, at that date, to Attica, or to Thessaly, or to both.

With the sources as they are, then, it is impossible to know where the myth began, or even whether its transfer from Thessaly to Athens or the other way around was something conducted by the community in question, or whether it is in fact just the result of confusion and conflation among scholiasts. What we appear to have in Thessaly and lack in Athens is any corroboration of the myth on coinage. Among the issues of the so-called Athenian Wappenmünzen[122] is one type showing the forepart of a leaping horse, bridled.[123] The posture is rather like that of Skyphios on Thessalian coinage, but unlike the Thessalian coins the Athenian ones do nothing to make it clear to the viewer that we are seeing a horse emerging from rock, rather than just a horse whose forepart only is in the frame. Moreover, leaping horse protomes are known from other areas in the same period, areas without – as far as we know – any relevant myths.[124] Without further evidence it seems most probable that the Athenians at some stage borrowed the myth from Thessaly in a bid to situate Kolonos, the centre of their Poseidon/horse connection, as the location of the first ever horse, not Tempe. One could speculate that, as their own cavalry increased in number and quality in the fifth century and their dependence on allied Thessalian cavalry decreased, they wished to signal their own equestrian credentials through such an act of competitive myth-appropriation. However, that must remain speculation.

That Thessalian Poseidon was associated with the excellence of the region's horses and horsemanship is clear from the bull-wrestling contest depicted on its coins, often with Poseidon's trident included to emphasise the connection. This is a clear similarity with the Attic and Korinthian cases, in which social groups for whom horses were an important signifier of status, whether in the cavalry or in racing, would have found in Poseidon's myths and cult an important reflection of their activities. The element of

122 Kroll (1981); Kroll and Waggoner (1984), 330–33 (on the dating of the Wappenmünzen). See also Van der Vin (2000).

123 Mack (2021), 114–16 suggests that in fact, if we read the horse on the Athenian coins as emerging from the ground, this may be evidence of competition between Athens and Thessaly – or between the Peisistratids and the Aleuadai? – to claim the first horse. She acknowledges, however, that reading the leaping horse as Skyphios is as speculative in Athens as it is in Thessaly.

124 Examples are Aiolian Kyme and the coins of Alexandros I of Macedon. Mack (2021, 115) plausibly suggests lines of stylistic influence between these coins and the horse-foreparts of Thessaly and Athens, but neither Macedon nor Kyme is known to have cultivated the myth of the first horse.

equestrian control found in Korinth in the cult of Athena Chalinitis may possibly have a Thessalian counterpart. There is a very small number of those coins on which the emerging horse appears to come from the rock ready-bridled, rather than wholly raw and unconstrained as most are. As Mack observes,[125] this departs from a strong ingredient in other Greek horse-myths, in which Poseidon creates the horse as a dangerously powerful natural force and then Athena employs *technē* (the bridle, the bit) to ensure its mastery and its usefulness to mankind. There is no sign that Athena had this role in Thessalian mythology; instead, the motif of bridled Skyphios suggests that Poseidon himself takes on both roles, producing the animal and ensuring it can be controlled. This is strengthened if we take the cult title Impsios as indicating that Poseidon was considered the yoker of horses, but that interpretation is not without difficulties.[126]

However, there is one substantial difference: in Thessaly, the extent to which Poseidon stood for social exclusivity, as he did in Korinth and Athens, is doubtful. Skyphios was the ancestor of all horses, not just an especially famous strain; and unlike in Athens, where the cavalry:hoplite ratio in armies taking the field tended to be roughly 1:10, in Thessaly it was typically 1:2. Horses in Thessaly had a socioeconomic range far wider than in most parts of Greece, despite the narrow oligarchies that dominated its political life, and the creation of the first horse may be seen as expressing an identity shared by the region as a whole, not singling out a small sub-section.

Poseidon and water management

In Korinth, Attica and elsewhere, the Poseidon–horse combination has a third element: the production of water sources. A stamp of Pegasos' hoof created the spring Hippokrene on Helikon, and another at Troizen; in Korinth itself Pausanias describes a fountain whose water gushed from the hoof of a sculpture of Pegasos, presumably a representation of the horse stamping and releasing spring waters.[127] In Athens, famously, the spring offered by Poseidon was rejected in favour of Athena's olive tree[128]

125 Mack (2021), 127–28.

126 The *epiklesis* is attested only in the Hellenistic period. Four dedications survive, all from the *chōra* of Larisa: *SEG* 42.511–14; Graninger (2006), 208–10. The connection with yoking is supplied by two entries of Hesychios' *Lexicon*: '<ἵμψας>· ζεύξας. Θετταλοί' and '<Ἴμψιος>· Ποσειδῶν ὁ ζύγιος' (see Kontogiannis 1992). However, the reference might just as well be to bulls. Kravaritou (2018, 12–13) suggests instead a connection to kourotrophy via the association between yoking and wedlock.

127 Helikon: Paus. 9.31.3; cf. Strabo 8.6.21. Troizen: Paus. 2.31.9. The Korinthian fountain: Paus. 2.3.5.

128 The earliest surviving mention of the contest between Poseidon and Athena at Athens is Hdt. 8.55. Typically, for a fuller account of the incident we are reliant on Apollodoros (*Bibl.* 3.14.1).

(though, interestingly, late sources make him offer a horse instead, perhaps a conflation with his Kolonos persona).[129] The rejection of Poseidon's spring is perhaps unsurprising since it was a spring of salt water, but in fact this incident is part of a wider motif in which the god loses a contest with another deity for prime position within a community. The anger which Poseidon typically feels upon losing these contests is connected, in the stories, with another of his key attributes: an association with water in its destructive rather than productive form. The *aition* of the cult of Poseidon Proklystios at Argos in the Peloponnese is a good example:

> There is there a sanctuary of Poseidon with the *epiklesis* Proklystios. For they say that Poseidon flooded much of the land, because Inachos and his fellow arbitrators decided that the land belonged to Hera rather than to him. It was Hera, indeed, who persuaded Poseidon to let the sea ebb back; and the Argives created the sanctuary of Poseidon Proklystios at the spot where the tide receded.[130]

Floodwaters caused (or simply not averted) by Poseidon, whether or not specifically of brine, are especially damaging or inconvenient for agriculture. Another Peloponnesian instance illustrates this. In the *chōra* of Matineia there was a plain called the Argon Pedion given to inundation by rainwater coming off the adjoining mountains; only a χάσμα γῆς, says Pausanias, prevents it from becoming a lake. The water, however, drains into the chasm, but then rises to the surface again at Genethlion on the shore of the Argolid, to form a miraculous flow of fresh water, called Dine, amid the brine of the sea. According to Pausanias, 'τὸ δὲ ἀρχαῖον καὶ καθίεσαν ἐς τὴν Δίνην τῷ Ποσειδῶνι ἵππους οἱ Ἀργεῖοι κεκοσμημένους χαλινοῖς' – 'In the old days the Argives would throw horses adorned

[129] Verg. *Georg.* 1.12–14 makes Poseidon strike the akropolis rock and bring forth a horse rather than a spring. The relative antiquity of this variant is unknowable, but it never achieved the currency among the Athenians that the spring version did. The horse version does not receive unambiguous corroboration from visual sources, either: a fourth-century Attic hydria showing the contest of Athena and Poseidon has the latter accompanied by a leaping horse, but it is not clear that it has emerged from the ground; all three deities shown (the third being Dionysos) are accompanied by their signature animals, Athena with snake and Dionysos with panther (St. Petersburg Hermitage, KAB6A).

[130] Paus. 2.22.4: 'ἐνταῦθα Ποσειδῶνός ἐστιν ἱερὸν ἐπίκλησιν Προσκλυστίου· τῆς γὰρ χώρας τὸν Ποσειδῶνά φασιν ἐπικλύσαι τὴν πολλήν, ὅτι Ἥρας εἶναι καὶ οὐκ αὐτοῦ τὴν γῆν Ἴναχος καὶ οἱ συνδικάσαντες ἔγνωσαν. Ἥρα μὲν δὴ παρὰ Ποσειδῶνος εὕρετο ἀπελθεῖν ὀπίσω τὴν θάλασσαν· Ἀργεῖοι δέ, ὅθεν τὸ κῦμα ἀνεχώρησεν, ἱερὸν Ποσειδῶνι ἐποίησαν Προσκλυστίῳ.' Likewise, baulked of possession of Athens, Poseidon floods the Thriasian Plain in Attika: Apollod. *Bibl.* 3.14.1.

with bridles into Dine for Poseidon.'[131] It seems likely that they did so to ensure the continued functioning of the crucial outlet, without which the adjoining plain would flood. Pausanias explains that the name Argos means 'fallow', 'untilled': 'Ἀργὸν καλούμενον, καθάπερ γε καὶ ἔστι' ('Called Argon, and indeed, *argon* it is!)'.[132] He goes on to say that rainwater coming down into the plains from the hills makes it too marshy for cultivation, but that far worse flooding would occur without the *chasma* leading out to Dine.[133]

Arkadia is especially noted for the strong hydrological aspect of its cults,[134] and Poseidon there sits alongside other divinities who, if suitably propitiated, help ward off the damaging effects of floodwater. A key example is Herakles. To him was attributed the creation of the massive drainage channel through the plain of Pheneos,[135] as well as the removal of the Stymphalian Birds, the avian embodiment of agriculture-harming inundations.[136] So it is especially interesting to find Diodoros attributing to Herakles the cleaving of Tempe also: 'Around the so-called Tempe the plain-land was marshy over a large area; he dug through the bordering area, and carrying off through the channel all the water of the marsh, he brought to light the plains which are in Thessaly along the Peneios river.'[137] Unlike Poseidon, Herakles has to toil, digging (though with hero-strength) rather than deploying a casual blow of the trident. In the Peloponnese his water engineering is clearly a way of accounting for the remains of Mycenaean drainage systems,[138] but that does not apply at Tempe; not only

[131] Paus. 8.7.2. For another Arkadian stream disappearing underground and re-emerging in the Argolid see 8.22.3 (Stymphalos). Sacrifice of living horses to the river-god Skamandros: Hom. *Il.* 21.130–31.

[132] In fact the meanings of *argos* are various. 'Fallow' and 'fruitless' are among them, but so are 'shining' and 'quick', which could apply to the water lying on the plain or rushing down the chasm. However, Pausanias' belief in the 'untilled' meaning probably derives from local tradition. Strabo thought *argos* essentially meant 'plain': Strabo 8.6.9.

[133] Mylonopoulos (2003), 110, noting the significance of the fact that a sanctuary of Poseidon stands at each end of the *chasma* – Poseidon Hippios on the Maintineian side, Poseidon Genesios in the Argolid. On the important cult of Poseidon Hippios at Mantineia see further Mylonopoulos (2003), 107–11.

[134] Balériaux (2019).

[135] Paus. 8.14.3.

[136] Paus. 8.22.3–9.

[137] Diod. 4.18.6: 'περὶ μὲν γὰρ τὰ καλούμενα Τέμπη τῆς πεδιάδος χώρας ἐπὶ πολὺν τόπον λιμναζούσης διέσκαψε τὸν συνεχῆ τόπον, καὶ κατὰ τῆς διώρυχος δεξάμενος ἅπαν τὸ κατὰ τὴν λίμνην ὕδωρ ἐποίησε τὰ πεδία φανῆναι τὰ κατὰ τὴν Θετταλίαν παρὰ τὸν Πηνειὸν ποταμόν.' It is interesting to note that immediately after this passage Herakles does the reverse at Boiotian Orchomenos, flooding the Minyan city there under (what would become) Lake Kopais.

[138] On Mycenaean water management in Arkadia and Boiotia see Knauss (1991); further

is Mycenaean engineering not in evidence, but in fact seismic activity – the domain of Poseidon, not Herakles – was genuinely an important factor behind the formation of the gorge; before this Thessaly was in reality substantially underwater.[139] It therefore seems highly likely that Peloponnesian myths of Herakles the engineer were extended to Thessaly (by Diodoros, his sources, or local communities in Thessaly, we cannot say), though the existing association between Thessaly and Herakles would have encouraged this development.

Throughout Greece, Poseidon above all other deities was used as a way of reflecting on a community's relationship with the natural space it occupied, in particular its water sources;[140] however, in each specific location myth and cult were shaped by the conditions – cultural, geographical – particular to that place. At least in the form in which they are attested in surviving sources, the actions of Thessalian Poseidon are strikingly different from the other versions discussed here. For a start he has no direct and explicit association with the sea.[141] His relationship to rivers has been noted; indeed, as Mili observes,[142] his creation of the plains entailed the creation of those rivers too. By the second century BC at any rate, he could be the recipient of the kind of hair-offering Achilles famously vowed to the Spercheios, at least for two young men of Phthiotic Thebes.[143] We find him in Larisa bearing the *epiklesis* Kranaios – 'of the spring'. An early fourth-century stele bearing the words ΠΟΤΕΙΔΩΝΙ ΚΡΑΝΑΙΩΙ ΠΥΛΑΙΩΙ was found *in situ* in the north-eastern part of modern Larisa, attesting to the cult. Pylaios presumably refers to one of the gates of the city, and Kranaios to a specific spring. There may be a connection to the nymph holding a hydria

on the connection with the Herakles myths see Knauss (1990). On Mycenaean water management in Boiotia see also Kalcyk and Weichenberger (1990). Indeed, the geology of both regions is genuinely conducive to flooding and to the phenomenon of rivers and streams passing underground and sometimes re-emerging.

139 Caputo and Helly (2000), 562.

140 This aspect of Poseidon in the Peloponnese: Mylonopoulos (2003), 397–98. For a discussion of Poseidon and landscape see de Polignac (2017a, b). The seismic activity with which Poseidon was also widely associated was indeed a major factor behind the formation of the Thessalian landscape and would have remained a periodic ingredient in the lives of its inhabitants. See Caputo and Helly (2000) and (2005), 199–211.

141 Votive dolphins from Prinos in western Thessaly are a rare marine element: Mili (2015), 42, n. 130.

142 Mili (2015), 42, n. 132.

143 See the famous stele bearing relief carvings of plaits of hair and the words Φιλόμβροτος Ἀφθόνητος Δεινομάχου Ποσειδῶν[ι] ('Philombrotos and Aphthonetos, sons of Deinomachos, [dedicated this] to Poseidon'. Presumably the setting up of the stele commemorated the act of hair dedication itself. The inscription: *IG* IX.2 146. The object as a whole: London BM 1839,0806.4. Discussion in Kravaritou (2018), 388–89.

beside a gushing fountain on fifth-century Larisaian coins,[144] especially if that nymph is Larisa, sometimes described as a lover of Poseidon.[145]

Not only is Thessalian Poseidon the god of helpful fresh water, he does not cause damaging inundation, or threaten to do so; instead, he removes waters that had previously always flooded the Thessalian basin. He is the solution, not the problem.[146] This is not to say that the landscape of Thessaly was in reality free from the baneful effects of unwanted water; flooding was a periodic problem there as in other parts of Greece.[147] No other deity has to intercede with him on behalf of mankind; there is no story of his anger. He does not have to compete for possession of Thessaly. He does not share the creation of Skyphios with a consort, unless one counts the inseminated Earth. He is the unchallenged creator and benefactor of the Thessalian land. That is not to say, however, that either he or his myths stand in isolation from parallel traditions, as will be discussed when we turn to focus specifically on the significance of Tempe as a complex mythological and religious space.

4. The wider importance of Tempe

So far this chapter has worked to situate the role of Poseidon within fifth-century Thessalian religion and mythology against a wider backdrop of his place in the region and beyond. Overall, while the god in his fifth-century forms does not emerge from nothing, we can identify some aspects of selection and adaptation by which he was fitted to the role of the chief deity of the Thessalian *ethnos*, and some ways in which the resulting cluster of ritual and mythology would have chimed with wider patterns in the god's character across Greece. One central theme is the way in which religion emphasised the importance of landscape in regional identity; cults celebrating the birth of Skyphios and the cleaving of Tempe celebrated, in effect, the creation of Thessaly as a geographical entity, just as the myth of

144 See, for example, *Nomos* 4, 60, no. 1112, dated to ca. 460–440 BC.

145 Larisa as lover of Poseidon: Dion. Hal. *Ant. Rom.* 1.17.3; for the possibility that this goes back to Hellanikos see Fowler (2013), 243–44.

146 Mili (2015), 238.

147 The Peneios was of fundamental importance in ensuring the drainage and control of water levels; however, in times of flood its waters could – according to travellers in the eighteenth and nineteenth centuries AD – flow into the Nessonis and Boibe lakes instead of debouching through Tempe. See Caputo et al. (1994), 224; Garnsey et al. (1984), 30–33. This tendency is mentioned by Strabo (9.5.19), who says that the waters pouring into Nessonis reduced Larisa's cultivable land; the Larisaians created embankments to prevent the inundation, but we cannot know the date of these works. Reference to the same project at Larisa is found in Pliny, *NH* 17.3, and Theophr. *CP* 5.14.2.

Fig. 12. The Peneios in the Tempe gorge. Photograph: author's own

the arriving Thessalids, or Thessaloi, came to represent the formation of the Thessalian *ethnos* as a human community. However, the religious significance of Tempe was not in fact limited to its connection with Poseidon, and in this final chapter section we turn to consider the implications of the emphasis on Tempe for our understanding of Thessaly as a symbolic and cultic space. See Fig. 12 for the gorge today.

a) Tempe and Deukalion's flood: markers of early myth-time

As we have seen, Poseidon was persistently associated with floods, their creation (outside Thessaly) and their dispersal. The theme of subsiding floodwaters has two major purposes in Greek myth. The first is to evoke and celebrate the fertility of a land by contemplating its opposite: floods ruin agriculture, and their removal facilitates it.[148] The second is to shape myth-time, to signal some kind of fresh start, since floods can remove

[148] The importance of the flood as a mythological motif and temporal marker may ultimately draw on the reality of flooding in Greece, not only localised seasonal inundations but also perhaps, as Knauss (1987) has argued, the meteorological conditions following the eruption on Thera ca. 1529 BC: ash clouds triggered exceptional rainfall while at the same time seismic activity caused the blocking of natural drainage channels

pre-existing populations and structures, and by disappearing leave the stage clear for a new set of actors. Two floods affected Thessaly: the original one removed by Poseidon, and the later one that Deukalion and Pyrrha survived (probably included in the *Ehoiai*, and mentioned in Chapter 2 above). Both episodes contain the two key themes, fertility and a new start, though the fertility theme is far more strongly represented in Poseidon's flood than in Deukalion's. Deukalion's flood works chiefly to bracket two successive ages and signal the start of the race of the Hellenes; Poseidon's draining of the water from the fields of Thessaly also constitutes a beginning, but places the emphasis not on a new population but on the creation – or rather the uncovering – of the natural landscape. Poseidon's flood comes first, in myth-time; Deukalion's threatens temporarily to undo the god's work.

Another important distinction concerns the geographical scope of each event. Poseidon's action is specific to Thessaly, whereas Deukalion's flood links Thessaly with adjoining regions and *ethnē*, as well as with the subsequently expanding network of the Hellenes. It is important to remember that few mythological inundations covered all of Greece, let alone the world; their range and application were more local. For example, a flood forced the hero Dardanos to move from Samothrace to Mount Ida, whence his grandson Tros descended to the plain below, braving the possibility of further inundations, and founded Troy.[149] Even Deukalion's flood, which seems to have derived from Near Eastern traditions of a worldwide deluge,[150] was made to accord with a large number of divergent local traditions, as Fowler describes.[151] As Chapter 2 made clear, though the myth of Hellen, son of Deukalion, was an important stage in the development of panhellenic thinking, the flood itself – even if it was included in the *Ehoiai*, which is not certain – was almost never thought of as obliterating humanity throughout Greece and producing a wholly clean slate; instead, its range was normally situated in the heartland of the original Hellenes, around the Spercheios valley and southern Thessaly, with Lokris also playing an especially important role.[152] Deukalion and Pyrrha made landfall either on Parnassos or on Othrys, signalling the variable location of the story's core.[153] The Tempe myth therefore shifted the geographical focus

in the karst systems of central Greece. Knauss situates this event around Lykoreia in the Parnassos area, a place associated with Deukalion's flood (e.g. Paus. 10.6.2).

149 Plato, *Laws* 3.702a; Strabo 13.1.25.

150 West (1997), 489–93 (though note that West does not believe the flood was included in the *Ehoiai*).

151 Fowler (2013), 114–17.

152 Lokris is peopled by the Leleges created when Deukalion and Pyrrha cast stones after the flood abates: Pind. *Ol.* 9.40–46; [Hes.] *Ehoiai* fr. 234 MW. For the geographically scattered traditions of the Leleges in Greek mythology see Descat (2001).

153 Parnassos: earliest in Pindar (*loc. cit.*); also Apollod. *Bibl.* 1.7.2. Othrys: Hellanikos

away from the heartland of the Hellenes and towards the northern edge of Hellas. Whereas Deukalion's flood, in one account, drained away from Thessaly southward,[154] the cleaving of Tempe released the trapped waters of that earlier inundation out of the north-eastern corner of the region. This difference has significant implications for how we see Thessaly's mythological orientation and character.

b) Tempe and Pelion: variations on the theme of primordial fertility

Poseidon does not have – and was never intended to have – a monopoly on Thessalian fertility; nor is Tempe the sole locus for that fertility's source and creation. In this section we shall examine a different – indeed strongly divergent – version of the Tempe myth, and a wholly different type of natural abundance. The former obliges us to confront the abiding puzzle of Baton of Sinope and the Thessalian Peloria.[155]

FGrH 4 F 117a. That Thessaly did take an active part, at some date, in claiming a share of the tradition is reflected in the fact that specific Thessalian communities were among several in Greece who displayed supposed tombs of Deukalion and Pyrrha, and place-names evoking them, in their territory: see Strabo 9.5.6. 'οἱ δ' ὕστερον τὴν Ἑλλάδα οἱ μὲν εἰπόντες χώραν διατετάσθαι φασὶν εἰς τὰς Θήβας τὰς Φθιώτιδας ἀπὸ Παλαιφαρσάλου [...] οἱ δ' εἰπόντες πόλιν Φαρσάλιοι μὲν δεικνύουσιν ἀπὸ ἑξήκοντα σταδίων τῆς ἑαυτῶν πόλεως κατεσκαμμένην πόλιν ἣν πεπιστεύκασιν εἶναι τὴν Ἑλλάδα καὶ δύο κρήνας πλησίον Μεσσηίδα καὶ Ὑπέρειαν, Μελιταιεῖς δ' ἄπωθεν ἑαυτῶν ὅσον δέκα σταδίους οἰκεῖσθαι τὴν Ἑλλάδα πέραν τοῦ Ἐνιπέως, ἡνίκα ἡ ἑαυτῶν πόλις Πύρρα ὠνομάζετο, ἐκ δὲ τῆς Ἑλλάδος ἐν ταπεινῷ χωρίῳ κειμένης εἰς τὴν ἑαυτῶν μετοικῆσαι τοὺς Ἕλληνας· μαρτύριον δ' εἶναι τὸν ἐν τῇ ἀγορᾷ τῇ σφετέρᾳ τάφον τοῦ Ἕλληνος τοῦ Δευκαλίωνος υἱοῦ καὶ Πύρρας. ἱστορεῖται γὰρ ὁ Δευκαλίων τῆς Φθιώτιδος ἄρξαι καὶ ἁπλῶς τῆς Θετταλίας.' ('As for later authorities, some, speaking of Hellas as a country, say that it stretches from Palaiopharsalos to Phthiotic Thebes. [...] As for those, however, who speak of Hellas as a city, the Pharsalians point out at a distance of sixty stadia from their own city a city in ruins which they believe to be Hellas, and also two springs near it, Messeïs and Hypereia, whereas the Melitaians say that Hellas was situated about ten stadia distant from themselves on the other side of the Enipeus, at the time when their own city was named Pyrrha, and that it was from Hellas, which was situated in a low-lying district, that the Hellenes migrated to their own city; and they cite as bearing witness to this the tomb of Hellen, son of Deukalion and Pyrrha, situated in their marketplace. For it is related that Deukalion ruled over Phthia, and, to put it simply, over Thessaly' (trans. Jones, adapted).

[154] Apollod. *Bibl.* 1.7.2: the flood is ended when the mountains of Thessaly part and release the waters over the Isthmos and the Peloponnese; these must therefore have been the region's southern mountains. Compare, however, Nonn. *Dion.* 6.373–76, in which the waters of Deukalion's flood are released by Poseidon cleaving a Thessalian mountain, an apparent conflation of the two events. However, the fact that the mountain in question is called μεσόμφαλον may possibly, through an oblique reference to Delphi, suggest the same location as in Apollodoros' account, to the south of Thessaly.

[155] Baton probably wrote in the later third or earlier second century BC: see Christesen

> At a public sacrifice which was being held by the Pelasgians, a certain man, whose name was Peloros, brought the news to Pelasgos that since the mountains called Tempe, with great earthquakes happening in Haimonia, were shattered and that since the water of the lake, having rushed through the aperture, was pouring into the stream of the Peneios, the entire territory, which had previously been marshy, was now bared to view and, as the waters dried up, plains wondrous in extent and beauty were appearing. Upon hearing (this news), Pelasgos set before Peloros a table which he himself had lavishly equipped. And the rest of the people showing kindness, each one brought what was best from among his possessions and set it on the table for the messenger, and Pelasgos himself devotedly waited on him, and among all the rest the distinguished men lent a hand, in whatever manner the opportunity to do so fell to each one of them.[156]

The passage goes on to explain that the myth of Pelasgos and Peloros was the *aition* of a festival considered a Greek version of the Roman Saturnalia, in which masters feasted their slaves. Certain aspects of this account are plainly problematic; in particular, the role-reversal ritual is described as the 'greatest festival' of the Thessalians 'ἔτι καὶ νῦν', and yet there is no other reliable evidence for its existence.[157] The fact that the god at the centre of the festival is Zeus is also puzzling. Poseidon's suitability is manifest, at least

(2011). His known works include treatises on tyrants, on Persian matters and on the poet Ion, as well as Attic history. For a discussion of Baton and of the Peloria against the backdrop of Hellenistic Thessaly's social and environmental changes see Graninger (2022), who makes a sound case for its essential veracity, despite problematic details.

156 Baton, *FGrH* 268 F5 (from his work *On Thessaly and Haimonia*): 'θυσίας κοινῆς τοῖς Πελασγοῖς γινομένης ἀπαγγεῖλαί τινα τῶι Πελασγῶι ἄνδρα, ὧι ὄνομα ἦν Πέλωρος, διότι ἐν τῆι Αἱμονίαι σεισμῶν μεγάλων γενομένων ῥαγείη τὰ Τέμπη ὄρη ὀνομαζόμενα καὶ διότι διὰ τοῦ διαστήματος ὁρμῆσαν τὸ τῆς λίμνης ὕδωρ ἐμβάλλοι εἰς τὸ τοῦ Πηνείου ῥεῖθρον, καὶ τὴν πρότερον λιμνάζουσαν χώραν ἅπασαν γεγυμνῶσθαι, καὶ ἀναξηραινομένων τῶν ὑδάτων πεδία θαυμαστὰ τῶι μεγέθει καὶ τῶι κάλλει ἀναφαίνεσθαι. ἀκούσαντα οὖν τὸν Πελασγὸν τὴν τράπεζαν ἀφθόνως αὐτῶι κεκοσμημένην τῶι Πελώρωι παραθεῖναι, καὶ τοὺς ἄλλους δὲ φιλοφρονουμένους ἕκαστον φέρειν ὅ τι ἔχοι παρ' αὑτῶι βέλτιστον καὶ παρατιθέναι ἐπὶ τὴν τράπεζαν τῶι ἀπαγγείλαντι, καὶ αὐτὸν τὸν Πελασγὸν προθύμως διακονεῖν καὶ τῶν ἄλλων τοὺς ἐν ἀξιώματι ὄντας ὑπηρετεῖν, καθότι ἑκάστωι ὁ καιρὸς παρέπιπτεν' (trans. Christesen).

157 Unreliable evidence: Arvanitopoulos' reconstruction of [τὰ Πελώρι]α in a fourth-century inscription (*Polemon* 1, 1929, 221, 426a); attempts to locate Zeus Peloris [*sic*] on the coins of Perrhaibian Phalanna in Moustaka (1983), 16; cf. Rakatsanis and Tziafalias (2004), vol. 2, 63. On the latter, almost all of the coins pressed into service as evidence have, in fact, the legend ΛΟΡΕΣ; though this has been taken as an abbreviated form of ΠΕΛΟΡΕΣ (in itself a difficult form of the name to explain), such a reading is highly questionable, not least because on the coins an abbreviation is not always spatially necessary. See, for example, *Nomos* 4, 101, no. 1261. The letters ΛΟΡΕΣ are squeezed under the head of the god (Zeus?), despite plenty of surrounding empty space.

on the superficial level of affinity: he is *the* earth-mover and water-redistributor; there seems to be an association between him and *pelor-* names, captured in enigmatic form in an Iliadic scholion;[158] he has Kronian qualities, noted below, which are relevant to the Golden Age imagery of the Peloria.[159] Zeus, on the other hand, hardly seems to fit. Not only is Poseidon wholly omitted, but the breaking apart of Tempe happens through, as far as Baton seems to have presented it, a natural event (an earthquake) rather than overtly divine agency. Zeus has little if anything to do with the miraculous event; he is just the deity the Thessalians chose to honour when celebrating it. He feels, in sum, a little extraneous.

There are various possible explanations. The whole passage may be a piece of fanciful Hellenistic invention, but, if so, it is one that accords remarkably strongly with key themes in Thessalian myth and cult. Baton (or Athenaios, for that matter) may have described the festival accurately, but made a mistake over the identity of the god. Or Zeus and Poseidon may have been joint recipients, and Baton (or Athenaios) fails to record that fact.[160] Finally, we might imagine variation either in place or time: perhaps one Thessalian community went out on a limb and associated the formation of Tempe with Zeus rather than Poseidon; or, in the Hellenistic Period, Zeus took over from Poseidon as the god associated with Tempe's creation, a change perhaps marked by a shift of focus from one religious site (Orthe?) to another. The first explanation, a simple error by Baton/Athenaios, seems most likely. Ultimately, however, we simply do not know.

Even with such uncertainties in play, it is obvious – and has been to many historians – that Baton's account chimes strongly with other elements in Thessalian religion and mythology, especially the Pelasgian aspect and the themes of water and food.[161] It has also been observed that there is strong resemblance between the Thessalian Peloria and the many local manifestations of Kronia festivals across Greece, hinging upon rituals of status-reversal and a celebration of natural plenty;[162] like them, the Peloria is connected, through its *aition*, with primordial myth-time through the figure

158 Schol. Hom. *Il.* 16.176: a pair of anecdotes about a Giant called Pelor; in one, he is struck by Poseidon's trident, leaps into the river Spercheios, and dies; in the other, he behaves remarkably like Poseidon in the *Ehoiai*, seducing one Polydora in the guise of the river Spercheios.

159 As Doyen argues (2011, 105–17), there is a tendency in Greek literature for Zeus and Poseidon to be represented as adversaries and as symbolically opposed; with Kronos, on the other hand, Poseidon shared certain key characteristics.

160 This is Robertson's favoured theory. 'It seems unlikely that a festival which commemorated these events omitted to honour the god of earthquakes and rivers,' he remarks (Robertson 1984, 8).

161 Helly (1992); Mili (2015), 239–41.

162 See, for example, Versnel (1993), 130 ('a typical reversal festival').

of Pelasgos, which certainly falls earlier than Deukalion.[163] While Kronos himself is not attested as a recipient of cult in Thessaly, Kronos has a position within Thessalian mythology that is obliquely relevant to the theme of agriculture. Unlike Zeus, he was not thought to have fathered offspring with anyone but his wife Rhea; however, the one known exception is his begetting of Cheiron with the nymph Philyra.[164] As Versnel notes, Cheiron's character is in keeping with the inherent contradictions of his father's;[165] as the *phēr theios*, both monster and teacher, he combines the orderly with the savage, the wild with culture. On Mount Pelion, Cheiron's cult involved a ritual that evoked primitive time through the wearing of raw fleeces, reinforcing the centaur's association with the distant past.[166] Though not mentioned by Baton, Cheiron constitutes another implicit link between the Peloria and attested Thessalian cult.

So Tempe was doubly linked to the theme of fertility, via the Petraia and the Peloria. Not only that, however: in the context of ancient narratives of the Persian Wars, Tempe assumed a crucial role in the articulation of Greek loyalty and belonging, charged themes in the characterisation of Thessaly and its place in Greece.

c) Tempe and Greek allegiance in the second Persian War

When, in 480 BC, Xerxes' forces were known to be approaching Greece, the Hellenic League, as it is conventionally called,[167] met at the Isthmos to discuss strategy, including the best place to make a concerted stand against the invaders.[168] At first it was decided to hold the pass at Tempe, and a force of 10,000 was sent there. Shortly afterwards, however, this force withdrew for reasons variously stated and imperfectly understood,[169] and a wholly

163 The Pelasgian phase was thought to have endured until either the Pelasgoi migrated away of their own accord, or were driven away by Deukalion, Deukalion's sons or some other aggressor. The Pelasgoi leave apparently of their own accord: Hdt. 1.57.1; Paus. 4.36.1. Driven out by Deukalion: Dion. Hal. *Ant. Rom.* 1.17.3. By Deukalion's sons: Diod. 5.60. By the Lapiths: Strabo 9.5.22. By Triopas: Kallim. *Hymns* 6.25.

164 Philyra goes back as far as Hesiod (*Theog.* 1001), but the earliest mention of Kronos as father is Pherekydes (*FGrH* 3 F 50: 'Φερεκύδης φησὶν ὅτι Κρόνος ἀπεικασθεὶς ἵππωι ἐμίγη {τῆι} Φιλύραι {τῆι} Ὠκεανοῦ καὶ διὰ τοῦτο διφυὴς ὁ Χείρων.') However, Fowler is surely right to assume that Kronos was considered the father *ab initio*. Fowler (2013), 23.

165 Versnel (1993), 110–11; cf. Mili (2015), 240.

166 Buxton (1994), 93–94.

167 For discussion of the name and of the nature of the organisation see Tronson (1991); Yates (2015).

168 Hdt. 7.172–75.

169 Westlake (1936); Robertson (1976); Graf (1979), 155–68; Helly (1995), 226–28. Herodotos says that the Greeks were warned by Alexandros I of Macedon that the oncoming Persians were simply too numerous to withstand, while at the same time they had doubts about the security of the pass as a place of defence, since another way

different approach was adopted: to hold out at Thermopylai instead, while the fleet was sent to nearby Artemision. The Persians were not stopped at Thermopylai, merely delayed. As for the Thessalians, the change of strategy had major repercussions for them, leaving them unsupported by their fellow Greeks and making their capitulation to Persia, in Herodotos' eyes at least, unavoidable. In Herodotos' account the incident is charged with meaning: the decision to hold Thermopylai rather than Tempe leaves the Thessalians out in the cold, in the grip of *anankē*, an important theme in the *Histories*.[170] Moreover, defending Thermopylai rather than Tempe leaves their position within the community of Greeks nearly as marginal and ambiguous as that of that of Alexandros of Macedon, who protests his philhellenism while working for Xerxes.[171]

It is true that questionable devotion to the resistance is not an accusation reserved for northerners in the *Histories*; even the Spartans receive a tar-dab from that brush, and some apparently staunch defenders of Greek freedom are shown up as motivated by dubious intentions.[172] However, Tempe and Thermopylai bracket Thessaly meaningfully, and the former is established as symbolically important in a number of ways. Crucially, Herodotos stages – surely, imagines – an excursion by sea made by Xerxes before entering Greece with his army. He goes ahead round the coast, taking his fleet but leaving his land forces in Makedonia, and views the mouth of the Peneios from the sea with great wonder.[173] Upon his enquiring, his guides tell him that this is the Peneios' only outlet into the sea; Herodotos breaks away briefly from the main story to recount Poseidon's cleaving of the ravine.[174] Xerxes' response to what his guides tell him is very striking:

through existed in the area of Perrhaibian Gonnoi. A different slant seems to have been put on the episode by Damastes of Sigeion, Herodotos' near-contemporary, however: that the Greek withdrawal was in response to suspicions regarding the Thessalians' loyalty (*FGrH* 5 F 4). Even more extreme is Diodoros' claim (11.2.3) that by the time the defence force was at Tempe the Thessalians and adjoining *ethnē* had already offered tokens of submission to the Persians. It is likely that in the aftermath of the war there were several divergent accounts of the incident competing for belief; certainly the energy with which Herodotos asserts the initial commitment of the Thessalians to opposing Xerxes suggests that his view did not have general acceptance.

170 Munson (2001); Baragwanath (2008), 205–10.

171 Alexandros and his ambiguous allegiance: see esp. Hdt. 9.45.

172 Herodotos claims that even Sparta might have medized had not Athens held firm: 7.139.4. The Phokians oppose Persia only because their Thessalian enemies do not: Hdt. 8.30.

173 On the passes between Macedon and Thessaly, and which one Xerxes chooses to use, see Helly (1973), vol. I, 8–12; Lazenby (1993), 115–16; van Rookhuijzen (2019), 110–13.

174 Herodotos' wording leaves it a little doubtful whether he himself credits the story of Poseidon's intervention or prefers a purely seismic explanation. Cf. Strabo 9.5.2,

> The Thessalians are wise; this was why, long before, they exercised caution and capitulated, their main reason being that their territory could be easily and speedily conquered. It would only have been a matter of making the river flow out over their land by barring the outlet with a dam and diverting it from its present channel, and the whole of Thessaly, with the exception of the mountains, would be under water.[175]

This episode is part of a wider characterisation of Xerxes in the *Histories* as a man who manipulates the very fabric of the Greek landscape – or rather, tries and threatens to do so – in a number of unnatural ways, and who represents a direct challenge to Thessaly's natural form and resources.[176] He is also an anti-Poseidon, threatening to undo the god's work, to un-make Thessaly in effect.[177] This ties in with the theme of Thessalian medism through necessity: Thessaly is especially vulnerable to Xerxes' aggression, in Herodotos' depiction.[178] And Tempe is doubly insecure: it cannot be safely defended by the Hellenic League forces and is, according to Xerxes' view, Thessaly's weak spot in terms of sheer survival. The very place whose formation brought Thessaly into the light of day has the potential to be its undoing.

Ultimately, in Herodotos' account, this reinforces the sense of Thessaly's unreliability. After all, even her famous horses are beaten in a race by those of the invading Persians.[179] Moreover, after the Persian fleet is badly damaged by storms off Cape Sepias, the Persians manage to induce calmer seas by sacrificing to Thetis.[180] They do so because they learn that Thetis has particular connections with that stretch of coast, having been carried off by Peleus there; however, she seems to have no particular loyalty to the land or

in which an earthquake alone is the cause of Tempe's creation, and Poseidon is not mentioned.

175 Hdt. 7.130.1–2: 'σοφοὶ ἄνδρες εἰσὶ Θεσσαλοί. ταῦτ' ἄρα πρὸ πολλοῦ ἐφυλάξαντο γνωσιμαχέοντες καὶ τἆλλα καὶ ὅτι χώρην ἄρα εἶχον εὐαίρετόν τε καὶ ταχυάλωτον. τὸν γὰρ ποταμὸν πρῆγμα ἂν ἦν μοῦνον ἐπεῖναι σφέων ἐπὶ τὴν χώρην, χώματι ἐκ τοῦ αὐλῶνος ἐκβιβάσαντα καὶ παρατρέψαντα δι' ὧν νῦν ῥέει ῥεέθρων, ὥστε Θεσσαλίην πᾶσαν ἔξω τῶν ὀρέων ὑπόβρυχα γενέσθαι' (trans. Godley, adapted).

176 Clarke (2018), 213–16, 238–53.

177 Clarke (2018), 193–95. She points out that, though Herodotos attributes the creation of Tempe to an earthquake, he calls the Thessalian belief in the involvement of Poseidon οἰκότα, reasonable, and therefore deliberately maintains the sense of Xerxes going against divine will.

178 On the vulnerability of the Thessalian and Perrhaibian landscapes see Baragwanath (2008), 206–08. See also van Rookhuijzen (2019), 107–10.

179 Hdt. 7.196.

180 Hdt. 7.191. The historian injects a small, not untypical, note of doubt as to the goddess' involvement: 'ἢ ἄλλως κως αὐτὸς ἐθέλων ἐκόπασε' ('or perhaps [the wind] abated of its own accord'). Mikalson (2003), 50; Clarke (2018), 252; van Rookhuijzen (2019), 122–36.

to Greece more generally, and can be easily suborned. Perhaps this is to be contrasted with Boreas, whose power was believed to have been behind the storm in the first place: the Athenians are able to call on him as a son-in-law because his wife's father was Erechtheus, and after his assistance they institute his cult beside the river Ilissos.[181] Thetis is the mother of Thessalian Achilles and has a cult in Pharsalos, but this does not prevent her supporting, as it were, the other side.[182] Ultimately, while the historian goes to some effort to indicate the innocence of most of the Thessalians from the charge of willing medism, he subtly undermines the loyalty of the region and of its very landscape, leaving a sense of inevitability that the main line of defence should move south and leave Thessaly undefended.

In Herodotos' account, then, Tempe is a boundary that is swiftly abandoned as being unstable and unreliable, and Thessaly shares this characterisation.[183] This reflects, but also distorts, Tempe's importance in Thessalian self-presentation, as the crux of their region's myth-history and natural character. But there are signs that Thessalian communities sought to influence, perhaps subvert, this discourse, using ritual to reinforce their importance in the cult of Apollo at Delphi, and therefore in the panhellenic community it represented.

d) Tempe and Delphi

Poseidon was not the only god strongly linked with Tempe in myth and ritual; Apollo also had this role. In fact Tempe played a part in the ritual calendar of Delphi that may seem at first to be so obscure as to be of interest only to committed antiquarians, but which actually constitutes a significant connection between the Greek panhellenic sanctuary and the northern edge of Thessaly.[184] This hinges upon an ill-attested but clearly important festival, the Septerion.[185]

The Septerion is given that name[186] only in the works of Plutarch, who

181 Hdt. 7.189.

182 It is also significant that Herodotos creates an implicit affinity between Xerxes and Thessalian Achilles, since both interfere with the flow of the river Skamandros (Hdt. 7.43). The Aiakidai (associated chiefly with Aigina) help the Greeks at Salamis, but Achilles himself might have a slightly less clear-cut allegiance. Bowie (2012), 275–76; Clarke (2018), 201. That said, there is certainly no overarching aim of making all Thessalian heroes problematic in the same way.

183 Compare Hdt. 7.176.4–5, discussed in Chapter 1, in which Thermopylai too becomes symbolically charged with the theme of Thessalian aggression, and the implicit alignment of their role as invaders with that of the Persians.

184 Mili (2015), 241–43.

185 Graninger (2006), 48–50.

186 On the form of the name – Septerion rather than the variant Stepterion – see Defradas (1954), 98. However, cf. Hesych. s.v. στεπτήρια; Hesychios explains this word

also draws upon his extensive personal knowledge of Delphic religious procedure to give us our most detailed surviving description of the rites. In the shorter and simpler of his two references, in the *Greek Questions*, Plutarch addresses the question of 'What was Charila among the Delphians' by explaining that Charila is one of three enneaeteric festivals the Delphians celebrate in order; the three in their proper sequence are Septerion, Herois and Charila. The Septerion is explained in the following terms:

> The Septerion seems to be an imitation of the god's battle with Python, and of the flight to Tempe after the battle, and of the pursuit. For some say that [Apollo] fled after the murder, seeking purification; others that he followed Python, who was wounded and fleeing along the road which we now call Sacred, and arrived shortly after his death. For he caught up with Python when the latter had lately died of his wound and been buried by his son, whose name was Aix, as they say. Therefore the Septerion is a representation of these events, or of other things of that nature.[187]

Despite the unhelpful vagueness of the final clause, we can accept a basic connection between the Septerion and Apollo's journey to Tempe after his fight with Python; it is likely that myths and rite were linked slightly differently depending on whom in the sanctuary one asked and which written authorities one consulted, but the essential theme is established. And it is corroborated by Plutarch's second reference to the rite, though the rhetorical complexity of this passage is greater. In the *On the Obsolescence of Oracles* the writer stages an elaborate discussion at Delphi[188] between a number of learned men, in the midst of which the Spartan Kleombrotos proposes a daring theory: that the less glorious deeds of gods were in fact carried out by *daimones* (demi-gods, immortal spirits). As part of this thesis he adduces Apollo's slaying of Python and subsequent search for purification: surely, he says, no true god would want or require formal

as meaning garlands or wreaths worn by suppliants. Kallimachos (fr. 89 Pf.) seems to have referred in the *Aitia* to Apollo donning a laurel wreath like a suppliant after killing the monster. There may, therefore, be a connection between the laurel, the theme of atonement and the name of the festival, however it should properly be spelled.

[187] Plut. *Quaest. Gr.* 12: 'τὸ μὲν οὖν Σεπτήριον ἔοικε μίμημα τῆς πρὸς τὸν Πύθωνα τοῦ θεοῦ μάχης εἶναι καὶ τῆς μετὰ τὴν μάχην ἐπὶ τὰ Τέμπη φυγῆς καὶ ἐκδιώξεως. οἱ μὲν γὰρ φυγεῖν ἐπὶ τῷ φόνῳ φασὶ χρῄζοντα καθαρσίων, οἱ δὲ τῷ Πύθωνι τετρωμένῳ καὶ φεύγοντι κατὰ τὴν ὁδόν, ἣν νῦν ἱερὰν καλοῦμεν, ἐπακολουθεῖν καὶ μικρὸν ἀπολειφθῆναι τῆς τελευτῆς· κατέλαβε γὰρ αὐτὸν ἐκ τοῦ τραύματος ἄρτι τεθνηκότα καὶ κεκηδευμένον ὑπὸ τοῦ παιδός, ᾧ ὄνομα ἦν Αἴξ, ὡς λέγουσι. τὸ μὲν οὖν Σεπτήριον τούτων ἢ τοιούτων τινῶν ἀπομίμησίς ἐστιν ἑτέρων' (trans. Babbitt, adapted).

[188] On the setting and the religious and philosophical thought in the *de Def. Or.* see Brenk (1977), 85–112. For a more general discussion of Plutarch's presentation of Delphi in the context of Roman rule see Stadter (2014), 82–97.

religious atonement after despatching a monster. In Kleombrotos' eyes, this contention does not invalidate the Septerion itself, but only the stories that accompany it, which therefore constitute a false *aition*. Importantly, the myths surrounding the Septerion are presented not just as the subject of informal fireside folklore but as part of the public and religious life of Delphi: we are told that the stories are recounted both in verse and in prose as part of the *agōnes* in the theatre.

As to the rites, they are described in the following terms:

> 'These rites,' he said, 'concerning the oracle, and in which the city lately initiated all the Greeks beyond Thermopylai, travelling as far as Tempe. For the structure which is set up here every eight years near the Threshing-floor is not a burrow-like nest of the serpent, but rather is a copy of the house of a tyrant or king. The attack on this structure is made in silence, via the so-called Dolonia, through which the Aioladai carrying torches lead the boy with both parents living; having set fire to the building and overturned the table they flee without looking back through the doors of the temple. Lastly, the wanderings and the servitude of the youth, and the purifications which take place around Tempe, hint darkly at guilt and at a reckless act.'[189]

In the fourth century we have further information about the festival, even though the word 'Septerion' is never used in our surviving sources. Ephoros, cited at length by Strabo, mentioned the burning of the Python-building at Delphi (he calls it a *skene*, which cannot here mean a tent but does suggest a simple, rather flimsy structure – after all, if it was designed to be burned every eight years it will hardly have been made in elaborate or permanent fashion), but did not, as far as we know, refer to the ritual journey to Tempe.[190] Hypothesis C to the scholia on Pindar's *Pythian Odes* seems to describe the ritual, without naming it, in connection (somehow) with the foundation of the Games by Eurylochos the Thessalian after the First Sacred War.[191] The

[189] Plut. *De Def. Or.* 15: 'τούτοις' ἔφη 'τοῖς περὶ τὸ χρηστήριον, οἷς ἄρτι τοὺς ἔξω Πυλῶν πάντας Ἕλληνας ἡ πόλις κατοργιάζουσα μέχρι Τεμπῶν ἐλήλακεν. ἥ τε γὰρ ἱσταμένη καλιὰς ἐνταῦθα περὶ τὴν ἅλω δι' ἐννέα ἐτῶν οὐ φωλεώδης τοῦ δράκοντος χειά, ἀλλὰ μίμημα τυραννικῆς ἢ βασιλικῆς ἐστιν οἰκήσεως· ἥ τε μετὰ σιγῆς ἐπ' αὐτὴν διὰ τῆς ὀνομαζομένης Δολωνίας ἔφοδος, μὴ αἰόλα δὲ τὸν ἀμφιθαλῆ κόρον ἡμμέναις δᾳσὶν ἄγουσι, καὶ προσβαλόντες τὸ πῦρ τῇ καλιάδι καὶ τὴν τράπεζαν ἀνατρέψαντες ἀνεπιστρεπτὶ φεύγουσι διὰ τῶν θυρῶν τοῦ ἱεροῦ· καὶ τελευταῖον αἵ τε πλάναι καὶ ἡ λατρεία τοῦ παιδὸς οἵ τε γιγνόμενοι περὶ τὰ Τέμπη καθαρμοὶ μεγάλου τινὸς ἄγους καὶ τολμήματος ὑποψίαν ἔχουσι.'

[190] Ephoros *FGrH* 70 F 31b.

[191] Davies (2007b), 67. For the date and nature of the Hypotheses' source material see Chapter 1, p. 46.

Thessalian end of the rite is described in lavish detail, however, in a section of Aelian's *Historical Miscellany* that almost certainly derives from Theopompos' *Philippika*.[192] 'The Thessalians say', we are told, that Apollo purified himself in the Peneios at Tempe after slaying Python and then returned triumphant to Delphi wearing a crown of Tempe laurel and carrying a *klados*, branch, presumably of the same material. The description continues:

> Here, indeed, the children of the Thessalians say that Pythian Apollo was purified according to the command of Zeus, when he shot dead the *drakōn* Pytho which guarded Delphi, when Gē still controlled the oracle. He then garlanded himself with a crown from the Tempe laurel and, taking a branch [of this same laurel] in his right hand he went to Delphi and took over the oracle as the son of Zeus and Leto. There is an altar at that place, where he was garlanded and took away the branch. And even now, every eight years, the Delphians send well-born boys and one of their own *architheōroi*. They take the road called 'Pythian'; it leads through Thessaly, Pelasgia, Oita, and the lands of the Ainianes, Malians, Dorians and western Lokrians. These people accompany the procession with singing and with reverence, no less than those who give reverence to those carrying the sacred objects of the Hyperboreans for the very same god. And furthermore they give crowns made from this same laurel to those who are victorious in the Pythian Games.[193]

Compared with our other accounts, whose chief focus is on the rituals carried out in Delphi, this passage is richly informative about the Thessalian participation in the Septerion. Although it is the Delphians who conduct the procession, we are given a clear picture of the inhabitants of lands along the route contributing to the festal procession. Plainly the effect would

192 Wilson (2014), n. 1 (citing earlier scholarship).

193 Theopompos *FGrH* 115 F 80.6–8: 'ἐνταῦθά τοί φασι παῖδες Θετταλῶν καὶ τὸν Ἀπόλλωνα τὸν Πύθιον καθήρασθαι κατὰ πρόσταγμα τοῦ Διός, ὅτε τὸν Πύθωνα τὸν δράκοντα κατετόξευσεν φυλάττοντα τοὺς Δελφούς, τῆς Γῆς ἔτι ἐχούσης τὸ μαντεῖον. στεφανωσάμενον οὖν ἐκ [ταύτης] τῆς δάφνης τῆς Τεμπικῆς καὶ λαβόντα κλάδον ἐς τὴν δεξιὰν χεῖρα [ἐκ τῆς αὐτῆς δάφνης] ἐλθεῖν ἐς Δελφοὺς καὶ παραλαβεῖν τὸ μαντεῖον τὸν Διὸς καὶ Λητοῦς παῖδα. ἔστι δὲ καὶ βωμὸς ἐν αὐτῶι τῶι τόπωι, ἐν ὧι καὶ ἐστεφανώσατο καὶ τὸν κλάδον ἀφεῖλε· καὶ ἔτι καὶ νῦν δι' ἔτους ἐνάτου οἱ Δελφοὶ παῖδας εὐγενεῖς πέμπουσι καὶ ἀρχιθέωρον ἕνα σφῶν αὐτῶν. οἳ δὲ παραγενόμενοι καὶ μεγαλοπρεπῶς θύσαντες ἐν τοῖς Τέμπεσιν ἀπίασι πάλιν στεφάνους ἀπὸ τῆς αὐτῆς δάφνης διαπλέξαντες, ἀφ' ἧσπερ οὖν καὶ τότε ὁ θεὸς ἐστεφανώσατο. καὶ τὴν ὁδὸν ἐκείνην ἔρχονται, ἣ καλεῖται μὲν Πυθιάς, φέρει δὲ διὰ Θετταλίας καὶ Πελασγίας καὶ τῆς Οἴτης καὶ τῆς Αἰνιάνων χώρας καὶ τῆς Μηλιέων καὶ Δωριέων καὶ Λοκρῶν τῶν Ἑσπερίων. οὗτοι δὲ καὶ παραπέμπουσιν αὐτοὺς σὺν αἰδοῖ καὶ τιμῆι οὐδὲν ἧττον ἤπερ οὖν ἐκεῖνοι, οἳ τοὺς ἐξ Ὑπερβορέων τὰ ἱερὰ κομίζοντας τῶι αὐτῶι θεῶι τούτωι τιμῶσι. καὶ μὴν καὶ τοῖς Πυθίοις ἐκ ταύτης τῆς δάφνης τοὺς στεφάνους τοῖς νικῶσι διδόασιν' (trans. Morison).

have been to enhance the interactions between the various communities, as they participate in turn in the festal activity accompanying the procession. As the passage itself makes clear, there is other processional activity in honour of Apollo, passing through the same territory: the carrying of the mysterious straw-wrapped offerings from the Hyperboreans, whose ultimate destination was in fact Delos rather than Delphi.[194] Moreover, the altar set up by the Peneios, where the laurel is harvested, is a permanent religious monument within the Thessalian landscape.[195] The sense of a shared religious space is enhanced by Aelian's admittedly rhapsodic description: 'πᾶς δὲ ὁ περίοικος λεὼς συνίασιν ἄλλοι ἄλλοις καὶ θύουσι καὶ συνουσίας ποιοῦνται καὶ συμπίνουσιν.' ('All the people living in the surrounding area come together and sacrifice with each other and hold feasts and drink together.')[196]

Inscriptions supply further clear signs of participation and interest in the Septerion. Four inscriptions testify to the presence of *dauchnaphoroi* ('laurel-bearers', *dauchna* being the epichoric form of *daphnē*). Two are from the later fifth century and come from Atrax and from near Larisa respectively. The Atragian text records a dedication by Εὔφορβος ἀρχιδαυχναφόρες κοἰ συνδαφναφόροι ('Euphorbos the *archidauchnaphorēs* and the *syndauchnaphoroi*.')[197] The Larisaian example also tells us the identity of the receiving deity:

> To Apollo Leschaios
> Aristion dedicated (this), he and his fellow *dauchnaphoroi*.[198]

The fact that the Apollo is here Leschaios rather than Pythios (or another explicitly Delphic form) should not deter us from seeing these 'laurel-bearers' as part of the Septerion procession. Another *archidauchnaphorēs*, one Sousipatros of Phalanna, explicitly connected with Delphi by claiming to have served as a *hieromnēmōn*, made his dedication to Apollo Kerdoios, an

194 Hdt. 4.33.1–3; Kallim. *Hymn* 4.282–90.

195 There is probable archaeological corroboration of this site, though the date of its inception is uncertain: the excavator, Theocharis, identified all remains found as Hellenistic (*AD* 16, 1960, *Chron.* 175), but cf. McDevitt (1970), 86, no. 638, identifying an inscription as fifth century BC. Dedications to Apollo Pythios and to Apollo Tempeitas are almost all Hellenistic: Mili (2015), Appendix 1, nos 47, 62, 67, 69, 70, 71; Rakatsanis and Tziafalias (2004), vol. 2, 72–76. For an overview of the religious landscape of the Tempe area see Kravaritou (2010), 422–23. For the dissemination of the *epiklesis* Pythios – in which, before the Hellenistic period, Thessaly formed an especially dense and significant cluster – see Davies (2007a), 59.

196 Note that the purification of Apollo at Tempe is also mentioned in Aristonoos' *Paian to Apollo*, included in a Delphic decree honouring the composer dated 334/3 BC and presumably intended for public display: *SIG* 449. Discussion of the hymn, its author and its historical and literary context: LeVen (2014), 294–96.

197 *SEG* 47.679.

198 *IG* IX.2 1027: Ἄπλονι Λεσχαίο[ι]/Ἀριστίον ὀνέθεκε κοἰ συνδαυχναφόροι.

important Thessalian form of the god.[199] Moreover, Helly has suggested that the *epiklesis* Leschaios is not wholly unconnected with the myth of Apollo's journey to Thessaly to achieve purification. As he points out, the word *leschē* can have associations with communal eating,[200] and a ritual meal was part of the Septerion, as we learn from Stephanos of Byzantium, s.v. Δειπνίας: 'Deipnias: a Thessalian village near Larisa, where they say Apollo had his first meal when he turned back from Tempe, purified. And it is customary for the boy who carries the laurel to go there to eat. Kallimachos in Book 4: "where Deipnias has welcomed him".'[201] Scholars place this brief quotation of Kallimachos (fr. 87) in the fourth book of the *Aitia*,[202] where we also find a description of Apollo washing his hands in the Peneios to cleanse himself after killing Python, and cutting laurel.[203] It is likely that the whole poem was an *aition* of the Septerion, and it is a great pity that so little of it survives. Despite the extreme obscurity of the name Septerion in our surviving sources, it plainly denoted a ritual with far-reaching significance in Thessaly and beyond. In the Septerion Thessaly, Tempe in particular, is cast as the source of purification and formal atonement. It is interesting at this point to return to Plutarch and recall that, according to him, the boy who burned Python's home at Delphi had subsequently to undergo ritual πλάναι and λατρεία, wanderings and servitude. Plutarch's character Kleombrotos pours scorn on the idea that the god himself should be so humbled (since the boy's experience is meant as a representation of the god's), but we can perhaps see it as part of a trend in Apollo's Delphic aspect. Following his killing of the Kyklopes, he was forced to atone by undergoing a period of servitude as herdsman for Admetos, ruler of Pherai.

Ascertaining the antiquity of the Septerion is no easy matter. Its earliest attestation is in the *Paians* of Pindar: X(a) certainly, and perhaps VIII also.[204] I have argued elsewhere[205] that, while the rite surely predated

199 *IG* IX.2 1234 (first century BC). The final inscription recording a *dauchnaphoros* is unpublished and is held in Volos Museum (inv. no. E 4519); it was found at Pherai.

200 Helly (1987), 141.

201 '<Δειπνιάς,> κώμη Θεσσαλίας περὶ Λάρισσαν, ὅπου φασὶ τὸν Ἀπόλλωνα δειπνῆσαι πρῶτον, ὅτε ἐκ τῶν Τέμπεων καθαρθεὶς ὑπέστρεψεν· καὶ τῷ παιδὶ τῷ διακομιστῇ τῆς δάφνης ἔθος εἰς τήνδε παραγενομένῳ δειπνεῖν. Καλλίμαχος δ' "Δειπνιὰς ἔνθεν μιν δειδέχαται.'

202 See, for example, Harder (2012), 715–18.

203 Fr. 89a.

204 X(a): Rutherford (2001a), 201–02. VIII: Harissis (2019), 115–17. Harissis puts forward the attractive suggestion that the four temples mentioned in *Paian* VIII were in fact portable shrines, one of which was the 'hut' ritually destroyed during the Septerion. Later authors misunderstood Pindar and turned the portable shrines into early temples of the god.

205 Aston (2019).

the fifth century, perhaps by a long way,[206] it was in the aftermath of the Persian Wars that its importance to the Thessalians appears most clearly.[207] The increased importance of Thessaly, and Tempe in particular, is visible if we examine the traditions regarding Delphic laurel, starting with its place in the famous myth of the early Apollo-temples.[208] In Pausanias' version, Tempe was the source of the laurel boughs out of which the first ever temple was constructed; this plainly accords to Tempe a highly significant role in the aetiology of Delphi, one that connects strongly with the Septerion and the use of Tempe laurel for the crowns in the Pythian Games.[209] In the ***Homeric Hymn to Apollo***, however, no mention is made of the laurel temple, or of its successor in Pausanias' account, a temple made of wax and feathers, or indeed of the third structure, made of bronze;[210] instead, we have mention only of the stone temple erected by Trophonios and Agamedes, both strongly associated with Boiotia.[211] Finally, even if we follow the contention of Bérard and of Auberson that at Euboian Eretria Apollo Daphnephoros had a temple of interlaced laurel branches, the inclusion of Tempe in the symbolic schema of this building is entirely hypothetical, and is based on a retrojection of much later mythological

[206] Cf. Rutherford (2018), who identifies four examples of a coherent type of purification ritual and suggests that the Septerion was the earliest.

[207] Cf. Defradas (1954), 101: he argues that the Septerion was sixth century in origin but appropriated elements of myth and ritual from a much earlier Kretan context.

[208] Sourvinou-Inwood (1979).

[209] Paus. 10.5.9.

[210] The laurel temple is absent also from Strabo 9.3.9.

[211] It should also be noted that in *HH* 3 Tempe is not a landmark mentioned in the account of Apollo's wanderings: 'Πιερίην μὲν πρῶτον ἀπ' Οὐλύμποιο κατῆλθες·/Λέκτον τ' ἠμαθοέντα παρέστιχες ἠδ' Ἐνιῆνας/καὶ διὰ Περραιβούς· τάχα δ' εἰς Ἰαωλκὸν ἵκανες,/ Κηναίου τ' ἐπέβης ναυσικλειτῆς Εὐβοίης.' ('To Pieria first you went down from Olympos and passed by sandy Lektos and the Enienes and through the land of the Perrhaiboi. Soon you came to Iolkos and set foot on Kenaion in Euboia, famed for ships … '. Lines 216–19.) Were Tempe strongly associated with the god and with his Delphic sanctuary at this time, it would surely have received at least a token mention. McInerney (2015a, 107) suggests that the inclusion of Pelion in the list of places visited by the pregnant Leto may reflect an association with the cult of Apollo Koropaios in the Pelion region; to that one might add that Iolkos could evoke the sanctuary of Apollo Pagasaios. Tempe, however, is wholly omitted. As Richardson observes (2010, 115), the *Hymn*'s account of Apollo's journey does not map exactly onto any known sacred route, but does include 'a number of places later associated with Apollo' – not, however, Tempe. Clay's suggestion (2006, 93) that the poet avoids reference to local cults and religious traditions in the interests of maintaining a panhellenic vision does not seem to sit easily with the oblique references that certainly are made (for example to the chariot ritual at Onchestos, lines 229–38). On the whole it is tempting to agree with Kolk that the inclusion of Tempe in Delphic processional ritual postdates the composition of the *Hymn*. Kolk (1963), 14.

narratives; it also overlooks the complete absence of Tempe from the *Homeric Hymn to Apollo*.[212]

The earlier temples are not a novelty of Pausanias' time; they certainly appear in what remains of Pindar's *Paian* 8, a work Rutherford considers to have been the probable source of Pausanias' description.[213] It is quite possible that Pindar invented the myth of the sequence of temples in its fully developed form, or that he combined in a single sequence rival myths from different communities, all trying to assert ownership over the origins of Apollo's cult at Delphi. In any case, Tempe laurel is notably absent from the pre-Classical texts;[214] this supports the argument that Tempe increased in importance in Delphic myth and ritual around the end of the sixth or the start of the fifth century BC.

A key factor was, I suggest, the second Persian War and its aftermath. Caution is required in identifying the post-Persian War years as a time of particularly abrupt and significant change. It is, however, undeniable that the war was a major catalyst for change in a way that had particular influence on the standing of Thessaly on the wider Greek stage, and in particular its perceived relationship with Hellenism, as the previous section identified. The invasion of Xerxes and its aftermath fuelled a shift by which the traditional basis of Hellenic identity on legendary descent was supplemented (though not replaced) by a growing emphasis on culture – on behaving like a Greek, and not like a *barbaros*. We shall see the Thessalians being presented as falling foul of this definition, in Chapter 6. While this discourse of oppositional identity – 'them and us' – took some decades to achieve momentum, the dust of the war had barely settled before Delphi, in particular, was being used as a prime location for the commemoration of opposition to Persia, and – as Scott argues – for the association of the name 'Hellenes' with the coalition of Greek states that actively resisted the Persians, in which body the Thessalians of course had no place.[215] As Rutherford says, the Septerion with its processional route up to Tempe and back constituted 'a linear celebration of

212 Bérard (1971), 67–70; Auberson (1974). The idea of a Tempe–Euboia–Delphi nexus is very tempting, but in fact Auberson's reconstruction of the Eretrian Daphnephoreion, and indeed the very identification of the building, are themselves now contested: see Walker (2004), 107.

213 Rutherford (2001a), 230–31. He argues that Pindar invented the myth of the temples in response to Delphic propaganda celebrating the construction of the Alkmaionid temple in the later sixth century.

214 Luce (1999, 990–91) argues that the importance of Tempe laurel goes back to the First Sacred War, in which he believes the Thessalians played a dominant role; however, the weaknesses of that theory were discussed in Chapter 1.

215 Scott (2010), 83–85.

North Greek identity'.[216] The meal at Deipnias is interesting too, in this regard. The Aiginetans may have dominated the provision of the sacred meal for the heroes in the Delphic Theoxenia, but the Thessalians, it would seem, claimed the greater honour of having fed Apollo himself, an event regularly re-enacted through the meal of the Delphian boy on his ritual journey.

So we find shades of possible competitive display aimed at the Aiginetans who dominated the cult of Neoptolemos at Delphi. Another ritual with which the Septerion may have interacted, whether or not in a spirit of competition, is the Theban Daphnephoria, in honour of Apollo Ismenios. Not only do the two festivals share certain ritual similarities (such as the key role of a boy with both parents living), but also, as Kowalzig argues, the mythology surrounding the foundation of the Daphnephoria was connected with the stories of the Thessalian origins of the Boiotoi.[217] It is likely that the Theban festival was in part influenced by the Septerion at Delphi, with its strong Thessalian dimension. Kowalzig suggests that shared Aiolian heritage was key to the Theban perception of an affinity with the Thessalians, and it is tempting to see this as lying behind the name choices of the Theban clan particularly prominent in the celebration of the Daphnephoria in the early fifth century: the so-called Aioladai.[218] Here there may exist the slightest trace of an actual ritual connection between the Septerion and the Theban Daphnephoria, in addition to the clear resemblance. In the passage from Plutarch's *On the Obsolescence of Oracles* quoted above, the poor condition of the manuscript exacerbates the inherent challenges of interpretation. In particular, the Greek phrase μὴ αἰόλα δὲ makes no sense. The best emendation (captured in the translation above) is ἧ Αἰολάδαι. We know from Hesychios that the Aioladai were παρὰ Δελφοῖς γένος τι. Hesychios does not say that the *genos* were Delphian but just that they were by or with (*para*) the Delphians. Does this suggest some kind of Theban involvement? Did the Theban Aioladai send representatives to take part in the Delphian part of the Septerion ritual *para Delphois* (alongside the Delphians)? Did this participation in the early fifth century lead to a particular group resident at Delphi being called, in commemoration, the Aioladai? It is a strong possibility.[219]

216 Rutherford (2018), 25.

217 Kowalzig (2007), 380–81. For further detailed discussion of the Daphnephoria in Theban society and in Pindar's works see Olivieri (2011), 170–92.

218 Celebrated in two poems of Pindar: see frs 94a and b Snell-Maehler.

219 Note, however, the alternative view of Schachter, who argues that the convergence of the Daphnephoria and the Septerion occurred in the fourth century at a time

As previously stated, it is impossible to argue that the Septerion did not exist significantly prior to the fifth century BC. However, the early fifth century is the date at which we have our first clear signs of its importance, from Pindar; Pindar too is our earliest source for the Theban Daphnephoria and the participation of the Aioladai. I have argued elsewhere[220] that the aftermath of the Persian Wars prompted the Thessalians to enhance their prestige at Delphi through an emphasis on the role of Tempe laurel in Delphic ritual; that the Daphnephoria of Thebes, another medising community, may have been connected to this rite forms a further strand in the wider historical context. As for Tempe, its significance as the source of Pythian laurel is not attested before the fifth century, but from that point on remains well established. Whether or not there was any practical interplay between Tempe's ritual significance in the cult of Poseidon, and its role in the cult of Apollo, cannot be ascertained. However, the two aspects together leave us in no doubt that in the fifth century it achieved a prime position in the identity of Thessaly as a landscape of myth and ritual.

5. Conclusions

In older scholarship the fifth century has sometimes been seen as a time of decline and disintegration in Thessaly;[221] however, this is absolutely not borne out by the available evidence. The Classical period as a whole has been identified by Kaczmarek as a time of significant population expansion in Thessaly, with new settlements established in previously underexploited territory.[222] The archaeological, epigraphic and numismatic records of the fifth century, combined, allow us to identify a significant number of sites that, if they did not come into being in the fifth century, achieved particular visibility at that time by, for example, the building of new monumental structures[223] or the inscribing of political decisions on stone.[224] Such traces

of substantial Theban influence in the Amphiktyony. See Schachter in *BNP* s.v. 'Daphnephoria'; Schachter (1981), 84–85.

220 Aston (2019).

221 See, for example, Sordi (1958), 90. She places the defeats at Keressos and in Phokis in the early fifth century, and sees them as triggering a period of 'decadenza', compounded by Thessalian medism and its repercussions. Cf. Keaveney (1995), 30.

222 Kaczmarek (2015), 76–84.

223 E.g. Pharkadon (modern Sykia), which received its first substantial fortifications in the fifth century. At (modern) Vlochos the earliest phase of fortification is certainly earlier than the fourth century BC: late Archaic? Early Classical? Late Archaic occupation is strongly suggested by imported pottery from the site. Vaïopoulou et al. (2020), 35–36, 68.

224 E.g., Thetonion and the important *IG* IX.2 257, the mid-fifth-century honorific inscription that mentions the local magistrates, titled Tagos and Hyloros.

in themselves strongly suggest a time when Thessalian communities were dynamic and active, and this wider picture accords with the findings of this chapter. The early fifth century saw the first coinage, both of several Thessalian poleis and in the name of the *ethnos* of the Thessalians (the first attested internal use of the ethnic). This coinage reflects the importance of the god Poseidon, in whose honour the bull-wrestling was probably conducted; as the creator of the first horse, Poseidon gave the region its most renowned animal resource, and as the cleaver of Tempe he caused the famous Thessalian plains to emerge from inundation and provide the arable and pastoral wealth for which Thessaly was famous. The coins celebrate both these myths, reflecting a drawing together of elements of the god's character that probably originated as local variants. The resulting cluster of myth and ritual celebrated the essence of Thessaly, its natural identity and its special character as a physical space. The greater importance of Tempe reinforced Thessaly's northern border, helping to shape the region into a unified and distinct religious space.

Thessalian Poseidon shares some salient aspects with the god in his manifestations in other parts of Greece, and this wider picture facilitates a fuller understanding of his role in Thessaly. Contrast is particularly illuminating: Thessalian Poseidon has no divine consort like Demeter in Arkadia; he does not use floodwaters to punish a people as he does in Argos and Troizen, but is placed solely in the role of benefactor. His character as shown in the fifth-century (and later) sources chimes with his appearances in earlier evidence, but appears to make some important modifications. Instead of being the ancestor of specific heroic lines, he becomes associated with the whole Thessalian *ethnos*; instead of giving prime horses to one clan he creates the ancestor of all horses. In a fundamental way this shift mirrors that identified in the previous chapter, from a focus on Thessalos as the ancestor of a west-Thessalian clan to his wider association with Thessalian elites to – finally – the myth of the arrival of the Thessaloi, the forerunners of the whole Thessalian *ethnos* in their occupations of the land that bore their name.

In Archaic literature Thessal- names are almost never mentioned; by the fifth century their use is widespread and entirely normal in prose and verse alike. Moreover, the myths about Thessaly and Thessalian heroes that populated early epic found a place in the prose mythography of the Classical period, as did the origin-myth of the Thessaloi, whether in Hekataios' account of the Thessalids[225] or the historians' story of the Thessaloi coming over the Pindos to secure a new homeland.[226] The precise interplay between internal and external processes – the Thessalians' own development of a shared mythological and religious identity, and the awareness of and

225 Hek. Fr. 137A Fowler.

226 Hdt. 7.176.4–5; Thuc. 1.12.3.

reference to that identity among other Greeks – cannot be reconstructed, but the two processes must have fed into each other. The role of the outsider view in the formation of a group's identity and self-perception should never be underestimated; in Chapter 6 we shall follow this theme to consider the increasingly hostile depiction of Thessaly from the later fifth century BC, and some of the ways in which Thessalians responded to that. First, however, we turn from religion and myth to co-operation on the political level, to examine the development of Thessaly as a political unit.

5

Political co-operation in Thessaly from the sixth to the fourth century

Up to this point, this book has followed a largely chronological trajectory to outline the emergence of Thessaly as an entity, and the Thessaloi as a self-defining *ethnos*, in myth and cult in the early fifth century. In Chapter 5, however, we take a broader synoptic view in order to fit into the picture the political dimension, how the Thessalians established connections and institutions across polis boundaries to achieve ends beyond the purposes of any single polis.

In the preceding two chapters we have identified a process by which, beginning in the late sixth century and proceeding through the fifth, myth and cult were used to shape an image of Thessaly as a region with certain defining natural attributes, and of the Thessaloi as a people with a particular relationship to and claim on the land. In the fourth century, in some ways, the expression of regional identity through myth and religion gave place to the expression of unique polis identities. In particular, coinage, used in the fifth century to emphasise shared practices and gods (especially horse-use, bull-wrestling, Poseidon) was instead turned more and more to the expression of unique polis identity with the proliferation of bronze issues. Though fourth-century coins do include one issue with the ethnic (ΠΕΤΘΑΛΩΝ), it is far scarcer than the ΦΕΤΑ/ΦΕΘΑ issues of the fifth century. At the same time, the regional cult of Poseidon seems to slip from our view in the fourth century. Chapter 5, however, will nip in the bud any sweeping notion of fourth-century 'fragmentation' or 'disunity' by showing that Thessaly's political trajectory is interestingly divergent from the pattern of ethnic expression established at this point. It will be argued that we would be mistaken in assuming formal political institutions on the regional level until the late fifth century, but that those are certainly discernible in the fourth.

Until relatively recently, the search for a Thessalian federal state dominated scholarly interest in the region, most importantly Sordi's *La Lega Tessala* (1958)[1] and Helly's *L'État thessalien* (1995). The valorisation of

[1] Her perspective on Thessalian unity is neatly captured by Welles (1960, 104):

political institutions arose from the implicit assumption that their absence amounted to chaos, fragmentation and a kind of failure. (We have met this sort of unconscious discontent already, motivating the search for the aggressive Archaic Thessaly in Chapter 1 and presenting Thessaly as the controller of Hellenism in Chapter 2.) Sordi's book is most explicit in its use of the language of success and failure, strength and decline, but the trend is certainly not limited to her.[2] More recent scholarship on Thessaly, however, has turned aside from such a single-minded quest for order and unity strictly defined, and even treatments of the Thessalian *koinon* have tackled the matter very differently, stressing the need to recognise change over time and the danger of trying to stitch the patchy ancient evidence into a convincing but misleading synthesis. The present chapter follows in the path of such developments, and adopts a pragmatic approach: rather than viewing Thessaly as falling short of – and periodically attaining – some abstract ideal of political cohesion, it assumes that the Thessalians co-operated in the ways, and to the extent, needed to carry out the collective actions they chose to undertake. Speculation on what they might have achieved had they arranged their affairs differently is fruitless and misguided. This chapter therefore focuses on the forms of political co-operation in which the Thessalians can be shown to have engaged and the types of organisation that would have allowed them to do so, depending on the conditions and circumstances of the time. By the end of the chapter we shall have encountered most of the 'normal' ingredients of the Greek federal state as theoretically conceived – a system of regional leadership; a decision-making mechanism with sub-regional representation; a federal military muster. However, these did not arise as a full bundle at the start; nor were they always present in the same forms or combinations through the period here covered. This should not surprise us; the Greeks were not designing their regional political systems with reference to a handbook or checklist, even though certain cases (such as the Boiotan *koinon*) may have been influential.[3] Even among theorists, the *koinon* seems to have been the subject of relatively little dedicated discussion or definition; that is a largely modern concern.[4] For the most part, we have to keep in mind an image

'While recognizing that Thessaly was only rather rarely a political unity, she feels that such occasions were the fulfillment of its destiny.'

2 For Larsen (1968), Thessalian unity is initially inherent, since the Thessaloi arrive as a tribe from Epeiros; this primordial cohesion is later sapped by various forces of fragmentation. Helly (1995), on the other hand, sees the Thessalian state as created, a process which he attributes in its most perfect form (a form dictated by advanced geometric and political principles) to Aleuas Pyrrhos.

3 See Beck (2000), who accepts Theban influence on Greek political developments but denies an 'export of federalism'.

4 Bearzot (2015).

of Greek communities as driven by pragmatic concerns that could change quickly.[5]

1. The Tetrads

Chapter 3 discussed the mythological significance of the creation of the tetrads; here we shall focus instead on the political circumstances and significance of this development. Its fundamental importance should not be overlooked. Though the tetrads themselves had, in many ways, limited impact on the lives of Thessalian communities, their formation constituted the earliest known articulation of the boundaries of Thessaly as distinct from the perioikic *ethnē* around it. As Chapter 1 observed, in the Archaic period the southern boundary of Thessaly in particular was highly fluid. In the Catalogue of Ships, Achilles' contingent overspills all later political borders, encompassing Thessaly, Achaia Phthiotis and indeed a little of later Lokris. Thessalian communities in the Iolkos zone, Euboian sites and communities along the Euboian Gulf participated in exchange networks in the Early Iron Age, partially building upon Bronze Age connections. At no point do political boundaries appear in, let alone hinder, such interactions, though the ethnic distinctions are at least as old as the Delphic Amphiktyony; the creation of the tetrads is the first sign that such boundaries even operate on the political level. It must have entailed a degree of co-operation between the Thessalians and the Achaians, one that sees the two *ethnē* 'sharing' the richly evocative name of Phthia in the differentiation of [Thessalia] Phthiotis and Achaia Phthiotis. The move must also have served some practical purpose; ancient communities did not generally undertake significant political actions for purely ideological reasons. Perhaps, as polis elites interacted and co-operated, it helped to define their 'spheres of influence' within the region. All we can say is that, before the 450s, they are invisible from an administrative perspective, and that, even after that, their utility and function are not readily apparent.

What can we say about the date of their formation? The earliest evidence for the names of all four is a fragment of Hellanikos, quoted by Harpokration in his *Lexikon* (s.v. τετραρχία):

[5] In viewing the topic in this way, I draw not only on recent Thessalography but also on the remarkable advances in the understanding of Greek *koina* in general. Salient pieces of scholarship on the theme as a whole include Beck (1997), Corsten (1999), Giovannini (2003); Rzepka (2002), Mackil (2013), McInerney (2013). It is significant that one of the most influential overviews of the topic now is a multi-authored volume rather than a monograph; this reflects the increased recognition of regional diversity in Greek political systems (Beck and Funke 2015).

> Thessaly was divided into four parts, each of which was called a tetrad, as Hellanikos says in his *Thessalian History* [*FGrHist* 4 F 52]: he says the names of the tetrads were Thessaliotis, Phthiotis, Pelasgiotis and Hestiaiotis. Aristotle in his *Thessalian Constitution* [fr. 497 Rose] says that the Thessalians were divided into four sections at the time of Aleuas Pyrrhos.[6]

Pelasgiotis on its own is named somewhat earlier, by Hekataios of Miletos,[7] and its inhabitants, the Pelasgiotai, by Simonides, if Strabo is to be believed.[8] Given the formal consistency of the -iotis ending of the tetrad names, it is very unlikely that Hekataios mentioned Pelasgiotis without being aware of the other three. It is therefore likely that by the early fifth century at least the tetrad names were well established. Histiaiotis and Phthiotis are used casually and without comment by Herodotos in his description of the migration of the Dorians; the fact that he is applying them to a set of events he regards as long distant in time suggests that he does not regard the names as a recent innovation.[9] Thucydides gives a similar impression. At 1.3.2 he describes the sons of Hellen as ruling in Phthiotis; he does not apply the name of the Homeric kingdom, Phthia, but rather instinctively applies the tetrad name, the one that in its adjectival form presupposes the existence of a regional whole (see below). This strongly suggests that by the fifth century the tetrad names had been in circulation long enough to have entered standard literary usage and to have lost all association with specific political developments. A date for their creation in the later sixth century is highly plausible.

The consistency of the tetrad names' endings is highly significant: it clearly reveals them to be the product of a process of systematic and highly considered reorganisation, whatever the authority behind it. In an article of lasting value, Gschnitzer demonstrated that the names follow a basic linguistic pattern.[10] They are all adjectival, with an ending in -iotis; according to Gschnitzer they derive from, and describe, not the name of an *ethnos* (Pelasgoi etc.) but – as indicated by the first iota in -iotis – the name of the land that took its name from the group believed to have inhabited

[6] 'τεττάρων μερῶν ὄντων τῆς Θετταλίας ἕκαστον μέρος τετρὰς ἐκαλεῖτο, καθά φησιν Ἑλλάνικος ἐν τοῖς Θετταλικοῖς. ὄνομα δέ φησιν εἶναι ταῖς τετράσι Θεσσαλιῶτιν Φθιῶτιν Πελασγιῶτιν Ἑστιαιῶτιν. καὶ Ἀριστοτέλης δὲ ἐν τῇ κοινῇ Θετταλῶν πολιτείᾳ ἐπὶ Ἀλεύα τοῦ Πυρροῦ διῃρῆσθαί φησιν εἰς δ μοίρας τὴν Θετταλίαν.'

[7] Hekataios, *FGrH* 1 F 133. Cf. also Hdt. 1.56.3: a mention of Histiaiotis, as an earlier location of the Dorians.

[8] Strabo 9.5.20.

[9] Hdt. 1.56.3. Note that Histiaiotis is called τὴν … καλεομένην Ἱστιαιῶτιν; had the historian wanted to indicate that the ancient name was any different, he would surely have called it τὴν νυν καλεομένην Ἱστιαιῶτιν, 'Histiaiotis as it is called now.'

[10] Gschnitzer (1954); see also Helly (1995), 159–61.

it. So we have, for example, the sequence Pelasgoi – Pelasgia – Pelasgiotis. The first is the name of the *ethnos*; the second is the name of the land inhabited by that *ethnos*; but what does the final stage indicate? If we take *tetras* to be the unexpressed feminine noun with which the -iotis adjective implicitly agrees, Pelasgiotis means 'the Pelasgian tetrad', Thessaliotis 'The Thessalian tetrad', Phthiotis 'the Phthian tetrad'. Alternatively, we may take the 'lurking' noun to be not *tetras* but Thessalia: 'Pelasgian Thessaly', etc. All is Thessaly, but the four tetrads are Thessaly in different forms, evoking different aspects of the region's mythology, as Chapter 3 established.

For all the coherence of the process, the creation of the tetrads should not necessarily be attributed to one man, Aleuas Pyrrhos. Sprawski has recently challenged the veracity of Aleuas' role, believing that in the fourth century, when Aristotle was writing, there was an attempt to exaggerate the significance of the Larisaian statesman, and that actually we ought to be sceptical of his contribution to the federal structure of Thessaly.[11] This goes against both Sordi and Helly who, in different ways, attribute to Aleuas region-wide reforms that are fundamental to the political and military coherence of Thessaly.[12] But in fact a more fundamental question lurks behind all such debate. Did any single author ever make Aleuas a creator of regional state structures? Seemingly not, in fact. In fragment 497, quoted above, Aristotle does not say that Aleuas divided Thessaly into four parts (that, is the tetrads); he merely says that this division took place ἐπὶ Ἀλεύα τοῦ Πυρροῦ, in the time of Aleuas (this use of ἐπὶ with the genitive is common and well attested). Aleuas was obviously important enough to be used thus to denote a time, but the fragment does not suggest that he was actually responsible for regional reform. (The same observation will be made with regard to his military reforms: see below.) Moreover, the evidence we have for how power was distributed and wielded in Thessaly gives a much stronger impression of collaborative elites than of any sole pan-Thessalian agency.

2. πατρώϊαι κεδναὶ πολίων κυβερνάσιες

When Pindar, in his *Pythian* 10, wished to complement the Larisaian aristocrats who had commissioned the praise-poem for young Hippokleas of Pelinna,[13] he did so in the following terms:

[11] Sprawski (2012).

[12] Sordi (1958), Helly (1995). For Aleuas' reforms as comprehensive and perfect see also Helly (2008). Already in 1924 Wade-Gery observed (p. 60) that 'Aleuas the Red is likely enough mythical', and this scepticism seems warranted as regards the possibility of reconstructing the details of his career, if not his very existence.

[13] Pindar was, in fact, probably made *proxenos* of the Thessalians: Piccinini (2017),

And I shall praise also his excellent brothers, since
Bearing on high the *nomos Thessalōn*
They increase it. Among good men lies
The careful hereditary governing of cities.[14]

'His' refers to Thorax, son of Aleuas; Thorax' brothers are Thrasydaios and Eurypylos. We know something of these men because they are mentioned by Herodotos: they are instrumental in his account of the invasion of Xerxes and how Thessaly behaved at that time. He refers to them collectively as the Aleuadai, but also calls them παῖδες Ἀλεύεω,[15] as indeed does Pindar,[16] and while παῖς can refer to members of an ethnic group or a class of people[17] this is far less common than the meaning 'son'. So in all likelihood the three men in Pindar and in Herodotos' narrative are the sons of Aleuas – a man important enough for his name to have supplied the collective designation of his sons – and that Aleuas is surely the same man to whom Aristotle seemingly attributes political reform in Larisa.

The Aleuadai tell us a great deal about how power was wielded in Thessaly at the end of the sixth century BC and the beginning of the fifth. Historians have sometimes tried to fit them into a schema of political institutions and bodies, in particular by suggesting that in its earliest form the federation was headed by a traditional leader, called the Tagos, with the Aleuadai the most prominent holders of that title.[18] There has also been a tendency to see the *koinon* as the development of a kind of primordial tribal unity, and its evolution as reflecting, in some ways, increasing tension between the traditional elites, whose power was pan-Thessalian, and the new power of the cities.[19] However, for the fifth century at least no such

115. We do not know, however, when he took up that role, and therefore whether he would also have had a good acquaintance with Thessalian society and politics when composing *Pythian* 10. Which came first, poem or proxeny? We cannot know.

[14] Lines 69–72:
ἀδελφεοῖσί τ' ἐπαινήσομεν ἐσλοῖς, ὅτι
ὑψοῦ φέροντι νόμον Θεσσαλῶν
αὔξοντες· ἐν δ' ἀγαθοῖσι κεῖνται
πατρώιαι κεδναὶ πολίων κυβερνάσιες

[15] Hdt. 9.58.2.

[16] *Pyth.* 10, line 5: 'Ἀλεύα ... παῖδες'.

[17] As in οἱ Λυδῶν παῖδες (meaning 'the Lydians') at Hdt. 1.27: see LSJ s.v. παῖς I.3.

[18] Wade-Gery (1924), 66; Rose (1995), 166. Robertson, on the other hand (1976, 106–07) argues that while the Aleuadai were *basileis*, the early Tagoi were all Pharsalian. This theory has, however, the fundamental weakness of applying the title of Tagos to individuals who are never named as such in the ancient sources.

[19] See, for example, Larsen (1968), 20–26: once the poleis start to acquire 'a corporate existence', manifested especially in the minting of coinage, they represent a challenge to the 'old guard'. Changes in the federal institutions reflected a desire to check the power

conflict between elites and poleis is discernible; in fact, the whole notion rests on the outdated supposition that urban development was backward in Thessaly, and there is no basis in the available evidence for any separation between regional and polis power. Certainly a sole pan-Thessalian ruler is impossible to identify before the second half of the fifth century. Rather, one can see Thessalian affairs as being pushed this way or that by various groups and individuals (none of whom is designated a Tagos), of whom the Aleuadai are simply the most visible.[20]

Their visibility to us results chiefly from their foreign contacts: they are hand in glove with the Peisistratidai of Athens, negotiate with two Persian kings, and have an interest in Macedonian affairs also.[21] Because of such connections they warrant mention in the non-Thessalian historical narratives in a way in which most other Thessalian individuals do not (though their bare names do occasionally surface). That said, they would genuinely have been participants in the inter-regional networks that tied together Greek elites. A neat example is Herodotos' account of the suitors of Agariste, daughter of Kleisthenes the tyrant of Sikyon.[22] Among those competing for Agariste's hand is a Thessalian, Diaktorides, a member of the Skopadai clan from Krannon, alongside men from south Italy, Aitolia, Epidamnos, Athens, Eretria, Elis, Arkadia, Argos and Molossia. While acknowledging the influence of Herodotos' own authorial purposes, Hornblower compares this tally with Olympic victor-lists to show a close correspondence; from this he plausibly concludes that the episode does capture important truths about who was prominent on the panhellenic stage in the sixth century, and the channels through which they interacted.[23]

of the traditional elite, in particular the replacement of *tetrarchoi* with *polemarchoi* and the Tagos with an Archon.

[20] Mitchell (2013), 92–96. As she further points out (109), the fourth century presents us with a number of Pheraian co-rulers (Polyphron and Polydoros, Teisiphonos and Lykophron, Lykophron and Peitholaos), which may be seen in part as a continuation of the family rule model used by the Aleuadai.

[21] As Graninger remarks (2010, 310), 'Near the turn of the fifth century, Amyntas I and "Thessalians", Aleuads most likely, each enjoyed a strong relationship with the Pisistratids of Athens (Hdt. 5.94) and it would not be surprising if the Argeads and Aleuads were at this time networking directly among themselves.' This suggestion is indeed corroborated by Mack (2021, 69–76), who detects strong iconographic similarities between the coinage of Alexandros I of Macedon and that of Larisa and posits significant interaction on that basis. Note also the argument of Robertson (1976, 119–20) that the Aleuadai and Alexandros were in cahoots at the time of Xerxes' invasion.

[22] Hdt. 6.126–27.

[23] Hornblower (2014).

Herodotos calls the Aleuadai Θεσσαλίης βασιλέες, but it has long since been recognised[24] that this does not mean that they ruled all of Thessaly: they are Thessalian kings, rather than kings of Thessaly. The same point applies to Pindar's statement that the *genos* of the Aleuadai rule (βασιλεύει), and also to a Thessalian *basileus* whom we find in Thucydides' account of the 450s BC. In a notoriously obscure episode in 454, the Athenians try to support the return from exile of one Orestes, son of 'Echekratidas the βασιλεύς Θεσσαλῶν'.[25] At first glance this may look like the attempted restoration of a pan-Thessalian ruler, inheriting his power from his father. However, Thucydides' account suggests a campaign focused on Pharsalos, and there is no reason to believe that Orestes is not simply being restored to power within his city, as one of its leading men.[26] The Thessalians, and Orestes himself of course, may well have hoped that, if his return was successful, he would dominate Thessalian affairs and help to steer them in directions advantageous to Athens. But neither Orestes nor his father Echekratidas provide convincing evidence of formalised pan-Thessalian rule in the mid-fifth century.

And indeed 'king' is a poor translation of *basileus* in the Herodotean context, since we are not dealing with monarchy: the sons of Aleuas – Thorax, Thrasydaios and Eurypylos – are all *basileis* at the same time. 'Lords' might be a better rendering. Moreover, the Aleuadai do not, in the *Histories*, rule Thessaly as kings would, by issuing orders to their subjects. Instead, they connive behind the scenes to achieve their larger goals, and meet with considerable resistance in the process. This is particularly clear in their role in the early stages of the invasion of Xerxes. Herodotos goes to great trouble to indicate that the Aleuadai do not have all the Thessalians behind them, and are not able – indeed, do not even try – to force compliance throughout the region. Instead, they privately encourage Xerxes to invade; the other Thessalians, says Herodotos, are set against such capitulation, but are forced to medise once the line of Greek resistance moved south from

[24] Robertson (1976), 107; Helly (1995), 124–25. The plurality of *basileis* in Greek culture generally is well established: see, for example, Hall (2014), 127–30; Mitchell (2013), 23–48. See also the useful summary of the term's various meanings in different periods in Carlier and Tinnefeld (2006).

[25] Thuc. 1.111.1. Helly (1995), 106.

[26] It is not wholly clear from Thucydides' account (1.111.1) whether Pharsalos is the polis to which Orestes' restoration is attempted or whether it is simply the location of the fiercest fighting. Wade-Gery and Morrison (1942) think the latter, believing that the Pharsalians checked the Athenian advance because they opposed their project – which they take to be the imposition of a pan-Thessalian ruler – and that Orestes was actually an Aleuad from Larisa. However, as I have said, it is more likely that Orestes' attempted restoration was as polis, not regional, ruler; moreover, the fact that we know of at least one Echekratidas of Larisa does not mean that all men of that name must be Larisaian.

Tempe to Thermopylai, leaving the Thessalians undefended by their fellow Hellenes.

We may be sceptical of Herodotos' claim that the Aleuadai actively encouraged Xerxes to invade in 485 BC,[27] but that a ruling family should, in the face of an imminent invasion that seemed to have every chance of succeeding, decide to throw in their lot with the aggressor, is inherently very believable.[28] They would stand to gain ascendancy over their political opponents at home, and wider influence throughout Thessaly.[29] They approached Xerxes as private individuals rather than as representatives of their *ethnos* (a fact Xerxes failed to understand, according to Herodotos);[30] moreover, there is no doubt that the advantage they hoped to gain from Xerxes, should his invasion succeed, is for themselves and not the whole of Thessaly (no doubt they expected to be puppet rulers once Thessaly, along with the rest of Greece, was incorporated into the Persian empire). They certainly aspired to regional influence, but their position does not seem to have been a formalised one. Coming back to the Pindar passage, this perspective is amply reinforced. *Agathoi* – nobles, aristocrats – rule by ancestral right, carefully and in accordance with the *nomos Thessalōn*, the custom or tradition of the Thessalians. They rule poleis.

There are other glimpses of the importance of kinship groups within the fabric of polis life in Thessaly, such as the Agathokleadai who appear in Bacchylides' fragmentary ode for Aristoteles of Larisa, who is praised in terms that chime strongly with *Pythian* 10, emphasising prosperity (*olbos*) and the city location as the basis of power:

[27] Hdt. 7.6.2, 7.130.3. Scholarly scepticism: Robertson (1976), 108; defence of Herodotos' view: Westlake (1936), 12–24. One form of evidence, however, adduced in the past to support Herodotos' picture of a strong connection between Larisa and Persia, has now been effectively challenged. Herrmann (1925) generated a long-held orthodoxy according to which the first issues of Larisaian coinage were minted on the Persian standard. See, for example, Westlake (1936), 12–13; Martin (1985), 34–35. Kagan (2004) has, however, largely demolished this theory.

[28] It is worth noting also that Damastes of Sigeion (*FGrH* 5 F 4) talks of the προδοσία (treachery) of 'Aleuas [sc. the Aleuadai] and the Thessalians'; however, because he does not specify which Thessalians, this may refer not to the rest of the *ethnos* as a whole but to those under the sway of the Aleuadai. Moreover, we only have Damastes' words briefly paraphrased by Speusippos. Westlake (1936); Robertson (1976); Graf (1979), 155–68; Helly (1995), 226–28.

[29] Keaveney (1995) discusses mixed motives among different Thessalian groups.

[30] Hdt. 7.130.3: δοκέων ὁ Ξέρξης ἀπὸ παντός σφεας τοῦ ἔθνεος ἐπαγγέλλεσθαι φιλίην ('Xerxes, thinking that they conveyed the friendship of their whole *ethnos* ... '). Note: Herodotos does not say – as he surely would have, had it been so – that the Aleuadai were working against a formal Thessalian *koinon*.

Hestia of the golden throne,
you increase the great wealth of those
glorious men, the Agathokleadai,
as you sit at the heart of the city streets
beside fragrant Peneios in the glens
of sheep-rearing Thessaly.[31]

A further instance of kinship as a major strand of polis organisation is the famous agreement of the Basaidai, in which *isotimia* and the *taga* are restricted to the members of the *syngeneia* (kinship group). While specific aspects of this text and its implications may be, and have been, debated, the close relationship between family and political or civic status is undeniable.[32] Such elites are pre-eminent in their own poleis, but through *philia* they cultivated connections – such as the Aleuadai's link with Pelinna[33] – and extended their influence more widely within Thessaly, even while they used *philia* to increase their clout on a wider stage.

As for 'the Thessalians', who oppose the policy of the Aleuadai, Herodotos gives us no signal that we should think of these as a federal body from which the Aleuadai had broken loose; instead, we should imagine that every Thessalian polis that did not wish to medise, and which viewed the Aleuadai as a threat to their future autonomy, sent their leading men to

31 Bacchyl. fr. 14B, lines 1–6:
'Εστία χρυσόθρον', εὐ-
δόξων Ἀγαθοκλεαδᾶν ἅτ' ἀφνε[ῶν
ἀνδρῶν μέγαν ὄλβον ἀέξεις
ἡμένα μέσαις ἀγυιαῖς
Πηνειὸν ἀμφ' εὐώδεα Θεσσαλία[ς
μηλοτρόφου ἐν γυάλοις·

For discussion of this poem, its imagery and its political context see Fearn (2009), who suggests that it may have celebrated the assumption by Aristoteles of the role of *hipparchos* within the polis; McDevitt (2009, 225) believes likewise, mentioning Pind. *Nem.* 11 as a parallel. Sceptical on some points: Mili (2015), 132–33. Further on the Agathokleadai see Helly and Tziafalias (2013), 152–55. On Thessalian patrons of *epinikia*: Stamatopoulou (2007a); Molyneux (1992), 117–45; Yatromanolakis (2001), 210–18.

32 Parker, in a re-evaluation of the text itself, argues that the *syngeneia* should not be taken as extremely narrow in its membership: it may not have contained only the Basaidai and the 'four families' (lines 2–3) (Parker 2010). Nonetheless, the use of kinship-based terminology – the patronymic name Basaidai and the word *syngeneia* – is significant. See also Helly (1970), 182–89; Helly (1995), 320–21; Zelnick-Abramovitz (2000), 113–18; Mili (2015), 60–69. The notion of *syngeneia* is discernible also in the tribal structure of Atrax: see Darmezin and Tziafalias (2007), 26–28.

33 Ntasios (2012), 52, suggests that in the fifth century Pelinna was subordinate first to Larisa and then to Pharkadon; this, however, is highly conjectural.

prepare and conduct the embassy that addressed the Greeks at the Isthmos council and proclaimed the disinclination of most Thessalians to capitulate to Persia. A high level of co-operation to meet the needs of a specific circumstance should not be mistaken for a Thessalian federal state at this early time. In fact, we see here a feature of Thessalian political life that will resurface later in this chapter: the role of an internal threat (here the conniving Aleuadai) in generating a surge of co-operation among the other Thessalians who feel their interests and prospects suddenly challenged.

3. Co-operative coinage

This picture of inter-polis co-operation, combined with an absence of formal federal structures, is supported by Thessalian coinage of the first half of the fifth century BC. It has now been well established that Thessalian poleis started to mint coins shortly after the Persian wars, on the Aiginetan standard.[34] The early issues show a remarkable degree of consistency between cities.[35] Larisa, Pherai, Krannon, Trikka, Pelinna, Pharkadon and Skotoussa all produced coins showing, on the obverse, a young man wrestling a bull, and on the reverse a horse or a head or forepart of a horse. A smaller number of cities, chiefly Skotoussa and Methylion, favoured a slightly different type, whose obverse was the forepart of a horse and whose reverse was an ear of grain. Across the board, cities labelled their coins with abbreviations of their polis names. Two things are clear: first, that cities minted on their own polis authority, and took pains to make that fact known; second, that, despite this, they collaborated on the choice of emblems.

It used to be assumed that the consistency of the early coin issues must indicate their status as a 'federal coinage'.[36] This is an unwarranted interpretation. Rather, we must remember that coinage was in its infancy in Thessaly in the early fifth century; the practice – the dies and other equipment, the technological expertise – spread between interconnected cities, as did emblems. Moreover, the choice of motifs is highly significant, so much so that they will reappear in various places through this book. The bull-wrestling almost certainly refers to an important festival *agōn*, and

[34] It used to be believed, following Herrmann (1925), that between ca. 500 and 479 BC Larisa minted coins on the Persian standard, a practice linked with her pro-Persian stance. However, this received an effective rebuttal by Kagan (2004).

[35] For discussion of, and scholarship on, the types in question, and for their religious significance see Chapter 4.

[36] E.g. Kraay (1976), 115. Martin, by contrast (1985, 35–36), argues that the coinage was not strictly federal, but does assume that a formal federation was in place at the time.

it is quite probable that this occasion, bringing Thessalians together from different poleis, was a catalyst to coin production and so influenced the choice of imagery. The role of regional festivals in dictating coin production and imagery is well attested in other regions.[37] The *aition* of the festival, moreover, concerned the river Peneios (specifically, its outflow into the sea at Tempe), and this corresponds with the distribution of the minting poleis, most of which lie on or near the Peneios or its major tributaries. The motifs of horses and grain celebrate the natural products that, more than anything else, expressed the shared nature and value of the region. The sharing of types between cities absolutely does not provide evidence for the weakness or backwardness of the polis in Thessaly; rather, it attests to the fifth century as a time when the articulation of regional identity was especially strong (as was discussed in Chapters 3 and 4).

However, it is important not to lose sight of the primarily practical and economic nature of coins, as Mackil and Van Alfen remind us in their authoritative study of 'co-operative coinages'.[38] They identify a long-standing and excessive tendency in scholarship to focus on the use of coins to make political and cultural statements rather than on their prime function, which was to facilitate economic interaction and transaction. This is surely the chief conclusion that the early coins of the Thessalian poleis should encourage us to reach: that these were communities strongly interlinked through trade. Mackil and van Alfen also stress, as others have done,[39] the correlation between co-operative coinage and military co-operation. As we shall see below, the poleis of Thessaly in the fifth century BC were clearly engaging in joint military ventures for which a consistent, convenient mode of payment for troops would have been highly beneficial. Nor should we see Larisa, for all her influential position, as having imposed her coin types on other poleis as a way of subjecting them to her political and economic will. There is no evidence at all for such strategies on her part; as described above, the Aleuadai, who steered Larisaian affairs, worked through informal behind-the-scenes methods and through traditional *philia*. If other poleis joined the co-operative, it will have been because it benefited them to do so.

37 For example, Nielsen has argued convincingly that the ΑΡΚΑΔΙΚΟΝ coinage of Arkadia was minted in connection with the sanctuary of Zeus on Mount Lykaion, and was not a federal issue in the commonly used sense of the word; as Pretzler comments, 'It seems more likely that the *Arkadikon* coinage represents the attempt by one or more individual powers to harness Arcadian symbols and sentiments for their own ends' (2009, 95); cf. Nielsen (1996) and (2002), 120–57.

38 Mackil and van Alfen (2006), 202–05.

39 E.g. Martin (1985), 36.

4. Military co-operation

As has been said, warfare involving contingents from different poleis is one mode of co-operation that we can clearly see in Thessaly. It produces more evidence than trade because wars tend to appear in the major historical narratives of the time. Two aspects of this topic will be considered: first, the clearly attested deployment of multi-polis Thessalian armies fighting outside Thessaly as part of their obligations to non-Thessalian *symmachoi*; and, second, the much murkier possibility of a federal muster based on formalised contributions from constituent poleis.

a) Thessalian armies abroad in the fifth century

Periodically the Thessalians waged war outside their own region in situations that required the participation of a number of poleis. Those in the Archaic period provide little of value for us here, because the sources tend to speak only of 'the Thessalians', or else to single out noteworthy individuals (such as Kleomachos of Pharsalos, in the Lelantine War), and give no information about the composition of the armies; certainly, it would be unwise to assume that a genuinely pan-Thessalian muster was involved, since such a thing is unattested in any sources that do supply more detail. As has already been established, we should be wary of seeing in Archaic Thessaly everything we think Classical Thessaly lacks (unity, strength and a concerted and aggressive foreign policy). Even fifth-century engagements tend to be described extremely briefly. These episodes are: the Thessalian aid rendered to the Peisistratidai against the Spartans in ca. 510 BC; the cavalry supplied by Menon of Pharsalos in (probably) 476 BC; the Thessalian involvement in the battle of Tanagra in 457 BC; and the Thessalian contingents sent to assist Athens against Sparta at the start of the Peloponnesian War in 431 BC. Of these, the Menon expedition was clearly an individual venture by a Pharsalian aristocrat favourable to Athens (or to some Athenians: see below). Regarding the others, of Tanagra we know only that Atrax was one of the contributing Thessalian poleis.[40] The only episode that produces anything like a muster-roll is that in 431, described by Thucydides:

> This aid of the Thessalians came to the Athenians according to the old alliance [that made in 461 BC], and there arrived from them Larisaians, Pharsalians, Krannonians, Pyrasians, Gyrtonians and Pheraians. Those

[40] Theotimos, whose death in the battle was commemorated on a stele set up in Larisa, was Atragian. The Larisaian location of the monument probably, as Helly (2004b, 25) suggests, also indicates Larisa's involvement, and perhaps also the role of Larisaians in co-ordinating the expedition.

> from Larisa were led by Polymedes and Aristonous, one from each *stasis*, and those from Pharsalos were led by Menon. And there were leaders of the others, city by city.[41]

Two things are immediately apparent here: first, that only certain poleis send troops; second, that there is no single commander-in-chief (or if there is, Thucydides does not consider him important enough to mention). As to the former, the inclusion of Pyrasos and Gyrton is hard to explain without a knowledge of the internal agreements that no doubt brought it about.[42] Pyrasos was located on the Bay of Pagasai, in Phthiotis but not far from Pherai, and Gyrton was on the southern bank of the Peneios towards the gorge of Tempe (though it is sometimes described as Perrhaibian rather than as part of Pelasgiotis).[43] There is no sense at all of a systematic selection of contributors, or of any desire to achieve regional representation; major poleis take part, and draw a couple of second-rankers with them, no doubt because of personal ties between the ruling elites. Does this suggest the absence of any formalised federal army at this time?

b) The Thessalian federal army

It was by no means unknown in Classical Greece for a *koinon* to develop a system for determining fixed contributions from member poleis to a combined muster. Such a system in early fourth-century Boiotia is described by the Oxyrhynchos Historian: the whole region was divided into eleven *merē* (parts, or districts), and 'ἐπετέτακτο δὲ καὶ στρατιὰ ἑκάστωι μέρει περὶ χιλίους μὲν ὁπλίτας, ἱππέας δὲ ἑκατόν' ('an army was established, around a thousand hoplites and a hundred cavalrymen [being contributed] by each *meros*').[44] This influential description has in effect inspired in historians of

41 Thuc. 2.22.3: 'ἡ δὲ βοήθεια αὕτη τῶν Θεσσαλῶν κατὰ τὸ παλαιὸν ξυμμαχικὸν ἐγένετο τοῖς Ἀθηναίοις, καὶ ἀφίκοντο παρ' αὐτοὺς Λαρισαῖοι, Φαρσάλιοι, Κραννώνιοι, Πυράσιοι, Γυρτώνιοι, Φεραῖοι. ἡγοῦντο δὲ αὐτῶν ἐκ μὲν Λαρίσης Πολυμήδης καὶ Ἀριστόνους, ἀπὸ τῆς στάσεως ἑκάτερος, ἐκ δὲ Φαρσάλου Μένων· ἦσαν δὲ καὶ τῶν ἄλλων κατὰ πόλεις ἄρχοντες.' In this context, as argued by Helly (1995, 234–35), the most plausible explanation of the word *stasis* is that it refers not to opposing political factions but merely to two contingents. Helly, however, develops the point in accordance with his theory that the expedition constitutes a muster of the Thessalian federal army as designed by Aleuas Pyrrhos: Aristinoos and Polymedes are leading, in his view, not just Larisaians but troops from the whole tetrad of Pelasgiotis.

42 It is likely that the involvement of Gyrton was a factor behind the Athenian honours paid to Kallippos, a citizen of that polis, in 422/1 (*IG* I³ 92); however, Lambert (https://www.atticinscriptions.com/inscription/IGI3/92#note-2) suggests that Kallippos may also have helped prevent the Spartan Rhamphias from passing through Thessaly in the winter of that year (see Thuc. 5.13).

43 Strabo 9.5.19; but cf. 9.5.22, in which he seems to categorise it as Pelasgiotic.

44 *Hell. Oxy. FGrH* 66 F 9. On the fourth-century Boiotian *koinon* and its earlier

Thessaly a desire to identify a comparable system in their own region. Two chief sources have been adduced as evidence: a fragment of Aristotle, and Xenophon's account of the plans of Jason of Pherai in the 370s.

The fragment of Aristotle is as follows: 'The *peltē* is a shield without a rim, as Aristotle says in his *Thessalian Constitution*, writing thus: "having divided the polis, Aleuas organised it by *klēros* so that each *klēros* should provide forty horsemen and eighty hoplites … ".'[45] Almost without exception, scholars have interpreted this brief passage as describing the creation and organisation of the Thessalian federal state by the late sixth-century Larisaian statesman Aleuas Pyrrhos.[46] Such a reading is of course encouraged by the attribution of the information to a work by Aristotle on *the Thessalian Constitution*.[47] The result of this interpretation has been extremely significant. The supposed fact of a late Archaic system for organising regional musters has underpinned all the major studies of the Thessalian state; moreover, Aristotle's comments have also had to be reconciled, sometimes rather forcibly, with the second source, Xenophon's account of Jason's situation and plans in around 375 BC.

Book 6 of Xenophon's *Hellenika* begins with the visit of Polydamas of Pharsalos to the Spartans (whose *proxenos* he is), with the purpose of warning them about the growing might and ambition of Jason. Polydamas reports a conversation he himself has had with Jason, in which the latter has enumerated his own strengths and resources, placing near-total emphasis on the military.[48]

> Well, then, this is plain to us, that if Pharsalos and the towns which are dependent upon you came over to me, I would easily be established as

forms and development see Schachter (2016), 51–65. He argues for very early origins for at least some elements of the federal system. On the earliest epigraphic attestation of the Boiotoi as a collective entity, see Beck (2014). More sceptical approaches to an early Boiotian *koinon* include that of Larson (2007), who believed that formal federation began in the mid-fifth century. If she is right, Thessaly would be following a roughly similar trajectory to that of Boiotia, by no means unfeasible in view of the influence suggested above in the area of coinage.

[45] Fr. 498 Rose: 'πέλτη ἀσπίς ἐστιν ἴτυν οὐκ ἔχουσα, καθάπερ φησὶν Ἀριστοτέλης ἐν Θεσσαλῶν πολιτείᾳ γράφων ὅυτως· διελὼν δὲ τὴν πόλιν Ἀλεύας ἔταξε κατὰ τὸν κλῆρον παρέχειν ἑκάστους, ἱππέας μὲν τεσσαράκοντα, ὁπλίτας δὲ ὀγδοήκοντα … '.

[46] Such an interpretation goes back at least to Meyer in 1909; see also Wade-Gery (1924); Sordi (1958), 65–68. Its fullest exponent is of course Helly (1995), who reiterates his views in summary in Bouchon and Helly (2015). Larsen (1968, 16–17) is sceptical about the historicity of Aleuas, but not the scope or nature of the reforms.

[47] On Aristotelian and other *Politeiai* see Thomas (2019), 358–73.

[48] On the military character of Xenophon's account of Jason's position see Beck (2001), 359–60; this reflects Xenophon's characterisation of Jason in general, and indeed the wider themes of the *Hellenika*, but it is a matter of historical reality that regional co-operation in Thessaly was typically galvanised by military needs.

> Tagos of all the Thessalians. Furthermore, whenever Thessaly is under a Tagos, her horsemen amount to six thousand and more than ten thousand men become hoplites. [9] And when I see both their bodies and their high spirit, I think that if one should deploy them well, there would be no *ethnos* to whom the Thessalians would deign to be subject. In addition, while Thessaly is an exceedingly flat land, all the surrounding *ethnē* are subject to her whenever a Tagos is established here; and almost all of the men there are javelin-men, so that it is likely that our force would be superior in peltasts also.[49]

It is immediately apparent that this situation is very different from Aristotle's remarks. Xenophon makes no mention of *klēroi*; it is the cities who are expected to furnish contingents to Jason's army. This difference was attributed by Wade-Gery to a major social shift in the region, as poleis develop (tardily) and come to supersede in importance the more traditional *ethnos*-organisation with which Aleuas was working.[50] But it is Helly who takes the most extreme and energetic measures to reconcile the Aleuas context with that of Jason. He rightly challenges the theory that poleis were originally unimportant and, with reference to Asklepiodotos' *Taktika*, develops a complex mathematical theory to explain that tetrads, *klēroi* and poleis were all integrated into a system for allocating troop contributions, a system based on Ionian geometry. The vulnerabilities of this theory are many;[51] here I shall focus solely on the unsuitability of the Aristotle fragment to be the lynchpin of such a reconstruction, and on the enormous methodological liberation to be gained from reading it as it really is.

[49] Xen. *Hell.* 6.1.8–9: 'οὐκοῦν τοῦτο μὲν εὔδηλον ἡμῖν, ὅτι Φαρσάλου προσγενομένης καὶ τῶν ἐξ ὑμῶν ἠρτημένων πόλεων εὐπετῶς ἂν ἐγὼ ταγὸς Θετταλῶν ἁπάντων κατασταίην· ὥς γε μήν, ὅταν ταγεύηται Θετταλία, εἰς ἑξακισχιλίους μὲν οἱ ἱππεύοντες γίγνονται, ὁπλῖται δὲ πλείους ἢ μύριοι καθίστανται. ὧν ἐγὼ καὶ τὰ σώματα καὶ τὴν μεγαλοψυχίαν ὁρῶν οἶμαι ἂν αὐτῶν εἰ καλῶς τις ἐπιμελοῖτο, οὐκ εἶναι ἔθνος ὁποίῳ ἂν ἀξιώσαιεν ὑπήκοοι εἶναι Θετταλοί. πλατυτάτης γε μὴν γῆς οὔσης Θετταλίας, πάντα τὰ κύκλῳ ἔθνη ὑπήκοα μέν ἐστιν, ὅταν ταγὸς ἐνθάδε καταστῇ· σχεδὸν δὲ πάντες οἱ ταύτῃ ἀκοντισταί εἰσιν· ὥστε καὶ πελταστικῷ εἰκὸς ὑπερέχειν τὴν ἡμετέραν δύναμιν' (trans. Brownson, adapted).

[50] Wade-Gery (1924), 60–61.

[51] A basic but immensely sensible point is made by Lasagni (2008), 377: that despite the existence of the regional level of organisation and governance, 'Il complesso di tali strutture non può essere infatti spiegato come un insieme coerente, ove i più piccolo raggruppamenti infrapoleici si raccordino alla polis e quindi ai distretti di livello federale attraverso una costruzione unitaria "a scatole cinesi".' In other words, rather than being integrated into a perfectly coherent whole, the different levels of Thessalian political life – regional, polis (and polis-clusters), tribes and households – constituted different kinds of organisation that worked differently and were sometimes in conflict with each other.

In the fragment, Aleuas is described as dividing not Thessaly as a whole but 'the city'. So determined have scholars been to extrapolate federal organisation that they have posited a number of emendations of τὴν πόλιν, so as to make the fragment say what they have wished it to say: that is, to describe the changes made not just to a city (singular) but to the whole of Thessaly.[52] But such manipulation of the text based on a preconception is unwarranted. In fact, the most logical reading of the passage as we have it is to see τὴν πόλιν as Larisa, Aleuas' home, and to see his military arrangements as being made there, and the fragment describing local measures. There is epigraphic evidence for careful and systematic land divisions within the *chōra* of Larisa, sometimes with a military dimension and plausibly of early date.[53] The reforms of Aleuas would make perfect sense within that context. If we try to apply them to the whole of fifth-century Thessaly, on the other hand, we find them fundamentally incompatible with the military expeditions discussed under (a) above, in which there is no sign of a formal system behind the composition and organisation of the contingents from several poleis that go to assist non-Thessalian *symmachoi*.

This does, however, leave us with the need to explain one striking feature of Xenophon's account: the fact that Jason describes the federal muster as one supported by long-standing tradition. The phrases ὅταν ταγεύηται Θετταλία and ὅταν ταγὸς ἐνθάδε καταστῇ, which occur in the passage above and later in the narrative,[54] plainly suggest that Thessaly was periodically, or at least occasionally, under the control of a Tagos, a single commander (the word *tagos* is connected with the verb τάσσω and its cognates, and relates to military organisation).[55] Under certain circumstances (here the emergence of an individual with indisputable regional influence), the combined armed forces of Thessaly could fall under the command of one man. The position of the Tagos had both precedent and a certain legitimacy. When, later in the account, Polydamas describes Jason being made Tagos, it is clear that, though force of arms may have prompted his election, the role was conferred on him ὁμολογουμένως, 'by agreement'. This makes the Tagos different from a *tyrannos*: Jason takes care to place his role on a legitimate footing, but the same cannot be said of Lykophron before him or of Alexandros after him, both of whom were strongly opposed in their attempts at pan-Thessalian rule.

52 Wade-Gery (1924), 58–59.

53 Helly and Tziafalias (2013) discuss the Larisaian system of ἱππότεια ἀρχαῖα, plots of public land traditionally allotted for growing of fodder-crops and therefore the maintenance of the cavalry.

54 Cf. 6.1.12: the *perioikoi* pay tribute to the Thessalians whenever there is a Tagos (ὅταν ταγεύηται τὰ κατὰ Θετταλίαν).

55 Helly (1995), 36–38.

Should we dismiss as false this picture created by Xenophon of the periodically centralised leadership of Thessalian military resources? If we choose to do so, it must be for one of two reasons: either Xenophon is misrepresenting the matter, deliberately or through ignorance, or Jason fabricated the custom of sole command to give his domination of the region a spurious legitimacy. Xenophon is fascinated by the figure of Jason, who in his hands does take on certain qualities typical of Xenophontic rulers (such as physical endurance and the maintenance of strict military rigour and honour among his soldiers);[56] his character is no doubt shaped and embellished to fit the mould. In addition, Xenophon is keen to emphasise the difference between Jason, who ruled in accordance with the *nomos Thessalōn*, and Alexandros, who ruled only by coercion: this may have led him to place greater weight on the Tageia as an established institution than it really deserved. Likewise it is quite plausible to imagine that Jason himself helped to diminish Thessalian resistance to his rule by referring to precedent of some kind. To see either Xenophon or Jason as actually fabricating Thessalian tradition, however, is excessive and unnecessary. Indeed, since we have reinterpreted Aristotle's remarks on Aleuas and the *klēroi* as applying only to Larisa we are free to see the Tageia, as Xenophon calls it, for what it is: the accepted possibility that the region's armies and certain revenues could be commanded by one man for the purposes of a particular campaign. All it required was that the Thessalians participating in the campaign accepted the temporary command of an individual agreed on by all. Nothing more elaborate, formal or institutionalised is required.

What of the names Tagos and Tageia? The challenges levelled by Helly against believing these to be traditional terms referring to a sole ruler, in widespread use in Thessaly before Jason, are serious and well-founded. In particular, it is true that when Tagos and the word *taga* (seemingly the Thessalian form of Tageia) occur in the region's inscriptions they do so almost without exception in a purely local manifestation, meaning not a regional commander but a local magistrate.[57] However, this does not rule out its use *also* to denote the commander of the region's joint armies. After all, the title Archon was, as will be discussed below, one with connections to regional rule, but it also occurs as a polis official, albeit in rather later documents.[58] All in all, it seems inadvisable to state that Tagos and *taga* could not denote regional command, just because in the extant documents they are always in a polis context. After all, we have no inscriptions

56 See esp. *Hell.* 6.1.5–6. Sprawski (1999), 9–12 (summarising earlier scholarship).

57 Most instances are Hellenistic, but for earlier uses see *SEG* 27.183 (*I.Atrax* 89, early fifth century) and *AE* (1934/35) 140 (Argoussa, late sixth or early fifth century).

58 See, for example, *IG* IX.2.215: three polis Archons in Thaumakoi.

expressly referring to pan-Thessalian command from before the fourth century, so we cannot know what terms they would have contained.

That sole military command was temporary and abnormal in Thessaly is immediately apparent, both from Xenophon's text and from a wider examination of Thessalian history. According to Polydamas, when there was a Tagos the *perioikoi* would serve as peltasts in the regional muster; elsewhere in *Hellenika* 6 we are told that Jason imposed on the *perioikoi* the tribute that was determined in the time of Skopas, another figure of the late sixth century. Once again there is a sense of tradition being revived, of a disused custom being dusted off, rather than the continuation of habitual practice. And the exploitation of the *perioikoi* by Jason would have interfered with the state of affairs that seems to have prevailed otherwise: that major cities would have strongly influenced adjoining perioikic regions (as, for example, Larisa did the Perrhaibians). So the existence of centralised command overrode the more localised power bases of individual cities and put a temporary check upon their influence. If this situation was in operation on more than a very occasional and *pro tem* basis, it would certainly have created disruption significant enough to come to our attention through the various ancient authors who inform us in passing about Thessalian events.

This explains the fierce resistance in Thessaly to Jason's successors. For Jason to engineer his Tageia may have been, despite initial resistance, just about acceptable:[59] he would have justified it with reference to the mighty deeds he intended to achieve with Thessaly's resources at his disposal, and his appropriation of Phokian territory – a blow in the long-standing hostility between Thessaly and Phokis – would have been popular with his fellow Thessalians. But it was a different matter after his death. The Tageia was not meant to last a man's lifetime, let alone extend to members of his family. It was not heritable or intended to be dynastic. Jason pushed it to its limits; Alexandros overstepped those limits entirely. It is also worth noting that, before Jason, Lykophron of Pherai also wanted 'ἄρξαι ὅλης τῆς Θετταλίας' – 'to rule the whole of Thessaly',[60] and was also met with vehement opposition. The intervention in Thessaly by the Macedonian king Archelaos some time in the last years of the fifth century may have been sparked by the rise of Lykophron and the subsequent conflict between Pherai and Larisa; such was probably the historical backdrop to both the *Peri Politeias* attributed (erroneously) to Herodes Atticus,[61] and Thrasy-

[59] Sprawski (2006), 138–39.

[60] Xen. *Hell.* 2.3.4.

[61] Text, commentary and discussion in Albini (1968). The work is most likely to contain authentically late fifth-century material, but to go so far as to attribute it to Kritias – as Wade-Gery and Morrison (1942) do – is perhaps a step too far. The text suggests political upheaval within Larisa as well as conflict between Larisa and Pherai: at

machos' highly fragmentary speech *On Behalf of the Larisaians.*[62] The Larisaian Aristippos who supported Kyros the Younger's bid for power may have been prompted to build up that Persian connection by his conflict with the Pheraian leader.[63] In all, as Sprawski suggests, there is no evidence that Lykophron ever gained lasting control over all of Thessaly.[64] The position of Jason, apparently elected to pan-Thessalian leadership, is all the more remarkable in the light of Lykophron's efforts and their results.

5. Archon, *archein*

So there appears to have been some custom in Thessaly whereby the region's military resources could be placed under the command of one man. This is hardly surprising: it is contingent on practical necessity. Electing a war-leader as the need arose does not amount to the permanent existence of structures of federal government, to a *koinon*. However, the evidence available to us also shows glimpses of a rather different kind of phenomenon, a rather different form of rule. The most important source in this regard is the set of inscriptions that accompanied the statues of the Daochos Monument at Delphi. As with the career of Jason, we face the task of assessing the balance of tradition and innovation. Like Jason, Daochos II lived amidst exceptional events in Thessaly, and cannot be regarded as a typical Thessalian. Like Jason, he seems to have realised that his position was unusual, and to have appealed to tradition in order to reinforce and to ratify it.

The Daochos Monument consisted of a structure walled on three sides and open on the fourth, possibly roofed but possibly hypethral, which housed a row of statues representing past and present members of the dedicator's

section 30 the creation of a short-lived hoplite oligarchy is mentioned. Sprawski (1999), 34–38.

62 In fact only one fragment survives, to be imagined as spoken by a Larisaian orator: 'Ἀρχελάῳ δουλεύσομεν Ἕλληνες ὄντες βαρβάρῳ;' ('Shall we, being Greeks, be slaves to the *barbaros* Archelaos?' – fr. B2 DK). This suggests that Archelaos' involvement in the conflict allowed him a dangerous degree of influence within Larisa itself. Borza (1990), 165; Müller (2016), 184–86.

63 Xen. *Anab.* 1.1.10 merely describes Aristippos as 'πιεζόμενος ὑπὸ τῶν οἴκοι ἀντιστασιωτῶν' ('hard-pressed by his political opponents at home') – these opponents may well have been Pheraian, though an opposing faction within Larisa is also possible.

64 Sprawski (1999), 39. Lykophron did not, however, disappear: he surfaces again in the narrative of Diodoros, engaged in war with another Larisaian leader, Medeios, who enlisted Boiotians and Argives as his allies (Diod. 14.82.5–6; discussion of the events and their chronology: Wade-Gery and Morrison (1942), 67–68; Andrewes (1971), 222; Munn (1997), 72–73; Sprawski (1999), 38–45; Buckler (2003), 82–84; Stamatopoulou (2007b), 221–22).

family, each figure accompanied by a short, mostly verse inscription describing his most noteworthy deeds. I have discussed the inscriptions and their ideological significance in detail elsewhere;[65] here the important aspect is certain claims made about the political roles of the dedicator, his grandfather (another Daochos, called 'Daochos I' for convenience), and his great-great-grandfather, Aknonios. The relevant inscriptions are as follows:

> Aknonios:
> Aknonios son of Aparos, *tetrarchos* of the Thessalians.
> Daochos I:
> I am Daochos son of Agias. My homeland was Pharsalos;
> I ruled all of Thessaly, not with force but with law,
> for twenty-seven years, and Thessaly burgeoned with
> great and fruitful peace, and with wealth.
> Daochos II:
> Increasing the virtues of my family's ancestors,
> I set up these gifts to lord Phoibos, honouring my family and my homeland –
> I, Daochos, possessed of glorious praise,
> *tetrarchos* of the Thessalians,
> *hieromnēmōn* of the Amphiktyons.[66]

There is one significant echo between this piece of evidence and Xenophon's Jason narrative, and that is the fundamental idea that Thessaly could be under the rule of a single individual, as claimed for Daochos I, and that this could be accomplished according to established and accepted custom. The expression οὐ βίαι ἀλλὰ νόμωι obviously removed from Daochos I any suspicion of having seized power in the manner of a Lykophron or an Alexandros, whose conduct (the latter especially) would have been fresh in the collective memory of most of those who viewed the Daochos Monument, not only in that of its Thessalian commissioner.

65 Aston (2012b); see also the discussion and references on pp. 325–28.

66 *FD* III 4.460, 1, 5 and 7:

> Ἀκνόνιος Ἀπάρου τέτραρχος Θεσσαλῶν.
>
> Δάοχος Ἀγία εἰμί, πατρὶς Φάρσαλος, ἁπάσης
> Θεσσαλίας ἄρξας vac. οὐ βίαι ἀλλὰ νόμωι,
> ἑπτὰ καὶ εἴκοσι ἔτη, πολλῆι δὲ καὶ ἀγλαοκάρπωι
> εἰρήνηι πλούτωι τε ἔβρυε Θεσσαλία.
>
> αὔξων οἰκείων προγόνων ἀρετὰς τάδε δῶρα
> στῆσεμ Φοίβωι ἄνακτι, γένος καὶ πατρίδα τιμῶν,
> Δάοχος εὐδόξωι χρώμενος εὐλογίαι,
> τέτραρχος Θεσσαλῶν
> ἱερομνήμων Ἀμφικτυόνων.

However, alongside this basic similarity, the Daochos inscriptions present us with an image strikingly divergent from that of Xenophon's Jason narrative. What that highlighted was the notion of the Tagos, the military commander able to muster and deploy Thessaly's armies in order to undertake specific campaigns. The Daochos inscriptions include neither this title nor this concept. Instead we have the verb ἄρχειν and the title *tetrarchos*, and a description of pan-Thessalian rule quite different from that of Xenophon's Tageia.

It is to be observed that Daochos I is no temporary war leader: quite the reverse. He is described as having ruled – ἄρξας – all of Thessaly for twenty-seven years of peace and prosperity. We are perhaps reminded of the formula κἐν ταγᾶ κἐν ἀταγία, which appears in two fifth-century decrees from Thetonion in Thessaliotis and which has sometimes been interpreted as a Thessalian equivalent of the stock formula 'both in war and in peace'.[67] Even though that meaning of the phrase is by no means secure,[68] we may recall the fact observed above, that a Tagos does seem only to have been chosen when military circumstances required it. It is impossible to date Daochos I's rule exactly, but if his claim of peace and prosperity is to have any credibility at all we must suppose that it predated the violent attempted seizure of pan-Thessalian power by Lykophron of Pherai in 404 BC; thus at the latest it must have begun in 431 BC, just as the Peloponnesian War was commencing. But why is no explicit mention made of Daochos in Thucydides' quite detailed account of Brasidas' crossing of Thessaly in 424 BC, an account in which several Pharsalians are named and Thessalian politics discussed?[69] Either the Daochos Monument substantially fabricates Thessalian history, or else Daochos I, despite ruling all Thessaly, was not sufficiently prominent in the Brasidas episode to warrant Thucydides' attention.

It is very hard to believe in the former idea. That Daochos II wished to emphasise and perhaps exaggerate the regional importance of his forebears is surely inevitable. His own position, which he must have owed at least in part to Philip, was open to question both inside and outside his homeland, and to corroborate it through the expression of family precedent is a natural step. Nonetheless, to suggest that he *invented* the fact that his forebears

[67] Mili (2015), 216–17.

[68] The inscription does not make it clear whether the condition described relates to all of Thessaly or just to the polis: as Helly has argued (1995, *passim*), the title of Tagos is most often found within the polis context, as a local magistrate. Moreover, the fact that both decrees are from Thetonion makes one suspect a local custom, its full nature and significance now irrecoverable. On the other hand, why would an individual polis have a condition of *atagia*, if Tagoi were routinely elected?

[69] Thuc. 4.78.

had regional influence is surely going too far, at least as regards Daochos I (Aknonios may have lived long enough ago to be open to significant manipulation). The Monument would have been viewed by Thessalians, who would surely be able to identify and object to substantial falsehood.

It may well be that Daochos exists behind Thucydides' account without being named. Let us look again at what the historian tells us about Thessalian reactions to Brasidas' arrival with his army of 1,700 hoplites:

> About the same time in the summer, Brasidas set out on his march for the Thracian places with seventeen hundred heavy infantry, and arriving at Herakleia in Trachis, from thence sent on a messenger to his friends at Pharsalos, to ask them to conduct himself and his army through the country. Accordingly there came to Meliteia in Achaia Panairos, Doros, Hippolochidas, Torylaos, and Strophakos, the *proxenos* of the Chalkidians, under whose escort he resumed his march, being accompanied also by other Thessalians, among whom was Nikonidas from Larissa, a friend of Perdikkas. It was never very easy to traverse Thessaly without an escort; and throughout all Hellas for an armed force to pass without leave through a neighbour's country, was a delicate step to take. Besides this the Thessalian people had always sympathized with the Athenians. Indeed if instead of *dynasteia* there had been *isonomia* in Thessaly, he would never have been able to proceed.[70]

What seems to be happening here is that Brasidas is being escorted by a small number of influential individuals who are his *philoi* (and a Larisaian *philos* of Perdikkas, king of Macedon). However, he meets resistance from 'different people who wanted the opposite things', ἄλλοι τῶν τἀναντία τούτοις βουλομένων, and the way in which this resistance is expressed is significant: it is, say the other (unnamed) Thessalians, unjust that he should travel through ἄνευ τοῦ πάντων κοινοῦ. How to translate this phrase? Of course the word *koinon* now tends to be used to denote the machinery

[70] Thuc. 4.78.103: 'Βρασίδας δὲ κατὰ τὸν αὐτὸν χρόνον τοῦ θέρους πορευόμενος ἑπτακοσίοις καὶ χιλίοις ὁπλίταις ἐς τὰ ἐπὶ Θρᾴκης ἐπειδὴ ἐγένετο ἐν Ἡρακλείᾳ τῇ ἐν Τραχῖνι καί, προπέμψαντος αὐτοῦ ἄγγελον ἐς Φάρσαλον παρὰ τοὺς ἐπιτηδείους, ἀξιοῦντος διάγειν ἑαυτὸν καὶ τὴν στρατιάν, ἦλθον ἐς Μελίτειαν τῆς Ἀχαΐας Πάναιρός τε καὶ Δῶρος καὶ Ἱππολοχίδας καὶ Τορύλαος καὶ Στρόφακος πρόξενος ὢν Χαλκιδέων, τότε δὴ ἐπορεύετο. ἦγον δὲ καὶ ἄλλοι Θεσσαλῶν αὐτὸν καὶ ἐκ Λαρίσης Νικονίδας Περδίκκᾳ ἐπιτήδειος ὤν. τὴν γὰρ Θεσσαλίαν ἄλλως τε οὐκ εὔπορον ἦν διιέναι ἄνευ ἀγωγοῦ καὶ μετὰ ὅπλων γε δή, καὶ τοῖς πᾶσί γε ὁμοίως Ἕλλησιν ὕποπτον καθειστήκει τὴν τῶν πέλας μὴ πείσαντας διιέναι· τοῖς τε Ἀθηναίοις αἰεί ποτε τὸ πλῆθος τῶν Θεσσαλῶν εὔνουν ὑπῆρχεν. ὥστε εἰ μὴ δυναστείᾳ μᾶλλον ἢ ἰσονομίᾳ ἐχρῶντο τὸ ἐγχώριον οἱ Θεσσαλοί, οὐκ ἄν ποτε προῆλθεν, ἐπεὶ καὶ τότε πορευομένῳ αὐτῷ ἀπαντήσαντες ἄλλοι τῶν τἀναντία τούτοις βουλομένων ἐπὶ τῷ Ἐνιπεῖ ποταμῷ ἐκώλυον καὶ ἀδικεῖν ἔφασαν ἄνευ τοῦ πάντων κοινοῦ πορευόμενον' (trans. Crawley, adapted). On this episode see Sprawski (1999), 26–28.

of federal government, but in antiquity it had a far more flexible range of meanings.[71] Even if we translate it more vaguely, however, as 'without the collective authorisation of all [Thessalians]', the words are still very suggestive. They seem to indicate that Brasidas should, and could, have obtained the permission of the Thessalians as a collective body, that relations with the Thessalians did not have to be conducted solely on the basis of *philia* between individuals, that more representative mechanisms were available and appropriate.

If so, perhaps we should consider Daochos as the leader (Archon?) of an early manifestation of the Thessalian *koinon*, though not one in which all the institutional features visible later had come into being. If we do adopt such a position, however, we are forced to concede that his power seems to have been seriously circumscribed. As has been said, Thucydides fails to name him (if indeed he knew his name); he does, however, name those powerful individuals in Pharsalos and Larisa who comprised what he calls the *dynasteia*, the narrow oligarchy.[72] This *dynasteia*, he tells us, called the shots in Thessalian politics; this is where the real power lay, and we are brought right back into the world of the elites celebrated by Pindar and Bacchylides. However, there are some signs of change. We absolutely cannot and should not see Daochos as offering any kind of democratic alternative to the influence of the nobles; that said, Thucydides does offer us a glimpse of contested control in late fifth-century Thessaly, and one may speculate that the development of more formalised regional government that comes to view in the fourth century went alongside some movement towards a broader involvement in civic life within the polis.[73] For the first

[71] See *LSJ* s.v. κοινός, II.2.c; Beck and Funke (2015), 14.

[72] On patterns and modes of oligarchy within Thessalian poleis see Mili (2015), 56–71. It is interesting that the (probably) Larisaian speaker in the *Peri Politeias* (on which see further below) contrasts the oligarchy of Sparta (in which political inclusion was extended to those able to bear arms for the state) with that of his own polis, which was much narrower. *Peri Politeias* 30–31; Wade-Gery and Morrison (1942), 69–71. The phenomenon of the double agora is often evoked as reflecting this political system, because artisans and farmers were apparently excluded from the 'free agora' unless specifically invited by the magistrates; Arist. *Pol.* 7.1331a (describing the phenomenon as typical of Thessalian cities, not just Larisa). However, given the importance of livestock in Thessalian poleis we might prefer to explain the phenomenon of the separate 'commercial agora' as driven by the need to keep a large, bustling, noisy, smelly cattle market away from civic and religious business. For possible locations of the two agorai in Larisa see Tziafalias (1994), 158–74.

[73] Our evidence tends to apply to Larisa. Aristotle talks of members of the oligarchy in Larisa courting the *ochlos* because it was by them that they were elected: Arist. *Pol.* 5.1305b 20. We also hear of the mass conferral of citizenship: Arist. *Pol.* 5.1275b, a passage sadly obscured by the inclusion of a topical joke about 'kettle-makers'. Such a politography may have been a mechanism for increasing support for the ruling faction

time, in Brasidas' crossing, we find a hint that *koinon* structures may have been viewed as an alternative to traditional elite power bases.

6. The **ΦΕΤΑ/ΦΕΘΑ** coins

The Thessalian *koinon* that came into being after 196 BC minted coins bearing the ethnic ΘΕΣΣΑΛΩΝ and the image of Athena Itonia. In this case, we can clearly identify a federal Thessaly as the political and economic authority behind the production and use of the coins. It is not possible, however, to assume that a similar situation pertained when the ethnic first appeared on Thessalian coins: the issues discussed in Chapter 4, bearing the legend ΦΕΤΑ/ΦΕΘΑ (that is, short for ΦΕΤΑΛΩΝ/ΦΕΘΑΛΩΝ, 'of the Thessalians'), and the image of the birth of Skyphios. Even if we follow those scholars who would down-date the coins to the second half of the fifth century, does this really change matters?[74] True, by the later fifth century there are other signs of increasingly formalised political co-operation in Thessaly, the *koinon* mentioned by Thucydides, and – not mentioned by Thucydides – the pan-Thessalian rule of the Archon Daochos I. But, even in that situation, can we be sure that the ΦΕΤΑ/ΦΕΘΑ coins were produced at the instigation of the *koinon*?

The alternative is that they were produced by a sub-group, polis or other, who had an interest in reinforcing their particular connection with the *ethnos* of the Thessalians. At first they were identified as coins of Pherai – abbreviated to ΦΕ – with the ΤΑ/ΘΑ being the first two letters of a magistrate's name.[75] It was Franke who first recognised that the letters stood for ΦΕΤΑΛΩΝ/ΦΕΘΑΛΩΝ, the ethnic in its dialect form; however, for him Pherai was still in the frame. Placing them concurrent with the bull-wrestling issues minted by individual poleis, he argued that they were minted by a small number of poleis dominated by Pherai.[76] For him, they represented a challenge to the grouping, centred on Larisa, producing the bull-wrestling coins: in effect, two rival mint-unions centred around dominant poleis. He was certain the ΦΕΤΑ/ΦΕΘΑ coins came from Pherai because, according to his dating, Pherai stopped producing other types for the duration of the ΦΕΤΑ/ΦΕΘΑ issues.[77] However, the idea that Pherai cannot possibly have ceased minting for a short period of time has been

(in a climate of sporadic stasis). Stasis in Larisa: Xen. *Hell.* 6.4.34; Arist. *Pol.* 5.1306a 20.

[74] Liampi (1996), 125; Psoma and Tsangari (2003), 114–15.

[75] E.g. Herrmann (1922).

[76] Franke (1970), 91–92.

[77] Franke (1973), 9.

questioned;[78] stronger reasoning comes in stylistic form, since there are good reasons for identifying Pherai as the producer of issues with a forepart or head of a horse on the obverse and an ear of grain on the reverse; the legend ΦΕ on these types has recently been interpreted as a shorter abbreviation of ΦΕΤΑ/ΦΕΘΑ, but it is well-attested as the abbreviation of ΦΕΡΑΙΩΝ on other issues whose Pheraian source is quite clear. Other possible minting poleis are Methylion, because it does also mint the Skyphios type in its own name, and Skotoussa because it produces a very similar type, but with the leaping forepart of a horse instead of a horse unambiguously emerging from rocks.[79]

Helly, for his part, has argued that the minting group – like the Petthaloi awarding *proxenia* and other honours on a fourth-century inscription more usually attributed to Pherai – were the *ethnos* of Epeirote origin who settled in Thessaliotis first before extending their presence and influence over the whole region over centuries up to the end of the Classical period.[80] While this theory of the narrow definition of Thessaloi/Petthaloi as an immigrant group leaves me unpersuaded, locating the ΦΕΤΑ/ΦΕΘΑ coins in Thessaliotis is attractive. We saw in Chapter 4 that Orthe is a likely centre for the cult of Poseidon. We also noted signs, such as the association between Kierion and Arne, that in the Classical period communities in that area were interested in reinforcing their traditional links with the myth of the arrival of the Thessalids/Thessaloi, a myth that gave their part of Thessaly a privileged relationship with the *ethnos* and its collective history.

In the fifth century – especially if we attach the ΦΕΤΑ/ΦΕΘΑ issues to the early to mid-400s[81] – it is more plausible to see coins minted in the name of the Thessalians not as federal issues per se but as coins produced by a subgroup, whatever their identity, interested in emphasising their affiliation to, and place within, the *ethnos*; on this model, being Thessalian is something to be claimed and perhaps competed for. However, a very short-lived version of the ΦΕΤΑ/ΦΕΘΑ coins appears in the mid-fourth century, this time in bronze and with an unabbreviated ethnic – ΠΕΤΘΑΛΩΝ – and on the obverse a laureate head of a bearded god, either Zeus or Poseidon, while Skyphios emerging from his rock has moved to the reverse. An explicit connection with Poseidon, regardless of the identity of the god on the obverse, is sometimes achieved by the inclusion of a trident in the field

[78] See, for example, Liampi (1996), 124–25; Mili (2015), 236.

[79] Liampi (1996, 125) sensibly eschews choosing a minting polis for the ΦΕΘΑ/ΦΕΤΑ coins: 'Ließe sich wohl am einfachsten annehmen, daß sie in Wirklichkeit im Namen aller Thessaler in eine traditionellerweise aktiven Münzstätte aus einem Anlaß geprägt wurden, der uns unbekannt ist.'

[80] Helly (1992), 85, n. 179; 91.

[81] Liampi (1996) dates the issues to the period 460–450 BC.

on the reverse, under the belly of the emerging horse.[82] By this date, as we shall see in the next section, we have unambiguous evidence of the existence of a Thessalian *koinon*, and this *koinon* may perhaps have been responsible for the production of the new Skyphios type, whose composition is, after all, very different from that of its fifth-century counterparts.[83] However, even the fourth-century Thessalian *koinon* was not straightforwardly representative of the whole *ethnos*, since it was generated as a coalition of poleis united by their shared opposition to Pherai.

7. A Thessalian *koinon* in the fourth century BC

In 361/0 a new alliance was drawn up between the Athenian state and the Thessalians. In fact, some form of alliance existed between Athens and Jason.[84] (This lends some credence to the restoration of Jason's name in the charter of the Second Athenian Confederacy formed in 378 BC,[85] a matter that has aroused heated debate.[86]) At first, Alexandros seems to have been able to inherit, or resume, the reasonably good relations with Athens that Jason had enjoyed; a treaty was contracted in 368.[87] However, this diplomatic cordiality did not survive the increasing involvement in Thessalian affairs of Athens' old enemies the Thebans, who sent their leading general Pelopidas into the region to thwart Alexandros' violent imposition of rule on Thessalian poleis;[88] after the Theban victory over Alexandros at Kynoskephalai in 364 BC, Theban influence in the north was massively increased, despite Pelopidas' death in the battle, and Alexandros was forced to become an ally of the Boiotians.[89] The Thessalians opposed to Alexandros' rule were so warmly inclined towards the Thebans that they mourned Pelopidas fervently and erected a statue in his honour at

[82] Mack (2021), 135–36.

[83] A sensible note of caution is struck by Martin, however (1985, 40), when speaking of attempts to situate the ΠΕΤΘΑΛΩΝ issue within the chronological framework of fourth-century Thessaly: 'these are only speculative dates established by supposed connections to historical events, and they have no special claim to authority.'

[84] [Demosth.] 49.10; Diod. 15.71.3–4; Xen. *Hell.* 7.1.28; Plut. *Pel.* 31.6; Sprawski (2006), 138; Buckler (2003), 256–57. Jason's more substantial alliance was with Thebes: Tuplin (1993), 119, n. 52; Sprawski (1999), 67–71.

[85] *IG* II^2 43; the problematic erasure occurs on line 111.

[86] E.g. Baron (2006), 390–91; Cawkwell (1981), 44–45; Mitchel (1984), 390–91; Sprawski (2020), 93–95.

[87] Diod. 15.71.3; this earlier alliance is mentioned in the record of the treaty of 361/0 between Athens and the Thessalian *koinon* (*IG* II^2 116, lines 30–40; see Bolmarcich 2007, 484–85).

[88] Buckler (2003), 319–27.

[89] Diod. 15.80.6.

Delphi.[90] Moreover, when the Thebans fought against the Spartans and the Athenians at Mantineia in 362, many Thessalians were ranged on the Theban side.[91] This is the backdrop to the alliance of 361/0 BC.[92] The Athenians faced an acute need to encourage resistance to Alexandros' rule, since the Pheraian had recently begun to menace Athenian interests in the Aegean with attacks on Tenos and Peparethos, going so far as to assault Panormos and Peiraious in Attica itself.[93]

The inscription recording the alliance, in combination with another closely related text, is the single most substantial piece of evidence for the workings of diplomatic relations between Classical Thessaly and another state. To understand how great a departure it seems to be from previous situations, we should step back for a moment and consider the earlier occasions on which Athens had conducted an alliance with 'the Thessalians'. On the face of it, the very fact of such alliances being possible speaks for the political existence of 'the Thessalians'. However, whereas this existence is certainly attested by the inscription of 361/0, the earlier cases give a very different impression.

a) Athenian alliances with 'the Thessalians' before 361/0

Diplomatic links between Athens and Thessaly start early, in the late sixth and early fifth centuries BC, as Herodotos reveals in describing how the Peisistratidai turned to the Thessalians for help when the Spartans under Anchimolios turned up to drive them out of Athens at the order of the Delphic oracle: 'The Peisistratidai found out about these things, and they called for help from Thessaly; for they had made an alliance with them. The Thessalians, at their request, reached a shared decision and despatched a thousand horsemen and their own *basileus* Kineas, a Koniaian man.'[94] This *summachia* raises many questions about the Thessalian side of

[90] Ostentatious Thessalian grief: Plut. *Pel.* 33. The dedicatory inscription recording the statue of Pelopidas – made by Lysippos, no less – set up at Delphi by the Thessalians after his death, survives: *SEG* 35.480. See Bousquet (1939) and (1963, 206–08). For this monument within the wider context of Boiotian dedicatory practices at Delphi at this time see Scott (2016), 111–12.

[91] Xen. *Hell.* 7.5.4: these comprised both supporters and opponents of the late Alexandros, in fact.

[92] *IG* II^2 116.

[93] [Demosth.] 50.4; Diod. 15.95.1–2; Polyain. 6.2.1. For a detailed discussion of Alexandros' actions against the backdrop of Pheraian maritime ambitions in the fourth century see Sprawski (2020).

[94] Hdt. 5.63.3: 'οἱ δὲ Πεισιστρατίδαι προπυνθανόμενοι ταῦτα ἐπεκαλέοντο ἐκ Θεσσαλίης ἐπικουρίην· ἐπεποίητο γάρ σφι συμμαχίη πρὸς αὐτούς. Θεσσαλοὶ δέ σφι δεομένοισι ἀπέπεμψαν κοινῇ γνώμῃ χρεώμενοι χιλίην τε ἵππον καὶ τὸν βασιλέα τὸν σφέτερον Κινέην ἄνδρα Κονιαῖον·'.

the agreement. Did it really constitute, as is suggested by the expression κοινῇ γνώμῃ, an alliance with the region as a whole? Who was Kineas 'the Koniaian', and how was he chosen to lead the Thessalian forces?

Herodotos is usually keen to identify the roles and contributions of specific individuals and sub-groups within the major events he describes, and it seems unlikely that when he talks of a 'common decision' he is simply inventing a consensus that had no historical reality at all. However, elsewhere in his narrative he makes it plain that the reins of Thessalian affairs are held with reasonable firmness by the Aleuadai of Larisa, who are particularly well-disposed towards the Peisistratidai. Peisistratos named one of his sons Thessalos, perhaps to mark the friendship;[95] his sons worked in concert with the Aleuadai, according to Herodotos, to solicit the invasion of Xerxes. This *philia* between the two families certainly underpinned the *summachia* that, after all, is anchored strongly to the Peisistratidai on the Athenian side: they, not their city, are described as having contracted it.[96]

Not only was the alliance between Athens and Thessaly at this time really just a formal expansion of a personal friendship; it actually supported and highlighted personal interests, even to the detriment of Thessaly on the one side and Athens on the other. When the Aleuadai joined with the Peisistratidai in encouraging the invasion of Xerxes in 480 BC, they did so, according to Herodotos, against the wishes of the majority of the Thessalians.[97] It is even possible that Aleuad influence in Perrhaibia influenced the Greek decision not to make Tempe their main line of defence, but to withdraw to Thermopylai, thus leaving the Thessalians exposed to the advancing Persians and leaving them no option but to submit.[98] For their part, the Peisistratidai tried to use their Thessalian friends to engineer

[95] In fact, even more significantly, the name Thessalos was added as a *parōnumion* to the son's existing name, Hegesandros: [Arist.] *Ath. Pol.* 17.3. Nagy suggests that this gesture was made when Peisistratos and his sons were cultivating a connection with Sigeion and its Achilles-cult, which the Aiolians also used as a way of evoking their supposed Thessalian origins: Nagy (2010), 148–49. This slightly different interpretation of the name also suggests a motive behind the Peisistratids' cultivation of Aleuad friendship: the 'cultural capital' that a Thessalian connection gave them in light of the region's epic credentials (see Chapter 2).

[96] Van Wijk (2017), 6–7. Compare, in their treatments of these treaties and their implications, Bouchon and Helly (2015), 232, and Mili (2019), esp. 227. Bouchon and Helly state that 'The numerous treaties between the Thessalians and the Athenians concluded between the sixth and the middle of the fourth century BCE showed that the *Thessaloi* formed a political entity which was able to negotiate alliances and treaties.' Mili, on the other hand, is rightly alert to the prime agency of individuals, especially on the Thessalian side, and to the dangers of assuming a formalised decision-making system behind those individuals.

[97] Hdt. 7.6.

[98] Robertson (1976).

their recall from exile and the suppression of domestic opposition. It is clear that, in the policy towards the Persians, the Aleuadai were following their own interests and those of their *philoi*, rather than representing Thessalian policy on a regional basis. In fact, it is likely that the *philia* was a triangular one, in which we should include Alexandros I, the king of Macedon.[99] Alexandros' advice to the Greek coalition contributed to the withdrawal from Tempe, and was therefore in keeping with the Aleuad policy. That he too was a friend of the Peisistratidai is suggested by the fact that he had, ca. 510, offered the exiled Hippias the site of Anthemon as a refuge, while the Aleuadai offered him Iolkos.[100] At the time of Xerxes' invasion he maintained a remarkable balancing act between friendship to Athens and submission to Persia.

The identity of Kineas, the leader of the allied Thessalian expedition, is as mysterious as the *koinē gnōmē*. Since he is leading a joint Thessalian military expedition, he must have been from a town of some significance, and yet no 'Konia' or similar, such as could have produced 'Koniaios', is known in Thessaly. This has sent scholars searching for emendations.[101] One possibility is to read 'Gonnaios' – Gonnaian, from Gonnoi.[102] This is rather tempting in some ways. Gonnoi, and Perrhaibia more generally, were within the ambit of Larisa and the Aleuadai at the time. It therefore makes sense for Kineas, as a citizen of Gonnoi, to lead an expedition to assist the Aleuadai's Athenian *philoi*. However, the city-ethnic Gonnaios is not attested. Gonneus is the usual form, at least in the inscriptions of the fourth century and later, and that would require quite a substantial emendation in Herodotos' text. The second possibility, sharing both the same historical appeal and the same basic objection, is Mondaieus, 'from Mondaia': Mondaia is another Perrhaibian town, and one with some links to Gonnoi, being therefore subject to Aleuad influence.[103] Sheer verbal similarity, however, has produced a rough scholarly consensus around the third suggestion: 'Kondaios', a man from Kondaia.[104] This town is attested as a polis only in the third century, and we know nothing about its status

[99] Graninger (2010), 310.

[100] Hdt. 5.94.

[101] Hornblower (2013), 188–89, for a summary of the suggestions made to date. The most intriguing is that Κονιαῖος is a patronymic adjective and that Kineas' father was Konas; however, with no comparable example of Thessalian patronymic adjectives finding their way into Herodotos (or any other Attic author), this seems unlikely.

[102] E.g. Lazenby (1993), 88. Helly's assertion (1973, vol. I, 74–75) that Herodotos would never have called a man from Perrhaibian Gonnoi a *Thessalos*, as he does Kineas, seems to assume a stricter use of the ethnic than might actually have prevailed.

[103] Gonnoi and Mondaia both participated, for example, in a dedication to Apollo Pythios in the early to mid-fourth century: see *SEG* 29.546.

[104] Robertson (1976), 106; Helly (1995), 221–22.

or activities in the fifth, but its location was almost certainly in Pelasgiotis, at no great distance from Larisa.[105] So once again Aleuad influence may be in the picture, and the expedition led by Kineas may plausibly be seen as motivated primarily not by the interests of the whole region but by those of a single influential family, able to sway the affairs of the *ethnos* to assist their friends.[106]

By 461, however, a formal condition of alliance existed between the Thessalians and the Athenians, as Thucydides tells us. The context is the aftermath of the Athenians' brusque dismissal by Sparta, to whom she had offered assistance in the struggle against the rebel helots on Ithome. Athens in her anger seeks other friends: 'When they arrived home, immediately they broke off the alliance which had been made against the Persians, and allied themselves with Sparta's enemy Argos; and by both of them the same oaths and the same alliance were contracted with the Thessalians.'[107] On the Athenian side, we are no longer in a situation where the family of a tyrant could dictate foreign policy (though of course the motivations of individuals would still have influenced the state's direction behind the scenes). A strategic rapprochement between the Peisistratidai and the Aleuadai has been replaced, for the Athenians at least, by a *summachia* contracted by the state. There are clear signs that diplomacy with Thessaly in the fifth century followed traditional modes of interaction; Athenian suspicion of lavish embassies to Thessaly will be discussed further in Chapter 6. The agreements were ostensibly contracted on behalf of, and for the benefit of, the Athenian people as a whole, and came under suspicion when they seemed not to be fulfilling this requirement. Excessive involvement of personal ambition or personal enrichment was regarded as inherently problematic; one cannot imagine the same attitude pertaining in Thessalian society.

What of the Thessalian side? Had the alliance achieved a greater formality there, too, and been placed on a political footing beyond the influence of a single clan? It cannot be overlooked that the very existence of an alliance would have required some degree or co-ordination among the Thessalians. The Athenians must have had individuals or a group to whom they could address their initial advances and their later embassies. They will not have

105 *IACP* s.v. 'Kondaia' (no. 399), 694.

106 This view differs significantly from that of Robertson (1976), who believes that we can in fact detect the workings of a proper Thessalian federation in the early fifth century: this organisation sends the Kineas expedition, and in fact operates in partial opposition to the power of the Aleuadai.

107 Thuc. 1.102.4: 'εὐθὺς ἐπειδὴ ἀνεχώρησαν, ἀφέντες τὴν γενομένην ἐπὶ τῷ Μήδῳ ξυμμαχίαν πρὸς αὐτοὺς Ἀργείοις τοῖς ἐκείνων πολεμίοις ξύμμαχοι ἐγένοντο, καὶ πρὸς Θεσσαλοὺς ἅμα ἀμφοτέροις οἱ αὐτοὶ ὅρκοι καὶ ξυμμαχία κατέστη.'

wandered speculatively through Thessaly seeking persons with whom to deal. They may have approached a figure such as Daochos, an Archon, when there was one. However, they need not have. They will have had friends and contacts among the leading men in Thessalian poleis, whom they could have approached. Rich friend and Archon may sometimes have been one and the same, but the existence of a formal *koinon* leader is not actually required for diplomatic connections to have been forged and maintained.

So we have the sense of Athens and Thessaly pulling apart – Athens' social and political fabric changes, that of Thessaly remains largely the same. It is also instructive to examine what their alliance with the Thessalians actually gave the Athenians, and what it did not. We first see the alliance being utilised by the Athenians at the battle of Tanagra in 457, and then at the outbreak of the Peloponnesian War, when the Athenians employ their Thessalian allies against invading Spartan forces. The two episodes have certain features in common. Together they reveal that having an alliance with the Thessalians did not secure either unwavering loyalty or pan-Thessalian involvement. The Thessalians who come to Athens' aid are listed by Thucydides as Larisaians, Pharsalians, Krannonians, Pyrasians, Gyrtonians and Pheraians. They are for the most part from large and significant communities who could spare the manpower and who were in any case accustomed to play a role in Greek affairs beyond Thessaly. So far so natural: we should hardly expect a pan-Thessalian muster, since all the Athenians required was a supplement of their own inadequate cavalry. More startling is the outcome of Thessalian allied assistance to Athens at the battle of Tanagra in 457 BC.

While in 431 BC Athens' Thessalian allies hardly covered themselves in glory, at Tanagra they were a distinct liability, changing sides halfway through the battle and surely thus contributing to the Spartan victory. That the opprobrium likely to have resulted from this dramatic defection was not lost on the Thessalians[108] is suggested by a remarkable verse epitaph from Larisa, which records the death of an Atragian, Theotimos, in the battle: strong emphasis is placed upon the honourable death the young man had sustained, fighting bravely among fellow Greeks and conferring glory on his homeland.[109] But why did the Thessalians perform this *volte*

[108] On the considerable influence of the battle in Athenian culture see Papazarkadas and Sourlas (2012), 603–04. The impact of the event in Thessaly is indicated by the dedication at Delphi discussed below.

[109] *SEG* 54.562:

οὔ τι καταισχύνας πόλεο̄ς κλέος ἐνθάδε κεῖαι
Ἄτραγος εὐρυχόρο̄ Θεσσαλίᾱ στέφανον
τεύχο̄ν, ὀ̄ Θεότιμε, Μενύλλου παῖ, σὺν ἀρίστο<ι>ς
ἀνδρ<ά>σιν Ἑλλέ̄νο̄ν ἐν Τανάγρας πεδίοῑ.

For discussion see Helly (2004b). See also the Introduction of this volume.

face? Thucydides says nothing by way of explanation,[110] and his silence has encouraged modern historians to theorise with varying degrees of plausibility. While the precise circumstances must remain unknown, it is surely right to suppose, as most have done, that the defection reflects internal division among the Thessalians themselves, resulting in a wavering of loyalty; Theotimos seems unlikely to have been among those who changed sides, given the emphasis on honour of his epitaph, and this suggests that the Thessalian contingent split.[111] The likelihood is made greater by the fact that Theotimos was plainly, to judge from his depiction on his grave stele, an infantryman, and the Thessalians who changed sides at Tanagra were cavalrymen.[112] Thus it is clear that, though a state could, on stone (so to speak), have an alliance with 'the Thessalians', the fact that the latter did not constitute a seamless political entity could cause damaging fluctuations in their allegiance.[113] Plainly Athens was trying to create and maintain a lopsided situation: an alliance between, on the one side, herself as a single community (for all the political dissent that naturally existed between its citizens) and, on the other, a region of many and various communities, quite capable of collective action when the need arose but not, at this time, operating within regular ***koinon*** structures.

[110] More detail is supplied by Diodoros (11.80), who claims that the Thessalians attacked the Athenian baggage-train and killed many of the Athenians before the latter realised they were hostile; the Thessalians themselves were then routed, with great loss of life. The Spartans, however, came to their aid. The latter suggests more than a sudden opportunistic desire, on the part of the Thessalians, to steal the Athenians' baggage; a shift of their loyalty towards the Spartans, which the latter reciprocated, is clearly implied.

[111] Wade-Gery and Morrison (1942), 62; Sordi (1958), 106–07.

[112] In addition to the literary testimonies, the Thessalian dedication at Delphi after the battle may be relevant in this regard: was the choice of statue – a horse – emblematic of the cavalry? Quite possibly. As for Theotimos, Sprawski (2014c) has put forward an attractive argument for identifying him, on the basis of his equipment, as a peltast rather than a hoplite, despite the prosperity of his family suggested by the quality of his monument. So perhaps two quite separate contingents of the Thessalian army at Tanagra parted company, with the cavalry displaying Spartan sympathies that the peltasts did not share.

[113] It may also be relevant to recall the complicated circumstances surrounding the battle. Sparta had, in 458, assisted the Dorians of Doris against the Phokians; given alleged anti-Phokian feeling in Thessaly, this may have inclined some to favour Sparta (Thuc. 1.107.2). Tanagra was followed by a spell of Spartan–Athenian wrangling for Delphic influence, exemplified by the so-called Second Sacred War in 449: Thuc. 1.112.5; Pownall (1998), 37–38; Sánchez (2002), 106–15. It is interesting, too, that Kimon, arriving at the battlefield, was unceremoniously driven away by the Athenians (Plut. *Kim.* 17.3–4, *Per.* 10.1; Kagan 1969, 91–92); if his Pharsalian friends (see below, n. 119) were among the Thessalians present, the spectacle could have influenced their defection.

This is not to say that Athens maintained her side of the alliance blamelessly. We may recall the mysterious 'Orestes incident' in 454 BC, in which Athens seemingly tried – and failed – to install in Pharsalos a leading man (Orestes son of Echekratidas) who had earlier been exiled.[114] The date of this bit of meddling in a Thessalian polis suggests that it may in part have been prompted by Tanagra, by resentment at the outcome of that event and by the desire to steer Thessalian opinion back to a more wholehearted support for Athenian interests. Of course the attempt was made at the polis level, but the interconnected nature of Thessalian polis elites would have made Orestes seem a useful puppet to manipulate, if he could be reintroduced into his community. The attempt backfired, and cannot have endeared Athens to the Thessalians – or at any rate to the Pharsalians – but the formal alliance remained intact and was called upon once again in 431 when, as noted above, allied Thessalian cavalry once more supplemented Athens' own military resources in her conflict against the Spartans. Neither side in the alliance felt the need to terminate it – neither the Athenians after Tanagra, nor the Thessalians after the 'Orestes incident' – which may attest, in part, to the Athenians' recognition of their weakness in cavalry and dependence on allied aid.[115]

The variability of Thessalian allegiances may be seen at various junctures in the Classical period: variability not only between, but also within, poleis. When the Spartan general Brasidas marched north in 424 BC on his way to attack Athens' holdings in the north Aegean, he found the crossing of Thessaly especially difficult. This might seem predictable: after all, Thessaly was Athens' ally, and had helped her against Spartan invaders in 431 BC; Sparta had moreover angered the Thessalians extremely by her foundation of Herakleia in Trachis only two years before Brasidas' arrival, in 426.[116] However, Thucydides' account of the episode reveals a far more confusing patchwork of agencies and motivations. Two factors are clearly important in this situation. The first is the role of personal relationships; and the second is the existence of divided attitudes among different sectors of the Thessalian population. We might take the episode to indicate that the cities of Pharsalos and Larisa were sympathetic towards the Spartans, whereas others were not: after all, we are told that Brasidas has friends in Pharsalos, and Nikonidas of Larisa is instrumental in assisting him. However, as

[114] Thuc. 1.111.1, hinting that the Athenians had other aims – also unrealised – beyond the immediate mission. Cf. Diod. 11.83, attributing the venture to the command of Myronides.

[115] That said, Bugh has argued that the Tanagra affair encouraged the Athenians to develop their own cavalry, in recognition of the undesirability of continued dependence on undependable Thessalians. Bugh (1988), 40–49; cf. Spence (1993), 9–15.

[116] Thuc. 3.92.

Sprawski argues, we cannot extrapolate stable policies from these personal friendships:[117] the very Nikonidas who helped Brasidas cross Thessaly was probably one of those who prevented a similar crossing by another Spartan army, led this time by Ischagoras on his way to aid Brasidas.[118] The reason for the change of direction lies with bonds of personal friendship: Nikonidas was the *philos* of the Macedonian king Perdikkas II, who wished Brasidas to arrive safely; this same Perdikkas did not want Ischagoras' army to reach Macedon, and used his Thessalian friends to prevent it. The policy at work here, then, is neither pro-Athenian nor pro-Spartan, but simply in accordance with the old principle of helping one's friends (with a generous admixture of expediency, no doubt).

Pharsalos likewise cannot simply be labelled 'pro-Spartan': after all, the influential family of the Menonids appear to have maintained a strongly pro-Athenian stance.[119] Indeed, it is probable that Menon of Pharsalos was assisting the Athenians at this very time, as has been established above. Within cities as within Thessaly as a whole, then, different groups, families and individuals would have maintained quite different attitudes towards various foreign powers. This state of affairs is even more visible, if anything, in the chaotic years around and after Athens' defeat by Sparta in 404 BC.[120] The people who interacted most effectively with the Thessalians – in particular, Philip of Macedon – were those who recognised this quality of Thessalian society and actually contrived to exploit it. This character was by no means dispelled in the fourth century by the development of more formalised machinery of regional government in Thessaly, to which we now turn.

[117] Sprawski (1999), 29–31.

[118] Thuc. 4.132.2. Ischagoras and a couple of colleagues make it through, but they realise that it is futile to try to take an army through.

[119] Stamatopoulou (2007b), 213–19. A Menon (called Menon I by historians for convenience) aided Kimon at Eion in 476/5 BC: Demosth. 23.199 and 13.23. The Pharsalian contingent fighting for the Athenians in 431 BC was led by Menon II: Thuc. 2.22.3. The Thucydides who was a *proxenos* of the Athenians in 411 BC was a member of the Menonid clan: Thuc. 8.92.8. Menon III's stay in Athens is recorded in Plato's *Menon*. Stamatopoulou's discussion gives a remarkable picture of a single family's consistently close ties – both political and cultural – with Athens.

[120] Aristippos of Larisa sought help from Kyros the Younger against his enemies at home: Xen. *Anab.* 1.1.10, 1.2.1; cf. Plato, *Men.* 78d, in which Sokrates calls Menon ὁ τοῦ μεγάλου βασιλέως πατρικὸς ξένος, 'the ancestral guest-friend of the Great King'. In 380 BC, when the Spartan king Agesipolis went north to deal with the aggressive behaviour of Olynthos, he was assisted by some Thessalians described by Xenophon (*Hell.* 5.3.9) as γνωσθῆναι τῷ Ἀγησιπόλιδι βουλόμενοι – 'wanting to become known to Agesipolis'. It was to Sparta that Polydamas of Pharsalos turned for help against Jason of Pherai in 375; however, in the ensuing decades different groups of Thessalians cultivated Macedonian and Athenian support.

b) Political institutions in the treaty of 361/0

The text of the treaty, in particular lines 14–36, floods the normally dark political landscape of Thessaly with sudden light. We have a mention of a *koinon*, indicating collective political authority with which another state could do business. We have an Archon, who is the chief presiding officer of the *koinon*; below him, we have *polemarchoi*, *hipparchoi*, *hieromnēmones* and other officials. These are the people who take oaths and contract alliances on behalf of the Thessalian *ethnos*. And the disparity between Thessaly and Athens in terms of diplomatic machinery is reduced: now Thessaly is operating not on the basis of personal *philia* (or not solely on that basis), but within the framework of formal political structures.

> Of the Athenians the
> generals and the Council and the *hipparchoi* and the cavalry
> shall swear this oath: 'I shall go in support with all my strength as far as
> possible if anybody goes against the federation of the Thessalians for
> war, or overthrows the Archon whom the Thessalians chose, or
> establishes a tyrant in Thessaly.' They shall swear the
> lawful oath. So that also the Thessalians shall swear to the
> city, the People shall choose five men from all
> Athenians, who shall arrive in Thessaly and administer this
> oath to Agelaos the archon and the *polemarchoi* and
> the *hipparchoi* and the cavalry and the *hieromnēmones*
> and the other officials who hold office on behalf of
> the *koinon* of the Thessalians: 'I shall go in support with all my
> strength as far as possible if anybody goes against the city of Athens
> for war or overthrows the People of the
> Athenians'.[121]

121 *IG* II² 116, lines 14–29:

ὀμόσαι δὲ Ἀ[θη]ναίων μὲν τὸς στρ-
[ατη]γὸς καὶ τ[ὴ]ν βολὴν καὶ τὸς ἱππάρχος καὶ τὸς ἱππέ-
[α]ς τόνδε τὸν ὅρκον· βοηθήσω π[α]ντὶ σθένει κατὰ τὸ δυ-
νατόν, ἐάν τι[ς] ἴηι ἐπὶ τὸ κοινὸν τὸ Θετταλῶν ἐπὶ πολ-
[έμ]ωι ἢ τὸν ἄρχοντα καταλύει, ὃν εἵλοντο Θετταλοί, ἢ
[τ]ύραννον καθ[ι]στῆι ἐν Θετταλίαι· ἐπομνύναι δὲ τὸν
[νό]μιμον ὅρκον. ὅπως δ' [ἂ]ν καὶ Θετταλοὶ ὀμόσωσι τῆι π-
[όλ]ει, ἐ[λ]έσθα[ι τὸ]ν δῆμον πέντε ἄν[δρ]ας ἐ[ξ] Ἀθηναίων ἁ-
πά[ν]των οἵτινες ἀφικόμενοι εἰς Θετταλία[ν] ἐξορκώ-
[σ]οσιν Ἀγέλαο[ν τ]ὸν ἄρχοντα καὶ τὸς [π]ολ[ε]μά[ρ]χος καὶ
τὸς ἱ[π]πάρχος καὶ τὸς ἱππέ[α]ς καὶ τὸ[ς ἱερ]ο[μν]ήμονας
καὶ τοὺς ἄλλο[ς] ἄρχοντας ὁπόσοι ὑπὲ[ρ] τõ κοινõ τõ Θε-
τταλῶν ἄρχοσ[ι]ν τόνδε τὸν ὅρκον· βο[η]θ[ήσ]ω παντὶ σθέ-
νει κατὰ τὸ δυνατόν, ἐάν τις ἴ[η]ι ἐπὶ τὴν πόλιν τὴν Ἀθ-
[ην]αίων ἐπὶ πολέμωι ἢ τὸν δῆμον καταλύει τὸν Ἀθηνα-

A second inscription relating to the same treaty must be brought in here, for it records in more detail the procedure whereby the Thessalian ambassadors swore the oaths, as follows:

> [...] summon the ambassadors
> Of the Thessalians to partake of hospitality in the Prytaneion
> Tomorrow. The following were chosen as ambassadors: [...]
> Empedos of Oe, Aischines [...]
> -oros the Acharnian, [...]
> The following Thessalians took the oath:
> *Polemarchoi*: of the Pelasgiotai, [...]
> Of the Phthiotai: Megalos. Of the Thettaliotai [...]
> Of the Hestiotai, Eiron. *Pezarchoi*: [...]
> Philippos, Polymides [...]
> Thibron, Kotimilas [...]
> Theodoros, Pameos [...]
> Dra-s, Philolaos [...]
> Hippokrates (vacat).[122]

The added significance here is the role of the tetrads: despite the lacunose state of the text, it is clear that oaths are sworn by representatives of the tetrads, who appear to be the *polemarchoi*. Therefore we learn that the *polemarchoi* were drawn from, or assigned to, the four tetrads of Thessaly, and ensured their representation in the working of the *koinon*. The major uncertainty, however, that attaches to these inscriptions is one that besets almost all the important evidence pertaining to the Thessalian state: to what extent are the arrangements visible part of an enduring system, which may

[ίων].
(trans. Lambert and Rhodes https://atticinscriptions.com/inscription/RO/44.).

122 *IG* II² 175:

> [— — — — — — — καλέσαι δὲ τοὺς πρέσβ]-
> ες τῶν Θετταλῶν ἐπὶ ξ[ένια ἐς τὸ πρυτανεῖον ἐ]-
> ς αὔριον ⁝ οἵδε ἡιρέ[θ]ησ[αν πρέσβες — — Ἔ]-
> [μ]πεδος Ὀῆθεν, Αἰσχίνη[ς — — — — — — — —]
> — ορος Ἀχαρνεύς, ΛΙΥ — — — — — — — — —
> [οἵδε] ὤμοσαν Θετταλῶν — — — — — — — —
> [π]ολέμαρχοι· Πελασγιωτ[ῶν — — — — — — — —]
> Φθιωτῶν· Μεγάλος. Θετ[ταλιωτῶν — — — —]
> [Ἑ]στ[ι]ωτ[ῶ]ν· Εἴρων. πέζαρχο[ι — — — — —]
> Φ[ί]λιππος, Πολυμίδης ⁝ Λ — — — — — — — —
> Θίβρων, Κοτιμίλας : Ύπ — — — — — — — — —
> Θεόδωρος, Παμε.ος, — — — — — — — — — — —
> Δρα...ς, Φιλόλαος, Οι — — — — — — — — — —
> Ἱπποκράτης vacat.

be read back into the fifth century at least, rather than new developments in the fourth century? We saw above that the tetrads themselves are sixth century in origin; we also saw that Daochos I in the late fifth century may have been an Archon, though this is not at all clear from the wording of the Daochos Monument. What of the *polemarchoi*?

That *polemarchos* did exist as a title in Thessaly in the mid-fifth century is known; what is harder to ascertain is its relation to regional political structures, in particular the tetrads. The key text is the inscription accompanying a dedication made at Delphi at some time shortly after 457 BC. The object dedicated was a horse; the statue itself does not survive, but its erstwhile presence is attested by the inscription on the base:

> 'The Thessalians dedicated the horse to Apollo as a tenth (i.e. of the plunder) from Tanagra.
> These men were *polemarchoi*:
> [There follow seven names.][123]

Here are the *polemarchoi*, certainly, but can we possibly see them as representatives of the tetrads, as they were in the fourth-century text? Two problems intrude. The first is that there are seven names, not four, and nothing in the arrangement of the inscription allows us to extract four names as constituting a particular group.[124] The second is the grammar: only two names are in the genitive case, and therefore part of the genitive absolute construction identifying the *polemarchoi*. The other five are nominative. Are Amyntas and Archagoras the *polemarchoi*, and the others merely 'Thessalians', agreeing with and qualifying 'Θεσσαλοὶ' on line 1? They are presumably the men of note who commissioned, paid for and set up the dedication. They made sure to identify themselves as 'Thessalians',

[123] *SEG* 17.243:

Θεσσαλοὶ τὸν *h*ίππον ἀνέθεν τὀπόλλονι δεκάταν τōν ἀ[π]ὸ Ταναγ[ρας]
πολεμαρχεόντōν τõνδε
Ἀμύντα Μέννες
Ἀρχαγόρō *h*υβρίλαος
ΚΑΙΣ Πολυδάμας
Προτέας
Εὐκρατίδας

For a different interpretation of τōν ἀ[π]ὸ Ταναγ[ρας] see Sordi (1958), 344–47. Discussion of the inscription and its restorations: Daux (1958); Helly (1995), 54–55; Schachter (2016), 110–11; Osborne and Rhodes (2017), 88–91.

[124] ΚΑΙΣ on line 5 is mysterious. Kais does exist as a personal name, but is attested only in the imperial period and in Asia Minor, and so the word seems unlikely to have that function here. If 'and' is meant, what of the sigma?

but this does not amount to a dedication by, or even on behalf of, the whole *ethnos*.

Polemarchoi are attested as polis figures, including within the Delphic context: compare a fourth-century dedication to Apollo by the Pharsalians.[125] *Polemarchoi* are mentioned, and here they are three; moreover, the fact that the inscription was set up by a polis dissuades us from interpreting these officials as part of a regional structure. Moving away from Delphi, Pherai in the later fourth century issued a proxeny decree bearing the πολεμαρχούντων formula and three names:[126] these men are also very unlikely to be *koinon* officials given the polis-based nature of the agreement. It is far more likely that the title was also deployed on the polis level (after all, it is both widespread and rather generic) as well as being used within the fourth-century *koinon*.[127] That said, the fact is that the Tanagra dedication makes no mention of any specific polis, and it is not impossible that as early as 457 each tetrad has a *polemarchos*. What we cannot know is their constitutional function, and whether they formed part of a regularised federal system or were primarily military in their role. In any case, it is only with the treaty of 361/0 that we can be sure of their inclusion in a fully developed *koinon*.

8. Thessaly under Macedonian rule

The date of Philip's first involvement in Thessalian affairs has been the subject of much debate.[128] In any case, Philip's first actions in Thessaly may not have been of an especially time-consuming kind. It is reasonable to place his marriage with the Larisaian Philinna, and perhaps also that with Nikesipolis of Pherai, especially if Satyros' list of Philip's wives preserves at least partly the correct chronological order of the associations: both Philinna and Nikesipolis are listed before Olympias, whom Philip married no later than 357.[129] Satyros explicitly says that Philip wished to forge a connection with the *ethnos Thettalōn*.[130] This may surely have been forward-looking diplomatic groundwork, before any more active and onerous involvement.

When Philip first operated militarily in Thessaly it was in the context of two concurrent and intertwined conflicts: first, the so-called Third Sacred

125 *SEG* 1.210; Daux (1958).

126 *SEG* 49.627. On *polemarchoi* as polis officials in Thessaly see Habicht (1999).

127 *Pace* Helly (1995), 258–60.

128 Ehrhardt (1967); Griffith (1970); Martin (1981). For an overview of the relationship between Philip and the Thessalians see Sprawski (2005). A useful survey of the early stages of his involvement is provided by Worthington (2012), 61–62.

129 Griffith (1970), 69–71; cf. Axenidis (1948), 11.

130 Satyros F21 Kumaniecki. For further discussion of the chronology and order of the marriages see Tronson (1984); Ogden (1999), 17–20.

War; and, second, the ongoing strife between the tyrants of Pherai and the rest of the Thessalians.[131] After the death of Alexandros of Pherai in 358 BC, Pherai had fallen under the rule of Lykophron II and Peitholaos. These became allies of the Phokian Onomarchos, who was leading the Phokian side in the Sacred War and who had all to gain should Thessaly, the most powerful member of the Delphic Amphiktyony, come under the control of a man friendly to his interests.[132] Ranged with Phokis also were the Athenians, Spartans and many other Peloponnesian communities; opposing them were the Boiotians, Thessalians, Dorians (of Doris in central Greece), Dolopians, Athamanians, Phthiotic Achaians, the Magnesians, Ainianians and some others.[133] When Philip was invited by the Thessalians, probably at the instigation of the Larisaian Aleuadai (ancestral *xenoi* of the Macedonian Argeads), to take on the struggle against Pherai,[134] he therefore obtained *carte blanche* to involve himself not only in Thessalian internal affairs but also in a wide-ranging Greek war with the crucial sanctuary of Delphi at its heart. He lost two battles to Onomarchos in 353 BC (defeats so severe that his army came near to mutiny), returned to Macedon over the winter to recoup and regather, and in 352 reversed his fortunes completely at the battle of the Krokos Plain, defeating the Phokians and their allies and killing Onomarchos himself.[135] Lykophron and Peitholaos left Pherai under a truce, and the city was in Philip's hands.[136] If he was made Archon of the Thessalians, it would have been shortly after this victory.

The Sacred War dragged on until 346; if the Thessalians had hoped that Philip would bring it to a swift conclusion they were disappointed, as this was plainly not among his priorities.[137] But in 346 it took only the presence of his armies on the threshold of Phokis to make the Phokian commander Phalaikos – who had previously held out stubbornly at Nikaia – surrender, and hand over to Philip the crucial Thermopylai corridor that led to the south.[138] Philip formally handed over to the Amphiktyony the task of deciding how matters should be finally resolved, but the importance of his Thessalian allies on the Amphiktyonic council guaranteed that the arrangements would be to his advantage, and indeed they were: Philip was

131 Worthington (2014), 39–49; Müller (2016), 252–62. Detailed discussion of the Sacred War in Sánchez (2002), 173–99.
132 Buckler (2003), 409–10; on the role of individuals rather than state interests in orchestrating the Sacred War see Londey (2010). On Philip's interaction with Peitholaos see Badian (1999).
133 Diod. 16.29.1.
134 Diod. 16.35.1; see Graninger (2010), 314.
135 Diod. 16.35.2–6. Worthington (2012), 105–08.
136 Diod. 16.37.3.
137 Errington (1990), 64–66.
138 Diod. 16.59.2–3; Buckler (2003), 449.

to take over the two votes previously held by the Phokians, to preside over the Pythian Games in collaboration with the Thessalians and Boiotians, and to enjoy *promanteia*, the right of consulting the oracle first.[139] As importantly, perhaps, he gained the opportunity to appear as the champion of Apollo, something he had exploited ever since the battle of the Krokos Plain when he ordered his men to wear chaplets of laurel to signify that they fought the Phokians on behalf of the god.[140]

For Philip's actions in Thessaly we are reliant on brief mentions in some of the least reliable texts that could be imagined: the hostile Demosthenes, trying to rouse the Athenians to oppose Philip energetically;[141] Isokrates, on the other side of the debate, presenting Philip as meritorious and a source of potential good;[142] and Theopompos, more interested in moral condemnation than in historical accuracy (though of course the selective transmission of Theopompos' work may well exacerbate this tendency).[143] Diodoros tells us little about internal Thessalian affairs. The overall picture, however, is one in which certain aspects emerge strongly. Analysing Philip's actions in Thessaly sheds light both on this crucial period of Thessalian political development and, here and there, on the traditional practices that predated it.

[139] Diod. 16.60.1–2. Hammond is right to stress that, formally, the two votes went to 'the Makedones', in keeping with the traditional representation of the Amphiktyons by *ethnos* (see Hammond 1994, 94). However, in inscriptions recording Amphiktyonic decrees there is a remarkable disjunction of syntax in the listing of Amphiktyons; whereas all other representatives are identified by the name of their *ethnos* in the genitive plural ('of the Thessalians', etc.), the Macedonian *hieromnēmones* are designated τῶμ παρὰ Φιλίππου, 'those from Philip' (see, for example, *CID* 2.36). *Promanteia*: Demosth. 9.32; Ellis (1976), 127–28; Hammond (1994), 92–97; Scott (2014), 155. Thessalian predominance at Delphi at this time, and how this benefited Philip: Roux (1979), 49, 52–53.

[140] Diodoros emphasises the extent to which his successful prosecution of the Third Sacred War allowed Philip to demonstrate piety: see, for example, Diod. 16.60.4 (cf. Just. *Epit.* 8.2.3).

[141] For an overview of the stages of Demosthenes' opposition to Philip (and to Aischines) see Worthington (2012), chs 6–8; Sawada (2019). See also Ryder (2000). On Demosthenes' conflict with Aischines regarding Philip: Buckler (2000). A detailed account of the events from Aischines' perspective is given by Harris (1995).

[142] For example, in his *Letter to Philip* (1.20), Isokrates commends Philip for having treated the Thessalians well and to their own advantage, and for having dealt deftly with them despite their traditional lack of docility and tendency towards truculence and sedition. See also Isok. 5.20. Isokrates clearly presented Thessaly as a perfect example of what Greeks elsewhere could hope to gain from co-operating with the Macedonian.

[143] For Theopompos' portrayal of Philip see Shrimpton (1991), *passim* but esp. 127–56; Flower (1994), 98–115.

a) Philip's own position in Thessaly

Until recently scholars took for granted that Philip was formally elected as the Archon of the Thessalian *koinon*. However, the evidence for such a supposition has recently received a significant challenge.[144] In particular, Sprawski has pointed out that the ancient text that at first seems to give us an unambiguous statement on the subject is in fact open to a wholly different interpretation. This is Justin 11.3, which describes how Alexander the Great, on his accession, had to persuade the Thessalians to support him by reminding them of the heroic ancestry they shared with the Argeads. Justin describes the Thessalians' reaction to Alexander's speech thus: 'Cupide haec Thessalis audientibus exemplo patris dux uniuersae gentis creatus erat.' ('The Thessalians listened to these things eagerly, and Alexander was made leader of the whole *gens* on the model of his father.') The *gens* in question has been taken to mean the Thessalians, and the sentence therefore to support the notion that Philip had the formal role of leader (that is, Archon) of the Thessalians, but Sprawski, by comparison with a passage of Diodoros, has shown that in fact the *gens universa* could mean the Greeks, whom Alexander sought to lead as hegemon of the League of Korinth.[145] In the Diodoros passage, the Thessalian *koinon* is important, but it gives Alexander its support in his bid for command of Greece, not command of Thessaly. Sprawski is right to note the very close correspondence of this text with Justin's claim, which suggests that Justin intended the same meaning. In sum, Sprawski argued that Philip's role in Thessaly was that of a very influential ally, into whose hands the Thessalians placed key aspects of their regional governance.

A less harmonious picture is suggested by Helly (2009), who argues that Philip worked to limit certain long-standing sources of Thessalian influence and prosperity, in particular by establishing his own command over certain key perioikic communities and over the maritime connections in the Gulf of Pagasai.[146] The kings of Macedon probably controlled the Perrhaibian Tripolis – the poleis of Azoros, Doliche and Pythion – since the early fourth

[144] Sprawski (2003). For a comparable view see Harris (1995), 175–76. Rebuttal of Harris' arguments: Buckler (2003), 420–21, n. 41.

[145] Sprawski (2003), 60. The passage of Diodoros is 17.4.1: 'πρώτους δὲ Θετταλοὺς ὑπομνήσας τῆς ἀρχαίας ἀφ' Ἡρακλέους συγγενείας καὶ λόγοις φιλανθρώποις, ἔτι δὲ μεγάλαις ἐπαγγελίαις μετεωρίσας ἔπεισε τὴν πατροπαράδοτον ἡγεμονίαν τῆς Ἑλλάδος αὐτῷ συγχωρῆσαι κοινῷ τῆς Θετταλίας δόγματι.' ('First he reminded the Thessalians of their ancient kinship from Herakles, and he raised their hopes by kind words and great promises; so he persuaded them to endorse, through a collective decision of [all] Thessaly, the hegemony of Greece which he had inherited from his father.'

[146] It is significant in this regard that in the treaty of the League of Korinth the perioikic *ethnē* are listed, alongside the Thessalians, in their own right: *IG* II3 1 318, lines 41, 48–50.

Fig. 13. Part of the 'Great Battery' at Goritsa; last quarter of the fourth century BC. Photograph: author's own

century BC.[147] Helly suggests that Philip extended this existing Macedonian dominion to encompass the rest of Perrhaibia, the crucial border zone between his kingdom and its southern neighbours.[148] He may also have brought about the migration of Magnesians from the edges of Pieria down to the Bay of Volos, in order to detach Pherai in particular from the sea access on which its prosperity and importance partly rested.[149] The site of Goritsa (Fig. 13) may provide archaeological evidence of his fortification of a key site overlooking the bay, and as for Pagasai, traditionally Thessaly's most important port, this he seems to have taken and held indefinitely.[150] For all that he was motivated by his own particular rhetorical purposes, Demosthenes may well be right in saying that the Thessalians resented the holding of Pagasai, the fortification of Magnesian sites and the exploitation of revenues for Philip's own ends rather than for the common use of the

[147] Helly (2009), 340–41.
[148] Helly (2009), 340–41.
[149] Helly (2006b), 165–73.
[150] Borza (1990), 220. For the (sensible) emendation of 'Pagai' to 'Pagasai' in Diod. 16.31.6 see Martin (1981), 192–95. Part of the impressive fortifications of Goritsa may be seen in Fig. 13.

Thessalian *koinon*.[151] In a sense, Philip's powers in Thessaly resemble those of the Tageia as exploited by Jason and his successors: commanding the Thessalian army, drawing on the region's revenues, exploiting the *perioikoi*. The ingredients of the Tageia were not fixed; Jason had shaped the role to suit his purposes, and it is certain that Philip did likewise. It was a role that was available to him after his defeat and displacement of Lykophron, the last Pheraian claimant.[152] It is also highly significant that his Pheraian bride, Nikesipolis, was the niece of Jason, cementing his association with that man's powers and prestige while helpfully bypassing the unpopular Alexandros and Lykophron.[153]

As Sprawski notes, if Philip was elected to the formal position of Archon, it is remarkable, indeed inexplicable, that this was not remarked on by either Demosthenes or Isokrates, both of whom would certainly have come to know of the fact. Demosthenes paints the Thessalians as people who sold their freedom to Philip in the hope of gain;[154] had they actually handed over to him the key magistracy of their *koinon*, this fact would have supplied the angry orator with wonderful ammunition. As for Isokrates, the same applies but for the opposite reason: he depicts the Thessalians as friendly towards, and benefiting from, Philip,[155] and so a formal election as Archon would also suit his rhetorical purpose. Absolute certainty in this matter is

151 Demosth. 1.22: 'καὶ γὰρ Παγασὰς ἀπαιτεῖν αὐτόν εἰσιν ἐψηφισμένοι, καὶ Μαγνησίαν κεκωλύκασι τειχίζειν. ἤκουον δ' ἔγωγέ τινων, ὡς οὐδὲ τοὺς λιμένας καὶ τὰς ἀγορὰς ἔτι δώσοιεν αὐτῷ καρποῦσθαι· τὰ γὰρ κοινὰ τὰ Θετταλῶν ἀπὸ τούτων δέοι διοικεῖν, οὐ Φίλιππον λαμβάνειν.' The speech was delivered in 349 BC. Three years later, in the aftermath of the Peace of Philokrates, Isokrates would speak of Philip having cultivated such a favourable attitude to him among the Thessalians 'ὥσθ' ἑκάστους αὐτῶν μᾶλλον ἐκείνῳ πιστεύειν ἢ τοῖς συμπολιτευομένοις' ('that they trusted him more than they did his fellow-citizens'). In truth, attitudes towards Philip in Thessaly are likely to have been very diverse. For example, Halos in Achaia Phthiotis opposed Philip and was punished harshly, but Pharsalos benefited from this development through the allocation of Halos' territory and sea-access to Pharsalian control: see Demosth. 11.1 and 19.39; Haagsma et al. (2019), 291–92.

152 Diod. 16.38.1.

153 Steph. Byz. s.v. Θεσσαλονίκη. See Carney (2000), 60–61.

154 E.g. Demosth. 8.62 (the *On the Chersonnese*, delivered in 341 BC): 'Θετταλοὺς πολλὰ δοὺς ὑπηγάγετ' εἰς τὴν νῦν παροῦσαν δουλείαν' ('To the Thessalians he gave many things, and so brought them into their present servitude').

155 See, for example, Isok. 5.20: 'τί γὰρ ἐλλέλοιπεν; οὐ Θετταλοὺς μὲν τοὺς πρότερον ἐνάρχοντας Μακεδονίας οὕτως οἰκείως πρὸς αὐτὸν διακεῖσθαι πεποίηκεν, ὥσθ' ἑκάστους αὐτῶν μᾶλλον ἐκείνῳ πιστεύειν ἢ τοῖς συμπολιτευομένοις' ('What has he not achieved? Has he not made the Thessalians, who previously controlled Macedon, so warmly inclined toward him that all of them trust in him more than in their fellow countrymen?' (Cf. Isok. *Epist.* 2.20, in which Isokrates praises Philip for winning popularity in Thessaly through his good treatment of them.)

of course impossible; Philip may have been Archon of Thessaly. But it is striking the extent to which ancient accounts use not the language of formal authority but far more flexible and general terms: those of persuasion, of popularity, of influence, of charisma. Philip seems to have operated not by direct decree, or through any visible federal mechanism, but through the kind of diplomatic manipulation of which he was a master. Again, this is not unlike Jason, who before he was formally Tagos cultivated, according to Xenophon, alliances with individual Thessalian cities.[156] Authors hostile to Philip and his methods could depict him as corrupt and corrupting, lavishing gifts, meals and favours on his stooges in order to sway them from their loyalty to their own land.[157] But behind the invective is an essential truth: that Philip's actions in Thessaly were conducted largely in a personal and informal manner, through the traditional mechanisms of *xenia* directed at individuals through whom he could steer wider affairs. His genius was to extend such relationships beyond the traditional Thessalian elite, so as to establish in positions of power men who owed their positions to him rather to inherited standing.

But if Philip was not Archon, but merely a highly influential ally with the backing of the Thessalian *koinon*, who *was* Archon? Was there one, or did the presence of Philip mean that the title lapsed? A great deal depends on one's view of the constitutional position of Daochos of Pharsalos, which will shortly be considered.

b) Daochos and other important individuals

Several names appear in the literary sources as Thessalian associates of Philip, often decried as puppets by Demosthenes and as dissolute drinking companions by Theopompos. These individuals, whose involvement with Philip tells us a great deal about his Thessalian policies, are as follows.

Simos and Eudikos of Larisa

In his speech *On the Crown*, delivered in 330 BC, Demosthenes lists individuals in various Greek cities who assisted Philip and were discarded once their usefulness was at an end. Among these are Simos and Eudikos of Larisa.[158] Eudikos remains otherwise unattested, but Aristotle mentions Simos as an Aleuad of political clout in Larisa.[159] With far less detail than one could wish, Aristotle describes how Simos and his fellow Aleuadai placed the affairs of Larisa in the hands of 'soldiers and a neutral leader' because of distrust between political factions within the city. Graninger

156 Xen. *Hell.* 6.1.5.

157 See, for example, Demosth. 18.295; Theopompos *FGrH* 115 F 81.

158 Demosth. 18.48.

159 Arist. *Pol.* 1306a.

suggests that this third party was Philip, and that Aristotle is referring to the Aleuadai handing control of Larisa over to the Macedonian king.[160] That is an attractive conjecture. Aristotle's description comes in the context of a discussion of how oligarchies fall, which, combined with Demosthenes' remark, suggests that Philip undertook régime change of some sort at Larisa once the Aleuadai had served the vital function of inviting him to take on the opposition to Pherai.[161] Diodoros' vague reference to Philip 'expelling tyrants from the cities'[162] suggests that this practice was not limited to Pherai; and in Polyainos we find a reference to Philip feigning illness in order to trick some Aleuadai into visiting him so that he could seize them (though the ruse was apparently unsuccessful).[163] Polyainos also tells us that Philip tended to support *demoi* – the general populace – in Thessalian cities; this may be taken as evidence that he wanted to disrupt the established *dynasteia*, the inherited power of the noble families, and that the Aleuadai may have fallen victim of this policy.

This would not be wholly surprising: it would be advantageous to Philip to establish in power individuals who were dedicated to his cause rather than to maintaining the traditional distribution of power in Thessalian society. And the Aleuadai, if unchecked, were likely to prove problematic for Philip. They will have hoped to gain enormously from his suppression of Pherai; would probably have expected that, on the basis of the ancestral *xenia* that existed between his family and theirs, he would allow them to dominate Thessalian politics once the Pheraian tyrants were out of the way. There is every sign that this hope was not fulfilled. It has been suggested that the suppression of the Aleuadai followed Simos' production of coinage in his own name in 344 BC, a sign of problematic political ambition.[164]

Agathokles

Theopompos tells us:

> Philip sent Agathokles, a slave and one of the Thessalian Penestai, who became very powerful as a result of his flattery and because when he joined in symposia he danced with him and provided laughter, to destroy the Perrhaibians and to oversee business there. The Macedonian (Philip) always had around him such men, with whom he spent much of his time

[160] Graninger (2010), 316.

[161] Cf. also Harpokration s.v. Σῖμος, which states that Simos was 'one of the Larisaians who seem to have collaborated with the Macedonian'.

[162] Diod. 16.69.8.

[163] Polyain. *Strat.* 4.2.11.

[164] Worthington (2014), 72. Though conjectural, this suggestion is appealing; previously, the Thessalian leader who minted coins in his own name most prolifically was Alexandros of Pherai, a wholly unpalatable precedent.

because of a love of drinking and buffoonery, and he often consulted and was advised (by them) about the most important matters.[165]

We may be suspicious of the description of Agathokles as a *penestēs*;[166] this feels like a rhetorical *reductio ad absurdum* of a basic truth, that he was not a member of any of the families that traditionally held sway in Thessaly. In any case, the mere fact of Philip imposing a ruler of his choice upon the Perrhaibians is significant. Perrhaibia of course was under the influence of Larisa, whose government Philip was, as we have seen, keeping on a tight rein. The imposition of Agathokles would have checked the city's power still further. Perrhaibia was, of course, especially important as being the march land between Thessaly and Macedon. And indeed the Thessalian *perioikis* was as important to Philip as the tetrads, in many ways. The garrisoning of Magnesia – continued despite Thessalian resentment – is further evidence of this, as is the control of Pagasai,[167] likewise the transfer of Halos in Achaia Phthiotis into Pharsalian control.[168] Controlling Pagasai removed the port from the ambit of Pherai, which had previously held sway over it, as well as allowing Philip to appropriate its revenues and vital sea access. Halos, an important city of the southern *perioikis*, was strategically placed on Philip's southward route, and that it should be under the domination of Pharsalos, a city friendly to his interests, was plainly important to his interests and ambitions.

Daochos of Pharsalos

Kineas, Thrasydaios and Daochos are three Thessalians who seem to have come in for particular opprobrium for having supported Philip – betrayed their country to the Macedonian, as Demosthenes presented it.[169] About

[165] *FGrH* 115 F 81: ''Αγαθοκλέα δοῦλον γενόμενον καὶ τῶν ἐκ Θετταλίας πενεστῶν Φίλιππος μέγα παρ' αὐτῶι δυνάμενον διὰ τὴν κολακείαν καὶ ὅτι ἐν τοῖς συμποσίοις συνὼν αὐτῶι ὠρχεῖτο καὶ γέλωτα παρεσκεύαζεν ἀπέστειλε διαφθεροῦντα Περραιβοὺς καὶ τῶν ἐκεῖ πραγμάτων ἐπιμελησόμενον. τοιούτους δ' εἶχεν ἀεὶ περὶ αὐτὸν ἀνθρώπους ὁ Μακεδών, οἷς διὰ φιλοποσίαν καὶ βωμολοχίαν πλείω χρόνον ὡς τὰ πολλὰ συνδιέτριβε καὶ συνήδρευε περὶ τῶν μεγίστων βουλευόμενος' (trans. Morison).

[166] Ducat (1994), 50–51.

[167] Garrisoning Magnesia and controlling Pagasai: Demosth. 1.22, 2.7 and 2.11. Demosthenes makes much of this matter because it seems to have rankled with the Thessalians; Philip apparently promised to return Magnesia to their control (2.7), and by 344/3 appears to have done so, if Demosth. 6.22 is anything to go by.

[168] [Demosth.] 11.1.

[169] Demosth. 18.295 (*On the Crown*, delivered in 330 BC): 'τῆς ἰδίας ἕνεκ' αἰσχροκερδίας τὰ κοινῇ συμφέροντα προΐεντο, τοὺς ὑπάρχοντας ἕκαστοι πολίτας ἐξαπατῶντες καὶ διαφθείροντες, ἕως δούλους ἐποίησαν, Θετταλοὺς Δάοχος, Κινέας, Θρασύδαος … ' ('For the sake of shabby private gain, they threw away the common good. All of them deceived and ruined the citizens who relied on them, and so made them into slaves. So

Kineas we know nothing; the name occurs in several Thessalian cities at various times, and we have no information about this particular individual's home, family or career. Thrasydaios (sometimes spelled Thrasydaos) emerges slightly further from the shadows because, along with Daochos, he served as a Delphic *hieromnēmōn* and in this capacity is listed in numerous inscriptions from the sanctuary. He was also – again with Daochos – sent by Philip to Thebes in 339 to try to persuade the Thebans not to side with the Athenians in opposing Macedon.[170] Because he and Daochos are so often operating together it might be assumed that Thrasydaios was a Pharsalian, as we know Daochos was, but this cannot be known for certain. The name Thrasydaios is attested in Larisa – in fact one of the Aleuadai known to Pindar and Herodotos held the name. It is therefore tempting to speculate that, when Simos and Eudikos were deposed in Larisa, a Thrasydaios (from a cadet branch of the same old family) was put in their place of influence within the city.[171] However, Pharsalian identity remains possible; to assume that a particular name could only be used within a single polis is obviously false.[172]

Of the three 'treacherous Thessalians', it is Daochos alone who emerges in detail, thanks to his own attention to his legacy and memorialisation: the Daochos Monument, discussed further in Chapter 6, contains a great deal of information, albeit full of puzzles, about his career and his political authority. We have discussed the presentation of Daochos I as a prosperous pan-Thessalian ruler; now it is as well to remind ourselves of what his grandson, Daochos II, says about himself.

> Increasing the virtues of my family's ancestors,
> I set up these gifts to lord Phoibos, honouring my family and my homeland –
> I, Daochos, possessed of glorious praise,
> *tetrarchos* of the Thessalians,
> *hieromnēmōn* of the Amphiktyons.[173]

Daochos, Kineas and Thrasydaos treated the Thessalians … '). Theopompos (*FGrH* 115 F 209) calls Thrasydaios 'μικρὸν μὲν ὄντα τὴν γνώμην, κόλακα δὲ μέγιστον' – 'small in intelligence, but an enormous flatterer'.

170 Plut. *Dem.* 18.2 (quoting the historian Marsyas, *FGrH* 135–36 F 20); Sánchez (2002), 239.

171 See, for example, Axenidis (1948), 24; Helly (1995), 62–64.

172 Note that in *CID* 2.8, a list of contributions to the temple-building funds at Delphi, the contribution of the Pharsalians is brought by a Thrasydaos (line 11), which might suggest that he was Pharsalian; however, he may just have conveyed the money because of his convenient association with the sanctuary (on the lists of this period see Davies 1998, 5).

173 *FD* III 4.460, 7.

Most of this inscription causes no problems of interpretation, though in light of the scathing comments of Demosthenes we may smile a little at the third line: plainly the *eulogia* did not extent to all quarters.[174] But the real difficulty lies in Daochos' description of himself as *tetrarchos Thessalōn*. To assess what exactly is meant by this phrase, we must look more closely at Philip's political reorganisation of Thessaly.

c) Political (re-)organisation

We have seen some of the ways in which Philip established control in Thessaly: overturning the tyranny of Pherai, installing new leading men in key cities, garrisoning Magnesia, controlling Pagasai and its revenues. However, he also directed his attention to the organisation of the Thessalian *koinon*, and some of his measures are reported, though briefly, in the ancient literature. Two excerpts, one of Theopompos and the other of Demosthenes, are especially important in this regard.

'That Philip established a ruler over each of these parts other authors have shown, including Theopompos in Book 44.'[175] Here Harpokration, in the same passage that reports the words of Hellanikos and Aristotle about the Thessalian tetrads, says that Theopompos, among others, wrote that Philip installed a ruler over each tetrad. This is not to say that Philip created the institution of tetradic rulers: we saw that in the 360s the oath of alliance between Athens and Thessaly was sworn, on the Thessalian side, by four *polemarchoi*, each representing a tetrad. If we had only this text we might assume that Philip just replaced existing *polemarchoi* with his own supporters, and made no institutional change. However, Demosthenes suggests otherwise: 'And as for Thessaly, what is the situation there? Has he not taken away their constitutions and their cities and established *tetrarchiai*, so as to enslave them not only city by city but also *ethnos* by *ethnos*?'[176] The context of this remark, in a speech delivered in 341 BC, is a list of the Greek states treated harshly or unjustly by Philip: some, such as Olynthos and Methone, have been obliterated, says the orator; others, such as Thessaly and Euboia, have had political change forced on them (in Euboia's case, the installation of *tyrannoi*). But it is still not clear that Demosthenes is really describing a substantial change of political system in Thessaly, rather than

[174] Note, however, Polybios' assertion that Demosthenes was unfairly scathing about Daochos and his fellow 'traitors': Polyb. 18.14.

[175] Theopompos *FGrH* 115 F 208 (= Harpokration s.v. τετραρχία): 'ὅτι δὲ Φίλιππος καθ' ἑκάστην τούτων τῶν μοιρῶν ἄρχοντα κατέστησε δεδηλώκασιν ἄλλοι τε καὶ Θεόπομπος ἐν τῆι μδ΄.'

[176] Demosth. 9.26: 'ἀλλὰ Θετταλία πῶς ἔχει; οὐχὶ τὰς πολιτείας καὶ τὰς πόλεις αὐτῶν παρῄρηται καὶ τετραρχίας κατέστησεν, ἵνα μὴ μόνον κατὰ πόλεις ἀλλὰ καὶ κατ' ἔθνη δουλεύωσιν'.

merely the imposition of new individuals in *koinon* roles. The verb καθίστημι in political contexts does not have to imply the creation of a new office; it can just as easily mean to appoint someone to an existing role.[177] The only explicit change of practice seems to relate to terminology, since there is no mention of *polemarchoi*. Theopompos as reported by Harpokration seems to have used the neutral term Archon; Demosthenes 9.26 as quoted above talked of *tetrarchiai* (implying the title *tetrarchos*). It might be tempting to assume that non-Thessalian authors were simply choosing the terms that seemed to them best suited to describing men who ruled tetrads, that they did not reflect Thessalian usage, and that we should not try to extrapolate Thessalian practice from their inconsistent and ill-informed accounts, were it not for the way in which Daochos describes himself in his monument at Delphi as a *tetrarchos Thessalōn*. Plainly at least one Thessalian did use the terminology reported by Demosthenes. But what role did the term *tetrarchos Thessalōn* actually denote?

There are two possible interpretations of the phrase. The first is to suggest that a *tetrarchos* was the ruler of a tetrad, and that therefore Daochos ruled Phthiotis, in which Pharsalos was the chief polis. This reading is supported by the manuscript of Demosthenes quoted above, in which Philip established *tetrarchiai* – if each tetrad had a *tetrarchia*, then it is easy to imagine that its presiding official was called a *tetrarchos*. The genitive plural *Thessalōn* is no hindrance: it would just have had descriptive force, as in the Herodotean *basileus Thessalōn* discussed above (p. 232). However, the quotation of Demosthenes 9.26 by Harpokration s.v. ἔθνος gives *tetradarchia*, a slightly different word, which is also used by Aelius Aristides, in describing how Philip controlled Thessaly 'φρουραῖς καὶ τετραδαρχίαις' ('with garrisons and *tetradarchai*').[178] Based on this alternative form, and on his observation that in extant Greek usage a *tetrarchos* (or *tetrarchēs*) means a ruler of a whole comprising four parts, not of a fourth part of a whole, Helly has suggested an alternative reconstruction: each tetrad was ruled by a *tetradarchos*, but the *tetrarchos* was the ruler of all four tetrads: that is, of all of Thessaly.[179] In this view Daochos would in fact be the Archon of all Thessaly, a far more powerful figure and Philip's most important agent within the Thessalian *koinon*.

This view is hard to accept. For a start, it underestimates the attestation of the word *tetrarchos* (or *tetrarchēs*, its exact synonym) meaning precisely the ruler of a fourth part.[180] It is true that other texts may be adduced in which

177 LSJ s.v. καθίστημι II.2.

178 Ael. Arist. 38.481.

179 Helly (1995), 45–58.

180 Strabo's description of the traditional political system of the Galatians (12.5) is a case in point. 'There were three *ethnē* which spoke the same language and were in no other

a *tetrarchos*/-*ēs* rules all four parts, such as Arrian's description of the military organisation in which a *tetrarchia* is a body of men comprising four *lochoi*, and the whole is commanded by a *tetrarchēs*.[181] So linguistic corroboration can plainly be found for both meanings, and cannot be used to decide between them. What is more probable in the Thessalian context? Surely if Daochos had been made ruler of all Thessaly Demosthenes would have known of it and made capital from the fact, singling Daochos out as the recipient of Philip's unmatched favour and as the arch-traitor of Thessalian affairs. As it is, Daochos merely appears in the list of stooges: 'Daochos, Kineas, Thrasydaos … '. No other ancient author mentions Daochos as a pan-Thessalian ruler either. It seems most sensible to assume that the Archon of Thessaly at the time of Philip was so unimportant compared with Philip himself and his supporters in the cities that his name has gone unrecorded; Daochos ruled Phthiotis, and his relative prominence, at the head of Demosthenes' list, results from the great importance of Pharsalos to Philip's designs. As for *tetradarchia*, this is just an alternative for *tetrarchia*, which some authors prefer but which was not used by the Thessalians themselves if the Daochos Monument is anything to go by.

More puzzling is Demosthenes' fleeting claim, otherwise entirely unattested, that Philip 'established a *dekadarchia* in Thessaly'.[182] The singular form prevents the obvious interpretation: that individual key cities were each placed in the hands of régimes of ten, rather like those established by the Spartan Lysandros. This would require the plural; it is unprecedented for the singular to be used in the sense of 'a system of *dekadarchia*', comprising several individual manifestations of the phenomenon. Instead, we have to assume that the *dekadarchia* extended over all of Thessaly, and it is difficult to see how such a system would have fitted with that of the *tetrarchiai*. One solution is to suppose that the *dekadarchia* actually replaced the Thessalian Archon, that instead of an elected pan-Thessalian leader the Thessalians were now ruled by a board of ten, chosen of course from among those loyal to Philip. This would tally with a trend discernible in Philip's Thessalian actions: an avoidance of centralisation, of placing ultimate

way different from each other. Each *ethnos* was divided into four parts (*merides*), and they called each part a *tetrarchia*. Each *tetrarchia* had its own *tetrarchēs*.' ('τριῶν δὲ ὄντων ἐθνῶν ὁμογλώττων καὶ κατ' ἄλλο οὐδὲν ἐξηλλαγμένων, ἕκαστον διελόντες εἰς τέτταρας μερίδας τετραρχίαν ἑκάστην ἐκάλεσαν, τετράρχην ἔχουσαν ἴδιον.')

181 Arr. *Takt.* 10.2; the same information is given in Ael. *Tact.* 9.2.

182 Demosth. 6.22 (from the *Second Philippic*, delivered in 344 BC): 'τί δ' οἱ Θετταλοί; ἆρ' οἴεσθ',' ἔφην, 'ὅτ' αὐτοῖς τοὺς τυράννους ἐξέβαλλε καὶ πάλιν Νίκαιαν καὶ Μαγνησίαν ἐδίδου, προσδοκᾶν τὴν καθεστῶσαν νῦν δεκαδαρχίαν ἔσεσθαι παρ' αὐτοῖς' ('What about the Thessalians? Do you think, I said, that when Philip was expelling their tyrants and giving them back Nikaia and Magnesia they expected that the *dekadarchia* which has now been established would exist among them?')

power in the hands of one man, and a preference for the cultivation of a clique of supporters.

Taking all the available evidence into account, it seems that Philip built on existing political mechanisms in Thessaly while conducting a really substantial change on the level of individual people, disrupting traditional power bases and installing men of his own choosing into key roles and locations. The tetrads were not his creation, nor was the possibility that each should be represented by a single official. However, the change in terminology from *polemarchos* to *tetrarchos* may well date from the period of his influence. Moreover, we cannot accurately gauge how the role and powers of the *tetrarchoi* differed from those of the *polemarchoi* in the 360s. In the case of the *polemarchoi* we have evidence only that they were authorised to swear an oath on behalf of their tetrad, and to represent it in negotiations with Athens. Philip's *tetrarchoi* must have had considerable power to direct the affairs of their tetrad, otherwise they would have been of little use to the Macedonian king.

d) Thessaly during the reign of Alexander the Great

Whether we think that Philip occupied the formal position of Archon in Thessaly, the elected head of the *koinon*, or whether we prefer, with Sprawski, to consider him instead an influential ally, nonetheless the massive practical utility of Thessaly to him – especially in the form of revenues and cavalry – is undeniable. This utility Alexander inherited with little disruption; according to Diodoros and Justin, he had only to remind the Thessalians of their shared heroic ancestry to quell the initial dissent in that quarter. Diodoros' wording makes it plain that what he primarily wanted from the Thessalian *koinon* was not confirmation as its head (though this is somewhat implied by Justin); instead, he needed their backing of his role as hegemon of Greece.[183] The same support he extracted from the neighbouring *ethnē* and, crucially, from the Delphic Amphiktyony, convened at a special assembly at Anthela; in light of Thessalian influence in the Amphiktyony at this time, its decision will have been a foregone conclusion.[184] So enthusiastic was Thessalian backing of his claim that they voted to march with Alexander to Athens; whether or not the army actually mustered or set out, its assistance was not required, as the Athenians ratified the king's hegemony without a blow struck.[185] From that point Alexander was hegemon of Greece (though not without significant challenges, especially from Athens and Thebes); this

183 Diod. 17.4.1.

184 Diod. 17.4.2.

185 Aischines 3.161: 'ἤδη δ' ἐψηφισμένων Θετταλῶν ἐπιστρατεύειν ἐπὶ τὴν ἡμετέραν πόλιν … ' ('When the Thessalians had already voted to march against our city … '). Athens agrees to Alexander's hegemony: Diod. 17.4.9.

larger, overarching power renders less important the question of whether he was also formally the leader of the Thessalian *koinon*.

The vigorous – if fruitless – participation by the Thessalians in the Lamian War after Alexander's death throws into relief their apparent lack of resistance to his hegemony. They did not take part in the revolt in Alexander's absence in 331 BC. Aischines depicts his enemy Demosthenes as having claimed to be working against Alexander by trying to stir up rebellion in Thessaly and Perrhaibia (the latter important in such a situation because of its strategic location on the passes between Thessaly and Macedon), but dismisses the claim as empty boasting.[186] Diodoros says that the revolt had some support outside the Peloponnese, but does not specify where;[187] surely if as important a Macedonian ally as Thessaly had tried to defect he would have mentioned as much. It is plain, then, that the Spartan instigators of the uprising found no support in Thessaly; around 2,000 Thessalians were serving as cavalrymen in Alexander's army at the time, which suggests a relationship of mutual dependence, with Alexander in possession of hostages to good Thessalian behaviour, but hostages on whose military assistance he relied strongly for the success of his campaign. Not only that, but as Martin points out, Alexander was surely using Thessalian revenues to fund his campaign.[188] The money that would otherwise go into the collective coffers of the Thessalian *koinon* now went east to fund Alexander's conquest of the Achaemenid Empire; this was certainly not a situation covered by the terms of the Korinthian League, which seems only to have imposed contributions of troops, rather than money, upon its members.[189] Nonetheless, it was not until Alexander's death that any overt resistance to Macedonian control in Thessaly manifested itself, and then the Exiles Decree of 324 BC may have been as significant a factor as any long-standing and cumulative resentment.[190] The terms of the Korinthian League prescribed that states be left with the political systems they had under Philip, and there are no signs that Alexander made any substantial adjustments to the Thessalian *koinon*.

186 Aischines 3.167.

187 Diod. 17.62.7.

188 Martin (1985), 118. Justin (*Epit.* 11.3.2) states that the Thessalians formally voted to hand over to Alexander the same revenues which Philip had previously controlled.

189 Smarczyk (2015), 453–58.

190 Diod. 18.8.2–5. For the possibility that this decree would have threatened political instability in Thessaly see Martin (1985), 132–33.

9. A Thessalian *koinon* in the early Hellenistic period?

The epigraphic record of the late fourth and the third century give ample proof of the Thessalians at least nominally operating as a collective body. It is true that in every instance we may challenge the extent to which 'the Thessalians' really represents a full cross section of the region's poleis; this is always the case, as we have seen. In early Hellenistic inscriptions the Thessalians are sometimes referred to as a *koinon*, sometimes as the '*ethnos* of the Thessalians', sometimes simply as 'the Thessalians'. An especially interesting example is an inscription from Aigai in the Troad, dating probably from between ca. 280 and ca. 250 BC, which we shall discuss further in Chapter 7. The text records the granting of thanks and honours by the Thessalians to the Aiolians, Koans and Magnesians on the Maiandros, and includes the following provision:

> The Thessalians have voted them
> freedom from duties on everything except on what
> they bring or export by way of trade, and
> citizenship for all of them wherever they wish in Thessaly,
> and that cities and cults and everything
> else be shared by them as they are by Thessalians.
> And the Aiolians, Koans and Magnesians from the
> Maiandros shall have marriage rights wherever they wish
> in Thessaly.[191]

On the one hand, as we shall see in Chapter 7, Larisa played a disproportionately large role in this particular set of transactions. On the other, the degree of regional co-operation suggested by the grant of rights is considerable. Giving *politeia*, partial *ateleia*, and *epigamia*, πᾶ νά κε βέλλουνθαι Πετθαλίας, would have been empty gestures had the other poleis, or a significant number, not been prepared to comply and honour the agreement. Moreover, the inscription goes on to identify religious sites

[191] Malay and Ricl (2009), 48–49 (lines 20–28):
ἐψάφισαν οἱ Πετθαλοὶ ἀτέ-
λειαν ἔμμεν αὐτοῖς πάντουν πλὰν εἰ πόσσα κ-
ε ἐπ ἐμπορία ἄγουνθι εἶ ἐξάγουνθι, καὶ πολι-
τείαν πάντεσσι πᾶ νά κε βέλλουνθαι Πετθαλί-
ας καὶ ἔμμεν αὐτοῖς καὶ πόλις καὶ ἱερὰ κοιν-
ὰ καὶ τὰ ἄλλα πάντα καττάπερ Πετθαλοῖς ἔνθι·
καὶ ἐπιγαμίαν ἔμμεν Αἰολείεσσι, Κούοις, Μα-
γνείτεσι τοῖς ἀπὺ Μαιάνδροι πᾶ νά κε βέλλο-
υνθαι Πετθαλίας.
(Trans. Parker, adapted.)

and occasions instrumental in publicising the decree on a regional level: the decree was originally proposed at the Thessalian Olympia festival, and the text is to be displayed in the sanctuary of Zeus Olympios in the territory of Larisa, at 'Itounos',[192] and in the sanctuary of Apollo Kerdoios in Larisa. We certainly cannot take the third century as a time when all political, diplomatic and religious activity in Thessaly was limited to the scope of the individual polis.

10. The primacy of the polis: citizenship in Thessaly

In this chapter we have observed that by the later fifth century, and in the fourth, political co-operation in Thessaly has taken on some formal manifestations, though they should not be regarded as steady and unchanging. However, it is important not to lose sight of the primary role played by the polis, throughout the period covered in this book, in most aspects of Thessalian political life. Federal structures, when they were employed, always overlaid the uneven texture of polis diversity, in which individual communities developed and maintained their own particular modes of civic activity.[193] Even more fundamentally, it should always be kept in mind that citizenship – the political rights, belonging and identity of the individual – remained almost wholly rooted in the polis. Except in very specific circumstances and ways, there was no such thing as a Thessalian citizen or a citizen of Thessaly. This is indicated by numerous things.

First, combinations of *politeia* and the rights that formed the citizenship 'bundle' (chiefly *ateleia*, *asylia*, *epinomia* and *epigamia*) were often conferred by one Thessalian polis on an inhabitant of another, showing that in normal circumstances, and without special dispensation, these rights were not transferable between poleis.[194] Second, we have formal mass enrolments of new citizens, most of them Thessalians from other poleis, as a way of boosting citizen numbers when the need arose; the most famous example is the Larisaian decree of ca. 215 BC in which the city, submitting with clear reluctance to an order from the Macedonian king Philip V, gives citizenship to a large number of Thessalians who had previously been living

192 Probably the sanctuary of Athena Itonia at Philia: see see further Chapter 7.

193 For a brief but insightful treatment of Thessalian polis institutions and bodies, and their role within regional organisation see Lasagni (2008), 382–83.

194 Mack (2015), 122–30. On *epinomia* specifically see Chandezon (2003), 351–89. He argues (380) that the right to pasture animals sat naturally alongside the other rights typically conferred to constitute the key aspects of settled life: 'Une maison, une terre à cultivar, un droit d'usage sue les pâturages communs formaient les trois éléments indispensables pour assurer une vie matérielle normale … .' ('A house, land to cultivate, the right to use the common pastures, these constituted the three essential elements to ensure a normal life in material terms.')

in Larisa with, in effect, the status of metics.[195] Third, when citizenship is granted to a non-Thessalian, it is normally the citizenship of a specific polis, and is almost never a blanket arrangement automatically including all of Thessaly. Finally, proxeny relationships are conducted between Thessalian poleis, which is significant because the role of the *proxenos* was essentially to provide support and security for outsiders not protected by the right of the citizen.[196] These conditions prevail throughout the period studied in this book; they also contrast significantly with what we know of the situation in other regions, at least from the fourth century BC, in which key citizen rights, reflecting important areas of economic and social interaction, were automatically extended between the member-poleis of the *koinon*.[197]

The exception that proves the rule is so deracinated as to have very limited utility to the historian trying to slot it into the overall picture of political progression. It is a proxeny decree whose letter-forms locate it in the fourth century, but for which no more precise dating is possible.

> To Euergetes the Chalkidian
> The Thessalians gave *pro-*
> *xenia* and *asylia* and
> *ateleia*, to him and to his
> family, when the Sorsikidaoi
> and Kotilidaoi were *prostatai*.[198]

It is remarkable to see 'the Thessalians' conferring the status of *proxenos*, along with some of the 'bundle' of rights associated with citizenship, on the honorand, and doing so with no reference to the polis: clearly the rights are to apply across Thessaly. Moreover, Euergetes of Chalkis would be

195 *IG* IX.2 517.

196 For example, in the corpus of Pheraian inscriptions on bronze tablets from the late fifth and the fourth centuries BC we find *proxenia* conferred by the city of Pherai not only on non-Thessalians but also on citizens of Proerna, Skotoussa and Krannon. See *SEG* 23.416, 419 and 421; Béquignon (1964), 403, 405, 407. This situation contrasts with that in Boiotia, where, from the fourth century, individual poleis did not appoint *proxenoi* of other poleis within the region: see Mackil (2015), 492. On the general nature and tendencies of the institution of *proxenia* see Mack (2015), 22–89.

197 Mackil (2013), 255–64.

198 MDAI(A) 59 (1934), 57, no. 15:

> Εὐεργέται Χαλκιδεῖ
> Πετθαλοὶ ἐδώκαιεν προ-
> ξενίαν καὶ ἀσυλίαν καὶ ἀ-
> [τέ]λειαν καὶ αὐτῶι καὶ γενε-
> ᾶ̣ι ̣προστατευόντων Σορ-
> ̣σικιδάων [κ]αὶ Κωτιλιδάων.

expected to safeguard the interests of any Thessalian who visited his home community.

We do not know where this decree was actually written and published, though Pherai is a good conjecture because the stone was seized by the Piraeus police along with others of certain Pheraian provenance.[199] Unfortunately, the (family?) groups named, the Sorsikidaoi and Kotilidaoi, are otherwise unattested and so cannot help us locate the document. The title of the *prostatēs* is likewise mysterious; as Graninger remarks, 'It is difficult to understand in what capacity these presumably corporate entities (families, tribes, etc.) could have served as *prostatai*', especially within the Thessalian state.[200] In Hellenistic Thessalian inscriptions the *prostatēs* is almost always an individual, normally described as the *prostatēs ekklesias*, clearly the president of the Assembly.[201] It is quite possible that the Sorsikidaoi and Kotilidaoi are in fact Pheraian, rather than pan-Thessalian, groups, since the decree may well have been enacted in Pherai, though it claimed to speak for all the Thessalians.

A Pheraian origin would be immensely significant, given that the date of the text may be established as fourth century on the basis of letter-forms. Surely the rule of Jason provides the most plausible context: at that time Pherai would be a highly suitable location for a decree of all the Thessalians, and it is not hard to imagine the Thessalians under Jason as having the political cohesion needed to give the document real validity. Moreover, Jason is known to have tried – albeit with little success – to cultivate connections in Euboia.[202] It could, however, have been created under Alexandros, though this would give the text a very different significance: in no real sense did Alexandros represent Thessalian wishes and intentions, and so the text becomes decidedly specious if we place it in that

[199] Graninger (2009), 23. A different suggestion is put forward by Helly in an as yet unpublished paper that he was kind enough to show me (forthcoming a): that the decree comes from Thessaliotis. He argues this on the basis of his theory that the Petthaloi are not the Thessalians in the normal expansive sense, but rather a restricted group in west Thessaly. Both this and the Pheraian interpretation amount to the same basic phenomenon, however: the agency of a specific community or group of communities rather than a truly pan-Thessalian political act.

[200] Graninger (2009), 22 n. 46.

[201] Another example of a group of concurrent *prostatai* is found in Helly (1973), II, no. 69, a decree of ca. 178 BC honouring judges from the Thessalian city of Mondaia. In this document we find the formula προστατευόντων δὲ τῆς ἐννόμου ἐκκλησίας κοινῇ τῶν ταγῶν πάντων ('when the *prostatai* of the lawful assembly were all the Tagoi, serving jointly'). Perhaps this is roughly comparable with the example under discussion.

[202] Diod. 15.30.3–5: Jason backs a puppet ruler in Hestiaia and its deme of Oreus, but he proves so unpopular that when the Spartans oust him the act wins them the enduring friendship of the people of the area.

time. There is no way of anchoring it securely in Thessalian history, so all we can do is acknowledge its exceptional nature. There is no comparable example up to the second century BC.

It is instructive to contrast this state of affairs with the situation post-196. From that point on, a new suite of epigraphic tendencies and formulae start to appear. A non-Thessalian can be designated as *proxenos Thessalōn*, representing the whole Thessalian state in a way that was not done previously except in the one instance discussed above.[203] As for conferrals of citizenship itself, *politeia*, these can be enacted by the *koinon* on a regional basis, though it is interesting to note the recurrence of the formula that the honorands should receive citizenship ἐμ πάσαις ταῖς ἐν Θεσσαλίαι πόλεσιν.[204] This does imply that, though the *koinon* could indeed grant region-wide citizenship, it still applied on a polis-by-polis basis, as a polis phenomenon, rather than constituting federal citizenship in the strict sense. In the first century BC, by contrast, we do find mention of the Thessalian *koinon* granting citizenship to two men of Chalkis without the formula about 'all the cities in Thessaly';[205] this may indicate that by that date (ca. 70 BC) federal *politeia* had become an entity in its own right.

The wider picture of *koina* and citizenship in Greece, within which the Thessalian example should be viewed, is varied. While it is no longer assumed that one of the essential ingredients of a true *koinon* was dual citizenship (that an inhabitant of a *koinon* region must be a citizen both of his member-polis and of the *koinon*), we do have evidence for dual citizenship in some places. In Chalkidike in the fourth century, all communities in the *koinon* enjoyed *epigamia* (the right to marry across polis boundaries) and *enktēsis* (the right to own property in another polis),[206] something alien to pre-196 Thessaly. (That said, Xenophon's description of the Chalkidian situation suggests that the shared rights were agreed upon as a special measure to give the *koinon* greater strength and unity, rather than being an automatic result of *koinon* status.) In Boiotia, individual poleis within the *koinon* do not appoint citizens of other Boiotian poleis as their *proxenoi*, indicating that formal representation was not needed between cities. This is significant: the role of a *proxenos* was normally to compensate for the difficulties that might be encountered when a citizen of one community visited another in which he was not protected by citizen status.

[203] A *proxenos Thessalōn*: *SEG* 55.608. Designations of individuals as '*proxenoi* and *euergetai* of the Thessalians' in *koinon* decrees: *SEG* 26.688 (ca. 179–165 BC); *SEG* 47.744 (ca. 150–130); *IG* IX.2 508 (ca. 49/48 BC).

[204] See, for example, *SEG* 34.558, lines 9–10. This is a decree of honours for foreign judges, ca. 150–130 BC.

[205] *SEG* 55.608.

[206] Xen. *Hell.* 5.2.12; Beck (2001), 360–62; Mackil (2013), 255–58; Zahrnt (2015).

11. Conclusions

Thessalian cities never operated in isolation. Geography, culture, linguistic habits (especially within Pelasgiotis), shared political tendencies: all these things made it all the more natural that various forms of co-operation occurred – social, economic, military (not to mention religious, such a significant aspect that it requires its own chapter). And none of these forms of co-operation should be regarded as lesser in significance – or as somehow a lesser achievement – than systems for regional decision-making such as might be encapsulated in the word *koinon*. And yet, such systems are important in their own right, and can be discerned – as long as we take seriously Mili's warning against trying to form the scattered fragments into a smooth historical narrative.[207] She is right that change and redesign are built into the fabric of Thessalian political life, and should not be brushed aside as an inconvenience for the historian, let alone as evidence of a 'failed state'. Nonetheless, this chapter has demonstrated the possibility of establishing certain phases and of considering their sequence, their interrelationship, as will now be summarised.

The earliest sign of formal centralised organisation is the tetrads, probably a late sixth-century creation. However, while a momentous development in some ways, this seems not to have had a significant discernible impact on political life until the fourth century; its primary significance was on the level of myth-historical identity. Indeed, formal political co-operation on the regional level is impossible to find in the earlier fifth century; instead we see elites (chiefly the Aleuadai), *basileis Thessalōn*, influencing Thessalian affairs through the more personal channel of *philia*. 'The Thessalians' in the early fifth century are, in effect, the ill-defined collective of polis leaders who opposed the plans of the Aleuadai, given temporary unity by this stance and by the need to seek external support.

There are glimpses of something rather different in the second half of the fifth century. The ΦΕΘΑ/ΦΕΤΑ coins of the mid-fifth century, whatever the circumstances of their creation, indicate a formal political authority funding and organising the production of coinage. This may well have been the *koinon* that opposed Brasidas' crossing; it may well have been led by an Archon, Daochos, who 'ruled all Thessaly for twenty-seven years, not by force but by law'. The appearance of the word *koinon* should not excite us unduly, for what – after all – does it really mean? A collective; however, we should not necessarily assume that all poleis were included, nor that within member poleis the *koinon* would really have affected the lives of most inhabitants. Given the narrow oligarchy that prevailed in Thessalian poleis, and the limited range of political enfranchisement, a great proportion of

[207] Mili (2019).

inhabitants were not full citizens anyway.[208] And we have no evidence for how the representation of poleis within the *koinon* was actually organised. It may well have followed traditional lines, with each member-poleis' leading family or families being its representatives. It should be noted and emphasised that nowhere, and at no point in the time period covered, do we find reference to any kind of *synedrion* where envoys of member-poleis gathered to vote their way through an agreed agenda.

In the fourth century three crucial episodes occur. The first is that Jason, in the 370s, dusts off and embellishes the traditional policy of a war-leader elected to muster and lead a military force drawn from across the region. Xenophon's Jason and Polydamas provide a detailed recipe for this command: contingents from Thessaly and the *perioikoi*, revenues set at fixed amounts by the shadowy Skopas.[209] However, the elaborate rigidity of the system was probably a product of Xenophon's creative desire to make Jason seem both meticulous and formidable. Xenophon also wished to portray him as legitimate, his authority backed by full precedent, chiefly so as to contrast him with Alexandros, who ruled not with *nomos* but with *bia*. Hence Xenophon's Jason appeals to the precedent both of Skopas and Aleuas. We discounted the idea that he was really resurrecting the military organisation of Aleuas Pyrrhos, however – this was shown to have been enacted only within Larisa. In sum, Jason in his ambitious plan to secure pan-Thessalian rule and extend Thessaly's power beyond its borders took a flexible tradition whereby Thessalian poleis could combine forces under a single military leader, should circumstances encourage it, into a federal military muster of new formality. In doing so he stayed true to certain Thessalian tendencies such as the hoplites:cavalry ratio of 2:1 in Thessalian armies,[210] but his role as an innovator should not be overlooked.

The second major fourth-century development is the treaty signed between 'the Thessalians' and Athens in 361/0. As is often the case, 'the Thessalians' clearly does not mean 'all the Thessalians': here it means 'all the Thessalians opposing Alexandros of Pherai', just as in 480 'the Thessalians' meant 'all the Thessalians opposing the Aleuadai'. The power of the internal aggressor to galvanise unity and co-operation was significant. Nonetheless, the inscription recording the alliance does reveal a remarkable amount of 'machinery'. We still have no central Thessalian *synedrion*, but

[208] On Thessalian oligarchy see Mili (2015), 54–60. It is interesting that the (probably) Larisaian speaker in the *Peri Politeias* (on which see further above) contrasts the oligarchy of Sparta (in which political inclusion was extended to those able to bear arms for the state) with that of his own polis, which was much narrower. *Peri Politeias* 30–31; Wade-Gery and Morrison (1942), 69–71.

[209] Xen. *Hell.* 6.1.7, 9, 12 and 19.

[210] Aston and Kerr (2018), 6–7.

we do have officials whose authority presumably exceeded the polis level, in particular the *polemarchoi*. We also have a glimpse of the tetrads playing a real role in political organisation for the first time.

This treaty marked a shift in the conduct of diplomacy by Thessalians. Its text reveals a degree of institutional formality supplementing (though surely not entirely replacing) the traditional modes of personal friendship. Those swearing the oath of alliance on behalf of the Thessalians did so because they occupied certain official roles, not because of any pre-existing personal ties with leading Athenians. At least on the face of it, the alliance brought Athens the co-operation of the whole Thessalian *koinon*, all four tetrads represented. Personal friendships and animosities were still no doubt working away beneath the surface, both within Thessaly and between Thessaly and Athens, but they are officially sidelined by the machinery of *koinon* governance. Whether they would have prevented a second Tanagra is unknown, since very soon the relationship between the two groups was overtaken by events: the Third Sacred War, and Philip's entry into Greek affairs. Philip's arrival on the scene is our third crucial episode.

However, the personal dimension did not disappear by any means; it is amply in evidence during the period of Philip's leadership of Thessaly, and inherited by Alexander. The fact that Philip did not, according to Sprawski's convincing argument, himself assume a formal role as Archon of the Thessalian *koinon* is significant here. He worked through influence rather than constitutional authority, and he worked through the agency of individuals, of individual *philoi*. Under his direction substantial changes were made to the Thessalian *koinon*, and yet it was not his main instrument; instead it allowed him to place key supporters in positions of legitimate power. By espousing the rhetoric of renewal, of restoration, Philip, like Xenophon's Jason, could present himself as taking Thessalian regional politics back to the 'good old days', a position reinforced by his 'restoration' of Thessaly's prime influence at Delphi. In fact, as has been said, Thessaly's pre-eminence in central Greece in the Archaic period is a mirage, but that would not have troubled Philip: the hazier the better, since it allowed him and his allies plenty of scope for invention.

What Philip really understood was the *nomos Thessalōn*. This was the traditional way of doing things in Thessaly.[211] It was maintained by consensus – often unspoken, always unwritten – among the elites. Individuals and groups might contend for power, tradition could always be evoked. When Jason took sole command of Thessalian armies and revenues in the 370s, he did so according to *nomos* – indeed, according to the *nomos Thessalōn*, if Xenophon's word order can be so interpreted.[212]

[211] Martin (1985), 81–88.

[212] Xen. *Hell.* 6.4.27: after the battle of Leuktra, we are told, when Jason returned

This legitimacy is contrasted with the rule of his successors, Polydoros and Polyphron, and then Alexandros. Plutarch includes Alexandros among τὰς παρανόμους καὶ βιαίους δυναστείας, which Pelopidas seeks to put down.[213] Diodoros also says that Alexandros established his rule παρανόμως καὶ βιαίως.[214] When the commissioner of the Daochos monument describes his ancestor's twenty-seven-year rule of all Thessaly, it is described as having been conducted οὐ βίαι ἀλλὰ νόμωι.

The occurrence of similar formulations in descriptions of Macedonian monarchy has led Mooren to suggest that a sense of tradition, of the 'done thing', was especially influential in northern Greek political life, where more formalised law-codes were absent.[215] It is not in fact clear that the north was any less well supplied with such law codes than most other areas of Greece; however, it is significant that both Macedonian kings and rulers of Thessaly – and, indeed, the leading men within Thessalian cities, as in Pindar's poem – were felt to be circumscribed by a traditional sense of legitimate and illegitimate behaviour. If Mooren is right, Philip would have come well equipped, through his own cultural background, to slip seamlessly into the Thessalian way of conducting politics, which – as Mili argues – was always a dynamic combination of the personal and the more formal.[216] Add in the fact that Philip could claim to share the Heraklid ancestry so crucial to Thessalian myth-history, and it is clear that the alignment of Philip and Thessaly was in many ways an ideal match. Alexander had to exert himself somewhat to inherit it, but it also served him well during his lifetime, most obviously on the battlefield at Gaugamela.

How has this chapter advanced our view of the development of Thessalian regional identity? It has compounded the picture built up so far, that in the Classical period Thessalian identity was manifest and important: we have seen that 'the Thessalians' did constitute a political unity from the formation of the tetrads. Also compatible with the previous two chapters, however, is the flexibility of that identity. In myth and cult we saw centralising elements (the figure of Thessalos, the cult of Poseidon), but they were never the whole picture, and so it is in the political sphere. Even when we can identify elements of regional organisation, these are dwarfed by other modes of political interaction: informal *philia*, and the

to Thessaly, 'μέγας μὲν ἦν καὶ διὰ τὸ τῷ νόμῳ Θετταλῶν ταγὸς καθεστάναι καὶ διὰ τὸ μισθοφόρους πολλοὺς τρέφειν περὶ αὐτὸν καὶ πεζοὺς καὶ ἱππέας.' The underlined portion may be translated either as 'because he had been chosen Tagos of the Thessalians, according to the law' or 'because he had been chosen Tagos, according to the law of the Thessalians'.

213 Plut. *Pel.* 31.4.

214 Diod. 15.61.2.

215 Mooren (1983), 206–25.

216 Mili (2019).

varied arrangements and customs of individual poleis. Moreover, like myth and cult, political co-operation shifted its forms and priorities as conditions changed.

Nor should we fail to notice ways in which the political picture differs from that of myth and cult. In Chapters 3 and 4, the end of the sixth century and the first half of the fifth emerged as a time when collective Thessalian identity was being expressed and advertised to a significant degree. In some ways such processes diminish in the fourth, in particular as coinage shifts to emphasise the myths, cults and imagery of individual poleis, and the Petraia – though no doubt it continues to be held – drops from our view, suggesting less emphatic advertisement. Politically, the picture is the reverse. In the earlier fifth century there is no convincing evidence of a formal *koinon*, whereas by the 360s that certainly has been formulated (even if we still cannot regard it as truly pan-Thessalian). Perhaps the existence of federal institutions removed some of the incentive for advertising cohesion through other channels. In the earlier fifth century the polis elites do not seem to have made use of formal decision-making structures or a system of regularised military muster if they wanted to undertake large-scale co-operative enterprises. They may have promoted shared identity as a way of encouraging 'buy-in'. The images and themes of Thessalian ethnogenesis – in particular, the natural land and its resources, gifts from Poseidon – provided a currency in more than one sense: iconographic material for the new coinage, but also a rationale for co-operation across polis boundaries. By promoting themselves as Heraklids, the Aleuadai claimed the right not only to be Thessalian but also to steer and dominate Thessalian affairs at a time when their power was not, as far as we can see, actuated through any institutional channels.

It must be stressed that this picture of Thessalian society in the early Classical period is not intended as a claim of peculiarity, let alone uniqueness. Such a claim would actually constitute an unconscious perpetuation of the discourse of alterity that still clings to Thessaly and its study. In fact, scholarship on the wider topic of elite power and its operation has achieved a recognition of the crucial importance of various kinds of 'cultural capital'. Rulers – whether monarchic or members of dominant groups – maintained their position by claiming *aretē*; this was done through assertion of heroic lineage and a special relationship with the divine, by commandeering key mythical narratives (such as an arrival myth), by demonstrating personal qualities of strength, intelligence, honour.[217] It is remarkable to see, in the early fifth century, various templates for achieving and controlling such cultural capital emerging among Thessalian polis elites; even more striking to see them being resurrected and embellished by new powers (Jason, Philip) in the fourth century.

[217] For a detailed exploration of this topic see Mitchell (2013), 57–73.

6

Thessaly moves to the margins

This book so far has charted the development in Thessaly of an ethnic identity consciously expressed and explicitly espoused by Thessalians themselves. By the early fifth century, Thessaly had been given a religious and myth-historical character that both unified it and set it apart from other *ethnē*; from that time, it formulated a political organisation on the regional level, though one of a highly flexible and variable nature. In dialogue with these developments, the external perspective has sharpened also: for the first time in the early fifth century non-Thessalian sources routinely speak of 'the Thessalians' as collective agents with a distinct identity, both from a myth-historical perspective – the arrival of the Thessaloi – and with reference to the *ethnos* in the authors' own time and experience. The Thessalians, *qua* Thessalians, have emerged.

The existence of something approaching a Thessalian stereotype does predate the Classical period; we have already noted, in Chapter 2, perceptions of Thessaly as rustic, old-fashioned and as the land left behind. In the Classical period, however – and particularly from the later fifth century – we begin to see a far more pejorative and critical discourse, in which Thessaly starts to represents aspects of the old-fashioned that have become unpalatable and out of keeping with the prevailing cultural and political climate. It might be assumed that a major factor behind this shift would be Thessalian medism in the second Persian invasion, but in fact the truth is not so simple. We should not imagine that the rhetoric of the later fifth century and beyond – in which the Persian Wars were couched in terms of good and bad, loyalists and traitors – was in play during the conflicts, or indeed immediately after them.[1] We always need to remember how few states – thirty-one in total – actively resisted; that the Persians would not have seemed to everyone the terrible bogeymen, utterly opposed to everything Greek, that they later became; that even within the Hellenic

[1] On the development of panhellenic ideology after the wars, rather than before or during them, see Yates (2019). On the evolution of Persian War narratives and the increasing emphasis on the image of Greek unity see Marincola (2007).

League there was dissent and rivalry, amply recorded by Herodotos.[2] Nor was medism promptly or systematically punished after the Persian defeat.[3]

Instead, medism gradually became one component in a system of disparaging Greeks who seemed not to accord with ethical and behavioural principles; the Thessalians were certainly tarred with this brush, but medism itself does not explain their disparagement. For that, in this chapter, we must consider what amounts to a subtle redrawing of the imaginary map of Greece, to relocate its centre and its periphery. It will be argued that, whereas in Archaic verse Thessaly had a certain symbolic centrality as close to the original Hellas, over the course of the Classical period it was increasing relegated to the margins, positioned as a northern 'debatable land', a reconfiguration primarily fuelled by the increasing alignment of the Thessalians with the Macedonians, both in reality and in the eyes of Greeks to the south, especially Athenians.

1. The hostile discourse in the later fifth and the fourth century

a) An exercise in ambiguity: Euripides' Alkestis

In representations of Thessalian society, wealth and hospitality tended to be closely connected. Pindar in *Pythian* 10, for example, emphasised not only the prosperity of his Thessalian patrons, but also their generosity, generosity manifest not in undignified cash payments but in the traditional motif of *xenia*. πέποιθα ξενίᾳ προσανέϊ Θώρακος ('I trust in the kindly hospitality of Thorax'), he says, incorporating the figure of the poet within this traditional aristocratic milieu of honourable exchange.[4]

There is a world of difference between a victory-ode written for an aristocratic patron, intended chiefly for performance within his social circle, and an Athenian drama designed to please the demographically mixed audience in the Theatre of Dionysos on the south slope of Athens' akropolis.[5] Little goes unquestioned and unchallenged in this new medium of drama;

[2] As Mitchell puts it (2007, 78), 'rather than actually creating unity, the Persian Wars came to *represent* unity and the idealized condition of the Hellenic community'.

[3] Aston (2019), 9–11; see also Schieber (1982).

[4] Pind. *Pyth.* 10.63. As Kurke (1991, 119–39) demonstrates, couching the poet/patron in such a way is by no means limited to odes for Thessalians; the Thessalians are not unusual, but are part of a certain category of elites with whom the poet claims equality. See also Sigelman (2016), 73–75.

[5] It is important to note that even praise-poetry for wealthy northern patrons could include an element of subtle admonishment. Simonides' poem for Skopas (fr. 542 *PMG*) seems to be in this mode. Even more interesting is Bacchylides 20B, for Alexandros I of Macedon, in which, as Fearn shows (2007, 27–86), the poet seems to allude delicately to the Macedonian association with drinking, and to the position of Macedonian allegiance between Greece and Persia. In this way, Bacchylides seems to prefigure, in

traditional views of heroes, gods and long-held ideals are held up for scrutiny, and political messages are rarely one-sided. In this environment it is unsurprising to see a more complex depiction of Thessalian mythological figures, especially when the playwright is Euripides, whose revisionist approach to old stories is well established. On the whole the Thessalian myths that held such a central position in Archaic epic and in Pindar's work are somewhat less in evidence in tragedy, displaced by the Theban Cycle in particular; nonetheless, for Euripides especially they provide important material, especially in the *Andromache* and the *Alkestis*.[6] The *Andromache* has been discussed above. Its perspective is complicated by the Molossian dimension, the playwright's clear intention to elucidate the Aiakid origins of the Molossian royal house; within this purpose, as has been said, Thessaly plays the role of origin-point and is especially connected with Thetis and her cult. In the *Medea*, Thessaly, as homeland of Jason, is in the background, but is not functionally or symbolically significant within the play. In the *Alkestis*, however (performed in 438 BC, Euripides' earliest surviving tragedy), we have a Thessalian setting for the whole drama, and one in which various key aspects of the perceived Thessalian character are important in the delineation of Admetos' behaviour in particular.[7]

On the face of it, the Thessalian characters in the play are uniformly admirable. Alkestis, of course, is the paradigm of the good wife, sacrificing herself to save her husband. But Admetos too is presented as ostensibly virtuous. That he is *hosios* – pious – is signalled in the opening lines by Apollo himself, and references to his goodness abound throughout.[8] Moreover, his goodness has a strongly traditional and strongly Thessalian flavour: he is the perfect *xenos*, or host.[9] That Thessaly was considered a place of

the early fifth century, the critical responses to northern Greek rulers that have become overt and scathing by the fourth century.

6 For northern Greek production contexts see the discussion of the *Andromache* in Chapter 2. Lost and fragmentary works also have to be taken into account; as Zapheiropoulos observes, for example, Aischylos' *Achilleis* and *Myrmidones* maintain the traditional importance of Phthia as a key locus of Thessalian mythology. Zapheiropoulos (2008), 153–54, provides a useful overview of the inclusion of Thessalian characters and places in Attic tragedy.

7 In various ways the play seems to be drawing upon Thessalian realities, such as the significant cult of Herakles in the region of Pherai, attested in particular by the excavation of a bronze *phiale* inscribed – in Archaic lettering – ΤΕΛΕΦΙΛΟΣ ΜΑΝΕΘΕΚΕΝ ΤΟΙ ΗΕΡΑΚΛΙ. See Stamelou and Doulgeri-Intzesiloglou (2010), 166. For a discussion of the Thessalian religious and mythological traditions on which the *Alkestis* seems to draw see Kravaritou and Stamatopoulou (2018).

8 Admetos as ὅσιος: line 10.

9 E.g. 566–67: 'τἀμὰ δ' οὐκ ἐπίσταται/μέλαθρ' ἀπωθεῖν οὐδ' ἀτιμάζειν ξένους.' ('My house does not know how to turn away or dishonour guests.' Admetos' hospitable generosity, the mainstay of his goodness in the play, is given as the reason why Apollo,

old-fashioned guest-friendship linking the elites of different regions is made clear, for example, by Xenophon's description of the Pharsalian Polydamas as φιλόξενός τε καὶ μεγαλοπρεπὴς τὸν Θετταλικὸν τρόπον ('hospitable and lavish, in the Thessalian manner').[10] The great wealth of Thessaly found its social outcome in generous hospitality, the cornerstone of aristocratic culture in Greece. Another key aspect of the Thessalian *mis-en-scène* in the play is the equestrian element; for example, the grief-stricken Admetos instructs his subjects: 'All you who harness four-horse chariots and single horses, cut the manes on their necks with an iron blade,'[11] a significant variation on the universal connection between mourning and the cutting of hair. This combination of horsemanship and hospitality finds its grisly inversion in the reason Herakles is travelling through Thessaly northward: he goes to capture the horses of Thracian Diomedes. Diomedes' mares are flesh-eating, and their master is as murderous as they, the antithesis of a good host.[12] In Thrace, horses and men share unnatural savagery; in Thessaly they combine to reinforce traditional *nomoi* of good behaviour, especially regarding guests. No doubt many, or most, of those watching the play at its first performance would not have seen anything problematic in Admetos' generosity.

However, Euripides does leave room for the king's virtue to be questioned. Leaving aside the central dilemma with which the playwright presents us – whether Admetos was justified in accepting his wife's self-sacrifice on his behalf – even his hospitality is problematic, because excessive. 'ἄγαν ἐκεῖνός ἐστ' ἄγαν φιλόξενος,' exclaims an anguished servant, with emphatic repetition.[13] This excessive regard for the rights of a guest leads Admetos to conceal his wife's death from the visiting Herakles; the result may be largely comic (Herakles carousing, unaware of the tragedy that has befallen the household and tipsily urging the distraught servants to cheer up),[14] and ultimately resolved by Alkestis' restoration to life and health, but it is genuinely problematic: by being too perfect a host, Admetos

when forced to undertake servitude as a herdsman on his lands, did so with a good grace, increasing his flocks and the wealth of his kingdom (lines 569–77: the Chorus speaks).

[10] On the traditional concept of *megaloprepeia* see Kurke (1991), 146–67 – she identifies the growing association, in the Classical period, between *megaloprepeia* and tyranny, and its incompatibility with key aspects of developing political discourse.

[11] Lines 428–29: 'τέθριππά θ' οἳ ζεύγνυσθε καὶ μονάμπυκας/πώλους, σιδήρῳ τέμνετ' αὐχένων φόβην.'

[12] At line 484 the Chorus asks Herakles, in horror, 'μῶν ἄπειρος εἶ ξένου;' ('Are you ignorant of the *xenos*?') – i.e. of what kind of *xenos* Diomedes is.

[13] Line 809: 'He is too, too hospitable!' On the theme of Thessalian hospitality in the play see Mili (2015), 266–67.

[14] Under the undoubted humour of Herakles' depiction lies a deep symbolic connection

unwittingly causes Herakles to infringe the correct conduct of a guest. The tone of the play is oddly light-hearted, and it certainly does not constitute a scathing critique of Thessalian *philoxenia*; rather, the traditional aristocratic principles that Thessaly so perfectly embodies are being held up to ridicule through the device of a *reductio ad absurdum*.[15]

b) Thessaly in Attic comedy

So the mythological material, drawn into the medium of tragedy, could be subjected to ambiguous treatments in the hands of a sophisticated playwright; nonetheless, tragedy offers no open attack on the values for which Thessaly stands. When we turn, however, to comedy, away from the world of gods and heroes, we find the region depicted in a far more politically pointed light, its problematic associations exposed. First and foremost, the long-standing connection between Thessaly and wealth (wealth with a pastoral foundation) is twisted into the ethically problematic theme of excessive consumption. Fragments of both Old and Middle Comedy contain numerous references to this theme, appearing to pay particular attention to the size of Thessalian food portions. Of course we must note the exaggerating effect of our chief source for these fragments: Athenaios' *Deipnosophistai*, whose preoccupation with food is inevitable and whose choice of quotation was no doubt affected by factors we cannot now ascertain. Nonetheless, it is plain that the Thessalians have a very strong

between drinking-cups and crossing the boundary between life and death: see Morin (2015).

[15] There is another highly significant depiction of problematic Thessalian *xenia*, but the impossibility of dating its inception prevents its full inclusion into the chronological picture of changing attitudes. This is the anecdote reported by Cicero (*de Oratore* 2.86; cf. Quint. *Inst.* 11.2.11–16) concerning Simonides' interaction with his Thessalian patron Skopas. Simonides composes an ode praising both Skopas and the Dioskouroi, and Skopas offers him half the agreed fee on the grounds that only half the poem is about him. Shortly afterwards, Skopas and his whole clan are wiped out when the roof of their dining hall collapses, and only Simonides, with his prodigious memory, can identify and name the mangled remains. This story is obviously full of symbolism and wholly apocryphal, but when did it arise? Its interest here lies in the fact that Skopas himself transgresses the honourable relationship between poet and patron – a relationship meant to rest on the image of *xenia* – by drawing crass attention to its monetary dimension; he is also parsimonious. In this he is the antithesis of Admetos and his excessive hospitality, but in their different ways both characters exploit the Thessalian stereotype in unflattering ways. The fact that the Thessalians are killed by their own dining hall, mid-feast, surely also employs their association with excessive consumption (on which see Aston 2012a). On the anecdote, its history and its mangled transmission see Slater (1972): he finds reason to date its inception before Kallimachos; cf. Kowerski (2008), who argues that it is Hellenistic.

showing among the *ethnē* described as gluttons in the text,[16] and that this *topos* derives chiefly from comic plays from the later fifth century BC, though it later becomes widespread.[17]

There was another aspect of this stereotype of Thessaly as a place of excessive consumption: that such abundance might be alluring, dangerously so, to other Greeks, including Athenians. In a 2012 article I discussed the stereotype of the Thessalians as purveyors of lavish hospitality, arguing that Thessalians came to symbolise, in the later fifth and the fourth century especially, a special danger for Athenians in contact with them – corruption, contamination, being lured away not only from self-discipline but also from loyalty to Athens. A key text for this is a choral ode in Aristophanes' *Wasps*, in which one Amynias is mocked for his conduct when on an embassy to Pharsalos:

> But once he went on an embassy to Pharsalos;
> and there he kept company,
> one on one, with the Penestai
> of the Thessalians, since he himself is
> a *penestēs* second to none.[18]

It is interesting to find this reference to an Athenian embassy to Pharsalos in a play first performed in 422. At this date the special importance of maintaining good relations with the Thessalians would have been clear to the Athenians. Two years earlier, Brasidas had made his way through the region thanks to his clever exploitation of *philia*; opposition was expressed by pro-Athenian Thessalians, but it was not enough to check him.[19] This may explain the renewed diplomatic effort, focused on the ever-useful Pharsalos, thanks to its position something of a gateway to the rest of the region. It may well have paid off, since in 422/1 – a little after *Wasps* was

[16] Athenaios' characters identify first certain individuals known for lavish eating, then the *ethnē* notorious for their consumption ('καὶ ἔθνη δὲ ὅλα εἰς πολυφαγίαν ἐκωμῳδεῖτο' – 10.417 b). In fact, the Boiotians and the Thessalians are the only two *ethnē* singled out here for detailed treatment, though in general the accusation of excess is directed widely through the *Deipnosophistai* and its source material.

[17] Comic fragments quoted in this regard include Aristophanes' *Frying-Pan Men* (fr. 507 KA), Krates' *Lamia* (fr. 21 KA) and Hermippos' *Fates* (fr. 42 KA).

[18] Aristoph. *Wasps* 1271–75:

> ἀλλὰ πρεσβεύων γὰρ ἐς Φάρσαλον ᾤχετ'·
> εἶτ' ἐκεῖ μόνος μόνοις
> τοῖς Πενέσταισι ξυνῆν τοῖς
> Θετταλῶν, αὐτὸς πενέστης
> ὢν ἐλάττων οὐδενός.

[19] Thuc. 4.78.

performed at the 422 Lenaia – the Spartan Rhamphias was prevented from passing north through Thessaly.[20]

As Bakola has established,[21] the joke in this passage is based on how ill-suited Amynias is to fit the normal type of the Athenian envoy in Thessaly. Because of his poverty he associates not with the wealthy Thessalians whose favour he is no doubt meant to be winning, but rather with their Penestai, their serfs, with whom he has a natural affinity. In a sense, the joke may also be at the expense of how the Athenian state has changed over the course of the fifth century: under the democracy, diplomacy has passed from the hands of its traditional practitioners – like the Peisistratidai – and beyond the elite into the hands of men whose resources are so scant that their only hope of social success in a place like Thessaly is to hobnob with the serfs. Behind it lies the basic reality: that ambassadorial service in Thessaly meant receiving lavish hospitality in – as Xenophon might put it – the old Thessalian manner.[22]

Being part of an embassy – no specific destination mentioned – is included among the signs of fine living promoted by Bdelykleon in the same play.[23] At 1245–47, shortly before the Amynias joke, Bdelykleon imagines a sophisticated symposiast singing the following ditty:

> Wealth and power
> for Kleitagora and me
> among the Thessalians … .[24]

While topical details are obscure, the basic message – wealth and power (are to be had) among the Thessalians – is not. *Bia*, which evokes force and violence rather than authority, is a politically charged word, often the direct antithesis of *nomos*/*nomoi*. On the Daochos Monument, Daochos II claimed to have ruled all Thessaly 'not with *bia* but with *nomos*'. In Pindar's *Pythian* 10, the Aleuadai were praised for enhancing the '*nomos* of the Thessalians'. In Athens, Thessaly had a reputation for *anomia*, lawlessness. So *bia*, the opposite of *nomos*, combined with wealth, is a neat encapsulation of what an Athenian might be expected to find there if bent upon self-enrichment and

[20] Thuc. 5.13.

[21] Bakola (2005).

[22] Xen. *Hell.* 6.1.3: Polydamas of Pharsalos is 'lavish and great-hearted, in the Thessalian manner'.

[23] *Wasps*, lines 1187–88.

[24] χρήματα καὶ βίαν
Κλειταγόρᾳ τε κἀμοὶ
μετὰ Θετταλῶν…

not fussy about the political company he kept.[25] Another sympotic ditty also has a Thessalian flavour: Bdelykleon asks his father Philokleon:

> But what about when Theoros, reclining at your feet,
> takes Kleon's right hand and sings,
> 'Friend, remember the story of Admetos, and love
> the *agathoi* ... '.[26]

The *agathoi* are of course not (merely) good men in the sense of private virtue, but men of the right class – the notables. It is interesting that in this context the myth should be used to embody the principle of *philia* between *agathoi*, surely a reference to the relationship of Admetos and Herakles. Once again, Thessaly is the home of traditional elite friendships, and it is into this milieu that Philokleon – supremely ill-suited as he is – is being introduced, with disastrous results. Aristophanes parodies not only the political culture that Thessaly represents to the Athenians, but also the pretension of those who hope to break into that culture from the outside. It is that desire that makes Thessaly dangerous, since it is not compatible with the ideals of the Athenian democracy.[27] Athenians may be drawn away from loyalty to their home state, and as a consequence Thessalian wealth is the object of both excoriation and envy.

c) Thessaly in philosophical circles

We might account for this development by reference to the particular perspective of comedy, which – though by no means straightforwardly 'poetry of the people' – tends to espouse a broader demographic point of view than other literary forms treated here. However, in fact the stereotype of the corrupt and corrupting Thessaly is not limited to comedy, especially as we move from the fifth century to the fourth. It appears also in the work of Plato, representing the antithesis to the character of Sokrates; Sokrates himself disdains to save his life by fleeing to Thessaly where

[25] An alternative MS reading has βίον instead of βίαν – this would signify 'livelihood', 'a means of making a living', even 'property'. If we accept this, the theme of enrichment prevails, though on this reading that of political violence is absent.

[26] Lines 1236–39:

> τί δ', ὅταν Θέωρος πρὸς ποδῶν κατακείμενος
> ᾄδῃ Κλέωνος λαβόμενος τῆς δεξιᾶς·
> "Ἀδμήτου λόγον, ὦταῖρε, μαθὼν τοὺς ἀγαθοὺς
> φίλει—"

[27] Participation in foreign embassies is problematic in general: cf. *Acharnians* 64–89, in which an ambassador reports on his visit to the Persian King and on the 'privations' he has suffered – lavish food and drink and extravagant comforts.

Kriton (naturally!) has guest-friends, saying that Thessaly offers nothing but lawlessness, disorder and endless dinners.[28]

Going to Thessaly, or refusing to go to Thessaly, were the subject of a certain amount of debate and antagonism within the philosophical world in the later fifth and earlier fourth centuries. It pitted Sokrates, symbolically, against prominent Athenians who *did* go to Thessaly. It may be that Plato had in the back of his mind the behaviour of Kritias, who, when exiled from Athens in ca. 410 BC, went to Thessaly and there involved himself somehow in Thessalian political discord.[29] Plato may not mention Kritias' Thessalian visit in contrast with Sokrates' refusal to take refuge there, but other authors play on the supposed relationship between Kritias' bad nature and the moral shortcomings of his new companions. Xenophon briefly but subtly suggests that Kritias was always bad – hence his choice of destination – but that exposure to Thessalians made him worse; moreover, it detached him from Sokrates, who had provided a virtuous antithesis to the negative influence of Thessaly.[30] Philostratus in his *Lives of the Sophists* picks up on this idea but subjects it to an interesting twist with the suggestion that, on balance, Kritias corrupted the Thessalians more than they did him.[31] It should be noted, however, that what little we have of Kritias' own writing is anything but favourable towards the Thessalians, so he himself does not seem to have expressed any affinity or sympathy with them.[32]

But the philosopher – or rather sophist – most famous for travelling to Thessaly and forming close connections there was Gorgias of Leontinoi, who resided at Larisa in the later period of his life and proved very influential among the nobles there. In Plato's *Gorgias* the yawning gulf between Gorgias and Sokrates is established, though no mention is made of the former's affiliation with Thessaly (perhaps because it is yet to commence?).[33] While Gorgias practises clever rhetoric, its purpose is as much about control and deception as about truth. Sokrates holds the key to real wisdom. In the *Menon* the Thessaly-connection is brought into the frame: their exposure to Gorgias and his craft has left the Larisaians addicted to sophistry and convinced of their own wisdom. However, Sokrates demolishes the philosophical pretensions of the Thessalian before him, young Menon of Pharsalos. He teases him openly, in the dialogue's opening lines, about the wisdom that Gorgias has supposedly imported into Thessaly, leaving

28 Plato, *Kriton* 53d–54c; Aston (2012a), 252–54.

29 Sprawski (1999), 31–34.

30 Xen. *Mem.* 1.2.24.

31 Philostratus, *Lives* 501–02.

32 Kritias, *FGrH* 338A F 8.

33 Dalfen (2004), 125–29; Cantarín and de Cerio Díez (2005), xxvi–xxxvii.

a 'drought' of wisdom in Athens;[34] his irony is entirely lost on the self-regarding young man. The supposed defection of Sophia from Athens to Thessaly is obviously part of the *topos* of Thessaly's ability to lure Athenians north; Sokrates says directly that 'κινδυνεύει ἐκ τῶνδε τῶν τόπων παρ' ὑμᾶς οἴχεσθαι ἡ σοφία' ('there's a risk that Wisdom is leaving this region to go to you').[35] The reference to the *auchmos* her departure causes evokes, of course, Thessaly's natural fertility contrasted with the relative aridity of Attica. But Plato's point is that Wisdom has not really left Athens: she remains because Sokrates, her perfect embodiment, remains (even when death threatens). Gorgias has not given Thessaly wisdom but only a second-rate facsimile, like the *eidolon* of Helen.[36]

If Plato's treatment of Menon of Pharsalos is critical, that of Xenophon is savage.[37] The *Anabasis*, which was probably composed and disseminated in the early 360s, shows signs of picking up elements of Menon's depiction in the *Menon*, and subverting them to turn grey to black. The context is the obituary of Menon included in the text after the betrayal and murder of the Greek generals by Tissaphernes. The Spartan Klearchos and the Boiotian Proxenos receive balanced character-portraits, shown to be laudable in some ways but blameworthy in others; by contrast, Menon is drawn as wholly bad. The criticism follows four basic strands:[38] he is motivated by excessive desire for wealth; he has no real loyalty to his friends, or staunch opposition to his enemies; he colludes with his men in their transgressions rather than setting them a moral example; and his sexual habits do not follow the approved pederastic customs of Greek society. On the one hand, this contains many of the stock ingredients of invective; on the other, it is slanted according to Thessalian stereotypes current at the time, and according to Plato's depiction in the *Menon*.

Xenophon himself gives us, in the *Hellenika*, a depiction of the ideal Thessalian, Polydamas of Pharsalos, whose virtue rests upon his conscientious use of wealth (for civic good), his loyalty to his *xenoi* (the Spartans, whose *proxenos* he is), and his *philotimia* and *megaloprepeia*, presented as typically Thessalian.[39] This chimes with Euripides' Admetos,

34 Plato, *Men.* 70a–71a; Klein (1965), 40–41; Ebert (2018), 50–54.

35 Plato, *Men.* 70c–71a.

36 Ionescu (2007), 4–6.

37 On the characterisation of Menon in the *Anabasis* see Brown (1986); Gray (2010), 75–77. Note that Ktesias' depiction of Menon also seems to have been hostile: see Bassett (2002), 452–56. On the *Anabasis* and Sokratic thought: Buzzetti (2014).

38 What follows summarises his obituary, Xen. *Anab.* 2.6.21–29. This section contains the distillation of Xenophon's hostility. Elsewhere the depiction is slightly more nuanced: in the conflict between Menon and the Spartan Klearchos, for example at 1.5.11, neither antagonist really emerges in a good light.

39 Xen. *Hell.* 6.1.2–3.

generous and hospitable to a fault, the ultimate *xenos*. Menon's greed and disloyalty obviously subvert these qualities entirely. The response of Plato, however, is subtler. In the Platonic dialogue, Menon is pressed to supply a definition of *aretē*.[40] At first he tries to establish separate definitions for different types of person (man, woman, child, slave), and at this stage his definition of virtue as applied to men seems admirable, if banal: 'First of all, if you take the virtue of a man, it is easily stated that a man's virtue is this – that he be competent to manage the affairs of his city, and to manage them so as to benefit his friends and harm his enemies, and to take care to avoid suffering harm himself.'[41] So far so Polydamas. When pushed, however, to give a universal definition, he offers a much starker and perhaps more honest formula: 'τί ἄλλο γ' ἢ ἄρχειν οἷόν τ' εἶναι τῶν ἀνθρώπων;' – 'What could it be but the ability to rule people?'[42] This is naked ambition laid bare – his true colours. However, Xenophon's Menon falls short of virtue according to both these definitions. He has left his polis far behind him; he is willing to harm his friends and to flatter his enemies, should it profit him to do so; he does indeed suffer appalling harm himself; and, most damning of all, he cannot even rule others well, since he is shown to be an ineffective leader. Thessaly, in Xenophon, is capable of conveying positive traditional values, but Menon entirely fails to live up to that quality.

Both Plato and Xenophon probably met Menon in Athens, and indeed his family was deeply connected with Athens.[43] The Menon who led the Pharsalian contingent on Athens' side in 431 BC – almost certainly the father of Plato's and Xenophon's Menon – did so as part of the alliance between Athens and Thessaly; however, there are also signs of private assistance rendered to Athens, when a Menon (probably an earlier one, but possibly the same)[44] led his own armed and mounted Penestai to help the Athenians at Eion. How exactly this enterprise fits within the alliance, whether it resulted from it or from an individual *xenia*-connection, we do not know, but the reward was civic: Menon was given either *ateleia* or full Athenian citizenship. If we date the Eion incident to the 420s, this would

40 For a summary of the *Menon*'s arguments see Merkelbach (1988), 5–10; for a more detailed analysis of the text: Scott (2006); Ionescu (2007). On the setting and context of the dialogue see Ebert (2018), 45–50. On the concept of *aretē* within the philosophical discourse of the time: Tarrant (2005), 20–23.

41 'πρῶτον μέν, εἰ βούλει ἀνδρὸς ἀρετήν, ῥᾴδιον, ὅτι αὕτη ἐστὶν ἀνδρὸς ἀρετή, ἱκανὸν εἶναι τὰ τῆς πόλεως πράττειν, καὶ πράττοντα τοὺς μὲν φίλους εὖ ποιεῖν, τοὺς δ' ἐχθροὺς κακῶς, καὶ αὐτὸν εὐλαβεῖσθαι μηδὲν τοιοῦτον παθεῖν.' Plato, *Menon* 71e (trans. Lamb, adapted.)

42 Plato *Men*. 73c; Klein (1965), 46–53; Thomas (1980), 81–95; Scott (2006), 23–32; Ionescu (2007), 10–19; Ebert (2018), 54–62.

43 On the particular prominence of Pharsalians in aristocratic networks outside Thessaly, and in Athenian affairs see Stamatopoulou (2007b).

44 *Pace* Coşkun (2013).

reinforce the particular intensity of Athens–Pharsalos interaction in the later fifth century, and the Menon of Plato and Xenophon becomes no chance visitor to Athens but one with strong recent ties to the city.[45] Either way, of all Thessalian poleis Pharsalos was the one with which the Athenians were most used to having dealings. Both Plato and Xenophon were writing about a man known to them and to many of their fellow countrymen, rather than about some distant figure residing in the imaginary north.[46] Real contact – diplomatic, personal, intellectual, military – brought Thessaly to greater Athenian notice and fuelled an increasingly ambivalent reception. However, this process can only be fully understood if we factor in a simultaneous development – the growing alignment between Thessalian and Macedonian affairs, and, at the same time, the increasing intrusion of Macedon into the Athenian consciousness at the end of the fifth century BC.

2. Thessaly and Macedon

a) Increasing alignment

Connections and affinities between Thessaly and Macedon are no sudden novelty in the period here discussed. We have described the porosity of Thessaly's southern border, leading into the Spercheios valley, and the same applies to some extent in the north. Passes pierced the highlands of Perrhaibia, allowing for traffic – famous armies passing through, but also, without doubt, the usual anonymous itinerants: merchants, herdsmen and the like. Towns situated on or near the passes show clear signs of influence from both sides, and of their liminal status. While ethnic boundaries – Thessaloi, Perrhaiboi, Magnetes, Makedones – were by no means unimportant, they did little to hinder practical interaction. Religious affinities are detectable between the Thessalians and the Macedonians, most visible in the Hellenistic period but certainly with far older origins.[47] And myth certainly crosses the marches. When Apollo descends from Olympos, going forth to found a new sanctuary, he goes through Pieria (later the

45 It is possible even that a Menon was resident in Athens, with Athenian citizenship. Osborne (1983), vol. 3, 20–23; Helly (1994). Osborne identifies this Menon as the Menon who held the position of Archon in Athens in 473/2; he was ostracised ca. 471. Intriguingly, one of the *ostraka* bearing his name adds the formula ἐκκ προ[δοτ]ῶ[ν], 'one of the traitors'. As Osborne observes (1983, 22), the date precludes a reference to the Thessalian defection at Tanagra; is this a glimpse of Athenian hostility towards medisers?

46 Klein (1965), 35–37; Ferrari (2016), 14–19.

47 Hatzopoulos (1994), 25–40. However, Graninger (2007) challenges some aspects of the proposed religious affinities.

grazing place of his sacred herds)[48] through Perrhaibia and down to Iolkos.[49] Nonetheless, a sharper sense of ethnic differentiation applies here in the Archaic period than it does on Thessaly's southern side. The Macedonians are not involved in the expedition to Troy, so in the Catalogue of Ships the Perrhaiboi constitute the northern edge of the combined Greek contingents. In the *Ehoiai*, the eponym Makedon is famously, for all his prestigious parentage,[50] separate from the lineage of Hellen.[51] If southern Thessaly and the Spercheios valley were seen as the crucible of Hellenism, Perrhaibia was certainly its edge.

Away from the border areas, we see plenty of political interaction between Thessaly and Macedon – the elites of both – as early as the late sixth and early fifth centuries. Herodotos' narrative makes it clear that key strategies of the Aleuadai aligned exactly with those of the Argead throne, though he omits any mention of Aleuadai and Argeadai communicating directly with each other, and it is possible that these events opened the door to future interactions rather than constituting them in their own right at the time. The first key event was the support offered to the exiled Peisistratid Hippias by both the Aleuadai and Amyntas I of Macedon; the second was the shared stance of the Aleuadai and Alexandros I when Xerxes invaded.[52] It is telling that Alexandros apparently warned the Hellenic League against trying to hold Tempe in 480 BC,[53] since this would certainly have assisted

[48] *HH* 4.191; Apollod. *Bibl.* 3.10.2. The fact that Apollo herds kine in Pieria and also in the lands of Admetos of Pherai is a further link between Thessaly and southern Macedon. In the Vulgate text of the *Iliad*, the horses of Eumelos also come from Pieria, where they were bred by Apollo. However, it is possible that this reading is a scribal error. But, even if it is, the error itself may have been triggered by a longstanding association between Apollo, herding, Pieria and Thessaly. Kirk (1985), 240–41.

[49] *HH* 3.216–18.

[50] Makedon as son of Zeus and Thyia: *Ehoiai* fr. 7 MW.

[51] Hall argues that this is a deliberate 'othering' of the Macedonians: Hall (2002), 168–70. Whether or not we should see this as an exclusionary gesture (and Sourvinou-Inwood 2002 does not), it certainly reflects a sense of ethnic distinction.

[52] In addition to short-term expedience, we should remember that both the Aleuadai and Alexandros were actively promoting Heraklid identity at this time. Whether doing so constituted a deliberate assertion of mutual connection, it is interesting to note the sense of solidarity between Heraklid elites in ancient Greece. A powerful – if later – reflection of this comes in the *Presbeutikos* in the Hippokratic pseudepigraphica, discussed in detail in the next chapter; here Thessalos son of Hippokrates, appealing to the Athenians not to continue their aggression against his homeland of Kos, warns that he may be forced to seek aid elsewhere: 'For others will help us if they behave properly: people in Thessaly, Argos, Sparta, the Macedonian kings, wherever other Heraklids or connections of the Heraklids live' (trans. Smith, adapted).

[53] Hdt. 7.173: here Alexandros' counsel is based on the size of the Persian force, while the Greeks follow it because of fear that the pass may be turned by way of an additional

the Aleuad desire to see Persian forces overrun Greece (and no doubt instal them as puppet rulers in Thessaly).[54] Alexandros' own motives are hard to gauge; Herodotos, of course, transmits a quantity of exculpation, presenting him as devoted to Greece though forced into collusion with the Persian foe, and in reality it would have been almost impossible for him to resist the invasion given that Macedon had been subject to Persia since 492 BC.[55] But, whatever the complexities of intention on either side, he and the Aleuadai found themselves closely aligned at this moment of crisis.[56]

In the 420s BC, *philia* between a Larisaian, Nikonidas, and the Argead king Perdikkas II was an influential factor in the activities of the Spartan Brasidas in the north. While Brasidas' relations with Perdikkas remained cordial he could also draw upon a certain amount of goodwill (though not unmixed) in Thessaly; when he and Perdikkas were at loggerheads, Thessaly also became a source of obstruction. We do not know that Nikonidas was an Aleuad, nor that Perdikkas' Thessalian connections were limited to that clan; Thucydides remarks of Perdikkas, in describing how he galvanised his Thessalian *xenoi* into hindering Brasidas' reinforcements, that he always cultivated the leading men; clearly expediency co-exists with, and may exceed, family loyalty.[57] In any case, *xenia*-networks have an expansive quality, and allowed a participant to draw on chains of association. It need hardly be said that at this period there was no such thing as a political alliance between the two regions; important though the connection was, it was conducted along the lines of individual friendships whose importance was discussed in Chapter 5.

Signs of heightened interaction appear with the reign of Archelaos. This important and ambitious king ruled in circumstances far removed from those of Perdikkas; whereas the latter had to contend defensively with the acquisitive interest of Athenians and Spartans in the north, Archelaos' reign coincided with Athens' defeat at Sparta's hands, which neutralised one major threat to the integrity of his kingdom and opened up new diplomatic and economic opportunities. He seems also, perhaps as a consequence of his broader ambitions, to have involved himself in Thessalian politics in a far more active

route. Damastes of Sigeion, however, says that Alexandros 'revealed the treachery of [the sons of] Aleuas and the Thessalians'. While this may seem to suggest that the king and the Aleuadai were opposed, in fact the former's action will still have suited the latter very well, however it was couched (Damastes, *FGrH* 5 F 4).

54 The Aleuadai (along with the Peisistratidai) actively encourage Xerxes to invade: Hdt. 7.6.2.

55 Hdt. 5.44; Borza (1990), 104–05.

56 Graninger (2010), 309–10; see also Müller (2016), 219–22.

57 Thuc. 4.132: 'παρασκευάσας τοὺς ἐν Θεσσαλίᾳ ξένους, χρώμενος αἰεὶ τοῖς πρώτοις' ('having readied his *xenoi* in Thessaly – for he always associated with the foremost men').

way than merely maintaining and exploiting traditional friendships. That he did maintain them, despite the cloud of uncertainty that seems to have hung over the legitimacy of his succession in some quarters, is made clear by the Aleuad identity of the man with whom he seems primarily to have been involved, Aristippos of Larisa. It would seem that Archelaos sponsored a bid by the Aleuadai, headed by Aristippos, to regain power in Larisa in the face of strong opposition;[58] Aristippos was installed, but at some cost, since Archelaos imposed a Macedonian garrison on Larisa and annexed land in Perrhaibia controlling the passes between the two regions. For details of the circumstances and outcome we are reliant upon the mysterious rhetorical work *Peri Politeias*, attributed (almost certainly falsely) to Herodes Atticus, and probably containing a decent acquaintance with events of the period in which it purports to have been delivered. The argument of Wade-Gery and Morrison that the author was Kritias is tempting, because if Kritias, in exile in Thessaly ca. 407 BC, was involved in the Larisaian stasis on the opposite side this may provide an explanation for Xenophon's otherwise wholly baffling claim that Kritias intrigued in Thessaly to establish a democracy, arming the Penestai against their masters.[59] Xenophon's comment – in the mouth of Theramenes – is condensed and offers no details, but Wade-Gery and Morrison may well be right that Kritias backed the more moderate oligarchic faction attempting to oust the Aleuadai from their long-standing control of Larisaian affairs. In any case, the basic historicity of Archelaos' involvement in the conflict is provided by a fragment of a speech written for the Larisaians – those opposed to Aristippos' faction – by Thrasymachos, in which Archelaos is branded a barbarian enslaving Greeks.[60] Moreover, Aristotle refers to one Hellanokrates, a young man of Larisa, to whom Archelaos promised restoration to his home polis; Archelaos reneged, and Hellanokrates was one of his assassins.[61]

Archelaos' actions in general triggered a complex set of responses in Athens.[62] On the one hand, he was granted honorific titles (*proxenos* and

[58] This must be the same Aristippos whose political woes are mentioned by Xenophon in the *Anabasis*; he sought help from Kyros the Younger – before the latter's attempted coup – as well as from Archelaos, and it is interesting to see the old Macedon–Thessaly–Persia triangle in operation again. Xen. *Anab.* 1.1.10 and 1.2.1.

[59] Xen. *Hell.* 2.3.36. Wade-Gery and Morrison (1942). The identity of Aristippos' enemies is unknown; Wade-Gery and Morrison (1942, 66) argue that the Pheraian Lykophron is meant, but equally Aristippos may have been ousted by a rival faction in Larisa.

[60] Thrasymachos, D18: [the Larisaian envoy speaks] 'Ἀρχελάῳ δουλεύσομεν Ἕλληνες ὄντες βαρβάρῳ;' ('Shall we, who are Greeks, be a slave to the *barbaros* Archelaos?').

[61] Arist. *Pol.* 5.1311b.

[62] Borza (1993), 242–44. For discussion of some broader aspects of the Macedonian stereotype in ancient sources see Müller (2016), 49–74.

euergetes) on the strength of his provision of timber to a beleaguered Athens after the Sicilian disaster. On the other, despite – or perhaps in some way because of – this formal goodwill, Archelaos seems to have aroused considerable hostility among the Athenian intelligentsia. Plato in particular used him as an emblem of the unjust, and therefore wretched, man, because of the violent and illegal means by which he supposedly attained the throne (though this may well reflect Athenian ignorance of Macedonian succession practices). At first glance condemnation of Archelaos – especially as it included speech-making against his involvement in the affairs of Larisa – would seem, if anything, to engender sympathy at Athens for the Thessalians: they are true Greeks, subject to the tyrannical impositions of a *barbaros*. But in fact it is not so simple. It is in the time of Archelaos that we start to see a certain symbolic alignment between Thessaly and Macedon, and in particular the characterisation of both as potentially appealing destinations which might draw Athenians away from their home and from their true identity.

It was established above that, in the later fifth century, going to Thessaly on an embassy was considered a risky business, opening the participant up to the allure of lavish hospitality. Archelaos' Macedon was similarly portrayed, though the emphasis among our surviving sources is less on official embassies than on the departure from Athens of artists and philosophers, drawn to the riches of the Macedonian court. Not all of these were Athenian, of course; the painter Zeuxis was from Herakleia, for example;[63] the musician Timotheos was from Miletos,[64] and the epic poet Choirilos was from Samos.[65] Archelaos seems to have succeeded in drawing Greeks to him from all over. But it is when an individual left Athens to go to Macedon that we have some critical, or at any rate pointed, treatment of the fact. Particularly significant is the pun, long-recognised, in Aristophanes' *Frogs*, when Dionysos is bewailing Athens' dire lack of good tragic poets. Some, such as Euripides, have died; others have left, among them Agathon, who has gone 'ἐς Μακάρων εὐωχίαν'. At first glance this seems to suggest that he too is deceased – the Blessed are the heroic dead who dwell in godlike eternal bliss in some such place as the island of Leuke, the White Isle. But in fact Agathon has gone to the Macedonian court, and Makarōn is a pun for Makedonōn. He is forever feasting among the Macedonians, at the court of Archelaos.[66]

[63] Ael. *Var. Hist.* 14.17. Here a typically hostile slant is put upon Zeuxis' commission: people visit Macedon only to see Archelaos' marvellous house and Zeuxis' paintings, not to visit the king himself (except those swayed by money).

[64] Plut. *De Alex.* 2; Steph. Byz. s.v. Μίλητος. Plant (2015), 389.

[65] Suda s.v. Χοιρίλος. Huxley (1969), 12–13.

[66] For discussion of Euripides at the court of Archelaos see Scullion (2003), who is highly sceptical; more credit is given to the idea by Duncan (2011).

This combination of feasting and death is very significant, for it is echoed just a few years after the *Frogs*' production in 405 BC when Sokrates refuses to escape to Thessaly in Plato's *Kriton*, probably published in 399 BC. Not only is life in Thessaly presented as limited to the consumption of food,[67] but the parallel between Thessaly and death is a strong theme in the dialogue. It is part of the argument that Sokrates presents to Kriton: to go to Thessaly is no better than death, amounts to the same thing in terms of the impact on friends and family.[68] The complete loss of identity that living in Thessaly would entail may be seen as tantamount to death. And, finally, Sokrates says that he knows the very day of his execution because it has been signalled to him obliquely by a beautiful woman in a dream, quoting to him the words from *Iliad* 9, 'ἤματί κεν τριτάτῳ Φθίην ἐρίβωλον ἵκοιο' ('On the third day you would come to fertile Phthia').[69] Phthia here signifies death, with its etymological connection with φθίω and φθίσις.[70] Moreover, its very fertility plays into the association, since natural abundance – as well as constant feasting – is a recurring theme in afterlife beliefs of the time.[71] While links between Thessaly and death have existed since the *Iliad*'s composition, it is in the early fourth century that they become drawn into the theme of Thessaly's power to tempt Athenians north, and the similarity to the depiction of Archelaos' Macedon is striking. Diogenes Laertios may be picking up on this alignment when he claims that 'He scorned Archelaos the Macedonian, Skopas the Krannonian and Eurylochos the Larisaian, and would neither accept money from them nor go away to live with them.' Archelaos, Skopas, Eurylochos: they are all lumped together as northern men with money and power but no wisdom, unsuitable hosts for Sokrates.[72]

67 Plato, *Kriton* 53e.

68 Plato, *Kriton* 54a.

69 Plato, *Kriton* 44b, quoting *Iliad* 9.363.

70 Mackie (2002), 172–73.

71 A particularly striking manifestation of this theme is the Totenmahl scene common in grave monuments in the Greek East and appearing from the Hellenistic period in Greece itself (Fabricius 1999). Even though, as Stamatopoulou observes (2016, 405–06), the full meaning of this motif would differ from region to region, it would surely have both drawn on and reinforced a strong connection between feasting/drinking and death. There also seems to be a persistent association between geographical extremity and feasting: see MacLachlan (1992) on the motif of feasting among the Aithiopes and Hyperboreans. Perhaps the position of the Thessalians at Greece's northern edge, and the Macedonians just beyond it, encouraged the perception of their lands as places of copious consumption.

72 Diog. Laer. *Lives* 2.5.25: 'ὑπερεφρόνησε δὲ καὶ Ἀρχελάου τοῦ Μακεδόνος καὶ Σκόπα τοῦ Κρανωνίου καὶ Εὐρυλόχου τοῦ Λαρισσαίου, μήτε χρήματα προσέμενος παρ' αὐτῶν,

Here we may mention Euripides' own associations with Thessaly and Macedon. The biographical tradition surrounding him is worth very little in terms of historical veracity, but is not without interest.[73] It links him with Magnesia, but the terms in which it does so are not convincing; if he really was the *proxenos* of the Magnetes, this would imply a degree of political co-ordination on the part of that *ethnos* not otherwise attested for the fifth century BC.[74] As for Macedon, it suggests that around 408 he left Athens altogether and went to Archelaos' court, where he wrote the *Archelaos* 'as a favour' (χαριζόμενος) to the king,[75] and where he later died.[76] As Scullion observes, it is virtually inconceivable that such a fact, if true, would not have been exploited in the *Frogs*, where it would have afforded enormous comic opportunities and where Agathon's defection was (subtly) noted. In all likelihood, the largely fictional biographical tradition draws on some background *realia*: that Euripides did have northern contacts, that he did spend time at Archelaos' court, and that his work is infused with northern themes and perspectives. The *cui bono* principle supports this. The choice of mythological detail in the *Andromache* only makes full sense if read as an aetiological advertisement of the Molossian ruling family (*illis bono*), and the same can be said of the *Archelaos* and the Macedonian king of that name. Thessalian themes have been described above. But the notion that Euripides died in Macedon is suggestive. Though it is unclear when the tradition began – its earliest attestation is third century[77] – it may well have been fuelled by the existing association between going north and dying.[78] The undignified nature of Euripides' reported behaviour in Macedon (in love with Archelaos' housekeeper; mocked for his bad breath; eventually torn apart by dogs) echoes

μήτε παρ' αὐτοὺς ἀπελθών.' This passage occurs, significantly, amid descriptions of Sokrates' self-restraint and austere style of life.

73 The source for these details is the *Vita* included in the Byzantine manuscripts of the plays, which draw, as Lefkowitz (1979, 188) observes, chiefly on comedy and on Euripides' tragedies themselves.

74 *Vita Eur.* 10.

75 *Vita Eur.* 11. On the circumstances of the composition of the *Archelaos* and its adaptation of Temenid mythology see further Harder (1985), 125–37; Jouan and Van Looy (1998), 275–91; Collard et al. (2004), 330–37; Moloney (2015), 59–63. See also the discussion of the play in Chapter 3.

76 *Vita Eur.* 21; for a collation of other ancient anecdotes regarding Euripides' death see Kovacs (1994), 64–67.

77 Hermesianax, *Leontion* 3.61–68.

78 It is interesting to note that both Timotheos and Choirilos were supposed to have died in Macedon: we seem to have here a literary *topos* in which Macedon is the land from which there is no return.

Sokrates' assertion that going to Thessaly will entail ridicule, status-loss and a kind of servitude.[79]

So there was already, by the early fourth century, a tendency to see Thessaly and Macedon in very similar terms, as northern destinations trying to lure Athenians into a life of corrupt excess. This discourse, however, is given new urgency with the emergence of a man who would bring the two regions into such a state of political entanglement that their histories could never subsequently be considered entirely apart from each other: Philip II of Macedon.

b) Philip: the culmination

Philip's father Amyntas III had various interactions with the Thessalians. When ousted from his kingdom in the 390s he took refuge with the Aleuadai;[80] later, restored, he formed an alliance with Jason.[81] The close relations of the two regions were therefore soundly established by the time Philip came to the throne in 359 BC. However, the circumstances of the Third Sacred War, and the Thessalian opposition to the tyrants of Pherai, gave Philip an opportunity to involve himself in Thessalian affairs to an unprecedented extent.

The Heraklid ancestry of the Argeads is first articulated (by Herodotos) in the context of Alexandros I's uneasy reign in the earlier fifth century.[82] At that time the genealogical exposition was needed, to persuade the Olympic

[79] The most scathing Athenian treatment of Archelaos' character is that of Plato in the *Gorgias* (470d–471d), in which Polos condemns Archelaos for having attained the Argead throne illegitimately by committing murder. See Dalfen (2004), 271–72; Ranasinghe (2009), 56–59. It is even possible that, to add extra piquancy to this treatment, Plato recycles and twists a sentiment in Euripides' *Archelaos*. Fr. 247 of the play reads τί δ' οὐκ ἂν εἴη χρηστὸς ὄλβιος γεγώς; ('Why would he not be good, since he is blessed/wealthy?'). This uses the evocative term ὄλβιος, associated with aristocratic prosperity; does Plato subvert the word and the sentiment when he has Polos say of Archelaos that since he is ἄδικος ('unjust') he must be ἄθλιος ('wretched'). Are ὄλβιος and ἄθλιος an ironic jingle? Is there, at any rate, a deliberate manipulation of the sentiment, if the mythological Archelaos must be good because wealthy and his real counterpart must be miserable because bad? Possibly. But to make the claim firmly we would need further context for the fragment; after all, we do not even know to whom the line refers.

[80] Diod. 14.92.3.

[81] Diod. 15.60.2; Sprawski (2020), 109–10. Amyntas seems to have had influence in, if not total control over, the march-land between Perrhaibia and Elimiotis. It is plausible that Pheraian support would have helped him to secure the southern borders of his kingdom: See Helly (1979). According to Diodoros, Jason himself took control of some of Perrhaibia: Diod. 15.57.2. On Perrhaibia as subject to some Macedonian control from the fourth century onwards see Helly (1973), vol. I, 81–87.

[82] Hdt. 5.22.

Hellanodikai to allow the king even to compete in the foot-race, since only Greeks could take part. Though the historicity of the incident is doubtful,[83] it serves to show how far Philip had changed the standing of his family: while his ancestor had had to undertake genealogical argumentation to be one among many competitors at a panhellenic sanctuary, Philip was *invited* to take his seat on the governing body of another, the sanctuary of Apollo at Delphi, in the role of saviour and champion. And this remarkable transition was greatly facilitated, if not actually made possible, by the Thessalians, in one of the great symbioses of history.[84]

Given the close alignment of two northern powers in the cradle of Greek history of culture, it is no wonder that we find a flurry of excoriation of both Thessalians and Macedonians from those especially bent upon disparagement, most notably Demosthenes and Theopompos. Demosthenes focuses on the treachery of individual Thessalians, selling out their own land as well as Greece more widely by colluding with Philip.[85] However, he also develops the idea that the Thessalians are inherently untrustworthy and faithless. He does so to serve a rhetorical purpose: persuading the Athenians that the coalition between Macedon and Thessaly was bound to break down – indeed, had cracks showing – because the Thessalians could never be relied upon to be staunch allies; therefore, he argues, Philip's position is weaker than it seems. The way in which he couches this is, however, interesting. In the *First Olynthiac*, delivered in 349 BC, he says: 'ταῦτα γὰρ [referring to τὰ τῶν Θετταλῶν] ἄπιστα μὲν ἦν δήπου φύσει καὶ ἀεὶ πᾶσιν ἀνθρώποις, κομιδῇ δ', ὥσπερ ἦν, καὶ ἔστι νῦν τούτῳ' ('Thessalian affairs were always inherently unreliable, as everyone found, and certainly Philip

83 Borza (1990), 111–12. Evidence for Alexandros actually having taken part in the contest, however, is marshalled by Remijsen (2019), 11–14.

84 Co-operation between Thessalians and Philip regarding Delphi took various forms. The Thessalians were instrumental in the allocation of the Phokians' confiscated votes to Philip in 346 BC: Demosth. 19.111 (Thessalian envoys try to persuade the Athenians to vote for Philip's enrolment in the Council); cf. Diod. 16.60.1; Roux (1979), 166. It was agreed that Philip was to organise the Pythian Games of 346 BC in concert with the Thessalians and the Boiotians: Diod. 16.60.2. Finally, as discussed in Chapter 5, the Thessalian *hieromnēmones* tended to be individuals favourable to Philip. Kottyphos, with his colleague Kolosimmos, appears in Amphiktyonic inscriptions between ca. 345 and 338 as one of the Thessalian *hieromnēmones*: see, for example, *CID* 2.34, 2.36, 2.43, 2.34. Roux (1979), 46–48. About them, however, we know little compared with the pair who took over from them: Daochos and Thrasydaios, whose work on Philip's behalf has been described above. The fact that Daochos is always listed first, of all twenty-four *hieromnēmones*, suggests that he led the Council. See, for example, *CID* 2.76 (335 BC).

85 E.g. Demosth. 18.295; on this speech and its context see Yunis (2005), 23–31 and 114–21; MacDowell (2009), 382–97. On Demosthenes' depiction of Philip see Harris (2018).

will find them just as they were').[86] This echoes a point made in 352, when Demosthenes wished to persuade the Athenians that Philip had been rash to put faith in the friendship of the Thessalians: 'You, Athenians, have never yet betrayed one of your friends, but as for the Thessalians, not one of their friends have they ever failed to betray.'[87]

What does Demosthenes have in mind – and expect his audience to have in mind – when he says this? Perhaps Thessalian medism; perhaps Thessalian conduct during the battle of Tanagra; perhaps a hazy sense of historical wrongdoing. Here we see state and individual pulling in different directions: as discussed above, the Thessalians were strongly associated with aristocratic *philia*/*xenia* between families, in the old manner, a quality of which Admetos is the extreme example. However, when attempts were made to shift from personal to state loyalty, the results were indeed patchy. Demosthenes, however, underestimates Philip's cunning: the king knew the value of forging personal friendships with individual Thessalians, and there is no evidence of any one of his Thessalian *philoi* ever turning against him. Indeed, what Demosthenes condemns as Philip luring the Thessalians into servitude by corrupting individuals with lavish gifts and the promise of power[88] can and should be seen as the use of traditional diplomatic methods, the forging of a *philia*-network independent of institutional structures, and the use of gift-giving and hospitality to cement it. Neither Thessalians nor Macedonians needed to worry about any ideological conflict between such practices and the principles of democracy, a conflict that of course fuelled Demosthenes' scathing depiction of their relationship.

Theopompos, on the other hand, makes full use of the rhetorical cliché current when he was writing, that of luxury, excess and lack of moderation, character flaws to which the Pharsalians, he claims, were prey even more than other Thessalians.[89] Significantly, he presents Philip and the Thessalians as natural allies because of their shared vices:

> Theopompos in the twenty-sixth (book) of the Histories says, 'Philip, recognizing that the Thessalians were dissolute and licentious in their lifestyle, prepared parties for them and endeavoured to please them in every way by dancing and partying and submitting to every sort of corruption—by nature he was a buffoon, getting drunk daily and delighting in the pursuits that lead to those things and to the so-called "men of wit" who tell

86 Demosth. 1.22.

87 Demosth. 23.112: 'ὑμεῖς μέν, ὦ ἄνδρες Ἀθηναῖοι, οὐδένα προὐδώκατε πώποτε τῶν φίλων, Θετταλοὶ δ' οὐδένα πώποθ' ὅντιν' οὔ.'

88 See esp. his rhetorical tour-de-force, 18.295. Discussion of the theme of corruption in Demosthenes' works: Nichols (2019).

89 Theopompos *FGrH* 115 F 49.

and make jokes— and he won over more of the Thessalians who associated with him by means of parties than by bribes.'[90]

The convergence between Thessalian and Macedonian character, identified as an increasing component in the Thessalian stereotype from the late fifth century onwards, is now complete.

The theme of consumption and the pernicious collaboration of Thessaly and Macedon finds especially piquant expression in a fragment of the poet of New Comedy, Mnesimachos. His play *Philip* was plainly a humorous attack on the king; in it, one character asks another (the identities of the *dramatis personae* being regrettably unknown), 'Did any of the Pharsalians come in order to eat the tables?' Eating so heartily that one consumes the very table is plainly a joke about gluttony, but the rest of the conversation quoted makes it clear that there is a stark political dimension. On being told no, the first speaker exclaims, 'εὖ γε δρῶντες. ἆρά που ὀπτὴν κατεσθίουσι πόλιν Ἀχαϊκήν' ('Good for them. Perhaps they're eating up a roasted Achaian polis?').[91] The image of Thessalians – more precisely, Pharsalians – colluding with Philip to destroy their fellow Greeks is entirely familiar from Demosthenes' accusations; that it should be presented as an act of greedy eating recycles the established stereotype of the gluttonous Pharsalian.

c) *Tryphē* and the 'othering' of Thessaly

Theopompos' assertion about the natural affinity of Philip and the Thessalians is the easiest to tie to a particular date and context – literary and historical – but this conjunction of Thessalians and Macedonians, united by the theme of *tryphē*, occurs piecemeal across the corpus of Greek literature from this time on.[92]

[90] *FGrH* 115 F 162: 'Θεόπομπος δ' ἐν ἕκτηι καὶ εἰκοστῆι Ἱστοριῶν 'τοὺς Θεσσαλούς' φησίν 'εἰδὼς ὁ Φίλιππος ἀκολάστους ὄντας καὶ περὶ τὸν βίον ἀσελγεῖς συνουσίας αὐτῶν κατεσκεύαζε καὶ πάντα τρόπον ἀρέσκειν αὐτοῖς ἐπειρᾶτο καὶ ὀρχούμενος καὶ κωμάζων καὶ πᾶσαν ἀκολασίαν ὑπομένων (ἦν δὲ καὶ φύσει βωμολόχος καὶ καθ' ἡκάστην ἡμέραν μεθυσκόμενος καὶ χαίρων τῶν ἐπιτηδευμάτων τοῖς πρὸς ταῦτα συντεῖνουσι καὶ τῶν ἀνθρώπων τοῖς εὐφυέσι καλουμένοις καὶ τὰ γέλοια λέγουσι καὶ ποιοῦσι), πλείους τε τῶν Θετταλῶν τῶν αὐτῶι πλησιασάντων ἥιρει μᾶλλον ἐν ταῖς συνουσίαις ἢ ταῖς δωρεαῖς' (trans. Morison, adapted).

[91] Fr. 8 KA. It seems likely that 'Achaian' here refers to Achaia Phthiotis, since Philip took Phthiotic Halos and gave it to the Pharsalians (handed it to them to gobble up).

[92] An example is the convoluted discussion in Athenaios (*Deipn.* 14.662f–664d) of something called the *mattyēs*, which apparently started as a simple barley meal but became a word for a very elaborate and indulgent dish. It is suggested in one place (663a) that the Thessalians in the time of Philip helped to popularise the dish in Athens; in another place (664b) this is attributed to the Macedonians. This confused bundle of

Thessaly's relationship with Macedon did not in fact cause her people to be openly branded as *barbaroi*. Though it was possible for Philip's detractors to call him a *barbaros*[93] – while simultaneously his supporters called on him to lead a panhellenic expedition against the Persians, the *real barbaroi* – the same accusation was never directly made against the Thessalians in the fourth century BC. They were incontestably Hellenes. However, we do see a growing tendency, no doubt fuelled by their close association with the Macedonians, to cast them as unsatisfactory Greeks, as meeting the ethnic criteria but falling short of expected ethical standards.[94] This is most starkly expressed by Kritias, reported to have said that their encouragement of the Persian invasion of 480 BC was motivated by a desire to obtain a share of Persian luxury for themselves.[95] This is a very similar sentiment to that of Theopompos about the Pharsalians and Philip: the accusation of a natural sympathy, founded on shared ethical shortcomings, between the Thessalians and a barbarian or semi-barbarian invader. Further, more oblique insinuations include the tradition concerning Thargelia, the hetaira from Miletos, who supposedly influenced the Thessalians to medise: here we have an expressive bundle of interlocking ideas, especially Eastern luxury and corruption and sexual indulgence.[96] We should recall Xenophon's Menon, too, not only a monster of greed but also enjoying unnatural relations (as a Greek would see it) with Ariaios and one Tharypas, the former a Persian, the latter bearing a Molossian name. Excessive intimacy with *barbaroi* and semi-*barbaroi* represents an extension of the same accusation of affinity with non-Greeks.[97]

assertions really amounts to a feeling that the luxurious food came from some rich and *tryphē*-loving people in the north.

93 E.g. Demosth. 9.31: 'οὐ μόνον οὐχ Ἕλληνος ὄντος οὐδὲ προσήκοντος οὐδὲν τοῖς Ἕλλησιν, ἀλλ' οὐδὲ βαρβάρου ἐντεῦθεν ὅθεν καλὸν εἰπεῖν, ἀλλ' ὀλέθρου Μακεδόνος, ὅθεν οὐδ' ἀνδράποδον σπουδαῖον οὐδὲν ἦν πρότερον πρίασθαι.' ('Not only is he no Greek, nor related to any Greek, but he isn't even a *barbaros* from anywhere with a decent name; no, he's a pestilent Macedonian, from somewhere it was never yet possible to buy a well-behaved slave.')

94 Pownall (2009).

95 Athen. *Deipn.* 12.527b and 14.663a. For the cultural dimension of medism see Graf (1984), 15, who claims 'Inherent in the term was the implication that collaborators with the Great King had rejected the peculiar manner of life characteristic of the Greek world in favor of the corrupting life-style of the East.' However, the idea that medism indicated a deep cultural affinity with the Persians did not fully develop during or immediately after the invasion itself. See Rung (2013), 71, 77.

96 Suda s.v. Θαργηλία; Plut. *Per.* 24.3. Note that in fact Persianism could be enacted – both publicly and privately – at Athens, despite the hostile discourse of dangerous alterity: see Miller (2017). Needless to say, Persian culture and style inspired as much fascination as it did revulsion.

97 Xen. *Anab.* 2.6.28: 'Ἀριαίῳ δὲ βαρβάρῳ ὄντι, ὅτι μειρακίοις καλοῖς ἥδετο, οἰκειότατος

What is especially striking is that accusations like Kritias' do not appear much earlier. For all the disapproval that must have attached to the Thessalians for their medism in the aftermath of the Persian Wars, suggested by Herodotos' great effort to exonerate the majority from full moral blame, we have no text from the first half of the fifth century openly accusing the Thessalians of being like the Persians in their style of life, conduct or character. Such would only come once the perceived ideological boundaries between them and us, traitor and loyalist, bad Greek and good, had become starkly defined in the later fifth century and the fourth. The fourth-century harpist Stratonikos is supposed to have been asked the jesting question, 'πότερα Βοιωτοὶ βαρβαρώτεροι τυγχάνουσιν ὄντες ἢ Θετταλοί' ('whether the Boiotians were more barbarian or the Thessalians'),[98] and though he confounded his questioner by answering 'The Eleans' because of a personal grudge against that community, the question itself shows that in this post-Classical context the two most notorious medisers could be lumped together as having *barbaros*-qualities.[99]

The development of the 'Thessalians are like Persians' motif in the late fifth century may also have drawn on a degree of genuine interaction at this time. Hyland has argued for an attempt by both Thessalians and Persians to renew, in the last decade of the fifth century, the *xenia* that had existed between them since the Persian invasion of 480. The earliest sign of this attempted *rapprochement* was the invitation made by Dareios II to the celebrity pankratist Poulydamas of Skotoussa; this Hyland connects with the involvement of Menon and Aristippos in the coup against Artaxerxes. While Persian connections with Greek communities at this time were by no means limited to Thessaly, in the case of Thessaly it may well have

ἔτι ὡραῖος ὢν ἐγένετο, αὐτὸς δὲ παιδικὰ εἶχε Θαρύπαν ἀγένειος ὢν γενειῶντα.' ('With Ariaios, a *barbaros*, he was on very intimate terms, since Ariaios liked attractive boys. And even when he was still in the bloom of youth, and beardless, he had Tharypas, who was bearded, as his lover.') Both these relationships cast Menon as the *erōmenos*, not a dignified role for a general to be associated with; however, the normal age relationships are distorted, because the bearded Tharypas plays the role of *paidika*. It is interesting to compare this accusation with Theopompos' claim that in the Argead court grown men chose to consort with other grown men, though themselves bearded: Theopompos *FGrH* 115 F 225b. Lane Fox (2004), 198–99.

98 Stratonikos, famous for his ascerbic wit, became a figure to whom pithy sayings attached, most of them probably spurious. See Gilula (2000).

99 The date of the anecdote is hard to ascertain, supposing it is not a fiction: Athenaios attributes it to Hegesandros, who probably worked in the second century BC, but even that is not known with certainty. Prandi (1989), 27–29.

reawakened old memories of medism and old accusations of fundamental disloyalty to Greece and its ideals.[100]

The *tryphē* theme is obviously a crucial part of that discourse, and continued to be so through successive centuries.[101] Living immoderately was an accusation that could be flung at anyone one wished to disparage, and no-one was immune. However, there is an undeniable tendency for it to cluster on the margins, so to speak, of the Greek world: the Lydians, the Sybarites, the tyrants of Syracuse, the Macedonians and the Thessalians.[102] As ever with stereotypes there are shreds of underlying truth. The high number of references to the gluttonous consumption by Thessalians of meat and cereals in particular reflects the region's abundance of pastoral and arable resources. However, it is of course massively distorted, and in some ways retrospective. It is no accident that when Theokritos wishes to conjure an image of rich Thessalians he does so with reference to the old families and using the past tense:[103] his Thessaly is the Thessaly Simonides

[100] Hyland (2015). It is interesting that Poulydamas seems to have emphasised his physical superiority to Dareios' best men, as if to maintain his integrity while engaging in close diplomatic relations. Lysippos was commissioned to sculpt a statue of him at Olympia, and the relief on the base shows him getting the better of an adversary while Dareios looks on. His epic combat against elite Persian warriors is described in Paus. 6.5.7.

[101] It is certainly true that, as Gorman and Gorman have argued, Athenaios' scattered references cannot be used to reconstruct a whole system of Hellenistic historiography founded upon *tryphē* as a key element of causation. They are, however, sufficient to show the theme at work in the hostile stereotyping of certain groups and individuals. See Gorman and Gorman (2007); also Pelling (2000) on the *tryphē*-discourse more generally.

[102] E.g. Plut. *Kim.* 14.2–3: Kimon contrasts rich Thessalians and Ionians with austere Spartans.

[103] Theokritos, *Idyll* 16.34–39:

πολλοὶ ἐν Ἀντιόχοιο δόμοις καὶ ἄνακτος Ἀλεύα
ἁρμαλιὴν ἔμμηνον ἐμετρήσαντο πενέσται·
πολλοὶ δὲ Σκοπάδαισιν ἐλαυνόμενοι ποτὶ σακούς
μόσχοι σὺν κεραῇσιν ἐμυκήσαντο βόεσσι·
μυρία δ' ἂμ πεδίον Κραννώνιον ἐνδιάασκον
ποιμένες ἔκκριτα μῆλα φιλοξείνοισι Κρεώνδαις·
Many Penestai in the halls of Antiochos and *anax*
Aleuas were allotted their monthly ration;
Many calves, along with horned cattle,
were driven lowing to the byres of the Skopadai;
ten thousand fine sheep the shepherds watched
on the plain of Krannon for the hospitable Kreondai.

That Theokritos' tone is laudatory rather than scathing is indicated above all by the adjective *philoxe(i)nos* in line 39; traditional hospitality is the good aspect of Thessalian wealth, while consumption and corruption are the bad.

visited.[104] The Thessaly of his own day was a far less suitable basis for his characterisation, for while the wealth of powerful individuals no doubt continued, the land as a whole suffered major economic damage from the near-constant warfare after the death of Alexander the Great.[105] The Penestai he mentions, so essential to the cliché of Thessaly's agricultural abundance, were probably undergoing a phase of enfranchisement at this time.[106] In the face of such changes, we see the manufacture of an imaginary Thessaly, full of nostalgia. This nostalgic Thessaly – an image in which the Thessalians actively participated – will be the subject of further discussion in the next chapter.

Now let us sum up the picture established thus far in this chapter. In terms of historical events, the later fifth century and the fourth have seen an increasing proximity between Thessalian interests and Macedonian ones. This coincides with, and contributes to, a shift in how Thessalians were perceived, a growing hostility in their perception. They are increasingly used as antitheses to emerging values of self-restraint and political moderation; going to Thessaly becomes an emblem of corruption, while refusing to go to Thessaly indicated steadfast loyalty to one's polis and one's own moral integrity. This pattern flows freely between literary genres, but has special clusters in Attic comedy and in philosophical writing. The close practical association between Philip and the Thessalians confirms, as it were, the suspicions of the Thessalians' detractors: they are revealed to be the *barbaroi*-sympathisers they had always been, and their medism in 480 BC – not a source of instant censure – is rediscovered as historical evidence of their unreliable allegiance. The *tryphē* motif aligns them not only with Macedon but more broadly with unsatisfactory Greeks, Greeks whose Greekness is suspect because of geographical marginality and supposed failure to behave as Greeks should.

In a sense, this trajectory has mapped out a process identified by Jonathan Hall in his work on Greek identity:[107] the increasing importance

[104] In this poem (and much more obliquely in *Id.* 22), Theokritos aligns himself with Simonides, famous for memorialising the Skopadai killed by a roof-fall in their feasting hall. The story of this incident, which contrasts Thessalian greed with Simonides' piety and moderation, seems to have Hellenistic origins: see n. 15 above. The fact that the Skopadai perish while feasting is of course a development of the semantic bundle of Thessaly, eating, death and obscurity.

[105] See Chapter 7, pp. 344–45.

[106] Ducat (1994), 105–13; in my view the process is likely to have been less abrupt than he envisages, and also to have followed different trajectories in different poleis. Sordi (1958, 325–27) dated the freeing of the Penestai much earlier, to the fifth century BC, but this is hard to support.

[107] Hall argues that from the late fifth century we can identify an Athenocentric emphasis on culture as the core ingredient of Hellenicity (Hall 2002, 189–220).

of culture as a criterion of (true) Greekness. When the main recipe of Hellenicity was genealogy – as it is, above all, in the *Ehoiai* – the Thessalians are unimpeachable. Whatever we think of their agency or lack of it in the formulation of such verse, it placed them close to the heart of Greekness. Over the course of the Classical period we see a major change. Genealogy does not cease to be important, far from it,[108] but the greater emphasis on culture is to the Thessalians' detriment because they are different, socially and politically, from the communities dominating the new discourse, in particular democratic Athens.

3. Thessalian/Macedonian responses

So far, the emphasis in this chapter has been on the external perspective. Now, however, we move to consider how, if at all, the Thessalians themselves tried to influence their perception by other Greeks during this period, when the articulation of their collective character was increasingly hostile. Particular attention will be paid to whether their self-presentation did anything to incorporate the relationship with Macedon that had proved so much to their detriment in the opinion of their detractors, and their increasing characterisation as lacking key criteria of the good Greek.

a) The First Sacred War

The First Sacred War is notoriously difficult to interpret, comprising a tangle of legends, contradictory variants and competitive myth-making wrapped around a probable core of truth.[109] In terms of sixth-century *realia*, one point can be made for sure: that the story of the war relates to the acquisition of a crucial piece of sacred land that thereafter was of enormous religious and strategic importance to the sanctuary. Though the details of the war are highly suspect, it is plausible to believe that Delphi's acquisition of the fertile Krisaian plain was an important stage in its history, probably in the early sixth century. It is possible that the *Homeric Hymn to Apollo* contains a veiled reference to conflict in its closing lines, which issue an

Subsequent scholarship (most powerfully perhaps Gruen 2011) has argued for a more variegated and nuanced picture, but the emergence of an increasing interest in defining Greekness in cultural terms – albeit as a strategy for contestation between communities rather than harmony – is undeniable. Hall himself returns to the matter and considers the arguments of some of his critics: Hall (2015), 24–27.

[108] Indeed, it is a major ingredient in the works of fifth-century historiographers such as Hellanikos (later fifth century), who moulds and reshapes aspects of the Hellenic stemma. For example, he makes Makedon a son of Aiolos, and therefore a blood descendant of Hellen, a significant alteration: *FGrH* 4 F 74.

[109] See Chapter 1. For a discussion of the very term and concept of the Sacred War see Pownall (1998).

obscure threat, that transgressive behaviour will result in subjection to 'other men' as *sēmantores* (leaders, rulers, overseers – a reference to the Amphiktyony?); however, this injunctions accords ill with the supposed circumstances of the First Sacred War, not least because the threat is issued to the priests of Delphi itself.[110] More fruitful discussion may be directed not at the Archaic period but at how the theme of sacred land and its use (and abuse) was also a topic of interest and tension in the fourth century, which helps to explain why it was at that time that stories of the First Sacred War began to be concertedly elaborated and circulated. Before the fourth century the war simply was not a matter of interest beyond (one assumes) Delphi and its immediate surrounds; neither Herodotos nor Thucydides mentions it.[111]

The very plurality of ancient traditions concerning the war is the crux of its symbolic importance, and no mere inconvenience to the historian. From the fourth century it had become available for adaptation, manipulation and reinvention, and the ways in which various groups and communities exploited its ideological potential is highly revealing. The traditions were summarised and tabulated on p. 45–47, and there we also noted the importance of recognising that Thessalian involvement in the War is by no means universal in the surviving ancient sources. Other communities also inserted their heroes into the narrative, or at least emphasised their contribution. From the point of view of the Thessalians, there are two important elements. The first is the fourth-century invention (as far as one can tell) of the Eurylochos tradition, which will be discussed here; the second is the remodelling of that tradition in the third century, under strong Koan influence, to which we return in Chapter 7.

Let us attempt to reconstruct the conditions in fourth-century Delphi that lay behind the Eurylochos tradition included in the works of Aristotle and Kallisthenes. Christesen argues that the composition and display of the *Pythionikai* must have taken place some time in the mid-330s BC, once Philip was established as influential at Delphi but before Kallisthenes left to join Alexander in Asia.[112] We know that the project received official endorsement from the Amphiktyons: the two authors were formally thanked and rewarded, and their catalogue of victors inscribed and displayed in the

[110] *HH* 3.540–44; see Chappell (2006), 331–34 for a critical treatment of the supposed relationship between the *Hymn* and the First Sacred War.

[111] See, however, Londey (2015), who argues that there are at least moments in the earlier fourth century when the traditions could have begun to be embellished, and that we should not see the process as connected only with the Third and Fourth Sacred Wars. Davies (1994) proposes earlier phases of the traditions' development; however, the silence of Herodotos and Thucydides remain a barrier to these suggestions.

[112] Christesen (2007), 179–95; see also Sánchez (2002), 19–20.

sanctuary for all to see.[113] And the context of the 330s, in the aftermath of the Third and Fourth Sacred Wars in which Philip and the Amphiktyons had collaborated, would certainly have provided a fertile setting for such myth-making. The details of the legendary conflict echo several of the strands of the fourth-century conflicts. In particular, the story of the First Sacred War would serve as a useful precedent in the following ways:

1. By reinforcing the sacred status of the Kirrhaian plain and the need for it to be preserved as such. The *aition* related by Aischines explains that the land was consecrated to Apollo after the transgressive behaviour of the Kirrhaians had led to its legitimate confiscation.[114] This sacred land was crucial in both fourth-century Sacred Wars. In the first, one of the charges levelled against the Phokians, which triggered their attack on the opposing Amphiktyonic forces and the outbreak of the war, was the illegal cultivation of the Krisaian plain.[115] In the second, Aischines in his *Against Ktesiphon* was able to turn Amphiktyonic censure away from the Athenians by condemning the misuse of the Krisaian plain by the Lokrians of Amphissa. Such situations would create a strong incentive for members of the Amphiktyony to emphasise that their actions to preserve the sacred land and punish its misuse had the backing of ancient precedent, not least because, in 356, the Phokians rounded upon their accusers for unjustly imposing a vast fine for the cultivation of a small piece of land.
2. By reinforcing the historical importance of the Amphiktyony as the body charged with the protection of the sanctuary as a whole. In the Third Sacred War the Phokians contested the legitimacy of Amphiktyonic control, claiming once to have had sole charge of the oracle and demanding a return to this arrangement.[116]
3. By emphasising the collective nature of Amphiktyonic action against the Kirrhaians, while especially glorifying individuals from certain Amphiktyonic communities. In particular, the Athenians initially supported Phokis in the Third Sacred War.[117] This will surely have given a particular incentive for such as Aischines to emphasise the role of Solon. When Kallisthenes and Aristotle produced their version of the

113 We have fragments of the inscription in which the two authors are awarded official praise and a crown: *FD* III 1 400. For discussion see Rhodes and Osborne (2003), no. 80, 394–95; Christesen (2007), 181–82. On the influential nature of Kallisthenes' work on the First Sacred War in particular see Pownall (1998), 47–49.

114 Aischines 2.107–09.

115 Diod. 16.23.2–3.

116 Diod. 16.23.5–6. Indeed, Londey (2015, 236–37) argues that the Phokians themselves would have used the stories of the First Sacred War to justify their seizure of Delphi during the Third Sacred War.

117 Diod. 16.27.5 and 29.1.

> myth for public display in the sanctuary, Solon was relegated to the role of advisor under the leadership of Eurylochos the Thessalian, but the fact that his contribution was included at all shows a willingness to use the story to reconcile the Athenians with their fellow Amphiktyons.

A further factor that has been the focus of scholarly attention is the way in which the First Sacred War tradition may have served to legitimise Philip's own involvement. Philip may have cast himself as Apollo's champion, but his actions were not universally commended even by those opposed to the Phokians. By 346 BC, probably realising that they could not win the war and faced by the approach of Philip with combined Thessalian and Macedonian forces, the Phokians appealed to the Athenians and the Spartans for help. The Athenians made no move to send aid, but instead negotiated with Philip the Peace of Philokrates, whose terms offered no protection to the desperate Phokians. Philip handed the punishment over to the Amphiktyons, a majority of whom certainly wished to see the Phokians punished with the greatest severity, as indeed they were. Demosthenes in his *On the Embassy*, delivered in 343 BC, gives a heart-rending description of the stricken land and towns of Phokis, and reflects the perception among many Athenians that Philip was as much a danger to the Athenians as to the Phokians, and that the desolation of Phokis might very well prove a grim prefiguring of Athens' treatment at Macedonian hands.[118]

In the aftermath of such a climate of fear and hostility directed against Philip, it is not implausible that he should have welcomed any chance to legitimise his actions around Delphi;[119] however, difficulties attend claims sometimes made about the Thessalian dimension of this propaganda. In particular, Robertson has argued that the Thessalian Eurylochos was intended to evoke a real-life Eurylochos, one of Philip's chief generals, and so was essentially a less-than-subtle stand-in for the Macedonian presence.[120] Eurylochos the Macedonian was one of Philip's representatives on the Amphiktyonic council in the late 340s, and therefore the name would have had Macedonian echoes in Delphic circles.[121] Perhaps this will have been a

118 Demosth. 19.65–66. The orator reminds the Athenians of the Phokians' past services to them; his larger purpose is to discredit the Peace of Philokrates and his rival Aischines. Because Diodoros' account of this time almost entirely omits mention of the Peace and the surrounding embassies, we are reliant on extrapolating events from the mutual excoriations of Demosthenes and Aischines. On this speech within the context of Demosthenes' work and career see MacDowell (2009), 314–42.

119 This is certainly a key element in Speusippos' *Letter to Philip* 8, in which Philip's acquisition of Amphiktyonic votes is directly corroborated by reference to the punishment of the Krisaians. Pownall (1998), 50–54.

120 Robertson (1978), 64–65.

121 See, for example, *CID* 2.36.

convenient coincidence for Philip, but to see the Thessalian Eurylochos as a mere proxy for Macedonian presence is unconvincing. Eurylochos was a name of long-standing currency among Thessalian elites,[122] and – though our earliest testimonies are fourth century – may have been attached to the First Sacred War in earlier narratives that have not survived.

Moreover, if we apply the *cui bono* principle to this situation, the answer is not solely Philip, or indeed Philip and the Thessalians. The Amphiktyony as a whole emerges from the two fourth-century conflicts in a far from wholly favourable light. In both conflicts it was unable to achieve a resolution without Philip's involvement. In the Third Sacred War, its allegiance was divided. The Athenians initially sided with the Phokians, then turned against them; then came to sympathise with them once more.[123] The Thessalians, so far from maintaining a solid opposition to Phokis, allowed them to be bribed into inaction by Onomarchos, and that is not to mention that the rulers of Pherai supported the Phokian side.[124] In the Fourth Sacred War, which blew up in 339 BC,[125] an air of near-farce and decided peculiarity hangs over the episode in which the Delphians, at the instigation of the Amphiktyonic council and of the Athenian *pylagoras* Aischines, decided to rush onto the Krisaian plain with mattocks and spades to destroy the buildings and installations the Amphissians had illegally erected on the sacred land, only to be chased away by the Amphissians.[126] Moreover, although an Amphiktyonic army under Kottyphos of Pharsalos, Thessalian *hieromnēmōn*[127] and perhaps council president,[128] was charged with the task of forcing the Amphissians to pay a fine for their misdeeds, the fine remained unpaid and the Amphissians unchastised until Philip

[122] Eurylochos as an aristocrat of Larisa: see Diog. Laer. 2.5.25 (discussed above, pp. 305–06).

[123] The Athenians revert to supporting the Phokians: Diod. 16.57.1.

[124] Bribery by Onomarchos: Diod. 16.33.3.

[125] On the outbreak and events of this conflict see Londey (1990); Sánchez (2001), 227–45.

[126] Aisch. 3.118–23. Aischines' accusations against the Amphissians are dismissed as an empty pretext by Desmothenes (18.149–50). Demosthenes calls Aischines' evocation of the First Sacred War 'λόγους εὐπροσώπους καὶ μύθους' ('outwardly attractive accounts and stories'): he seems to be questioning not only the applicability of the ancient conflict to the contemporary one, but also – very obliquely – its historical veracity.

[127] Kottyphos, with his colleague Kolosimmos, appears in Amphiktyonic inscriptions between ca. 345 and 338 as one of the Thessalian *hieromnēmones*: see, for example, *CID* 2.34, 2.36, 2.43, 2.34.

[128] This is described in Aischines' *Against Ktesiphon*, 3.124 and 3.128 (cf. Demosth. 18.151). The formula used of Kottyphos is ὁ τὰς γνώμας ἐπιψηφίζων, quite in keeping with political terminology of the time.

returned from campaigning in Skythia (whereupon the Amphissians paid up meekly).[129]

In sum, the fourth-century traditions concerning the First Sacred War seem to preclude the singling out of a single figure or group as the dominant agent. Instead, they emphasise solidarity and collaboration, a closing of ranks against the transgressor. However, within this picture the role of Thessaly is obviously important, and it is clear that the traditions were developed to encompass and reflect the new level of influence Thessalians held within the sanctuary. As has been argued, we should not leap to see in this a return of past Thessalian glories, to the power and prestige they enjoyed at Delphi in the Archaic period. But this does not mean that the theme of restoration was unimportant at the time. The stories of the First Sacred War certainly served to endorse Thessalian power by reference to its age and precedents. Moreover, story-telling was not the sole medium through which the message of traditional entitlement was disseminated: physical structures also had a role to play.

b) The Daochos Monument

The Thessalians were not, on the whole, particularly lavish or conspicuous dedicators at Delphi. In fact, Amphiktyonic communities in general tended to show up slightly less than others in certain spheres of activity, such as in the commissioning of monumental dedications and in contributions to the temple-building fund in the fourth century BC, at least after the Third Sacred War.[130] Both patches of absence have been explained by reference to the fact that most Amphiktyonic states, being geographically relatively close to the sanctuary and having a conspicuous role by virtue of their *hieromnēmones* (among whom the Thessalians were especially prominent in the time of Philip II), had less need than others to make visible and lasting records of their presence within the sanctuary.[131] We also have the usual difficulties of ascertaining position and date of Thessalian dedications. Two are given fairly secure historical context at least by their inscriptions, the collective dedication of spoils after Tanagra[132] (see Chapter 5) and the statue

129 Buckler (2003), 491–93.

130 Rutherford (2004) points out that only post-War can a proper comparison between Amphiktyons and others be made, since the War changed the system of payments: the payment of the *oboloi*, required of Amphiktyonic states, was discontinued after the War; from that point, only voluntary *eparchai* were given, and these could come from any community.

131 Scott (2010), 55, remarking on the prevalence in the sixth century of 'dedicators from the margins of the Greek world' and the relative lack of Amphiktyonic dedicators; see also pp. 88–91. Cf. Rutherford (2004), 114, on the lack of Amphiktyonic donors in the records of the fourth-century temple building fund.

132 *SEG* 17.243.

of Pelopidas put up after the latter's death at Kynoskephalai in 364 BC.[133] We also, however, have an epigraphically attested dedication whose exact date is unknown.[134]

A number of further Thessalian dedications are mentioned in Pausanias' description of the site, with no information as to date and position. For example, a small statue of Apollo given by one Echekratidas of Larisa was regarded by the Delphians as the first dedication ever made on the site;[135] this suggests considerable antiquity, but obviously tells us more about the stories told by the locals in the second century AD than about the object itself. An equestrian group dedicated after a Pheraian cavalry victory over the Athenians is tantalising because we would like to know more about the event that generated it.[136] Vague as he is, however, Pausanias' value lies in giving the perspective of a visitor to the sanctuary describing monuments that existed in clusters in certain areas of the site. Sometimes their dates are very disparate, but at other times their juxtaposition allows glimpses of what Scott (2010) has called 'spatial politics': the symbolic choice of space to make visual gestures and reply to the visual gestures of others. A Thessalian example occurs at 10.13.4–7:

> Opposite the bronze head of the bison [dedicated by the mid-third century Paionian king Dropion] is a statue of a man wearing a breastplate, on which is a cloak. The Delphians say that it is an offering of the Andrians, and a portrait of Andreus, their founder. The images of Apollo, Athena, and Artemis were dedicated by the Phokians from the spoils taken from the Thessalians, their enemies always, who are their neighbours except where the Epiknemidian Lokrians come between. The Thessalians too of Pharsalos dedicated an Achilles on horseback, with Patroklos running beside his horse: the Macedonians living in Dion, a city at the foot of Mount Pieria, the Apollo who has taken hold of the deer; the people of Kyrene, a Greek city in Libya, the chariot with an image of Ammon in it. The Dorians of Korinth too built a treasury, where used to be stored

133 *SEG* 22.460; Scott (2010), 115.

134 *SEG* 1.210: the Pharsalians dedicated the votive, whatever it was, to Apollo, but two men of Atrax are named as its creators. Helly (1995, 258) argues that the inscription dates from the period of Theban influence in Thessaly, perhaps roughly contemporary with the monument for Pelopidas. It is interesting that, when a record was made in 329/8 of the conferral of proxeny on two Pharsalians by the Delphians (*SEG* 22.462), this record was inscribed on the same block, exploiting existing Pharsalian visibility. Unfortunately the original location of the block is unknown; it was found incorporated in a later wall near the entrance of the *temenos*. See Pomtow (1921), 13–14.

135 Paus. 10.16.8.

136 Paus. 10.15.4. As Scott remarks (2010, 98), the placement of the Pheraian dedication is significant: it was situated next to an earlier Athenian offering, an aggressive gesture given the victory it apparently celebrated.

> the gold from Lydia. The image of Herakles is a votive offering of the Thebans, sent when they had fought what is called the Sacred War against the Phokians. There are also bronze statues, which the Phokians dedicated when they had put to flight the Thessalian cavalry in the second engagement. The Phliasians brought to Delphi a bronze Zeus, and with the Zeus, an image of Aigina. The Mantineians of Arkadia dedicated a bronze Apollo, which stands near the treasury of the Korinthians. Herakles and Apollo are holding onto the tripod and are preparing to fight about it. Leto and Artemis are calming Apollo, and Athena is calming Herakles. This too is an offering of the people of Phokis, dedicated when Tellias of Elis led them against the Thessalians. Athena and Artemis were made by Chionis, the other images are works shared by Diyllos and Amyklaios. They are said to be Korinthians.[137]

The mention of the Korinthian treasury situates us, in all probability, somewhere below the north-east end of the temple terrace. Two features of Pausanias' list stand out here: a cluster of northern communities (Thessaly, Macedon, Paionia) and repeated references to conflict between Thessalians and Phokians. As has been said (Chapter 1), it is very unlikely that the Phokian dedications here really date to the sixth century; it is more likely that they were created after the Third Sacred War,[138] commemorating victories that by that time had achieved legendary status and magnitude in Phokian history.[139] The fact that Thebes chose this space for a monument

[137] 'τοῦ βίσωνος δὲ τῆς κεφαλῆς καταντικρὺ τῆς χαλκῆς ἀνδριάς ἐστι θώρακά τε ἐνδεδυκὼς καὶ χλαμύδα ἐπὶ τῷ θώρακι· Ἀνδρίων δὲ ἀνάθημα οἱ Δελφοὶ λέγουσιν Ἀνδρέα εἶναι τὸν οἰκιστήν. τό τε ἄγαλμα τοῦ Ἀπόλλωνος καὶ Ἀθηνᾶς τε καὶ Ἀρτέμιδος Φωκέων ἀναθήματά ἐστιν ἀπὸ Θεσσαλῶν ὁμόρων τε – πλὴν ὅσον οἱ Λοκροὶ σφᾶς οἱ Ἐπικνημίδιοι διείργουσι – καὶ ἀεὶ πολεμίων ὄντων. ἀνέθεσαν δὲ καὶ οἱ ἐν Φαρσάλῳ Θεσσαλοὶ καὶ Μακεδόνων οἱ ὑπὸ τῇ Πιερίᾳ πόλιν Δῖον οἰκοῦντες Κυρηναῖοί τε τοῦ Ἑλληνικοῦ τοῦ ἐν Λιβύῃ, οὗτοι μὲν τὸ ἅρμα καὶ ἐπὶ τῷ ἅρματι ἄγαλμα Ἄμμωνος, Μακεδόνες δὲ οἱ ἐν Δίῳ τὸν Ἀπόλλωνα ὃς εἰλημμένος ἐστὶ τῆς ἐλάφου, Φαρσάλιοι δὲ Ἀχιλλέα τε ἐπὶ ἵππῳ καὶ ὁ Πάτροκλος συμπαραθεῖν οἱ καὶ τῷ ἵππῳ. Κορίνθιοι δὲ οἱ Δωριεῖς ᾠκοδόμησαν θησαυρὸν καὶ οὗτοι· καὶ ὁ χρυσὸς ὁ ἐκ Λυδῶν ἀνέκειτο ἐνταῦθα. τὸ δὲ ἄγαλμα τοῦ Ἡρακλέους ἀνάθημά ἐστι Θηβαίων, ὅτε Φωκεῦσιν ἐπολέμησαν τὸν ἱερὸν καλούμενον πόλεμον. εἰσὶ καὶ εἰκόνες χαλκαῖ Φωκέων ἀναθέντων, ἡνίκα δευτέρᾳ συμβολῇ τὸ ἱππικὸν ἐτρέψαντο τὸ ἐκ Θεσσαλίας. Φλιάσιοι δὲ ἐκόμισαν ἐς Δελφοὺς Δία τε χαλκοῦν καὶ ὁμοῦ τῷ Διὶ ἄγαλμα Αἰγίνης. ἐκ δὲ Μαντινείας τῆς Ἀρκάδων Ἀπόλλων χαλκοῦς ἐστιν ἀνάθημα· οὗτος οὐ πόρρω τοῦ Κορινθίων ἐστὶ θησαυροῦ. Ἡρακλῆς δὲ καὶ Ἀπόλλων ἔχονται τοῦ τρίποδος καὶ ἐς μάχην περὶ αὐτοῦ καθίστανται· Λητὼ μὲν δὴ καὶ Ἄρτεμις Ἀπόλλωνα, Ἀθηνᾶ δὲ Ἡρακλέα ἐπέχουσι τοῦ θυμοῦ. Φωκέων καὶ τοῦτό ἐστιν ἀνάθημα, ὅτε σφίσιν ἐπὶ τοὺς Θεσσαλοὺς Τελλίας ἡγήσατο Ἠλεῖος. τὰ μὲν δὴ ἄλλα ἀγάλματα Δίυλλός τε ἐν κοινῷ καὶ Ἀμυκλαῖος, τὴν δὲ Ἀθηνᾶν καὶ Ἄρτεμιν Χιονίς ἐστιν εἰργασμένος· Κορινθίους δὲ εἶναί φασιν αὐτούς' (trans. Jones and Ormerod, adapted).

[138] Franchi and Proietti (2015), 239–42.

[139] Cf. Paus. 5.24.1–2: he describes a Thessalian dedication at Olympia set up as a tithe

celebrating their victory over the Phokians in the Third Sacred War shows that this area became a space for the competitive demonstration of triumph and defiance, with the Phokians seeking to restore their collective prestige by reference to the shadowy late Archaic conflict in which they, not the Thessalians, had ultimately triumphed.[140] Demosthenes' description of the desolation of Phokis after the Third Sacred War suggests how potent the legend of Phokian Desperation could have been at such a time, reminding the Phokians and other Greeks that they had previously come to the brink of total annihilation, only to win through to stunning victory over the northern foe.

It is also interesting to observe the use of Herakles in this flurry of 'spatial politics'. One of the monuments commemorating Phokian triumph over the Thessalians is a group showing the fight over the Delphic tripod; in this, Herakles might be taken to signify Thessaly, since he is the aggressor against the Delphic god and his sacred property. After the Sacred War, to cast another community as the despoiler of Delphi in this way would have been especially useful – if blatant – propaganda. However, the Theban dedication of an image of Herakles makes a contrary claim: that Herakles was their hero, and that he was implicitly involved in their victory at the Phokians' expense, a victory that left the Thebans, along with the Thessalians, in a position of great power within the sanctuary.[141] In light of this back-and-forth, it seems logical to connect the Pharsalian dedication mentioned in the passage with the same context, and suggest that the Pharsalians – Philip's most important ally among the Thessalians – were taking this opportunity, having achieved high standing in the sanctuary at the expense of the Phokians in particular, to remind all Greeks visiting Delphi of their own special connection with Achilles. It is significant that they place Achilles – famous for the fleetness of his own feet, after all – on a horse, giving him an immediately recognisable Thessalian flavour, and one in keeping with other Thessalian dedications on the site.

However, we are on a different level of both size and preservation with the Daochos Monument (Fig. 14).[142] This was a structure designed to catch

of plunder taken from the Phokians. He denies that it could have come from the Third Sacred War, and instead suggests vaguely that it came from a conflict between the Thessalians and Phokians before the invasion of Xerxes. It could indeed have derived from some conflict of the late Archaic period, but equally an Archaic monument whose origins had become obscure could have had new explanations – to do with an earlier conflict – attached to them in the period after the Third Sacred War.

[140] Scott (2010), 126–27.

[141] Thebans and Thessalians as the immediate beneficiaries of Philip's settlement of the war: Diod. 16.59.4t–60.2; Demosth. 19.50.

[142] For an overview of the monument and its reconstruction see Keesling (2017), 108–11. It should also be noted that, within Thessaly itself in the fourth century, other

Fig. 14. Statues of the Daochos Monument, Delphi; 330s BC. Delphi Archaeological Museum. Photograph: author's own

the eye – whether or not it was roofed[143] – as one ascended to the entrance of the temple. If unroofed it would have allowed all those in the vicinity an instant view of the statue-series and therefore a powerful impression of the dedicator's lineage in all its splendour. The use of such an *epiphanēs topos* certainly indicates the influence of the man who commissioned the work, though the mechanisms by which space was allocated are largely unknown. The monument itself was influential.[144] The statue group itself

communities took pains to evoke Delphic connections. For example, when the polis of Pherai commissioned a new temple of Zeus Thaulios and Ennodia in the late fourth century, the building strongly echoed the temple of Apollo at Delphi built in the 330s, a project in which the Thessalians were strongly involved. See Østby (1994), 141–42; Canlas (2021), 361–64.

143 The argument for a roofed structure is put forward by Jacquemin and Laroche (2001), who also suggest that it occupied and embellished the site of a somewhat earlier (ca. 360 BC) Thessalian treasury. Partida (2011, 233) observes that marble statues at Delphi did tend to be within roofed structures, whereas those in the open air were normally of bronze. Nonetheless, the matter is inconclusive in the case of the Daochos Monument.

144 For example, Kosmetatou (2004, 234–36) makes a case for its influence on the

'quoted' a pre-existing monument at Pharsalos: a bronze statue of Agias by Lysippos. It is interesting that Daochos (for presumably it was he) first chose to advertise one of his significant forebears within his home polis, and then to incorporate a copy both of the effigy and – with some adjustments – of the accompanying inscription,[145] within the much grander arrangement in the panhellenic shrine. Partida notes examples of monuments within poleis referring to originals at Delphi, but the Agias case is the other way around.[146] At Pharsalos he commissioned a visual reminder of one ancestor; at Delphi the focus was on dynastic continuity, and on the cumulative magnitude of the family's achievements over the generations.

That the monument as a whole confers powerful *aretē* on its dedicator, Philip's associate Daochos of Pharsalos,[147] need hardly be said. The effect of an ancestor group is to give the dedicator the advantage of collective virtues, all of which enhance his own character. This explains the variety of the group: plainly the sculptor or sculptors wished to encompass different modes of excellence – the athlete, the warrior, the statesman. However, there is more to the function of precedent than that. The fact that we lack all but the feet of the dedicator's own image means that for this aspect the inscriptions are our first port of call when considering how he was made to echo key aspects of his forebears' roles and achievements. Scholars have noted the degree of care and linguistic nuance in the inscriptions, designed

presentation of family relationships in Poseidippos' *Hippika*. It may also have influenced the Philippeion at Olympia, though that depends on the relative dating of the two monuments: see Schultz (2009), 129–31.

145 The Pharsalian text (*IG* IX.2 249) has three largely missing opening lines, different from the Delphic text. Then it contains the four verse lines about Agias' victories in the pankration.

146 Partida (2011), 231. For discussion of the two statues of Agias see Stewart (1978), 309–13, who argues that the Delphi Agias is a rather imprecise copy of the Lysippan original.

147 As I have argued elsewhere, Geominy's alternative dating of the monument (Geominy 1998), to make Daochos I Philip's ally and the dedicator, Daochos II, his grandson in the early third century, is not ultimately persuasive, chiefly because the third-century Daochos has no attestation, epigraphic or otherwise. See Aston (2012b), 47–48. However, certainty is not possible, and we certainly cannot use the identification of the Agias as a work of Lysippos to corroborate the earlier dating: as von Steuben (1999) observes, the Lysippan image may have been considerably older than the others, set up alone both at Delphi and (its duplicate) at Pharsalos. Again, however, Lysippos' long *floruit* would allow for this time difference even if we maintain the earlier dating of the Monument. Perhaps the Agias statue, alone, was included in the Thessalian treasury, ca. 360, proposed by Jacquemin and Laroche (2001) as the forerunner of Daochos' creation (on which see n. 143 above).

to achieve subtle intertexts between them and therefore bind them together as a family while establishing particular connections between individuals.[148]

The inscriptions attached to Aknonios, Agias and Daochos I are especially significant for our purposes here.

> Aknonios son of Aparos, *tetrarchos* of the Thessalians.
>
> (The epigrams for the athletes Agias, Telemachos and Agelaos follow here.)
>
> I am Daochos son of Agias. My homeland was Pharsalos;
> I ruled all of Thessaly, not with force but with law,
> for twenty-seven years, and Thessaly burgeoned with
> great and fruitful peace, and with wealth.
>
> Increasing the virtues of my family's ancestors,
> I set up these gifts to lord Phoibos, honouring my family and my
> homeland –
> I, Daochos, possessed of glorious praise,
> *tetrarchos* of the Thessalians,
> *hieromnēmōn* of the Amphiktyons.[149]

First and most obviously, Daochos takes the trouble to tell the viewer that the role he holds, that of *tetrarchos*, has been held by another in his family. While there is no evidence that the role was formally heritable, this certainly works to assert his suitability. If there is any truth to the

[148] See esp. Day (2018), 81: 'The cross-referencing, framing, and intertextuality caused each statue to be viewed and each text to be read in reference to others, thereby complicating viewers' initial perceptions and constructing syntactical relationships. Readers and viewers entered into a complex conversation about Daochus' family with images and texts that created a unified monument out of a multiplicity of elements.' Cummins (2009, 328–34) focuses on the epigrams of the three athletes to show the cumulative layering of praise and interlinking between the verses.

[149] *FD* III 4.460, 1, 5 and 7:

> Ἀκνόνιος Ἀπάρου τέτραρχος Θεσσαλῶν.
>
> Δάοχος Ἀγία εἰμί, πατρὶς Φάρσαλος, ἁπάσης
> Θεσσαλίας ἄρξας vac. οὐ βίαι ἀλλὰ νόμωι,
> ἑπτὰ καὶ εἴκοσι ἔτη, πολλῆι δὲ καὶ ἀγλαοκάρπωι
> εἰρήνηι πλούτωι τε ἔβρυε Θεσσαλία.
>
> αὔξων οἰκείων προγόνων ἀρετὰς τάδε δῶρα
> στῆσεμ Φοίβωι ἄνακτι, γένος καὶ πατρίδα τιμῶν,
> Δάοχος εὐδόξωι χρώμενος εὐλογίαι,
> τέτραρχος Θεσσαλῶν
> ἱερομνήμων Ἀμφικτυόνων.

Athenian accusations that Daochos owed his position to Philip (and, indeed, even if Philip did not confer it, he at least refrained from taking it away), then proving his inherent suitability would have been important. Referring to Aknonios is an especially effective way of doing so, because a long family tradition would deflect the accusation of his role being merely a Macedonian creation; instead, the viewer – perhaps a fellow Thessalian sceptical of his credentials – is invited to consider that Daochos is merely reclaiming an ancestral distinction. The fact that the position of *tetrarchos* is not attested for the period in which Aknonios would have operated (later sixth to early fifth century),[150] but may well in fact have been brought in as part of Philip's political reforms, suggests a degree of retrojection and even fabrication that would accord well with other fourth-century examples, such as Jason's use of the title Tagos. At the same time, Daochos is able to exceed his ancestors' achievements. The expression αὔξων οἰκείων προγόνων ἀρετὰς does not suggest that his own *aretai* are themselves superlative, merely that he adds them to the family stock and so increases the quantity in total. However, the closing two lines – partially extra-metrical[151] – which echo the Aknonios text but add a further element, achieve a combination of continuity and innovation. There is no evidence that any member of his family was previously a *hieromnēmōn*; that position belongs to him alone.

Daochos I, however, is described as possessing a role Daochos II could not: that of Archon of all Thessaly. As has been said, it is possible, though unlikely, that Philip himself occupied this position; possible also that it did not exist at the time, if we believe that Thessaly as a whole was directed by a Board of Ten (the *dekadarchia*). If Philip was Archon of Thessaly, it is interesting to see Daochos the *tetrarchos* – a subordinate local ruler – laying indirect claim, through his ancestor, to a position the Macedonian king held. The gesture is all the more subtle because of the tone of nostalgia in which it is couched. The twenty-seven years of peace and prosperity attached to Daochos I, the Archon, are hard to square with the conditions of the dedicator's own time, which saw turbulence regionally and within Pharsalos itself,[152] thanks chiefly to the Pheraian rulers' attempts to establish and hold control over Thessaly, as well as embroilment in the Third Sacred

150 For the dating of the various family members see Smith (1910).

151 Taken together they roughly approximate to an iambic pentameter but their division between lines is significant.

152 Pharsalos was in fact seized by Medeios of Larisa in 395 BC. Medeios was helped by the Greeks who had lately concluded a treaty against Sparta, and Medeios' attack on Pharsalos removed a Spartan garrison in the city. However, when Diodoros says that he then τοὺς ἐν αὐτῇ κατοικοῦντας ἐλαφυροπώλησεν ('sold the inhabitants of the city into slavery'), this must refer to the Pharsalians themselves. (Diod. 14.82.5–6.) Just over twenty years later Pharsalos came under the control of Jason of Pherai (Xen. *Hell.* 6.1.18).

War. Daochos I rules over a Golden Age Thessaly; his is the ideal pan-Thessalian rule, to which no contemporary reality could match up, set before the rise of Pherai at the end of the fifth century. Reaching back past the turbulent phase of Pherai's rise, dominance and eventual subjection would have been especially beneficial in light of the threat Pheraian rulers had sometimes posed to southern Greece and Delphi in particular. As I have suggested elsewhere,[153] the Daochos I epigram was intended to 'live down' certain events in Thessalian history: the impressive career of Jason, who is depicted in Xenophon as harbouring ambitions to control the Delphic sanctuary and perhaps even extend Thessalian hegemony further south;[154] and the notorious Alexandros, who certainly ruled with *bia*, not with *nomos*. Instead, virtues recognised by all Greeks are emphasised.[155] That phase of Thessaly's violent recent past was not absent from the sanctuary: the statue of Pelopidas attested to the Thessalians' gratitude for Theban assistance against the Pheraian threat. Does the epigram of Sisyphos I, with its emphasis on martial valour, make oblique reference to a time of turmoil? Perhaps – but it is *very* oblique. The retrospective flavour of the Monument, its focus on the more distant past, would also have been enhanced by its significant recycling of language and themes from Pindar's *Pythian* 10,[156] and perhaps also from Bacchylides.[157]

Unsurprisingly, the Daochos Monument makes no direct reference to Daochos II's close connection with Philip. Macedonian backing for his power as *tetrarchos*, or indeed for his position as *hieromnēmōn*, was not something Daochos wished to advertise. However, in more subtle ways a cultural and religious affinity is suggested between Thessaly and Macedon. The first – the link with Neoptolemos achieved through the location of the Monument beside his shrine – will be considered further below. Here we shall ask whether the visual effect of the statues evokes a shared northern Greek culture, and would have been recognised as doing so by the viewer;

153 Aston (2012b).

154 Xen. *Hell.* 6.4.27–31. Note especially the reference to Jason's possible appropriation of Delphic treasure – the old fear – at 6.4.30.

155 On the Monument embodying the qualities of the ideal ruler expressed by authors such as Xenophon and Isokrates see Fehr (1979), 64–66.

156 Aston (2012b), 58. Note also that Pavlou (2022) sees *Pythian* 10 as being directed in part towards an Amphiktyonic audience; this would mean that the Daochos Monument was drawing on a text *already* imbued with Delphic connections. Her argument on this point is weakened by a questionable claim that Thessaly dominated the Amphiktyony in the early fifth century; nonetheless, the Pythian victory of Hippokleas may have been enough to give the poem some exposure at Delphi.

157 *Ep.* 14B contains the theme of increase (ἀέξεις, line 3), which echoes, or is echoed by, depending on its date, Pind. *Pyth.* 10, line 71(αὔξοντες), and the αὔξων in the inscription attached to Daochos II.

detecting such an affinity would be significant, as it would suggest a strong desire on Daochos' part to use the public 'stage' of Delphi to affirm as a positive phenomenon the connection between Thessaly and Macedon that had become such a toxic ingredient in pejorative rhetoric at the time. This brings us to confront the matter of clothing, and in particular of Thessalian and Macedonian cloaks.

The short *chlamys* was strongly associated with Thessaly; that much is certain. Late lexicographers identify a particular shape as especially Thessalian: the presence of outward-projecting corners, resembling, and therefore called, wings.[158] In fact this description probably relates to style of wearing as much as shape, and perhaps draws on a long history of visual depictions of the Thessalian horseman, his short cloak blowing back as his horse surges forward.[159] In other words, clothing evokes activities and style of life, and so in this case is intimately linked with the Thessalians' reputation for horsemanship. Such garments and such activities were not of course exclusive to Thessaly; riders, warriors and huntsmen wear short cloaks on Athenian pots too. But the Thessalian flavour of the garment is to be found as early as Bacchylides' time, when the poet gives the young Theseus a specifically Thessalian *chlamys* in order to emphasise his youthful, dashing, warlike character.[160]

Three of the statues in the Daochos Monument wear *chlamydes*:

[158] E.g. *Et. Magn.* s.v. Θετταλικὰ πτερά: τοῦτο εἴρηται διὰ τὸ πτέρυγας ἔχειν τὰς Θετταλικὰς χλαμύδας. <Πτέρυγες> δὲ καλοῦνται αἱ ἑκατέρωθεν γωνίαι, διὰ τὸ ἐοικέναι πτέρυξι. ('Thessalian wings: this saying comes from the fact that Thessalian *chlamydes* have wings. The corners on each side are called 'wings' because they resemble wings.')

[159] In particular, the bull-wrestling coins of the earlier fifth century established the image within the consciousness of the Thessalians themselves, and would have been viewed widely outside the region too. The manipulation of characteristically Thessalian garments and accessories is a specific but interesting aspect of Thessalian coinage: see, for example, the head of a young man wearing a *petasos* on the coins of the Pheraian Alexandros. These were small denomination, allowing little room for the design, and emblems were sought that evoked Thessalian identity in a tiny space: the *petasos* was one, the hoof and lower leg of a horse was another (see, for example, *Nomos* 4, 116, no. 1312).

[160] Bacchyl. *Dith.* 18.52–59:

στέρνοις τε πορφύρεον
χιτῶν' ἄμφι, καὶ οὔλιον
Θεσσαλὰν χλαμύδ'· ὀμμάτων δὲ
στίλβειν ἄπο Λαμνίαν
φοίνισσαν φλόγα· παῖδα δ' ἔμμεν
πρώθηβον, ἀρηΐων δ' ἀθυρμάτων
μεμνᾶσθαι πολέμου τε καὶ
χαλκεοκτύπου μάχας ...

('A purple tunic covers his chest, and a woollen Thessalian cloak. Bright red Lemnian

Aknonios, Daochos I and Daochos II. Two others, Sisyphos I and II, hold *chlamydes*; in the case of the former, the artist has gone to pains to emphasise his masculinity through the obvious outline of his genitals, and the fact that the *chlamys* is held rather than worn facilitates this while stopping short of the athletic nudity of Agias and his brothers; Sisyphos I is a soldier rather than an athlete. As for Sisyphos II, the lack of an epigram suggests that he was too young to have accumulated *aretai* of his own, and the held *chlamys* might suggest potential, a mantle he will come to don. So what does the worn *chlamys* signify? In the Daochos Monument it is a very different article from the flying cloak of the Thessalian horseman. It is pinned on one shoulder so that it hangs rather stiffly and nearly closed, only one arm and shoulder uncovered. It is austere and statesmanlike, but it is still a *chlamys* rather than the *himation*, or mantle, that we might expect senior men of authority to wear. It is interesting that a garment that had such a strong association in Athens with contexts of riding, hunting and youth need not have any of those properties in this Thessalian sculpture-group.[161] Nonetheless, its repeated depiction within the group conferred a strong Thessalian flavour, surely deliberately.

It has been suggested that in fact the *chlamydes* in the Daochos Monument are not Thessalian at all, but Macedonian. This is posited on grounds of design: the *chlamydes* in the Daochos Monument have no wings and so cannot be Thessalian; instead, they must be Macedonian, since the *chlamydes* of Macedon are sometimes associated with a more rounded shape.[162] However, there is no attestation of the rounded Macedonian *chlamys* before the end of the fourth century or even the start of the third.[163] Moreover, it is by no means clear that the garments in the Daochos Monument *are* rounded;[164] the 'wings' characteristic of the Thessalian version would in

fire flashes from his eyes. He is a boy in the prime of youth, intent on the playthings of Ares: war and battles of clashing bronze.')

161 Fascinatingly, Pollux (*Onom.* 7.46) says that the word ἐνθετταλίζομαι means 'to wear a *chlamys*' (i.e. to dress as a Thessalian), a sense repeated in Steph. Byz. s.v. Θεσσαλία; this usage seems to occur in Eupolis (fr. 215 KA), though there the context is unknown. Cf. Phil. *Her.* 10.5 (describing the young Thessalian hero Protesilaos): χλαμύδα ἐνῆπται, ξένε, τὸν Θετταλικὸν τρόπον ('He wears a *chlamys*, visitor, in this Thessalian manner').

162 Alexandria in Egypt was said to have been planned in a semi-circular shape like that of a *chlamys*: see, for example, Plut. *Alex.* 26.5. Even though the anecdote is factually unconvincing, it does give insight into the perceived shape of the garment in its Macedonian form at this time.

163 Lattimore (1975), 88.

164 *Pace* Saatsoglou-Paliadeli (1993), 143–44. Aristotle (fr. 500 Rose) can only be securely identified as saying that the *chlamys* and the *chlaina* were different shapes; the idea that the *chlamys* was rounded may come from Ammonius (*de Dif. Voc.* 147 Valck).

fact not be in evidence with the garments wrapped and fastened as they are in the monument.[165] Given the strong association between the *chlamys* and Thessaly there does not seem any certainty, or indeed probability, that the sculptor(s) of the Monument intended to evoke a Macedonian element explicitly. It is possible that southern Greeks would have elided ethnic distinctions to consider the short cloak a more generally northern phenomenon,[166] but most probable that those viewing the monument would simply have seen it as a Thessalian garment on figures of Thessalian men. Costume, then, does not support the idea that the monument was trying to suggest a cultural affinity, sympathy even, between Thessaly and Macedon; rather, we see an emphasis on Thessalian identity, which tallies with the emphasis in the inscriptions on Thessaly as well as on Pharsalos. Plainly, in terms of the visual impression intended, Daochos wished to restore his own homeland to full prominence after its *de facto* take-over by Philip, with his own help.

One of the most significant aspects of the Daochos Monument is in fact its location. In addition to its prominence, it was placed next to, and perhaps even connected with, the shrine of Neoptolemos. This is striking because, as noted in Chapter 2, there is no earlier evidence of active Thessalian involvement in the cult of Neoptolemos at Delphi; indeed, Thessalian interest in the Aiakidai was chiefly directed to Thetis. Pharsalos held the Thetideion in its territory; it makes sense for a Pharsalian to feel a connection to her grandson, but there are no signs of the connection being meaningful before. We should perhaps connect the Daochos Monument with the statue group of Achilles and Patroklos mentioned above, though its dating is problematic.

Why would this period see a sudden expression of Thessalian interest in Neoptolemos at Delphi? There are bound to be factors we cannot detect, including the practical (availability of suitable building space within

[165] When the *pteruges* appear in Thessalian art the context tends to be such as to emphasise movement, youth, or both. On coins, the young bull-wrestlers often wear *chlamydes* with *pteruges*: see, for example, the mid-fifth-century hemidrachm from Pelinna, *Triton* XV 222, no. 509.1. The funerary stele of a young man in the Diachronic Museum of Larisa (mid-fifth century, from Larisa itself) shows the deceased standing in a *chlamys* with *pteruges*, and wearing in addition the *petasos* popular in, though by no means exclusive to, Thessaly. There is no movement here, but the youth of the subject is certainly emphasised. Fougères 1888, 179–81. For a *petasos* on a young man's grave stele see Doulgeri-Intzesiloglou 2000, 79–80 and pl. 35 – Larisa, earlier fifth century BC.

[166] It is interesting that Strabo (7.7.8) includes the *chlamys* among cultural habits that the Macedonians and the Epeirotes have in common: 'ἔνιοι δὲ καὶ σύμπασαν τὴν μέχρι Κορκύρας Μακεδονίαν προσαγορεύουσιν, αἰτιολογοῦντες ἅμα ὅτι καὶ κουρᾷ καὶ διαλέκτῳ καὶ χλαμύδι καὶ ἄλλοις τοιούτοις χρῶνται παραπλησίως … '.

the sanctuary, for example) and the wider historical context (had Aigina diminished its own involvement in Neoptolemos's cult by this time?). One aspect, however, that is important to consider is the way in which the figure of Neoptolemos in particular might have worked to express genealogical connections between Thessaly and Macedon, and indeed between Thessaly, Macedon and Molossia. I have argued elsewhere for the former relationship.[167] Philip's wife Olympias is said to have cultivated a strong sense of her Aiakid descent and to have passed that on to her son Alexander; no doubt her status at Philip's court drew on the fact that she had added descent from Neoptolemos to the Heraklid ancestry the Argeads already possessed. Olympias may have lost her influence over the climate and priorities of the Argead court after 337 BC, when she quarrelled with Philip and departed for her Molossian homeland; however, Philip continued to cherish diplomatic connections with the Molossian kingdom.[168] When Alexander needed, after his father's assassination, to remind the Thessalians of the ancient *syngeneia* between his family and them, he was able to cite not only Herakles but also the Aiakidai.[169] In fact he was bending strict genealogy here: Neoptolemos had no Thessalian progeny, and at no point did Aiakid descent pertain to the whole Thessalian *ethnos*. But in such diplomatic contexts such details seem to have been unimportant. The incident reveals the way in which a sprawling heroic lineage could be evoked to express connections between regions and communities, and it is plausible that Daochos intended the location of his monument to gratify his Macedonian associates' interest in the figure of Neoptolemos. This is strongly reinforced by the designation of the Thessalian Eurypylos, in Aristotle's and Kallisthenes' account of the First Sacred War, as the New Achilles. In that, the 'new' is as significant as the 'Achilles': the sense is one of renovation, of rediscovery, of the Thessalians – in their alliance with Philip – recovering a heroic standing that they had previously lost. In such a climate the location of the Daochos Monument makes sense as part of the Thessalian/Macedonian use of Delphi to enact their ancestral proximity.

c) Aleuas, Delphi and Dodona

The dusting off and exploiting of old myth-historical traditions of this kind was not limited to Pharsalos in its relationship with Macedon. We find further glimpses if we look at the development at this time of the character of Aleuas, the legendary statesman of Larisa. For the first time we find his

167 Aston (2012b).

168 In 342 he had installed Olympias' brother Alexandros on the Molossian throne, and to this man he married his daughter Kleopatra in 336 to ensure that the relationship remained strong despite his estrangement from Olympias. Diod. 16.91.4.

169 Just. *Epit.* 11.3.1–2; cf. Diod. 17.4.1, in which only Herakles is mentioned.

Fig. 15. Silver drachma from Larisa; ca. 400–340 BC. Obv: head of Aleuas; rev.: eagle with thunderbolt. Photograph: © The Trustees of the British Museum

by-name Pyrrhos. It is impossible to rule out the possibility that this was conferred on the historical Aleuas in his lifetime, but it is more likely that it was attached to his name when he achieved legendary status as founder of the Larisaian political system (see Chapter 5). While the ancients sometimes connected the word with his hair colour,[170] it is impossible not to see in it an echo of the other name for Neoptolemos, especially as the practice of calling Neoptolemos Pyrrhos also attained greater popularity in the fourth century.[171] Perhaps giving Aleuas the surname Pyrrhos was equivalent to calling Eurypylos the New Achilles, an attempt to tie important figures in Thessalian myth-history to heroes of the Homeric age.

Relevant to this matter of Aleuas' fourth-century standing is a notoriously enigmatic coin type issued in relatively small numbers by the city of Larisa some time in the fourth century (Fig. 15). The type bears on the obverse the head of Aleuas, surely Aleuas Pyrrhos, in a conical helmet; on the reverse is an eagle perched upon a horizontal thunderbolt. On the obverse the legend is ΑΛΕΥ (which allows us to identify Aleuas with reasonable certainty, though the abbreviation leaves one uncertain whether the man or the family is referred to). On the reverse we find ΕΛΛΑ and ΛΑΡΙΣΑΙΑ. ΕΛΛΑ in particular has generated much debate, and may possibly be the abbreviation of the name of a local magistrate under whose

[170] Hegemon *FGrH* 110 F 1.

[171] Only the name Neoptolemos is known in Homer, though both names seem to have been used in the *Kypria* (fr. 19 West), probably dating from the later sixth century BC. Apart from the *Kypria*, the first text to use the name Pyrrhos for Neoptolemos is Theopompos *FGrH* 115 F 355.

aegis the coins were minted.[172] On the other hand, some scholars have argued that the word relates to 'Hellas', whether as an abbreviation of that or of one of its cognates.[173]

What would this represent? A basic statement of Greekness? Surely not; nobody at this time actually impugned the Hellenicity of the Thessalians, despite poor opinion in some quarters of their character. More likely is some reference to one of the sanctuaries in which Hellenic identity and terminology were especially strongly represented. Delphi is a possibility in this regard; the strong analogy between the Amphiktyony and the concept of the Hellenes certainly continued in the fourth century, and the legends that surround Aleuas' youth include a Delphic element, the famous story by which his kingly power was ratified by the Pythia (who, in the process, drew special attention to his nickname).[174] However, the eagle and thunderbolt on the coin recall Molossian issues of the same period, including some minted by Alexandros, Olympias' brother.[175] In the case of the Molossian issues the link with Dodona is reinforced by the obverse: a head of Zeus with oak-leaf chaplet. Neither Zeus nor thunderbolt were exclusive to Dodona, of course, but here the ΕΛΛΑ legend comes back into the frame. Dodona was saturated with Hell- names and terms (Selloi/Helloi, Hellopia etc.), but the most direct identification is with *hella*, which meant (according to Hesychios) 'Διὸς ἱερὸν ἐν Δωδώνῃ', 'the sanctuary of Zeus at Dodona'. This, combined with the eagle and thunderbolt, strongly suggests that the Larisaian coin was making an explicit reference to the famous north-western oracle, while at the same time creating an unparalleled portrait of its legendary nomothete.[176]

172 Sordi (1956). Note that Lorber (2008, 128–29) uses the evidence of hoards to show that Sordi's dating of the coin to the beginning of the reign of Alexander the Great is too late.

173 Von Sallet (1878), 99–101 (suggesting that the head on the obverse is actually Hellas herself); Wade-Gery (1924), 64, arguing that 'Hellas' here refers specifically to the Delphic Amphiktyony.

174 Plut. *De Fraterno Amore* 21. The episode serves as a kind of *aition* of the name Pyrrhos, since the Pythia uses it adjectivally to clarify whom the oracle denotes ('I mean the *pyrrhos* one … ').

175 Meyer (2013, 120) links these coins with Alexandros of Epeiros' payment of soldiers for his campaign in south Italy from 334 BC. Raynor (2017) argues convincingly that Epeirote (rather than Molossian) ethnogenesis was a significant element of Alexandros' rule, and that in this regard he set the stage for the later activities of Pyrrhos. It is interesting that the Thessalian interest in Dodona at this time may have been in part a response to energetic Molossian self-advertisement, just as it was in the third century. For the unification of Epeiros even before Alexandros see Pascual (2018), 65–71.

176 Sordi (1956). She argues that the coin type was minted at the instigation of Alexander the Great, with the aim of linking Macedon, Thessaly and Molossia. For Badian, on the other hand (1999, 115–16), the coin was minted by Philip II as Larisaian citizen

This Larisaian reference to Dodona obliges us to consider the antiquity of Thessalian involvement in the sanctuary and its surrounding mythology. Past scholarship has tended to claim that an active link was very early, drawing, for its starting point, on the fact that in the *Iliad* Zeus of Dodona is called *Pelasgikos*, Pelasgian.[177] The link between Dodona and the Pelasgoi is also to be found in Hesiod, Ephoros, and later authors.[178] Kowalzig, who argues energetically that Thessaly cultivated an association with Dodona in the Archaic period,[179] suggests that the designation of Dodonaian Zeus as 'Pelasgian' drew on a Thessalian claim to have founded Dodona.[180] This theory should, however, be treated with some caution. Although – as was discussed in Chapter 3 – the Pelasgians did come to be associated particularly strongly with Thessaly, they were never limited in scope to that region; parcels of them could and did crop up all over the Greek world. And if we ask what Homer would have meant by 'Pelasgian', the answer is not straightforward. It is true that 'Pelasgian Argos' seems to refer, in the *Iliad*, to part or most of Thessaly; however, the reference to the Pelasgoi who fight for the Trojans is more problematic. They are from Larissa, and are under the command of Hippothoos and Pylaios, sons of Lethos. Kowalzig uses them to support her theory concerning the identification of 'Pelasgian' with 'Thessalian' by supposing that this Larissa is the Thessalian one,[181] but that is hard to credit, despite the tempting Amphiktyonic flavour of 'Pylaios': the contingent fights for Troy, and none of the other Trojan allies hails from any further west than Thrace. Hippothoos and Pylaios are surrounded by Thracian and Hellespontine communities; the placement of a Thessalian

and Tagos of the Thessalians, and the ΕΛΛΑ legend refers to his foundation of the Hellenic League in 337 BC. Prentzas (2004), in a recent reconsideration of the type, is, however, surely right to argue that Larisaian agency should be considered uppermost, not Macedonian, and to point to stylistic reasons for an earlier date. He argues that the coin reflects close Thessalian/Macedonian relations in the time of Alexandros II, and specifically dates it to 370/69, after Alexandros II's intervention in Thessaly in support of the Larisaians against Alexandros of Pherai (Diod. 15.61.3–5.) While this is a persuasive suggestion, it seems unnecessary and unwise to remove all reference to Dodona in the eagle motif, and perhaps from ΕΛΛΑ too. Further discussions of the coin type include Herrmann (1925), 63–66; Wade-Gery (1924), 63–64.

177 Hom. *Il.* 16.233. Parke (1967), 1–4, 36.

178 Hes. fr. 319 MW; Ephoros, *FGrH* 70 F 142; Strabo 5.2.4 and 7.7.10.

179 This relates to her wider argument that Boiotians' ritual activity at Dodona – a space imbued with Thessalian resonances – constituted an enactment of the collective memory of their Thessalian origins (Kowalzig 2007, 341–52). Castelnuovo (2017), by contrast, argues that the Boiotian *tripodephoria* had a later date of inception and was not primarily a reference to the Thessalian connection.

180 Kowalzig (2007), 346–47.

181 Kowalzig (2007), 346.

contingent here, away from the other groups from that region, would be very odd. There were several Larissai (and Larisai) in the ancient Greek world, as Strabo remarks; he is surely right to say that Homer's Larisa must be one of the ones in western Asia, near Troy.[182] In the *Odyssey* the Pelasgoi are in Krete. So it is by no means the case that 'Pelasgian' may be treated as a synonym of Thessalian in Homer. Right from the start, the Pelasgoi are mysterious, scattered, impossible to pin down to a single location.

Before moving on, we should note a further apparent link between Dodona and Thessaly in the *Iliad*, this time in the Catalogue of Ships.[183] There occurs in the Catalogue a geographical elision of Thessaly and Epeiros that has baffled both ancient commentators and modern historians. The poet says:

> And Gouneus led from Kyphos twenty-two ships.
> There followed him the Ainianes staunch in battle, and the Perrhaiboi,
> Those who made their homes in the region of harsh-wintered Dodona,
> And those who worked the lands around lovely Titaressos
> Which sends its fair-flowing water into Peneios;
> But it does not mingle with Peneios of the silver eddies,
> But rather flows over the top of it like olive oil.
> For Titaressos is a branch of the water of Styx, that terrible oath.[184]

Scholars have puzzled over the apparent placement of the Perrhaiboi in the region of Dodona.[185] The oddity is resolved somewhat by assuming that the poet intended to define the Perrhaiboi and the Ainianes as inhabiting two distinct regions: the Perrhaibians are around the river Titaressos, and the Ainianes are in the Dodona region. This makes perfect sense from a grammatical perspective. But the fact remains that the scope of Gouneus' command is an odd one, encompassing peoples dwelling far

182 Strabo 13.3.2.

183 N.b. Dodona is mentioned in the *Odyssey* (14.327, 19.296), but with no reference to Thessaly.

184 Hom. *Il.* 2.747–55:

> Γουνεὺς δ' ἐκ Κύφου ἦγε δύω καὶ εἴκοσι νῆας·
> τῷ δ' Ἐνιῆνες ἕποντο μενεπτόλεμοί τε Περαιβοὶ
> οἳ περὶ Δωδώνην δυσχείμερον οἰκί' ἔθεντο,
> οἵ τ' ἀμφ' ἱμερτὸν Τιταρησσὸν ἔργα νέμοντο
> ὅς ῥ' ἐς Πηνειὸν προΐει καλλίρροον ὕδωρ,
> οὐδ' ὅ γε Πηνειῷ συμμίσγεται ἀργυροδίνῃ,
> ἀλλά τέ μιν καθύπερθεν ἐπιρρέει ἠΰτ' ἔλαιον·
> ὅρκου γὰρ δεινοῦ Στυγὸς ὕδατός ἐστιν ἀπορρώξ.

185 E.g., Parke (1967), 5–6.

from each other, and separated by the Pindos range. It is likely that ancient puzzlement over the domain of Gouneus helped to foster the theory that the oracle of Zeus started in Thessaly (see Chapter 7). Strabo, for all his scathing treatment of Souidas and Kineas, his sources, seems to endorse their theory that Dodona used to be near Skotoussa, and his motive may well be to resolve the apparent problem of Gouneus' domain.[186]

If we want grounds for seeing Gouneus' command as compatible with some basic aspects of historical reality, we might turn to the suggestion of Gounaris,[187] that the contingents in the Catalogue of Ships reflect not fixed political boundaries but mobile pastoral populations spanning apparently inchoate geographical ranges. The theme of migration that pervades the myths of Thessaly was especially intense in the trans-Pindos zone that Gouneus' lands seem to straddle; mobile populations constantly traversed it, and, in reality, it is likely to have been an area of transhumant pastoralism, communities wintering their flocks at lower level on one side or the other and then driving them up into high pastures for summer grazing.[188] On the other hand, Homer's allocation of different groups and places to Gouneus may also reflect, in the poet's rather patchy knowledge of Thessalian geography, a loose traditional association of Dodona with Thessaly, also manifest in Achilles' reference to the oracle. The Dodona/Thessaly link may also be suggested by the inclusion of magical Dodonan oak-wood in the construction of the Argo, though the provenance of the timber and its explicitly mantic properties are only attested from the fifth century BC.[189]

However, none of this quite signals the deliberate incorporation of Dodona by the Thessalian into their collective self-expression; such a thing is not clearly attested before the later fourth century.[190] What seems

[186] Strabo 9.5.20.

[187] Gounaris (2012).

[188] Indeed, Chapinal-Heras (2021, 208–10) makes a good case for the likelihood that Dodona itself was a centre for stockbreeding and herding activity. His study of the several routes connecting Dodona with other regions identifies the significance of the Metsovo route in connecting Dodona with Thessaly (see his pages 141–43). It is also worth noting *SEG* 15.384, an inscription of 370–68 BC, listing *damiorgoi* [*sic*] involved in, as Meyer argues, the administration of Dodona; they are listed with their ethnics, and the range of some of the tribal *ethnē* – in particular the Kelaithoi and the Genoaioi – extend, as Meyer observes, close to the edge of Thessaly, near the Metsovo pass. Meyer (2013), 47–56 (on the nature of the text) and 91–98 (the territorial extent).

[189] The Argo is mentioned in the *Odyssey* (12.69–70) but without reference to the timber or Dodona; for these we wait until Pherekydes *FGrH* 3 F 111a and Aischylos, fr. 20 Radt (from the *Argo*, or *Rowers*): the former has the Argo refusing to carry Herakles because of his weight; the latter refers to the timber 'groaning'; neither says as much, but it is reasonable to assume Dodona was the source, given later accounts such as Apollod. *Bibl.* 1.9.16.

[190] The text that seems to come closest to suggesting Thessalian involvement is a

most likely is that – as the evidence clearly shows[191] – the Boiotians were actively cultivating a connection with Dodona in both ritual and myth; they incorporated a Thessalian element in the myth-making because it accorded with the migration tradition that was central to their shared identity, and perhaps encouraged by the 'Pelasgian' label given to the sanctuary by Homer, and by the Pelasgian/Thessalian association. The association did not, however, require active involvement by the Thessalians.[192]

In the fourth century that is beginning to change. Our earliest securely attested Thessalian consultation of the oracle at Dodona is dated to 400–375: the polis of Pherai enquired concerning the community's *sōtēria*, safety (as well they might given the turbulence of that time for Pherai).[193] However, there is a difference between a community or an individual making use of a religious resource in time of need, and any suggestion that Dodona was considered a symbolically meaningful component of Thessalian identity. The latter really begins with our Aleuas coin. In Chapter 7 we shall see a surge in deliberate references to the connection, driven by new political circumstances in the third century, but the fourth-century backdrop is formative. There are signs at this time that Dodona may have been renewing its claim to a privileged role in the origins of Hellenicity. In Aristotle, for example, we find a striking assertion that Deukalion's flood especially affected the region around Dodona: 'This took place chiefly in the Greek world and in it especially about ancient Hellas, the country about Dodona and the Acheloos, a river which has often changed its course. Here the Selloi dwelt and those who were formerly called Graikoi

fragment of Pindar, probably part of a *Paian*, which clearly described elements of the Dodona sanctuary, including the Helloi. The word *Thessaloi* also appears, but as an interlinear scholion. Did the poem describe Thessalian links to Dodona and, most importantly, was it composed for the Thessalians, in connection with some ritual occasion? Possibly, but it cannot be proved. See Piccinini (2017), 111–18.

191 Piccinini (2017), 102–15, for discussion of the literary sources. Especially important is Ephoros *FGrH* 70 F 119, relating the *aition* of a Boiotian *tripodephoria*, a story bound up with the myth of the Boiotian migration from Thessaly.

192 Piccinini (2017, 119–22) claims that it was the 'program of Aleuas' at the end of the sixth century to weave together Aiakid and Heraklid origin-stories and so reconcile the tradition of the Thessalian invaders with those of the region's pre-existing populations. While there are some elements of truth in this (in particular the naming of the tetrads as a way of combining old mythological ingredients into a regional system), Piccinini shows no caution about the dates of her sources and accepts wholesale Sordi's arguments about Thessalian cultivation of the Neoptolemos-cult at Delphi in the sixth and fifth centuries, as well as the dubious reality of Aleuas as a lawgiver single-handedly reforming Thessalian society.

193 DVC 2940B, accessed from *Dodona Online* at https://dodonaonline.files.wordpress.com/2022/03/ciod_dvc_2940b2937a.pdf (accessed 4 May 2022).

and now Hellenes.'[194] Dodona and Greek identity had, by this stage, a long and complex history, for all its location in the midst of non-Greek peoples.[195] *hell-* words and names attach to the area early (for example, Hellopia in Hesiod),[196] and it is even possible that, as Parke suggests,[197] the -enes ending of Hellenes suggests a north-western origin for the name, which then moved (though cultural transfer or the physical migration of population groups) down to the Spercheios valley, its Iliadic location. In other words, we cannot be sure that Dodona's connection with Hellenism was secondary to that of central Greece and the ambit of the Delphic Amphiktyony, its core territory in the *Ehoiai*, although the *Iliad* does give it a different myth-historical niche: by calling it Pelasgian, it designates Dodona pre-Greek, originating before the birth of Hellen, and so gives it primordial status and a certain archaic alterity. The term Graikoi, of course, is strongly associated with Epeiros; as Malkin has demonstrated, it came to be the word by which neighbouring peoples (Illyrian, Messapian, Italiot) designated the Epeirotes, and it spread from there, just as Hellenes may have spread outwards from an original central Greek nucleus.[198] Whether the Selloi – the priests of Dodona mentioned in the *Iliad* – really shared etymology with the *hell-* root, by Pindar's time it was possible to replace Selloi with Helloi[199] and so claim such a link. And at this very time, of course, the Molossian royal family, closely associated with Dodona, was advertising its Greek credentials through Aiakid origins, thereby linking themselves not only with famous Greek heroes but with the part of Greece considered the 'original Hellas', the territory of Peleus and Achilles. Pindar helps to convey this identification in *Nemean 7*, when – having recounted the death of Neoptolemos at Delphi[200] – he says, 'An Achaian man, a dweller beyond the Ionian sea, happening to be nearby, will not blame me.'[201] 'Achaian',

[194] Aristotle, *Met.* 1.352a–b: 'καὶ γὰρ οὗτος περὶ τὸν Ἑλληνικὸν ἐγένετο τόπον μάλιστα, καὶ τούτου περὶ τὴν Ἑλλάδα τὴν ἀρχαίαν. αὕτη δ' ἐστὶν ἡ περὶ Δωδώνην καὶ τὸν Ἀχελῷον· οὗτος γὰρ πολλαχοῦ τὸ ῥεῦμα μεταβέβληκεν· ᾤκουν γὰρ οἱ Σελλοὶ ἐνταῦθα καὶ οἱ καλούμενοι τότε μὲν Γραικοὶ νῦν δ' Ἕλληνες.'

[195] See, for example, Thuc. 2.68: Greeks and *barbaroi* in and around Amphilochian Argos.

[196] Strabo (7.7.10) and the scholion on Soph. *Trach.* 1167a quote several lines of the *Ehoiai* (fr. 240 MW) describing the oracle, its visitors from all over the world, its oak tree and the rich land of Hellopia on whose edge Dodona is located.

[197] Parke (1967), 8; see also Lhôte (2006), x–xi.

[198] Malkin (1998), 146–49; see also Kittelä (2013), 33–34.

[199] Pind. fr. 59.3 Snell.

[200] On the possibility that *Nem.* 7 refers to the treatment of Neoptolemos in *Paian* 6 see Burnett (2005), 199–200.

[201] Pind. *Nem.* 7.64–65: 'ἐὼν δ' ἐγγὺς Ἀχαιὸς οὐ μέμψεταί μ' ἀνὴρ/Ἰονίας ὑπὲρ ἁλὸς οἰκέων'. It is tempting to follow Piccinini (2017, 116) in taking this to be a man from

here, does not, of course, refer to Peloponnesian Achaia but, most probably, to one of the Homeric designations for all the Greeks at Troy, that is, Greek. The Molossian rulers are *andres Achaioi* on the basis of their descent from one of the foremost Homeric Achaioi.

Very hard to fit into the picture is a further branch of the linguistic bundle *hell-/sell-*, the figure of Hellos. Hellos does seem to consolidate the link with Thessaly, but when to date his invention? A Homeric scholiast explains the Helloi of Dodona as 'ἀπὸ Ἕλλοῦ τοῦ Θεσσαλοῦ' – 'descended from Hellos the son of Thessalos', or 'descended from Hellos the Thessalian'.[202] We might prefer the latter translation except for a myth recorded by Hyginus in his *Fabulae*, concerning one Thessalus, who founded the temple of Jupiter Dodonaeus in the land of the Molossians.[203] So we seem to have a myth whereby the sanctuary of Zeus at Dodona is established by one Thessalos, whose son Hellos is the ancestor of the priests, the Helloi or Selloi, who thereafter serve the oracle. It should be noted that this Thessalos is wholly separate from Thessalos the son of Aiatios; however, as the latter entered Thessaly from Thesprotia, his Epeirote connection may have helped to fuel the invention of the other Thessalos, the Dodonaian one. But when did Thessalos father of Hellos come on the scene? Quite probably not until the flurry of revisionist myth-making in the third century, which we shall examine in Chapter 7.

Aristotle's assertions are unlikely to emerge from nowhere. Probably a privileged place in the early history of Hellenism was one of the instruments used from the Archaic period in the competitive interaction between Dodona and Delphi.[204] Still, it is truly remarkable to find, in Aristotle, the description of the area round Dodona as ἡ Ἕλλας ἡ ἀρχαία, an unambiguous claim of primacy over the Spercheios area. It is also striking to find Deukalion's flood focused on Dodona; where does that leave Dodona's Pelasgian identity, established in the *Iliad*? Washes it away, presumably: the flood allows for a clean slate, for the introduction of Hellenic rather than pre-Hellenic identity. With his close relationship with the Argead court, Aristotle himself may have been influenced by Olympias'

the Homeric kingdom of Achaia on the southern edge of Thessaly, and therefore as an implicit suggestion that the contemporary inhabitants of Achilles' homeland might take an interest in the depiction of his son. However, the description Ἰονίας ὑπὲρ ἁλὸς οἰκέων ('living above the Ionian sea') is hard to square with Achaia Phthiotis. For the Molossian identification see further Burnett (2005), 194–96.

202 Schol. Hom. *Il.* 16.234.

203 Hyg. *Fab.* 225.

204 As Eidinow (2014) and more recently Piccinini (2018) have argued, however, historians have tended to overstate the amount of mutual disparagement between oracular sanctuaries in ancient Greece.

intense personal interest in Dodona,[205] evidence of which is provided by an incident reported in Hypereides' *In Defence of Euxenippos*, composed between 330 and 324 BC. Olympias apparently objected to the Athenians' embellishing the statue of Dodona, and wrote to remind them ὡς ἡ χώρα εἴη ἡ Μολοττία αὐτῆς, ἐν ᾗ τὸ ἱερόν ἐστιν ('that the country of Molossia, in which the sanctuary lies, was hers').[206] This incident presumably took place after, having fallen out with her son's regent Antipatros, she once again moved from Macedon to Molossia and effectively co-ruled with Aiakides after the death on campaign of her brother Alexandros. So at the time when Aristotle was probably writing the *Meteorologika* we have strong connections between Macedon, Molossia and the sanctuary of Dodona, and strong interests in promoting its importance as a northern bastion of Hellenic identity. The Aleuas coin with its reference to Dodona tends to be dated between the early and the mid-fourth century, but the stylistic grounds on which this is done are very shaky indeed, and we certainly cannot rule out the possibility that it coincided with the circumstances described above.

In any case, we can see some familiar patterns emerging. Once again, Thessaly's role in Hellenism is a significant once. In the Archaic period Delphi seems to have been the key ritual node in this process. Now Dodona is strongly in the frame. This is because of its increasing implication in the programme of the Molossian rulers, asserting their own Greek credentials as well as the panhellenic status of 'their' oracle. The former was achieved through genealogical association with a dynasty central to the conception of the 'other' Hellas, the Hellas of Peleus and Achilles; this is the side of Hellenicity that, in the fifth century, the Aiginetan elites were so energetic in claiming. Pharsalos stood in a sense between Delphi and Dodona, with the Aiakids the tie between the two sanctuaries, but the evidence only supports its active involvement with Delphi. The Aleuas coin is Larisaian, which is highly significant; were the Larisaians perhaps trying to claim religious and symbolic territory in which the Pharsalians did not have a stake? If so, the trend does not end there; in the next chapter we shall see other Pelasgiotic sites fostering links with Dodona in the time of Pyrrhos.

The importance of Aiakid identity to the Molossian rulers shows that heroic genealogy never lost its importance in the articulation of belonging to the Greek *ethnos*. However, as has been said, the bulky presence of the barbarian in the Greek imagination had worked to combine this traditional discourse with that of cultural opposition between Greek and non-Greek, us and them. We have seen this work to the Thessalians' disadvantage, as they came to be increasingly cast as falling short of Greek standards of character and conduct, in part because of their increasing association with

205 Kittelä (2013), 42–44.
206 Hyper. 4.25–26.

Macedon in the southern imagination. Reinforcing traditional connections with Delphi and Dodona, cradles of Hellenism from the Archaic period, were perhaps intended to offset this hostility.

4. Conclusions

The early fifth century brought us clear signs of Thessalian identity being forged from within through the development of myths and cults expressing the nature of the region and its people; in non-Thessalian texts the Thessalians and their land became part of the common parlance as unified entities, whose political manifestations – variable, shifting as circumstances shifted – were surveyed in Chapter 5. The present chapter has taken the story forward by placing the focus on the external perspective as its starting point. It has pursued the increasing hostility of non-Thessalian sources – Athenians especially – and identified the increasing use of Thessaly to evoke unpalatable modes of life and society. Shades of suspicion in the aftermath of the Persian Wars become downright condemnation in the fourth century, and the close association between the Thessalians and Philip II of Macedon was shown to put the nail in the coffin of Thessalian acceptability, in the eyes of many. This process may be summarised as the formulation of a negative Thessalian stereotype.

In this process the Thessalians did not remain passive, though their voices are quieter than those of their detractors. Thessalian self-presentation may be seen to respond to pejorative characterisation in two main ways. First, alignment with Macedon was, for the most part, embraced; the Daochos Monument saw the expression of a northern identity that enfolded both regions, and the renewed importance of Dodona drew in Molossian links too. Second, through their increased prominence at Delphi, though this in itself helped to arouse resentment, the Thessalians were able to present themselves as benefactors of the sanctuary and of Greece more generally, especially through manipulation of the traditions of the First Sacred War. However, their greatest opportunity for reputation-enhancement was yet to come, and would again involve their close association with Macedon. In the next chapter we shall see how Thessalians travelling with Alexander were able to present themselves as in some ways correcting a well-established accusation against the character of their *ethnos*, that it had more in common with *barbaroi* than with true Hellenes.

7

Re-creations of Thessaly in the early Hellenistic period

More than ever before, Thessaly in the Hellenistic period was subject to the influence – largely disruptive – of foreign powers. Macedonian control continued, but no longer unchallenged; in particular, the Aitolian presence is an important one. From 279 BC, the Aitolians – who had defeated Galatian invaders and thereafter basked in the role of defenders of Delphi[1] – swiftly became the most powerful *ethnos* in Central Greece, and in the process detached Achaia Phthiotis and other *ethnē* on Thessaly's southern border from Thessalian control.[2] When the Macedonian king Demetrios II died in 229 BC, the Aitolians seized control of large portions of Thessaly itself,[3] and while most of this territory was taken back by Antigonos Doson, Achaia Phthiotis remained in subjection to the Aitolians.[4] When Philip V re-established full Macedonian control over Thessaly, Phthiotic Thebes was an especially sharp and difficult thorn in his flank, though he did successfully take it.[5] When the Romans made peace with the Aitolians and the Macedonians after Kynoskephalai in 197 BC they refused to restore any Thessalian territory to the Aitolians, apart from allowing them to take back Phthiotic Thebes and Pharsalos.[6] In the Third Macedonian War, which went on until 168 BC, Thessaly was one of the key territories whose possession was contested between Perseus and Rome.[7] As for Macedonian

[1] The potency of this incident in Greek – especially Delphic – memory is conveyed by the detailed narrative in Paus. 10.19–23. Scholten (2000), 31–45.

[2] As early as 290 BC Aitolian occupation of the routes into Delphi led Demetrios to take the unprecedented step of celebrating the Pythian Games at Athens instead, essentially relinquishing Macedonian involvement in the sanctuary. Plut. *Dem.* 40.4; Grainger (1999), 91.

[3] Scholten (2000), 164–70; Grainger (1999), 100–12. For the geographical extent of the Aitolians' expansion into Thessaly and its neighbours see Helly (2009), 368, fig. 3.

[4] Scholten (2005), 153.

[5] Polyb. 5.97, 99–100. Scholten (2000), 170–80.

[6] Polyb. 18.38 and 47.

[7] See esp. Livy 42.55–67: the Romans defeat Perseus at Kallinikos in Perrhaibia in 171 BC; they cannot take Gonnoi because of the strength of its position, but make some

control in Thessaly, this was, as Helly stresses, not applied in a uniform manner; it differed from polis to polis, with *epistatai* – governors – rarely imposed on the poleis of 'Thessaly proper' but installed quite frequently in the poleis of the *perioikis*.[8] Helly believes that the official status of the Macedonian rulers in Thessaly was that of *symmachoi* rather than formal leaders of the *koinon*; even if this is so, however, it is probable that they continued to avail themselves of the region's revenues as their Argead forerunners had.[9] It is hard not to regard as essentially accurate Polybios' statement that, though Thessaly was not stripped of its own pre-existent political system, in effect it was entirely under Macedonian control, except when that control was disrupted by other foreign powers.[10]

Largely as a result of her involvement in this near-continuous chain of conflicts and upheavals, the populations of several of Thessaly's cities were severely depleted and her famous agricultural resources consequently sapped. Underpopulation of cities, resulting especially in an inability to exploit fully the surrounding agricultural land, emerge strongly from the epigraphic evidence. A *locus classicus* on this matter, mentioned in the Introduction, is the pair of letters recorded in a single inscription, which were sent to the city of Larisa by Philip V in 217 and 215 BC.[11] In the first letter the king stipulates the creation of new citizens, a measure necessary 'because of the wars' (διὲ τὸς πολέμος), which had obviously taken their toll on population numbers. Philip's main aim is said to be to ensure that Larisa's land should be more fully cultivated – τὰν χούραν μᾶλλον ἐξεργασθείσεσθειν. This picture of neglected and unworked or under-worked land is corroborated by a recently published inscription, also from Larisa, which deals with the sale of parcels of land called *hippoteia* and supposedly allocated for the growing of fodder crops for horses. In this text, also late third century in date, the parcels of land being sold are those that have been allowed to slip out of proper cultivation, and though the causes are not made clear the editors Helly and Tziafalias make a plausible link

gains in Perrhaibia, and then move into Achaia Phthiotis, where they take Antron and Pteleon and receive the surrender of Larisa Kremaste.

8 Helly (2009), 351.

9 Helly (2009), 347–48.

10 Polyb. 4.76.2: 'Θετταλοὶ γὰρ ἐδόκουν μὲν κατὰ νόμους πολιτεύειν καὶ πολὺ διαφέρειν Μακεδόνων, διέφερον δ' οὐδέν, ἀλλὰ πᾶν ὁμοίως ἔπασχον Μακεδόσι καὶ πᾶν ἐποίουν τὸ προσταττόμενον τοῖς βασιλικοῖς.' ('Ostensibly the Thessalians conducted their politics according to their laws and were in a very different situation from that of the Macedonians. In fact, however, they were in no way different, but suffered just what the Macedonians did and obeyed every order given them by the kings.')

11 *IG* IX.2 517; discussion of the text and its context in Habicht (1970). On the identity of the new citizens see Oetjen (2010). Note that both Philip V and his son Perseus helped to fund a new gymnasion in Larisa: *SEG* 13.390 and Habicht (1983).

Fig. 16. A section of the fortifications of New Halos, between the north-west and south gates; late fourth to early third century. Photograph: author's own

with the circumstances of the letters from Philip: the city's manpower is not sufficient to ensure proper agricultural activity.[12] Nor was this *oliganthropia* limited to Larisa: both Pharsalos and Phalanna in the third century also created significant numbers of new citizens, as inscriptions attest.[13]

There are also signs that conditions in Hellenistic Thessaly prompted some shifts in the pattern of settlement and urban configuration. On the

[12] Helly and Tziafalias (2013), 247–49; Reger (2005), 334–36.

[13] Kaczmarek (2015), 234–37. On the agriculture impact of war in the Hellenistic period see Chaniotis (2011), 128–29, noting especially a case of grain shortage in Gonnoi in the early second century BC. Chronic debt in second-century Krannon: Chaniotis (2011), 133. Economic hardship in late third century Larisa: Salviat and Vatin (1974), 254–56; Helly (1973), vol. I, 118–19. Even before the difficult conditions of the third and second centuries, Thessaly – for all its famous arable and pastoral abundance – was by no means immune to periodic food shortages, as is shown by the inclusion of some Thessalian poleis in the famous grant of grain by Kyrene ca. 330 BC (*SEG* 9.2). Diplomacy played a role in such matters as well as agricultural necessity; in the early third century the Thessalian *koinon* was able to provide grain to Kos (*IG* XII.4 1:133; see further below). One should not overlook the advantage to the donor in terms of prestige: see Bresson (2011), 89–93, on the role of the grain donations in Kyrene's prosperity and self-presentation in the later fourth century.

one hand, Kaczmarek, taking a broad-brush approach to Thessaly as a whole, identifies an increase in the number of fortified rural sites of modest size; plainly those without the protection of a large town took steps to improve their security.[14] On the other, Haagsma, Surtees and Chykerda, focusing specifically on Achaia Phthiotis and in particular the survey data from New Halos, note a tendency to consolidate settlement in the town of New Halos itself, a withdrawal from rural sites. This they combine with the instances of synoecism in the late fourth and the third century, and suggest that both were responses to the turbulence of the times.[15] If one takes into account the increase in very substantial urban fortifications at this time, a coherent picture does emerge of communities trying to bolster themselves against the violence of the time (Fig. 16).

Thessaly was of course not alone in feeling the strain as the struggles of the Hellenistic age raged back and forth. However, her crucial strategic position and natural resources[16] did make her the setting for a disproportionately large amount of fighting and concomitant upheaval. Nor did the advent of the Romans initially make matters better; Flamininus officially declared the Thessalians free in 197 BC, a gesture greeted with rapturous applause,[17] but the wars went on until 148 BC, and while they were in progress the Roman presence was sometimes a burden to the Thessalians: we read frequently of Roman armies wintering in Thessaly and of course living off the land.[18] In addition, a combination of crippling debt and Macedonian destabilisation brought about a spate of political upheavals in Thessalian poleis, and surges of popular discontent.[19] However, the Romans were in the end the source of peace in Thessaly, and Thessaly lived under Roman rule with unusual placidity, in a condition of peace that they would have been hard put to gain for themselves without determined outside agency.[20]

As has long been recognised by historians, however, neither hardship nor the imposition of external control discernibly reduced cultural life in

14 Kaczmarek (2015), 90.

15 Haagsma et al. (2019), 295–96.

16 Livy (31.41.7) calls her fields *opimos ad praedam* – 'excellent for plunder'.

17 Polyb. 18.46.5; Plut. *Flam.* 10.4; Livy 33.32.5. For discussion of the declaration see Walsh (1996); for the significance of its setting see Gebhard (1993), 168–70.

18 E.g., Livy 42.64 (Roman forces harvesting Thessalian crops for their own use after the battle of Kallinikos against Perseus in 171 BC). Perseus had done much the same thing, including appropriating large numbers of livestock, shortly before the battle: 42.56.8.

19 Mendels (1982), 104–06.

20 According to Livy (34.51), Flamininus' policy was to choose as federal (and perhaps some polis) magistrates men of wealth and property who would see to it that dissent was stamped down and the *status quo* maintained. See Derow (2005), 63.

Greek communities. Turbulence and uncertainty seem, if anything, to have galvanised forms of collective self-expression. Rulers permitted and even encouraged the vibrant religious and cultural activity that allowed communities to express their identities and their shared myth-histories despite the curtailment of their freedoms. This is the Golden Age of 'kinship diplomacy', communities often far distant from each other in miles forging or renewing ties through assertions of shared heroic ancestry.[21] With their stock of famous myths the Thessalian were well supplied with the raw material for such exchanges, but we do not always find them being conducted by the most obvious contenders. Although the ultimate power of the various Hellenistic rulers overlaid all aspects of life in the Greek world, beneath this existed a dense mesh of connections identified by Ma in terms of a 'peer polity network'. In this, a claim on significant myth-historical credentials could equip small and relatively obscure communities to interact with far larger and more influential ones and, for that matter, with rulers, in a strikingly non-hierarchical arrangement of 'horizontal' associations.[22] All in all, we have a new range of ways to articulate Thessalian identity, new audiences for doing so and new opportunities for previously marginal groups to participate in the process.

1. East with Alexander

The end of Chapter 6 left the Thessalians in a peculiar position within the wider Greek world. On the one hand, their increasing alignment with Macedon under Philip II – an alignment both real and strongly perceived – had brought to a head the process of cultural marginalisation, among disapproving, especially Athenian, elites, which had been in progress since the last quarter of the fifth century. On the other hand, the practical upshot of their association with Philip was to place them centre-stage in Greek affairs, and especially at Delphi, the traditional heartland of Hellenicity. This was accompanied by a strong discourse of *restoration*, of recovering glorious past deeds, which found its narrative focus in the stories of the First Sacred War. Thessaly deserved to be at the heart of Delphic affairs because it had held a key role in the sanctuary's preservation against the Krisaioi and Kraugalidai, the creation of its sacred land, and the inauguration of the Pythian Games. The fact that this tradition rested on very shaky grounds, historically, did not reduce its potency. With Alexander's

[21] For discussion of the ways in which Hellenistic communities responded to and manipulated the mythological, and in particular the epic, past see Alcock (1997). On the expansion of diplomatic connections between Thessalian and non-Thessalian poleis in the Hellenistic period see Kaczmarek (2015), 187–95.

[22] Ma (2003); see also Renfrew (1986).

accession, the pack was shuffled and the cards dealt again, though the pack was the same. Suddenly, the Thessalians with Alexander were engaged in a massive collective enterprise against *barbaroi*. At least in its early stages, the campaign was presented by Alexander as a panhellenic one. Macedonians and Thessalians, so recently dismissed by their detractors as, respectively, northern *barbaroi* and their adherents, led the conquest of the Persians some fifty years after Persian troops under Xerxes had made the journey the other way.[23]

The Thessalians who accompanied Alexander's Asian expedition were both numerous and, in many cases, occupying significant roles.[24] Strootman has calculated that around 2,000 Thessalian cavalrymen fought in Alexander's army: the same number, significantly, as the Macedonian cavalry.[25] Moreover, we find several Thessalians in the king's immediate ambit, among his *hetairoi* or as similarly high-ranking individuals. There are signs also that the Thessalians regarded their participation in the campaign as a very important event. For example, in a Pheraian inscription of the early second century listing *gymnasiarchoi* of the polis, the list is headed with the formula 'The following became *gymnasiarchoi* after our citizens returned from campaigning in Asia with Alexander.'[26] For this polis at least, going east with Alexander constituted a major historical milestone, by which subsequent events could be dated, and retained this status for generations to come. Returning to the time of the expedition itself, it is telling, as Strootman notes, that after Alexander formally dismissed his allied Greek troops in 330 BC, 130 Thessalians chose to re-enlist as mercenaries.[27] The

23 On Alexander's exploitation of the Persian Wars as a precursor to his own panhellenic campaign see Kremmydas (2013). On his panhellenism see Flower (2000a). On his exploitation of the key concepts of *eleutheria* and *autonomia* (and what they really meant in the actualities of his campaign) see Dmitriev (2011), 90–107. On the particular application of the concepts to the Greeks of Asia: Seager and Tuplin (1980); Seager (1981).

24 The important roles played by Thessalians travelling with Alexander do not, of course, reflect a condition of perfect contentment in Thessaly itself. We hear of at least one attempted revolt during Alexander's reign, though we have no information on whether it was ever really actuated: Aischines (3.167) refers to a claim made (falsely, as he alleges) by Demosthenes to have stirred up a rebellion in Perrhaibia and Thessaly. The Thessalians sustained economic hardships as a result of money and men flowing east to fuel the campaign of conquest: Martin (1985), 153–65.

25 Strootman (2010–2011), 57–60; see also Wallace (2016), 21–23.

26 *SEG* 29.552, lines 1–2. For discussion of the text, its context and its reconstructions see Helly et al. (1979). They calculate (pp. 232–36) that the list of *gymnasiarchoi* runs from 330 (the return from Asia) until 189 BC, on the basis that normally there are two *gymnasiarchoi* per year. In this regard they improve upon the interpretation in Habicht (1976).

27 Arr. *Anab.* 3.25.4; Strootman (2010–2011), 66. They were in fact dismissed in the

starting point of this close relationship is the bond Philip forged with the Thessalians, on which Alexander in his turn was able to draw as long as it suited him.

Alexander's expedition marked a seminal phase in the development of the Greek view of their interaction with non-Greek peoples. It was seen as settling the score after the Persian invasions of Greece, not only by orators such as Isokrates[28] but also, apparently, by Alexander himself. The discourse was inherited from Philip's reign,[29] and both kings stood to benefit from the shift the expedition would facilitate in their standing within the Greek world: though detractors might have branded Philip a *barbaros*, he planned, and his son carried out, a panhellenic campaign against a common Persian foe. If we take the ethnic discourse of the time at its starkest and most basic, we can say that the expedition reclassified the Macedonian kings from 'them' to 'us'.[30]

Of course, the reality, even on the level of perceptions, was not so simple. Lane Fox has cautioned against assuming that the Macedonians themselves saw their mission as the suppression of a racially inferior 'other'. He draws attention to a striking feature of the way in which the campaign connected with traditional mythology. Time and again, Alexander encounters physical relics of mythical events and casts himself as the re-enactor – or more often the surpasser – of heroic achievements in the same territories through which he and his armies tramp.[31] He does so not to put the seal on his own superiority over conquered peoples, but to create a sense of *affinity*: Alexander is returning to places his heroic forebears visited, and encountering landscape features reminiscent of, and indeed shaped to resemble, those of his homeland. The lands and peoples Alexander acquires are not rendered 'Other', but rather familiar.[32] This does not, of course,

following year, a move Strootman connects with the killing of Parmenion, to whom they may have been loyal. However, individuals remained with the expedition. For a possible Thessalian name attested at Ai Khanoum see Mairs (2015), 78–79.

[28] Perlman (1969); Flower (2000b), 68–69. As the latter remarks (p. 69), in Greek attitudes 'The notion of profit … is inseparable from that of revenge. The Greeks would exact vengeance by enriching themselves at the expense of Persia.'

[29] On the revenge motif in accounts of Philip's and Alexander's actions see Low (2018), 456.

[30] On the panhellenism of this period as pinned to the theme of attacking Persia see Low (2018), 455–57. Fourth-century panhellenism and its response to the Persian Wars: Marincola (2007).

[31] To take one example among many: according to a (rather sceptical) Arrian, he captured the Aornos Rock even though Herakles himself had failed to do so. Arr., *Anab.* 4.28.1–2.

[32] Lane Fox (2018). Cf. by contrast Gruen (2011), 224–26, who sees such use of myth as 'cultural thievery'.

prevent the process being essentially one of possession: the very pre existing connections between the newly acquired territories and the Macedonian homeland justify their addition to the empire.

Some at least of the Thessalians travelling with Alexander seem to have approached the experience of conquest and exploration in a similar vein. It is interesting to note first of all that the main narratives of Alexander's travels do not mention any Thessalian involvement in Alexander's close personal association with Achilles or with Herakles, the two heroes with whom he and the Thessalians were jointly connected. Scholars have used the remarkable description in Philostratus' *Heroikos* to argue that Alexander's own fervent interest in Achilles and his cult caused a revitalisation of the cult among the Thessalians;[33] however, reading this text as a record of real events is problematic, and there remains no direct and reliable evidence that when Alexander paid his respects at Achilles' tomb the Thessalians were involved in any way.[34] It is not unlikely that Alexander's fervent interest in Achilles stimulated subsequent Thessalian cult (see section 6 below), but we cannot claim that the Thessalians accompanying the king used Achilles as a way of viewing their own eastward journey, or as a Homeric precedent for their own military achievements. Perhaps Alexander's intense personal association with the hero made their identification with him difficult or even politically inexpedient.

They seem instead to have found a different mythic paradigm, one in which the Macedonian king had no claim of his own: Jason. Medea and her son Medeios[35] had long been implicated in how the Greeks perceived, and made sense of, lands east of the Hellespont.[36] Perseus as ancestor of

[33] Ghisellini (2017), 83; Bouchon and Helly (2013), 212–14.

[34] Arr. *Anab.* 1.12.1–2.

[35] Sometimes spelled Medos: see, for example, Apollod. *Bibl.* 1.9.28; Diod. 10.27.1. It is interesting that in the *Theogony* the myth is strongly Thessalian in flavour: Medeios is the son of Jason and Medea and is raised by Cheiron upon their return to Thessaly. By contrast, other later texts make Medeios the son of Medea and Aigeus. This may reflect an Athenian appropriation of the story in the aftermath of the Persian Wars; cf. the connection between Aigeus and the name of the Aegean Sea, manufactured in the fifth century to articulate and justify Athenian maritime supremacy (see Ceccarelli 2012).

[36] Medea as eponym of the Medes: Hdt. 7.62.1. Medeios (son of Medea) as eponym of the Medes goes back to Hes. *Theog.* 1001. This has provoked some discussion: some scholars think that a reference to the Medes is implausible before the sixth century, which risks playing havoc with the dating of the *Theogony*; one solution is to propose a later date for its final section. See West (1966), 430; West (1985, 130) also includes the presence of Medeios among his reasons to date the *Ehoiai* to the sixth century. However, Fowler (2013, 16) notes earlier evidence of Greek awareness of the Medes, and cautions against assuming that only the conditions of the sixth century can have produced a desire to incorporate the Medes in the mythological landscape.

the Persians goes back to Herodotos at least.[37] We saw also, in Chapter 2, the use of the Argonauts' voyage as a mythic forerunner of exploration and colonisation by Greeks in western Asia. At that stage, however, no active Thessalian participation in such use of the myths was discernible. With Alexander, this changes markedly. Strabo cites substantial portions of the work of two Thessalians who accompanied Alexander, Medeios of Larisa and Kyrsilos of Pharsalos, whose myth-historical interpretation of Armenia in particular is very striking.[38] Medeios is a well-attested member of Alexander's entourage.[39] Kyrsilos is far more obscure;[40] however, the name is more strongly attested in Thessaly than any other part of Greece. The father of one of the *gymnasiarchoi* listed in the Pheraian inscription mentioned above was a Kyrsilos. In addition, a fourth-century Kyrsilos is known from an unpublished Pheraian proxeny decree in which he is named as one of the polis' *polemarchoi*;[41] perhaps he was the same man who served as *hieromnēmōn* at Delphi in 324/3.[42] Whether these Pheraian Kyrsiloi had any family relationship with Kyrsilos of Pharsalos the author, we cannot know; certainly families extended between poleis. In any case, the authentic Thessalian identity of the name is secure.

Returning to Medeios, before examining the text itself, we should pause and note how significant the name itself might be. Epigraphic and literary sources reveal a Larisaian family in the fourth century that favoured Medeios (which some authors spell Medios) as a name for its sons. Although the name becomes widespread in the third and second centuries, in the fourth it is far less widely attested, with – in addition to our Larisaians and one Atragian[43] – one example from Athens and one from Hagnous.[44] The first Larisaian Medeios we know of is described by Diodoros as 'Μηδίου δὲ τοῦ τῆς Λαρίσσης τῆς ἐν Θετταλίᾳ δυναστεύοντος' ('Medeios who was powerful in Larisa in Thessaly'); he opposed the power of Lykophron of Pherai, with southern Greek assistance. His son Eurydamas allegedly consorted with Neaira.[45] This Medeios seems to have been the grandfather of Alexander's companion. So already in the second half of the fifth century

37 Hdt. 7.150.2. Note that the idea is here placed in the mouth of Xerxes, who is using it to win the Argives over to his way of thinking; the extent to which it was believed to be true, by Herodotos or any other Greek (let alone Persian!) of the time, is debatable.

38 Bernard (1997); Lücke (2000), 121–22; Traina (2016), 111–12.

39 Heckel (2006), 158.

40 Heckel (2006), 101.

41 *SEG* 49.627, dated to the second half of the fourth century; this could actually be our author, following his return from Asia.

42 *CID* 2.102. Lefèvre (1998), 24.

43 *SEG* 32.584 (with spelling Meideios).

44 *LGPN* s.v. Medeios. For the Larisaian family see Habicht (1970), 265–68.

45 Demosth. 59.108.

a ruling family of Larisa was making the decision to name its scion in such a significant way. What would the name actually have entailed? Would it have evoked the Medes, or Medeia, or a combination of the two?[46] We cannot know. In any case, it suggests a background that might have shaped how his grandson saw his eastward travels and the peoples he encountered, and the mythical lens through which he regarded them.

So rich in detail is Strabo's account, taken from these two Thessalian sources, that it warrants quoting in full.

> There is an ancient story of the Armenian race to this effect: that Armenos of Armenion, a Thessalian city, which lies between Pherai and Larisa on Lake Boibe, as I have already said, accompanied Jason into Armenia; and Kyrsilos the Pharsalian and Medeios the Larisaian, who accompanied Alexander, say that Armenia was named after him … . They also say that the clothing of the Armenians is Thessalian, for example, the long tunics, which in tragedies are called Thessalian and are girded round the breast; and also the cloaks that are fastened on with clasps, another way in which the tragedians imitated the Thessalians, for the tragedians had to have some alien decoration of this kind; and since the Thessalians in particular wore long robes, probably because they of all the Greeks lived in the most northerly and coldest region, they were the most suitable objects of imitation for actors in their theatrical make-ups. And they say that their style of horsemanship is Thessalian, both theirs and alike that of the Medes. To this the expedition of Jason and the Jasonian monuments bear witness, some of which were built by the sovereigns of the country, just as the temple of Jason at Abdera was built by Parmenion. It is thought that the Araxes was given the same name as the Peneios by Armenos and his followers because of its similarity to that river, for that river too, they say, was called Araxes because of the fact that it 'cleft' Ossa from Olympos, the cleft called Tempe. And it is said that in ancient times the Araxes in Armenia, after descending from the mountains, spread out and formed a sea in the plains below, since it had no outlet, but that Jason, to make it like Tempe, made the cleft through which the water now precipitates, and that in consequence of this the Araxene Plain, through which the river flows to its precipitate descent, was relieved of the sea.[47]

[46] Decourt and Tziafalias (2007) tentatively propose that Medeios reflected pro-Persian sympathies, especially since the name Mardonios also occurs. However, Mardonios is attested only much later (time of Augustus: *I.Atrax* 31 and 37). Interestingly, the female name Medeia is virtually unattested, in Thessaly or elsewhere. Did her deeds make a direct association unpalatable when a family was naming a daughter?

[47] Strabo 11.14.12–13: 'ἀρχαιολογία δέ τίς ἐστι περὶ τοῦ ἔθνους τοῦδε τοιαύτη· ἄρμενος ἐξ Ἀρμενίου πόλεως Θετταλικῆς, ἣ κεῖται μεταξὺ Φερῶν καὶ Λαρίσης ἐπὶ τῇ Βοίβῃ, καθάπερ εἴρηται, συνεστράτευσεν Ἰάσονι εἰς τὴν Ἀρμενίαν· τούτου φασὶν ἐπώνυμον τὴν Ἀρμενίαν οἱ περὶ Κυρσίλον τὸν Φαρσάλιον καὶ Μήδιον τὸν Λαρισαῖον, ἄνδρες συνεστρατευκότες

Strategies typical of such mythological analogies abound in this passage. Names are pressed into service: Armenos is created, probably, for this purpose, but Armenia is presented as a form of the name Ormenion, included among the Thessalian sites in the Homeric Catalogue of Ships.[48] Likewise, the hero Armenos is a version of Ormenos, the *oikistēs* of the Homeric Ormenion. Thus the new myths are able to draw upon, and adapt, the authoritative tradition of Homer, while accommodating the real place-name Armenia. Customs also contribute: the Armenians cultivate a Thessalian style of dress and a Thessalian style of riding (the latter surely the essence of the perceived Thessalian character). Traces of Jason's expedition, which Armenos accompanied, are also discovered: the Jasonia, shrines of Jason, which were extrapolated, it has been argued, from the Old Persian word for 'sanctuary', *yāzayan*.[49] To a Greek on the look-out for echoes of his own myth-history, the inexact phonetic match would be unimportant. Finally, and perhaps most strikingly, we find a resurrection of the old Thessalian myth of the cleaving of Tempe. The Araxes has no outlet; Jason, wishing to make it resemble the Peneios of his homeland, creates a channel through which it may escape. In so doing he manufactures a second Thessaly by reference to the mythical tradition which, from the fifth century, provided the 'recipe' for the natural character of Thessaly. He takes on, in effect, the miraculous power of Poseidon; thus Alexander's campaign gives man god-like agency (just as Alexander himself surpassed the deeds of the *hēmitheoi*, and indeed cultivated divine status).

Ἀλεξάνδρῳ... καὶ τὴν ἐσθῆτα δὲ τὴν Ἀρμενιακὴν Θετταλικήν φασιν, οἷον τοὺς βαθεῖς χιτῶνας οὓς καλοῦσιν Θετταλικοὺς ἐν ταῖς τραγῳδίαις, καὶ ζωννύουσι περὶ τὰ στήθη καὶ ἐφαπτίδας, ὡς καὶ τῶν τραγῳδῶν μιμησαμένων τοὺς Θετταλούς· ἔδει μὲν γὰρ αὐτοῖς ἐπιθέτου κόσμου τοιούτου τινός, οἱ δὲ Θετταλοὶ μάλιστα βαθυστολοῦντες, ὡς εἰκός, διὰ τὸ πάντων εἶναι Ἑλλήνων βορειοτάτους καὶ ψυχροτάτους νέμεσθαι τόπους ἐπιτηδειοτάτην παρέσχοντο μίμησιν τῇ τῶν ὑποκριτῶν διασκευῇ ἐν τοῖς ἀναπλάσμασιν· καὶ τὸν τῆς ἱππικῆς ζῆλόν φασιν εἶναι Θετταλικὸν καὶ τούτοις ὁμοίως καὶ Μήδοις. τὴν δὲ Ἰάσονος στρατείαν καὶ τὰ Ἰασόνια μαρτυρεῖ, ὧν τινα οἱ δυνάσται κατεσκεύασαν παραπλησίως ὥσπερ τὸν ἐν Ἀβδήροις νεὼν τοῦ Ἰάσονος Παρμενίων. τὸν δὲ Ἀράξην κληθῆναι νομίζουσι κατὰ τὴν ὁμοιότητα τὴν πρὸς τὸν Πηνειὸν ὑπὸ τῶν περὶ τὸν Ἄρμενον ὁμωνύμως ἐκείνῳ· καλεῖσθαι γὰρ Ἀράξην κἀκεῖνον διὰ τὸ ἀπαράξαι τὴν Ὄσσαν ἀπὸ τοῦ Ὀλύμπου ῥήξαντα τὰ Τέμπη· καὶ τὸν ἐν Ἀρμενίᾳ δὲ ἀπὸ τῶν ὀρῶν καταβάντα πλατύνεσθαί φασι τὸ παλαιόν, καὶ πελαγίζειν ἐν τοῖς ὑποκειμένοις πεδίοις οὐκ ἔχοντα διέξοδον, Ἰάσονα δὲ μιμησάμενον τὰ Τέμπη ποιῆσαι τὴν διασφάγα, δι' ἧς καταράττει νυνὶ τὸ ὕδωρ εἰς τὴν Κασπίαν θάλατταν· ἐκ δὲ τούτου γυμνωθῆναι τὸ Ἀραξηνὸν πεδίον, δι' οὗ τυγχάνει ῥέων ἐπὶ τὸν καταράκτην ὁ ποταμός (trans. Jones, adapted).

[48] Bernard argues convincingly that the two are one and the same rather than separate settlements, and that Armenos and Ormenos are essentially identical. Bernard (1997), 137–38.

[49] Traina (2017), 94.

So, the Thessalians travelling with Alexander thought they were finding a second Thessaly, created in the heroic age of Jason; as Lane Fox puts it, their voyage was a symbolic *nostos*, since in a sense they were coming to a (second) home. We immediately have to temper this image with some caution: we cannot, for example, be sure that either author went in person to Armenia, either with or after Alexander. Another Thessalian, however, almost certainly did: Menon (presumably Pharsalian, given the name), whom Alexander sent to Armenian Syspiritis to inspect the gold-mines there.[50] Menon was conducted to the mines by locals, whose account of the region's culture and legends may well have fed into the stories of the hero Armenos and his Thessalian origins; perhaps his hosts, wishing to cultivate a good working relationship with Alexander's representative, would even have suggested ancestral connections. No doubt Menon could also have seen the landscape around the upper reaches of the Araxes, heard about its outlet, having joined the river Kyros, into the Caspian Sea, and about the fertile valley to which its waters contributed (now in Azerbaijan).[51] Autopsy is not unimportant. However, though Menon was no doubt an important conduit of information about Armenia, the elaborate analogy with Jason's expedition can probably be attributed largely to the significantly named Medeios, predisposed to find Argonautic associations. The fact that Medeios was close to Alexander would also have been important. As has been said, Alexander himself saw the lands he occupied through the lens of myth, finding traces of the earlier presence of his heroic relations – Herakles, Achilles, Midas and others – in the landscapes and customs he encountered.

The use of travelling heroes to legitimise conquest and colonisation through precedent is of course a very old one – indeed, it is a motif that surfaced when we looked at Thessaly's place in Archaic epic, in Chapter 2. Then, however, the Thessalians were rarely discernible as active producers of the epic narratives that survive to be read today; and they were not participants in the major colonising phase of the seventh and sixth centuries. Instead, stories created in Thessaly at an earlier stage, at the tail end of the Bronze Age and in the Early Iron Age, supplied material for composition by other Greeks looking for ways to articulate and reinforce their own voyages and territorial acquisitions. Now, however, as we move to the end of the fourth century and into the third, the Thessalians are more active both in travelling and in story-telling.

[50] Strabo 11.14.9; see Hammond (1996), 134–35.

[51] Great interest in landscape, geography and natural history is shown by the surviving fragments of the work of Polykleitos of Larisa, who also travelled east with Alexander. See *FGrH* 128, esp. F 5–7 and 9–11.

The impossibility of knowing quite when Medeios and Kyrsilos formulated their accounts of Armenia prevents precise placing, but they undoubtedly form a symbolic hinge between the Classical period and the Hellenistic. The fifth century began in Thessaly with, among other things, the Aleuadai welcoming Xerxes' forces into Greece; now in the later fourth century another Larisaian – as well as many Thessalians from other poleis – takes part in an expedition of conquest against the Persians, doing so, moreover, in concert with a ruler from the Macedonian dynasty from whose compliance Xerxes had also benefited. Between these two 'bookends' lies a clear evolution of perceptions. This evolution took Thessaly from the core of Hellenism to its periphery, from being the heartland of Hellas to barely Hellas at all, allied and aligned with *barbaroi*, resembling them in style of life and in moral shortcomings. With Alexander, however, a massive shift commences. Thessalian participation in a panhellenic expedition eastwards is just the start of it; the map of Hellenism is redrawn yet again. However, the Thessalians never escape their association, in the eyes of other Greeks, with decadence and excess. Medeios exemplifies this: he is given a key role in luring Alexander to his doom, pressing him to attend the fatal symposium that brought on his final illness.[52] Alexander himself is presented in all the ancient narratives as losing his attachment to his Macedonian (and in the wider sense, Greek) identity, and instead taking on the trappings of the peoples he conquers; in this process, the cabal of 'flatterers' around him, Medeios included, is seen as central. The lure of Eastern *tryphē* is not, of course, limited to Macedonians and Thessalians in the ancient imagination – it is a trap into which any Greek may fall. But wealthy northerners are seen as especially vulnerable to its appeal, as Chapter 6 made clear. The Thessalian participation in Alexander's campaign does nothing to change this; if anything, it exacerbates the stereotype.

There is no doubt, however, that Alexander's conquest of the Persian Empire caused a radical change to the recipe of Hellenicity. Certainly, the ability of Athens to dominate definitions of Greekness faded as the boundaries of the Greek world expanded. Diverse ethnic groups as far from Greece as Baktria and Pakistan could opt into selected aspects of Greek culture: architecture, visual imagery, language and names, and so on; multicultural and polyglot society flourished in the great hubs of Alexandria and Pergamon; Greekness became a phenomenon widely and variously

[52] Plut. *Alex.* 75; Arr. *Anab.* 7.25.1. Elsewhere (*Adulator* 24) Plutarch depicts Medeios as the leader of a group of flatterers around Alexander whose bad influence led him to reject good men like Parmenion and Philotas and turn instead to people who encouraged his growing love of finery and growing pretension to divinity. While this obviously represents a historiographic *topos* about the corrupting effects of autocratic power, it also recycles the old association between Thessalians and the decadent East.

enacted outside its traditional boundaries. At the same time, communities within 'Greece proper' experienced a new infusion of influences from non-Greek cultures. Thessaly was by no means apart from these processes, as is most startlingly attested, in the earlier second century BC, by the now famous sacred law from Marmarini, about fifteen kilometres to the north-east of Larisa.[53] This remarkable text reveals the worship of a combination of Greek and non-Greek deities at a sanctuary housing a mystery cult. The non-Greek aspects of the cult are themselves not uniform in origin, apparently encompassing Syrian, Anatolian, Mesopotamian and some Egyptian elements; only one of the several non-Greek deities is attested elsewhere. There is a degree of self-consciousness in the inscription itself regarding the combination of Greek and non-Greek elements; one of the provisions allows for the worshippers to θύειν ... τῆι θεῶι Ἑλληνικῶι νόμωι ('sacrifice in the Greek manner') should they wish to. We do not know who these worshippers were, what their ethnicities were, or how the cult came to be established in Thessaly, but its presence in (probably) Pelasgiotis must have changed the religious landscape of the surrounding area considerably. Never in fact isolated, in the Hellenistic period Thessaly was plainly as receptive to the trans-Aegean exchange of customs, beliefs and practices as was any region of Greece.[54]

2. Dodona

The outward-looking focus of much Thessalian activity at this time did not, however, diminish the importance of the traditional cultural centres in Greece itself. Throughout this book, the relationship between Thessaly and Delphi has been shown to be central to the perceived position of Thessaly within Greek identity and its articulation. In the world mapped out in the *Ehoiai*, the Hellenic stemma had its roots on the southern edge of Thessaly, within the heartland of the Delphic Amphiktyony. Inclusion in the Amphiktyony, even though it did not amount to the oft-claimed domination until the mid-fourth century BC, certainly gave Thessaly a key role within one of the cradles of Hellenicity. Under Philip, the Thessalians could once again be presented as serving Apollo's shrine in the interests of Hellas more widely. The third century, however, saw a radical shift, as between ca. 278 and 178 BC the Aitolian dominance of the Amphiktyony

[53] Decourt and Tziafalias (2012) and (2015); Parker and Scullion (2016); Bouchon and Decourt (2017).

[54] Another striking instance of Thessalian religious connectivity before the Hellenistic period is the incidence of 'Orphic' gold tablets and related texts in the region. See Parker and Stamatopoulou (2004); for the intersection between Thessalian eschatology and philosophy see Avagianou (2002).

displaced the Thessalians from the Amphiktyony.[55] This occlusion may well be a factor behind the increased Thessalian interest in Dodona clearly visible at the relevant time (and perhaps also behind other increases in Thessalian activity at panhellenic sanctuaries, such as the enthusiasm for horse and chariot racing: see below, Section 3). In addition to achieving general visibility in a prestigious oracular sanctuary, this association allowed Thessalians to situate themselves within another of the key mainland foci of Hellenicity, although the religious, mythological and political environment was quite different.

While Thessalian interest in Dodona was stirring in the fourth century, it is the figure of Pyrrhos (ruler of Epeiros between 306 and 302 BC, and then, after a period of exile, from 297 to 272), who seems to have been the main factor behind this resurgence in the association.[56] Pyrrhos had a Thessalian mother, Phthia, the daughter of the Menon of Pharsalos who played a distinguished role in the Lamian War;[57] Pyrrhos himself occupied Thessaly in 292 while making war on Demetrios Poliorketes, and overran the region again in 274 after defeating Antigonos Gonatas. After this success, he dedicated captured arms from Antigonos' Gallic soldiers in the temple of Athena Itonia,[58] with the following dedicatory inscription:

> These shields, taken from the brave Galatians, Pyrrhos
> the Molossian hung up as a gift for Itonian Athena,
> having overpowered the whole army of Antigonos. No great wonder:
> the Aiakidai were always spearmen, now and in days past.[59]

55 Sánchez (2002), 270–301.

56 For a comprehensive, if not recent, account of the career of Pyrrhos see Lévêque (1957). On Pyrrhos and Dodona: Piccinini (2016).

57 On Pyrrhos' family background see Plut. *Pyrrh.* 1; Lévêque (1957), 83–89. Thessalian participation in the Lamian War: Diod. 18.15.

58 There is some debate about the location of the sanctuary. At 1.13.2, Pausanias describes it as 'between Pherai and Larisa', which seems to rule out either the Philia site or one in Achaia Phthiotis. Graninger (2011a, 52–54) argues for the existence of a sanctuary of the goddess in Pelasgiotis, but – while his assertion of more than one cult site of the goddess is surely correct – the lack of all other attestation for a Pelasgiotic one makes his theory hard to accept. The fact that Pausanias visited Larisa in person (9.30.9) does not guarantee a perfect recall of Thessalian geography and landmarks. Pyrrhos surely would have made the dedication in the same location visited by the Koan ambassadors, probably Philia (see 4(a) below).

59 Paus. 1.13.3:

> τοὺς θυρεοὺς ὁ Μολοσσὸς Ἰτωνίδι δῶρον Ἀθάνᾳ
> Πύρρος ἀπὸ θρασέων ἐκρέμασεν Γαλατᾶν,
> πάντα τὸν Ἀντιγόνου καθελὼν στρατόν. οὐ μέγα θαῦμα·
> αἰχμηταὶ καὶ νῦν καὶ πάρος Αἰακίδαι.

Cf. Plut. *Pyrrh.* 26.5 and Diod. 22.11, both of whom repeat the inscription.

The last line of this inscription is especially significant: it harks back to Pyrrhos' family legends, and the reference to mighty Aiakid spearmen of the past would have been especially effective near the homeland of Achilles. It was as a descendant of Achilles that Pyrrhos approached this major Thessalian sanctuary.

Pausanias adds an important detail: that while the Galatian shields were dedicated at the sanctuary of Athena Itonia, those from the Macedonian troops were instead taken to the sanctuary of Zeus at Dodona and there dedicated with a further verse inscription. Thus by his two-part offering Pyrrhos twinned Dodona with the Thessalian sanctuary, and Zeus with Athena Itonia. Pyrrhos' interest in Dodona also manifested itself in a considerable programme of building and augmentation in the sanctuary of Zeus at Dodona, which Pyrrhos had plainly decided to designate as his kingdom's religious centre.[60]

Two Thessalian authors seem to have been associated with Pyrrhos and to have responded in their writing to his interest in connecting Thessaly and Dodona. At the lacunose end of what remains of Book Seven, Strabo says:

> But Souidas [*FGrH* 602 F 11a], pandering to the Thessalians with fabulous tales, says that the sanctuary was moved to there [i.e. Dodona] from Pelasgia which surrounds Skotoussa (Skotoussa is in Thessalian Pelasgiotis), and that most of the women from whom the present prophetesses are descended moved along with it; and it is because of this that Zeus is called 'Pelasgian'. Kineas is even more of a fable-monger.[61]

The fragmentary nature of the text unfortunately prevents us from learning about the fictions of Kineas, but Stephanos of Byzantium's dictionary of ethnics, s.v. Δωδώνη, fills in the gaps to some extent, surely consulting Strabo but having access to a part of the work now lost to us:

> And Souidas says [*FGrH* 602 F 11c] that the sanctuary of Zeus Phegonaios [i.e. Zeus 'of the oak'] was in Thessaly, and that it was this that [Achilles] invoked. Others write 'Bodonaios', for there is a polis called Bodone where he is honoured. And Kineas says that the polis was in Thessaly and the oak-tree and the oracle of Zeus were moved [from there] to Epeiros.[62]

60 Kittelä (2013), 44–45.

61 Strabo 7.7.12: 'Σουίδας μέντοι Θετταλοῖς μυθώδεις λόγους προσχαριζόμενος ἐκεῖθέν τέ φησιν εἶναι τὸ ἱερὸν μετενηνεγμένον ἐκ τῆς περὶ Σκοτοῦσσαν Πελασγίας (ἔστι δ' ἡ Σκοτοῦσσα τῆς Πελασγιώτιδος Θετταλίας), συνακολουθῆσαί τε γυναῖκας τὰς πλείστας, ὧν ἀπογόνους εἶναι τὰς νῦν προφήτιδας· ἀπὸ δὲ τούτου καὶ Πελασγικὸν Δία κεκλῆσθαι· Κινέας δ' ἔτι μυθωδέστερον.'

62 'καὶ Σουίδας δέ φησι Φηγωναίου Διὸς ἱερὸν εἶναι ἐν Θεσσαλίαι, καὶ τοῦτον ἐπικαλεῖσθαι. ἕτεροι δὲ γράφουσι Βωδωναῖε· πόλιν γὰρ εἶναι Βωδώνην, ὅπου τιμᾶται.

Exactly what makes Kineas (*FGrH* 603 F 2a and b) ἔτι μυθωδέστερος is not quite clear from these brief descriptions; perhaps it was the transplantation of the sacred oak to which Strabo objected. In any case, we seem to have two authors, Souidas and Kineas, who both told the same basic story: that the oracle of Zeus used to be in Pelasgiotis, near Skotoussa, until it was (in the distant past) moved thence to Molossia.

Whether there is any truth in this at all we cannot know. What is interesting, however, is that these particular authors apparently chose to propagate the story of the oracle's Thessalian origins. Strabo thought that Souidas did so to please the Thessalians, who would indeed stand to gain honour from having a prior claim on the important oracle. However, Kineas' motives may have been slightly different. While Souidas' identity is obscure, light is shed on Kineas by Plutarch's *Life of Pyrrhos*, which describes how Kineas, a Θεσσαλὸς ἀνήρ and an accomplished orator, was used by the Epeirote king for many diplomatic missions.[63] Here, then, we have a Thessalian in the employ of Pyrrhos, who must surely have supported the king's policy of achieving religious connections between the two regions; Kineas' claim about the origin of the oracle must have been designed to please both communities, Thessalian and Molossian.[64] For claiming Thessalian origins was absolutely in keeping with the tenor of Pyrrhos' self-representation in general, a policy which he inherited from his royal predecessors with their Thessaly-infused names.[65]

As for Souidas, we are entirely lacking in information about him apart from what we can glean from his name and work. The fact that he wrote a *Thessalika* does not of course mean he must have been Thessalian himself, but his name indicates that very strongly; all fourteen known instances of the name recorded in the *Lexicon of Greek Personal Names* are from Thessaly

Κινέας δέ φησι πόλιν ἐν Θεσσαλίαι εἶναι, καὶ φηγὸν καὶ τὸ τοῦ Διὸς μαντεῖον εἰς Ἤπειρον μετηνεχθῆναι.'

[63] Θεσσαλὸς ἀνήρ; great eloquence: Plut. *Pyrrh.* 14.1–2. Ambassadorial services: 18.2–3, 21.3, 22.3. Kineas is clearly no mere messenger; he undertakes complex diplomacy on Pyrrhos' behalf.

[64] It is interesting, in this regard, to note that Skotoussa has a Heleneion in its territory, in the second century at least: see *SEG* 43.311, line 47. Was this a sanctuary of Helenos, son of Neoptolemos, as Helly (2018, 369) suggests? If so, it would suggest that the polis cultivated the Aiakid links so crucial to Pyrrhos' self-presentation; while the date of the sanctuary's creation cannot be known, the third century, when authors close to Pyrrhos seem to have promoted Skotoussa's connection with Dodona, would have provided a favourable context. However, cf. Missailidou-Despotidou (1993), 197, suggesting that the Heleneion is likely to have been a sanctuary of Helen.

[65] In this matter I disagree with Parke (1967), 36–39, who argues that Molossians and Thessalians were contending with each other, through such accounts, to claim the original ownership of the sanctuary.

or (in one case, Hypata in Ainis its immediate environs). His date too is uncertain, but I suggest that, since his claim regarding Dodona is so similar to Kineas', we should consider him to be contemporary with Kineas or to have lived and worked not long after him.[66]

3. Thessalian horsemanship in new settings

In Chapter 4, Poseidon held centre-stage as a god of horses and horsemanship. As Petraios he was the god honoured with the unique Thessalian contest of the bull-wrestling, depicted on the first 'co-operative coinage' of the Thessalian poleis in the earlier fifth century BC. His horse-offspring Skyphios was chosen as the key motif on the coins minted in the name of the Thessalian *ethnos*. The Skyphios motif reappears in the fourth century on the coins of Orthe and on the ΠΕΤΘΑΛΩΝ issue; thereafter we lose all evidence of its religious importance on the regional basis. Instead, we have private dedications to Poseidon in a number of horse-related forms. Does this mean that his worship devolved to the polis level entirely?

In all likelihood yes. The only faint suggestion of its continuity in the third century comes from Apollonios' *Argonautika*, in which Aietes driving his chariot is likened to Poseidon driving from one to another of his cult-sites; in the list of places he visits is included 'Haimonian Petra', or 'the Haimonian rock', which the scholiast explains as the site of a festival of Poseidon Petraios. Apollonios uses the present tense, ostensibly the present tense of the poet's own day, but the poet is hardly situating himself in the contemporary reality of his own or his reader's day; his is the bardic voice of epic,[67] and we cannot extrapolate an acquaintance with a flourishing Thessalian Poseidon-festival. That said, the other cult sites listed were active in the third century, and the list does not have a flavour of deliberate archaism or obsolescence. Perhaps, then, we should contemplate the possibility that the Petraia with its bull-wrestling continued in Thessaly in a reduced state.[68] Some quite significant rupture is strongly suggested by the fact that, when the bull-wrestling is incorporated within regional equestrian contests in the second century BC, it is in a wholly different religious setting.

66 Williams (2012).

67 On Apollonios' adaptation of literary traditions see Green (1997), 62–71.

68 There are later glimpses of a Poseidonia festival in Thessaly – see, for example, *IG* IX.2 614b, a lacunose inscription from Larisa, dated to the first century AD, which seems to mention 'the Poseidonia of the Thessalians'. This festival appears to have included equestrian contests, though there is no evidence of bull-wrestling. Perhaps Poseidon continued to receive equestrian contests only on the local level, without much publicisation, while the Eleutheria was the main setting for such events, but then regained a regional festival by the first century AD. See Graninger (2006), 208.

Poseidon has disappeared; instead we have Zeus Eleutherios, and a new festival, the Eleutheria, celebrating the declaration of Greek freedom by Flamininus at the Isthmos in 197 BC. Moreover, though the *taurotheria* must be essentially the same activity as that enacted at the Petraia for Poseidon, the composition of the festival seems different. In non-equestrian events at least, non-Thessalians take part, even Romans. As Graninger has demonstrated in detail, the festival systematically displayed Thessalian identity – in which horsemanship is a crucial ingredient – in a forum not limited to Thessalians, thus ensuring its wider dissemination.[69]

What, however, of the third century, and the curious gap between the apparent effacement of the Petraia and the inauguration of the Eleutheria? In fact, that is just the period in which we see a striking trend: a major surge in Thessalian equestrian victories in the records of victories in the four major panhellenic Crown Games. To understand the significance of this, we must note that, contrary to every reasonable expectation, the Thessalians in the Archaic and Classical periods do not make an especially strong showing in these contests. As noted in Chapter 4, this is not to say that Thessalians were simply not involved in the Crown Games. Seventy Thessalian victories are known from the period between 648 and 84 BC. Among these, the pankration appears as the most popular event, with fifteen known victories; however, there is artificial inflation of this figure by the extraordinary claimed successes of Agias of Pharsalos, recorded in the Daochos Monument discussed in the previous chapter. The same is true of wrestling: in fact, all fourteen attested Thessalian victories in this event are claimed for Agias' brother Telemachos. Without this distortion the most frequently attested event is without doubt the stadion, but again we cannot treat this statistic at face value: the stadion was by far the most frequently recorded event in our surviving victor lists, and so leaves an unnaturally copious record. However, this inflation of the figures for certain events does not remove the significance of the relatively slight equestrian showing.

[69] Graninger (2011a), 74–85. It is interesting to note that the bull-wrestling, thus advertised, seems to catch on. Not only did the Romans under Claudius incorporate the spectacle into their programme of public entertainment (Suet. *Div. Claud.* 21), but the event, called the *taurokathapsia*, appears several times in the epigraphic and visual record of Roman Asia Minor: see Robert (1940). Note, however, that the Eleutheria had a more locally restricted counterpart, the festival – perhaps called the Stena – established to commemorate the battle against Perseus in 172/1 BC. Here the participation seems to be limited to Thessalians, and, in addition to a wide array of equestrian and other contests, there was a performance of commemorative poetry, perhaps recounting recent achievements as well as more ancient ones. See Petrovic (2009), 205–09; on the programme and nature of the Stena see Graninger (2006), 124–32. As Graninger observes, the Stena's programme is the more idiosyncratic, suiting its wholly Thessalian audience.

The disinclination of the famous horsemen of Greece to exploit a seemingly prime opportunity for self-advertisement has been discussed in detail elsewhere.[70] There Kerr and I argue that one important reason was the relationship between the prestige of horses and their social and economic exclusivity. Being able to afford to breed or to buy horses – especially a team for the *tethrippon*, which also entailed the expense of the chariot – was rare in most Greek states, in which the landscape did not sustain large-scale pastoralism, and *hippotrophia* represented a wasteful deployment of scarce natural resources, one only the richest could afford to do. Thessaly, on the other hand, was different: not only did the land allow for extensive grazing, but the military importance of horses made their use far more central to the fabric of communities than they tended to be elsewhere. Because horses were demographically far less exclusive they did not have the special cachet of scarcity, and so were less potent as a means of self-advertisement by a narrow elite. This situation changed, however, in the Hellenistic period, when economic hardship and growing social inequality contributed to a decline in the cavalry and a concomitant interest in racing among the ruling elite.[71]

We may also, however, view the matter from a more positive angle and ask what the Thessalians racing their horses at Crown Games in the Hellenistic period hoped to achieve by doing so, in terms of self-advertisement and other, more tangible benefits. In terms of the former, the poems of Poseidippos are our most important resource, since they allow us to glimpse how Thessalian victors wanted their achievements to be viewed, and in what terms they were couched. The verses in the *Hippika*, a section in the so-called 'New Poseidippos' found in 1992 and published in 2002, have revolutionised our understanding of Thessalian self-presentation and equestrian participation in the third century BC.[72]

At this point we must pause to consider the nature of Poseidippos' work.[73]

[70] Aston and Kerr (2018). For a comparable survey of the fluctuating popularity of racing within a particular community, against the backdrop of shifting political ideology, see Golden (1997).

[71] The best illustration of these conditions comes from the third-century inscription discussed in Helly and Tziafalias (2013). The text records the sale, at Larisa, of public lands traditionally allocated for the growing of fodder-crops for horses, surely cavalry horses. By the time the sale is held, the land is being used for different purposes (to build on, to grow crops for human consumption); the old system of polis investment in horse maintenance has broken down. The polis sells off the plots of land to raise emergency revenue in a time of shortage, to meet immediate military needs.

[72] On the circumstances and impact of the discovery see Bing (2009).

[73] Poseidippos himself is epigraphically attested, first in a proxeny decree from Delphi, dating to the mid-270s (*FD* III 3 192), and second in a proxeny decree from Aitolian Thermon, dating to some time 262–236 BC (*IG* IX.1² 1:17), in which he

The *Hippika* take the form of epigrams, most of them short, purporting to be written to accompany statues commemorating the victories to which the texts refer. In other words, they are very different from the long *epinikia* of Pindar, Bacchylides and Simonides at the end of the sixth century and the beginning of the fifth. They are to be viewed more in the tradition of Greek verse inscriptions; but this begs the question of whether they were ever inscribed. Nothing in their content precludes the notion that they were indeed commissioned by victors to accompany the kinds of statue (often equestrian) that were set up in sanctuaries and sometimes in the home town of the victor. However, none has ever been found *in situ*, on stone, and it is likely that their epigraphic form is merely a poetic trope.[74] In any case, from the poet's point of view the most significant stage of dissemination must have been when the poems were collected in papyrus form, and circulated thus in third-century Alexandria and beyond.[75] In other words, though the *Hippika* may possibly have been commissioned to accompany statues, their life was never limited to stone: they travelled freely on more portable material, and would have been read alongside Poseidippos' other works, by readers not especially interested in the victories or the victors.[76]

Even if never inscribed in stone, the *Hippika* certainly do record real victories. We know this because many of them laud famous individuals, especially the Ptolemies, to whose victories ten out of the eighteen poems in the group are dedicated.[77] The majority of these victories are those won by the chariot of one Berenike, who is most plausibly identified as the daughter of Ptolemy II Philadelphos and sister of Ptolemy III Euergetes, she who was later called 'Syra' because she married Antiochos II Theos, the Seleukid king. (However, in the poems she is still unmarried, a *parthenos* and princess.)[78] These victories sit among a notable enthusiasm

is actually referred to as Πο̣[σ]ε̣ιδ̣ί̣ππωι τῶι ἐπιγραμματοποιῶι Πελλαίωι, Poseidippos of Pella, the epigrammatist (line 24). Bing (2009), 182–84: he makes the point that Poseidippos' public recognition, and his designation as ἐπιγραμματοποιός, strongly suggest that he did indeed create verses for public monuments. On inscribed epigram and public oral performance see Petrovic (2009), esp. 203–12.

74 A dissenting voice: De Rossi (2019), who argues that the epigrams praising Thessalian horses would have accompanied statues set up in a stud in Thessaly and used to advertise Thessalian breeding stock. This is a tempting suggestion, but no activity of such a kind is otherwise attested.

75 On the structure and artistry of the arrangement see Fantuzzi (2004).

76 Kosmetatou (2004) demonstrates that they build on a long tradition of victory commemoration, in the form of both monuments and *epinikia*, but that they do so in accordance with the poetic tendencies of the third century.

77 Remijsen (2009).

78 Note, however, the argument of Clayman that we should not read too literally the descriptions of Berenike as a *parthenos* – she was an 'honorary virgin'. Clayman (2014),

for – and success in – racing on the part of the Ptolemies, a habit that allowed them to combine the traditional Pharaonic interest in racing with an appeal to traditional Greek and Macedonian ideals of equestrian accomplishment.[79] Nor was it otherwise unheard of for them to employ the services of a poet to commemorate their successes. Kallimachos, for example, lauded the chariot victory of another Berenike, the wife of Ptolemy III Euergetes, at Nemea in the 240s.[80] One of Poseidippos' poems records a victory by the chariot of Polykrates of Samos, admiral of the Ptolemaic fleet and important member of the court circle.[81] Kallimachos would go on to record a victory of Sosibios, chief minister of Ptolemy IV Philopatōr, reinforcing the impression that important associates of the ruling dynasty were included in their enthusiasm for racing and in their commemorative strategies.[82] Poseidippos' subjects therefore have the ring of historical veracity, and it is inconceivable that his non-Ptolemaic *laudandi* are, by contrast, simply invented.

Among these non-Ptolemaic *laudandi*, the most numerous group are the Thessalians, who receive four epigrams celebrating seven victories. (A narrow Thessalian defeat is also mentioned in AB 74.) The chance survival of this corpus of verse, which was discovered in the wrappings of a mummy in Milan, and first published in 2001, must to some extent skew our data and contribute to the peak in Thessalian hippic victories in the period 300–250 BC. However, we have sufficient other sources – in particular the anonymous chronicle of Olympic victories, *FGrHist* 257a (P.Oxy. XVII 2082) – to indicate that the trend is not an artificial one. The anonymous chronicle lists four Thessalian hippic victories, all between 296 and 268/7 BC. By contrast, in the period 300–250 BC only two non-hippic victories by Thessalians are known. This reverses the pattern of the Archaic and Classical periods, in which athletic victories substantially outnumbered equestrian ones in the Thessalian tally. Why did the Thessalians become so interested in participating in hippic victories at that very specific time?

152. Dating the victories commemorated by Poseidippos therefore defies absolute certainty.

[79] Fantuzzi (2005), 250–51. In addition to family members in the strict sense, note the victories of Bilistiche, supposedly the mistress of Ptolemy II Philadelphos: *FGrHist* 257a F 6; Paus. 5.8.11; Plut. *Amat.* 9; Euseb. *Chron.* 1.207; Athen. 13.596E. For discussion of the racing craze of Hellenistic dynasts see Van Bremen (2007). Bilistiche: Ogden (2008), 365–79.

[80] Van Bremen (2007), 349–50.

[81] Bing (2002–2003), 244.

[82] Fr. 384 Pfeiffer.

Remijsen and Scharff have drawn attention to some important features of the poems' presentation of Thessalian ethnicity.[83] The following verse illustrates some of the salient themes:

> This victorious horse, exalted for its speed, I, Amyntas,
> have brought from my own herd
> to you, Pisan Zeus, and I did not make an end of
> my Thessalian fatherland's ancient fame for horses.[84]

The poem emphasises the fact that Amyntas has brought his winning racehorse from his *patris*, Thessaly: this is significant because Thessaly is being presented as a land with a traditional reputation – *doxa* – for horses. In a sense, this tradition is a manufactured one, in that, as has been said, Thessaly did not have an especially substantial past record of racing. However, the poet is instead drawing on a more general association between Thessaly and horses, established as early as the *Iliad*[85] and enjoying regular repetition and allusion through the span of ancient literature. Racing at the Crown Games obviously provided Hellenistic Thessalians with the opportunity to revive that traditional association and to press it into service with specific reference to racing in a way that had not been done before. The fact that horses and horsemanship were always a feature of the regional stereotype rather than being linked to any particular polis connects with the observation of Remijsen and Scharff that Poseidippos, unlike Pindar, leaves the polis out of the picture altogether. In the panhellenic milieu that Poseidippos is evoking, the broad-brush 'Thessalian' is evocative, the polis simply insignificant.[86] It is interesting to consider, as Remijsen does,[87] some reflection of wider contemporary practice, since inscribed victor lists of the third century seem somewhat more inclined to omit the polis ethnic than do their fourth-century or indeed their second-century counterparts. However, the data are not copious or consistent enough to allow for genuine chronological comparison.

[83] Remijsen and Scharff (2015).

[84] Poseidippos AB 85:

> ἀθλοφόρο]ν ταχυτᾶτι διάκριτον ἵππον Ἀμύντας
> τοῦτον ἀ]π' οἰκείας ἀγαγόμαν ἀγέλας
> πρὸ[ς] σ[έ, Ζε]ῦ Πισᾶτα, καὶ οὐ κατέλυσα παλαιᾶς
> δόξας [εἰν] ἵπποις πατρίδα Θεσσαλίαν.

(Trans. Kosmetatou and Acosta-Hughes, https://chs.harvard.edu/english-hippika, adapted.)

[85] Hom. *Il.* 2.761–70.

[86] As Scharff (2016) notes, whereas in early Classical epinikian the identity of the victor's polis is emphasised alongside regional identity, in this Hellenistic verse the polis is omitted and all the focus is on Thessaly.

[87] Remijsen (2019), 36–37.

Let us return to the factors that may have prompted the rise in Thessalian equestrian victories in the first half of the third century especially. One possible benefit would be contact with the Ptolemies, or at least with their representatives. It must have been clear in the earlier third century that Philadelphos and Euergetes and their families were investing their energies in the panhellenic Games; if one wanted to cultivate some acquaintance, or at least gain their notice, then participating in those Games would have been a promising way of going about it. Here it is important to note the decided Thessalian preference at this time for the *kelēs teleios*, or jockey-race for full-grown horses.[88] This was not wholly new,[89] but now it took on a fresh strategic value. In networking terms, it would have been decidedly counter-productive to compete constantly against the Ptolemies in their own favoured event of the *tethrippon*, and risk beating them. The *kelēs teleios* allowed the Thessalians to display their equestrian credentials without encroaching on royal preserve. In terms of expenditure, display and glamour, it was a lesser event than the *tethrippon*. But it still allowed them a certain proximity to the Ptolemies: both groups flourishing their *hippotrophia*, without direct competition.

Though it is impossible to prove beyond doubt that Thessalians and Ptolemies (or their agents) actually made use of the prime networking opportunity of the Games, the presence of Thessalians at Alexandria – some in very significant positions of cultural influence – suggests that a complete lack of interaction is very unlikely. In particular, two of the chief priests in Alexandria's official cult of the deified Alexander were Thessalians: in 263/2, Kineas son of Alketas, and in 257/6, Antiochos son of Kebbas.[90] This would have placed them in a central role in maintaining the asserted link between the Ptolemies and the Argead dynasty whose legitimate successors they claimed to be.[91] As the third century progresses we find more

[88] Examples in Poseid. *Hipp.* 71, 83, 84, 85; one each in POxy XVII 2082 = *FGrH* 257a F 4 and F6. On the categories of competition in operation by the mid-third century see Mann and Scharff (2022).

[89] In 648 BC, a Thessalian called Krauxidas was apparently the first winner of the *kelēs teleios* upon the introduction of the event into the Olympic programme: Paus. 5.8.8. One Echekratidas of Thessaly apparently won the same event in 464 BC: Pliny, *NH* 10.180.

[90] Kineas: Clarysse and Van der Veken (1983), 6, no. 28; Antiochos: page 8, no. 34. Kineas is especially interesting: in 267 BC he was an athletic victor at the Basileia festival in Alexandria (see *SEG* 27.1114). The contest is not equestrian, but once again *agōnes* are plainly instrumental in links between Thessaly and Ptolemaic Egypt. Remijsen (2019), 36; Koenen (1977), 19–28.

[91] In 272/1 BC the priest of Alexander was the very Kallikrates of Samos celebrated in Poseidippos AB 74: in that poem his horses are described as winning against a Thessalian chariot, so we know that the Ptolemies' admiral would have been at the

Thessalians, and not only illustrious individuals. The military presence of Thessalians in Hellenistic Egypt was especially significant. The formula 'the cavalry-command [*hipparchia*] of the Thessalians and of the other Greeks' is a stock phrase in the papyri of the period when identifying the unit to which a person belongs, and while it is unlikely that membership of the 'Thessalian *hipparchia*' was actually limited to Thessalians by this time, the expression conveys the importance of the Thessalian cavalry within the Ptolemaic armies.[92] Funerary monuments – both their style of decoration and their inscriptions – reveal a desire by Thessalian cavalrymen in fourth- and third-century Alexandria to emphasise their ethnic origin as well as their equestrian identity.[93]

One more practical motivation remains to be considered. As Fantuzzi observes, the Ptolemies took pains to present themselves as Macedonian, and as the true inheritors of the Heraklid identity of the Argead dynasty.[94] This may have fuelled their interest in Kos, another setting where – as we shall see in Section 4 – Thessalian connections constituted important cultural capital. For the Thessalians, they would surely have presented a far more palatable model of Macedonian ethnicity than the Antigonids, who controlled their region by force. Moreover, during the earlier third century, the Ptolemies would have seemed to offer Greece – including Thessaly – a genuine possibility of challenging Antigonid rule. Ptolemy II Philadelphos supported Athens and Sparta against Macedon in the Chremonidean War (267–261 BC), which ended in failure and in a defeat for the Egyptian fleet sent out to assist the Athenians.[95] Ptolemy III Euergetes did not risk direct military engagement with the Antigonids' forces, but continued his father's strategy of supporting their opponents: the Achaian League (from the late

same festival, and in the same event, as a Thessalian team: could he have been a link between the Thessalians and the Ptolemies? It is quite possible, though it cannot be proved.

92 On the Ptolemaic cavalry and its use of different ethnic contingents see Fischer-Bovet (2014), 126–27, 173–74, 177, 192–93. In addition to the rank and file, two Thessalians occupied important positions in the Ptolemaic army during the Syrian Wars in the reign of Ptolemy IV Philopator, ca. 219–217. One was Echekrates, who trained the mercenary cavalry and fought at the battle of Raphia: see Polyb. 5.65. The other was Hippolochos, who actually deserted from Ptolemy to Antiochos and ended up fighting at Raphia on the Seleukid side: Polyb. 5.70, 71, 79.

93 Cole (2019).

94 Fantuzzi (2005), 251–52. See also Scharff (2019).

95 Grabowski (2020) questions whether Ptolemy II ever had any serious intention of wresting control of Greece away from the Antigonids; however, the Thessalians would not necessarily have been aware of the limits of his ambitions. For an overview of the events see Buraselis (1982), 155–60; Gabbert (1997), 45–53; on the war's dates and the motives behind it see O'Neil (2008).

240s to 226/5), the Spartans and – following the accession of Antigonos Doson – the Aitolians, who saw their growing control over Thessaly threatened by this formidable new ruler.[96]

So the sudden surge of Thessalian hippic victories at the major Crown Games in the first half of the third century BC is best explained as an attempt to cultivate Ptolemaic connections at a time when these seemed to offer an attractive possibility of weakening Macedonian influence in northern Greece. Both the Thessalians and the Ptolemies could present horse/chariot racing as part of their inherited tradition, even if, as has been said, this claim had a slightly shaky basis on the Thessalian side: Amyntas linked equestrian excellence with the long-standing *doxa* of his *patris*, Thessaly; Berenike's victories are presented as a continuation of the accomplishments of her forebears, whose Macedonian identity is emphasised. The *agōnes hippikoi* provided a prestigious context in which representatives of the two *ethnē*, Thessalian and Macedonian, could meet and evoke a glorious past that they shared and from which others were excluded. In a sense, this is reminiscent of the role of Delphi in the fourth century BC, allowing Philip and his Thessalian allies (especially Daochos) to reinforce their shared mythical heritage through reference to the Aiakid Neoptolemos.[97]

Our evidence suggests that the Thessalians withdrew almost entirely from the panhellenic Crown Games from the mid-third century onwards, but this does not mean that their athletes, or their horses, were idle. Instead, they found new opportunities for competition, especially at certain of the regional festivals that arose, or were enlarged and revived, at this time. The vagaries of the survival of victor lists prevents a complete picture of the ebbs and flows of Thessalian participation, but it is clear that Boiotia was a favourite destination for Thessalian athletes and horses. In the case of the Amphiaraia at Oropos, we have a sizable gap between an inscription of 329/8 BC in which Thessalians feature[98] and a more substantial corpus of records from the period 80–50 BC in which Thessalians again appear.[99] The

[96] Mackil (2013), 111.

[97] See Aston (2012b) and Chapter 6 above.

[98] *Epigr. tou Or.* 520: a Thessalian (polis not indicated) wins the men's kithara contest; a Larisaian wins the boys' diaulos; a Pharsalian wins the men's pentathlon. Nielsen (2014), 107–08.

[99] *Epigr. tou Or.* 522, most of which is legible: Larisaians win the men's stadion, the men's diaulos, the men's *hippios* (a foot-race), the men's boxing. Larisa is the only Thessalian polis represented. *Epigr. tou Or.* 528: one Thessalian, a Larisaian again, who wins the boys' pentathlon. 529: suddenly a greater variety of Thessalian poleis are present, with a Pelinnaian winning the *kelēs pōlikos*, Krannonians winning the *harma pōlikon* and the *harma teleion* and a Larisaian winning the *kelēs teleios*. When all three lists are considered together, imperfect record though they are, it is clear that Thessalians are not, as a group, choosing to specialise either in athletic or hippic *agōnes*.

lacuna is in the availability of lists – perhaps reflecting a period of decline in the festival – rather than in the participation of Thessalians. Elsewhere in Boiotia, we find a Thessalian as victor in the *synōris teleios* (chariot race for two mature horses) in a list from the second-century Basileia festival at Lebadeia (unfortunely a more precise dating is impossible).[100] In the early first century a Thessalian from Kierion won the trumpeters' contest at the Mouseia in Thespiai.[101]

These Boiotian instances, and the scattering of Thessalians in the records of other festivals, confirm the picture of an outgoing, connected Thessaly using festivals to ensure inclusion in a wide range of regional and inter-regional religious networks. Although no Thessalians appear in the surviving victor lists of Athenian festivals,[102] that Thessaly was included in the circuit of the Athenian festival announcers, proclaiming the Panathenaia and the Eleusinia, is clear from an inscription from Gonnoi concerning the selection of a *theorodokos*.[103] Though their relatively short-lived enthusiasm for the *agōnes hippikoi* at the four major Crown Games may have waned, the Thessalians of the later period plainly continued to cultivate the connections that festival participation could supply.

To sum up, this section has established the continued relevance of horses and horsemanship in religious contexts in which Thessalians were active participants. However, whereas in the Classical period panhellenic festivals were apparently of little interest compared with the Thessalian festival of the Petraia – at which a unique regional contest allowed for the articulation of what made Thessaly Thessaly – in the first half of the third century we see the panhellenic Crown Games achieving more significance for purposes of display. There, the Thessalians could demonstrate the equestrian excellence with which their region was firmly associated on the wider stage, and build important networks in the process. They did not wholly depart from traditional practices, such as the preference for horse races over chariot races. But they were operating as Greeks among Greeks, rather than as Thessalians among Thessalians. Only in the second century would the special Thessalian contest of the *taurotheria* regain its centrality for the Thessalians, and then it would have quite a different character from that of the Petraia, with audiences including Greeks from outside

[100] *SEG* 3.367.
[101] *IG* VII.1760.
[102] The Pharsalian pentathlete mentioned in Plut. *Per.* 36.3 may, as Nielsen observes (2014, 113), have competed in the Panathenaia at a much earlier date. A Panathenaic amphora from Larisa dating to the 440s indicates another instance of Thessalian participation in the festival: see Stamatopoulou (2007a), 335–36. However, no Hellenistic instances survive.
[103] Helly (1973), vol. II, 109.

Thessaly, and even Romans. Once again, special Thessalian skills would be demonstrated, but this time before a more diverse range of spectators.

4. Thessalos: an eponym abroad

a) The hero reappears

The same combination of continuity and innovation is discernible with regard to the figure of Thessalos, who reappears in the third century thanks to the important inscription from Aigai in the Troad, mentioned above – the only clear attestation, to date, of the hero-cult of Thessalos himself.[104] In Chapter 3 it was shown that the myth of the Heraklid Thessalos and his family was probably first cultivated in western Thessaly, before being appropriated and disseminated in the leading poleis of Pelasgiotis in the late sixth and early fifth centuries. By the mid-fifth century the tradition of the Thessalids' arrival over the Pindos had started to be replaced by that of the Thessaloi, an invading *ethnos*, which could be adapted to provide a charter-myth for all Thessalians, rather than just narrow elites. However, it must be remembered that the figure of Thessalos is first attested earlier, in the *Iliad*. There his sons lead contingents from Kos and surrounding areas. At that stage, we considered the possibility of both Koan and Thessalian agency in the formulation of the myths. However, in our third-century context there is no doubt that we have a dialogic situation in which Thessalos is of interest on both sides of his story's geographical range. So important is the inscription revealing this that it is worth quoting in full.

> Speudoun the priest (proposes a decree expressing) the gratitude of the Thessalians at the Olympia which the Thessalians conduct. Since Speudoun the priest of Zeus Olympios reported the goodwill which the Aiolians, Koans and Magnesians from the Maeander displayed towards the Thessalians – for all the cities performed a rite and sacrifice to Olympian Zeus and the hero Thettalos and the other gods and invoked in common for all the Thessalians and for their own people safety, good fortune, good offspring – the Thessalians have voted them freedom from duties on everything except on what they bring or export by way of trade, and citizenship for all of them wherever they wish in Thessaly, and that cities and cults and everything else be shared by them as they are by Thessalians. And the Aiolians, Koans and Magnesians from the Maeander shall have marriage rights wherever they wish in Thessaly. Speudoun the priest shall write up the decree on stone stelai and (set them up) in the Olympion and in Itounos and in Lassa [i.e. Larisa] in the shrine of Apollon Kerdoios. And let there be inscribed there also the names of all the cities

[104] Bouchon and Helly (2013), 209–10; Mili (2015), 248–54.

participating in the sacrifice to Zeus Olympios and the competition. The decree was proposed at the Olympia, when Speudoun was priest of the Olympian for the second time, and in Lassa Timounidas son of Alexias, Astonoos son of Lagetas, Hipparchos son of Soukrateis, Hippodromos son of Pantaponos, Klearchos son of Deinippos were tagoi.[105]

As Parker has observed, Larisa is visibly dominant on the Thessalian side of this exchange.[106] The festival of the Olympia and the sanctuary called the Olympion were probably in their territory, though its precise

[105] *SEG* 59.1406 B:

Σπεύδουν ὁ λείτορας τὰν εὐχαριστίαν Πετ-
θαλοῦν ἐν Ὀλυμπίοις τοῖς Πετθαλοῖ ἀγοῦσι·
ὀπειδεὶ ἐξάγγελλε Σπεύδουν ὁ λείτορας τ-
οῖ Διὸς τοῖ Ὀλυμπίοι τὰν εὔνοιαν τὰν εἴχοιε-
ν ποτὶ Πετθαλὸς Αἰολεῖες, Κοῦοι, Μάγνειτες
οἱ ἀπὺ Μαιάνδροι – τοῦ τε γὰρ Δὶ τοῦ Ὀλυμπίου
καὶ εἴρουϊ Πετθαλοῦ καὶ τοῖς ἄλλοις θεοῖς
τελετὰν καὶ θυσίαν πεποεῖσθαι τὰς πόλις π-
άνσας καὶ εὔξασθαι Πετθαλοῖς πάντεσσι καὶ
τοῦ δάμου τοῦ ἑαυτοῦν κοινᾶ σουτειρίαν, εὐ-
τυχίαν, εὐγονίαν –, ἐψάφισαν οἱ Πετθαλοὶ ἀτέ-
λειαν ἔμμεν αὐτοῖς πάντουν πλὰν εἰ πόσσα κ-
ε ἐπ ἐμπορία ἄγουνθι εἶ ἐξάγουνθι, καὶ πολι-
τείαν πάντεσσι πᾶ νά κε βέλλουνθαι Πετθαλί-
ας καὶ ἔμμεν αὐτοῖς καὶ πόλις καὶ ἱερὰ κοιν-
ὰ καὶ τὰ ἄλλα πάντα καττάπερ Πετθαλοῖς ἔνθι·
καὶ ἐπιγαμίαν ἔμμεν Αἰολείεσσι, Κούοις, Μα-
γνείτεσι τοῖς ἀπὺ Μαιάνδροι πᾶ νά κε βέλλο-
υνθαι Πετθαλίας· ὀνγράψαι μὰ τὸ ψάφισμα Σπ-
εύδονα τὸν λείτοραν ἐν στάλας λιθίας καὶ
[. .]ΤΕΘΕΙΜΕΝ ἐν Ὀλύμπιον καὶ ἐν Ἴτουνον καὶ
ἐν Λάσσαν ἐν [τὸ ἱε]ρὸν τοῖ Ἄπλουνος τοῖ Κερδ-
οίοι· ἐγγράφειμεν αὐτ[εῖ]καὶ πολίουν τὰ ὀνύ-
ματα πανσᾶν τᾶν κοινανενσᾶν τᾶς θυσίας Δι-
ὸς τοῖ Ὀλυμπίοι καὶ τοῖ ἀγοῦνος· ἐγράφει τὸ
ψάφισμα ἐν Ὀλυμπίοις, λειτορεύοντος δὶς τ-
οῖ Ὀλυμπίοι Σπεύδουνος, ταγευόντουν ἐν Λά-
σσα Τιμουνίδα Ἀλεξία, Ἀστονόοι Λαγέτα, Ἱππ-
άρχοι Σουκράτεος, Ἱπποδρόμοι Πανταπόνοι,
Κλεάρχοι Δεινίπποι.

Text: Malay and Ricl (2009); trans. Parker (2011).

[106] Parker (2011), 113–15; cf. Bouchon and Helly (2013): at p. 223 they make the broader observation that 'L'État fédéral de l'époque héllenistique et romaine se présente désormais comme une organisation qui a été centralisée et contrôlée à partir de Larisa.' The prominence of the polis in regional and supra-regional religious activity is therefore a reflection of this political centrality.

location is unknown; their sanctuary of Apollo Kerdoios was one of the three Thessalian locations in which the decree was to be posted up. However, the reference to Itounos (Itonos) as another publication site is significant. This was also the destination of Koan ambassadors coming to Thessaly to announce the Asklepieia a few decades later (see below),[107] and the place where Koan ambassadors formally announced the honours paid to the Thessalians as a reward for supplying grain to Kos in a time of shortage.[108] Debate surrounds the location of this site: should we take it as referring to the sanctuary of Athena Itonia at Philia in Thessaliotis,[109] or to the site in Achaia Phthiotis, related perhaps to Iton in the Catalogue of Ships, where there may have been a second shrine of the goddess?[110] The latter would perhaps have the merit of relative convenience for visitors from across the Aegean. However, given the strong and long-standing resonance between Thessalid mythology and the Philia site,[111] the Thessaliotis location is somewhat preferable. This would make for significant implications: otherwise, it is only in the second century, after the establishment of the new Thessalian *koinon*, that we find Philia acting as the repository of collective Thessalian decrees and exercising a religious role as a true federal sanctuary. It seems that the second-century *koinon* continued a pattern emerging at the latest in the century before, rather than innovating *ex nihilo*.

As for the actors on the other side, the 'Aiolians, Koans and Magnesians from the Maiandros', the combination is fascinating. Each group severally did cultivate Thessalian connections in the Hellenistic period, as we shall see, and in each case those connections were founded upon the very flexible concept of *syngeneia* – kinship – but this basic truth should not make us overlook the diversity of their motivations. The Koans and Magnesians will be discussed in more detail below; here let us consider the Aiolians. At first glance their interest seems completely predictable. From the fifth century BC, if not earlier, there was a well-established ancient perception that the 'original Aiolis' – that is to say, the original homeland of the Aiolians of Asia Minor – was somewhere in northern Greece, whether Aitolia (as

107 *IG* XII.4 1:207.

108 *IG* XII.4 1:133, ca. 294–288 BC. See Segre (1934); Garnsey et al. (1984), 35–36; Bosnakis and Hallof (2010), 330–41. It seems likely that in the *Epibomios*, one of the ancient biographical pastiches of the Hippokratic corpus and a close companion of the *Presbeutikos* in purpose and composition context, Hippokrates is to be imagined in the same sanctuary of Athena Itonia when he appeals to the Thessalians for help in the face of Athenian aggression against Kos; he says explicitly that the altar he is standing at is Athena's, though her cult title Itonia is not used. On this text see Smith (1990), 4–6.

109 For the use of the name Itonos for this sanctuary see Tziafalias and Helly (2004–2005), 397.

110 Strabo 9.5.14. See Intzesiloglou (2006), 235–42; Graninger (2011a), 55–64.

111 See Chapter 3.

Thucydides thought) or Thessaly (as in Herodotos); the very vagueness reflects the fact that these are traditions developed by the Aiolians of the eastern Greek world, whose acquaintance with northern Greece will no doubt have been slight.[112] This built upon the Archaic tradition placing Aiolos and his descendants primarily in central and northern Greece, in which Thessalian agency was, as has been argued, questionable. However, the apparent simplicity of the connection between the Aiolians and the Thessalians should in this context be scrutinised: after all, what interest had the Aiolians in Thessalos? The arrival of the Thessalids in Thessaly marked a rupture in Thessalian myth-historical identity, away from the compendious Aiolid stemma; the sanctuary at Philia was connected with this myth, and the elite of Larisa tended to identify as Heraklid rather than Aiolid, inasmuch as one can ascertain their mythic identification at all. We are alerted thus to a key feature of these Hellenistic religious interactions, one that will recur several times in this chapter: that they are 'baggy' enough to encompass a variety of different motivations and interests on the part of the actors, and that the concept of *syngeneia* is rarely applied with strict regard to precise heroic lineage. The activity attested in the Aigai inscription was not limited to the rite and sacrifice for Thessalos, in any case; the Olympia, with its supremely generic name and recipient, will have ensured that there was something on offer for everyone.

The involvement of Kos, on the other hand, is different. Not only did they have an early link with the hero Thessalos, as reflected in the Catalogue of Ships, but in the early and mid-third century they deepened their specific connection with Thessalian communities and placed diplomacy with Thessaly at the heart of their mythological and religious identity. This had two aspects: first, their diplomatic interest was directed broadly at a number of Thessalian communities, both tetradic and perioikic; second, there are signs that two poleis, Larisa and Trikka, were particular recipients of Koan attention.

b) Thessalian communities and the Koan asylia *bid*

The third century BC was the heyday of the Koan Asklepios cult.[113] The sanctuary itself underwent a programme of new building, and in 242 it

[112] Compare the Dorian homeland in central Greece, a subject of great ignorance among most of the Greeks positing its role as the origin-point of the Dorians. Beck (2019), 396; Rousset (2015), 222–25.

[113] It should be noted that none of the excavated remains of the sanctuary of Asklepios on Kos pre-dates the mid-fourth century BC, and it is likely that the cult began during the phase of its rapid diffusion across Greece, from the late fifth century onwards, a process driven by the importance of Epidauros. Riethmüller (2005), 206–07 and 229–40. For an overview of the sanctuary and the cult see Paul (2013), 167–87.

was formally granted the condition of *asylia* – ritual inviolacy.[114] This was the culmination of a process of energetic diplomacy in which ambassadors travelled through the Greek world obtaining the agreement of many communities for *asylia* to be granted;[115] the inscriptions recording these agreements, which were set up in the sanctuary, provide a significant insight into the religious network within which the Asklepieion operated, even though not every text is extant or published.[116] In the corpus we do have, several texts from Thessaly and its *perioikis* are included.[117] On a single piece of stone (*SEG* 53.850) are recorded the decrees of Phthiotic Thebes, Gonnoi and Homolion (as well as Megara). There is a second inscription, sadly lacunose, on which *asylia* grants by two further Thessalian cities (names missing, but with unmistakeable Thessalian dialect) are recorded.[118]

By bitter ill-fortune, whenever the text in *SEG* 53.850 indicates explicitly the name of the *ethnos* of which the granting city was part, the name of the *ethnos* has fallen prey to damage to the stone. The inscriptions from Gonnoi and Homolion contain a formula indicating that the connection forged was *both* between the two poleis (Kos and its northern Greek counterpart) *and* between Kos and the *ethnos* as a whole; however, in every case the name of the *ethnos* is illegible. Rigsby chose to restore καὶ τῶι ἄλλωι ἔθνει τῶι Θεσσαλῶν,[119] which would suggest that, for the Koans at least, perioikic communities were considered part of the Thessalian *ethnos*. However, Helly puts forward arguments for restoring instead the names of perioikic *ethnē*: Περραιβῶν in the case of Gonnoi, and Μαγνητῶν in the case of Homolion. His reasoning is largely historical rather than strictly epigraphic: he simply believes it to be inaccurate to consider either Gonnoi or Homolion as part of Thessaly. In this he is substantially justified, but we have to take into account both the external perspective of the Koans (who largely dictated the text of the inscriptions)[120] and the slight ambiguity of the wording. This latter is illustrated by

114 Rigsby (1996), 106–11.

115 For their possible itinerary see Bosnakis and Hallof (2003), 233–34; Rigsby (2004), 11–12.

116 For discussion of the *asylia*-bid and of the inscriptions see Rigsby (1996), 106–11.

117 As Rigsby observes (2004, 12), while the Thessalian poleis were included within a much wider campaign, the special significance they held for the Koans is indicated by other inscriptions recording diplomatic interaction: *IG* XII.4 1:133, discussed above, in which the Thessalians are honoured for having provided grain in a time of shortage in the early third century; and *IG* XII.4 1:55, of 168 BC, in which a Larisaian doctor is praised by the Koans (precise reason unknown). Both texts mention *syngeneia*.

118 *SEG* 53.851[1]; Bosnakis and Hallof (2003), 229–34.

119 Rigsby (2004). Note, however, that in Rigsby (1996), 133, he stops short of a restoration, and also notes the possibility that the inscription concerned Demetrias 'with its *ethnos* the Magnesians'.

120 This is strongly suggested by the consistency of formulation across the four

the wording of the Gonnoi example. While it is true that the Perrhaiboi are mentioned as the group to which the people of Gonnoi belong, it should be considered as possible that the Koans were recording their friendship *both* with them *and* with the Thessalians as a whole. On line 4, it is φιλίαν καὶ ... συγγένειαν that seem to be being expressed towards Gonnoi and the *ethnos* whose name is obliterated; this formula, though heavily restored, is supported by the wording in the Homolion text.[121] On the other hand, φιλίαν καὶ συμμαχίαν (military alliance) are evoked in the case of the Perrhaiboi. Helly dismisses this distinction with the suggestion that συμμαχίαν may be an erroneous reading, but there is an alternative interpretation.[122] On what grounds could the people of Gonnoi be said to have συγγένεια with the Koans? Probably only by enveloping them in the Thessalian *ethnos* (whose kinship links with Kos were being emphasised at this time: see below). I think we should consider the possibility that the Koans were, in the Gonnoi and Homolion cases, exercising a certain ingenious and profitable flexibility both in their diplomacy and in its linguistic formulation. They expressed a condition of shared kinship with 'the Gonneans/Homolions and the rest of the *ethnos* of the Thessalians', eliding the ethnic distinction between Thessalians and Perrhaibians/Magnesians; the Gonneans and Homolians allowed this blurring of ethnic lines because the *syngeneia* with Kos was diplomatically advantageous to them.

The second inscription, *SEG* 53.851[1],[123] obviously derives from cities in tetradic Thessaly rather than the *perioikis*, since it deploys full Thessalian dialect, which the perioikic communities do not. In fact, linguistic features suggest Pelasgiotis. The first two lines of fragment B read [— — — τὰν φιλίαν καὶ τὰν συγγένειαν δια]φυλάσσει τὰν ἐ̣[ξ ἀρχᾶς ὑπάρχονσαν]/[τᾶ πόλι τοῦν Κούουν κοινᾶ πὸτ τὸ ἔθνος τ]ὸ̣ Πετθαλοῦν ('... preserves the friendship and kinship existing from the very beginning[124] between the polis of the

examples on the same stele: although the decrees are those of the cities in question, the inscriptions were carved and set up in the sanctuary on Kos, and surely follow the Koans' stipulated wording.

121 Ὁμολιέων·
ἀγαθῆι τύχηι· ἐφ' ἱερέως τοῦ Ἀσκληπιοῦ Φιλοξένου, ἐπιστα-
τοῦντος δὲ Ἀνδρονίκου τοῦ Ἀντιφίλου· παραγενομένων πα-
ρὰ τῆς πόλεως τῆς Κώ[ι]ων ἀρχιθεώρου μὲν Ἀριστολόχου
Ζμένδρωνος καὶ θε[ωροῦ] Μακα{κα}ρέως {Μακαρέως} Ἀράτου καὶ ἐμφανιζόν-
[των τήν] τ̣ε φιλίαν κ[αὶ τὴν] συγγένειαν τὴν ὑπάρχουσαν ταῖς
π̣όλεσιν ἐξ ἀρχῆς αὐ[ταῖς] πρὸς αὐτὰς καὶ τῶι ἄλλωι ἔθνει τῶ[ι]
[Θεσσαλῶν] ...

122 Helly (2004a), 99.

123 Bosnakis and Hallof (2003), 234–36.

124 This is one of several instances in the corpus of *asylia* inscriptions in which the antiquity of the relationship is emphasised: see Nelson (2013), 252.

Koans as a whole, and the *ethnos* of the Thessalians'). There are other indications that Koan diplomacy was directed to the Thessalian *ethnos* at this time too. In the early third century the Thessalians had supplied the Koans with grain at a time of shortage, and had been formally thanked, praised and rewarded as a result; the Koan inscription recording this directs its gratitude to 'the *ethnos* of the Thessalians and the several cities'.[125] (Plainly some kind of collective Thessalian action was involved, but perhaps the grain contributions were organised on a polis-by-polis basis.) On line 95 a *koinon* is mentioned; the ethnic is missing, but Θεσσαλῶν is most likely, since the Koans could not be referred to in this way. So by the time of the *asylia* bid the Koans had already established strong ties with the Thessalians as a collective body.

We have noted some of the individual poleis that seem to have taken important roles in the Kos–Thessaly connection. There are two, however, that deserve further attention: one is Trikka and the other is Larisa.

c) Asklepios and Trikka

Trikka is a tantalising site. On the one hand, Strabo calls its Asklepios-sanctuary τὸ ἀρχαιότατον καὶ ἐπιφανέστατον, 'the oldest and most famous (sc. in the Greek world)';[126] on the other, archaeological investigation has not provided corroboration, and even the sanctuary's location is not certain.[127] Mili notes that none of the remains at the site tentatively identified with the Trikka Asklepieion dates from before the Hellenistic period, and that the spread of the god's cult in Thessalian towns took place in the fourth century BC, at the same time that the same trend was occurring elsewhere in Greece.[128] The fourth century is also when Trikka starts to place Asklepios on its coins; earlier issues were dominated by bull-wrestling motifs.

A clear sign of outsider interest in Trikka comes in the inscription of Isyllos' *Paian*, posted up in the Epidaurian Asklepieion and dedicated to Apollo Maleatas and Asklepios.[129] On lines 29–31 we are told that 'οὐδέ κε Θεσσαλίας ἐν Τρίκκηι πειραθείης / εἰς ἄδυτον καταβὰς Ἀσκληπιοῦ, εἰ μὴ ἀφ' ἁγνοῦ / πρῶτον Ἀπόλλωνος βωμοῦ θύσαις Μαλεάτα' ('Not even in Thessalian

[125] *IG* XII.4 1:133; the formula quoted is on line 129.

[126] Strabo 9.5.17.

[127] Riethmüller (2005), 91–98. At 8.6.15 Strabo makes the tantalising observation that Trikka, like Epidauros and Kos, displayed in its temple the records of successful cures. A set of Trikkan Miracle Inscriptions? This would suggest a degree of dynamic self-advertisement, but of course no such text has been found.

[128] Mili (2015), 145–47.

[129] For an overview of the *Paian* and its date and context see Fantuzzi (2010), 183–89; as he observes, it belongs to the reign of a Philip, which may possibly be Philip II but is more likely to be Philip III or V – this would situate it either in the 310s or the 210s. The impossibility of more accurate dating is unfortunate.

Trikka would you make an attempt, having gone down to the *adyton* of Asklepios, without first sacrificing on the holy altar of Apollo Maleatas').[130] Not only does this suggest a well-known sanctuary (perhaps with a subterranean chamber) of Asklepios at Trikka at this time, but the element of competition is also significant. The *Paian* stakes a vigorous claim, on behalf of Epidauros, on the birth and upbringing of Asklepios, to the detriment of Thessaly's claim, and the reference to a preliminary sacrifice to Apollo Maleatas in Trikka should be seen in the light of this: since Maleatas is presented as an Epidaurian deity, his role at Trikka gives that sanctuary too a heavy debt to Epidauros. This suggests that in the third century the Trikka Asklepieion was considered significant enough for rival Asklepios-centres to wish to disparage subtly, or play down.

We certainly have to acknowledge the possibility that, while the connection of Asklepios with Trikka is a very early one in Greek literature,[131] and while there may well have been a modest cult site there from an early time, the fame and distinction to which Strabo alludes are really a Hellenistic phenomenon for the most part. This possibility is interesting in view of the strong evidence for external interest in Trikkaian Asklepios in the Hellenistic period. It seems to have been at this time that the cult gained wide and significant renown, no doubt encouraged by its Homeric credentials. This would accord very well with the tendencies of the age: a basis of ancient tradition, but a great deal of religious innovation and adaptation laid over that.[132]

There is evidence that the sanctuary of Asklepios on Kos considered itself to have been founded from Trikka, that the god himself came from his Thessalian homeland to establish the cult on the island (rather as he was thought to have arrived in person in Athens to found his cult there: he was very much a god of tangible arrivals).[133] This is reflected in a *Mimiambos* of Herodas, a text that strongly suggests the mesh of Thessalian associations Kos was cultivating in the third century BC. *Mimiambos* 2 is narrated by a brothel-keeper, Battaros, protesting in a Koan lawcourt against ill-treatment by a Phrygian, Thales. Battaros ends his speech with an impassioned plea

130 Detailed discussion of the hymn may be found in LeVen (2014), 317–28.

131 Hom. *Il.* 2.729–33: the sons of Asklepios lead the contingent from Trikka, Ithome and Oichalia. There was a contest to be Asklepios' birthplace among the major sites of his worship, and no way of determining for certain which had prior claim, but the Thessalian birthplace tradition is certainly early: it appears in *Ehoiai* fr. 59 MW and in Pindar (*Pythian* 3). On the competing birthplace traditions see Aston (2004); Riethmüller (2005), 37–46.

132 A brief note in Strabo (8.4.4) seems to suggest that the temple of Asklepios at Gerenia was modelled on the one at Trikka – another case of influence, but sadly not amenable to precise dating.

133 *IG* II^3 4 665; Clinton (1994).

for the rights of resident foreigners to be taken seriously, supporting his point with a subtle reference to the important role played by outsiders in Kos' legendary past:

> Now [i.e. by judging in my favour] you will show the strength of Kos and Merops,
> And the fame held by Thessalos and by Herakles,
> And how Asklepios came here from Trikka,
> And why Phoibe gave birth to Leto here.[134]

This plainly shows the belief that Asklepios – a god remarkable for his physical travels and migrations – came to Kos from Trikka.[135] However, what is remarkable is the dense bundle of mythic allusions that both Herodas and the character Battaros could expect their audiences to understand. Merops was a legendary early king of Kos and may in a sense be a synonym of the island in this text. The final line of the excerpt refers to a local Koan belief that Leto, mother of Apollo, was born on the island. Thessalos is of course the son of Herakles and the Koan princess Chalkiope, daughter of king Eurypylos whom Herakles killed.[136] So we see a two-way transfer and a mythical interdependence: Thessaly supplies Kos with its healing god, but Kos gives Thessaly the hero who will bring about its renaming and its new collective identity sixty years after the Trojan War.

It might reasonably be asked at this point whether Herodas actually reflects Koan beliefs, or whether they are artificially evoked. Some caution is needed: none of the *Mimiamboi* really creates a detailed Koan mis-en-scène, though two of the poems are set on the island,[137] and we cannot take the undoubted significance of Kos in the poems as evidence that the poet originated or worked there; indeed, nothing specific about his life is known with any certainty.[138] What we can say, however, is that his poems are infused with an awareness of, and respect for, Ptolemaic authority, whether

134 Herod. *Mim.* 2.95–98:
νῦν δείξετ' ἡ Κῶς κὠ Μέροψ κόσον δραίνει
κὠ Θεσσαλὸς τίν' εἶχε κἠρακλῆς δόξαν,
κὠσκληπιὸς κῶς ἦλθεν ἐνθάδ' ἐκ Τρίκκης,
κἤτικτε Λητοῦν ὧδε τεῦ χάριν Φοίβη.

135 Riethmüller (2005), Bd. I, 91–93.

136 Pherekydes *FGrH* 3 F 78.

137 *Mimiamboi* 2 and 4. The latter is set in an Asklepieion, almost certainly that on Kos (Zanker 2009, 104; but cf. Cunningham 1966, 115–17), and dwells at length on the works of art in the sanctuary. It also begins with references to Trikka and to Podaleirios and Machaon, reinforcing the Thessalian connection.

138 Cunningham (1971), 1–3.

or not he actually worked at Alexandria.[139] This – and perhaps a desire to please the reigning Ptolemy[140] – certainly helps to explain the appearance of Kos in the poems. The Ptolemies were well aware of the Koan drive to publicise and enhance their Asklepieion. Among his various interactions with the island, Ptolemy II – who was actually born on the island, in 308/7 BC – wrote a letter to Kos concerning the sanctuary of Asklepios, a small portion of which survives.[141] Ptolemy III Euergetes formally recognised the sanctuary's *asylia*.[142] In addition to such tangible contacts, there are signs that Kos was important to the self-presentation of the Ptolemies, especially Ptolemy II. In Kallimachos' *Hymn to Delos*, the infant Apollo, still *in utero*, forbids his mother to give birth to him on Kos, because that island is destined to become the birthplace of another god, Ptolemy.

Kos, then, including its Asklepieion, was of considerable interest to the Ptolemies, in whose milieu Herodas seems to have operated;[143] it is very unlikely that Herodas' second *Mimiambos* would have deviated significantly from the traditions about the island that were widely espoused at the time.[144] Moreover, as will be discussed below, the reference to Herakles also ties in with both contemporary Thessalian and Ptolemaic preoccupations; it is noteworthy how often those seem to coincide (on which see further the section on *agōnes hippikoi*, pp. 360–68). What we cannot find is any clear sign that Trikka – its citizens, or indeed the religious personnel of its Asklepieion – was actively pursuing the external associations here discussed, with Kos or indeed with anywhere else. This is very likely to reflect scant evidence rather than a genuine indifference, but the fact remains that for active Thessalian participation in the Asklepios-cult beyond the region's boundaries we have to look to another polis, namely Larisa.

139 As Cunningham remarks (1971, 2–3), the Ptolemaic references are 'exactly what one would expect in an author of this date', given the cultural importance of Alexandria.

140 Most likely to be Ptolemy II Philadelphos: see Rist (2016), 2.

141 Rigsby (1996), 124–26; the identification of Ptolemy II as the sender is probable but not certain; it might be Euergetes.

142 Rigsby (1996), 112, no. 8.

143 Nelson (2005), 218–19. Elsewhere, however (2013, 248), he notes that 'The island's association with Alexandria was shaken by Antigonus Gonatas' naval victory just off Cos around 258 BC.'

144 Traces of such traditions of Thessalian origins include Philitas fr. 55 Lightfoot = Hesych. s.v. Θεσσαλαί. Such scraps, and certain occurrences of shared names between Kos and Thessaly, have in the past encouraged historians to believe that Kos was founded by Thessalian migrants, but a wholesale settlement of this kind is not on the whole likely. This is not, however, to deny the strong probability of early contact, reflected in Homer. See Riethmüller (2005), 206–11.

d) Larisa and Kos

The fact that Larisa features quite prominently as the homeland of invalids mentioned in the Hippokratic corpus[145] should perhaps not be considered overly significant: as the region's most prominent and best-connected city, Larisa is far more likely than other Thessalian poleis to have come to the notice of medical writers and practitioners outside Thessaly. However, there are strong indications that a direct connection between Larisa and the figure of Hippokrates was fostered both by the Koans and by the Larisaians, in the third century BC especially. So much so that in the Greek anthology a verse purporting to be the epitaph of Hippokrates could describe him as 'Thessalian Hippokrates'.[146]

On the Koan side, the key evidence comes from the *Presbeutikos*, an anonymous oration purporting to have been delivered at Athens by Hippokrates' son Thessalos in ca. 407 BC, arguing for a cessation of the Athenian campaign against Kos. That Hippokrates had a son called Thessalos is very likely and in itself highly significant, but the *Presbeutikos* is certainly a later fabrication, though a most interesting one – in fact, its very mendacity is arguably more meaningful in this context than authenticity would have been. As Nelson has persuasively argued,[147] the work should be seen in the context of the *asylia* bid and its embassies in the 240s BC, a process in which, as we have seen, Thessalian communities were involved.[148] The close connection between Kos and Thessaly is reflected in various ways in the text. For a start, the work is extremely flattering to the Thessalians: it replaces other existing traditions concerning the First Sacred War with one in which the heroes' roles are shared by the Thessalian Eurylochos (probably, as we have seen, a fourth-century invention) and the Koan healers Nebros

145 For example, note its appearances in *Epidemics* 4 and 12 (as well as one by Thessalian Meliboia in *Epidemics* 16); for discussion see Wee (2016), 145.

146 'Θεσσαλὸς Ἱπποκράτης, Κῷος γένος, ἐνθάδε κεῖται,/Φοίβου ἀπὸ ῥίζης ἀθανάτου γεγαώς … ' ('Thessalian Hippokrates, of Koan descent, lies here, born of the stock of immortal Phoibos … ' – *Anth. Gr.* VII.135).

147 Nelson (2007), expanding and augmenting the suggestions of Nelson (2005). He argues that the *Presbeutikos* replicates the third-century *History of Kos* by Makareus, and from the speeches of Koan ambassadors engaged in the *asylia*-bid.

148 Cf. Nelson (2013), 250: 'the Coan *asylia* decrees paint a picture of a co-ordinated programme of rhetorical and diplomatic strategies aimed at particular audiences and regional interests'. Of these audiences and regional interests, Thessaly was plainly one. On the role of ambassadorial speeches in Hellenistic diplomacy and culture see further Amendola (2019). It should be noted, however, that a diplomatic relationship existed between the Asklepiadai and the polis – and sanctuary – of Delphi, from the first half of the fourth century BC, and it is possible that the myth of Nebros and Chrysos existed then, being rediscovered in the third century. See *CID* 1.11 and 1.12; Bousquet (1956), 579–94; Smith (1990), 16.

and Chrysos.[149] In addition, it presents the Thessalians and the healers of Kos as sharing heroic ancestry: as Nelson observes, the latter derived their descent not only from Asklepios himself, but also from Herakles;[150] the Heraklid ancestry of elite Thessalians (though as we saw in Chapter 3 it is by no means the only, or even the dominant, version of their mythic origins in all contexts and periods) is emphasised in this text in order to reinforce the sense of deep-seated cohesion between Kos and Thessaly. For Nelson, the text draws upon far more extensive family histories developed by Koan elites to articulate and advertise their illustrious and significant genealogy, in which Thessalian connections were plainly central.

Even though Larisa is not explicitly mentioned in the *Presbeutikos*, it is noteworthy that the city claimed to have the tomb of Hippokrates in its territory.[151] Moreover, there is no doubt that of all Thessalian communities it was the most active in cultivating the figure of Thessalos, the Heraklid hero who links Kos and Thessaly. In the Aigai decree mentioned above, Larisa is triply important: first, as Parker argues, the festival called the Olympia (otherwise unattested) is likely to have been held in the city's vicinity; second, one of the three locations for the publication of the decree – in addition to the Olympion (headquarter of the Olympia festival) and the regional sanctuary of Itonos (the sanctuary of Athena Itonia) – is the sanctuary of Apollo Kerdoios at Larisa; third, Larisaian Tagoi are used as a dating formula in the final few lines.[152] These features may chiefly reflect the simple fact that Larisa was the most prominent city in Thessaly at the time in terms of political and religious organisation,[153] but a more specific interest in the hero Thessalos is suggested by the strong fashion,

149 *Presb.* 2–4; for discussion of the First Sacred War variants see Chapter 7.

150 It is worth noting that in the *Presbeutikos* Heraklid ancestry is used as a way of reaching out to the Antigonid rulers of Macedon; this sits awkwardly (at first glance) alongside the close relations between Kos and the Ptolemies, who were themselves staking a claim to privileged Argead (and therefore Heraklid) descent. But, as Buraselis notes, in the turbulent conditions of the third century Kos could not afford to alienate either power (Buraselis 2004), and genealogy perhaps supplied the means of appealing to both.

151 Soranus, *Vit. Hippok.* 11: Hippokrates dies at Larisa and is buried between Larisa and Gyrton, where his tomb may be viewed to this (i.e., the author's) day. (Cf. Souda s.v. Ἱπποκράτης.) It is also intriguing to note that in interaction between Kos and Larisa, the former was not alone in medical practice: Larisa produced a doctor praised by the Koans for his *eunoia* towards them in 168 BC (*IG* XII.4 1:55). His name, was not, alas, Thessalos.

152 Parker (2011), 113–15.

153 It is significant that, at some point in the first half of the third century, the polis of Larisa invested in the construction of a new theatre large enough to seat 10,000 people, and this despite the economic difficulties of the time. This certainly suggests an ambitious cultural programme. See Tziafalias (2011); Mili (2015), 117–18.

in third- and second-century Larisa, for naming sons Thessalos (or dialect equivalents). Moreover, this trend is, very significantly, shared with Kos during the third century especially.

The personal name Thessalos (including its variants) is in fact a wildly popular toponymic/ethnonymic personal name in antiquity, outstripping all but 'Athenaios'.[154] Thessaly-related names had flexible and enduring currency, for their distribution in both time and place is very wide. In almost no cases, however, is it possible to know anything of the motives behind the choice of name. The exceptions to this state of affairs are those where a son is named Thessalos to evoke and compliment a region with which the father enjoyed some meaningful relationship, especially one of *xenia* – the sons of Peisistratos and of the younger Kimon are the most famous examples. However, in addition to these individual cases where our knowledge of context explains the choice of name, we can identify some significant clusters of usage where we might be able to assess the relationship with local institutions, customs and concerns. The most prominent example of the latter is Kos, which provides seventeen Thessaloi (in all forms of the name), of which eight belong to the third century BC. This is a striking concentration when the data are viewed as a whole.

When a Koan man named his son Thessalos, a reference to the hero Thessalos was probably not the only – or even necessarily the chief – resonance he was aiming for. The famous healer Hippokrates named his son Thessalos mainly, we may assume, as a reference to the contacts he enjoyed with that region. (This is very similar to the cases of Kimon and Peisistratos.) Thereafter, when the healing sanctuary grew to new importance in the third century, calling a son 'Thessalos' may in some cases have been a way of asserting a link with the medical credentials of the community. Some at least of the individuals bearing the name must have been related to each other by family ties, which their use of the same names reflected. It is instructive, however, to compare the popularity of the name Thessalos on Kos with that of Hippokrates: the latter has fifteen known instances in all, of which two are fifth century BC (including the famous one), two are fourth century, four are third century, three are either third or second, two are second century (and the rest are undated). We would expect the numbers to rise because of the increase in epigraphic material in the Hellenistic period compared with the earlier periods. Unlike Thessalos, the name Hippokrates displays a slight spike in popularity only in the third century BC. This suggests that the popularity of Thessalos is not related solely to a desire to evoke medically significant names, since that would affect the popularity of Hippokrates equally. Even if recurrences of

154 The data behind this pattern are derived from the *Lexicon of Greek Personal Names* and its online search facility at http://clas-lgpn2.classics.ox.ac.uk.

the name Thessalos are in some cases due to the use of family names, the increase in usage is still very noteworthy.

This leaves two possibilities: first, that the name was a way of evoking the region of Thessaly, which as we have seen was important for the Koans – especially their healers – as the supposed origin of the Asklepios-cult, as well as being linked by the hero Thessalos, whose sons migrated to Thessaly after the Trojan War. Second, the name may indeed have been a direct reference to Thessalos. We cannot know this for certain, and it is perhaps more realistic to see both name and hero as a way of reinforcing connections with an important region on the Greek mainland, whose ancestral affiliation the Koans were especially keen to cultivate in the third century.

So much for the Koans – why did the people of Thessalian Larisa show such enthusiasm for naming their sons Thessalos in the third and second centuries BC? If all the variants of the name are counted together in the first instance,[155] Larisa returns fourteen examples, two dated to either the fourth or the third century BC, four to the third century, six to the second century and one to the first century (the remaining cases are undated). The peak of popularity is therefore a century or so later than it is on Kos – however, it should be acknowledged that the paucity of the evidence makes such variations statistically insignificant, especially when we take into account the growing numbers of extant inscriptions between the fourth and the first centuries BC. We cannot refine the data sufficiently to show an irrefutable correlation between Thessalos-use in Kos and in Larisa, but it seems significant that the two communities most enthusiastic in their use of the name in the Hellenistic period are two who also share the worship of a hero of that name. As with the Koan instances, Thessalian uses of the name Thessalos must in part refer to ethnic identity, a linguistic gesture significant in itself, but, once again, hero-name, human name and ethnicity constitute overlapping circles in a cultural Venn diagram.

Despite the particular connections between Larisa and Hippokrates, and despite Larisa's energetic involvement in the Thessalos cult as witnessed by the Aigai inscription, the primarily regional focus of Kos' Thessaly-interest should be noted. In order to conduct her *asylia* campaign it was logistically necessary to approach and interact with individual poleis. However, the *ethnos* of the Thessaloi was always evoked, in the diplomatic language of inscriptions, in the popularity of the personal name Thessalos,

155 Apart from a couple of rare variants (one Thessalia and one Petthalokrates) all the known instances are either Thessalos or Petthalos. Since the latter is a dialect form of the former, and since the choice between them is essentially determined by whether the inscription containing the name is in dialect or koine, they cannot really be treated as different names.

and in the cult of the hero Thessalos. There is little sign of a particular Koan cultivation of Larisa, much as the latter might have wished it. Trikka was the place of Asklepios' birth; Thessaly was the land that Pheidippos, Antiphos and their descendants appropriated. Larisa was not a name to conjure with. It is not in the Catalogue of Ships; it has no role in the earliest stratum of recorded Thessalian mythology. And yet – or perhaps, therefore – it was, as ever since the late sixth century, the most energetic manufacturer of its own mythological credentials and connections.

5. Further cases of Thessalian *syngeneia*

In the case of Kos and its Asklepieion, we observed a two-sided situation. On the one hand, the *asylia*-bid depended upon the range, scope and size of its application: many Greek communities, as well as individuals, were approached, and in Thessaly itself not only were various poleis included but also little if any distinction seems to have been made between tetradic and perioikic Thessaly, with the latter probably encompassed within the banner of the *ethnos Thessalōn*. On the other hand, within this scattergun method, we can identify a special status for Thessaly, as the source of Asklepios and the recipient of the Thessalids. A similar combination of general and specific is to be found in the famous publicity campaign on the part of Magnesia on the Maiandros.

Near the end of the third century BC the Greek community of Magnesia on the Maiandros undertook a process of self-advertisement whose intricacy and visibility (the latter thanks in large part to the survival of some key inscriptions) have made it famous among instances of Hellenistic religious embellishment.[156] The polis obtained an oracle from Delphi in 220/19 BC to institute a festival, with stephanitic games, in honour of local goddess Artemis Leukophryene. It also, as Kos had done not long before, made a bid for the sanctuary to enjoy the status of *asylia*, inviolacy.[157] As in Kos, this process was accompanied by – or, rather, rested on – the assertion of significant legendary connections with the Greek mainland, in particular Thessaly. Unlike in the Koan case, from Magnesia we actually have a public record of the myth at the centre of these connections: the narrative was inscribed on a stele in the agora, where the documents from the *asylia* bid were also presented.[158] Somewhat damaged though it is, the inscription

[156] Sumi (2004). On the Magnesian *asylia*-bid: Rigsby (1996), 179–85; Chaniotis (1999), 54–58; Sosin (2009).

[157] *Asylia* was successfully secured in 208, but there was an earlier, failed bid: see Thonemann (2007).

[158] Slater and Summa (2006). On the spatial and archaeological context of the festival's site and that of the inscriptions' display see Jürgens (2017); Hammerschmied (2018).

(*I.Magn.* 17 = *FGrH* 482 F 3) allows us to piece together the main points of the story. The Magnetes who fight at Troy are for some reason (the text here is missing) unable to return to their home; instead, they establish a city on Krete, between Gortyn and Phaistos, but retain a hankering to return to Thessaly. An omen – the sighting of a white raven – encourages the descendants of the founders to hope for a return eighty years after the original settlement, but when they send to Delphi for corroboration of this plan they are told by the Pythia that, so far from going back to Thessaly, they must move on again to another foreign land. The oracle points out their chief founder, Leukippos, previously unknown to them, who is instructed by the god to lead the Thessalians to the future site of Magnesia on the Maiandros.[159]

As in the Koan case, we have here a recycling and augmentation of pre-existing traditions. Prinz has exhaustively identified and analysed the various strands of the story upon which the Magnesian record drew, and established some of its key phases.[160] The Magnetes of course are included in the Catalogue of Ships,[161] but have the slightest possible role in the plot of the *Iliad* itself. There are, however, traces of the development of a post-Homeric tradition regarding their attempted *nostos* and a shipwreck off the coast of Libya. By the time of Aristotle, as he convincingly argues, they have been incorporated into an 'official' foundation myth for Magnesia on the Maiandros, which the third-century account somewhat modified. The fourth-century version may be reconstructed in outline as follows. Apollo serves Admetos, king of Pherai, as a herdsman by way of penalty for his killing of the Kyklopes (this is a tradition drawn from the *Ehoiai*).[162] In gratitude for Apollo's service Admetos sends to Delphi a tithe of men (ἀνθρώπων ἀπαρχή)[163] that the god despatches as colonists to Asia Minor under the leadership of Leukippos, not himself Magnesian but rather a

[159] Leukippos is sometimes identified on the coins of Magnesia minted in the fourth, third and second centuries: the obverse bears a horseman with a 'Boiotian' helmet, a spear and a short cloak; on the reverse is a bull, head lowered (see, for example, *SNG* München 586). While this specific identification seems insecure, it is plausible to detect an evocation of Thessalian numismatic imagery; for example, the horseman is very similar to the cavalryman on the silver coinage of Pherai in the fourth century: see examples in *Nomos* IV, 114–15.

[160] Prinz (1979), 111–37.

[161] Hom. *Il.* 2.756–59.

[162] West (1985), 69.

[163] Aristotle fr. 631 Rose. Athenaios mangles the cited text somewhat, so that the Magnesians become Delphian colonists; however, as Prinz points out, this is inherently implausible; Delphi ratifies colonies but does not send out her own people in this way. Prinz (1979), 113; see also Thomas (2019), 217–18

descendant of Bellerophon.[164] The main development of the third-century version is the incorporation of the Kretan element; the idea of a Kretan Magnesia may in fact originate with Plato, perhaps our earliest surviving source.[165] So, as Prinz demonstrates, the Magnesian inscription represents the synthesis of several pre-existing strands, but one that takes care to maintain the Thessalian connection current from at least the century before. It has been observed that the claim of Thessalian origins trumped the earlier idea that Magnesia on the Maiandros was settled by Ionians and therefore closely connected with the Athenians; in fact, the myth of colonisation from Thessalian Magnesia represents an earlier myth-historical phase, and so undermines and supplants the Ionian alternative completely. It also gives the Magnesians primacy over the Ionian poleis in their vicinity, making them the earliest Greeks to settle in the region. There may well have been specific aspects of the political climate of the late third century that encouraged Magnesia to reject Ionian affiliation,[166] but since the Thessalian origin-myth certainly existed in the time of Aristotle it was not invented *ex nihilo* for such short-term motives.[167]

As for the other side of the transaction, can we identify any signs of Thessalian participation in, or response to, the claim on their ancestral role by the Magnesians on the Maiandros? It is perhaps dangerous to make too much of the inscription in which the people of Gonnoi agree to the conferment of *asylia* on the sanctuary of Artemis Leukophryene.[168] On the one hand, the text contains the clause ἐπειδὴ Μάγνητες οἱ ἐπὶ Μαιάν/δρου φίλοι ὄντες καὶ συγγενεῖς Γοννέων ('Since the Magnesians on the Maiandros are friends and relations of the Gonneans … '), and also refers to the fact that the Magnesians ἀνενεώσαντο τὴν ἐξ ἀρχῆς / ὑπάρχουσαν φιλίαν καὶ οἰκειότητα Μάγνησίν τε καὶ / Γοννεῦσιν ('renewed the friendship and close connection that existed between the Magnesians the Gonneans from the very beginning'). On the other, we have to note that terms such as *sungeneia* and *oikeiotēs* (and their other forms) were used widely in the records of the *asylia* grants made by a number of other communities approached by the

164 As Jürgens observes (2017, 94–95), Leukippos' family tree was situated at the heart of genealogical Hellenicity, since he was a direct descendant of Hellen and his son Aiolos.

165 At any rate, in the *Laws* we find a new settlement on Krete called Magnesia, implicitly evoking the connection between the Thessalian Magnesia and Krete. Prinz (1979), 125.

166 Dušanić (1983), 35.

167 For further discussion of the various strands of tradition and their incorporation into the Magnesian inscriptions see Biagetti (2010).

168 Copy displayed at Magnesia on the Maiandros: *I.Magn.* 33. Copy at Gonnoi: Helly (1973), vol. II, 111. The only other Thessalian case surviving is *I.Magn.* 26, a badly damaged inscription in which the name of the granting polis is lost, but the dialect certainly Thessalian. On this text see further below.

Magnesians. It can reasonably be argued that the Thessalians have an especially good claim on *syngeneia* in its strict sense of kinship through the foundation-myth of the Thessalians settlers, and no doubt such traditions were in the minds of the Magnesians when they approached Gonnoi, and in the minds of the Gonneans when they responded favourably. However, it is essential not to imagine any kind of spurious exclusivity in this situation: concepts such as *syngeneia* were flexible enough to allow the Magnesians to establish a network of contacts, and a network was what they wanted rather than a unilateral connection with any Thessalian polis.[169]

That said, it is possible that a particular expression, the claim that *syngeneia/oikeiotēs* had existed between two communities *ex archēs*, from the beginning, is more restrictive or exclusive in sense. Although it appears on a number of Hellenistic inscriptions in which two communities are reinforcing supposedly primordial connections,[170] within the corpus of *asylia* texts from Magnesia it appears only in the Gonnoi inscription.[171] More significantly still, the same expression appears in the Koan *asylia* texts only in connection with Thessalian communities.[172] It would seem that this particular formula was used by both sanctuaries, a mere few decades

169 Considerable debate surrounds the precise meaning and implications of the term *syngeneia* in diplomatic contexts, and in particular whether it always referred to consanguinity in the strict sense. For example, Curty (2005) makes a strong counter-argument to that of Lücke (2000, 15–27, himself challenging Curty 1995), for whom the consanguinity existing in individual and family relationships cannot be taken to apply with equal consistency on the state level. Patterson (2010), on the other hand, deliberately steps back from the specifics of terminology and its meaning to consider *syngeneia* in the light of the larger question of how mythological traditions could be adapted, augmented and sometimes overlooked to support the assertion of connections between individuals and groups.

170 See, for example, *IG* VII 4130, a late second-century BC text in which '*syngeneia* existing from the beginning' is recorded between Larisa and the Boiotians, presumably on the basis of the belief that the Boiotoi were driven out of Thessaly by the family of Thessalos: this is not true kinship, but illustrates the flexibility of the term and its application. Other examples, not involving Thessaly: *FD* III 2.18 and 2.19 (Delphi, third century BC); *IG* IX.1² 2:583 (Akarnanian decree from Olympia, 216 BC).

171 See n. 168 above. In a different context Magnesia does use the formula to describe Gortyn in Crete (*I.Magn.* 65a + 75) but, again, this is significant given Gortyn's role in the Magnesian foundation myth.

172 See *SEG* 53.850, a stele containing the *asylia* verdicts from Gonnoi, Homolion, Phthiotic Thebes and Megara (discussed above). *Ex archēs* formulae occur in the first two. The Megara text includes the expression διὰ τὰν προϋπάρχουσ[αν] ọἰκειότατα (variants of which occur elsewhere in the corpus and elsewhere), but the force of this phrase is different: it simply means 'pre-existing', rather than 'from the beginning'. See also *SEG* 53.851[1], a very lacunose inscription, discussed above, in which two Thessalian cities grant *asylia*; the *ex archēs* formula has been plausibly restored in line 2 of fragment B.

apart, to signal a special status for Thessaly as related from the beginning – that is, from the moment of foundation. (As has been noted, in the Koan case Thessaly is the colony of Kos; in the Magnesian case, Magnesia is the colony of Thessaly.) Furthermore, Rigsby notes a significant term in *I.Magn.* 26, an *asylia* decree from a Thessalian city whose name is lost.[173] Rather than the more widespread – and vague – *syngeneia*, this document speaks of *homogeneia* between the city and Magnesia on the Maiandros. This term indicates identical origins, rather than shared origins – a fine but important shade of distinction, not employed in any of the other surviving documents (or indeed, anywhere else in published epigraphic material, as far as I have been able to ascertain).

We may have here a case of Thessalian poleis vying with each other to express a special status vis-à-vis the Magnesian visitors. One polis seems to have been deliberately deviating from the well-established language of Hellenistic kinship diplomacy, with a possible view to exceeding other poleis' claims on a special relationship with Magnesia. But which polis? Rigsby follows Kern in positing Larisa.[174] His claim rests on features in the text, in particular the mention of more than one treasurer and of the provision of a boat to the *theoroi*. But while the flexible state of *syngeneia* could reasonably pertain to any Thessalian – or, as we have seen, perioikic – community, what grounds would Larisa have for claiming identical origins with the Magnesians? Is she simply bending mythic tradition to suit her purposes? The only specific Thessalian polis implicated in the mythology surrounding the Magnesian foundation is Pherai, as noted above, whose king Admetos is the source of the 'tithe of men': could Pherai have been the city claiming *homogeneia* with the Magnesians, having in mind the tradition of Admetos' role?

Serious practical problems confront this possibility. Rigsby is right to draw attention to the fact that the polis in the inscription has more than one *tamias*, treasurer, something well-attested in Larisa and a few other Thessalian cities, but not in Pherai. The mention of supplying a boat for the Magnesian visitors is also problematic. It is true that in citing epigraphic evidence for a river harbour at Larisa Rigsby misinterprets the word λιμένα in *IG* IX.2 517,[175] but nonetheless this feature is an obstacle to a Pheraian origin: Pherai controlled the port of Pagasai for much of the Classical period, but lost this possession largely in the time of Philip II, and wholly after the foundation of Demetrias in 294 BC.[176] In general Pherai

[173] Rigsby (1996), 200–02.

[174] Rigsby (1996), 201.

[175] The word there is in its unique Thessalian sense of 'market-place'.

[176] Marzolff (1980), 5–42; Bakhuizen (1987), 332–33; Cohen (1996), 111–14. For a useful recent summary of the site and its remains see Stamatopoulou (2018). Its

was rather a spent force in the third century BC, and does not play a very visible role in the interstate religious diplomacy that concerns us here. It is more likely that Larisa was exercising a degree of creativity in putting herself forward as uniquely well connected with the Magnesians; after all, the Koan case revealed her domination of the Thessalian involvement in the cult of Thessalos, even though her connections to that hero were far less strong than those of other parts of Thessaly.

The records of Thessalian communities' inclusion in networks of *syngeneia* and closely related forms of connection continue, and perhaps slightly increase, in the second century BC. Curty's catalogue contains links between Larisa and Boiotian Akraiphia,[177] Larisa and Peparethos,[178] and the Thessalian *koinon* and Teos,[179] as well as an inscription mentioning *sungeneia*, *oikeiotēs* and *philia* between Larisa and Skotoussa.[180] Curty asserts the basic principle that *syngeneia* in particular was only cited if a very specific connection – namely, a shared hero-ancestor – was believed to exist between the two communities. In most cases this is surely so; it is highly plausible that behind the stark text of the inscriptions lie reserves of local legend that both communities would know and which did not require inclusion. For example, the relationship between Larisa and Skotoussa is surely something more specific than the fact that both communities are Thessaloi.

However, the flexibility of the use of mythology should not be overlooked; this is illustrated very well by the *syngeneia* cited between Larisa and 'all the Boiotians' (the repetition of that phrase in the text is striking) in the inscription concerning Akraiphia. There were ancient myths that gave shared descent to Larisaians and Boiotians, such as the story reported by Dionysios of Halikarnassos that some of the Pelasgoi, offspring of Poseidon and the nymph Larisa, who had settled in Thessaly and were later driven out, moved thence to Boiotia;[181] or else because Boiotos was a son of Poseidon and Arne (see Chapter 3). But while such legends may well have been pressed into the service of interstate diplomacy, the extent

strategic importance was massive. As Gabbert (1997, 40) remarks, 'It was the door to Macedonia, while the other garrisons in Greece were the outer fences.'

177 *IG* VII 4130; Curty (1995), no. 9. The date of the inscription is some time after 171 BC. It records Akraiphia's use of arbitrators from Larisa, 'ἥτις ὑπάρχει συγγενὴς πᾶσιν Βοιωτοῖς', 'which is kin to all of the Boiotians' (line 7, repeated line 11).

178 *SEG* 26.677; Curty (1995), no. 18. The inscription is late second century; *syngeneia*, *philia* and *eunoia* are all cited.

179 Curty (1995), no. 19; Daux (1975). Once again we have references to *syngeneia*, *philia* and *eunoia*.

180 *IG* IX.2 519; Curty (1995), no. 17. Late second century BC.

181 Dion. Hal. *Ant. Rom.* 1.17–18.

to which they were undeviatingly espoused by everyone in the participant communities is very questionable. Larisa had other *aitia* – for example, the Heraklid descent of its elite, which contradicted Pelasgian and Aiolian identity – not strictly compatible with the idea of shared descent with the Boiotians. These could clearly be set aside when the occasion demanded it. The many cases known of this type where a creative recollection, adaptation or even invention of tradition served specific needs in the immediate term are quite different from the spate of myth-fuelled diplomacy between Kos and Thessaly in the third century, where the connections were deeper and more substantial.

How *syngeneia* might actually be articulated is vividly illustrated by the well-known Larisaian decree from ca. 160–150 BC recording honours for two citizens from Alexandreia in the Troad. The first of these, Bombos son of Alpheios, is rewarded for having visited Larisa and given a remarkable live performance:

> … since
> Bombos son of Alpheios, the Aiolian from Alexandreia, staying
> in the city and making performances in the
> gymnasion, recorded in his compositions and
> readings the glorious things that befell the
> Larisaians, and the *syngeneia* and *philia* existing
> between the cities, and renewed the goodwill existing
> between the Aiolians and the polis of the Larisaians … .[182]

There is evidence that such performances were also a feature of third-century kinship diplomacy. They generally support Curty's argument that *sungeneia* rested upon specifics rather than a vague sense of commonality, for Bombos – like others of his ilk[183] – must have had particular stories to tell. What would they have been in this case, to substantiate the *syngeneia* of the Larisaians and the Aiolians? Helly remarks that 'Bombos avait beaucoup

182 The text is that of Helly (2006a), lines 12–19; he discusses the inscription in detail.

… ὀπειδεὶ
[Β]όμβος Ἀλφεί[οι] Αἰολεὺς [ἀπ' Ἀλεξαν]δρείας παρεπιδαμεί-
σας ἐν τᾶ πόλε[ι καὶ ἐποιεισάμε]νος ἐπιδείξις ἐν τοῦ γ[υ]-
[μ]νασίο[υ συνεμναμονεύσατο ἔ]ν τε τοῖς πεπραγματευμένοις
αὐτοῦ καὶ ἀκροάεσσι τοῦν γεγενειμένουν ἐνδόξουν Λα-
ρισαίοις καὶ τάν τε συγγενείαν καὶ φιλίαν ταῖς πολίεσσι π[ὸ]-
θ' εὐτὰς, ὀνενε[ούσατο] καὶ τὰ φιλάνθρουπα τὰ ὑπάρχοντα
Αἰολείεσσι πὸτ τὰν πόλιν τὰν Λαρισαίουν … .

183 Chaniotis (2009), esp. 259–62. On the relationship between wandering poets and local history see Petrovic (2009). For travelling poets in Hellenistic Larisa in particular see Santin (2018).

à raconter d'histoires et de légendes de voyages et de fondations pour évoquer les liens entre les Thessaliens et les Éoliens d'Asie'[184] – presumably he envisages chiefly (as does Chaniotis also)[185] the story of the original settlement of Aiolis by settlers from Thessaly. If so, this again reveals how little the Heraklid claims of the Larisaian elite served to exclude alternative myth-historical affiliations. The Asklepiadai of Kos could use shared Heraklid lineage to enhance their Thessalian ties, and the Larisaians could respond enthusiastically, but when an Aiolian link was sought instead a different aspect, ingredient or stage of the Thessalian story could be called upon. When, in the later sixth century, Heraklid identity achieved ascendance among the elites of Pelasgiotis it allowed them to create a distinction between the Aiolid identity of other Thessalians and of other ethne such as the Boiotians. By the Hellenistic period, by contrast, all versions of Thessalian myth-history swirled together in a variegated melting pot of possibilities from which diplomats could pick and choose as circumstances dictated.[186]

To sum up our observations so far: for all the significant change and innovation the age after Alexander brought, we see the recurrence of familiar motifs, such as the hero Thessalos. This time, however, their setting is radically altered: it is the multiform network of kinship diplomacy that served to link communities across great geographical distances and despite discrepancies in their size, power and political affiliations. In such a diverse corpus of documents as the inscriptions attesting to this network, Thessalian communities were only a small group of known players within the large number participating. Nonetheless, in selected cases discussed here they offered something special for the non-Thessalian community or communities involved. Moreover, the active participation of the Thessalians in each case moves us away from ancient scholarly speculation about

184 Helly (2006a), 199, n. 73 ('Bombos had much to recount of the histories and legends of voyages and foundations, to evoke the connections between the Thessalians and the Aiolians of Asia.'). Helly also asserts shared ritual between the two in the form of the offerings to Achilles made in the Troad by the Thessalians according to Philostratus, *Heroikos*. For the largely fictional or symbolic nature of this account, however, see the Epilogue. Helly's use of Philostratus in this case is challenged on different grounds by Jones (2010), 37–38, who reasserts the importance of kinship rather than ritual as the source of the communities' connection.

185 Chaniotis (2009), 261: he suggests that the events narrated might have spanned from the mythical to the more recent, to include Thessalian actions in the Macedonian Wars.

186 I am indebted to Rosanagh Mack (pers. comm.) for the observation that the coins of Alexandreia from the third and second centuries, showing a grazing horse, may draw on the important Larisaian issues of the fourth century. This would suggest that the awareness of Thessalian culture in the Troad was anything but limited and superficial.

Thessaly as a place of origins and point of departure: important in the past but no longer active in maintaining links. When Herodotos calls Thessaly the original Aiolis we are given no real suggestion that the Thessalians saw or promoted themselves as such; they are just the recipients of a theory imposed from without. In the third and second centuries, by contrast, perhaps because of the new epigraphic sources available, the Thessalians step into the frame to a newly increased extent as interested exploiters of their own traditions.[187]

6. Heroes in the *perioikis*

Chapter 2 introduced the observation that, although Thessaly was clearly one of the crucibles in which the source material of early epic was formed, active Thessalian involvement in the production of the stories as we know them – in the form in which we have them – appears to have been slight. In the *Iliad*, Thessaly is the land left behind, a theme that extends to other works as Thessalian heroes fail to complete their *nostos*. Thessaly was the origin-point of epic heroes, not their most assiduous 'owner'. Thessalian heroes are diasporic. They were claimed by communities wishing to situate their own beginnings in Thessaly; Thessaly was one of the regions associated with the primordial, with Pelasgoi, with Deukalion, with Hellen. The idea of Thessaly as a place of origins continued in the historiography of the Classical period – as, for example, in Herodotos' assertion that Thessaly was the original Aiolis – without any clear sign that the Thessalians themselves actively exploited the potential of this characterisation to enhance their standing in the Greek world.

It is significant that when the Thessalians manufactured a shared tradition of mythic origins they chose a very different story: not Hellen, not Aiolos and his descendants, not the Aiakidai, not heroes who left but heroes who arrived, Heraklid conquerors from across the mountains and across the sea. Placing the sandal of Jason – if that is how the motif should be interpreted – on the early coins of Larisa takes the hero away from his Iolkian roots, but apart from this we just see glimpses of the heroes of epic as local figures, with no wider incorporation into myth or cult on a regional basis. The games of Protesilaos, Pharsalos' Thetideion, the cult of Zeus Laphystios at Halos in which the figure of Phrixos was central: these are the idiosyncratic local aspects of the famous stories, probably of great age and owing little to the development of epic on the panhellenic level. They are

[187] This is not to say that we can detect Thessalian participation in every such tradition. The Chians had, among their various origin-stories, the claim to have been settled by Pelasgoi from Thessaly, and this is not a tradition of which the Thessalians seem to have made any use. See Mac Sweeney (2013), 80; Thomas (2019), 208–09.

too firmly rooted in particular Thessalian communities or sub-regions to be suitable material for the manufacture of the *ethnos*' charter-myth.

In the Hellenistic period the significance, resonances and indeed location of the heroes of epic underwent unsurprising shifts. There are perhaps signs of change in the last quarter of the fourth century: a case has been made that Pharsalos in particular responded to Alexander the Great's own interest in his Aiakid heritage by stepping up its cultivation of the figures of Achilles and Thetis.[188] This is of course amply possible, and would represent a logical development of the move made at Delphi by Daochos to align his own family's history with the Aiakid stemma by locating the Daochos Monument next to the shrine of Neoptolemos.[189] However, Pharsalos' interest in Achilles is founded upon some problematic evidence, as has been said, in particular the use of Philostratus' *Heroikos* as evidence for ritual activity in the Troad, and the interpretation of divinities on votive reliefs as Achilles and Thetis despite the lack of epigraphic corroboration. By contrast, later fourth- and third-century coinage from perioikic communities present us with some irrefutable signs of interest and give new insights into how poleis in Magnesia and Achaia Phthiotis wished to present themselves to each other, to other Thessalians, and to the Macedonians who were an increasingly important presence from Philip II on.

For the Magnesians and the Phthiotic Achaians, the involvement of Macedon in the affairs of Thessaly and its surrounds brought new opportunities. The check placed upon the regional influence of Pherai, first by Philip II and then, in the early third century, by Demetrios Poliorketes, had repercussions for southern Magnesia mirrored in Achaia Phthiotis by the reduction of Pharsalos. It is fascinating to observe that when the power balance between Thessalian polis and adjoining *perioikis* shifted in this way, the perioikic communities moved to reclaim the special connections with the myths and the characters of epic.

188 Ghisellini (2017).

189 Aston (2012b); note also the Pharsalians' dedication, in the fourth century, of a statue of Homer: *IG* IX.2 246; Decourt (1995), no. 56, p. 73. It is also significant that the Menon of Pharsalos who fought with distinction in the Lamian War of 323/2 chose to name his daughter 'Phthia'. Small signs of growing interest in Achilles in the fourth century are not limited to Pharsalos: see, for example, the curious anecdote about the Larisaian ruler Simos dragging an enemy, Eurydamas, round the tomb of his brother, clearly in imitation of Achilles. Kallim. fr. 588 Pfeiffer; Aristotle fr. 166 Rose; discussion in Hughes (1991), 58. Euphorion's reference to the Thessalian leader of the Amphiktyonic forces in the First Sacred War as the New Achilles might also be relevant in this regard, though whether the soubriquet goes back to Aristotle and Kallisthenes – as Robertson (1978, 64) thought – or is a third-century invention, cannot ultimately be known; if the former, it would accord well with Daochos' association with Neoptolemos.

a) The Argo returns to Iolkos

Whether we identify early Iolkos with Dimini or with a cluster of sites in that area, it was certainly part of the important Mycenaean zone around the Bay of Pagasai and inland to Velestino (Pherai). It was pivotal in early myth, founded by the Aiolid Kretheus (the brother of Salmoneus, king of Elis) and the launching point of the Argo when she left Greece with her crew of heroes to recover the Golden Fleece. And yet from the Classical period the name Iolkos was attached to a polis relatively unimportant in terms of its impingement on wider Thessalian affairs.[190] This obscurity is chiefly a result of the nature and limitations of our sources: literary accounts favour moments at which local communities slotted into major Hellenic events, such as the much-cited offer of Iolkos to Hippias by the Aleuadai;[191] and the excavation and publication of archaeological material from Magnesia at any rate cannot compare with that in Pelasgiotis. All this leaves a misleading impression of unimportance, no doubt. However, this does not negate the significance of the fact that in the second half of the fourth century a polis called Iolkos emerged from the shadows and began to mint coins with a clear reference to the Argo myth.

As Liampi records, the fact that Iolkos minted coins at all was unknown until relatively recently, when a small number in a private collection came to scholarly view; the legend ΙΩΛΚΙΩΝ makes their provenance secure (Fig. 17).[192] Less secure is their dating; Liampi places them around the mid-fourth century on stylistic grounds, but certainty is not possible. Their obverse bears the head of Artemis Iolkia. Arvanitopoulos thought that he had identified remains of a Classical-period temple of Artemis Iolkia in Iolkos, though the attribution of the dislocated fragments to this particular cult is not supported by epigraphic evidence.[193] In the third century her cult was incorporated into Demetrias, whose coins she also decorated;[194] by

[190] Helly (2006b, 160) makes the plausible suggestion that this polis was a new foundation of the Classical period, expressly naming and presenting itself as the successor to the Mycenaean Iolkos. Cf. Intzesiloglou (1994, 34–42), who argues that Iolkos was Dimini in the Late Bronze Age, and that the name switched to Kastro in the Protogeometric period.

[191] Hdt. 5.94.

[192] Liampi (2005), 24.

[193] *PAE* 66 (1911) 305–12; see also Boehm (2018), 156.

[194] For an example see *Triton* XV, 44, no. 61. Though he does not use her specific *epiklesis*, Apollonios surely has Artemis Iolkia (as worshipped in Iolkos and subsequently also in Demetrias) in mind when he speaks of 'νηοσσόον εὐπατέρειαν/Ἄρτεμιν, ἣ κείνας σκοπιὰς ἁλὸς ἀμφιέπεσκεν/ῥυομένη καὶ γαῖαν Ἰωλκίδα' ('Ship-protecting Artemis of the noble father, whose protection encompasses those peaks by the sea [lit. 'look-outs of the sea'] and the Iolkian land' – Ap. Rhod. *Arg.* 1.570–72). Mili (2015, 203) argues that the cult of Artemis Iolkia in Demetrias took precedence, at least from the reign of

Fig. 17. Reverse of a bronze chalkous from Iolkos, showing the prow of the Argo; late fourth century BC. Private coll. Drawing by Rosemary Aston. © Rosemary Aston 2023

the second century at least she formed a local triad with Zeus Akraios on Mount Pelion and Apollo Koropaios on the Pelion promontory.[195] On the reverse of the Iolkian coins is the prow of a ship. Demetrias also combines the obverse Artemis with the ship's prow; if Liampi is right to place the Iolkian coins in the fourth century, then we may see this as a striking case of iconographic borrowing on the part of the new Macedonian foundation. However, Liampi argues that while the ship on the Demetrias issues is a reference to the polis' genuine naval power and strategic significance, in the case of Iolkos the image is of a specific mythological vessel, the Argo.[196]

It is hard to imagine that the authorities in Demetrias would not also

Antigonos Gonatas: 'Artemis Iolkia might have continued to receive some cult back at Iolkos, but the headquarters of the cult was clearly now the new sanctuary in the sacred agora closely connected with the palace.'

195 See, for example, *IG* IX.2 1109, on which see Daux (1959). On Korope see Adrymi-Sismani (2012), 177–79.

196 Liampi (2005), 27–29. Further discussion of the prow motif on the coins of Demetrias: Kron and Furtwängler (1983).

have wished to evoke the Argo, as a mythological parallel to the naval importance of the polis in the present day. However, it is certainly true that the ship on the Iolkian coins has a detail that makes it far less generic: an odd formation of the prow post. Liampi suggests that this represents the famous speaking timber from Dodona that was incorporated into the Argo's fabric,[197] but, if so, the die-cutter has done a very poor job of representing an oak-leaf (something ancient die-cutters were perfectly able to depict when they wished to).[198] Instead, an ingenious suggestion has been made to me:[199] that the prow post is in semi-anthropomorphic form, female, with one arm extended forward (urging the ship on its way, one supposes) while the other is crooked back.[200] In examples where the edge of the flan is not too worn, the shape of the figure's head can be clearly seen. That the speaking timber of the Argo might be depicted in such a way is supported by the Attic red figure column-krater from ca. 470–460 BC in which the Argo has a semi-anthropomorphic stern post; the design is very different, but the essential idea – that part of the Argo had a female form – is the same.[201] As for numismatic parallels, the closest are the coins of Demetrios Poliorketes in which a winged, trumpet-playing Nike stands in the prow of a galley; the Iolkian design is very similar, but incorporates the female form within the very fabric of the ship. Thus the identification of the vessel is assured.

The traditional way of describing the historical context of these developments is with reference to Philip II's changes to the distribution of regional power in Thessaly. Up to the mid-fourth century, although the date of commencement is uncertain, the Pagasai region was under the control of Pherai, which profited greatly from the access to the sea thus provided. Philip, however, needed to reduce Pherai's power as well as ensuring that his control of Thessaly served his own strategic aims and the Pagasitic area was freed from Pheraian control, while the port's revenues were redirected into the Macedonian royal coffers. While this picture is substantially accurate, a more radical view has been put forward by

197 Liampi (2005), 29.

198 See, for example, *SNG* Manchester University Museum 861 (the Epeirote League, ca. 230–170 BC): one can clearly see the shape of the oak leaves in the wreath, small as they are. Philip V of Macedon also minted elaborate oak-wreath designs: e.g. *SNG* Lockett Collection 1531.

199 R. Mack, pers. comm.

200 Alternatively, the arm not extended forward could be holding a shield, its concave interior towards the viewer. There are other coin images in which a goddess holds a shield with its upper rim close to her body and its lower rim elevated outwards: see, for example, *SNG* Manchester University Museum 857, an octobol of Pyrrhos showing a standing Athena.

201 New York Met. Mus. 34.11.7.

Helly, who argues that in fact Philip facilitated a movement of population whereby the Magnetes, previously based on and around Mount Ossa to the north, extended their range southwards to inhabit also the region around the gulf.[202] This would give added significance to the energetic numismatic self-presentation we see in Iolkos and elsewhere, and to the (re-)creation of a sub-regional identity around the new polis of Demetrias in the third century BC. Rather than involving merely the appropriation or reappropriation of mythological elements by communities with a long history in the region, it would involve a newly arrived group trying to forge for itself a myth-historical sense of belonging in territory recently acquired. The fact that so much emphasis appears to have been placed on the oldest known myths from the region becomes especially interesting seen in this light, as an appeal to long-standing tradition by an immigrant population.[203]

Whether one agrees with Helly's argument, however, becomes less important after the foundation of Demetrias.[204] Whether or not Magnetes were installed in the region in the later fourth century BC, from ca. 294 the synoecism caused undeniable change. Existing local populations shifted: some poleis seem to have lost their inhabitants to the new settlement, while others remained in place but became satellites of Demetrias.[205] Moreover,

[202] Helly (2006b). The theory is developed in more detail in Helly (2013). His assertions concerning population movements in the fourth century convince somewhat, less so the suggestion that they were initiated by a late phase of the territorial encroachment of the invading Thessaloi.

[203] In many ways Demetrias was not culturally integrated within the surrounding landscape, but retained its special identity and unusual degree of multiculturalism. This is reflected in its famous painted grave stelai, which do not replicate Thessalian funerary norms of the time: see Stamatopoulou (2016), 438; Stamatopoulou (2018), 363–65.

[204] On the site and its urban formation see Marzolff (1996).

[205] The two categories are strongly suggested by Strabo (9.5.15): 'τῆς δὲ Δημητριάδος ἑπτὰ σταδίους ὑπέρκειται τῆς θαλάττης Ἰωλκός. ἔκτισε δὲ Δημήτριος ὁ πολιορκητὴς ἐπώνυμον ἑαυτοῦ τὴν Δημητριάδα μεταξὺ Νηλείας καὶ Παγασῶν ἐπὶ θαλάττῃ τὰς πλησίον πολίχνας εἰς αὐτὴν συνοικίσας, Νήλειάν τε καὶ Παγασὰς καὶ Ὀρμένιον, ἔτι δὲ Ῥιζοῦντα Σηπιάδα Ὀλιζῶνα Βοίβην Ἰωλκόν, αἳ δὴ νῦν εἰσι κῶμαι τῆς Δημητριάδος.' ('Iolkos is situated seven stadia from Demetrias, overlooking the sea. Demetrias, which is on the sea between Neleia and Pagasai, was founded by Demetrios Poliorketes, who named it after himself, settling in it the inhabitants of the nearby towns, Neleia and Pagasai and Ormenion, and also Rhizos, Sepias, Olizon, Boibe, and Iolkos, which are now villages belonging to Demetrias.') The survival of Iolkos as a political entity in its own right, at least for a few decades, is indicated by an inscription dated between 276 and 239, in which are recorded decrees of the *dēmos* of the Iolkians (with the formula 'ἔδοξεν τῶι δήμωι τῶι Ἰωλ̣κ[ίων') – see Graninger (2011b), who describes it as a 'sub-πόλις entity' (p. 122). It is unrealistic to imagine that Demetrios would have wished to empty the

new citizens from Macedon and even farther afield came, in time, to settle in Demetrias.[206] The arrival of the Magnetes in the region over a century before would probably have paled into relative insignificance compared with this new upheaval. And, as Kravaritou in particular has identified, the new conditions of the third century would have created a powerful need to unify the area – Demetrias and its surrounding territory – and to mesh together religious and mythological traditions with the new circumstances of the time.[207] Artemis Iolkia was, as we have seen, part of this process of incorporation and unification, drawing on an important element of the Jason story. Nor were other major epic myths neglected; after all, Demetrias had within its territory the single most important node in the Thessalian myth-historical landscape – the cave of Cheiron.

b) Cheiron on Pelion

The importance of Cheiron to early Thessalian myth cannot be overstated. As nurse and educator, he tied together all the major sub-regional clusters of early Thessalian mythology: the interlocking clans of Phthia, Iolkos and Pherai, and the Asklepios bundle linking the Dotion Plain with Trikka. There is no doubt that he represents one of the oldest and most fundamental elements of Thessalian mythology, and his place within the schema of Thessalian fertility was discussed in Chapter 4. There has been a tendency in past scholarship to see Cheiron's cult on Pelion also as a very early part of the area's religious milieu,[208] but it is important not to ignore the fact that his cult on Pelion is tied almost exclusively to Hellenistic sources, or the clear signs of his special importance to that area in the context of third-century historical developments.

Attempts to push the cult back even into the Classical period rely on the identification of a site explored and documented by Arvanitopoulos on the Pliasidi peak of Pelion (Fig. 18).[209] This was almost certainly a sanctuary: the oval shape of 'Building A' suggests a small temple, and many of the small objects found have the quality of dedications. Three pieces of dedicatory stelai were also discovered. The site also incorporated a cave, and it is this that prompted the identification of the site as that described by Herakleides: according to Arvanitopoulos

area entirely; rather, he needed to move enough people to stock his new town, while creating a dependent network of surrounding settlements. The fact that Artemis Iolkia had a sanctuary within Demetrias, as well as her Classical shrine in Iolkos itself, suggests a process of religious integration rather than straightforward centralisation: see Kravaritou (2016), 134–36.

206 Batziou-Efstathiou (1996), 16.

207 Kravaritou (2011). See also Boehm (2018), 151–61; Canlas (2021), 366–70.

208 See, for example, Papachatzis (1984), 136–41; Gorrini (2006).

209 Arvanitopoulos in *Praktika* 1911, 305–12.

Fig. 18. View east from the Pliasidi peak of Mount Pelion. Photograph: author's own

and most subsequent historians, the cave found is the Cheironion and 'Building B' the temple of Zeus Akraios.[210] However, this identification is not unproblematic. There is no clear epigraphic evidence. Moreover, Pelion is not short of caves (the Pelion Cave Project identified over 150 caves and rock shelters on the mountain),[211] so it is not impossible that the Cheironion was elsewhere on Mount Pelion. However, looking at the matter from another angle, if the Pliasidi remains are not those of the sanctuary of Zeus Akraios and Cheiron, one is left with the task of ascertaining what they *were*, and no suitable candidate is forthcoming based on our knowledge of the cults active in the region at the time. The

[210] Mili (2015), 203. Wiznura and Williamson (2018–2020, 92–93) assume that Cheiron's cult on the site was of great (though unspecified) antiquity, and that of Zeus Akraios a relatively late addition, but Cheiron's early role in mythology does not necessarily translate into ritual practice in Thessaly. Like Achilles, he may have been brought into – or at least greatly enhanced in – Thessalian cult in the Classical or even Hellenistic periods.

[211] Andreasen et al. (2009).

matter is an ongoing mystery.[212] One can, however, say with certainty that Cheiron was of religious importance in Thessaly in the fourth century BC, since he is included in the long metrical inscription in the cave of the nymphs near Pharsalos, though in that context it should be noted that he is one of a large number of deities worshipped in the site.[213]

The third century is a different matter: then the cult on Pelion comes alive before our eyes, the focus of a famous and remarkable annual pilgrimage by the young men of Demetrias, as described by the third-century geographer Herakleides Kritikos:[214]

> On the topmost peak of the mountain is a cave, called the Cheironion, and a sanctuary of Zeus Aktaios to which, at the rising of the Dog Star and in the time of greatest heat, the most distinguished citizens and those in the prime of life ascend. They have been chosen in the presence of the priest, and they are wrapped round the waist with new fleeces – so great does the cold on the mountain happen to be.[215]

It is clear that Demetrias is unique in its ethnic mixture and in the circumstances of its creation. That said, this energetic performance of ritual at the Cheironion must have served symbolic purposes relevant to

212 The dating of the Pliasidi finds is doubly puzzling when compared with Herakleides' text. They give a fifth-century date for the inception of the sanctuary and attest to considerable activity in the fourth century; thereafter the material record wanes, presumably indicating a lessening in ritual activity. How are we to reconcile this with Herakleides' suggestion of a cult flourishing in the third century?

213 Decourt (1995), no. 73, 90–94; Aston (2011), 91–92; Aston (2015); Wagman (2016), 66–93.

214 On Herakleides and his work see Arenz (2006), who notes on pp. 46–47 that Thessaly has a special role in the text. Not only does the Thessaly section bulk large, it also has religious information lacking elsewhere. Most interestingly, it provokes Herakleides, unusually, to switch into the first person. All these observations encourage Arenz to say that 'Eine biographische Verortung des Autors nach Thessalien, vielleicht sogar als Bürger von Demetrias, ist daher plausibel.' ('A biographical origin in Thessaly, perhaps as an inhabitant of Demetrias, is plausible.') If true, this would certainly give Herakleides a level of insight into Thessalian customs unique among surviving authors of the period. On the dating of the text and the backdrop of the Chremonidean War: pp. 54–55.

215 *FGrH* 369A F 2.8: 'ἐπ' ἄκρας δὲ τῆς τοῦ ὄρους κορυφῆς σπηλαιόν ἐστι τὸ καλούμενον Χειρώνιον καὶ Διὸς Ἀκταίου ἱερὸν, ἐφ' ὃ κατὰ κυνὸς ἀνατολὴν κατὰ τὸ ἀκμαιότατον καῦμα ἀναβαίνουσι τῶν πολιτῶν οἱ ἐπιφανέστατοι καὶ ταῖς ἡλικίαις ἀκμάζοντες, ἐπιλεχθέντες ἐπὶ τοῦ ἱερέως, ἐνεζωσμένοι κώδια τρίποκα καινά· τοιοῦτον συμβαίνει ἐπὶ τοῦ ὄρους τὸ ψῦχος εἶναι.' With good reason, it has become conventional to amend this to 'Akraios' on the basis of epigraphic evidence from the area and of the *epiklesis*' occurrence elsewhere: see Wiznura and Williamson (2018–2020), 91. Note: throughout, the translation of Herakleides used is that of McInerney (adapted).

all the constituent elements of Demetrias: Macedonians, Magnetes and Thessalians from other parts of the region.[216] And in fact we may see it as offering a powerful boost to Magnesian identity and self-respect, and perhaps countering some aspects of the region's marginality over the foregoing two centuries. Cheiron is a fitting recipient of such a gesture. On the one hand he is integral to the network of Thessalian heroic mythology. As the tutor of Achilles, Herakles, Jason, Asklepios and others, he links the great stories of northern Greece: all these heroes and more began their careers in his mountain cave before going on to fulfil their glorious and difficult destinies. By (re-)claiming Cheiron, the Magnesians could claim a stake in epic narratives that resounded beyond Thessaly, through the Greek-speaking world. At the same time, Cheiron is profoundly marginal – physically, with his hybrid form; spatially, in his Pelion eyrie; and existentially, as a being both godlike and death-prone.[217] This is part of his essentially Kronian identity (see Chapter 4) and integral to his character; it contributes, however, to his special utility in the ambit of third-century Demetrias.

Burkert identified a strong connection between the fleece ritual on Pelion and a sacrifice made on the island of Keos by the hero Aristaios to ward off pestilence caused by the Dog-star Sirius.[218] The connections are various: the fleece ritual on Pelion is timed according to Sirius and its parching heat; Aristaios was a Thessalian hero, son of Apollo by the nymph Kyrene, the granddaughter of Peneios;[219] he was one of Cheiron's charges and protégés;[220] both Aristaios and Cheiron could deflect sickness.[221] For Burkert, the two cults, on Pelion and on Keos, are part of a number, in different parts of the Greek world, whose purpose was to protect agricultural fertility from various forms of natural harm, in particular damaging wind and pestilence. It is interesting to note that both were couched in the language of panhellenic utility: Aristaios' Kean sacrifice was 'on behalf of all Greeks';[222] Cheiron was a 'friend to

[216] On the importance of Zeus Akraios to the religious self-presentation of Demetrias and Magnesia more widely see Wiznura and Williamson (2018–2020), 93–96.

[217] On the mortality and death of Cheiron as central to his characterisation see Aston (2006).

[218] Burkert (1983), 109–16.

[219] Pindar's *Pythian* 9 is our most detailed early description of the story in which Apollo woos Kyrene with the help of Cheiron. However, the story of Apollo, Kyrene and the birth of Aristaios goes back to the *Ehoiai*: fr. 215 MW; West (1985), 85–89.

[220] Ap. Rhod. *Arg.* 2.509–10.

[221] Ap. Rhod. *Arg.* 2.518–19.

[222] Diod. 4.82.2.

mankind'.[223] The former in particular cannot but remind us of Aiakos' sacrifice to Zeus Hellanios on Aigina.

However, it is striking that all our secure and detailed evidence for the Pelion cult and for the interlinked activity of Aristaios on Keos is third century in date (or later). This encourages the suggestion that the religious reshaping of the Pelion region under the aegis of Demetrias included a reassertion of the importance of Cheiron's cult in the maritime network of agriculturally important ritual. Apollonios, for example, who shows other signs of being aware of and responsive to Thessalian epichoric cult,[224] includes in his *Argonautika* a detailed description of the birth and upbringing of Aristaios, and his subsequent religious role on Keos:[225]

> There [in north Africa] she bore Phoibos' son, Aristaios, whom the Haimonians, rich in wheat fields, call Agreus and Nomios. For in his love for her the god made her a long-lived nymph in that land and a huntress, whereas he took their infant son to be raised in Cheiron's cave. And when he grew up, the divine Muses arranged his marriage and taught him healing and prophecy, and they made him keeper of all their sheep that grazed on the Athamantian plain of Phthia and around steep Othrys and the sacred stream of the Apidanos river. But when from the sky Seirios was scorching the Minoan islands, and for a long time the inhabitants had no relief, then they summoned him on the instructions of the Far-Shooter to ward off the pestilence. And he left Phthia at the command of his father and settled in Keos, having gathered the Parrhasian people who are of the lineage of Lykaon. And he built a great altar to Zeus Ikmaios and duly performed sacrifices on the mountains to that star Seirios and to Zeus himself, son of Kronos. And for this reason the Etesian winds sent by Zeus cool the land for forty days, and still today in Keos priests make sacrifices before the Dog Star rises.[226]

223 Pind. *Pyth.* 3.5.

224 This is not to say that he had any personal contact with Thessaly. As Librarian at Alexandria he would have had access to unparalleled academic resources; furthermore, his work served the perspective and cultural ideology of the Ptolemaic court (probably during the reign of Ptolemy III Euergetes). See Stephens (2008), 98–104, who makes the interesting point that, in alluding extensively to Pindar's *Pythian* 4, Apollonios is emphasising traditional connections with north Africa. In other words, once again early Thessalian mythology is used in the partial fabrication of tradition, and as a way of anchoring disparate communities to the Greek mainland and its myth-history.

225 On Apollonios within the intellectual and political context of Ptolemaic Alexandria see Hunter (1993), 152–62; Mori (2008), 19–41.

226 Ap. Rhod. *Arg.* 2.506–27:

ἔνθα δ' Ἀρισταῖον Φοίβῳ τέκεν, ὃν καλέουσιν
Ἀγρέα καὶ Νόμιον πολυλήιοι Αἱμονιῆες.
τὴν μὲν γὰρ φιλότητι θεὸς ποιήσατο νύμφην

So Aristaios' Thessalian identity is reinforced through his role as keeper of the region's famous herds, and through his cult titles, suggestive of a hero-cult (otherwise unattested in the region). Whatever its origins, the trans-Aegean nature of the Cheiron–Aristaios ritual complex certainly suits the outward-looking perspective of Demetrias, a node in a network of Antigonid strongholds, as well as restoring the far-flung connections that, in the earliest surviving Greek mythology, Thessalian figures certainly had.

For all Demetrias' power and the importance of the sea-link, however, within Thessaly Magnesia did not enjoy significant ownership of the one resource for which the region was famous: extensive well-irrigated plains suited to the large-scale cultivation of crops and flocks. From a modern tourist's perspective the beauty and distinction of Thessaly's eastern seaboard are unmatched; in practical terms, however, and from the ancient viewpoint, it was second-rate land compared with the plains spread out on view to the west. Whereas, as we have seen, the fifth-century self-presentation of the Thessalians along the Peneios and its tributaries rested upon the twin products of horses and grain, Magnesia could boast no such resources in any real measure. What is more, Magnesia and the Magnetes are repeatedly linked with tales of defeat and subjugation. Pelion was the home of the Centaurs, driven from its peaks by the Lapiths who also appropriated key territory along the course of the Peneios.[227] One ancient account of the origins of the Penestai, Thessaly's serf population, claims that they were in fact the Magnetes, reduced to servile status by the

αὐτοῦ μακραίωνα καὶ ἀγρότιν· υἷα δ' ἔνεικεν
νηπίαχον Χείρωνος ὑπ' ἄντροισιν κομέεσθαι.
τῷ καὶ ἀεξηθέντι θεαὶ γάμον ἐμνήστευσαν
Μοῦσαι, ἀκεστορίην τε θεοπροπίας τ' ἐδίδαξαν·
καί μιν ἑῶν μήλων θέσαν ἤρανον, ὅσσ' ἐνέμοντο
ἂμ πεδίον Φθίης Ἀθαμάντιον ἀμφί τ' ἐρυμνὴν
Ὄθρυν καὶ ποταμοῦ ἱερὸν ῥόον Ἀπιδανοῖο.
ἦμος δ' οὐρανόθεν Μινωίδας ἔφλεγε νήσους
Σείριος, οὐδ' ἐπὶ δηρὸν ἔην ἄκος ἐνναέτῃσιν,
τῆμος τόν γ' ἐκάλεσσαν ἐφημοσύνῃς Ἑκάτοιο
λοιμοῦ ἀλεξητῆρα. λίπεν δ' ὅ γε πατρὸς ἐφετμῇ
Φθίην, ἐν δὲ Κέῳ κατενάσσατο, λαὸν ἀγείρας
Παρράσιον, τοί πέρ τε Λυκάονός εἰσι γενέθλης·
καὶ βωμὸν ποίησε μέγαν Διὸς Ἰκμαίοιο,
ἱερά τ' εὖ ἔρρεξεν ἐν οὔρεσιν ἀστέρι κείνῳ
Σειρίῳ αὐτῷ τε Κρονίδῃ Διί. τοῖο δ' ἕκητι
γαῖαν ἐπιψύχουσιν ἐτήσιοι ἐκ Διὸς αὖραι
ἤματα τεσσαράκοντα, Κέῳ δ' ἔτι νῦν ἱερῆες
ἀντολέων προπάροιθε Κυνὸς ῥέζουσι θυηλάς (trans. Race, adapted).

227 See, for example, Strabo 9.5.19

invading Thessaloi.[228] The fact that we have challenged the historicity of this story of invasion and displacement does not remove the ancient characterisation of the Magnetes as subject to defeat and displacement.

The cult of Cheiron and Zeus Akraios gave the Magnesians, in particular those incorporated within the polis of Demetrias, a way of being marginal with pride. As Buxton has noted, the fleeces worn by the men making their annual pilgrimage to the cave are the garments of the shepherd and the hunter, those who pursue their lives and livelihoods on the peaks that neither arable nor the husbandry of bovines or horses can reach.[229] They are enacting the symbolic life of the mountain that forms the core of their territory, and they do so in such a way as to emphasise, rather than play down, the extremity of the location: they move from the flaming heat of the Dog-days at low altitude to the cold of the mountain, thus symbolically connecting the extremes of their variegated territory. This is very different from the plains around the Peneios' banks, and the difference is being positively emphasised.

However, when we begin to think of Pelion as a marginal area, second-best land, we must remember that it was not like the bare crags of many other parts of Greece. Even today, the thick scrub of oak and beech that clothes the mountains' tops is very striking to an eye more accustomed to arid rock. Even in Homer, the lushness of Pelion was expressed in its epithet, *einosiphyllon*,[230] and this characterisation continues in Herakleides' almost rhapsodic descriptions. The trees and plants of Pelion, however, are not merely decorative: some bear edible fruit, but the majority are noted for their healing properties, as in the following passage.

> The mountain is rich in medicinal plants that possess a great variety of healing powers for those who can recognize them and can use them. It has one in particular with properties unlike any other. The bush grows to a height of no more than a metre above the ground, and is black; the root, however, grows just as deep below the ground.
>
> When the root is ground fine and applied as a poultice, those suffering gout lose their pain and it prevents their ligaments from swelling. The bark is also ground up and drunk with wine, an effective treatment for bowel complaints. The leaves, too, are ground up and the salve is applied to the linen bandages of those suffering eye disease. This salve gently dries up the constant mucous flow, giving relief to those who suffer from the discharge and are in danger of losing their sight, so that the discharge is no longer produced in the eyes.

228 Theopompos *FGrH* 115 F 122; discussion in Ducat (1994), 52–53 and 94.
229 Buxton (1994), 93–94.
230 Hom. *Il.* 2.757.

> One clan among the citizens knows this power; this clan is said to be descended from Cheiron. Father hands down and shows the power to son, and thus it is guarded, so that none other of the citizens knows it. And it is sacrilegious for those who understand the medicines to help the afflicted for payment, but they must do so for free.[231]

As in 2.8, the 'citizens' in question are those of Demetrias, and another important element is added to our picture of that city's relationship to the Cheiron cult: a family from the city claims descent from Cheiron[232] and practises herbal medicine in that capacity, free of charge.[233] We know nothing about this family (they must, at least, be local to the area, rather than Macedonian or from elsewhere, for their genealogical claim to have any weight); nonetheless, we can see that their connection with Cheiron allowed them to present themselves as the authorised exploiters of Pelion's most valued natural resources. These resources are the opposite of those on the plains – rare, semi-magical herbs rather than waving corn and herds of horses and cattle. But they are valuable in their own way, their value conveyed in the care with which access to their power is controlled.

[231] *FGrH* 369A F 2.10–12: 'τὸ δὲ ὄρος πολυφάρμακόν τέ ἐστι καὶ πολλὰς ἔχον καὶ παντοδαπὰς δυνάμεις τάς τε ὄψεις αὐτῶν γινώσκουσι καὶ χρῆσθαι δυναμένοις. μίαν δέ τινα ἔχει καὶ ἄλλας δυνάμεις ἀνομοίους. φύεται δὲ τὸ δένδρον τῶι μεγέθει μὲν οὐ πλέον ἢ πήχεος τοῦ ὑπὲρ γῆς φαινομένου, τῆι δὲ χρόαι μέλαν. ἡ δὲ ῥίζα ἕτερον τοσοῦτόν ἐστι κατὰ γῆς πεφυκυῖα.

'τούτου δὲ ἡ μὲν ῥίζα τριφθεῖσα λεῖα καὶ καταπλασθεῖσα τῶν ποδαγρώντων τοὺς πόνους ἀφίστησι καὶ κωλύει τὰ νεῦρα φλεγμαίνειν. ὁ δὲ φλοιὸς λειανθεὶς καὶ μετ' οἴνου ποθεὶς τοὺς κοιλιακοὺς ὑγιαίνει. τὰ δὲ φύλλα τριφθέντα καὶ ἐγχρισθέντα εἰς ὀθόνιον τῶν ὀφθαλμιώντων καὶ ὑπὸ τοῦ ῥεύματος κατατεινομένων καὶ κινδυνευόντων ῥαγῆναι τὴν ὄψιν τὴν ἐπιφορὰν τοῦ ῥεύματος ἀναστέλλει πραιέως καὶ ὡσανεὶ παραιτούμενα μηκέτι ἐπὶ τοὺς ὀφθαλμοὺς φέρεσθαι τὸ ῥεῦμα.

'ταύτην δὲ τὴν δύναμιν ἓν τῶν πολιτῶν οἶδεν γένος· ὃ δὴ λέγεται Χείρωνος ἀπόγονον εἶναι. παραδίδωσι δὲ καὶ δείκνυσι πατὴρ υἱῶι, καὶ οὕτως ἡ δύναμις φυλάσσεται, ὡς οὐδεὶς ἄλλος οἶδεν τῶν πολιτῶν· οὐχ ὅσιον δὲ τοὺς ἐπισταμένους τὰ φάρμακα μισθοῦ τοῖς κάμνουσι βοηθεῖν ἀλλὰ προῖκα.'

[232] It is significant to see Cheiron being made an ancestor in his own right: in Archaic and Classical traditions he trained heroes but was rarely an ancestor in the strict sense (bearing only daughters, none of whose offspring are ever mentioned: Pind. *Pyth.* 4.1–2–103). Note also the seemingly innovative claim by the Thessalian author Souidas (probably third century BC) that Cheiron was the father of Thetis and grandfather of Achilles, a move that gives him influential progeny (Souidas *FGrH* 602 F 7 – see further discussion below).

[233] Cf. Plutarch, *Quaest. Conv.* 3.1: the Magnesians offer to Cheiron the roots of plants that have been efficacious on a patient, considering him the first practitioner of the art. A strong association of Cheiron with Pelion's healing herbs is to be found in Theophrastos, *Peri Phytōn Historia* 9.11.1–7 and Nikandros, *Theriaka* 500–05. See Aston (2009), 94.

There may be one final aspect of the healing theme that further explains the value of the Cheiron cult to Magnesia – in particular, here, to Demetrias. Magnesia was involved, as noted above, in the *asylia*-bid made by the Koans on behalf of their Asklepieia in the 240s BC. The Magnesian polis to which the Koan ambassadors directed their address was Homolion, on the northern flank of Ossa, overlooking the mouth of the Peneios. This is interesting given the dominant role of Demetrias by that time: one might have expected Demetrias, not Homolion, to be the Magnesian polis that hosted and responded to the Koan *theōroi*.[234] But not so. While religious processes such as the *asylia* bid were largely above, or outside, political allegiances of the time, we might explain the role of Homolion by recalling that Kos was at this time under Ptolemaic control.[235] For its *theōroi* to approach Demetrias, an Antigonid stronghold, may have been too problematic even within the sphere of interregional religious diplomacy. If an appeal to *Realpolitik* is not persuasive, one might note instead the poliadic importance of Homolion's own Asklepios cult, whose priests played a prominent civic role – this would have constituted helpful conditions for the Koan *theōroi* to work in. The Asklepios cult of Demetrias seems, by contrast, to be of later date.[236]

In either case, the apparent[237] non-involvement of Demetrias in the Koan relationship may help further to explain the role and value of Cheiron's cult in Demetrias. The Koan healers claimed the identity of Asklepiadai, descendants of Asklepios, whose worship, they believed, came to their island from Thessalian Trikka. But the healers of Demetrias make a bold counter-claim: they are descended from Asklepios' teacher, and therefore

234 On the subordination of Magnesian communities to the authority of Demetrias, both in the third and the second century BC, see Intzesiloglou (1996).

235 Rigsby (2004). For an opposing view see Buraselis (2004), who argues that the *asylia*-claim by Kos was indeed a political gambit, designed to obtain Antigonid favour in particular.

236 The secure evidence for this (coins and inscriptions) is all from the Roman period: see, for example, *IG* IX.2, 1124. See Mili (2015), 143. The Magnesian *koinon* was reshaped under Roman influence in the early second century and became an autonomous political body, free from Thessalian domination and based in Demetrias; at this time, Asklepios was placed on the federal coinage of Magnesia. See, for example, Rogers (1932), 354, 356; for the new *koinon* structures see Intzesiloglou (1996), 101–02.

237 It is necessary to stress the *apparent*, because of the patchy nature of the evidence. However, the inscription recording the grants of *asylia* from northern Greek cities seems to follow a geographical order, corresponding with the journey of the *theōroi*: the order is Gonnoi – Homolion – Phthiotic Thebes – Megara, and the omission of Demetrias from its proper location in that southward-moving list is significant. It is also noteworthy that Homolion seems to be treated as representing the *ethnos* of the Magnesians, a daring claim that does seem to exclude Demetrias deliberately in, one would think, a spirit of competition for local cultural standing.

have a sort of technical primacy. They could therefore establish their own unique place in the network of healing cults and mythology without being overshadowed either by Kos or by the Asklepieion at Trikka in western Thessaly. This does not mean that Asklepios himself was unimportant in Magnesia: when the *ethnos* had a formal *koinon* in the second century BC, the god was placed on their federal coinage. In the third century, however, with numerous major Greek sanctuaries competing energetically for a stake in Asklepios' birth, life, death and legacy, Cheiron provided Demetrias with a refreshing alternative. Once again, a certain religious marginality (matching the marginality of his cult location and physical anatomy) was in fact advantageous rather than a weakness to his worshippers.

Finally, Cheiron was a suitable deity for a polis as outward-looking and as connected as Demetrias. He anchored in Thessalian mythology heroes whose actions and travels actually reached out over the Aegean: Achilles to the Troad, Jason to the Black Sea. Cheiron was never as insular as he might seem: his image turns up at Lefkandi, testifying to cultural traffic between southern Thessaly and Euboia in the tenth century, long before the first appearance of surviving epic verse (Fig. 2). While this aspect was important in early Thessalian mythology, when the Thessalians come to manufacture their collective religious and mythological persona in the fifth century they turn aside from it somewhat to focus on Poseidon's creation of their landscape and their horses, a myth-cluster redolent of autochthony. Magnesia has no share in that theme and with a renewed interest in Cheiron we see the citizens of Demetrias recovering the earlier strand, focused on the relationship between Pelion and the Bay of Iolkos and the networks and connections that lay beyond.

c) Aiakids, Athamids and others in Achaia Phthiotis

As in Magnesia, where the subduing of Pheraian power and later the foundation of Demetrias brought about a radical shake-up in myth and religion and their use to articulate regional identity, so in Achaia Phthiotis the renewed focus on old myths can only be understood by reference to external factors.[238] As Haagsma, Surtees and Chykerda have demonstrated, the reduction of Pharsalian power combined with the turbulent conditions of the wars between Macedonians, Aitolians and Romans proved fertile ground for a new sense of ethnic solidarity among the poleis of Achaia Phthiotis.[239] While, as they show, various aspects of material culture can

[238] For further manifestations of the energetic appropriation of tradition in Hellenistic Achaia Phthiotis see Canlas (2021), 339–42, who focuses on the construction of small, simple temples as a deliberately archaising tendency.

[239] Haagsma et al. (2019). See also Boehm (2018), 68: there was a 'wholesale Antigonid reorganization of Achaia Phthiotis' under Demetrios. Boehm also follows Reinders

shed light on this process, coinage is absolutely key. The emergence of a monogram ☧ on the coins of Peuma, New Halos and Larisa Kremaste is significant: while not certain in its meaning, this symbol is most plausibly interpreted as an abbreviation of ΑΧΑΙΩΝ; and indeed, whatever its meaning its recurrence between poleis reflects a strong co-operative element at work.[240] Even more telling are the images on the coins.

Between the fourth and the second century BC – a remarkable consistency over time – Larisa Kremaste minted bronze coins whose reverse shows Thetis, carrying armour – certainly bound for Achilles – and riding a hippocamp (see Fig. 19).[241] The AX monogram is also included, on the shield carried by Thetis. It is even possible that this motif appeared on a state seal of the polis, though this is based upon the identification – indeed, the very authenticity – of a mysterious object, a bronze disc just under five centimetres in diameter with the Thetis motif, strikingly similar to the coins, on one side and a Skylla on the other.[242] Somewhat in favour of a civic function is the abbreviation ΛΑ on the outer edge of the side bearing Thetis. However, accounting for the presence of Skylla on an object of such major collective importance is tricky; there is no other evidence for her significance to this community. It is perhaps safer to assume that the object merely confirms the popularity of the emblem in this place in the fourth century (and later); Miller notes its presence on various items of jewellery.[243] Coinage was no doubt partly responsible for encouraging the dissemination of the image beyond official representations and into the private domain.

Pharsalos had an important sanctuary of the goddess Thetis, and Larisa Kremaste's enthusiastic appropriation of her image, with the implicit Achilles-connection conveyed by the weapons, should certainly be seen in part as a response to the reduction of Pharsalian power by Demetrios Poliorketes at the end of the fourth century.[244] However, we should not overlook the fact that Achaia Phthiotis forms the heart of Achilles' territory in the Catalogue of Ships; rather than staging an audacious claim on myths

(2009, 372–73) in believing that Demetrios created a political *koinon* of the Phthiotic Achaians, based on the AX monogram on the coinage of several poleis. It is not in fact certain whether we are looking at a formal *koinon*, a mint union, or just intense economic co-operation, but in any case, the increased cohesion of the region is clear.

240 Reinders et al. (2016) give an overview of the issues and emphasise the prosperity and significance of Achaia Phthiotis in the early Hellenistic period.

241 Note that a strikingly similar type was minted by Pyrrhos of Epeiros in the period 300–270 BC; see, for example, *SNG* Lockett Collection 1651. It is likely that the Epeirote coin drew inspiration from its Larisaian counterpart, given other evidence of Pyrrhos' interest in Thessaly.

242 Robinson (1934).

243 Miller (1979), 18–19.

244 Diod. 20.110.2.

Fig. 19. Bronze alloy trichalkon from Larisa Kremaste; ca. 302–286 BC. Obv.: head of a young man (Achilles?); rev.: Thetis on a hippocamp carrying shield. Photograph: © The Trustees of the British Museum

'belonging' to another polis, Larisa Kremaste was merely indicating a new desire and ability, through coinage, to remind the region and the wider Greek world of the myth's original range. We do not, of course, have enough evidence to be sure how much of an innovation this really represented; it is amply possible that the stories of Achilles and Thetis circulated in the region throughout the intervening centuries.[245] But it is indeed important that when, in the early Hellenistic period, Larisa Kremaste joined the co-operative minting trend, it was the Thetis story she selected, a clear reassertion of her epic credentials.[246]

A stronger sense of the maintenance of tradition is available to us in the case of New Halos. We call this Hellenistic polis 'New' because it was a refoundation, in 302, of an earlier Halos at Magoula Plataniotiki; the new

[245] A revisionist Thessalian approach to Achilles and his mythology in the Hellenistic period may also be suggested by Souidas' presentation of him, in his work the *Thessalika*, as the son of Thetis and grandson of Thetis' father Cheiron (Souidas *FGrH* 602 F 7; Tufano 2019, 350–52). However, positing Souidas as a deliberate innovator relies on a knowledge of local Thessalian traditions that we do not in fact possess. We also cannot be absolutely sure that Souidas was Thessalian, though the name is linked to the region.

[246] It is possible that the young male head on the coins of Peuma – which also bear the AX monogram, dominant and emphatic, on the reverse – should be interpreted as Achilles: see Reinders et al. (2016), 59 (sceptical); Moustaka (1983), 62–63 (less so).

Fig. 20. Hellenistic theatre at Phthiotic Thebes. Photograph: author's own

settlement was short-lived, being destroyed by an earthquake ca. 265 BC.[247] We do have a few coins of the Classical city, which were presumably minted before Parmenion destroyed the polis in 346 BC and gave its territory to Pharsalos.[248] These Classical coins show Zeus on the obverse and on the reverse Helle seated on the Golden Ram in flight. When New Halos resumes minting after 302, it uses a near-identical design: Zeus on the obverse and the Golden Ram on the reverse; now, however, the ram's occupant is not Helle but her brother Phrixos.[249] It is impossible to account for this peculiar little change, but one should note the closer connection thereby created with a long-standing cult of the area: that of Zeus Laphystios. This cult of Halos, in whose *aition* Phrixos was central and to whose ritual he continued to be

[247] Reinders (2003), 231–47.

[248] Reinders (1988), 158–64.

[249] Reinders (1988), 164–66, 236–51; Reinders (2003), 138–45, 320–26. Helle, however, remained a subject of some interest within the community of New Halos, as a mould-made terracotta of her sitting sideways on the ram suggests: Van Boekel and Muldner (2003), 113–14; Athamas also appears, labelled, on a mould-made bowl from the south-east gate. For discussion of both objects see Haagsma et al. (2019), 303, 312–13 and figs 12 and 13.

related, is described in some detail by Herodotos; supposedly the Persian king Xerxes encountered it during his invasion of Greece.[250] We do not know what happened to the sanctuary of Zeus Laphystios when the old site of Halos was destroyed; neither in the old nor the new site was the sanctuary actually located by archaeological investigation. However, it is reasonable to assume that the people of New Halos continued to worship the god, since they placed him on their coins, and the inclusion on the coins of Phrixos may have been a way of ensuring cultic continuity in highly disrupted circumstances. Here, in any case, we plainly have a case not of Hellenistic innovation but of the painstaking maintenance of tradition in the face of enormous turbulence.

The third polis to mint with the monogram AX in this period is Phthiotic Thebes. Interestingly, Thebes included the monogram occasionally, if our surviving sample is anything to go by, and then only rather unobtrusively.[251] A range of types was minted in the third century, their obverses unified with the motif of a veiled female head (interpreted as Demeter), their reverses bearing various motifs, among them the galley prow with a male figure striding forth before it, armed and in martial pose. This can only be Protesilaos, famous for dying just after his enthusiastic disembarkation on the shore of Troy.[252] Thus a third polis of Achaia Phthiotis used coinage in the Hellenistic period to restore its ownership of a Homeric hero.[253] As with Halos, there is a background of ritual continuity here. From the fifth century at least, games of Protesilaos were celebrated at Phylake, and it is believed, with good reason, that in the fourth century Thebes was created through the synoecism of Phylake with Pyrasos.[254] Thus it stood on or near a site of Homeric and Classical importance, strongly connected with the hero Protesilaos, but its ownership of the myth needed assertion because of the new name and organisation in the fourth century BC.

Further glimpses of the re-emergence of characters from early myth also come from the epigraphic record. Especially significant in this regard is a recently published verse inscription from New Halos, excavated in 1999 and probably dating to the early third century BC.[255] However, this text is very different in its nature and implications from the coin motifs this

[250] Hdt. 7.197.

[251] For example, in *Triton* XV, 306, no. 761, the small monogram is so marginal that it has largely slipped off the edge of the flan thanks to a slight mis-strike. In no. 762 it is tucked away between the legs of a prancing horse. Often it is simply not included.

[252] Reinders (2003), 143.

[253] Cultural activity in Phthiotis Thebes in the third century is also attested by the construction of a theatre, possibly on the site of an earlier (fourth century) structure: Fig. 20. See Adrymi-Sismani (2011).

[254] *IACP* s.v. Thebai (no. 444), 717.

[255] Harder et al. (2017); Haagsma et al. (2019), 304. For the wider picture of literary composition, verse and prose, in Thessaly see Bouvier (1979).

sub-section has dealt with up to now. It is anything but local. Its long lists of (mainly) heroic names appears to be cataloguing some of the main branches of early Thessalian mythological genealogy, including the sons of Tyro and Kretheus, including Pheres, and Pheres' son Admetos and grandson Eumelos. Even more strikingly, however, considerable space is given to the Aiolids who left Thessaly to settle Messenia and, subsequently, Athens and Asia Minor; the verse is celebrating not only heroes who resided in Thessaly, but also, implicitly, Thessaly's role as the origin-point of stemmata spreading out over the Greek world. This is a remarkable reassertion, in the early Hellenistic period, of Thessaly's importance in early epic as an origin-point in the stories of Greek migration and resettlement. The fact that the text was created and displayed in New Halos is interesting. Though part of the perioikic region of Achaia Phthiotis, New Halos plainly felt ownership of, and wished to celebrate, Thessalian mythology as a whole and its wider ramifications.

Harder, Van Nijf and Nikolaou connect the text with the popularity, rising to a peak in the Hellenistic period, of heroic catalogues advertising the heritage of a region, often both performed and inscribed.[256] This is important; other such compositions celebrating Thessaly are indeed known from the third and second centuries BC. An especially well-documented case is that of Bombos son of Alpheios, from Alexandreia in the Troad, mentioned above, who won honours from Larisa as a reward for celebrating the city's glorious past in performances in the gymnasion with the aim of cementing the *syngeneia* between the two communities.[257] However, it also responds, perhaps, to the fact that several other Greek communities were, at this time, claiming Thessalian origins with renewed enthusiasm. The Koan drive to establish the Thessalian origins of their Asklepios-cult was discussed above, as was the case of Magnesia on the Maiandros and its complex myth of Thessalian migration. The conditions – cultural, historical – were plainly right for a resurrection of the Archaic image of Thessaly as a place of origin with offshoots across the Aegean. Once again, Thessaly plays an important role as a cradle of Hellenism as the Aiolid stemma is dusted off and celebrated afresh. The New Halos inscription, however, is no *Ehoiai*. It combines the famous genealogies of the epic tradition with some names whose obscurity left the editors partially or totally baffled, which can only be local heroes and figures of legend, and others that seem to suggest connections between Thessaly and other regions, but connections that are by no means canonical or well established.[258] The poem seems also to include characters we would classify as historical rather than

256 Harder et al. (2017).

257 Helly (2006a).

258 In this category fall Antaios, Byzes and Gordios: see Harder et al. (2017), 41.

mythological, including Aleuas[259] and Daochos.[260] So Thessaly's glorious past has become an amalgam of epic material, obscure local legend and significant Thessalian statesmen, a combination ranging from the entirely panhellenic to the intensely epichoric.

7. Conclusions

In a sense, the third century BC has brought us full circle, but with so much changed. The later fifth century and most of the fourth saw Thessaly increasingly 'othered' as ethically unsatisfactory and even imperfectly Greek. The conquests of Alexander and their long aftermath changed that. Alexander himself took Thessalians east with him and provided them with opportunities for donning the mantle of the triumphant Hellenes marching against *barbaroi*. In the hyperconnected world of the Hellenistic age, Greek communities across the Aegean found in Thessaly and in Thessalian traditions a powerful source of cultural capital, restoring a sense of the region as a crucial origin-point in the shared myth-history of the Hellenes. As Hellenism diffused over a vast geographical range and diversity of ethnic groups,[261] Thessaly lost the sense of marginality that had attached to it in a period when Athens reformulated the recipe for Greekness in the decades after the Persian Wars.

There is no better illustration of this shift than a portion of the surviving work of the geographer Herakleides Kritikos, whose account of Cheiron's cult was discussed above:

> Regarding, therefore, the Peloponnese as its beginning, I set the boundary of Greece at the small outlet of Magnesia. Some may say that we are mistaken reckoning Thessaly part of Greece, but it is they who are ignorant of the truth of the situation. For Greece (Hellas) was once just a town in olden days, named for Hellen, the son of Zeus, and founded by him, being part of the territory of Thessaly, lying between Pharsalos and the city of the Melitaians. So Hellenes are those who are descended from Hellen and speak the Hellenic language inherited from Hellen.[262]

[259] That is, if we read, as the editors tentatively suggest, 'Ἀλ⟨ε⟩ύαν τ'α[' at the end of line 5: the stone is badly worn at this point.

[260] 'Δαιάοχον', line 19. It may be relevant here to note the hero-cult of Alexandros of Pherai which, according to Boehm (2015), was maintained in Hellenistic Demetrias. If Boehm is right, this would constitute another significant link with a notable figure from Thessaly's political history.

[261] Strootman (2020), 202–04.

[262] Herakleides *FGrH* 369A F 3, 3.1–3.2: 'τὴν μὲν οὖν Ἑλλάδα ἀπὸ Πελοποννήσου τὴν ἀρχὴν λαβὼν μέχρι τοῦ Μαγνήτων ἀφορίζω στομίου. τάχα δὲ φήσουσίν τινες ἡμᾶς ἀγνοεῖν τὴν Θετταλίαν τῆς Ἑλλάδος καταριθμοῦντας, ἄπειροι τῆς τῶν πραγμάτων ὄντες ἀληθείας.

At this point the author dwells at some length upon the two Archaic traditions concerning the Hellenes, their Iliadic location to the south of Thessaly and their descent from Hellen. He then resumes, in summary:

> What is presently called Greece is a word, but not a reality, for I maintain that 'to hellenize' or 'speak Greek' is not a matter of correct pronunciation but concerns the language's descent. This speech is from Hellen. Hellas lies in Thessaly. Accordingly we say that those men inhabit Hellas, and, with respect to their speech, they 'hellenize' or 'speak Greek'. If, specifically with respect to its origins, Hellas is part of Thessaly, it is also right that since 'Hellenes' is now the designation in wide use, then Thessaly should be considered part of Hellas.[263]

This passage has several significant and striking features. The first and most obvious is that Herakleides has to defend himself for including Thessaly in Greece at all. Despite the symbolic importance of Thessaly within the discourse of Hellenism at this time, Herakleides plainly felt that his readers needed a reminder of its unique original links with Hellas and the Hellenes, perhaps because the especially close connection between Thessaly and Macedon that had prevailed since the time of Philip II had made Thessaly seem, in the eyes of some, part of Greece's blurry northern periphery rather than its heart. However, language plays a major role in the author's argument. Elsewhere in the fragment he mentions a claim by the Athenians that theirs is the true Greek language; the implication is that the Thessalian dialect, still active at this time, is not.[264] In other words, Greek identity is, as ever, contestable: particular communities may claim a privileged connection for themselves while disparaging the position of others. Herakleides has recourse to Archaic traditions to rediscover and reassert the original Hellas and its inhabitants, restoring Thessaly's credentials in the matter; he tries to pull the diverse and complex discourse of Greekness back to its local origins. As Arenz suggests, 'Hier spricht ein Thessaler gegen ein athenozentrisch formulierte griechische Identität.'[265]

ἡ γὰρ Ἑλλὰς, τὸ παλαιὸν οὖσά ποτε πόλις, ἀφ' Ἕλληνος τοῦ Διὸς ἐκλήθη τε καὶ ἐκτίσθη, τῆς τῶν Θετταλῶν οὖσα χώρας, ἀνὰ μέσον Φαρσάλου τε κειμένη καὶ τῆς τῶν Μελιταιέων πόλεως. Ἕλληνες μὲν γάρ εἰσιν τῶι γένει καὶ ταῖς φωναῖς ἑλληνίζουσιν ἀφ' Ἕλληνος.'

263 Herakleides *FGrH* 369A F 3, 3.5–3.6: 'ἡ δὲ καλουμένη νῦν Ἑλλὰς λέγεται μὲν, οὐ μέντοι ἐστί. τὸ γὰρ ἑλληνίζειν ἐγὼ εἶναί φημι οὐκ ἐν τῶι διαλέγεσθαι ὀρθῶς ἀλλ' ἐν τῶι γένει τῆς φωνῆς. αὕτη <δ'> ἐστὶν ἀφ' Ἕλληνος. ἡ δὲ Ἑλλὰς ἐν Θετταλίαι κεῖται. ἐκείνους οὖν ἐροῦμεν τὴν Ἑλλάδα κατοικεῖν καὶ ταῖς φωναῖς ἑλληνίζειν. εἰ δὲ καὶ κατὰ τὸ ἴδιον τοῦ γένους τῆς Θετταλίας ἡ Ἑλλάς ἐστι, δίκαιον καὶ κατὰ τὸ κοινὸν, ὡς νῦν ὀνομάζονται Ἕλληνες, τῆς Ἑλλάδος αὐτὴν εἶναι.'

264 Herakleides *FGrH* 369A F 3, 3.5–3.7.

265 Arenz (2005), 173. ('Here speaks out a Thessalians against an Athenocentric

But he was not the only one in the third century to recognise Thessaly's importance. The communities outside the Greek heartland that saw in Thessaly their primordial home similarly had recourse to centuries-old stories in which Thessaly played a significant role. But they manipulated them to suit their own circumstances, as we would expect, and for their part the Thessalians responded in new ways, fitting their traditions to new purposes and, in the case of horse-racing, evoking traditions that were not actually very strong in the first place.[266]

formulation of Greek identity.') His discussion of the importance of Thessaly in Herakleides' articulation of Greekness: pp. 162–73.

266 Needless to say, Thessalian responses to the key themes discussed in this chapter did not stop at the end of the third century. The creation/embellishment of the cult of Zeus Eleutherios after 197 BC is an interesting example of the persistence of implicit evocations of the Persian Wars. Though Graninger (2008, 92–94) does identify a small number of instances of this form of the deity elsewhere in Greece, the *epiklesis* applied to Zeus is actually rather rare, and must surely have recalled the two most famous cults: that at Plataia supposedly founded after the victory against the Persians in 497 (Thuc. 2.71.2; Strabo 9.2.31), which was accompanied by a festival called the Eleutheria; and that in Athens, where the stoa dedicated to the god after 479 was one of the chief monuments in the Agora (Paus. 1.3.2–3). By their selection of this form of the deity and of the name of the festival, therefore, the Larisaian authorities were obliquely suggesting an analogy between the Macedonians and the Persians, and between the Thessalians and the Greeks who fought them off.

Concluding remarks

This book has followed the articulation of Thessalian regional identity through many centuries of changing circumstances. In essence, the end of the sixth century BC and the early fifth were identified as the time during which the Thessalians began to use myth, cult and the early stages of political co-operation to define their collective identity as an *ethnos*, separate from other Greeks in their origins, customs, religious priorities and natural resources.

Chapters 1 and 2 considered the Archaic conditions out of which the process of purposeful identity formation arose. Chapter 1 argued against seeing the Thessalians as an *ethnos* with a primordial tribal unity, or as a hegemonic power in central Greece, dominating the Delphic Amphiktyony and launching concerted invasions of Phokis and Boiotia. In fact, it was suggested that the conditions of much of central Greece were more conducive to ethnogenesis than those in Thessaly. Moreover, to reduce Thessaly's relations with her southern neighbours to the traditional motif of aggression is to ignore the picture that emerges more and more from the archaeological record: that in the Late Bronze Age and the Early Iron Age, and continuing into the Archaic, a network of connections, both maritime and inland, linked south-eastern Thessaly with (in particular) Euboia, Lokris, Phokis and Boiotia. In these circumstances, the political boundaries between *ethnē* that we see gaining importance in the Classical period seem to have had little or no meaning. Conflict, when it occurred, is likely to have been on a local scale, over, for example, grazing rights and access to passes; such conflicts are more likely to have arisen between the small *ethnē* around the Spercheios valley than between the Thessalians *qua* Thessalians and their southern neighbours. It is possible that in the late Archaic period this changed somewhat; perhaps strengthening ethnic divides started to disrupt traditional connectivity; perhaps the Thessalians (whose process of political cohesion was underway, at the end of the sixth century, with the creation of the tetrads) did start to constitute a more concerted threat. However, to read this back into the seventh and earlier sixth centuries is not supported by the available evidence. We also risk simplifying the role of Delphi, its Amphiktyony in particular, by casting it as an instrument of Thessalian imperialist aggression, rather than (for the most part) as a forum for the negotiation of co-existence and co-operation between many adjoining *ethnē*.

Chapter 2 focused on a specific aspect of Thessaly's place in Archaic Greece: its role in early epic, especially the *Iliad*, probably composed in the seventh century, and the *Ehoiai*, probably composed in the early sixth. Overall, the chapter's aim was to question the extent to which either poem can really be thought to encapsulate Thessalian perspectives. Regarding the *Iliad*, it was argued that even the most prominent Thessalian hero, Achilles, presents an ambiguous situation: Thessaly may be his homeland, but it is also the land to which he cannot return, since doing so would constitute the destruction of his *kleos*. This was argued to be a special manifestation of a wider theme: that of Thessaly as the land left behind. The narrative importance of Thessalian heroes probably reflects the oral development of major myth-cycles (Achilles and his family; the Iolkos Cycle; the voyage of Jason) in the region in the Late Bronze or Early Iron Age. However, by the time the epics poems were composed in the form in which we have them, the main actors behind them are not Thessalian. The poet of the *Iliad* seems to have had an Ionian perspective; the Argo's story too is drawn into the east Greek context, as a reflection of colonising activities (of Milesians and Athens especially) around the Troad and the Black Sea. From such a perspective, Thessaly is an important homeland, but thereby consigned to past time. As for the *Ehoiai*, here the site of production may be a little closer to Thessaly, since strong Amphiktyonic fingerprints are discernible on what remains of the work. It was argued, however, that to read 'Thessalian' for 'Amphiktyonic' is a grave error, not only because the veracity of Thessaly's Delphic dominance is so questionable but also because the whole tenor of the poem works against any simplistic appropriation by a single group. It is a poem about connections: heroic dynasties sprawl between regions, and the central figures of Deukalion, Pyrrha and Hellen are themselves 'shared' by being situated imprecisely in the area around the Amphiktyonic shrine at Anthela. Like the Amphiktyony itself, the *Ehoiai* is a co-operative project. This aspect connects closely with one feature of the *Iliad*: the fact that Hellas and the Hellenes cannot be located using a pin in a map. The symbolic origins of Greeks and Greekness are placed within the ambit of Delphi, but not placed so that any one community could make an incontestable claim of ownership.

The picture shifts significantly at the end of the Archaic period, and Chapters 3 and 4 chart the changes. Chapter 3 analysed the development and evolution of the Thessalids tradition, and its scion the Thessaloi tradition. These present a major break from the content and priorities of the *Ehoiai*. They supply an Heraklid origin for the Thessalians, declining to reuse the Aiolid stemma that dominated the Thessalian portions of the *Ehoiai*. They constitute a story of arrival, not of departure: suddenly Thessaly is the land attained, not the land left behind. And, for the first time, especially with the Thessaloi tradition, myth is used to confer a special identity on a whole *ethnos*, to give it both internal cohesion and a clear distinction from other *ethnē*. By the mid-fifth century the Thessaloi were strongly established as a group unified by shared origins, a shared journey into their homeland, and by the routine use of the ethnic, both in non-Thessalian texts and internally in the form of coin legends. Being Thessalian was kept latent in the *Iliad*, insignificant in the *Ehoiai*; by the fifth century it has taken centre stage in the representation and self-representation of the Thessalians. Chapter 4 explored its consolidation in religion, through the development of a bundle of myths and rituals dominated by the figure of Poseidon, which expressed the shared properties of the Thessalian land and the shared qualities of its people. At the same time, pre-existing strands of mythology were carefully incorporated, most notably in the naming of the tetrads.

At no point, however, and in no way, did the creation of *ethnos* myths and cults discourage variety and dissent. Sub-groups could and did strike out on different tracks of self-definition, and of course individual poleis maintained their own unique customs and traditions. Even the *ethnos* myths were subject to adaptation and contestation, by, for example, rewriting the parentage of Thessalos to promote a particular polis. Their variability mirrors that of the modes of political co-operation studied in Chapter 5. While a picture of increasing formalisation is visible from our available evidence, we have to recognise that the Thessalian *koinon* changed in composition and organisation to meet new historical events and conditions, and in response to internal and external pressures. It was also only one facet of political life in Thessaly. It never displaced the influence of elite individuals and families; nor did it prevent the polis from retaining its primacy as the key unit of citizenship and civic identity.

The emergence of the Thessalians as a clear self-defining group, with shared myths, cults and an existence, however labile, as a political unit, seems to have stimulated external responses and judgements. From the later fifth century in particular, a set of Thessalian stereotypes crystallise; they also grow more pejorative, twisting traditional characteristics into a hostile discourse. Chapter 6 followed this process, viewing it against a key contributing factor: the increasing alignment (both real and perceived) between Thessaly and Macedon, culminating in the collaboration with Philip II, a collaboration largely staged in the charged setting of Delphi. Condemnation of Thessalians could take various forms, but at the heart of the process was the changing articulation of Greekness. Were the Thessalians good Greeks? Did they display the characteristics of good Greeks, or did they belong with northern *barbaroi*? In Archaic culture Thessaly occupied an important position: the original Hellas, after all, was on its southern margins. It was strongly integrated into the heroic genealogies of which Hellenism was largely composed. By contrast, in the Classical period, the Thessalians increasingly fell short, in Athenian eyes especially, of the standards of character and conduct presented as central to Greek identity. They joined the Macedonians on the questionable northern fringes, in an imaginary border-zone of excess, political corruption and disloyalty to the principles of Hellas.

Chapter 6 identified some signs of Thessalian rebuttal of such a characterisation, but it was in the Hellenistic period, discussed in Chapter 7, that a substantial revision of Thessalian self-presentation was accomplished, against a backdrop of radically changed historical conditions. In this period, many of the traditional themes of Thessalian identity returned: the land as a place of origins, as important to articulations of Greekness, as wealthy, as producer of prized and prize-winning horses. These characteristics caused it to be valued afresh by new actors: by the Ptolemies, by the Asklepiads of Kos, by the communities of Aiolis, by those promoting the cult of Artemis Leukophryene in Magnesia on the Maiandros. In some ways Chapter 7 brought the trajectory of the book around to where it began, as the stories and heroes of epic resumed their prominence and took on new meaning in the poleis of Magnesia and Achaia Phthiotis, and as the characterisation of Thessaly as a corrupt northern backwater was subsumed by the new cultural complexity of the expanded Greek world. More than any other time, the early Hellenistic period showed us Thessalian communities actively engaging with new and renewed networks of interaction to assert their contribution to the history and traditions of Greece.

Epilogue

In his *Heroikos*, Philostratus describes an elaborate ritual carried out annually by the Thessalians in honour of Achilles:

> The Thessalian offerings which came regularly to Achilles from Thessaly were decreed for the Thessalians by the oracle at Dodona. For indeed the oracle commanded the Thessalians to sail to Troy each year to sacrifice to Achilles and to slaughter some sacrificial victims as to a god, but to slaughter others as for the dead. At first the following happened: a ship sailed from Thessaly to Troy with black sails raised, bringing twice seven sacred ambassadors, one white bull and one black bull, both tame, and wood from Mount Pelion, so that they would need nothing from the city. They also brought fire from Thessaly, after they had drawn both libations and water from the river Sperkheios.[1]

The text goes on to describe subsequent elements of ritual: a hymn to Thetis, invocation of Achilles and an invitation to Patroklos, and then the culmination, a dual sacrifice in which a black bull is sacrificed as to a hero (its throat cut, the meat burned) and a white one is sacrificed as to a god. The flesh from the latter is carried away and later eaten.[2]

It is not unknown for this work to be mined for information on Thessalian religious customs, but in fact that is to misunderstand its nature and purpose entirely.[3] The rituals are no longer carried out at the time of narration – that is, when the informative vine-dresser is passing on to his

[1] Phil. *Her.* 53.8–9: 'τὰ δὲ Θετταλικὰ ἐναγίσματα φοιτῶντα τῷ Ἀχιλλεῖ ἐκ Θετταλίας ἐχρήσθη Θετταλοῖς ἐκ Δωδώνης· ἐκέλευσε γὰρ δὴ τὸ μαντεῖον Θετταλοὺς ἐς Τροίαν πλέοντας θύειν ὅσα ἔτη τῷ Ἀχιλλεῖ καὶ σφάττειν τὰ μὲν ὡς θεῷ, τὰ δὲ ὡς ἐν μοίρᾳ τῶν κειμένων. κατ' ἀρχὰς μὲν δὴ τοιάδε ἐγίνετο· ναῦς ἐκ Θετταλίας μέλανα ἱστία ἠρμένη ἐς Τροίαν ἔπλει, θεωροὺς μὲν δὶς ἑπτὰ ἀπάγουσα, ταύρους δὲ λευκόν τε καὶ μέλανα, χειροήθεις ἄμφω, καὶ ὕλην ἐκ Πηλίου, ὡς μηδὲν τῆς πόλεως δέοιντο· καὶ πῦρ ἐκ Θετταλίας ἦγον καὶ σπονδὰς καὶ ὕδωρ τοῦ Σπερχειοῦ ἀρυσάμενοι' (trans. Maclean and Aitken).

[2] Phil. *Her.* 53.11–13.

[3] Detailed discussion of the text and its purposes: Dué and Nagy (2002); Maclean and Aitken (2002).

Phoinikian the precious and startling knowledge concerning heroes that he has obtained directly from his confidant Protesilaos. Quite the reverse: the Thessalians have reduced them in scale and complexity, in successive ignoble stages.[4] The full version was carried out at some unspecified time, before the rule of the 'Aiakidai' in Thessaly was replaced by that of *tyrannoi.* Once the tyrants took control, a messy situation prevailed: some towns sent the offerings, others not, and the rites no longer worked as a collective enterprise by the whole *ethnos*. Punished with a drought by the angry hero, the Thessalians reinstated the offerings but in a lopsided form, carrying out only the sacrifice for Achilles in his hero aspect, omitting the rite for a god. Even this unsatisfactory half-measure was abandoned again when Xerxes invaded. When the Thessalians went east with Alexander, himself an Achilles-enthusiast, they briefly recovered their cult fervour and performed a new kind of rite, a mock cavalry battle followed by sacrifices (their nature unspecified). However, their motivation was chiefly to secure the hero's aid for their campaign, and once Dareios had been killed they let their devotion flag yet again and the rites went neglected.

And that is as far as the story goes. There is no further resumption of the sacrifices. The Thessalians are punished, in a decidedly banal way (with swingeing fines for the illegal manufacture of murex-dye),[5] but this does not prompt them to reinstate the rites. And that is how the matter is allowed to rest. Even the personal intercession of Protesilaos on behalf of his fellow countrymen cannot move Achilles from his implacable *mēnis*. The Thessalians have permanently squandered his goodwill.

To treat this passage as conveying accurate information about Thessalian religion is inadvisable. The learned Philostratus certainly injected his fantasy with grains of truth, including the cult of Protesilaos at Thessalian Phylake,[6] and we cannot prove that the Thessalians never made offerings to Achilles in the Troad, even though all other evidence is lacking. This should not blind us, however, to what Philostratus is really offering us. The *Heroikos* is in part a text about things going wrong. Palamedes is unjustly slighted; Protesilaos dies prematurely, as does Achilles; Homer is a good poet but he makes mistakes and distorts the record. Most of these wrongs can be righted, with the benevolent intervention of Protesilaos and by the

[4] Phil. *Her.* 53.14–17.

[5] Phil. *Her.* 53.22. This seems to be a realistic touch: Lucretius mentions Thessalian murex-fishing as if it is famous (associated especially with Meliboia), at *de Rer. Nat.* 2.500–01. For the legal aspects of the punishment see Huvelin (1925).

[6] Phil. *Her.* 16.5; cf. Pind. *Isth.* 1.58. Jones (2001) identifies the cult of Protesilaos at Elaious in the text as particularly imbued with realism. See also Rutherford (2009), entertaining the possibility that some foundation of historical fact – sporadic Thessalian offerings at Troy? – lay behind the literary elaboration of the work.

magical pen of Philostratus himself: Protesilaos can enjoy joyful meetings with his wife Laodike in the underworld; Achilles can live in wedded bliss on Leuke with Helen; Palamedes' reputation can be repaired and Homer's errors corrected. But one thing cannot be repaired: the Thessalians' hopeless failure to maintain their own religious traditions.[7] In fact, they sabotage resolution. The original sacrifices to Achilles were in themselves a healing of division. The two victims, white and black, drew together the two parts of Achilles' fractured nature, mortal and god. The spatial aspects reconciled, somewhat uneasily, the homeland Phthia with the final resting place in Asia.[8] Though Achilles still did not go home, Thessaly obtained a share of him.

The relevance of this to the current book is clear. In fact, in a sense, the *Heroikos* provides a commentary on the fluctuating status and reputation of the Thessalians. The initial glory of the heroic age; the tyrants and a time of disunity; the blow of Xerxes' arrival; a surge of respect (and perhaps self-respect) under Alexander; the tarnishing of the glory of Issos and Gaugamela. This is, of course, about perceptions, not the reality of Thessalian life; much of the book has been dedicated to challenging the discourse of loss and decline. But Philostratus encapsulates crucial elements of Thessaly's shifting character in the eyes of other Greeks. He also prefigures some scholarly responses to the region: the quest for primordial glory days; the disgruntlement when those days seem to end in disunity.

He was not the only one. We might think of Strabo's struggles to make the Thessaly of his own time fit the Thessaly of Homer. 'ἐοίκασιν οὖν διὰ τὰς συνεχεῖς μεταστάσεις καὶ ἐξαλλάξεις τῶν πολιτειῶν καὶ ἐπιμίξεις συγχεῖν

[7] Cf., however, the *Life of Apollonios of Tyana* 4.16.1–3 and 4.23: Achilles tells Apollonios of his anger at the Thessalians for neglecting the rites, and employs him as an ambassador to approach them at a meeting of the Delphic Amphiktyony and frighten them into resuming the offerings. The Thessalians do so. This might encourage us to believe that at some time in the first century AD there was a burst of Thessalian ritual activity in Achilles' honour in the Troad. In this case the story of the rites' neglect and the hero's anger would be a convincing aition, very like that associated with the cult of Demeter Melaina at Phigaleia (see Paus. 8.42.3–7), which is similarly dominated by motifs of neglect and punishment. Even if so, however, it does not supply any reliable evidence for the existence of the ritual in its earlier phases. Moreover, the fact that the *Heroikos* leaves Achilles angry and the rites lapsed casts the reality of their first-century performance into doubt too. Note that rites for Achilles *do* seem to have been performed by Caracalla in AD 213, an event to which Philostratus must be obliquely referring (see Rutherford 2009, 237–38). None of the ancient descriptions of Caracalla's venture mention Thessalian involvement.

[8] The sense of unease is conveyed by the fact that the Thessalians deliberately abstain from feasting in enemy territory: they carry the carcass of the white bull away with them rather than eating it on the Trojan shore (53.13).

καὶ τὰ ὀνόματα καὶ τὰ ἔθνη, ὥστε τοῖς νῦν ἔσθ' ὅτε ἀπορίαν παρέχειν',[9] he remarks peevishly when trying to identify the historical Krannonians and the Gyrtonians in the Catalogue of Ships, something he accomplishes only by saying that the Krannonians used to be called Phlegyai and the Gyrtonians Ephyroi. At 9.5.3 he remarks that in Thessaly overall few towns have kept their ancient glory. (The exception is Larisa, omitted from Homer but subsequently mighty.) As Wallace remarks, Strabo views Thessaly and Boiotia through the Homeric lens more than any other region, and in neither case does the perspective make him approve of the region's condition in his own day.[10] Even when explicit authorial comments of this kind are not made, a tone of nostalgia is often adopted in descriptions of Thessaly. When Theokritos in *Idyll* 16 describes the vast herds of cattle and serfs over which the Thessalian lords held sway, he was looking back to the time of Simonides; the Thessaly of his own day was sadly diminished. But such attitudes were not new in the Hellenistic period; as we saw in Chapter 2, even in Homer Thessaly is the land of the hero's youth, to be consigned to the past as the hero moves away to his *aristeia* and his glorious death and burial in another land.

This is not to say that Thessaly was considered unimportant; on the contrary, it came to have considerable symbolic power, which could be returned to in a wide variety of different times and contexts. Heliodoros, for example, in his novel the *Aithiopika*, makes Thessalian identity and traditions central to the characterisation of his young hero Theagenes: Theagenes wrestles bulls, when the occasion demands it; he takes part in a *theōria* to the shrine of Neoptolemos at Delphi; he claims descent from Achilles (albeit via a rather oblique genealogical route).[11] He is not actually Thessalian, in the strict sense: he is from Ainis, in the Spercheios valley. Is he being extra Thessalian, because the ethnic claim is a little fictitious? Whitmarsh has argued so,[12] but another way of viewing the matter, with Mili,[13] is to recall that Ainis in the Roman period was an important region

[9] Strabo 9.5.21: '[Later writers] seem to have mixed up the names and the tribes, because of the constant revolutions and population-movements; and this sometimes causes despair for the writers of today.'

[10] Wallace (1979), 171. Perhaps Strabo is also unconsciously echoing Thuc. 1.2.3: Thessaly and Boiotia have been subject to many changes of population because of the fertility and desirability of their land.

[11] Bull-wrestling: 10.28–30; *theōria* to Neoptolemos and claim on Achilles: see esp. 2.34. This passage also refers to the Ainianes' claim of direct descent from Hellēn. The association with Achilles is presented as surprising because Phthia is conventionally associated with the area around Pharsalos; however, the Ainianes assert that it properly refers to the land around the Malian Gulf. Nobili (2020), 27–29.

[12] Whitmarsh (1998).

[13] Mili (2011); cf. Graninger (2011a), 153–58.

of central Greece, not the backwater that Whitmarsh envisages, and that there are other signs that its people espoused grandiose and ancient traditions; Theagenes may reflect those circumstances accurately. Nor was his pose wholly fake. Ainis had just as strong a claim on Achilles and Neoptolemos as did Thessaly, perhaps better. In any case (and without over-stressing ethnic boundaries that may not have mattered much when Heliodoros was writing), the fervour of the Ainianes in the *Aithiopika* is a corrective to the apathy of the Thessalians in the *Heroikos*,[14] and reminds us not to see the matter too much through a single text.

These presentations of Thessaly from outside the region have their roots, of course, in what the Thessalians said about themselves. The central question of this book has been how the Thessalians themselves presented being Thessalian, and the stories they told about their own shared identity. It has sought to recover Thessalian voices, while recognising that those voices were often raised in response to the voices of others. It has also tried to avoid seeking a Thessaly that never really existed, or becoming drawn into implicit narratives of nostalgia and dissatisfaction. It has not, however, produced the only version of Thessaly that there was, is, or can ever be. The spate of recent PhD theses approaching Thessalian regional identity primarily from the perspective of material culture certainly point the way to an important new direction, with potential to gain fresh insights into the Thessalians' conscious symbolic deployment of buildings, monuments and objects, but also into the realities of their daily lives, identity as lived rather than as projected. The florescence of Thessaly studies since the research for this book began just over a decade ago is striking and heartening. It is to be hoped that Achilles – who must in any case have enjoyed the ceremonial unveiling of his statue in 2012 in the town square of Farsala – is now finally mollified.[15]

[14] Indeed, as Rutherford notes, there are strong signs in the *Aithiopika* that Heliodoros was responding to Philostratus' text: Rutherford (2009), 245–47.

[15] See Fig. 21.

Fig. 21. Statue of Achilles in the main square of Farsala. Photograph courtesy of Margriet Haagsma

Bibliography

Acosta-Hughes, B. and C. Cusset. 2012. *Euphorion: Œuvre poétique et autres fragments*. Paris: Les Belles Lettres.

Adrymi-Sismani, V. 1999–2001. 'Μυκηναϊκή Ιωλκός.' *AAA* 32–34, 71–100.

—. 2006. 'The Palace of Iolkos and Its End.' In S. Deger-Jalkotzy and I.S. Lemos eds, *Ancient Greece: From the Mycenaean Palaces to the Age of Homer* (Edinburgh: Edinburgh University Press), 465–81.

—. 2008. 'Το Διμήνι και η παρουσία των Μυκηναίων στη Θεσσαλία.' In L. Gklegkle ed., *1° Διεθνές Συνέδριο Ιστορίας και Πολιτισμού της Θεσσαλίας. Πρακτικά Συνεδρίου 9–11 Νοεμβρίου 2006*, vol. 1 (Thessaloniki: Περιφέρειας Θεσσαλίας), 85–97.

—. 2011. 'Το αρχαίο θέατρο των Φθιοτίδων Θηβών.' In V. Adrymi-Sismani ed., *Αρχαία Θέατρα στη Θεσσαλία* (Athens: Diozoma), 49–66.

—. 2012. 'Φεραί (Βελεστίνο)'; 'Μαγνησία.' In E. Nikolaou and S. Kravaritou eds, *Αρχαίες Πόλεις Θεσσαλίας και Περίοικων Περιοχών* (Larisa: Π.Ε.Δ. Θεσσαλίας), 120–28; 140–63.

—. 2020. 'The Destruction of Mycenaean Centres in Eastern Thessaly.' In G.D. Middleton ed., *Collapse and Transformation: The Late Bronze Age to Early Iron Age in the Aegean* (Oxford: Oxbow Books), 23–33.

Adrymi-Sismani, V., M.F. Guerra and Ph. Walter. 2009. 'The Mycenaean Tomb of Kazanaki (Volos) and the Myth of the Golden Fleece.' *Archaeosciences* 33, 135–41.

Agnousiotis, D. 2014. 'Το Βελεστίνο και η ευρύτερη περιοχή κατά τη Μέση Εποχή Χαλκού.' *ΥΠΕΡΕΙΑ* 6, 59–74.

Albini, U. 1968. Peri Politeias *di Erode Attico. Introduzione, testo critico e commento*. Firenze: F. Le Monnier.

Alcock, S.E. 1997. 'The Heroic Past in a Hellenistic Present.' In P. Cartledge, P. Garnsey and E. Gruen eds, *Hellenistic Constructs: Essays in Culture, History, and Historiography* (Berkeley: University of California Press), 20–34.

Allan, W. 2000. *The* Andromache *and Euripidean Tragedy*. Oxford: Oxford University Press.

Allen, A. 1993. *The Fragments of Mimnermus: Text and Commentary*. Stuttgart: Franz Steiner.

Allen, T. 1921. *The Homeric Catalogue of Ships*. Oxford: Clarendon.

Ambühl, A. 2016. 'Epyllion as Idyll or Enigma? Thessaly as a Mythico-literary Landscape of War in Catullus 64 and in Callimachus' *Hymn to Delos*.' *Aitia* 6, https://journals.openedition.org/aitia/1459.

Amendola, D. 2019. '*Presbeutikoi* and *Enteuktikoi Logoi* in Hellenistic Interstate Relations. Some Further Thoughts from an Epigraphical Perspective (c. 306–205 B.C.).' *Ktèma* 44, 87–103.

Andersen, L. 1969. 'The *Shield of Heracles:* Problems of Genesis.' *Classica et Mediaevalia* 30.1, 10–26.

Anderson, J.K. 1995. 'The Geometric Catalogue of Ships.' In J. Carter and S. Morris eds, *The Ages of Homer* (Austin: University of Texas Press), 181–91.

Andreasen, N.H., N. Pantzou and D.C. Nielsen. 2009. 'The Pelion Cave Project: An Ethno-archaeological Investigation of the Human Use of Caves in the Early Modern and Modern Period in East Thessaly.' In E. Hallager and S. Riisager eds, *Proceedings of the Danish Institute at Athens VI* (Athens: Danish Institute at Athens), 175–87.

Andrewes, A. 1971. 'Two Notes on Lysander.' *Phoenix* 25.3, 206–26.

Apostolopoulou-Kakavogianni, O. 1990. ''Ενα νέο ιερό στις Φερές.' *Υπέρεια* 1, 57–70.

—. 1992. 'Ευρήματα της πρωτογεομετρικής και γεομετρικής περιόδου από τις Φερές.' In *Διεθνές Συνέδριο για την αρχαία Θεσσαλία: στη μνήμη του Δημήτρη Ρ. Θεοχάρη. Πρακτικά* (Athens: Ταμείο Αρχαιολογικών Πόρων και Απαλλοτριώσεων), 312–20.

Arachoviti, P. 1994. 'Θολωτός πρωτογεωμετρικός τάφος στην περιοχή των Φερών.' In *Θεσσαλία. Δεκαπέντε Χρόνια Αρχαιολογικής Έρευνας, 1975–1990. Αποτελέσματα και Προοπτικές* (Athens: Kapon), 125–38.

Arachoviti, P., A. Doulgeri-Intzesiloglou and M. Tsigara. 2012. 'Ναός Θαυλίου Διός Φερών. Νέα δεδομένα.' In A. Mazarakis Ainian ed., *Αρχαιολογικό Έργο Θεσσαλίας και Στερεάς Ελλάδας* 3, vol. 1 (Volos: Εργαστήριο Αρχαιολογίας Πανεπιστημίου Θεσσαλίας & Υπουργείο Πολιτισμού, Παιδείας και Θρησκευμάτων), 451–58.

Archibald, Z.H. 2009. 'Northern Greece.' In K.A. Raaflaub and H. van Wees eds, *Companion to Archaic Greece* (Chichester: Blackwell), 294–313.

Arenz, A. 2006. *Herakleides Kritikos «Über die Städte in Hellas»: Eine Periegese Griechenlands am Vorabend des Chremonideischen Krieges*. Munich: Herbert Utz.

Arjona, M. 2013. 'Θάλαττα Λοκρῶν: Plying the Sea of the Locrians.' In J. Pascual and M.-F. Papakonstantinou eds, *Topography and History of Ancient Epicnemidian Locris* (Leiden: Brill), 361–92.

Arrington, N.T. 2016. 'Talismanic Practice at Lefkandi: Trinkets, Burials and Belief in the Early Iron Age.' *Cambridge Classical Journal* 62, 1–30.

Arvanitopoulos, A. 1929b. 'Θεσσαλικαί ἐπιγραφαί.' *Polemon* 1, 201–26.

Aston, E.M.M. 2004. 'Asclepius and the Legacy of Thessaly.' *Classical Quarterly* 54, 18–32.

—. 2006. 'The Absence of Chiron.' *Classical Quarterly* 56, 349–62.
—. 2009. 'Thetis and Cheiron in Thessaly.' *Kernos* 22, 83–107.
—. 2011. *Mixanthrôpoi: Animal-Human Hybrid Deities in Greek Religion. Kernos* Suppl. 25. Liège: Centre International d'Étude de la Religion Grecque Antique.
—. 2012a. 'Friends in High Places: The Stereotype of Dangerous Thessalian Hospitality in the Later Classical Period.' *Phoenix* 66.3–4, 247–71.
—. 2012b. 'Thessaly and Macedon at Delphi.' *Electrum* 19, 41–60.
—. 2015. '"Welcome, Visitors": Religious Inclusivity in a Pharsalian Cave-cult.' In A. Mazarakis Ainian ed., *Αρχαιολογικό Έργο Θεσσαλίας και Στερεάς Ελλάδας* 4, vol. 1 *Θεσσαλία* (Volos: Εργαστήριο Αρχαιολογίας Πανεπιστημίου Θεσσαλίας & Υπουργείο Πολιτισμού, Παιδείας και Θρησκευμάτων), 223–27.
—. 2017. 'Centaurs and Lapiths in the Landscape of Thessaly.' In G. Hawes ed., *Myths on the Map: The Storied Landscapes of Ancient Greece* (Oxford: Oxford University Press), 83–105.
—. 2019. 'ἐμήδισαν προθύμως οὐδ'ἔτι ἐνδοιαστῶς: Thessalian Medism and Its Repercussions.' *Hermathena* 204–05, 7–40.
Aston, E.M.M. and J. Kerr. 2018. 'Battlefield and Racetrack: The Role of Horses in Thessalian Society.' *Historia* 67.1, 2–35.
Auberson, P. 1974. 'La reconstitution de Daphnéphoréion d'Érétrie.' *Antike Kunst* 17, 60–68.
Avagianou, A.A. 2002. 'Physiology and Mysticism at Pherai: The Funerary Epigram for Lykophron.' *Kernos* 15, 75–89.
Axenidis, Th.D. 1948. *Η Μακεδονική Ηγεμονία εν Θεσσαλία, και η Θέσις της Λαρίσης εν Αυτή*. Athens: A. Sideri.
Babbitt, F.C. 1936. *Plutarch's Moralia*, vol. 4. Cambridge, MA: Harvard University Press.
Bader, F. 1999. 'Homère et le pèlasge.' In A. Blanc and A. Christol eds, *Langues en contact dans l'antiquité: aspects lexicaux* (Nancy: ADRA; Paris: de Boccard), 15–56.
—. 2009. 'Le nom des Vénètes et leur expansion.' In F. Biville and I. Boehm eds, *Autour de Michel Lejeune. Actes des journées d'étude organisées à l'Université Lumière-Lyon 2-Maison de l'Orient et de la Méditerranée, 2–3 février 2006* (Lyon: Maison de l'Orient et de la Méditerranée-Jean Pouilloux), 31–77.
Badian, E. 1999. 'Philip II and the Last of the Thessalians.' *Αρχαία Μακεδονία* 1, 109–22.
Bakhuizen, S.C. 1987. 'Magnesia unter makedonischer Suzeränität.' *Demetrias* V, 319–38.
Bakola, E. 2005. 'A Missed Joke in Aristophanes' *Wasps* 1265–1274.' *Classical Quarterly* 55.2, 609–13.
Baladié, R. 1996. *Strabon:* Géographie, *Tome VI (Livre IX)*. Paris: Les Belles Lettres.
Balériaux, J. 2019. 'Mythical and Spatial Landscapes of Poseidon Hippios in Arcadia.' *Kernos* 32, 81–99.

Baragwanath, E. 2008. *Motivation and Narrative in Herodotus*. Oxford: Oxford University Press.

Baron, C.A. 2006. 'The Aristoteles Decree and the Expansion of the Second Athenian League.' *Hesperia* 75, 379–95.

Bassett, S.L. 2002. 'Innocent Victims or Perjurers Betrayed? The Arrest of the Generals in Xenophon's *Anabasis*.' *Classical Quarterly* 52, 447–61.

Batziou-Efstathiou, A. 1996. 'Δημητριάδα.' In E.I. Kontaxi ed., *Αρχαία Δημητριάδα. Η Διαδρομή της στο Χρόνο* (Volos: Δ.Η.Κ.Ι.), 11–46.

Baurain-Rebillard, L. 1998. 'Des peintres linguistiques?' *Métis* 13, 75–105.

Bearzot, C. 1997. 'P.Oxy. 3985: Considerazioni sulla data e sull'ispirazione dell'elegia di Simonide per la battaglia di Platea.' In B. Kramer, W. Luppe and H. Maehler eds, *Akten des 21. Internationalen Papyrologenkongresses, Berlin, 13.-19.8. 1995*, vol. 1 (Stuttgart: Teubner), 71–79.

—. 2015. 'Ancient Theoretical Reflections on Federalism.' In H. Beck and P. Funke eds, *Federalism in Greek Antiquity* (Cambridge: Cambridge University Press), 503–11.

Beck, H. 1997. *Polis und Koinon. Untersuchungen zur Geschichte und Struktur der griechischen Bundesstaaten im 4. Jahrhundert v. Chr.* Stuttgart: Franz Steiner.

—. 2000. 'Thebes, the Boiotian League, and the Rise of Federalism in Fourth Century Greece.' In P.A. Bernardini ed., *Presenza e funzione della città di Tebe nella cultura greca. Atti del Convegno Internazionale, Urbino 7–9 luglio 1997* (Pisa and Rome: Istituti Editoriali e Poligrafici Internazionali), 331–44.

—. 2001. '"The Laws of the Fathers" versus "The Laws of the League": Xenophon on Federalism.' *Classical Philology* 96.4, 355–75.

—. 2014. 'Ethnic Identity and Integration in Boeotia: The Evidence of the Inscriptions (6th and 5th Centuries BC).' In N. Papazarkadas ed., *The Epigraphy and History of Boeotia* (Leiden: Brill), 19–44.

—. 2019. 'The Aiolians: A Phantom *ethnos*?' In H. Beck, K. Buraselis and A. McAuley eds, *Ethnos and Koinon* (Stuttgart: Franz Steiner), 385–404.

—. 2020. *Localism and the Ancient Greek City-State*. Chicago, IL: University of Chicago Press.

Beck, H. and P. Funke. 2015. 'An Introduction to Federalism in Greek Antiquity.' In H. Beck and P. Funke eds, *Federalism in Greek Antiquity* (Cambridge: Cambridge University Press), 1–29.

Beck, H. and A. Ganter. 2015. 'Boiotia and the Boiotian League.' In H. Beck and P. Funke eds, *Federalism in Greek Antiquity* (Cambridge: Cambridge University Press), 132–57.

Béquignon, Y. 1937a. *Recherches archéologiques à Phères de Thessalie*. Paris: Les Belles Lettres.

—. 1937b. *La vallée du Spercheios des origines au IVe siècle, études d'archéologie et de topographie*. Paris: De Boccard.

—. 1958. 'La question de l'homérique Phthia et du site de Pharsale.' *Revue Archéologique* 1, 93–95.

—. 1964. 'Études thessaliennes, XI.' *Bulletin de Correspondance Hellénique* 88, 400–12.

Bérard, C. 1971. 'Architecture érétrienne et mythologie delphique.' *Antike Kunst* 14, 59–73.

Bernard, P. 1997. 'Les origines thessaliennes de l'Arménie vues par deux historiens thessaliens de la génération d'Alexandre', *Topoi Supplement* 1, 131–216.

Bernstein, F. 2019. '"Ionische Migration" vs. "Große Kolonization der Griechen": Kategorien und Konsequenzen.' *Historia* 68.3, 258–84.

Biagetti, C. 2010. 'Richerche sulle tradizione di fondazione di Magnesia al Meandro. Un aggiornamento.' *Klio* 92, 42–64.

Billows, R.A. 2016. 'Hellenika Oxyrhynchia (66).' In I. Worthington ed., *Jacoby Online. Brill's New Jacoby, Part II.* Leiden: Brill. http://dx.doi.org/10.1163/1873-5363_bnj_a66.

Bing, P. 2002–2003. 'Posidippus and the Admiral: Kallikrates of Samos in the Milan Epigrams.' *Greek, Roman, and Byzantine Studies* 43, 243–66.

—. 2009. *The Scroll and the Marble: Studies in Reading and Reception in Hellenistic Poetry.* Ann Arbor: University of Michigan Press.

Biraschi, A.M. 2005. 'Strabo and Homer: A Chapter in Cultural History.' In D. Dueck, H. Lindsay and S. Pothecary eds, *Strabo's Cultural Geography: The Making of a Kolossourgia* (Cambridge: Cambridge University Press), 73–85.

Blome, D.A. 2020. *Greek Warfare beyond the Polis: Defense, Strategy, and the Making of Ancient Federal States.* Ithaca: Cornell University Press.

Blümel, W. 1982. *Die aiolischen Dialekte: Phonologie und Morphologie der inschriftlichen Texte aus generativer Sicht.* Göttingen: Vandenhoeck & Ruprecht.

Blundell, S. 2019. 'One Shoe Off and One Shoe On: The Motif of Monosandalism in Classical Greece.' In S. Pickup and S. Waite eds, *Shoes, Slippers, and Sandals: Feet and Footwear in Classical Antiquity* (Oxford and New York: Routledge), 216–28.

Boehm, R.A. 2015. 'Alexander, "Whose Courage Was Great": Cult, Power, and Commemoration in Classical and Hellenistic Thessaly.' *Classical Antiquity* 34.2, 209–51.

—. 2018. *City and Empire in the Age of the Successors: Urbanization and Social Response in the Making of the Hellenistic Kingdoms.* Oakland: University of California Press.

Bolmarcich, S. 2007. 'The Afterlife of a Treaty.' *Classical Quarterly* 57.2, 477–89.

Bommeljé, S. 1988. 'Aeolis in Aetolia: Thuc. III 102, 5 and the Origins of the Aetolian Ethnos.' *Historia* 37, 297–316.

Borza, E.N. 1990. *In the Shadow of Olympus: The Emergence of Macedon.* Princeton, NJ: Princeton University Press.

—. 1993. *The Philhellenism of Archelaus. Αρχαία Μακεδονία* 5, vol. 1, 237–44.

Bosnakis, D. and K. Hallof. 2003. 'Alte und neue Inschriften aus Kos I.' *Chiron* 33, 203–62.

—. 2010. 'Alte und neue Inschriften aus Kos IV.' *Chiron* 40, 323–58.

Bouchon, R. 2008. 'L'ère auguste: ébauche d'une histoire politique de la Thessalie sous Auguste.' *Bulletin de Correspondance Hellénique* 132, 427–71.

—. forthcoming. 'Lieux des cultes et concours de Thessalie en l'honneur de Poséidon.'

Bouchon, R. and J.-C. Decourt. 2017. 'Le règlement religieux de Marmarini (Thessalie): nouvelles lectures, nouvelles interprétations.' *Kernos* 30, 150–86.

Bouchon, R. and B. Helly. 2013. 'Construire et reconstruire l'état féderal thessalien (époque classique, époque hellénistique et romaine).' In P. Funke and M. Haake eds, *Greek Federal States and their Sanctuaries: Identity and Integration* (Stuttgart: Franz Steiner), 205–26.

—. 2015. 'The Thessalian League.' In H. Beck and P. Funke eds, *Federalism in Greek Antiquity* (Cambridge: Cambridge University Press), 231–49.

Bousquet, J. 1939. 'Une statue de Pélopidas à Delphes signée de Lysippe.' *Revue Archéologique* 14, 125–32.

—. 1956. 'Inscriptions de Delphes.' *Bulletin de Correspondance Hellénique* 80, 547–97.

—. 1963. 'Inscriptions de Delphes.' *Bulletin de Correspondance Hellénique* 87.1, 188–208.

—. 1965. 'Convention entre Myania et Hypnia.' *Bulletin de Correspondance Hellénique* 89.2, 665–81.

Bouvier, H. 1979. 'Poètes et prosateurs de Thessalie dans les inscriptions.' In B. Helly ed., *La Thessalie: Actes de la Table-Ronde 21–24 Juillet 1975, Lyon* (Paris: de Boccard), 257–64.

Bowden, H.H. 2003. 'The Functions of the Delphic Amphictyony before 346 BCE.' *Scripta Classica Israelica* 22, 67–83.

Bowie, A.M. 2012. 'Mythology and the Expedition of Xerxes.' In E. Baragwanath and M. de Bakker eds, *Myth, Truth, and Narrative in Herodotus* (Oxford: Oxford University Press), 69–286.

Braund, D. 1996. 'The Historical Function of Myth in the Cities of the Eastern Black Sea Coast.' In O. Lordkiparidze and P. Lévêque dirs, *Sur les traces des Argonautes: actes du 6e symposium de Vani (Colchide) 22–29 septembre 1990* (Paris: Les Belles Lettres), 11–19.

Bremmer, J.N. 2007. 'The Myth of the Golden Fleece.' *Journal of Ancient Near East Religions* 6, 9–38.

—. 2008. *Greek Religion and Culture, the Bible and the Ancient Near East.* Leiden: Brill.

Brenk, F.E. 1977. *In Mist Apparelled: Religious Themes in Plutarch's* Moralia *and* Lives. Lugduni Batavorum: Brill.

Bresson, A. 2011. 'Grain from Cyrene.' In Z.H. Archibald, J.K. Davies and V. Gabrielsen eds, *The Economies of Hellenistic Societies, Third to First Centuries BC* (Oxford: Oxford University Press), 66–95.

Brixhe, C. and G. Vottéro. 2004. 'L'alternance codique ou quand le choix du code fait sens.' In R. Hodot ed., *La koiné grecque antique V: Alternances codiques et changements de code* (Nancy: ADRA; Paris: de Boccard), 7–44.

Brown, T.S. 1986. 'Menon of Thessaly.' *Historia* 35.4, 387–404.

Brownson, C.L. 1921. *Xenophon,* Hellenica, vol. 2. Cambridge, MA: Harvard University Press.

Bubeník, V. 1989. *Hellenistic and Roman Greece as a Sociolinguistic Area.* Amsterdam: J. Benjamins.

Buck, C.D. 1913. 'The Interstate Use of the Greek Dialects.' *Classical Philology* 8.2, 133–59.

—. 1955. *The Greek Dialects: Grammar, Selected Inscriptions, Glossary.* Chicago, IL: University of Chicago Press.

Buck, R.J. 1972. 'The Formation of the Boeotian League.' *Classical Philology* 67.2, 94–101.

Buckler, J. 1989. *Philip II and the Sacred War.* Leiden: Brill.

—. 2000. 'Demosthenes and Aeschines.' In I. Worthington ed., *Demosthenes: Statesman and Orator* (London: Routledge), 114–58.

—. 2003. *Aegean Greece in the Fourth Century BC.* Leiden: Brill.

Buckler, J. and H. Beck. 2008. *Central Greece and the Politics of Power in the Fourth Century BC.* Cambridge: Cambridge University Press.

Bugh, G.R. 1988. *The Horsemen of Athens.* Princeton, NJ: Princeton University Press.

Buraselis, K. 1982. *Das hellenistische Makedonien und die Ägäis. Forschungen zur Politik des Kassandros und der drei ersten Antigoniden (Antigonos Monophthalmos, Demetrios Poliorketes und Antigonos Gonatas) im Ägäischen Meer und in Westkleinasien.* Munich: C.H. Beck.

—. 2004. 'Some Remarks on the Koan Asylia (242 BC) against Its International Background.' In K. Höghammer ed., *The Hellenistic Polis of Kos* (Uppsala: Acta Universitatis Upsaliensis), 15–20.

Burgess, J.S. 2009. *The Death and Afterlife of Achilles.* Baltimore, MD: Johns Hopkins University Press.

Burkert, W. 1983. *Homo Necans: The Anthropology of Ancient Greek Sacrificial Ritual and Myth.* Translated by P. Bing. Berkeley: University of California Press.

Burnett, A.P. 2005. *Pindar's Songs for Young Athletes of Aigina.* Oxford: Oxford University Press.

Bury, J.B. 1895. 'The History of the Names Hellas, Hellenes.' *Journal of Hellenic Studies* 15, 217–38.

Buxton, R. 1994. *Imaginary Greece: The Contexts of Mythology.* Cambridge: Cambridge University Press.

Buzzetti, E. 2014. *Xenophon the Socratic Prince: The Argument of the* Anabasis of Cyrus. New York: Palgrave Macmillan.

Cameron, A. 2004. 'The *Garland* of Philip.' *Greek, Roman, and Byzantine Studies* 21.1, 43–62.

Canlas, G.R.L. 2021. *Sacred Space and Community Identities: Sanctuaries in Broader Thessaly from the Archaic to the Early Imperial Periods*. DPhil thesis, University of Alberta.

Cantarín, R.S and M.D. De Cerio Diéz. 2005. *Platón:* Gorgias. *Edición crítica, traducción, introducción y notas*. Madrid: Consejo Superior de Investigaciones Científicas.

Caputo, R. and B. Helly. 2000. 'Archéosismicité de l'Égée: étude des failles actives de la Thessalie.' *Bulletin de Correspondance Hellénique* 124, 560–88.

—. 2005. 'Archaeological Evidences of Past Earthquakes: A Contribution to the SHA of Thessaly, Central Greece.' *Journal of Earthquake Engineering* 9.2, 199–222.

Caputo, R., J.-P. Bravard and B. Helly. 1994. 'The Pliocene Quaternary Tecto-Sedimentary Evolution of the Larissa Plain (Eastern Thessaly, Greece).' *Geodinamica Acta* 7.4, 219–31.

Carbon, J.-M. and J.P.T. Clackson. 2016. 'Arms and the Boy: On the New Festival Calendar from Arkadia.' *Kernos* 29, 119–58.

Carlier, P. and F. Tinnefeld. 2006. 'Basileus.' In H. Cancik, H. Schneider and C.F. Salazar eds, *Brill's New Pauly*. http://dx.doi.org/10.1163/1574-9347_bnp_e213150.

Carney, E. 2000. *Women and Monarchy in Macedonia*. Normal: University of Oklahoma Press.

Cassio, A.C. 1998. 'La cultura euboica e lo sviluppo dell' epica greca.' In B. D'Agostino and M. Bats eds, *Euboica: L'Eubea e la presenza euboica in Calcidica e in Occidente* (Napoli: Centre Jean Bérard), 11–22.

Castelnuovo, L.M. 2017. 'Fra acqua e fuoco: la tripodeforia dei Beoti a Dodona.' *Quaderni Urbinati di Cultura Classica* 116.2, 107–26.

Cawkwell, G. 1981. 'Notes on the Failure of the Second Athenian Confederacy.' *Journal of Hellenic Studies* 101, 40–55.

Ceccarelli, P. 2012. 'Naming the Aegean Sea.' *Mediterranean Historical Review* 27.1, 25–49.

Chandezon, C. 2003. *L'élevage en Grèce, fin V[e]–fin Ier siècle a.C.: l'apport des sources épigraphiques*. Pessac: Ausonius.

Chaniotis, A. 1999. 'Empfängerformular und Urkundenfälschung: Bemerkungen zum Urkundedossier von Magnesia am Mäander.' In R.G. Khoury ed., *Urkunden und Urkundenformulare im Klassischen Altertum und in den orientalischen Kulturen* (Heidelberg: C. Winter), 51–70.

—. 2009. 'Travelling Memories in the Hellenistic World.' In R. Hunter and I.C. Rutherford eds, *Wandering Poets in Ancient Greek Culture: Travel, Locality and Pan-Hellenism* (Cambridge: Cambridge University Press), 249–69.

—. 2011. 'The Impact of War on the Economy of Hellenistic *Poleis*: Demand-Creation, Short-Term Influences, Long-Term Impacts.' In Z.H. Archibald, J.K. Davies and V. Gabrielsen eds, *The Economies of Hellenistic Societies, Third to First Centuries BC* (Oxford: Oxford University Press), 122–41.

Chapinal-Heras, D. 2021. *Experiencing Dodona: The Development of the Epirote Sanctuary from Archaic to Hellenistic Times*. Berlin: De Gruyter.

Chappell, M. 2006. 'Delphi and the *Homeric Hymn to Apollo*.' *Classical Quarterly* 56.2, 331–48.

Chatziangelakis, L. 2008. 'Η εποχή του Χαλκού στη δυτική Θεσσαλία.' In L. Gklegkle ed., *1° Διεθνές Συνέδριο Ιστορίας και Πολιτισμού της Θεσσαλίας. Πρακτικά Συνεδρίου 9–11 Νοεμβρίου 2006*, vol. 1 (Thessaloniki: Περιφέρειας Θεσσαλίας), 362–71.

Christesen, P. 2007. *Olympic Victor Lists and Ancient Greek History*. Cambridge: Cambridge University Press.

—. 2011. 'Baton of Sinope (268).' In I. Worthington ed., *Jacoby Online. Brill's New Jacoby, Part III*. Leiden: Brill. http://dx.doi.org/10.1163/1873-5363_bnj_a268.

Chrysostomou, P. 1998. *Η Θεσσαλική θεά Εν(ν)οδία η Φεραία θεά*. Athens: Υπουργείο Πολιτισμού.

Clarke, K. 1999. *Between Geography and History: Hellenistic Constructions of the Roman World*. Oxford: Clarendon.

—. 2018. *Shaping the Geography of Empire: Man and Nature in Herodotus'* Histories. Oxford: Oxford University Press.

Clarysse, W. and G. Van der Veken, with the assistance of S.P. Vleeming. 1983. *The Eponymous Priests of Ptolemaic Egypt (P.L. Bat. 24.)* Leiden: Brill.

Clay, J.S. 2005. 'The Beginning and End of the Catalogue of Women and Its Relation to Hesiod.' In R. Hunter ed., *The Hesiodic Catalogue of Women: Constructions and Reconstructions* (Cambridge: Cambridge University Press), 25–34.

—. 2006. *The Politics of Olympus: Form and Meaning in the Major Homeric Hymns*. 2nd ed. London: Duckworth and Bristol Classical Press.

—. 2010. *The Politics of Olympus: Form and Meaning in the Major Homeric Hymns*. London: Bloomsbury.

—. 2011. *Homer's Trojan Theater: Space, Vision, and Memory in the* Iliad. Cambridge: Cambridge University Press.

Clayman, D.L. 2013. *Berenice II and the Golden Age of Ptolemaic Egypt*. Oxford: Oxford University Press.

Clinton, K. 1994. 'The Epidauria and the Arrival of Asklepios in Athens.' In R. Hägg ed., *Ancient Greek Cult Practice from the Epigraphical Evidence: Proceedings of the Second International Seminar on Ancient Greek Cult, Organized by the Swedish Institute at Athens, 22–24 November 1991* (Stockholm: Svenska institutet i Athen and P. Åströms), 17–34.

Cohen, G.M. 1996. *The Hellenistic Settlements in Europe, the Islands, and Asia Minor*. Berkeley: University of California Press.

Coldstream, N. 2003. *Geometric Greece, 900–700 BC*. 2nd ed. London and New York: Routledge.

Cole, S.E. 2019. 'Ptolemaic Cavalryman on Painted Alexandrian Funerary Monuments.' *Arts* 8.2, 58.

Collard, C., M.J. Cropp and J. Gibert. 2004. *Euripides: Selected Fragmentary Plays*, vol. II. Oxford: Oxbow (Aris & Phillips).
Corsten, T. 1999. *Vom Stamm zum Bund: Gründung und territoriale Organisation griechischer Bundesstaaten*. Munich: Oberhummer Gesellschaft.
Corvisier, J.-N. 1991. *Aux origines du miracle grec: peuplement et population en Grèce du Nord*. Paris: Presses Universitaires de France.
Coşkun, A. 2013. 'Die Menoniden von Pharsalos: Proxenoi der Athener im 5. Jh.' *Hermes* 141, 142–54.
Crawley, R. 1910. *Thucydides: History of the Peloponnesian War*. London: J.M. Dent & Sons.
Crielaard, J.-P. 1995. 'Homer: History and Archaeology. Some Remarks on the Date of the Homeric World.' In J.-P. Crielaard ed., *Homeric Questions: Essays in Philology, Ancient History and Archaeology, Including the Papers of a Conference Held by the Netherlands Institute at Athens (15 May 1993)* (Amsterdam: J.C. Gieben), 201–88.
—. 2006. '*Basileis* at Sea: Elites and External Contacts in the Euboean Gulf Region from the End of the Bronze Age to the Beginning of the Iron Age.' In S. Deger-Jalkotzy and I.S. Lemos eds, *Ancient Greece: From the Mycenaean Palaces to the Age of Homer* (Edinburgh: Edinburgh University Press), 271–97.
—. 2009. 'The Ionians in the Archaic Period: Shifting Identities in a Changing World.' In A.M.J. Derks and N.G.A.M. Roymans eds, *Ethnic Constructs in Antiquity: The Role of Power and Tradition* (Amsterdam: Amsterdam University Press), 37–84.
Cromey, R.D. 2006. 'Apollo Patroos and the Phratries.' *L'Antiquité Classique* 75, 41–69.
Cummins, M.F. 2009. 'The Praise of Victorious Brothers in Pindar's *Nemean Six* and on the Monument of Daochus at Delphi.' *Classical Quarterly* 59, 317–34.
Cunningham, I.C. 1966. 'Herodas 4.' *Classical Quarterly* 16.1, 113–25.
—. 1971. *Herodas:* Mimiambi. *Edited with Introduction, Commentary and Appendices*. Oxford: Clarendon.
Curty, O. 1995. *Les parentés légendaires entre cités grecques: catalogue raisonné des inscriptions contenant le terme syngeneia et analyse critique*. Genève: Librairie Droz.
—. 2005. 'Un usage fort controversé: la parenté dans le langage diplomatique de l'époque hellénistique.' *Ancient Society* 35, 101–17.
Cuscunà, C. 2009. 'Ethne, mito e storia nei Thessalica di Riano Cretese.' In E. Lanzillotta, V. Costa and G. Ottone eds, *Tradizione e trasmissione degli storici greci frammentari. In ricordo di Silvio Accame. Atti del II Workshop Internazionale Roma, 16–18 febbraio 2006* (Tivoli: Edizioni TORED), 447–82.
Dakoronia, P. 1994. 'Spercheios Valley and the adjacent area in Late Bronze Age and Early Iron Age.' In *Θεσσαλία. Δεκαπέντε Χρόνια Αρχαιολογικής Έρευνας, 1975–1990. Αποτελέσματα και Προοπτικές* (Athens: Kapon), 233–42.

Dalfen, J. 2004. *Platon:* Gorgias. *Übersetzung und Kommentar.* Göttingen: Vanderhoeck & Ruprecht.

Dandrow, E. 2017. 'Ethnography and Identity in Strabo's *Geography*.' In D. Dueck ed., *The Routledge Companion to Strabo* (London and New York: Routledge), 113–24.

Darmezin, L. and A. Tziafalias. 2007. 'The Twelve Tribes of Atrax: A Lexical Study.' In E. Matthews ed., *Old and New Worlds in Greek Onomastics* (Oxford: Oxford University Press), 21–27.

Daux, G. 1957. 'Remarques sur la composition du Conseil amphictionique.' *Bulletin de Correspondance Hellénique* 81, 95–120.

—. 1958. 'Dédicace thessalienne d'un cheval à Delphes.' *Bulletin de Correspondance Hellénique* 82, 329–34.

—. 1959. Daux G. 'Sur les décrets de Démétrias relatifs au sanctuaire d'Apollon Coropaios (*SIG*^{3} 1157 = *IG* IX.2 1109).' *Bulletin de Correspondance Hellénique* 83, 285–87.

—. 1975. 'Note sur un décret thessalien pour des juges étrangers.' *Zeitschrift für Papyrologie und Epigraphik* 16, 37–38.

Daverio Rocchi, G. 2011. *Frontiere del Parnasso: Identità etnica e dinamiche locali nella Focide antica.* Alessandria: Edizioni dell' Orso.

—. 2013. 'Ethnic Identity, Cults and Territorial Settlement: East and West Lokrians.' In P. Funke and M. Haake eds, *Greek Federal States and Their Sanctuaries: Identity and Integration* (Stuttgart: Franz Steiner), 139–61.

—. 2015. 'The Lokrians and Their Federal Leagues.' In H. Beck and P. Funke eds, *Federalism in Greek Antiquity* (Cambridge: Cambridge University Press), 179–98.

Davies, J.K. 1994. 'The Tradition of the First Sacred War.' In S. Hornblower ed., *Greek Historiography* (Oxford: Oxford University Press), 193–212.

—. 1998. 'Finance, Administration, and *Realpolitik*: The Case of Fourth-Century Delphi.' In M. Austin, J. Harries and C. Smith eds, *Modus Operandi: Essays in Honour of Geoffrey Rickman* (London: Institute of Classical Studies), 1–14.

—. 2007a. '*Pythios* and *Pythion*: The Spread of a Cult Title.' *Mediterranean Historical Review* 22.1, 57–69.

—. 2007b. 'The Origins of the Festivals, Especially Delphi and the Pythia.' In S. Hornblower and C. Morgan eds, *Pindar's Poetry, Patrons and Festivals: From Archaic Greece to the Roman Empire* (Oxford: Oxford University Press), 47–69.

Day, J.W. 2018. 'The "Spatial Dynamics" of Archaic and Classical Greek Epigram: Conversations among Locations, Monuments, Texts, and Viewer-Readers.' In A. Petrovic, I. Petrovic and E. Thomas eds, *The Materiality of Text: Placement, Perception, and the Presence of Inscribed Texts in Classical Antiquity* (Hoboken: Wiley), 73–104.

Decourt, J.-C. 1995. *Inscriptions de Thessalie I: Les cités de la vallée de l'Enipeus.* Athens: Ecole Française d'Athènes.

—. 2011. 'Caïnis-Caïneus et l'occupation humaine de la plaine orientale de Thessalie.' *Revue des Études grecques* 111.1, 1–41.

Decourt, J.-C. and B. Helly. 2015. 'Thessalie.' *Revue des Études Grecques: Bulletin Épigraphique* 128, 513–40.

Decourt, J.C. and A. Tziafalias. 2007. 'Mythological and Heroic Names in the Onomastics of Atrax.' In E. Matthews ed., *Old and New Worlds in Greek Onomastics* (Oxford: Oxford University Press), 9–20.

—. 2012. 'Un nouveau règlement religieux de la région de Larissa.' In A. Mazarakis Ainian ed., *Αρχαιολογικό Έργο Θεσσαλίας και Στερεάς Ελλάδας* 3, vol. 1 (Volos: Εργαστήριο Αρχαιολογίας Πανεπιστημίου Θεσσαλίας & Υπουργείο Πολιτισμού, Παιδείας και Θρησκευμάτων), 463–73.

—. 2015. 'Un règlement religieux de la région de Larissa: cultes grecs et "orientaux".' *Kernos* 28, 13–51.

Defradas, J. 1954. *Les thèmes de la propagande delphique.* Paris: Librairie C. Klincksieck.

Deger-Jalkotzy, S. 1999. 'Elateia and Problems of Pottery Chronology.' *Periphery* I, 195–202.

—. 2004. 'Elateia-Alonaki: The Mycenaean and Early Iron Age Pottery and the History of the Cemetery.' *Mycenaean Seminar 2002–03, 19th March 2003, Special Elateia Day* (*BICS* 47), 187–88.

De Polignac, F. 2017a. 'Détroits, isthmes, passages: paysages «sous le joug» de Poséidon.' *Kernos* 30, 67–83.

—. 2017b. 'Détroits, isthmes, passages … : Addendum.' *Kernos* 30, 1–2, https://journals.openedition.org/kernos/2488?lang=en.

De Rossi, F.C. 2019. 'Identification of Some Winners in the *Keles* Race in Posidippus' Epigrams.' In J.-C. Moretti and P. Valavanis eds, *Les hippodromes et les concours hippiques dans la Grèce antique. BCH* Supplement 62 (Athens: EFA), 335–40.

Derow, P. 2005. 'The Arrival of Rome: From the Illyrian Wars to the Fall of Macedon.' In A. Erskine ed., *A Companion to the Hellenistic World* (Oxford and Malden, MA: Blackwell), 51–70.

Desborough, V.R.d'A. 1972. *The Greek Dark Ages.* London: Ernest Benn.

Desborough, V., R. Nicholls and M. Popham. 1970. 'A Euboean Centaur.' *Annual of the British School at Athens* 65, 21–30.

Descat, R. 2001. 'Les traditions grecques sur les Lélèges.' In V. Fromentin and S. Gotteland eds, *Origines Gentium* (Bordeaux: Édtions Ausonius), 169–77.

Detienne, M. 1971. 'Athena and the Mastery of the Horse.' Translated by A.B. Werth. *History of Religions* 11.2, 168–84.

Detienne, M. and P. Vernant. 1978. *Cunning Intelligence in Greek Culture and Society.* Translated by J. Lloyd. Hassocks: Harvester Press.

Dillery, J. 1995. *Xenophon and the History of His Times.* London: Routledge.

Di Salvatore, M. 1994. 'Ricerche sul territorio di Pherai. Insediamenti, difese, vie e confini.' In *Θεσσαλία. Δεκαπέντε Χρόνια Αρχαιολογικής Έρευνας, 1975–1990. Αποτελέσματα και Προοπτικές* (Athens: Kapon), 93–124.

Dmitriev, S. 2011. *The Greek Slogan of Freedom and Early Roman Politics in Greece*. Oxford: Oxford University Press.

Domínguez, A.J. 2015. 'Eastern Locris between Thessaly and Phocis.' In A. Mazarakis Ainian ed., *Αρχαιολογικό Έργο Θεσσαλίας και Στερεάς Ελλάδας* 4, vol. 2 (Volos: Εργαστήριο Αρχαιολογίας Πανεπιστημίου Θεσσαλίας & Υπουργείο Πολιτισμού, Παιδείας και Θρησκευμάτων), 883–92.

—. 2018. 'New Developments and Tradition in Epirus: The Creation of the Molossian State.' In A.J. Domínguez ed., *Politics, Territory and Identity in Ancient Epirus* (Pisa: Edizioni ETS), 1–42.

Domínguez Monedero, A.J. 2008. '*Ethnos*, *Koinon* and *Polis* among the Locrians.' In M. Lombardo and F. Frisone eds, *Forme sovrapoleiche e interpoleiche di organizzione nel mondo greco antico. Papers from the International Conference at Lecce 17–20 September 2008* (Lecce: Congedo), 322–30.

Donati, J.C., A. Sarris, N. Papadopoulos, T. Kalaycı, F.-X. Simon, M. Manataki, I. Moffat and C. Cuenca-García. 2017. 'A Regional Approach to Ancient Urban Studies in Greece through Multi-Settlement Geophysical Survey.' *Journal of Field Archaeology* 42.5, 450–67.

Donnellan, L. 2017. 'The "Euboean" Koine: Reassessing Patterns of Cross-Cultural Interaction and Exchange in the North-Western Aegean Region.' In S. Handberg and A. Gadalou eds, *Material Koinai in the Greek Early Iron Age and Archaic Period. Acts of an International Conference at the Danish Institute at Athens, 30 January–1 February 2015* (Åarhus: Åarhus University Press and the Danish Institute at Athens), 43–63.

Doulgeri-Intzesiloglou, A. 1994. 'Οι νεότερες αρχαιολογικές έρευνες στην περιοχή των αρχαίων Φερών.' In *Θεσσαλία. Δεκαπέντε Χρόνια Αρχαιολογικής Έρευνας, 1975–1990. Αποτελέσματα και Προοπτικές* (Athens: Kapon), 76–83.

—. 1996. 'Περιοχή Βελεστίνου (αρχαίων Φερών).' *AD* 51 *Chron.*, 342–45.

—. 1997. 'Βελεστίνο (αρχ. Φεραί).' *AD* 52 *Chron.*, 467–70.

—. 2000. *Θεσσαλικές Επιγραφές σε Τοπικό Αλφαβήτο*. PhD thesis, Aristotelian University of Thessaloniki.

Doulgeri-Intzesiloglou, A. and P. Arachoviti. 2009. 'Η αρχαία πόλη των Φερών: Πορίσματα ερευνώντης τελευταίας εικοσιπενταετίας (1980–2005).' In L. Gklegkle ed., *1ο Διεθνές Συνέδριο Ιστορίας και Πολιτισμού της Θεσσαλίας. Πρακτικά Συνεδρίου 9–11 Νοεμβρίου 2006*, vol. 1 (Thessaloniki: Περιφέρειας Θεσσαλίας), 233–43.

Dowden, K. 2006. 'The Epic Tradition in Greece.' In R. Fowler ed., *The Cambridge Companion to Homer* (Cambridge: Cambridge University Press), 188–205.

Doyen, C. 2011. *Poséidon souverain: contribution à l'histoire religieuse de la Grèce mycénienne et archaïque*. Bruxelles: Académie royale de Belgique.

Drews, R. 1979. 'Argos and Argives in the *Iliad*.' *Classical Philology* 74.2, 111–35.

Dubois, L. 2014. 'Cinq questions d'onomastique et de lexicologie dialectales.' *Revue de Philologie* 88, 65–78.

Ducat, J. 1964. 'Le Ptoion et l'histoire de la Béotie a l'époque archaïque.' *Revue des Études Grecques* 11, 283–90.

—. 1994. *Les pénestes de Thessalie*. Paris: Les Belles Lettres.

Dué, C. and G. Nagy. 2002. 'Preliminaries to Philostratus's *On Heroes*.' In J.K.B. Maclean and E.B. Aitken, *Flavius Philostratus:* On Heroes. *Translated with an Introduction and Notes* (Atlanta, GA: Society of Biblical Literature), xv–xli.

Duncan, A. 2011. 'Tragedians at the Courts of Tyrants.' In D. Carter ed., *Why Athens? A Reappraisal of Tragic Politics* (Oxford: Oxford University Press), 69–84.

Dušanić, S. 1983. 'The ΚΤΙΣΙΣ ΜΑΓΝΗΣΙΑΣ, Philip V, and the PanHellenic Leukophryena.' *Epigraphica* 45, 11–48.

Easterling, P.E. 1994. 'Euripides outside Athens: A Speculative Note.' *Illinois Classical Studies* 19, 73–80.

Ebert, T. 2018. *Platon:* Menon. Berlin: de Gruyter.

Eder, B. 2009. 'The Northern Frontier of the Mycenaean World.' In A. Mazarakis Ainian ed., *Αρχαιολογικό Έργο Θεσσαλίας και Στερεάς Ελλάδας* 2, vol. 1 *Θεσσαλία* (Volos: Εργαστήριο Αρχαιολογίας Πανεπιστημίου Θεσσαλίας & Υπουργείο Πολιτισμού, Παιδείας και Θρησκευμάτων), 195–205.

Edmunds, L. 1984. 'Thucydides on Monosandalism (3.22.2).' In A.L. Boegehold ed., *Studies Presented to Sterling Dow on His Eightieth Birthday* (Durham, NC: Duke University), 71–75.

Edwards, A. 1985. 'Achilles in the Underworld: *Iliad*, *Odyssey*, and *Aethiopis*.' *Greek, Roman, and Byzantine Studies* 26.3, 215–27.

Ehrhardt, P. 1967. 'Two Notes on Philip of Macedon's First Interventions in Thessaly.' *Classical Quarterly* 17.2, 296–301.

Eidinow, E. 2014. 'Oracles and Oracle-Sellers. An Ancient Market in Futures.' In D. Engels and P. Van Nuffelen eds, *Religion and Competition in Antiquity. Latomus* 434 (Bruxelles: Éditions Latomus), 55–95.

Ellinger, P. 1993. *La légende nationale phocidienne: Artémis, les situations extrêmes et les récits de guerre d'anéantissement*. Paris: de Boccard.

Ellis, J.R. 1976. *Philip II and Macedonian Imperialism*. London: Thames & Hudson.

Errington, R.M. 1990. *A History of Macedonia: Hellenistic Culture and Society*. Translated by C. Errington. Berkeley: University of California Press.

Fabricius, J. 1999. *Die hellenistischen Totenmahlreliefs: Grabrepräsentation und Wertvorstellungen in ostgriechischen Städten*. Munich: F. Pfeil.

Fantuzzi, M. 2004. 'The Structure of the *Hippika* in P.Mil.Vogl. VIII 309.' In B. Acosta-Hughes, E. Kosmetatou and M. Baumbach eds, *Labored in Papyrus Leaves: Perspectives on an Epigram Collection Attributed to Posidippus (P.Mil.Vogl. VIII 309)*, Hellenic Studies Series 2 (Washington, DC: Center for Hellenic Studies), 212–24.

—. 2005. 'Posidippus at Court: The Contribution of the *Ἱππικά* of P. Mil. Vogl.VIII 309 to the Ideology of Ptolemaic Kingship.' In K.J. Gutzwiller ed., *The New Posidippus: A Hellenistic Poetry Book* (Oxford: Oxford University Press), 249–68.

—. 2010. 'Sung Poetry: The Case of Inscribed Paeans.' In J.J. Clauss and M. Cuypers eds, *A Companion to Hellenistic Literature* (Chichester and Malden, MA: Blackwell), 181–96.

Fearn, D. 2007. *Bacchylides: Politics, Performance, Poetic Tradition.* Oxford: Oxford University Press.

—. 2009. 'Oligarchic Hestia: Bacchylides 14B and Pindar *Nemean* 11.' *Journal of Hellenic Studies* 129, 23–38.

Fehr, B. 1979. *Bewegungsweisen und Verhaltensideale: Physiognomische Deutungsmöglichkeiten der Bewegungsdarstellung an griechischen Statuen des 5. und 4. Jhs. v. Chr.* Bad Bramstedt: Moreland Editions.

Felsch, R.C.S. 2007. 'Zur Stratigraphie des Heiligtums.' In R.C.S. Felsch ed., *Kalapodi II* (Mainz am Rhein: Philipp von Zabern), 1–27.

Ferrari, F. 2016. *Platone,* Menone*: Introduzione, traduzione e commento.* Milan: BUR Rizzoli.

Feuer, B. 1983. *The Northern Mycenaean Frontier in Thessaly.* Oxford: BAR.

—. 2016. *Boundaries, Borders and Frontiers in Archaeology: A Study of Spatial Relationships.* Jefferson, NC: McFarland & Company.

Figueira, T.H. 1991. *Athens and Aigina in the Age of Imperial Colonization.* Baltimore, MD and London: Johns Hopkins University Press.

Finkelberg, M. 2005. *Greeks and Pre-Greeks: Aegean Prehistory and Greek Heroic Tradition.* Cambridge: Cambridge University Press.

—. 2018. 'Lesbian and Mainland Greece.' In J.K. Giannakis, E. Crespo and P. Filos eds, *Studies in Ancient Greek Dialects from Central Greece to the Black Sea* (Berlin: de Gruyter), 447–56.

Fischer-Bovet, C. 2014. *Army and Society in Ptolemaic Egypt.* Cambridge: Cambridge University Press.

Flower, M. 1994. *Theopompus of Chios: History and Rhetoric in the Fourth Century BC.* Oxford: Clarendon.

—. 2000a. 'Alexander the Great and Panhellenism.' In A.B. Bosworth and E.J. Baynham eds, *Alexander the Great in Fact and Fiction* (Oxford: Oxford University Press), 96–135.

—. 2000b. 'From Simonides to Isocrates: The Fifth-Century Origins of Fourth-Century Panhellenism.' *Classical Antiquity* 19.1, 65–101.

—. 2002. 'The Invention of Tradition in Classical and Hellenistic Sparta.' In A. Powell and S. Hodkinson eds, *Sparta beyond the Mirage* (London: Classical Press of Wales and Duckworth), 191–217.

Fontenrose, J. 1960. *The Cult and Myth of Pyrros at Delphi.* Berkeley: University of California Press.

Forrest, G. 1956. 'The First Sacred War.' *Bulletin de Correspondance Hellénique* 80, 33–52.

Forsdyke, S. 2012. '"Born from the Earth": The Political Uses of an Athenian Myth.' *Journal of Ancient Near Eastern Religions* 12, 119–41.

Fossey, J.M. 1986. *The Ancient Topography of Eastern Phokis.* Amsterdam: J.C. Gieben.

—. 1990. *The Ancient Topography of Opountian Lokris.* Amsterdam: J.C. Gieben.

Fougères, G. 1888. 'Bas-reliefs de Thessalie.' *Bulletin de Correspondance Hellénique* 12, 179–87.

Fowler, R. 1998. 'Genealogical Thinking, Hesiod's *Catalogue*, and the Creation of the Hellenes.' *Proceedings of the Cambridge Philological Society* 44, 1–19.

—. 2013. *Early Greek Mythography*, vol. 2. Oxford: Oxford University Press.

—. 2018. 'The *nostoi* and Archaic Greek Ethnicity.' In S. Hornblower and G. Biffis eds, *The Returning Hero:* Nostoi *and Traditions of Mediterranean Settlement* (Oxford: Oxford University Press), 43–64.

Franchi, E. 2016. *Die Konflikte zwischen Thessalern und Phokern: Krieg und Identität in der griechischen Erinnerungskultur des 4. Jahrhunderts.* Munich: Herbert Utz.

—. 2017. 'Migration in Greek Origin Stories and Oracular Tales: The Phocian Ghost Soldiers Revisited.' *Metis* 15, 181–202.

—. 2020a. 'Genealogies and Violence: Central Greece in the Making.' In F. Marchand and H. Beck eds, *The Dancing Floor of Ares: Local Conflict and Regional Violence in Central Greece. Ancient History Bulletin* Suppl. 1, 138–67, https://ancienthistorybulletin.org/wp-content/uploads/2020/10/Ch-4-Tufano.pdf.

—. 2020b. 'The Ambivalent Legacy of the Crisaeans: Athens' Interstate Relations (and the Phocian Factor) in 4th-Century Public Discourse.' *Klio* 102.2, 509–35.

Franchi, E. and G. Proietti. 2015. 'Commemorating War Dead and Inventing Battle Heroes: Heroic Paradigms and Discursive Strategies in Ancient Athens and Phocis.' In G. Lee, H. Whittaker and G. Wrightson eds, *Ancient Warfare: Introducing Current Research, vol. 1* (Cambridge: Cambridge Scholars), 229–51.

Franke, P.R. 1970. 'ΦΕΘΑΛΟΙ – ΦΕΤΑΛΟΙ – ΠΕΤΘΑΛΟΙ – ΘΕΣΣΑΛΟΙ: Zur Geschichte Thessaliens im 5. Jarhhundert v. Chr.' *Archäologischer Anzeiger* 85, 85–93.

—. 1973. 'Numismatic Evidence on the Existence of a Thessalian Confederacy in the Fifth Century BC.' *Νομισματικά Χρονικά* 2, 5–12.

Fraser, P.M. 2009. *Greek Ethnic Terminology*. Oxford: Oxford University Press.

Freitag, K. 2007. 'Ethnogenese, Ethnizität und die Entwicklung der griechischen Staatenwelt in der Antike.' *Historische Zeitschrift* 285, 373–99.

—. 2013. 'Die Akarnanen: Ein Ethnos ohne religiöses Zentrum und gemeinsame Feste?' In P. Funke and M. Haake eds, *Greek Federal States and Their Sanctuaries: Identity and Integration* (Stuttgart: Franz Steiner), 65–83.

Fritzilas, S.A. 2019. '*Samphoras* and Koppatias: The Brand-name Horses of Sikyon and Corinth.' In J.-C. Moretti and P. Valavanis eds, *Les hippodromes et les concours hippiques dans la Grèce antique. BCH* Supplement 62 (Athens: EFA), 307–23.

Funke, P. 2007. 'Die Perser und die griechischen Heiligtümer in der Perserkriegzeit.' In B. Bleckmann ed., *Herodot und die Epoche der Perserkriege: Realitäten und Fiktionen. Kolloquium zum 80. Geburtstag von Dietmar Kienast* (Köln: Böhlau), 3–19.

—. 2013. 'Greek Amphiktyonies: An Experiment in Transregional Governance.' In H. Beck ed., *A Companion to Ancient Greek Government* (Chichester: Wiley), 451–65.

Funke, P. and M. Haake eds. 2013. *Greek Federal States and Their Sanctuaries: Identity and Integration*. Stuttgart: Franz Steiner.

Gabbert, J.J. 1997. *Antigonus II Gonatas: A Political Biography*. London: Taylor & Francis.

Galanakis, Y. and M. Stamatopoulou. 2012. 'A Preliminary Report on the Archival Material from the Excavations of the Tholos Tomb at Ano Dranista (Ano Ktimeni) in Thessaly by A.S. Aravanitopoulos (1911).' In A. Mazarakis Ainian ed., *Αρχαιολογικό Έργο Θεσσαλίας και Στερεάς Ελλάδας* 3, vol. 1 (Volos: Εργαστήριο Αρχαιολογίας Πανεπιστημίου Θεσσαλίας & Υπουργείο Πολιτισμού, Παιδείας και Θρησκευμάτων), 205–18.

Ganter, A. 2013. 'A Two-Sided Story of Integration: The Cultic Dimension of Boiotian Ethnogenesis.' In P. Funke and M. Haake eds, *Greek Federal States and Their Sanctuaries: Identity and Integration* (Stuttgart: Franz Steiner), 85–105.

—. 2014. 'Ethnicity and Local Myth.' In J. McInerney ed., *A Companion to Ethnicity in the Ancient Mediterranean* (Chichester: Wiley Blackwell), 228–40.

García-Ramón, J.L. 1975. *Les origines postmycéniennes du groupe dialectal éolien: étude linguistique*. Salamanca: Universidad de Salamanca.

Gardiner, E.M., K.K. Smith and W.B. Dinsmoor. 1909. 'The Group Dedicated by Daochus at Delphi.' *American Journal of Archaeology* 13.4, 447–76.

Garnsey, P., T. Gallant and D. Rathbone. 1984. 'Thessaly and the Grain Supply of Rome in the Second Century B.C.' *Journal of Roman Studies* 74, 30–44.

Gebhard, E.R. 1993. 'The Evolution of a Pan-Hellenic Sanctuary: From Archaeology towards History at Isthmia.' In N. Marinatos and R. Hägg eds, *Greek Sanctuaries: New Approaches* (London and New York: Routledge), 154–77.

Gehrke, J.-H. 1994. 'Mythos, Geschichte, Politik. Antik und Modern.' *Saeculum* 45, 239–64.

Geominy, W. 1998. 'Zum Daochos-Weihgeschenk.' *Klio* 80, 369–402.

Georganas, I. 2000. 'Early Iron Age Tholos Tombs in Thessaly (c. 1100–700 BC).' *Mediterranean Archaeology* 13, 47–54.

—. 2008. 'Between Admetus and Jason: Pherai in the Early Iron Age.' In C. Gallou, M. Georgiadis and G.M. Muskett eds, *DIOSKOUROI: Studies Presented to W.G. Cavanagh and C.B. Mee on the Anniversary of their 30-Year Contribution to Aegean Archaeology* (Oxford: Archaeopress), 274–80.

—. 2009. 'Dying in Early Iron Age Thessaly.' In A. Mazarakis Ainian ed., *Αρχαιολογικό Έργο Θεσσαλίας και Στερεάς Ελλάδας* 2, vol. 1 *Θεσσαλία* (Volos: Εργαστήριο Αρχαιολογίας Πανεπιστημίου Θεσσαλίας & Υπουργείο Πολιτισμού, Παιδείας και Θρησκευμάτων), 195–205.

—. 2011. 'The Transition from the Late Bronze to the Early Iron Age in Thessaly: Some Thoughts.' In A. Mazarakis Ainian ed., *The Dark Ages Revisited, International Conference in Memory of W.D.E. Coulson, University of Thessaly, Volos, 14–17 June 2007* (Volos: University of Thessaly Press), 627–33.

Georgiou, E. 2015. 'The Coinage of Orthe.' In U. Wartenberg and M. Amandry eds, *ΚΑΙΡΟΣ: Contributions to Numismatics in Honor of Basil Demetriadi* (New York: American Numismatic Society), 55–82, pls 1–5.

Ghisellini, E. 2017. 'Rilievi votive dalla Tessaglia per Achille e Teti.' *Rendiconti*, 28, 29–103.

Gilula, D. 2000. 'Stratonicus, the Witty Harpist.' In D. Braund and J. Wilkins eds, *Athenaeus and His World: Reading Greek Culture in the Roman Empire* (Exeter: University of Exeter Press), 423–33.

Giovannini, A. 1969. *Étude historique sur les origines du Catalogue des Vaisseaux*. Bern: Éditions Francke.

—. 2003. 'Genèse et accomplissement de l'État fédéral de la Grèce antique à la Constitution américaine de 1787–1789.' In K. Buraselis and K. Zoumboulakis eds, *The Idea of European Community in History,* vol. 2, *Aspects of Connecting Poleis and Ethne in Ancient Greece* (Athens: National Kapodistrian University of Athens), 143–76.

Godley, A.D. 1922. Herodotus: *The Persian Wars, Volume III: Books 5–7.* Cambridge, MA: Harvard University Press.

Golden, M. 1997. 'Equestrian Competition in Ancient Greece: Difference, Dissent, Democracy.' *Phoenix* 51, 327–44.

—. 2008. *Greek Sport and Social Status.* Austin: University of Texas Press.

Gorman, R.J. and Gorman, V.B. 2007. 'The Tryphê of the Sybarites. A Historiographical Problem in Athenaeus.' *Journal of Hellenic Studies* 127, 38–60.

Gorrini, M.E. 2006. 'Healing Heroes in Thessaly: Chiron the Centaur.' In Mazarakis Ainian ed., *Αρχαιολογικό έργο Θεσσαλίας και Στερεάς Ελλάδας. Πρακτικά επιστημονικής συνάντησης Βόλος, 27.2–2.3.2003* (Volos: Εργαστήριο Αρχαιολογίας Πανεπιστημίου Θεσσαλίας & Υπουργείο Πολιτισμού, Παιδείας και Θρησκευμάτων), vol. 1, 283–95.

Gounaris, A.P. 2012. 'Το θεσσαλικόν απόσπασμα του Νηῶν Καταλόγου: τεκμήριο Μυκηναϊκής οικιστικής ή πρωτοϊστορικής ανθρωπολογίας.' In A. Mazarakis Ainian ed., *Αρχαιολογικό Έργο Θεσσαλίας και Στερεάς Ελλάδας* 3, vol. 1 *Θεσσαλία* (Volos: Εργαστήριο Αρχαιολογίας Πανεπιστημίου Θεσσαλίας & Υπουργείο Πολιτισμού, Παιδείας και Θρησκευμάτων), 251–68.

Gow, A.S.F. and D.L. Page. 1968. *The Greek Anthology: The* Garland of Philip, *and some Contemporary Epigrams.* Cambridge: Cambridge University Press.

Grabowski, T. 2020. 'The Activity of Ptolemy II's Fleet in the Aegean Sea.' *Electrum* 27, 131–48.

Graf, D. 1979. *Medism: Greek Collaboration with Achaemenid Persia.* Ann Arbor: University of Michigan Press.

—. 1984. 'Medism: The Origin and Significance of the Term.' *Journal of Hellenic Studies* 104, 15–30.

Grainger, J.D. 1999. *The League of the Aitolians.* Leiden: Brill.

Graninger, D. 2006. *Regional Cults of Thessaly.* PhD thesis, Cornell University.

—. 2007. 'Studies in the Cult of Artemis Throsia.' *Zeitschrift für Papyrologie und Epigraphik* 162, 151–64.

—. 2009. 'Apollo, Ennodia, and Fourth-Century Thessaly.' *Kernos* 22, 109–24.

—. 2010. 'Macedonia and Thessaly.' In J. Roisman and I. Worthington eds, *A Companion to Ancient Macedonia* (Oxford: Wiley-Blackwell), 306–25.

—. 2011a. *Cult and* Koinon *in Hellenistic Thessaly.* Leiden: Brill.

—. 2011b. '*IG* IX 2 1099B and the *komai* of Demetrias.' *Zeitschrift für Papyrologie und Epigraphik* 177, 119–22.

—. 2022. 'Environmental Change in a Sacred Landscape: The Thessalian Peloria.' *Journal of Ancient History and Archaeology* 9.1, 87–92.

Gray, V.J. 2010. *Xenophon's Mirror of Princes: Reading the Reflections.* Oxford: Oxford University Press.

Gregory, J. 2018. *Cheiron's Way: Youthful Education in Homer and Tragedy.* Oxford: Oxford University Press.

Griffith, G.T. 1970. 'Philip of Macedon's Early Interventions in Thessaly (358–352 B.C.).' *Classical Quarterly* 20.1, 67–80.

Green, P. 1997. *Apollonius:* Argonautica. *Translated, with Introduction, Commentary, and Glossary.* Berkeley: University of California Press.

Gruen, E. 2011. *Rethinking the Other in Antiquity.* Princeton, NJ: Princeton University Press.

Gschnitzer, F. 1954. 'Namen und Wesen der Thessalischen Tetraden.' *Hermes* 82.4, 451–64.

Guillon, P. 1963. *Études béotiennes: le bouclier d'Héraclès et l'histoire de la Grèce centrale dans la période de la première guerre sacrée.* Aix-en-Provence: Éditions Ophrys.

Gutzwiller, K. 2010. 'Heroic Epitaphs of the Classical Age: The Aristotlian Peplos and Beyond.' In M. Baumbach, A. Petrovic and I. Petrovic eds, *Archaic and Classical Greek Epigram* (Cambridge: Cambridge University Press), 219–49.

Haagsma, M. 2014. 'Ten Years of Archaeological Research at Kallithea: An Overview.' *The Bulletin of the Canadian Institute in Greece*, 33.

Haagsma, M., S. Karapanou and L. Surtees. 2015. 'Greek-Canadian Fieldwork at Kastro Kallithea 2006–2012.' In A. Mazarakis Ainian ed., *Αρχαιολογικό Έργο Θεσσαλίας και Στερεάς Ελλάδας*, vol. 1 (Volos: Εργαστήριο Αρχαιολογίας Πανεπιστημίου Θεσσαλίας & Υπουργείο Πολιτισμού, Παιδείας και Θρησκευμάτων), 195–205.

Haagsma, M., L. Surtees and M. Chykerda. 2019. 'Ethnic Constructs from Inside and Out: External Policy and the *ethnos* of Achaia Phthiotis.' In H. Beck, K. Buraselis and A. McAuley eds, *Ethnos and Koinon* (Stuttgart: Franz Steiner), 285–319.

Habicht, Ch. 1970. 'Epigraphische Zeugnisse zur Geschichte Thessaliens unter der makedonischen Herrschaft.' *Ancient Macedonia* I (Thessaloniki: Institute for Balkan Studies), 265–79.

—. 1976. 'Hellenistische Gymnasiarchenliste aus Pherai.' *Demetrias* I (Bonn: Habelt), 181–99.

—. 1983. 'Makedonen in Larisa?' *Chiron* 13, 21–32.

—. 1999. 'Städtische Polemarchen in Thessalien.' *Hermes* 127.2, 254–56.

Hall, J.M. 1995. 'How Argive Was the "Argive" Heraion? The Political and Cultic Geography of the Argive Plain, 900–400 B.C.' *American Journal of Archaeology* 99.4, 577–613.

—. 1997. *Ethnic Identity in Greek Antiquity*. Cambridge: Cambridge University Press.

—. 2002. *Hellenicity: Between Ethnicity and Culture*. Chicago, IL: University of Chicago Press.

—. 2014. *A History of the Archaic Greek World, ca. 1200–479 BCE*. 2nd ed. Chichester: Wiley-Blackwell.

—. 2015. 'Ancient Greek Ethnicities: Towards a Reassessment.' *Bulletin of the Institute of Classical Studies* 58.2, 15–29.

Hammerschmied, K. 2018. 'The Panhellenic Festival of Artemis Leukophryene in Magnesia-on-the-Meander: A Spatial Analysis of a Hellenistic Procession.' In U. Luig ed., *Approaching the Sacred: Pilgrimage in Historical and Intercultural Perspective* (Berlin: Edition Topoi), 91–127.

Hammond, N.G.L. 1931–1932. 'Prehistoric Epirus and the Dorian Invasion.' *Annual of the British School at Athens* 32, 131–79.

—. 1967. *Epirus: The Geography, the Ancient Remains, the History and Topography of Epirus and Adjacent Areas*. Oxford: Clarendon.

—. 1994. *Philip of Macedon*. London: Duckworth.

—. 1996. 'Alexander and Armenia.' *Phoenix* 50.2, 130–37.

Hampe, R. 1951. *Die Stele aus Pharsalos im Louvre*. Berlin: de Gruyter.

Hard, R. 2004. *The Routledge Handbook of Greek Mythology*. London: Routledge.

Harder, A. 1985. *Euripides'* Kresphontes *and* Archelaos*: Introduction, Text and Commentary*. Leiden: Brill.

—. 2012. *Callimachus:* Aetia. *Introduction, Text, Translation, and Commentary*. Oxford: Oxford University Press.

Harder, A., O. van Nijf, E. Nikolaou, T. Dijkstra and S. Kamphorst. 2017. 'Inscriptions from Halos.' *Pharos* 23.2, 33–65.

Hardie, A. 2006. 'The Aloades on Helicon: Music, Territory and Cosmic Order.' *Antike und Abendland* 52, 42–71.

Harris, E.M. 1995. *Aeschines and Athenian Politics*. Oxford: Oxford University Press.

—. 2018. 'The Stereotype of Tyranny and the Tyranny of Stereotype.' In M. Kalaitzi, P. Paschidis, C. Antonetti and A.-M. Guimier-Sorbets eds, *Βορειοελλαδικά: Tales from the Lands of the Ethne. Essays in Honour of Miltiades B. Hatzopoulos* (Athens: National Hellenic Research Foundation and the Institute of Historical Research), 167–78.

Harissis, H. 2019. 'Pindar's Paean 8 and the Birth of the Myth of the First Temples of Delphi.' *Acta Classica* 62, 79–124.

Hatzopoulos, M. 1994. *Cultes et rites de passage en Macédoine.* Athens: Κέντρον Ελληνικής και Ρωμαϊκής Αρχαιότητος του Εθνικού Ιδρύματος Ερευνών.

Hauptmann, A. 2011. 'Gold in Georgia I: Scientific Investigations into the Composition of Gold.' In Ü. Yalçın ed., *Anatolian Metal V* (Bochum: Deutsches Bergbau-Museum), 173–86.

Heckel, W. 2006. *Who's Who in the Age of Alexander.* Oxford and Malden, MA: Blackwell.

Hedreen, G. 1991. 'The Cult of Achilles in the Euxine.' *Hesperia* 60.3, 313–30.

—. 2010. 'The Trojan War, Theoxenia, and Aegina in Pindar's Paean 6 and the Aphaia Sculptures.' In D. Fearn ed., *Aegina: Contexts for Choral Lyric Poetry. Myth, History, and Identity in the Fifth Century BC* (Oxford: Oxford University Press), 323–70.

Helly, B. 1970. 'La convention des Basaidai.' *Bulletin de Correspondance Hellénique* 94, 161–89.

—. 1973. *Gonnoi*, 2 vols. Amsterdam: Hakkert.

—. 1979. 'Une liste des cités de Perrhébie dans la première moitié du IVe siècle avant J.-C.' In B. Helly ed., *La Thessalie: Actes de la Table-ronde, 21–24 Juillet 1975, Lyon* (Lyon: Maison de l'Orient; Paris: de Boccard), 165–200.

—. 1987. 'Le «Dotion Pedion», Lakéreia et les origines de Larisa.' *Journal des Savants* 3–4, 127–58.

—. 1991. 'Premiers agriculteurs de Thessalie: mythe des origies à la lumière de la philologie, de l'archéologie et de la linguistique.' In M.-C. Cauvin ed., *Rites et rythmes agraires. Séminaire de recherche sous la direction de Marie-Claire Cauvin* (Lyon: Maison de l'Orient et de la Méditerranée Jean Pouilloux), 135–47.

—. 1992. 'Incursions chez les Dolopes.' In I. Blum, L. Darmezin, J.-C. Decourt, B. Helly and G. Lucas eds, *Topographie antique et géographie historique en pays Grec* (Paris: Centre National de la Recherche Scientifique), 49–91.

—. 1994. 'La glose d'Hésychius ΜΕΝΩΝΙΔΑΙ: pénestes thessaliens ou ostracisés Athéniens?' *Revue de Philologie de Littérature et d'Histoire Anciennes* 68.1, 135–46.

—. 1995. *L'État Thessalian: Aleuas le Roux, les Tétrades et les Tagoi.* Lyon: Maison de l'Orient Méditerranéen.

—. 1999. 'Modèle, de l'archéologie des cités à l'archéologie du paysage.' In M. Brunet ed., *Territoires des cités grecques* (*BCH* Suppl. 34), 99–124.

—. 2004a. 'Décrets de cités thessaliennes à Cos.' *Chiron* 34, 87–107.

—. 2004b. 'Epigramme funéraire pour Théotimos, fils de Ményllos, d'Atrax (457 av. J.-C.).' *Zeitschrift für Papyrologie und Epigraphik* 148, 15–28.

—. 2006a. 'Décret de Larisa pour Bombos, fils d'Alkaios, et pour Leukios, fils de Nikasias, citoyens d'Alexandrie de Troade (ca 150 av. J.-C.).' *Chiron* 36, 171–203.

—. 2006b. 'Un nom antique pour Goritsa?' In A. Mazarakis Ainian ed., *Αρχαιολογικό Έργο Θεσσαλίας και Στερεάς Ελλάδας* 1, vol. 1 (Volos: Εργαστήριο Αρχαιολογίας Πανεπιστημίου Θεσσαλίας & Υπουργείο Πολιτισμού, Παιδείας και Θρησκευμάτων), 155–79.

—. 2007. 'Le dialecte thessalien, un autre modèle de développement.' In I. Hajnal ed., *Die altgriechischen Dialekte: Wesen und Werden. Akten des Kolloquiums Freie Universität Berlin 19.–22. September 2001* (Innsbruck: Institut für Sprachen und Literaturen der Universität Innsbruck), 177–222.

—. 2008. 'Éléments pour une histoire de la distribution des territoires en Thessalie de l'époque Néolithique à la fin de l'Antiquité.' In L. Gklegkle ed., *1º Διεθνές Συνέδριο Ιστορίας και Πολιτισμού της Θεσσαλίας. Πρακτικά Συνεδρίου 9–11 Νοεμβρίου 2006*, vol. 1 (Thessaloniki: Περιφέρειας Θεσσαλίας), 194–205.

—. 2009. 'La Thessalie au 3e siècle av. J.-C.' In A. Mazarakis Ainian ed., *Αρχαιολογικό Έργο Θεσσαλίας και Στερεάς Ελλάδας* 2, vol. 2 (Volos: Εργαστήριο Αρχαιολογίας Πανεπιστημίου Θεσσαλίας & Υπουργείο Πολιτισμού, Παιδείας και Θρησκευμάτων), 339–68.

—. 2013. *Géographie et Histoire des Magnètes de Thessalie.* Sainte-Colombe-sur-Gand: La Rumeur Libre Éditions.

—. 2018. 'Some Materials for a Historical Grammar of the Thessalian Dialect.' In J.K. Giannakis, E. Crespo and P. Filos eds, *Studies in Ancient Greek Dialects from Central Greece to the Black Sea* (Berlin: de Gruyter), 351–74.

—. 2019. 'Les datifs en et dans les dédicaces et épitaphes thessaliennes en alphabet épichorique (VIe–Ve s. av. J.-C.).' *Revue de Philologie, de Littérature et d'Histoire Anciennes* 93, 95–112.

—. forthcoming, a. 'Des génitifs en -ō dans le décret de Thétônion pour Sôtairos de Corinthe (*IG* IX 2, 257, Thessaliotide, Ve s. av. J.-C.).'

—. forthcoming, b. 'Poséidon Kouérios, 'celui qui sort du creux du rocher.' In C. Morgan and M. Stamatopoulou eds, *Sanctuaries and Cults in Ancient Thessaly.*

Helly, B. and A. Tziafalias. 2013. 'Décrets inédits de Larisa organisant la vente de terres publiques attribuées aux cavaliers.' *Topoi* 18, 135–249.

Helly, B., G.J. Te Riele and J.A. Van Rossum. 1979. 'La liste des gymnasiarques de Phères pour les années 330–189 av. J.-C.' In B. Helly ed., *La Thessalie: Actes de la Table-Ronde 21–24 Juillet 1975, Lyon* (Paris: de Boccard), 220–52.

Herrmann, F. 1922. 'Die thessalische Münzunion im 5. Jahrhundert.' *Zeitschrift für Numismatik* 33, 33–43.

—. 1925. 'Die Silbermünzen von Larissa in Thessalien.' *Zeitschrift für Numismatik* 35, 1–69.

Hope Simpson, R. and J.F. Lazenby. 1970. *The Catalogue of Ships in Homer's Iliad.* Oxford: Clarendon.

Hornblower, S. 2007. '"Dolphins in the Sea" (*Isthmian* 9.7): Pindar and the Aiginetans.' In S. Hornblower and C. Morgan eds, *Pindar's Poetry, Patrons, and Festivals from Archaic Greece to the Roman Empire* (Oxford: Oxford University Press), 287–308.

—. 2009. 'Did the Delphic Amphiktiony Play a Political Role in the Classical Period?' In I. Malkin, C. Constantakopoulou and K. Panagopoulou eds, *Greek and Roman Networks in the Mediterranean* (London and New York: Routledge), 39–56.

—. 2011. *The Greek World, 479–323 BC.* 4th ed. London and New York: Routledge.

—. 2013. *Herodotus:* Histories *Book V.* Cambridge: Cambridge University Press.

—. 2014. 'Agariste's Suitors.' In A. Moreno and R. Thomas eds, *Patterns of the Past: Epitēdeumata in the Greek Tradition* (Oxford: Oxford University Press), 217–32.

Howe, T. 2003. 'Pastoralism, the Delphic Amphiktyony and the First Sacred War: The Creation of Apollo's Sacred Pastures.' *Historia* 52.2, 129–46.

—. 2008. *Pastoral Politics: Animals, Agriculture and Society in Ancient Greece.* Claremont, CA: Regina Books.

Howgego, C. 1995. *Ancient History from Coins.* London: Routledge.

Hughes, D.D. 1991. *Human Sacrifice in Ancient Greece.* London: Routledge.

Hunter, R.L. 1993. *The* Argonautica *of Apollonius: Literary Studies.* Cambridge: Cambridge University Press.

Huvelin, P. 1925. 'Appendice: ΛΙΘΟΙ 'ΕΠΙΚΡΕΜΑΝΤΑΙ.' In G. Radet, *Notes sur l'histoire d'Alexandre* (Bordeaux: Feret et Fils), 17–20.

Huxley, G. 1969. 'Choirilos of Samos.' *Greek, Roman, and Byzantine Studies* 10, 12–29.

Hyland, J.O. 2015. 'The Prince and the Pancratist: Persian–Thessalian Relations in the Late-Fifth Century B.C.' *Greek, Roman, and Byzantine Studies* 55, 315–28.

Intzesiloglou, B.G. 1994. 'Ιστορική τοπογραφία της περιοχής του κόλπου του Βόλου.' In B. Helly ed., *La Thessalie. Quinze années de recherches archéologiques, 1975–1990. Bilans et perspectives. Actes du colloque international, Lyons, 17–22 Avril 1990* (Athens: Kapon), 31–56.

—. 1996. 'Ο συνοικισμός και η πολιτική οργάνωση της Δημητριάδας και του Κοινού των Μαγνήτων κατά την ελληνιστική περίοδο.' In E.I. Kontaxi ed., *Αρχαία Δημητριάδα. Η Διαδρομή της στον Χρόνο* (Volos: Δημοτικό Κέντρο Ιστορικών Ερευνών), 91–111.

—. 2000. 'A Newly Discovered Archaic Bronze Statue from Metropolis (Thessaly).' In C.C. Mattusch, A. Brauer and S.E. Knudsen eds, *From the Parts to the Whole: Acta of the 13th International Bronze Congress, Held at Cambridge, Massachusetts, May 28th–June 1st, 1996* (Portsmith, RI: *Journal of Roman Archaeology*), 65–68.

—. 2002a. 'The Archaic Temple of Apollo at Ancient Metropolis (Thessaly).' In M. Stamatopoulou and M. Yeroulanou eds, *Excavating Classical Culture: Recent Archaeological Discoveries in Greece* (Oxford: Archaeopress), 109–15.
—. 2002b. 'Aiatos et Polycléia. Du mythe à l'histoire.' *Kernos* 15, 289–95.
—. 2006. 'Η Ιτωνία Αθηνά και το Θεσσαλικό ομοσπονδιακό ιερό της στη Φίλια Καρδίτσας.' In A. Mazarakis Ainian ed., *Αρχαιολογικό Έργο Θεσσαλίας και Στερεάς Ελλάδας* 1, vol. 1 (Volos: Εργαστήριο Αρχαιολογίας Πανεπιστημίου Θεσσαλίας & Υπουργείο Πολιτισμού, Παιδείας και Θρησκευμάτων), 231–47.
Ionescu, C. 2007. *Plato's* Meno*: An Interpretation.* Lanham, MD: Lexington Books.
Irwin, E. 2010. 'Herodotus on Aeginetan Identity.' In D. Fearn ed., *Aegina: Contexts for Choral Lyric Poetry. Myth, History, and Identity in the Fifth Century BC* (Oxford: Oxford University Press), 373–425.
Jacquemin, A. and D. Laroche. 2001. 'Le monument de Daochos ou le trésor des Thessaliens.' *Bulletin de Correspondance Hellénique* 125, 305–32.
Janko, R. 1982. *Homer, Hesiod and the Hymns.* Cambridge: Cambridge University Press.
—. 1986. 'The Shield of Heracles and the Legend of Cycnus.' *Classical Quarterly* 36.1, 38–59.
Jasnow, B., C. Evans and J.S. Clay. 2018. 'Poetic and Geographical Organization in the Catalogue of Ships.' *Transactions of the American Philological Society* 148.1, 1–44.
Jeffery, L.H. 1990. *The Local Scripts of Archaic Greece: A Study of the Origin of the Greek Alphabet and its Development from the Eighth to the Fifth Centuries B.C.* Revised 2nd ed. Oxford: Clarendon.
Johnston, A. 2021. 'Dodona and the Concept of Local Scripts.' In R. Parker and P.M. Steele eds, *The Early Greek Alphabets: Origin, Diffusion, Uses* (Oxford: Oxford University Press), 107–18.
Jones, B. 2012. 'Relative Chronology and an "Aeolic Phase" of Epic.' In Ø. Andersen and D.T.T. Haug eds, *Relative Chronology in Early Greek Epic Poetry* (Cambridge: Cambridge University Press), 44–64.
Jones, C.P. 2001. 'Philostratus' *Heroikos* and Its Setting in Reality.' *Journal of Hellenic Studies* 121, 141–49.
—. 2010. 'Kinship (συγγένεια) in Two Cities of the Troad.' *Chiron* 40, 29–40.
Jones, H.L. 1924. *The Geography of Strabo.* Cambridge, MA: Harvard University Press.
Jones, W.H.S. and H.A. Ormerod. 1918. *Pausanias: Description of Greece, in 4 Volumes.* Cambridge, MA: Harvard University Press.
Jost, M. 1985. *Sanctuaires et cultes d'Arcadie.* Paris: J. Vrin.
—. 2007. 'The Religious System in Arcadia.' In D. Ogden ed., *A Companion to Greek Religion* (Oxford and Malden, MA: Blackwell), 264–79.
Jouan, F. and H. Van Looy. 1998. *Euripide, Tome VIII: Fragments 1re partie, Aigeus-Autolykos.* Paris: Les Belles Lettres.

Jürgens, K. 2017. 'Pilgrimage and Procession in the Panhellenic Festivals: Some Observations on the Hellenistic Leukophryena in Magnesia-on-the-Meander.' In T.M. Kristensen and W. Friese eds, *Excavating Pilgrimage: Archaeological Approaches to Sacred Travel and Movement in the Ancient World* (London and New York: Routledge), 87–105.

Kaczmarek, C. 2015. *A Name and a Place: Settlement and Land Use Patterns, Identity Expression, and Social Strategies in Hellenistic and Roman Thessaly.* PhD thesis, University of Leicester.

Kagan, D. 1969. *The Outbreak of the Peloponnesian War.* Ithaca, NY: Cornell University Press.

Kagan, J. 2004. 'The So-Called Persian Weight Coins of Larissa.' In L. Kypraiou ed., *Ὀβολός 7: Coins in the Thessalian Region: Mints, Circulation, Iconography, History Ancient, Byzantine, Modern* (Athens: Friends of the Numismatic Museum), 79–86.

Kalcyk, H. and J. Weichenberger. 1990. 'Die Katawothren am ehemaligen Kopaissee in Böotien, Grld. Vorläufiger Bericht über die Untersuchungen in den Jahren 1985–1988.' In A. Schachter ed., *Essays in the Topography, History and Culture of Boiotia, Teiresias Supplement* 3 (Montreal: Dept. of Classics, McGill University), 27–32.

Kalligas, P.G. 1992. 'Θεσσαλία και Εύβοια κατά την πρώιμη εποχή του σιδήρου.' In *Διεθνές Συνέδριο για την Αρχαία Θεσσαλία: στη Μνήμη του Δημήτρη Ρ. Θεοχάρη. Πρακτικά* (Athens: Ταμείο Αρχαιολογικών Πόρων και Απαλλοτριώσεων), 298–307.

Kaplan, P. 2014. 'Ethnicity and Geography.' In J. McInerney ed., *A Companion to Ethnicity in the Ancient Mediterranean* (Chichester: Wiley Blackwell), 298–311.

Karagiannopoulos, C. 2017–2018. 'Revealing Geometric to Classical Thessaliotis.' *Archaeological Reports* 64, 113–31.

Karamitrou-Mentessidi, G. 2011. 'Aiani – Historical and Geographical Context.' In R. Lane Fox ed., *Brill's Companion to Ancient Macedon: Studies in the Archaeology and History of Macedon, 650 BC–300 AD* (Leiden: Brill), 93–112.

Karantzali, E. 2013. 'Mycenaeans within the Spercheios Valley: The Inhabitations at Frantzis and Lygaria.' In G. Graziado, R. Guglielmino, V. Lenuzza and S. Vitale eds, *Φιλική Συναυλία. Studies in Mediterranean Archaeology for Mario Benzi* (Oxford: Archaeopress), 139–53.

Karouzou, E. 2017. 'Thessaly from the Protogeometric to the Early Archaic Period.' In A. Mazarakis Ainian, A. Alexandridou and X. Charalambidou eds, *Regional Stories: Towards a New Perception of the Early Greek World. Acts of an International Symposium in Honour of Professor Jan Bouzek, Volos 18–21 June 2015* (Volos: University of Thessaly Press), 343–80.

—. 2018. *Thessaly, from the Late Bronze Age to the Early Iron Age (c. 1600–700 BC).* DPhil thesis, Oxford University.

—. 2020. 'Thessaly.' In I.S. Lemos and A. Kotsonas eds, *A Companion to the Archaeology of Early Greece and the Mediterranean*, vol. 2 (Hoboken, NJ: Wiley Blackwell), 883–912.

Kase, E.W., G.J. Szemler, N.C Wilkie and P.W. Wallace eds. 1991. *The Great Isthmus Corridor Route: Explorations of the Phokis-Doris Expedition*, vol. 1. Dubuque IA: Kendall Hunt.

Katakouta, S. 2012. 'Τα Φάρσαλα στην Πρώιμη Εποχή του Σιδήρου.' In A. Mazarakis Ainian ed., *Αρχαιολογικό Έργο Θεσσαλίας και Στερεάς Ελλάδας* 3, vol. 1 (Volos: Εργαστήριο Αρχαιολογίας Πανεπιστημίου Θεσσαλίας & Υπουργείο Πολιτισμού, Παιδείας και Θρησκευμάτων), 241–50.

Keaveney, A. 1995. 'The Medisers of Thessaly.' *Eranos* 93, 30–38.

Keesling, C.M. 2017. *Early Greek Portraiture*. Cambridge: Cambridge University Press.

Kennell, N.M. 2017. 'Spartan Cultural Memory in the Roman Period.' In A. Powell ed., *A Companion to Sparta* (Oxford and Malden, MA: Blackwell), 643–62.

Kern, O. 1900. *Die Inschriften von Magnesia am Maeander*. Berlin: W. Spemann.

Kilian, K. 1975. *Fibeln in Thessalien von der Mykenischen bis zur Archaischen Zeit*. Munich: Beck.

Kilian-Dirlmeier, I. 2002. *Kleinfunde aus dem Athena Itonia-Heiligtum bei Philia (Thessalien)*. Mainz: Verlag des Römisch-Germanischen Zentralmuseums.

Kirk, G.S. 1985. *The* Iliad*: A Commentary*, vol. 1. Cambridge: Cambridge University Press.

Kittelä, S.-I. 2013. 'Dodona and Neoptolemos: Heroic Genealogies and Chains of Ethnicity.' In M. Kajava ed., *Studies in Ancient Oracles and Divination* (Rome: Institutum Romandum Finlandiae), 29–47.

Klein, J. 1965. *A Commentary on Plato's* Meno. Chapel Hill: University of North Carolina Press.

Knauss, J. 1987. 'Deukalion, Lykoreia, die große Flut am Parnaß und der Vulkanausbruch von Thera (im Jahr 1529 v. Chr.?).' *Antike Welt* 18.3, 23–40.

—. 1990. 'Der Graben des Herakles im Becken von Pheneos und die Vertreibung der stymphalischen Vögel.' *Athenische Mitteilungen* 105, 1–52.

—. 1991. 'Arkadian and Boiotian Orchomenos, Centres of Mycenaean Hydraulic Engineering.' *Irrigation and Drainage Systems* 5, 363–81.

Knodell, A.R. 2013. *Small-World Networks and Mediterranean Dynamics in the Euboean Gulf: An Archaeology of Complexity in Late Bronze Age and Early Iron Age Greece*. PhD thesis, Brown University.

—. 2017. 'A Conduit Between Two Worlds. Geography and Connectivity in the Euboean Gulf.' In Z. Tankosić, F. Mavridis and M. Kosma eds, *An Island Between Two Worlds: The Archaeology of Euboea from Prehistoric to Byzantine Times. Proceedings of an International Conference, Eretria, 12–14 July 2013* (Athens: Norwegian Institute at Athens), 195–208.

—. 2021. *Societies in Transition in Early Greece: An Archaeological History.* Oakland: University of California Press.

Koenen, L. 1977. *Eine agonistische Inschrift aus Ägypten und frühptolemäische Königsfeste.* Meisenheim am Glan: Hain.

Kôiv, M. 2011. 'A Note on the Dating of Hesiod.' *Classical Quarterly* 61.2, 355–77.

—. 2016. 'Communities and Rulers in Early Greece: Development of Leadership Patterns in Euboia and Argolis (12th–6th Centuries BC).' In T.R. Kämmerer, M. Kôiv and V. Sazonov eds, *Kings, Gods and People: Establishing Monarchies in the Ancient World* (Münster: Ugarit-Verlag), 293–354.

Kolk, D. 1963. *Das pythisches Apollonhymnus als aitiologische Dichtung.* Meisenheim am Glan: Anton Hain.

Kontogiannis, A. 1985. 'Παρατηρήσεις στην *IG*, IX 2 580 (και σε άλλες στοιχηδόν επιγραφές της Λάρισας).' In K. Gallis, I. Sakellion and K. Spanos eds, *Πρακτικά του Α' Ιστορικού–Αρχαιολογικού Συμποσίου Λάρισα – Παρελθόν και Μέλλον: 26–28/4/1985* (Larisa: Δήμος Λαρίσας), 111–32.

—. 1992. ''Ίμψιος: Ποσειδών ο Ζύγιος.' In *Διεθνές Συνέδριο για την Αρχαία Θεσσαλία: στη Μνήμη του Δημήτρη Ρ. Θεοχάρη. Πρακτικά* (Athens: Ταμείο Αρχαιολογικών Πόρων και Απαλλοτριώσεων), 381–91.

Kosmetatou, E. 2004. 'Constructing Legitimacy: The Ptolemaic *Familiengruppe* as a Means of Self-Definition in Posidippus' *Hippika*.' In B. Acosta-Hughes, E. Kosmetatou and M. Baumbach eds, *Labored in Papyrus Leaves: Perspectives on an Epigram Collection Attributed to Posidippus (P.Mil.Vogl. VIII 309)*, Hellenic Studies Series 2 (Washington DC: Center for Hellenic Studies), 225–46.

Kottaridi, A. 2011. 'The Palace of Aegae.' In R. Lane Fox ed., *Brill's Companion to Ancient Macedon* (Leiden: Brill), 297–333.

Kounouklas, P. 2018. 'Marine Installations at the Site of Kynos.' In M.P. Papakonstantinou, Ch. Kritzas and I.P. Touratsoglou eds, *Πύρρα: Μελέτες για την Αρχαιολογία στην Κεντρική Ελλάδα προς Τιμήν της Φανουρίας* Δακορώνια (Athens: ΣΗΜΑ), 233–47.

Kovacs, D. 1994. *Euripidea.* Leiden: Brill.

—. 1995. *Euripides: Children of Heracles, Hippolytus, Andromache, Hecuba.* Cambridge, MA: Harvard University Press.

Kowalzig, B. 2007. *Singing for the Gods: Performances of Myth and Ritual in Archaic and Classical Greece.* Oxford: Oxford University Press.

Kowerski, L.M. 2005. *Simonides on the Persian Wars: a Study of the Elegiac Verses of the 'New Simonides'.* London and New York: Routledge.

Kraay, C.M. 1976. *Archaic and Classical Greek Coins.* London: Methuen.

Krahtopoulou, A., A. Dimoula, A. Livarda and N. Saridaki. 2018. 'The Discovery of the Earliest Specialised Middle Neolithic Pottery Workshop in Western Thessaly, Central Greece.' *Antiquity* 92.362 e5, 1–7.

Kramer-Hajos, M. 2012. 'The Land and the Heroes of Lokris in the "Iliad".' *Journal of Hellenic Studies* 132, 87–105.

—. 2016. *Mycenaean Greece and the Aegean World: Palace and Province in the Late Bronze Age*. Cambridge: Cambridge University Press.
—. 2020. 'The Euboean Gulf.' In G.D. Middleton ed., *Collapse and Transformation: The Late Bronze Age to Early Iron Age in the Aegean* (Oxford: Oxbow Books), 77–85.
Krapf, T. 2018. 'Sovjan (Korçë): First Remarks about the Late Bronze Age Pottery.' In G. Karamitrou-Mentessidi ed., *Το Αρχαιολογικό Έργο στην Άνω Μακεδονία*, 3, vol. A (Aiani: Αρχαιολογικό Μουσείο Αιανής), 115–30.
Kravaritou, S. 2010. 'Αρχαίες λατρείες και μύθοι της περιοχής των εκβολών του Πενειού.' In S.G. Gouloulis and S. Sdrolia eds, *Άγιος Δημήτριος Στομίου* (Larisa: Νομαρχιακή Αυτοδιοίκηση Λάρισας), 419–32.
—. 2011. 'Synoecism and Religious Interface in Demetrias (Thessaly).' *Kernos* 24, 111–35.
—. 2012. 'Μηχανισμοί διαμόρφωσης εθνικής ταυτότητας στη Θεσσαλία και Βοιωτία των κλασικών και Ελληνιστικών χρόνων.' In A. Mazarakis Ainian ed., *Αρχαιολογικό Έργο Θεσσαλίας και Στερεάς Ελλάδας* 3 (Volos: Εργαστήριο Αρχαιολογίας Πανεπιστημίου Θεσσαλίας & Υπουργείο Πολιτισμού, Παιδείας και Θρησκευμάτων), 505–14.
—. 2016. 'Sacred Space and the Politics of Multiculturalism in Demetrias (Thessaly).' In M. Melfi and O. Bobou eds, *Hellenistic Sanctuaries: Between Greece and Rome* (Oxford: Oxford University Press), 128–51.
—. 2018. 'Cults and Rites of Passage in Ancient Thessaly.' In M. Kalaitzi, P. Paschidis, C. Antonetti and A.-M. Guimier-Sorbets eds, *Βορειοελλαδικά: Tales from the Lands of the Ethne. Essays in Honour of Miltiades B. Hatzopoulos* (Athens: National Hellenic Research Foundation and the Institute of Historical Research), 377–96.
Kravaritou, S. and M. Stamatopoulou. 2018. 'From Alkestis to Archidike: Thessalian Attitudes to Death and the Afterlife.' In G. Ekroth and I. Nilsson eds, *Round Trip to Hades in the Eastern Mediterranean Tradition: Visits to the Underworld from Antiquity to Byzantium* (Leiden: Brill), 124–62.
Kremmydas, C. 2013. 'Alexander the Great, Athens, and the Rhetoric of the Persian Wars.' *Bulletin of the Institute of Classical Studies Supplement* 124, 199–211.
Kroll, J.H. 1981. 'From *Wappenmünzen* to Gorgoneia to Owls.' *American Numismatic Society Museum Notes* 26, 1–32, pls 1–2.
Kroll, J.H. and N.M. Waggoner. 1984. 'Dating the Earliest Coins of Athens, Corinth and Aegina.' *American Journal of Archaeology* 88.3, 325–40.
Kron, U. and A. Furtwängler. 1983. 'Demetrios Poliorketes, Demetrias und die Magneten: zum Bedeutungswandel von Siegel- und Münzbild einer Stadt.' *Αρχαία Μακεδονία* 3, 147–68.
Kühr, A. 2006. *Als Kadmos nach Boiotien kam: Polis und Ethnos im Spiegel thebanischer Gründungsmythen*. Hermes Einzelschriften 98. Stuttgart: Franz Steiner.

Kullmann, W. 2012. 'The Relative Chronology of the Homeric Catalogue of Ships and of the Lists of Heroes and Cities within the Catalogue.' In Ø. Andersen and D.T.T. Haug eds, *Relative Chronology in Early Greek Epic Poetry* (Cambridge: Cambridge University Press), 210–23.

Kurke, L. 1991. *The Traffic in Praise: Pindar and the Poetics of Social Economy.* Ithaca, NY: Cornell University Press.

—. 2012. *Aesopic Conversations: Popular Tradition, Cultural Dialogue, and the Invention of Greek Prose.* Princeton, NJ: Princeton University Press.

Kurke, L. and R. Neer. 2019. *Pindar, Song, and Space: Towards a Lyric Archaeology.* Baltimore, MD: Johns Hopkins University Press.

Lalonde, G.V. 2020. *Athena Itonia: Geography and Meaning of an Ancient Greek War Goddess.* Leiden: Brill.

Lamb, W.R.M. 1925. *Plato, in Twelve Volumes,* Vol. 2: *Laches, Protagoras, Meno, Euthydemus.* Cambridge, MA: Harvard University Press.

Lane Fox, R. 2004. 'Sex, Gender and the Other in Xenophon's *Anabasis*.' In R. Lane Fox ed., *The Long March: Xenophon and the Ten Thousand* (New Haven: Yale University Press), 184–214.

—. 2018. 'Macedonians and *Nostoi*.' In S. Hornblower and G. Biffis eds, *The Returning Hero:* Nostoi *and Traditions of Mediterranean Settlement* (Oxford: Oxford University Press), 198–203.

Langlotz, E. 1951. 'Die Larisa des Telephanes.' *Museum Helveticum* 8, 157–70.

Larsen, J.A.O. 1960. 'A New Interpretation of the Thessalian Confederacy.' *Classical Philology* 55.4, 229–48.

—. 1963. 'The Thessalian Tetrades in Plutarch's *Moralia* 822E.' *Classical Philology* 58.4, 240.

—. 1968. *Greek Federal States: Their Institutions and History.* Oxford: Clarendon.

Larson, J. 2000. 'Boiotia, Athens, the Peisistratids, and the *Odyssey*'s Catalogue of Heroines.' *Greek, Roman and Byzantine Studies* 41, 193–222.

—. 2001. *Greek Nymphs: Myth, Cult, Lore.* Oxford: Oxford University Press.

—. 2007. *Tales of Epic Ancestry: Boiotian Collective Identity in the Late Archaic and Early Classical Periods.* Stuttgart: Franz Steiner.

—. 2019. 'Hermes and Heracles.' In J.F. Miller and J.S. Clay eds, *Tracking Hermes, Pursuing Mercury* (Oxford: Oxford University Press), 49–64.

Lasagni, C. 2008. 'Raggruppamenti locali e organizzazione territoriale in Tessaglia.' In M. Lombardo and F. Frisone eds, *Forme sovrapoleiche e interpoleiche di organizzazione nel mondo greco antico: Atti del convegno internazionale, Lecce, 17–20 Settembre 2008* (Lecce: Congedo Editore), 377–87.

Latacz, J. 2004. *Troy and Homer: Towards a Solution of an Old Mystery.* Oxford: Oxford University Press.

—. 2006. 'Rhianus.' In H. Cancik, H. Schneider and C.F. Salazar eds, *Brill's New Pauly.* http://dx.doi.org/10.1163/1574-9347_bnp_e1022460.

Lattimore, S. 1975. 'The Chlamys of Daochos I.' *American Journal of Archaeology* 79.1, 87–88.

Lavelle, B.M. 2005. *Fame, Money, and Power: The Rise of Peisistratos and 'Democratic' Tyranny at Athens.* Ann Arbor: University of Michigan Press.

Lazenby, J.F. 1993. *The Defence of Greece, 490–479 B.C.* Warminster: Aris & Phillips.

Lefèvre, F. 1998. *L'Amphictionie pyléo-delphique: histoire et institutions.* Paris: de Boccard.

Lefkowitz, M.R. 1979. 'The Euripides *Vita*.' *Greek, Roman, and Byzantine Studies* 20.2, 187–210.

Lehmann, G.A. 1980. 'Der "Erste Heilige Krieg": Eine Fiktion?' *Historia* 29.2, 242–46.

—. 1983. 'Thessaliens Hegemonie über Mittelgriechenland im 6. Jh. v. Chr.' *Boreas* 6, 35–43.

Lemos, I. 1998. 'Euboea and Its Aegean Koine.' In B. D'Agostino and M. Bats eds, *Euboica: L'Eubea e la presenza euboica in Calcidica e in Occidente* (Napoli: Centre Jean Bérard), 45–58.

—. 2002. *The Protogeometric Aegean.* Oxford: Oxford University Press.

—. 2011–2012. 'Euboea and Central Greece in the Postpalatial and Early Greek Periods.' *Archaeological Reports* 58, 19–27.

Leone, B. 2012. 'A Trade Route Between Euboea and the Northern Aegean.' *Mediterranean Archaeology* 25, 229–42.

LeVen, P.A. 2014. *The Many-Headed Muse: Tradition and Innovation in Late Classical Greek Lyric Poetry.* Cambridge: Cambridge University Press.

Lévêque, P. 1957. *Pyrrhos.* Paris: de Boccard.

Lévy, E. 1991. 'Apparition des notions de Grèce et de Grecs.' In S. Said ed., *ἙΛΛΗΝΙΣΜΟΣ: Quelques jalons pour une histoire de l'identité grecque. Actes du colloque de Strasbourg 25–27 octobre 1989* (Leiden: Brill), 49–69.

Lhôte, É. 2006. *Les lamelles oraculaires de Dodone.* Genève: Librairie Droz.

Liampi, K. 1996. 'Das Corpus der Obolen und Hemiobolen des Thessalischen Bundes und die politische Geschichte Thessaliens im 2. Viertel des 5. Jahrhunderts v. Chr.' In W. Leschhorn, A.V.B. Miron and A. Miron eds, *Hellas und der griechische Osten: Studien zur Geschichte und Numismatik der griechischen Welt. Festschrift für Peter Robert Franke zum 70. Geburtstag* (Saarbrücken: SDV Saarbrücker Druckerei und Verlag), 99–126.

—. 2005. 'Iolkos and Pagasai: Two New Thessalian Mints.' *Numismatic Chronicle* 165, 23–40.

—. 2015. 'A Hoard from Thessaly Containing Aeginetan Staters and Thessalian Issues of the 'Taurokathapsia' Type.' In P.G. Van Alfen, G. Bransbourg and M. Amandry eds, *Fides: Contributions to Numismatics in Honor of Richard B. Witshonke* (New York: American Numismatic Society), 1–19.

Lightfoot, J. 2017. 'Man of Many Voices and of Much Knowledge; or, In Search of Strabo's Homer.' In D. Dueck ed., *The Routledge Companion to Strabo* (London and New York: Routledge), 251–62.

Lis, B. and Š. Ruckl. 2011. 'Our Storerooms Are Full: Impressed Pithoi from Late Bronze/Early Iron Age East Lokris and Phokis and Their Socio-Economic Significance.' In W. Gauß, M. Lindblom, R. Angus,

K. Smith and J.C. Wright eds, *Our Cups Are Full: Pottery and Society in the Aegean Bronze Age. Papers Presented to Jeremy B. Rutter on the Occasion of His 65th Birthday* (Oxford: Archaeopress), 154–68.

Livieratou, A. 2009. 'The Transition from the Late Bronze to the Early Iron Age in East Phokis and Lokris.' In A. Mazarakis Ainian ed., *Αρχαιολογικό Έργο Θεσσαλίας και Στερεάς Ελλάδας* 2, vol. 2 (Volos: Εργαστήριο Αρχαιολογίας Πανεπιστημίου Θεσσαλίας & Υπουργείο Πολιτισμού, Παιδείας και Θρησκευμάτων), 951–73.

—. 2012. 'Phokis and East Lokris in the Light of Interregional Contacts at the Transition from the Late Bronze Age to the Early Iron Age.' In M. Iacovou ed., *Cyprus and the Aegean in the Early Iron Age: The Legacy of Nicholas Coldstream* (Nicosia: Bank of Cyprus Cultural Foundation), 77–128.

—. 2020. 'East Lokris-Phokis.' In G.D. Middleton ed., *Collapse and Transformation: The Late Bronze Age to Early Iron Age in the Aegean* (Oxford: Oxbow Books), 97–105.

Londey, P. 1990. 'The Outbreak of the 4th Sacred War.' *Chiron* 20, 239–60.

—. 2010. 'Phokian Desperation: Private and Public in the Outbreak of the 3rd Sacred War.' In A.J. Turner, J.H.K.O. Chong-Gossard and F.J. Vervaet eds, *Private and Public Lies: The Discourse of Despotism and Deceit in the Graeco-Roman World* (Leiden: Brill), 29–38.

—. 2015. 'Making Up Delphic History: The 1st Sacred War Revisited.' *Chiron* 45, 221–38.

—. 2020. 'War and Memory in Central Greece: Phokis, Thessaly and Persia.' *Όρμος – Ricerche di Storia Antica* 12, 87–108.

Loptson, P. 1981. 'Pelasgikon Argos in the Catalogue of Ships (681).' *Mnemosyne* 34, 136–38.

Loraux, N. 1993. *The Children of Athena: Athenian Ideas about Citizenship and the Division between the Sexes.* Translated by C. Levine. Princeton, NJ: Princeton University Press.

Lorber, C.C. 2008. 'Thessalian Hoards and the Coinage of Larissa.' *American Journal of Numismatics* 20, 119–42.

Lordkiparidze, O. 1996. 'La geste des Argonautes dans les premières epopées grecques sous l'angle des premiers contacts du monde grec avec le littoral pontique.' In O. Lordkiparidze and P. Lévêque dirs., *Sur les traces des Argonautes: actes du 6e symposium de Vani (Colchide) 22–29 septembre 1990* (Paris: Les Belles Lettres), 21–49.

—. 2001. 'The Golden Fleece: Myth, Euhemeristic Explanation and Archaeology.' *Oxford Journal of Archaeology* 20, 1–38.

Lorenz, B. 2019. *Griechische Grabgedichte Thessaliens.* Heidelberg: Winter.

Low, P. 2018. 'Panhellenism without Imperialism? Athens and the Greeks before and after Chaeronea.' *Historia* 67.4, 454–71.

Luce, J.-M. 1999. 'Le paysage delphique du XIIe à la fin du Ve siècle av. J.-C.' *Comptes-rendus des séances de l'année. Académie des inscriptions et belles-lettres* 3, 975–95.

—. 2007. 'Géographie funéraire et identités ethniques a l'âge du fer en Grèce.' In J.-M. Luce ed., *Les identités ethniques dans le monde grec*, *Pallas* 73 (Toulouse: Presses Universitaires du Mirail), 39–51.

—. 2014. 'Les modes funéraires et la parole dans la Grèce de l'âge du fer ancien.' In C. Müller and A.-E. Veïsse eds, *Identité ethnique et culture matérielle dans le monde grec: actes de la table ronde organisée à Paris (INHA) les 10 et 11 décembre 2010* (Besançon: Presses universitaires de Franche-Comté), 37–51.

Lücke, S. 2000. *Syngeneia: Epigraphisch-historische Studien zu einem Phänomen der antiken griechischen Diplomatie*. Frankfurt am Main: Marthe Clauss.

Lund, A.A. 2005. 'Hellenentum und Hellenizität: Zur Ethnogenese und zur Ethnizität der antiken Hellenen.' *Historia* 54.1, 1–17.

Luraghi, N. 2002. 'Becoming Messenian.' *Journal of Hellenic Studies* 122, 45–69.

—. 2009. *The Ancient Messenians: Constructions of Ethnicity and Memory*. Cambridge: Cambridge University Press.

—. 2014. 'The Study of Greek Ethnic Identities.' In J. McInerney ed., *A Companion to Ethnicity in the Ancient Mediterranean* (Chichester: Wiley Blackwell), 213–27.

Ma, J. 2003. 'Peer Polity in the Hellenistic Age.' *Past & Present* 180, 9–39.

McDevitt, A. 1970. *Inscriptions from Thessaly: An Analytical Handlist and Bibliography*. Hildesheim and New York: Georg Olms.

—. 2009. *Bacchylides: The Victory Poems. Translation with Introduction and Commentary*. Bristol: Bristol Classical Press.

MacDowell, D.M. 2009. *Demosthenes the Orator*. Oxford: Oxford University Press.

McInerney, J. 1997. 'The Phokikon and the Hero Archegetes.' *Hesperia* 66.2, 193–207.

—. 1999. *The Folds of Parnassos: Land and Ethnicity in Ancient Phokis*. Austin: University of Texas Press.

—. 2001. 'Ethnos and Ethnicity in Early Greece.' In I. Malkin ed., *Ancient Perceptions of Greek Ethnicity* (Washington DC: Center for Hellenic Studies), 51–74.

—. 2006. 'On the Border: Sacred Land and the Margins of the Community.' In I. Sluiter and R. Rosen eds, *City, Countryside, and the Spatial Organization of Value in Classical Antiquity* (Leiden: Brill), 33–59.

—. 2010. *The Cattle of the Sun: Cows and Culture in the World of the Ancient Greeks*. Princeton, NJ: Princeton University Press.

—. 2011. 'Delphi and Phokis: A Network Theory Approach.' *Pallas* 87, 95–106.

—. 2013. '*Polis* and *koinon*: Federal Government in Greece.' In H. Beck ed., *A Companion to Ancient Greek Government* (Malden, MA: Wiley-Blackwell), 466–79.

—. 2014. 'Pelasgians and Leleges: Using the Past to Understand the Present.' In J. Ker and C. Pieper eds, *Valuing the Past in the Greco-Roman World* (Leiden: Brill), 25–55.

—. 2015a. 'From Delos to Delphi: How Apollo Comes Home.' In L. Käppel and V. Pothou eds, *Human Development in Sacred Landscapes* (Göttingen: V & R Press), 103–20.

—. 2015b. 'Phokis.' In H. Beck and P. Funke eds, *Federalism in Greek Antiquity* (Cambridge: Cambridge University Press), 199–221.

Mack, R. 2021. *The Role of the Horse on Thessalian Coinage, ca. 479–320 BC*. PhD thesis, University of Reading.

Mack, W. 2015. *Proxeny and Polis: Institutional Networks in the Ancient Greek World*. Oxford: Oxford University Press.

MacKay, P.A. 2002. '"The Great Isthmus Corridor Route": Evidence from Ottoman and Early Modern Itineraries.' In H.R. Goette ed., *Ancient Roads in Greece: Proceedings of a Symposium Organized by the Cultural Association Aigeas (Athens) and the German Archaeological Institute (Athens) with the Support of the German School at Athens, November 23, 1998* (Hamburg: Dr. Kovač), 103–44.

Mackie, C.J. 2002. 'Homeric Phthia.' *Colby Quarterly* 38.2, 163–73.

Mackil, E. 2013. *Creating a Common Polity: Religion, Economy, and Politics in the Making of the Greek Koinon*. Berkeley: University of California Press.

—. 2015. 'The Economics of Federalism in the Ancient Greek World.' In H. Beck and P. Funke eds, *Federalism in Greek Antiquity* (Cambridge: Cambridge University Press), 487–502.

Mackil, E. and P. van Alfen. 2006. 'Cooperative Coinage.' In P. Van Alfen ed., *Agoranomia: Studies in Money and Exchange Presented to John H. Kroll* (New York: American Numismatic Society), 201–46.

MacLachlan, B. 1992. 'Feasting with Ethiopians: Life on the Fringe.' *Quaderni Urbinati di Cultura Classica* 40.1, 15–33.

Maclean, J.K.B. and E.B. Aitken. 2002. *Flavius Philostratus:* On Heroes. *Translated with an Introduction and Notes*. Atlanta, GA: Society of Biblical Literature.

Mac Sweeney, N. 2013. *Foundation Myths and Politics in Ancient Ionia*. Cambridge: Cambridge University Press.

Maehler, H. 1968. *Bacchylides: Lieder und Fragmente*. Berlin: Akademie-Verlag.

Mairs, R. 2015. 'Heroes and Philosophers? Greek Personal Names and Their Bearers in Hellenistic Bactria.' In N.W. Mariko and J.P. Ito-Adler eds, *The Silk Road: Interwoven History 1. Long-Distance, Trade, Culture, and Society* (Cambridge: Cambridge Institutes Press), 71–100.

Malay, H. and M. Ricl. 2009. 'Two New Hellenistic Decrees from Aigai in Aiolis.' *Epigraphica Anatolica* 42, 39–47.

Malkin, I. 1998. *The Returns of Odysseus: Colonization and Ethnicity*. Berkeley: University of California Press.

—. 2018. 'Returning Heroes and Greek Colonists.' In S. Hornblower and G. Biffis eds, *The Returning Hero:* Nostoi *and Traditions of Mediterranean Settlement* (Oxford: Oxford University Press), 83–104.

Mann, C. and S. Scharff. 2022. 'Horse Races and Chariot Races in Ancient Greece: Struggling for Eternal Glory.' In S.W. Bell, C. Jaser and C. Mann eds, *The Running Centaur: Horse-Racing in Global-Historical Perspective* (Oxford and New York: Routledge).

Marinatos, S. 1940. *Bericht über den VI. Internationalen Kongress für Archäologie, Berlin 21–26 August*. Berlin: de Gruyter.

Marincola, J. 2007. 'The Persian Wars in Fourth-Century Oratory and Historiography.' In E. Bridges, E. Hall and P.J. Rhodes eds, *Cultural Responses to the Persian Wars: Antiquity to the Third Millennium* (Oxford: Oxford University Press), 105–26.

Marks, J. 2012. 'Ἀρχοὺς αὖ νεῶν ἐρέω: A Programmatic Function of the Iliadic Catalogue of Ships.' In F. Montanari, A. Rengakos and C.C. Tsagalis eds, *Homeric Contexts: Neoanalysis and the Interpretation of Oral Poetry* (Berlin: de Gruyter), 101–12.

Martin, R.P. 2005. 'Pulp Epic: the *Catalogue* and the *Shield*.' In R. Hunter ed., *The Hesiodic Catalogue of Women: Constructions and Reconstructions* (Cambridge: Cambridge University Press), 153–75.

Martin, T.R. 1981. 'Diodorus on Philip II and Thessaly in the 350s B.C.' *Classical Philology* 76.3, 188–201.

—. 1985. *Sovereignty and Coinage in Classical Greece*. Princeton, NJ: Princeton University Press.

Marzolff, P. 1980. *Demetrias III: Demetrias und seine Halbinsel*. Bonn: Habelt.

—. 1996. 'Η πολεοδομική εξέλιξη και τα κυριότερα έργα της περιοχής.' In E.I. Kontaxi ed., *Αρχαία Δημητριάδα. Η Διαδρομή της στον Χρόνο* (Volos: Δ.Η.Κ.Ι.), 47–73.

Mazarakis Ainian, A. 1997. *From Rulers' Dwellings to Temples: Architecture, Religion and Society in Early Iron Age Greece*. Jonsered: Paul Åströms.

—. 2009. Ανασκαφή Ιερού των αρχαϊκών-κλασσικών χρόνων στη θέση «Σωρός» (2004–2005) [Παράρτημα: Ψωμά, Σελήνη, Ο μικρός «θησαυρός»].' In A. Mazarakis Ainian ed., *Αρχαιολογικό Έργο Θεσσαλίας και Στερεάς Ελλάδας* 2, vol. 1 (Volos: Εργαστήριο Αρχαιολογίας Πανεπιστημίου Θεσσαλίας & Υπουργείο Πολιτισμού, Παιδείας και Θρησκευμάτων), 269–94.

—. 2012. 'Ανασκαφικές έρευνες στο ιερό του Απόλλωνος στο Σωρό (2006–2008).' In A. Mazarakis Ainian ed., *Αρχαιολογικό Έργο Θεσσαλίας και Στερεάς Ελλάδας* 3, vol. 1 (Volos: Εργαστήριο Αρχαιολογίας Πανεπιστημίου Θεσσαλίας & Υπουργείο Πολιτισμού, Παιδείας και Θρησκευμάτων), 287–98.

Mendels, D. 1982. 'Polybius and the Socio-Economic Revolution in Greece (227–146 B.C.).' *L'Antiquité Classique* 51, 86–110.

Merkelbach, R. 1988. *Platons* Menon*: Herausgegeben, übersetzt und nach dem Inhalt erklärt*. Frankfurt: Athenäum.

Meyer, E. 1909. *Theopomps Hellenika: mit einer Beilage über die Rede an die Larisaeer und die Verfassung Thessaliens.* Halle: M. Niemeyer.

Meyer, E.A. 2013. *The Inscriptions of Dodona and a New History of Molossia.* Stuttgart: Franz Steiner.

Middleton, G. 2010. *The Collapse of Palatial Society in LBA Greece and the Postpalatial Period.* Oxford: Archaeopress.

Mikalson, J.D. 2003. *Herodotus and Religion in the Persian Wars.* Chapel Hill: University of North Carolina Press.

Mili, M. 2011. 'The Thessalian Ainians or the Ainians of Thessaly? Dedications and Games of Identity in Roman Thessaly.' *Zeitschrift für Papyrologie und Epigraphik* 176, 169–76.

—. 2015. *Religion and Society in Ancient Thessaly.* Oxford: Oxford University Press.

—. 2019. 'Ἄπιστα τὰ τῶν Θετταλῶν: The Dubious Thessalian State.' In H. Beck, K. Buraselis and A. McAuley eds, *Ethnos and Koinon* (Stuttgart: Franz Steiner), 271–84.

Miller, M.C. 2017. 'Quoting "Persia" in Athens.' In R. Strootman and M.J. Versluys eds, *Persianism in Antiquity* (Stuttgart: Franz Steiner), 49–68.

Miller, S.G. 1974. 'The Altar of the Six Goddesses in Thessalian Pherai.' *California Studies in Classical Antiquity* 7, 231–56.

—. 1979. *Two Groups of Thessalian Gold.* Berkeley: University of California Press.

Minchin, E. 2001. *Homer and the Resources of Memory.* Oxford: Oxford University Press.

Minon, S. 2009. 'La stèle diglosse de Sigée en Troade (IG I 3 1508, ca 550 a. C.).' In B. Bortolussi, M. Keller, S. Minon and L. Sznajder eds, *Traduire, transposer, transmettre dans l'Antiquité gréco-romaine* (Paris: Picard), 1–14.

Missailidou-Despotidou, V. 1993. 'A Hellenistic Inscription from Skotoussa (Thessaly) and the Fortifications of the City.' *Annual of the British School at Athens* 88, 187–217.

Mitchel, F. 1984. 'The Rasura of *IG* 11^2 43: Jason, the Pheraian Demos, and the Athenian League.' *Ancient World* 9, 39–58.

Mitchell, L.G. 2006. 'Greeks, Barbarians and Aeschylus' *Suppliants.*' *Greece & Rome* 53.2, 205–23.

—. 2007. *Panhellenism and the Barbarian in Archaic and Classical Greece.* London: Bloomsbury.

—. 2013. *The Heroic Rulers of Archaic and Classical Greece.* London: Bloomsbury.

Moloney, E. 2015. 'Neither Agamemnon nor Thersites, Achilles nor Margites: The Heraclid Kings of Ancient Macedon.' *Antichthon* 49, 50–72.

Molyneux, J.H. 1992. *Simonides: A Historical Study.* Wauconda, IL: Bolchazy-Carducci.

Mooren, L. 1983. 'The Nature of the Hellenistic Monarchy.' In E. Van 't Dack, P. Van Dessel and W. Van Gucht eds, *Egypt and the Hellenistic World* (Leuven: Studia Hellenistica), 206–40.

Moreau, A. 1994. *Le mythe de Jason et Médée: Le va-nu-pied et la sorcière*. Paris: Les Belles Lettres.

Morgan, C. 1990. *Athletes and Oracles: The Transformation of Olympia and Delphi in the 8th century BC*. Cambridge: Cambridge University Press.

—. 2001. 'Ethne, Ethnicity, and Early Greek States, ca. 1200–480 B.C.: An Archaeological Perspective.' In I. Malkin ed., *Ancient Perceptions of Greek Ethnicity* (Washington DC: Center for Hellenic Studies), 75–112.

—. 2003. *Early Greek States Beyond the Polis*. London and New York: Routledge.

—. 2006. '*Ethne* in the Peloponnese and Central Greece.' In S. Deger-Jalkotzy and I. Lemos eds, *Ancient Greece: From the Mycenaean Palaces to the Age of Homer* (Edinburgh: Edinburgh University Press), 233–54.

—. 2009a. 'Ethnic Expression on the Early Iron Age and Early Archaic Greek Mainland: Where Should We Be Looking?' In T. Derks and N. Roymans eds, *Ethnic Constructs in Antiquity: The Rise of Power and Tradition* (Amsterdam: Amsterdam University Press), 11–36.

—. 2009b. 'The Early Iron Age.' In K.A. Raaflaub and H. van Wees eds, *Companion to Archaic Greece* (Chichester: Blackwell), 43–63.

Mori, A. 2008. *The Politics of Apollonius Rhodius'* Argonautica. Cambridge: Cambridge University Press.

Morin, B. 2015. 'Σκύφος ετ Σκάφος: La «vaisselle» de l'ivresse d'Hérakles a-t-elle à voir avec le «vaisseau» qui transporte Alceste sur l'Achéron?' *Revue de philologie* 89.2, 33–51.

Morison, W.S. 2011. 'Pherekydes of Athens (3).' In I. Worthington ed., *Jacoby Online. Brill's New Jacoby, Part I*. Leiden: Brill. http://dx.doi.org/10.1163/1873-5363_bnj_a3.

—. 2014. 'Theopompos of Chios (115).' In I. Worthington ed., *Jacoby Online. Brill's New Jacoby, Part II*. Leiden: Brill. http://dx.doi.org/10.1163/1873-5363_bnj_a115.

Morpurgo-Davies, A. 1968. 'Thessalian Patronymic Adjectives.' *Glotta* 46, 85–106.

—. 1987. 'The Greek Notion of Dialect.' *Verbum* 10, 7–27.

Moustaka, A. 1983. *Kulte und Mythen auf thessalischen Münzen. Beiträge zur Archäologie* 15. Würzburg: Konrad Triltsch.

Müller, S. 2016. *Die Argeaden: Geschichte Makedoniens bis zum Zeitalter Alexanders des Großen*. Paderborn: Ferdinand Schöningh.

—. 2017. 'The Symbolic Capital of the Argeads.' In S. Müller, T. Howe, H. Bowden and R. Rollinger eds, *The History of the Argeads: New Perspectives* (Wiesbaden: Harrassowitz), 183–98.

Munn, M. 1997. 'Thebes and Central Greece.' In L.A. Tritle ed., *The Greek World in the Fourth Century: From the Fall of the Athenian Empire to the Successors of Alexander* (London and New York: Routledge), 66–106.

Munson, R.V. 2001. '*Ananke* in Herodotus.' *Journal of Hellenic Studies* 121, 30–50.

Mylonopoulos, I. 2003. *Heiligtümer und Kulte des Poseidon auf der Peloponnes. Kernos* Supplement 13. Liège: Centre International d'Étude de la Religion Grecque Antique.

Nafissi, M. 2017. 'Lykourgos the Spartan "Lawgiver": Ancient Beliefs and Modern Scholarship.' In A. Powell ed., *A Companion to Sparta* (Oxford and Malden, MA: Blackwell), 93–123.

Nagy, G. 1990. *Greek Mythology and Poetics*. Ithaca, NY: Cornell University Press.

—. 1999. *The Best of the Achaeans: Concepts of the Hero in Archaic Greek Poetry*. Revised 2nd ed. Baltimore, MD and London: Johns Hopkins University Press.

—. 2010. *Homer the Preclassic*. Berkeley: University of California Press.

—. 2011a. 'Asopos and His Multiple Daughters: Traces of Preclassical Epic in the Aeginetan Odes of Pindar.' In D. Fearn ed., *Aegina: Contexts for Choral Lyric Poetry: Myth, History, and Identity in the Fifth Century BC* (Oxford: Oxford University Press), 41–78.

—. 2011b. 'The Aeolic Component of Homeric Diction.' In S.W. Jamison, H.C. Melchert and B. Vine eds, *Proceedings of the 22nd Annual UCLA Indo-European Conference* (Bremen: Ute Hempen Verlag), 133–79.

Neer, R.T. 2001. 'Framing the Gift: The Politics of the Siphnian Treasury at Delphi.' *Classical Antiquity* 20.2, 273–344.

Nelson, E.D. 2005. 'Coan Promotions and the Authorship of the *Presbeutikos*.' In P.J. Van der Eijk ed., *Hippocrates in Context: Papers Read at the XIth International Hippocrates Colloquium, University of Newcastle upon Tyne, 27–31 August 2002* (Leiden: Brill), 209–36.

—. 2007. 'Hippocrates, Heraclids, and the "Kings of the Heracleidai": Adaptations of Asclepiad History by the Author of the *Presbeutikos*.' *Phoenix* 61.3/4, 234–46.

—. 2013. 'Coan *Asylia*: Small-State Diplomacy and the Hippocratic Legend.' In F. de Angelis ed., *Regionalism and Globalism in Antiquity* (Leuven: Peeters), 247–66.

Nichols, R.J. 2019. 'Corruption.' In G. Martin ed., *The Oxford Handbook of Demosthenes* (Oxford: Oxford University Press), 167–78.

Niehoff-Panagiotidis, J. 1994. *Koine und Diglossie*. Wiesbaden: Harrassowitz.

Nielsen, T.H. 1996. 'Was There an Arkadian Confederacy in the Fifth Century?' In M.H. Hansen and K. Raaflaub eds, *More Studies in the Ancient Greek Polis* (Stuttgart: Franz Steiner), 39–62.

—. 2000. 'Epiknemidian, Hypoknemidian, and Opountian Lokrians: Reflections on the Political Organisation of East Lokris in the Classical Period.' In P. Flensted-Jensen ed., *Further Studies in the Ancient Greek* Polis, *Historia* Einzelschriften 138 (Stuttgart: Franz Steiner), 91–120.

—. 2002. *Arkadia and Its Poleis in the Archaic and Classical Periods*. Göttingen: Vandenhoeck & Ruprecht.

—. 2014. 'Foreign Entrants at Minor Athletic Festivals in Late-Archaic and Classical Greece.' *Nikephoros* 27, 91–158.

Niemeier, W.-D. 2013. *Das Orakelheiligtum des Apollon von Abai/Kalapodi: Eines der bedeutendsten griechischer Heiligtümer nach den Ergebnissen der neuen Ausgrabungen*. Wiesbaden: Harrassowitz Verlag.

—. 2017. 'The Oracle Sanctuary of Abai/Kalapodi from the Bronze to the Iron Age.' In A. Mazarakis Ainian, A. Alexandridou and X. Charalambidou eds, *Regional Stories: Towards a New Perception of the Early Greek World. Acts of an International Symposium in Honour of Professor Jan Bouzek, Volos 18–21 June 2015* (Volos: University of Thessaly Press), 323–42.

Nikolaou, E. 2012. 'Εστιαιώτις (Part 2)'; 'Θεσσαλιώτις.' In E. Nikolaou and S. Kravaritou eds, *Αρχαίες Πόλεις Θεσσαλίας και Περίοικων Περιοχών* (Larisa: Π.Ε.Δ. Θεσσαλίας), 59–70; 71–98.

Nobili, C. 2020. 'The Sanctuary of Delphi in Heliodorus' *Aethiopica*: Between Material Culture and Intertextuality.' *Ancient Narrative* 16, 15–36.

Ntasios, P. 2012. 'Εστιαιώτις (Part 1).' In E. Nikolaou and S. Kravaritou eds, *Αρχαίες Πόλεις Θεσσαλίας και Περίοικων Περιοχών* (Larisa: Π.Ε.Δ. Θεσσαλίας), 47–58.

Oetjen, R. 2010. 'Antigonid Cleruchs in Thessaly and Greece: Philip V and Larisa.' In G. Reger, F.X. Ryan and T. F. Winters eds, *Studies in Greek Epigraphy in Honor of Stephen V. Tracy* (Paris: de Boccard), 237–93.

Ogden, D. 1997. *The Crooked Kings of Ancient Greece*. Bristol: Bristol Classical Press.

—. 1999. *Polygamy, Prostitutes and Death: The Hellenistic Dynasties*. London: Duckworth and the Classical Press of Wales.

—. 2008. 'Bilistiche and the Prominence of Courtesans in the Ptolemaic Tradition.' In P. McKechnie and P. Guillaume eds, *Ptolemy II Philadelphos and His World* (Leiden: Brill), 353–86.

—. 2011. *Alexander the Great: Myth, Genesis and Sexuality*. Exeter: University of Exeter Press.

Olivieri, O. 2011. *Miti e culti Tebani nella poesia di Pindaro*. Pisa and Rome: Fabrizio Serra.

O'Neil, J.L. 2008. 'A Re-Examination of the Chremonidean War.' In P. McKechnie and P. Guillaume eds, *Ptolemy II Philadelphos and His World* (Leiden: Brill), 65–90.

Orengo, H.A., A. Krahtopoulou, A. Garcia-Molosa, K. Palaiochoritis and A. Stamati. 2015. 'Photogrammetric Re-Discovery of the Hidden Long-Term Landscapes of Western Thessaly.' *Journal of Archaeological Science* 64, 100–209.

Orfanou, V. 2015. 'Early Iron Age Greece, Ancient Pherai, and the Archaeo-metallurgy of Copper.' In Z.T. Polychroniadis and D. Evely eds, *Aegis: Essays in Mediterranean Archaeology Presented to Matti Egon* (Oxford: Archaeopress), 107–16.

Ormand, K. 2014. *The Hesiodic* Catalogue of Women *and Archaic Greece*. Cambridge: Cambridge University Press.

Osborne, M.J. 1983. *Naturalization in Athens*, vol. 3. Brussels: AWLSK.
Osborne, R. and P.J. Rhodes. 2017. *Greek Historical Inscriptions, 478–404 BC*. Oxford: Oxford University Press.
Østby, E. 1994. 'A Reconsideration of the Classical Temple at Pherai.' In B. Helly ed., *La Thessalie. Quinze années de recherches archéologiques, 1975–1990. Bilans et perspectives. Actes du colloque international, Lyons, 17–22 Avril 1990* (Athens: Kapon), 139–42.
Ostroverkhov, A.S. and S. B. Okhotnikov. 1996. 'Les sources historiques et archéologiques de l'île Leuké.' In A. Fraysse, E. Geny and T. Khartchilava eds, *Sur les traces des Argonautes. Actes du 6e Symposium de Vani (Colchide)*, 22–29 septembre 1990 (Paris: Les Belles Lettres), 271–75.
Palaima, T.G. 2009. 'Continuity from the Mycenaean Period in an Historical Boeotian Cult of Poseidon (and Erinys).' In D. Danielidou ed., *Δώρον. Τιμητικός Τόμος για τον Σπύρο Ιακωβίδη* (Athens: Academy of Athens), 527–36.
Panagiotopoulou, E. 2020. 'Protogeometric Thessaly: An Integrated Study of Burial Practices and Isotope Analysis of Human Remains.' In N. Dimakis and T.M. Dijkstra eds, *Mortuary Variability and Social Diversity in Ancient Greece: Studies on Ancient Greek Death and Burial* (Oxford: Archaeopress), 7–13.
Pantou, P.A. 2010. 'Mycenaean Dimini in Context: Investigating Regional Variability and Socioeconomic Complexities in late Bronze Age Greece.' *American Journal of Archaeology* 114, 381–401.
Papachatzis, N.D. 1984. 'Μύθοι και αρχαιότερες λατρείες της Θεσσαλικής Μαγνησίας.' *Αρχαιολογική Εφημερίς* 1984, 130–50.
Papadimitriou, N. 2008. 'Both Centre and Periphery? Thessaly in the Mycenaean Period.' In A. Tziafalias ed., *First International Congress on the History and Culture of Thessaly 9–11 November 2006* (Athens: Εκδόσεις Αλεξανδρος), 99–113.
Papadopoulos, J. 1997. 'Phantom Euboians.' *Journal of Mediterranean Archaeology* 10.2, 191–219.
—. 2011. '"Phantom Euboeans" a Decade on.' In D. Rupp and J. Tomlinson eds, *Euboea and Athens: Proceedings of a Colloquium in Memory of Malcolm B. Wallace. Athens, 26–27 June 2009* (Athens: Canadian Institute in Greece), 113–33.
Papadopoulou, Z. 2017. 'The Funerary and Habitation Evidence of Central Greece: A Discussion on the Early Iron Age Social Organisation.' In A. Mazarakis Ainian, A. Alexandridou and X. Charalambidou eds, *Regional Stories: Towards a New Perception of the Early Greek World. Acts of an International Symposium in Honour of Professor Jan Bouzek, Volos 18–21 June 2015* (Volos: University of Thessaly Press), 293–322.
Papazarkadas, N. and D. Sourlas. 2012. 'The Funerary Monument for the Argives Who Fell at Tanagra (*IG* I^3 1149): A New Fragment.' *Hesperia* 81.4, 585–617.

Parke, H.W. 1967. *The Oracles of Zeus: Dodona, Olympia, Ammon*. Cambridge, MA: Harvard University Press.

Parke, H.W. and Boardman, J. 1957. 'The Struggle for the Tripod and the First Sacred War.' *Journal of Hellenic Studies* 77.2, 276–82.

Parker, H.N. 2008. 'The Linguistic Case for the Aiolian Migration.' *Hesperia* 77.3, 431–64.

Parker, R. 2010. 'The Convention of the Basaidai and the Four Families.' *Zeitschrift für Papyrologie und Epigraphik* 173, 87–88.

—. 2011. 'The Thessalian Olympia', *Zeitschrift für Papyrologie und Epigraphik* 177, 111–18.

Parker, R. and S. Scullion. 2016. 'The Mysteries of the Goddess of Marmarini.' *Kernos* 29, 1–52.

Parker, R. and M. Stamatopoulou. 2004. 'A New Funerary Gold Leaf from Pherai.' *Αρχαιολογική Εφημερίς* 143, 1–32.

Parker, V. 1997. *Untersuchungen zum Lelantischen Krieg und verwandten Problemen der frühgriechischen Geschichte*. Historia Einzelschriften 109. Stuttgart: Franz Steiner.

Partida, E.C. 2011. 'The Nexus of Inter-Regional Relations Established by Creators and Artisans in the Ancient Sanctuary and the Town of Delphi.' *Pallas* 87, 223–42.

Pascual, J. 2018. 'From the Fifth Century to 167 B.C.: Reconstructing the History of Ancient Epirus.' In A.J. Domínguez ed., *Politics, Territory and Identity in Ancient Epirus* (Pisa: Edizioni ETS), 43–100.

Patterson, L.E. 2010. *Kinship Myth in Ancient Greece*. Austin: University of Texas Press.

Paul, S. 2013. *Cultes et sanctuaires de l'île de Cos*. *Kernos* Suppl. 28. Liège: Centre d'Étude de la Religion Grecque Antique.

Pavlou, M. 2022. 'Localizing Pindar's *Pythian* 10: Some Thoughts on the Ode's Political Undertones.' *Mnemosyne* 75, 1–19.

Peek, W. 1960. *Griechische Grabgedichte*. Berlin: Akademie-Verlag.

Pelling, C.B.R. 2000. 'Fun with Fragments: Athenaeus and the Historians.' In D. Braund and J. Wilkins eds, *Athenaeus and His World: Reading Greek Culture in the Roman Empire* (Exeter: University of Exeter Press), 171–90.

Pendleton, E.J. 2004. 'Six Centuries of Thessalian Horses on Coins.' In L. Kypraiou ed., *Ὀβολός 7: Coins in the Thessalian Region: Mints, Circulation, Iconography, History Ancient, Byzantine, Modern* (Athens: Friends of the Numismatic Museum), 23–32.

Pentedeka, A. 2012. 'Δίκτυα ανταλλαγής της κεραμικής στη Νεολιθική Θεσσαλία: κόμβοι και σύνδεσμοι, οικισμοί και σχέσεις.' In A. Mazarakis Ainian ed., *Αρχαιολογικό Έργο Θεσσαλίας και Στερεάς Ελλάδας* 3, vol. 1 (Volos: Εργαστήριο Αρχαιολογίας Πανεπιστημίου Θεσσαλίας & Υπουργείο Πολιτισμού, Παιδείας και Θρησκευμάτων), 45–56.

Perlman, S. 1969. 'Isocrates' *Philippus* and Panhellenism.' *Historia* 18, 370–74.

Petrakos, B.Ch. 1997. *Οι Επιγραφές του Ωρωπού*. Athens: Η εν Αθήναις Αρχαιολογικής Εταιρεία.

Petrovic, A. 2009. 'Epigrammatic Contests, *Poeti Vaganti* and Local History.' In R. Hunter and I.C. Rutherford eds, *Wandering Poets in Ancient Greek Culture: Travel, Locality and Pan-Hellenism* (Cambridge: Cambridge University Press), 195–216.

Piccinini, J. 2016. 'Renaissance or Decline? The Shrine of Dodona in the Hellenistic Period.' In M. Melfi and O. Bobou eds, *Hellenistic Sanctuaries: Between Greece and Rome* (Oxford: Oxford University Press), 152–69.

—. 2017. *The Shrine of Dodona in the Archaic and Classical Ages: A History*. Macerata: Edizioni Università di Macerata.

—. 2018. 'The Relationships among Greek Oracular Sanctuaries: Rivalry, Cooperation or Desistance?' In A.J. Domínguez ed., *Politics, Territory and Identity in Ancient Epirus* (Pisa: Edizioni ETS), 171–92.

Pikoulas, Y.A. 2008. 'Οδικό δίκτυο και άμυνα στη δυτική ορεινή Θεσσαλία.' In L. Gklegkle ed., *1ο Διεθνές Συνέδριο Ιστορίας & Πολιτισμού της Θεσσαλίας. Πρακτικά Συνεδρίου 9–11 Νοεμβρίου 2006*, vol. 1 (Thessaloniki: Περιφέρειας Θεσσαλίας), 328–39.

—. 2009. 'Διασχίζοντας τον Όλυμπο: οδικό δίκτυο και άμυνα στην Περραιβία. Η έρευνα του 2009.' In P. Adam-Beleni and K. Tsakalou eds, *Αρχαιολογικό Έργο στη Μακεδονία και τη Θράκη* 23, vol. 1 (Thessaloniki: ΥΠΑΙΘΠΑ/ Αριστοτέλειο Πανεπιστήμιο Θεσσαλονίκης), 135–39.

—. 2012. 'Τα προγράμματα του ΠΘ/ΙΑΚΑ 1. «Διασχίζοντας την Πίνδο. Διαβάσεις και άμυνα». *Η έρευνα στη Θεσσαλία*: 2006. 2. «Διασχίζοντας τον 'Ολυμπο: Οδικό δίκτυο και άμυνα στην Περραιβία» (2008).' In A. Mazarakis Ainian ed., *Αρχαιολογικό Έργο Θεσσαλίας και Στερεάς Ελλάδας* 3, vol. 1 (Volos: Εργαστήριο Αρχαιολογίας Πανεπιστημίου Θεσσαλίας & Υπουργείο Πολιτισμού, Παιδείας και Θρησκευμάτων), 277–86.

Plant, I. 2015. 'Thucydides, Timotheus and the Epitaph for Euripides.' *Classical Journal* 110.4, 385–96.

Polinskaya, I. 2013. *A Local History of Greek Polytheism: Gods, People and the Land of Aigina, 800–400 BCE*. Leiden: Brill.

Pomtow, H. 1921. 'Pharsalica I.' *Philologus* 77, 194–99.

Pownall, F.S. 1998. 'What Makes a War a Sacred War?' *Echos du monde classique: Classical Views* 42.1, 35–55.

—. 2009. 'The Decadence of the Thessalians: A Topos in the Greek Intellectual Tradition from Critias to the Time of Alexander.' In P. Wheatley and R. Hannah eds, *Alexander and His Successors: Essays from the Antipodes* (Claremont, CA: Regina Books), 237–60.

—. 2016. 'Hellanikos of Lesbos (4).' In I. Worthington ed., *Jacoby Online. Brill's New Jacoby, Part I*. Leiden: Brill. http://dx.doi.org/10.1163/1873-5363_bnj_a4.

—. 2017. 'The Role of Greek Literature at the Argead Court.' In S. Müller, T. Howe, H. Bowden and R. Rollinger eds, *The History of the Argeads: New Perspectives* (Wiesbaden: Harrassowitz), 215–29.

Prandi, L. 1989. 'Perché «Guerra Cremonidea»? Egesandro di Delfi (*FHG* IV, p. 415, frg. 9) e la fortuna di un nome.' *Aevum* 63.1, 24–29.

Prentzas, K. 2004. 'A New Interpretation of the Aleuas Coin.' In B. Mimica, J. Dobrinić and D. Mandić eds, *Proceedings of the 4th International Numismatic Congress in Croatia, September 20–25, 2004* (Rijcka: Tiskara Venerus), 207–15.

Pretzler, M. 2009. 'Arcadia: Ethnicity and Politics in the Fifth and Fourth Centuries BCE.' In P. Funke and N. Luraghi eds, *The Politics of Ethnicity and the Crisis of the Peloponnesian League*. Hellenic Studies Series 32 (Washington DC: Center for Hellenic Studies), 86–109.

Prignitz, S. 2014. 'Zur Identifizierung des Heiligtums von Kalapodi.' *Zeitschrift für Papyrologie und Epigraphik* 189, 133–46.

Prinz, F. 1979. *Gründungsmythen und Sagenchronologie*. Munich: Beck.

Pritchett, W.K. 1958. 'New Light on Thermopylai.' *American Journal of Archaeology* 62.2, 203–13.

Psoma, S. and D. Tsangari. 2003. 'Monnaie commune et états fédéraux. La circulation des monnayages frappés par les états fédéraux du monde grec.' In K. Buraselis and K. Zoumboulakis eds, *The Idea of European Community in History*, vol. 2, *Aspects of Connecting Poleis and Ethne in Ancient Greece* (Athens: National Kapodistrian University of Athens), 111–42.

Raaflaub, K.A. 2015. 'Forerunners of Federal States: Collaboration and Integration through Alliance in Archaic and Classical Greece.' In H. Beck and P. Funke eds, *Federalism in Greek Antiquity* (Cambridge: Cambridge University Press), 434–51.

Race, W.H. 2009. *Apollonius Rhodius: Argonautica*. Cambridge, MA: Harvard University Press.

Rakatsanis, K. and A. Tziafalias. 1997. *Λατρείες και Ιερά στην Αρχαία Θεσσαλία. Α' Πελασγιώτις*. Ioannina: University of Ioannina Press.

—. 2004. *Λατρείες και Ιερά στην Αρχαία Θεσσαλία. Β' Περραιβία*. Ioannina: University of Ioannina Press.

Ranasinghe, N. 2009. *Socrates in the Underworld*. South Bend, IN: St Augustine's Press.

Raynor, B. 2017. 'Alexander I and the Creation of Apeiros.' *Chiron* 47, 243–70.

Redfield, J.M. 2003. *The Locrian Maidens: Love and Death in Greek Italy*. Princeton, NJ: Princeton University Press.

Reger, G. 2005. 'The Economy.' In A. Erskine ed., *A Companion to the Hellenistic World* (Oxford and Malden, MA: Blackwell), 331–53.

—. 2014. 'Ethnic Identities, Borderlands, and Hybridity.' In J. McInerney ed., *A Companion to Ethnicity in the Ancient Mediterranean* (Chichester: Wiley Blackwell), 112–26.

Reinders, H.R. 1988. *New Halos: A Hellenistic Town in Thessalía, Greece*. Utrecht: HES.

—. 2003. 'The Coins'; 'Catalogue of Coins'. In H.R. Reinders and W. Prummel eds, *Housing in New Halos: A Hellenistic Town in Thessaly, Greece* (Lisse: Swets & Zeitlinger), 138–45; 320–26.

—. 2009. 'The Hellenistic City of New Halos: A Creation of Demetrios Poliorketes?' In A. Mazarakis Ainian ed., *Αρχαιολογικό Έργο Θεσσαλίας και Στερεάς Ελλάδας* 3, vol. 1 (Volos: Εργαστήριο Αρχαιολογίας Πανεπιστημίου Θεσσαλίας & Υπουργείο Πολιτισμού, Παιδείας και Θρησκευμάτων), 369–79.

Reinders, H.R. and W. Prummel. 1998. 'Transhumance in Hellenistic Thessaly.' *Environmental Archaeology* 3.1, 81–95.

Reinders, H.R., E. Asderaki-Tzoumerkioti and M. Vaxevanopoulos. 2016. 'Copper Production and Coinage in Achaia Phthiotis.' *Pharos* 22.2, 43–85.

Remijsen, S. 2009. 'Challenged by Egyptians: Greek Sports in the Third Century BC.' *International Journal of the History of Sport* 26.2, 246–71.

—. 2019. 'Only Greeks at the Olympics? Reconsidering the Rule against Non-Greeks at "Panhellenic" Games.' *Classica et Mediaevalia* 67, 1–61.

Remijsen, S. and S. Scharff. 2015. 'The Expression of Identities in Hellenistic Victor Epigrams.' Classics @ 13, https://classics-at.chs.harvard.edu/classics13-remijsen-and-scharff/.

Renfrew, C. 1986. 'Introduction: Peer-Polity Interaction and Socio-Political Change.' In C. Renfrew and J.F. Cherry eds, *Peer-Polity Interaction and Socio-Political Change* (Cambridge: Cambridge University Press), 1–18.

Rengakos, A. 2015. '*Aethiopis*.' In M. Fantuzzi and C. Tsagalis eds, *The Greek Epic Cycle and Its Reception: A Companion* (Cambridge: Cambridge University Press), 306–17.

Rhodes, P.J. and R. Osborne. 2003. *Greek Historical Inscriptions: 404–323 BC*. Oxford: Oxford University Press.

Richardson, N. 2010. *Three Homeric Hymns to Apollo, Hermes and Aphrodite: Hymns 3, 4, and 5*. Cambridge: Cambridge University Press.

Riethmüller, J.W. 2005. *Asklepios: Heiligtümer und Kulte*. Heidelberg: Archäologie und Geschichte.

Rigsby, K.J. 1996. *Asylia: Territorial Inviolability in the Hellenistic World*. Berkeley: University of California Press.

—. 2004. '*Theoroi* for the Koan Asklepieia.' In K. Höghammer ed., *The Hellenistic Polis of Kos* (Uppsala: Acta Universitatis Upsaliensis), 9–14.

Rist, A. 2016. *The* Mimiambs *of Herodas. Translated into an English 'Choliambic' Metre with Literary-Historical Introductions and Notes*. London: Bloomsbury.

Robbins, E. 1975. 'Jason and Cheiron: The Myth of Pindar's Fourth Pythian.' *Phoenix* 29.3, 205–13.

Robert, L. 1940 *Les gladiateurs dans l'Orient grec*. Paris: E. Champion.

—. 1973. 'Les juges étrangers dans la cite grecque.' In E. von Caemmerer, J.H. Kaiser, G. Kegel, W. Müller-Freienfels and H.J. Wolff eds, *ΞΕΝΙΟΝ. Festschrift für Pan. J. Zepos*, I (Athens: Katsikalis), 765–82.

Robertson, N. 1976. 'The Thessalian Expedition of 480 BC.' *Journal of Hellenic Studies* 96, 100–20.

—. 1978. 'The Myth of the First Sacred War.' *Classical Quarterly* 28.1, 38–73.
—. 1980. 'The Dorian Migration and Corinthian Ritual.' *Classical Philology* 75.1, 1–22.
—. 1984. 'Poseidon's Festival at the Winter Solstice.' *Classical Quarterly* 34.1, 1–16.
Robinson, D.M. 1934. 'The Bronze State Seal of Larissa Kremaste.' *American Journal of Archaeology* 38.2, 219–22.
Roesch, P. 1982. *Études béotiennes*. Paris: de Boccard.
Rogers, E. 1932. *The Copper Coinage of Thessaly*. London: Spink and Sons.
Rop, J. 2019. 'The Phocian Betrayal at Thermopylae.' *Historia* 68.4, 413–35.
Rose, B. 2008. 'Separating Fact from Fiction in the Asian Migration.' *Hesperia* 77.3, 399–430.
Rose, P.W. 1995. *Sons of the Gods, Children of Earth: Ideology and Literary Form in Ancient Greece*. Ithaca, NY: Cornell University Press.
Rousset, D. 2002. *Le territoire de Delphes et la terre d'Apollon*. Paris: de Boccard.
—. 2015. 'Microfederalism in Central Greece: The Dorians and Oitaians.' In H. Beck and P. Funke eds, *Federalism in Greek Antiquity* (Cambridge: Cambridge University Press), 222–30.
Roux, G. 1979. *L'Amphictionie, Delphes et le temple d'Apollon au IVe siècle*. Paris: de Boccard.
Roy, J. 2011. 'On Seeming Backward: How the Arkadians Did It.' In S.D. Lambert ed., *Sociable Man: Essays on Ancient Greek Social Behaviour in Honour of Nick Fisher* (Swansea: Classical Press of Wales), 67–85.
Rung, E. 2013. 'Herodotus and Greek Medism.' In A. Mehl, A. Makhlayuk and O. Gabelko eds, *Ruthenia Classica Aetatis Novae: A Collection of Works by Russian Scholars in Ancient Greek and Roman History* (Stuttgart: Franz Steiner), 71–82.
Russo, C.F. 1950. *Hesiodi* Scutum*: Introduzione, testo critico e commento con traduzione e indici*. Firenze: 'La Nova Italia'.
Rusten, J. and J. König. 2014. *Philostratus*, vol. 5: *Heroicus, Gymnasticus, Discourses 1 and 2*. Cambridge, MA: Harvard University Press.
Rusyaeva, A.S. 2003. 'The Temple of Achilles on the Island of Leuke in the Black Sea.' *Ancient Civilizations from Scythia to Siberia* 9.1–2, 1–16.
Rutherford, I.C. 2001a. *Pindar's* Paeans*: A Reading of the Fragments with a Survey of the Genre*. Oxford: Oxford University Press.
—. 2001b. 'The New Simonides: Towards a Commentary.' In D. Boedecker and D. Sider eds, *The New Simonides: Contexts of Praise and Desire* (Oxford: Oxford University Press), 33–54.
—. 2004. 'The Keian Theoria to Delphi: Neglected Data from the Accounts of the Delphic Naopoioi (CID 2.1–28).' *Zeitschrift für Papyrologie und Epigraphik* 147, 107–14.
—. 2005. 'Mestra at Athens: Hesiod fr. 43 and the Poetics of Panhellenism.' In R. Hunter ed., *The Hesiodic Catalogue of Women: Constructions and Reconstructions* (Cambridge: Cambridge University Press), 99–117.

—. 2009. 'Black Sails for Achilles: The Thessalian Pilgrimage in Philostratus' *Heroicus*.' In E.L. Bowie and J. Elsner eds, *Philostratus* (Cambridge: Cambridge University Press), 230–50.

—. 2012. 'The *Catalogue of Women* within the Greek Epic Tradition: Allusion, Intertextuality and Traditional Referentiality.' In Ø. Andersen and D.T.T. Haug eds, *Relative Chronology in Early Greek Epic Poetry* (Cambridge: Cambridge University Press), 152–67.

—. 2018. 'Delphi, Primeval Purification and Theoria: In Search of a Schema.' In A. Kavoulaki ed., *Πλειών: Papers in Memory of Christiane Sourvinou-Inwood. Ariadne* suppl. 1 (Rethymno: School of Philosophy, University of Crete), 21–32.

—. 2020. *Hittite Texts and Greek Religion: Contact, Interaction, and Comparison*. Oxford: Oxford University Press.

Ryder, T.T.B. 2000. 'Demosthenes and Philip II.' In I. Worthington ed., *Demosthenes: Statesman and Orator* (London: Routledge), 45–89.

Rzepka, J. 2002. 'Ethnos, Koinon, Sympoliteia and Greek Federal States.' In T. Derda, J. Urbanik and M. Wecowski eds, *Ευεργεσίας Χάριν: Studies Presented to Ewa Wipszycka and Benedetto Bravo by Their Disciples* (Warsaw: Fundacaja im. Rafała Taubenschlaga), 225–47.

Saatsoglou-Paliadeli, C. 1993. 'Aspects of Ancient Macedonian Costume.' *Journal of Hellenic Studies* 113, 122–47.

Sacks, D. 2005. *Encyclopedia of the Ancient Greek World*. Rev. ed. (revised L.R. Brody). New York: Facts on File Inc.

Sakellariou, M.B. 2009. *Ethne grecs à l'âge du bronze*. 2 vols. Paris: de Boccard.

Salviat, F. and C. Vatin. 1974. 'Le cadastre de Larissa.' *Bulletin de Correspondance Hellénique* 98, 247–62.

Sammons, B. 2010. *The Art and Rhetoric of the Homeric Catalogue*. Oxford: Oxford University Press.

Sánchez, P. 2001. *L'Amphictionie des Pyles et de Delphes. Recherches sur son rôle historique, des origines au IIe siècle de notre ère*. Stuttgart: Franz Steiner.

Sánchez-Moreno, E. 2013. 'Communication Routes in and around Epicnemidian Locris'; 'Mountain Passes in Epicnemidian Locris.' In J. Pascual and M.-F. Papakonstantinou eds, *Topography and History of Ancient Epicnemidian Locris* (Leiden: Brill), 279–336; 337–60.

Santin, E. 2008. 'Nuova lettura dell'epigramma funerario per Diokleas (*IG* IX 2, 255, *Agios Georgios Pharsalôn*, Tessaglia).' *Zeitschrift für Papyrologie und Epigraphik* 166, 73–79.

—. 2018. 'Poeti e conferenzieri stranieri in Tessaglia in età ellenistica: l'epigramma funerario per Herillos figlio di Herodoros di Kalchedon.' In F. Camia, L. Del Monaco and M. Nocita eds, *Munus Laetitiae. Studi miscellanei offerti a Maria Letizia Lazzarini*, vol. 2 (Rome: Sapienza Università Editrice), 223–49.

Santin, E. and A. Tziafalias. 2013. 'Épigrammes signées de Thessalie.' *Topoi Orient-Occident* 18.1, 251–82.

Sawada, N. 2019. 'Allies and Foes (1): Aeschines, Hyperides, Lycurgus.' In G. Martin ed., *The Oxford Handbook of Demosthenes* (Oxford: Oxford University Press), 337–51.

Schachermeyr, F. 1950. *Poseidon und die Entstehung des grieschen Götterglaubens*. Munich: L. Lehnen.

Schachter, A. 1981. *Cults of Boiotia, Vol. 1: Acheloos to Hera*. London: Institute of Classical Studies.

—. 1986. *Cults of Boiotia, Vol. 2: Herakles to Poseidon*. London: Institute of Classical Studies.

—. 2016. *Boiotia in Antiquity: Selected Papers*. Cambridge: Cambridge University Press.

Scharff, S. 2016. 'Das Pferd Aithon, die Skopaden und die πατρὶς Θεσσαλία. Zur Selbstdarstellung hippischer Sieger aus Thessalien im Hellenismus.' In C. Mann, S. Remijsen and S. Scharff eds, *Athletics in the Hellenistic World* (Stuttgart: Franz Steiner), 209–29.

—. 2019. 'Virtual Halls of Fame: Imagined Communities of Equestrian Victors in the Hellenistic Period.' In J.-C. Moretti and P. Valavanis eds, *Les hippodromes et les concours hippiques dans la Grèce antique. BCH* Supplement 62 (Athens: EFA), 341–52.

Schieber, A.S. 1982. 'Leotychidas in Thessaly.' *L'Antiquité Classique* 51, 5–14.

Schmitt, H.-O. 2007. 'Die Angriffswaffen.' In R.C.S. Felsch ed., *Kalapodi II* (Mainz am Rhein: Philipp von Zabern), 423–551.

Schneider, H. 1979. 'Histoire géologique du bassin néogène et quaternaire de la Thessalie.' In B. Helly ed., *La Thessalie: Actes de la Table-Ronde 21–24 Juillet 1975, Lyon* (Paris: de Boccard), 43–50.

Scholten, J.B. 2000. *The Politics of Plunder: Aitolians and their Koinon in the Early Hellenistic Era, 279–217 BC*. Berkeley: University of California Press.

—. 2005. 'Macedon and the Mainland, 280–221.' In A. Erskine ed., *A Companion to the Hellenistic World* (Oxford and Malden, MA: Blackwell), 134–58.

Schultz, P. 2009. 'Divine Images and Royal Iconography in the Philippeion at Olympia.' In J.T. Jensen, G. Hinge, P. Schultz and B. Wickkiser eds, *Aspects of Ancient Greek Cult: Context, Ritual and Iconography, Åarhus Studies in Mediterranean Antiquity* 8 (Åarhus: Åarhus University Press), 125–94.

Scodel, R. 1982. 'The Achaean Wall and the Myth of Destruction.' *Harvard Studies in Classical Philology* 86, 33–50.

Scott, D. 2006. *Plato's* Meno. Cambridge: Cambridge University Press.

Scott, M. 2010. *Delphi and Olympia: The Spatial Politics of Panhellenism in the Archaic and Classical Periods*. Cambridge: Cambridge University Press.

—. 2014. *Delphi: A History of the Center of the Ancient World*. Princeton, NJ: Princeton University Press.

—. 2016. 'The Performance of Boiotian Identity at Delphi.' In S. Gartland ed., *Boiotia in the Fourth Century BC* (Philadelphia: University of Pennsylvania Press), 99–120.

Scullion, S. 2003. 'Euripides and Macedon, or the Silence of the "Frogs".' *Classical Quarterly* 53.2, 389–400.

Seager, R. 1981. 'The Freedom of the Greeks of Asia: From Alexander to Antiochus.' *Classical Quarterly* 31.1, 106–12.

Seager, R. and C. Tuplin. 1980. 'The Freedom of the Greeks of Asia: On the Origins of a Concept and the Creation of a Slogan.' *Journal of Hellenic Studies* 100, 141–54.

Segre, M. 1934. 'Grano di Tessaglia a Coo.' *Rivista di Filologia* 12, 169–93.

Severin, T. 1986. *The Jason Voyage: The Quest for the Golden Fleece.* London: Simon and Schuster.

Shaw, P.-J. 2001. 'Lords of Hellas, Old Men of the Sea: The Occasion of Simonides' Elegy on Plataea.' In D. Boedecker and D. Sider eds, *The New Simonides: Contexts of Praise and Desire* (Oxford: Oxford University Press), 164–81.

Sherratt, A. and S. Sherratt. 1991. 'From Luxuries to Commodities: The Nature of Mediterranean Bronze Age Trading Systems.' In N.H. Gale ed., *Bronze Age Trade in the Mediterranean. Papers Presented at the Conference Held at Rewley House, Oxford, in December 1989* (Jonsered: P. Åströms), 351–86.

Shrimpton, G.S. 1991. *Theopompus the Historian.* Montreal: McGill-Queen's University Press.

Siewert, P. 1979. 'Poseidon Hippios am Kolonos und die athenischen Hippeis.' In G.W. Bowersock, W. Burkert and M. Putam ed., *Arktouros: Hellenic Studies Presented to Bernard M.W. Knox on the Occasion of his 65th Birthday* (Berlin: de Gruyter), 280–89.

Sigelman, A.C. 2016. *Pindar's Poetics of Immortality.* Cambridge: Cambridge University Press.

Simon, E. 1962. 'Otos und Ephialtes.' *Antike Kunst* 5.1, 43–44.

Sivignon, M. 1979. 'Place géographique de la Thessalie dans l'ensemble hellénique.' In B. Helly ed., *La Thessalie: Actes de la Table-Ronde 21–24 Juillet 1975, Lyon* (Paris: de Boccard), 37–42.

Slater, W.J. 1972. 'Simonides' House.' *Phoenix* 26.3, 232–40.

Slater, W.J. and D. Summa. 2006. 'Crowns at Magnesia.' *Greek, Roman, and Byzantine Studies* 46, 275–99.

Slatkin, L.M. 1991. *The Power of Thetis: Allusion and Interpretation in the* Iliad. Berkeley: University of California Press.

Smarczyc, B. 2015. 'The Hellenic Leagues of Late Classical and Hellenistic Times and Their Place in the History of Greek Federalism.' In H. Beck and P. Funke eds, *Federalism in Greek Antiquity* (Cambridge: Cambridge University Press), 452–70.

Smith, K.K. 1910. 'The Olympic Victory of Agias of Thessaly.' *Classical Philology* 5.2, 169–74.

Smith, W.D. 1990. *Hippocrates: Pseudepigraphic Writings.* Leiden: Brill.

Snodgrass, A.M. 1980. *Archaic Greece: The Age of Experiment.* Berkeley: University of California Press.

Sordi, M. 1956. 'La dracma di Aleuas e l'origine di un tipo monetario di Alessandro Magno.' *Annali del Istituto Italiano di Numismatica* 3, 9–22.
—. 1958. *La lega tessala fino ad Alessandro Magno.* Rome: Istituto Italiano per la Storia Antica.
—. 1966. 'Mitologia e propaganda nella Beozia arcaica.' *Atene e Roma* 11, 14–24. Reproduced in M. Sordi 2002, *Scritti di storia greca* (Milan: V&P Università), 271–84.
—. 1979. 'Aspetti della propaganda tessala a Delfi.' In B. Helly ed., *La Thessalie: Actes de la Table-Ronde 21–24 Juillet 1975, Lyon* (Paris: de Boccard), 157–64.
Sosin, J.D. 2009. 'Magnesian Inviolability.' *Transactions of the American Philological Society* 139.2, 369–410.
Sourvinou-Inwood, C. 1979. 'The Myth of the First Temples at Delphi.' *Classical Quarterly* 29.2, 231–51.
—. 2002. 'Greek Perceptions of Ethnicity and the Ethnicity of the Macedonians.' In L.M. Castelnuovo ed., *Identità* e *prassi storica nel Mediterraneo greco* (Milan: Et), 173–203.
—. 2003. 'Herodotos (and Others) on Pelasgians: Some Perceptions of Ethnicity.' In P. Derow and R. Parker eds, *Herodotus and His World: Essays from a Conference in Memory of George Forrest* (Oxford: Oxford University Press), 103–44.
Spence, I.G. 1993. *The Cavalry of Classical Greece: A Social and Military History with Particular Reference to Athens.* Oxford: Clarendon.
Sprawski, S. 1999. *Jason of Pherae: A Study on History of Thessaly in Years 431–370 BC.* Kraków: Jagiellonian University Press.
—. 2003. 'Philip II and the Freedom of the Thessalians.' *Electrum* 9, 56–66.
—. 2005. 'All the King's Men: Thessalians and Philip II's Designs on Greece.' In D. Musial ed., *Society and Religions: Studies in Greek and Roman History* (Toruń: Wydawnictwo Uniwersytetu Mikołaja Kopernika), 31–49.
—. 2006. 'Alexander of Pherae: *Infelix* Tyrant.' In S. Lewis ed., *Ancient Tyranny* (Edinburgh: Edinburgh University Press), 135–47.
—. 2008. 'Thessalians and Theirs [*sic*] Neighbours in the Classical Period.' In L. Gklegkle ed., *1º Διεθνές Συνέδριο Ιστορίας & Πολιτισμού της Θεσσαλίας. Πρακτικά Συνεδρίου 9–11 Νοεμβρίου 2006*, vol. 1 (Thessaloniki: Περιφέρειας Θεσσαλίας), 131–37.
—. 2012. 'Remarks on Aristotle's *Thettalon Politeia.*' *Electrum* 19 (2012), 137–47.
—. 2014a. 'Thessalos, Son of Jason and Medea: Pheraian Myths and Local Identity.' *Υπέρεια* 6, 267–72.
—. 2014b. 'A Land Apart: The Description of Thessaly in the Homeric Catalogue of Ships.' In K. Twardowska ed., *Within the Circle of Ancient Ideas and Virtues: Studies in Honour of Professor Maria Dzielska* (Krakow: Historia Iagellonica), 85–95.
—. 2014c. 'Peltasts in Thessaly.' In N.V. Sekunda and B. Burliga eds, *Iphicrates, Peltasts and Lechaion* (Gdańsk: Foundation for the Development of Gdańsk University), 95–112.

—. 2020. 'The Maritime Policy of the Tyrants of Pherae.' *Electrum* 27, 89–115.
Stadter, P. 2014. *Plutarch and His Roman Readers*. Oxford: Oxford University Press.
Stählin, F. 1924. *Das Hellenische Thessalien: Landeskundliche und geschichtliche Beschreibung Thessaliens in der hellenischen und römischen Zeit*. Stuttgart: J. Engelhorns.
Stamatopoulou, M. 2004–2009. 'Το Αρχείο του Αποστόλου Σ. Αρβανιτόπουλου (1874–1942).' *Horos* 17–21, 635–47.
—. 2007a. 'Thessalian Aristocracy and Society in the Age of Epinikian.' In S. Hornblower and C. Morgan eds, *Pindar's Poetry, Patrons, and Festivals from Archaic Greece to the Roman Empire* (Oxford: Oxford University Press), 309–42.
—. 2007b. 'Thessalians Abroad, the Case of Pharsalos.' *Mediterranean Historical Review* 22.2, 211–36.
—. 2011–2012. 'Thessaly (Prehistory to Roman).' *Archaeological Reports* 58, 75–95.
—. 2012–2013. 'Thessaly (Prehistory to Roman).' *Archaeological Reports* 59, 35–55.
—. 2016. 'The Banquet Motif on the Funerary Stelai from Demetrias.' In C.M. Draycott and M. Stamatopoulou eds, *Dining and Death: Interdisciplinary Perspectives on the 'Funerary Banquet' in Ancient Art, Burial and Belief* (Leuven: Peeters), 405–79.
—. 2018. 'Demetrias: The Archaeology of a Cosmopolitan Macedonian Harbour.' In M. Kalaitzi, P. Paschidis, C. Antonetti and A.-M. Guimier-Sorbets eds, *Βορειοελλαδικά: Tales from the Lands of the Ethne. Essays in Honour of Miltiades B. Hatzopoulos* (Athens: National Hellenic Research Foundation and the Institute of Historical Research), 343–76.
—. 2019. 'Μάκαιρα Θεσσαλία; Η Θεσσαλία κατά την αρχαϊκή περίοδο.' In S. Katakouta and D. Palaiothodoros eds, *Τοπική Κεραμική της Θεσσαλίας (από τον 7ο στον 5ο Αι. π.Χ.). Πρακτικά Ημερίδας Λάρισα, 24 Νοεμβρίου 2017* (Larisa: Petasos), 21–39.
—. 2021. 'A New Look at Old Finds: The Bronze Handle NAM X15463 from Thessaly and the Sanctuary of Athena Polias at Phthiotic Thebes.' In A. Sphyroera, T. Panagou, M. Koutsoumpou and X. Charalampidou eds, *Έξοχος ἄλλων. Τιμητικός τόμος για την καθηγήτρια Εύα Σημαντώνη-Μπούνια* (Athens: Οργανισμός Διαχείρισης και Ανάπτυξης Πολιτίστικων Πόρων), 673–92.
Stamatopoulou, M. and S. Katakouta. 2020. 'Monumental Funerary Architecture in Thessaly in the Classical and Hellenistic Periods: An Overview.' In C. Berns and C. Huguenot eds, *Griechische Monumentalgräber: Regionale Muster und ihre Rezeption im ägäischen Raum in klassischer und hellenistischer Zeit* (Düren: Shaker Verlag), 147–74.
Stamatopoulou, Z. 2014. 'Hesiodic Poetry and Wisdom in Plutarch's *Symposium of the Seven Sages*.' *American Journal of Philology* 135, 533–58.

Stamelou, E. and A. Doulgeri-Intzesiloglou. 2010. 'Ιερό Ηρακλή αρχαϊκών χρόνων στην αρχαία οδό Φερών-Παγασών.' *Υπέρεια* 5, 161–80.

—. 2019. 'Κεραμική αρχικών χρόνων από το ιερό του Ηρακλή στη θέση "Σπαρτιάς-Λατομείο" στην περιοχή του Σέσκλου.' In S. Katakouta and D. Palaiothodoros eds, *Τοπική Κεραμική της Θεσσαλίας (από τον 7ο στον 5ο Αι. π. Χ). Πρακτικά Ημερίδας Λάρισα, 24 Νοεμβρίου 2017* (Larisa: Petasos), 95–115.

Starikova, A.O. 2019. 'Corinth and Ephyra in Simonides' Elegy (fr. 15–16 West, Plut. *De malign.* 872D-E).' *Philologia Classica* 14, 8–19.

Stephens, S. 2008. 'Ptolemaic Epic.' In T.D. Papanghelis and A. Rengakos eds, *Brill's Companion to Apollonius Rhodius* (Leiden: Brill), 95–114.

Stevens, P.T. 1971. *Euripides:* Andromache. *Edited with Introduction and Commentary*. Oxford: Clarendon.

Stewart, A.F. 1978. 'Lysippan Studies 2: Agias and Oilpourer.' *American Journal of Archaeology* 82.3, 301–13.

Stewart, E. 2017. *Greek Tragedy on the Move: The Birth of a Panhellenic Art Form c. 500–300 BC*. Oxford: Oxford University Press.

Stöllner, T. and I. Gambashidze. 2011. 'Gold in Georgia II: The Oldest Gold Mine in the World.' In Ü. Yalçin ed., *Anatolian Metal V* (Bochum: Deutsches Bergbau-Museum), 87–200.

Strootman, R. 2010–2011. 'Alexander's Thessalian Cavalry.' *Talanta* 42–43, 51–67.

—. 2020. 'Hellenism and Persianism in Iran.' *Dabir* 7, 201–28.

Suárez de la Torre, E. 1997. 'Neoptolemos at Delphi.' *Kernos* 10, 153–76.

Sumi, G. 2004. 'Civic Self-Representation in the Hellenistic World: The Festival of Artemis Leukophryene in Magnesia-on-the-Maeander.' In S. Bell and G. Davies eds, *Games and Festivals in Classical Antiquity: Proceedings of a Conference Held in Edinburgh 10–12 July 2000* (Oxford: Archaeopress), 79–88.

Szemler, G.J., W.J. Cherf and J.C. Kraft. 1996. *Thermopylai: Myth and Reality in 480 BC*. Chicago, IL: Ares Publishers.

Szidat, S. 2001. *Poseidon als Erdeschütterer*. Munich: Hieronymus Buch-reproduktions.

Taplin, O. 1999. 'Spreading the Word through Performance.' In S. Goldhill and R. Osborne eds, *Performance Culture and Athenian Democracy* (Cambridge: Cambridge University Press), 33–57.

Tarrant, H. 2005. *Recollecting Plato's* Meno. London: Duckworth.

Tausend, K. 1992. *Amphiktyonie und Symmachie: Formen zwischenstaatlicher Beziehungen im archaischen Griechenland. Historia* Einzelschriften 73. Stuttgart: Franz Steiner.

Teffeteller, A. 2001. 'The Chariot Rite at Onchestos: *Homeric Hymn to Apollo* 229–38.' *Journal of Hellenic Studies* 121, 159–66.

Thomas, C.G. 2005. *Finding People in Early Greece*. Columbia and London: University of Missouri Press.

Thomas, J.E. 1980. *Musings on the* Meno*: A New Translation with Commentary.* The Hague: Martinus Nijhoff.

Thomas, R. 2019. *Polis Histories, Collective Memories and the Greek World.* Cambridge: Cambridge University Press.

Thonemann, P. 2007. 'Magnesia and the Greeks of Asia (*I.Magnesia* 16.16).' *Greek, Roman, and Byzantine Studies* 47, 151–60.

Traina, G. 2016. 'Traditions on Armenia in Submerged Greek Literature: Preliminary Considerations.' In G. Colesanti and L. Lulli eds, *Submerged Literature in Ancient Greek Culture*, vol. 2 (Berlin: de Gruyter), 111–23.

—. 2017. 'Strabo and the History of Armenia.' In D. Dueck ed., *The Routledge Companion to Strabo* (London and New York: Routledge), 93–101.

Tronson, A. 1984. 'Satyrus the Peripatetic and the Marriages of Philip II.' *Journal of Hellenic Studies* 104, 116–26.

—. 1991. 'The Hellenic League of 480 B.C.: Fact or Ideological Fiction?' *Acta Classica* 34, 93–110.

—. 2000. *"The Hellenes" as a Political Concept: The Development of a Hellenic Ideology in Greece from Archaic Times down to the End of the Fifth Century B.C.* PhD thesis, Harvard University.

Tsetskhladze, G.R. 1998. 'Greek Colonisation of the Black Sea Area: Stages, Models, and Native Population.' In G.R. Tsetskhladze ed., *The Greek Colonisation of the Black Sea Area: Historical Interpretation of Archaeology* (Stuttgart: Franz Steiner), 9–68.

Tufano, S. 2019. *Boiotia from Within: The Beginnings of Boiotian Historiography.* Münster: Universitäts- und Landesbibliothek Münster.

Tuplin, C. 1993. *The Failings of Empire: A Reading of Xenophon* Hellenica *2.3.11–7.5.27.* Stuttgart: Franz Steiner.

Tziafalias, A. 1988. 'Ασκληπιείο Τρίκκης. Μύθος η πραγματικότητα.' *Τρικαλινά* 8, 171–218.

—. 1994. 'Δεκαπέντε χρονιά ανασκαφών στην αρχαία Λάρισα.' In B. Helly ed., *La Thessalie. Quinze années de recherches archéologiques, 1975–1990. Bilans et perspectives. Actes du colloque international, Lyons, 17–22 Avril 1990* (Athens: Kapon), 153–78.

—. 2011. 'Ανακάλυψη αρχαίων θεάτρων Λάρισας.' In V. Adrymi-Sismani ed., *Αρχαία Θέατρα στη Θεσσαλία* (Athens: Diozoma), 23–32.

Tziafalias, A. and B. Helly. 2004–2005. 'Deux décrets inédits de Larisa.' *Bulletin de Correspondance Hellénique* 128–29, 377–420.

—. 2013. 'Décrets inédits de Larisa organisant la vente de terres publiques attribuées aux cavaliers', *Topoi* 18.1, 135–249.

Tziafalias, A., R.A. Bouchon, L. Darmezin, J.-C. Decourt, B. Helly, G. Lucas and I. Pernin. 2016. *Corpus des inscriptions d'Atrax en Pélasgiotide (Thessalie). Études épigraphiques*, 7. Paris: de Boccard.

Ulf, C. 1996. 'Griechische Ethnogenese versus Wanderungen von Stämmen und Stamstaaten.' In C. Ulf ed., *Wege zur Genese griechischer Identität: die Bedeutung der früharchaische Zeit* (Berlin: Akademie Verlag), 240–79.

—. 2015. 'Deukalion und (k)ein leeres Land – Wanderungen der Ioner und Dorier – Hellenengenealogie, oder: Die Hellenen kommen aus Hellas.' In M. Asche and U. Niggemann eds, *Das leere Land: historische Narrative von Einwanderergesellschaften*. Historische Mitteilungen, Beihefte, vol. 92 (Stuttgart: Franz Steiner), 31–45.

Vaïopoulou, M., H. Whittaker, R. Rönnlund, F. Tsiouka, J. Klange, D. Pitman, R. Potter, L. Shaw, J. Hagen, E. Siljedahl, M. Forsénn, S. Chandrasekaran, S. Dandou, V.F. Ljungdahl, A. Pavilionytė, H. Scott-Pratt, H. Schlager and H. Manley. 2020. 'The 2016–2018 Greek–Swedish Archaeological Project at Thessalian Vlochos, Greece.' *Opuscula* 13, 7–72.

Van Boekel, G.M.E.C. and B. Muldner. 2003. 'Terracotta Figurines.' In H.R. Reinders and W. Prummel eds, *Housing in New Halos: A Hellenistic Town in Thessaly, Greece* (Lisse: Swets & Zeitlinger), 106–18.

Van Bremen, R. 2007. 'The Entire House Is Full of Crowns: Hellenistic Agones and the Commemoration of Victory'. In S. Hornblower and C. Morgan eds, *Pindar's Poetry, Patrons and Festivals: From Archaic Greece to the Roman Empire* (Oxford: Oxford University Press), 345–75.

Van der Vin, J.P.A. 2000. 'Coins in Athens during the Time of Peisistratos.' In H. Sancisi-Weerdenburg ed., *Peisistratos and the Tyranny: A Reappraisal of the Evidence* (Amsterdam: J.C. Gieben), 147–53.

Vanicelli, D. 1989. 'Il nome Ἕλληνες in Omero.' *Rivista di Filologia e di Istruzione Classica* 117, 34–48.

Vannicelli, P. 2012. 'The Mythical Origins of the Medes and Persians.' In E. Baragwanath and M. de Bakker eds, *Myth, Truth, and Narrative in Herodotus* (Oxford: Oxford University Press), 255–68.

Van Rookhuijzen, J.Z. 2019. *Herodotus and the Topography of Xerxes' Invasion*. Berlin: de Gruyter.

Van Wees, H. 2003. 'Conquerors and Serfs: Wars of Conquest and Forced Labour in Archaic Greece.' In N. Luraghi and S.E. Alcock eds, *Helots and Their Masters in Laconia and Messenia: Histories, Ideologies, Structures* (Cambridge, MA: Harvard University Press), 33–80.

Van Wijk, R. 2017. 'Athens, Thebes and Plataia and the End of the Sixth Century BCE.' *Journal of Ancient History* 5.2, 1–26.

Versnel, H. 1993. *Inconsistencies in Greek and Roman Religion, 2: Transition and Reversal in Myth and Ritual*. Leiden: Brill.

Vidal-Naquet, P. 1986. *The Black Hunter: Forms of Thought and Forms of Society in the Greek World*. Translated by A. Szegedy-Maszak. Baltimore, MD: Johns Hopkins University Press.

Visser, E. 1997. *Homers Katalog der Schiffe*. Stuttgart: Teubner.

Von Sallet, A. 1878. 'Zur griechischen Numismatik.' *Zeitschrift für Numismatik* 5, 92–109.

Von Steuben, H. 1999. 'Zur Komposition des Daochos-Monuments.' In H. von Steuben ed., *Antike Porträts: Zum Gedächtnis von Helga von Heintze* (Paderborn: Bibliopolis), 35–38.

Vottéro, G. 1996. 'Koinès et koinas en Béotie à l'époque dialectale (VIIe–IIe s. av. J.-C.).' In C. Brixhe ed., *La koiné grecque antique II: La concurrence* (Nancy: ADRA; Paris: de Boccard), 43–92.

Wade-Gery, H.T. 1924. 'Jason of Pherai and Aleuas the Red.' *Journal of Hellenic Studies* 44.1, 55–64.

Wade-Gery, H.T. and J.S. Morrison. 1942. 'Meno of Pharsalus, Polycrates, and Ismenias.' *Classical Quarterly* 36.1, 57–78.

Wagman, R.S. 2016. *The Cave of the Nymphs at Pharsalus: Studies on a Thessalian Country Shrine*. Leiden: Brill.

Walker, K.G. 2004. *Eretria: A Political and Social History from the Earliest Times to 490 BC*. London and New York: Routledge.

Wallace, P. 1979. *Strabo's Description of Boiotia: A Commentary*. Heidelberg: Carl Winter.

Wallace, S. 2016. 'East and West: Lines of Communication between Alexander and the Greeks.' *Hermathena* 200/201, 15–72.

Walsh, J.J. 1996. 'Flamininus and the Propaganda of Liberation.' *Historia* 45.3, 344–63.

Wathelet, P. 1975. 'L'origine du nom des Hellènes et son développement dans la tradition homérique.' *Les Études Classiques* 43, 119–28.

Wee, J.Z. 2016. 'Case History as Minority Report in the Hippocratic *Epidemics* 1.' In G. Petridou and C. Thumiger eds, *Homo Patiens: Approaches to the Patient in the Ancient World* (Leiden: Brill), 138–65.

Welles, B. 1960. 'Review of *La lega Tessala fino ad Alessandro Magno* by Marta Sordi.' *American Journal of Archaeology* 64.1, 104–06.

West, M.L. 1966. *Hesiod:* Theogony. *Edited with a Prolegomena and Commentary*. Oxford: Clarendon.

—. 1985. *The Hesiodic Catalogue of Women: Its Nature, Structure, and Origins*. Oxford: Clarendon.

—. 1988. 'The Rise of the Greek Epic.' *Journal of Hellenic Studies* 108, 151–72.

—. 1997. *The East Face of Helicon: West Asiatic Elements in Greek Poetry and Myth*. Oxford: Clarendon.

—. 2005. '*Odyssey* and *Argonautica*.' *Classical Quarterly* 55.1, 39–64.

—. 2011. *The Making of the* Iliad: *Disquisition and Analytical Commentary*. Oxford: Oxford University Press.

—. 2012. 'Towards a Chronology of Early Greek Epic.' In Ø. Andersen and D.T.T. Haug eds, *Relative Chronology in Early Greek Epic Poetry* (Cambridge: Cambridge University Press), 224–41.

—. 2014. *The Making of the* Odyssey. Oxford: Oxford University Press.

Westlake, H.D. 1935. *Thessaly in the Fourth Century BC*. London: Methuen.

—. 1936. 'The Medism of Thessaly.' *Journal of Hellenic Studies* 56.1, 12–24.

Whitmarsh, T. 1998. 'The Birth of a Prodigy: Heliodorus and the Genealogy of Hellenism.' In R. Hunter ed., *Studies in Heliodorus. PCPS* Suppl. 21 (Cambridge: Cambridge Philological Society), 93–124.

Williams, M.F. 2012. 'Souidas of Thessaly (602).' In I. Worthington ed., *Jacoby Online. Brill's New Jacoby, Part III*. Leiden: Brill. http://dx.doi.org/10.1163/1873-5363_bnj_a602.

Williams, R.T. 1972. *The Silver Coinage of the Phokians*. London: Royal Numismatic Society.

Wilson, N.G. 2014. *Aelian:* Historical Miscellany. Cambridge, MA: Harvard University Press.

Wiznura, A. and C.G. Williamson. 2018–2020. 'Mountains of Memory: Triangulating Landscape, Cult and Regional Identity through Zeus.' *Pharos* 24, 77–112.

Worthington, I. 2012. *Demosthenes of Athens and the Fall of Classical Greece*. Oxford: Oxford University Press.

—. 2014. *By the Spear: Philip II, Alexander the Great, and the Rise and Fall of the Macedonian Empire*. Oxford: Oxford University Press.

Yates, D. 2015. 'The Tradition of the Hellenic League against Xerxes.' *Historia* 64.1, 1–25.

—. 2019. *States of Memory: The Polis, Panhellenism, and the Persian War*. Oxford: Oxford University Press.

Yatromanolakis, D. 2001. 'To Sing or to Mourn? A Reappraisal of Simonides 22 W^2.' In D. Boedecker and D. Sider eds, *The New Simonides: Contexts of Praise and Desire* (Oxford: Oxford University Press), 208–25.

Yunis, H. 2005. *Demosthenes, Speeches 18 and 19. Translated with Introduction and Notes*. Austin: University of Texas Press.

Zahrnt, M. 2015. 'The Chalkidike and the Chalkidians.' In H. Beck and P. Funke eds, *Federalism in Greek Antiquity* (Cambridge: Cambridge University Press), 341–57.

Zanker, G. 2009. *Herodas:* Mimiambs. *Edited with a Translation, Introduction and Commentary*. Oxford: Oxbow (Aris & Phillips).

Zapheiropoulos, Ch. 2008. 'Η γη του «αλλόκοτου»: η Θεσσαλία στην αθηναϊκη τραγωδία του 5ου αιώνα π.Χ.' In L. Gklegkle ed., *1° Διεθνές Συνέδριο Ιστορίας & Πολιτισμού της Θεσσαλίας. Πρακτικά Συνεδρίου 9–11 Νοεμβρίου 2006*, vol. 1 (Thessaloniki: Περιφέρειας Θεσσαλίας), 152–60.

Zelnick-Abramovitz, R. 2000. 'The Xenodokoi of Thessaly.' *Zeitschrift für Papyrologie und Epigraphik* 130, 109–20.

Ziskowski, A. 2014. 'The Bellerophon Myth in Early Corinthian History and Art.' *Hesperia* 83, 81–102.

Index

Printed and bound by CPI Group (UK) Ltd, Croydon, CR0 4YY

27/02/2024

14459834-0001